MOSES AND PHARAOH

Other books by Gary North

Marx's Religion of Revolution, 1968
An Introduction to Christian Economics, 1973
Foundations of Christian Scholarship (editor), 1976
Unconditional Surrender, 1981
Successful Investing in an Age of Envy, 1981
The Dominion Covenant: Genesis, 1982
Government By Emergency, 1983
The Last Train Out, 1983
Backward, Christian Soldiers?, 1984
75 Bible Questions Your Instructors Pray You Won't Ask, 1984
Coined Freedom: Gold in the Age of the Bureaucrats, 1984
Negatrends, 1985
The Sinai Strategy, 1986
Conspiracy: A Biblical View, 1986
Unholy Spirits: Occultism and New Age Humanism, 1986

MOSES AND PHARAOH

Dominion Religion Versus Power Religion

Gary North

Institute for Christian Economics
Tyler, Texas

Published by
The Institute for Christian Economics
P. O. Box 8000
Tyler, Texas 75711

This book is dedicated to

Robert A. Nisbet

who taught me to ask two crucial
questions: "What is the nature
of social change?" and "What
is so natural about it?"

TABLE OF CONTENTS

No one, in our time, believes in any sanction greater than military power; no one believes that it is possible to overcome force except by greater force. There is no "law," there is only power. I am not saying that that is a true belief, merely that it is the belief which all modern men do actually hold. Those who pretend otherwise are either intellectual cowards, or power-worshippers under a thin disguise, or have simply not caught up with the age they are living in.

George Orwell*

* George Orwell, "Rudyard Kipling," *Horizon* (Feb. 1942); in *The Collected Essays, Journalism and Letters of George Orwell*, 4 vols. (New York: Harcourt, Brace & World, 1968), II, p. 185.

PREFACE

This book is the first section of volume 2 of my series, *An Economic Commentary on the Bible*. It is Part 1 of *The Dominion Covenant: Exodus*. Volume 1 was *The Dominion Covenant: Genesis* (Institute for Christian Economics, 1982). The focus of this commentary is on those aspects of the Book of Exodus that relate to economics. Nevertheless, it is broader than a narrowly defined economic analysis, for biblical economics is broader than strictly economic analysis. The early nineteenth-century term, "political economy," is closer to the biblical norm for economics; the late eighteenth-century term, "moral philosophy," is closer yet.

It would be unwise for me to repeat the foundational material that I covered in *Dominion Covenant: Genesis*. In that book, I made the strongest case that I could for the existence of a uniquely Christian economics, especially with respect to epistemology: "What can we know, and how can we know it?" This book is based on the epistemological foundation laid down in volume 1. For those who are uninterested in epistemology — and there are a lot of you in this category — I can only restate my original position: it is not that there is a meaningful Christian economics among all other economic schools of thought; it is that there is *only* Christian economics. There is no other sure foundation of true knowledge except the Bible. The only firmly grounded economics is Christian economics. All non-Christian approaches are simply crude imitations of the truth — imitations that cannot be logically supported, given their own first principles concerning God, man, law, and knowledge. Biblical economics is therefore at war with all other economic systems.

We can see this in the conflict between Moses and Pharaoh. This conflict was a conflict which involved every aspect of life, including economics. We need to understand the theological issues that divided Egypt from Israel in order to understand similarly divisive approaches to economics and political theory today. Economic disagreements today are closely related to the same theological divisions that separated Moses from Pharaoh.

There is no doubt that Pharaoh knew some things about economics. If we do not assume this, we can make no sense of his actions. He also knew a great deal about biblical law. But this knowledge only led to his condemnation, just as it does in the case of all other forms of non-Christian knowledge. The anti-Christians have enough knowledge to condemn them eternally, but not enough to construct a progressive long-term civilization. They have occasionally constructed long-term static civilizations, most notably Egypt and China, but only through the imposition of tyranny.[1]

Using Humanists to Defeat Humanism

Similarly, modern economists have considerable knowledge about the workings of the market, and the failures associated with all forms of central economic planning. But again and again, the officially neutral, value-free economists appeal to biblical notions of peace and prosperity. The idea of value-free science is a myth. So it is time to take up where Moses left off: with a challenge to humanistic economics.

Readers will find that I cite the writings of many economists and social thinkers. I use their insights — insights that are *stolen from the Bible* when they are correct. When men come to conclusions that are also the conclusions of the Bible, we should use their discoveries. These discoveries are our property, not theirs. God owns the world; the devil owns nothing. We are God's adopted children; they are God's disinherited children. Therefore, I am quite willing to cite secular scholars at length, since I know that most readers have neither the time nor access to the sources to follow up on every idea. I do not expect the majority of my readers to master the intricate details of every scholar's argument, nor master my refutations or applications of their insights.

When we read Christian refutations of this or that writer in books written a generation ago, let alone a century or a millennium ago, we find that the reading is slow going. "Why did the authors

---

1. Karl Wittfogel, *Oriental Despotism: A Comparative Study of Total Power* (New Haven, Connecticut: Yale University Press, 1957), reprinted in 1981 by Vintage Books.

spend so much space dealing with such dead issues?" we ask ourselves. The answer is simple: because when the books were written, those issues were not dead. Similarly, a hundred years from now, any readers who may stumble across this book will skim over most of its extended quotations. Few works of scholarship in one generation survive into the next, and the writers I cite or refute will be long-forgotten for the most part. Indeed, many of them are not well-known today. I am not devoting time simply to refute every erroneous idea in sight; I am using these citations as examples, as springboards to introduce explicitly biblical interpretations. The scholars I cite are very often foils for me; I want readers to know that such ideas exist and need refuting or reinterpreting.

The most important thing is how well I integrate such humanistic insights into my biblical reconstruction of economics, without 1) losing the importance of these insights or 2) becoming a slave of the humanist presuppositions which officially undergird such insights. But this is the most important task in any field. Every Christian faces this problem. We buy and sell with pagans in many marketplaces, and one of these marketplaces is the marketplace for ideas. We must use their best ideas against them, and we must expose their worst ideas in order to undermine men's confidence in them. In short, in God's universe, it is a question of "heads, we win; tails, they lose."

The Outrage of the Christian Classroom Compromisers

It is important to understand from the beginning that the perspective expounded in this book is unpopular in academic Christian circles. Two economic ideas dominate the thinking of the twentieth century: the idea of central economic planning, and the idea of the "mixed economy," meaning interventionism by the civil government into the economy: Keynesianism, fascism, or the corporate state. Men have had great confidence in the economic wisdom of the State, at least until the 1970's. Most Christian academics in the social sciences still go along enthusiastically with some variant of this statist ideology. Thus, when they are confronted with what the Bible *really* teaches in the field of political economy, they react in horror.

Most amusingly, one of these interventionists has accused me of holding Enlightenment ideas,[2] not realizing that he and his associ-

---

2. Ronald Sider, *Rich Christians in an Age of Hunger* (rev. ed.; Downers Grove, Illinois: Inter-Varsity Press, 1984), p. 102.

ates are the true heirs of the dominant Enlightenment tradition, the tradition which exalts the State. When these "radical Christian" critics think "Enlightenment," they think "Adam Smith." They obviously do not understand the Enlightenment. When we look at the historical results of the Enlightenment, we should think "French Revolution, Russian Revolution, and President Franklin Roosevelt's New Deal." We should think "the glorification of the State."

The Enlightenment had its right wing, of course, and Adam Smith was in it, but he was heavily influenced by the moral ideals of Deism, which were in turn a pale reflection of Christian theism.[3] But this individualistic tradition barely survived the revolutionary and statist Enlightenment heritage. What the successful bearers of the torch of the Enlightenment did was to set Europe on fire—in the name of liberty, fraternity, and equality. James Billington's book has described it well: *Fire in the Minds of Men* (1980). It was the left wing of the Enlightenment which triumphed. When men deify mankind, they almost always wind up deifying the State, the highest collective of mankind, the apotheosis of man's power. They become adherents of the power religion.

I reject all Enlightenment thought. This is why I reject most of what is taught in your typical Christian college. The baptized humanism of the modern Christian college classroom, especially in the social sciences and humanities, has led many people astray. This is one reason why I wrote my little book, *75 Bible Questions Your Instructors Pray You Won't Ask* (P.O. Box 7999, Tyler, Texas: Spurgeon Press, 1984; $4.95). It is subtitled, "How to Spot Humanism in the Classroom and the Pulpit." There is a lot of it to spot. The book is an antidote to baptized humanism.

What the typical Christian college course in the social sciences teaches is left-wing Enlightenment thought: naive Kantianism, warmed-over Darwinism, armchair Marxism (especially his theory of class consciousness and the innate disharmony of interests), and the discarded economic policies of some Presidential administration of a decade and a half earlier. It is all taught in the name of Jesus, in the interests of "Christian social concern" and "relevant Christianity." They fight that great bugaboo of 1880-1900, Social Darwinism (which hardly anyone has ever believed in), in the name of Christian-

---

3. Adam Smith, *The Theory of Moral Sentiments* (1759), with a new introduction by E. G. West (Indianapolis, Indiana: Liberty Classics, 1976).

ity, but they do so by means of the same arguments that the founders
of the dominant intellectual stream, Darwinian central planning,
used against the Social Darwinists.[4] They peddle the conclusions of
the really dangerous brand of Darwinism — the Darwinism of the
planning elite[5] — in the name of Christianity.

The hue and cry against my explicitly revelational Christian economics has now been raised in the unread little journals of the Christian academic community.[6] What has offended them most is the
heavy reliance I place on Old Testament law. On this point, they are
in agreement with the antinomian pietists: all such laws are no
longer binding.[7]

Why this hostility to Old Testament law, or even New Testament
"instructions"? Because Old Testament law categorically rejects the
use of taxes to promote statist social welfare programs. It categorically rejects the idea of State power in coercive wealth-redistribution
programs. Samuel warned the people against raising up a king, for
the king would take ten percent of their income (I Sam. 8:15, 17). He
promised that the State would, in short, extract the equivalent of
God's tithe from the hapless citizenry. And in the twentieth century,
most modern industrial civil governments extract four to five times
God's tithe. The tax policies of the modern welfare State are therefore immoral. More than this: they are demonic.

"Proof texting, proof texting!" cry the church-attending Dar-

---

4. The best introduction to the history of this subject is Sidney Fine, *Laissez Faire
and the General-Welfare State: A Study of Conflict in American Thought, 1865-1901* (Ann Ar-
bor: University of Michigan Press, 1956).

5. Gary North, *The Dominion Covenant: Genesis,* Appendix A: "From Cosmic Purposelessness to Humanistic Sovereignty."

6. See, for example, the essay by Thomas E. Van Dahm, professor of economics
at Carthage College (which I had never before heard of), "The Christian Far Right
and the Economic Role of the State," *Christian Scholars Review,* XII (1983), pp. 17-36.
He peddled another diatribe, this time against the biblical case for the gold standard, to *The Journal of the American Scientific Affiliation,* XXXVII (March 1984): "The
Christian Far Right and Economic Policy Issues." This journal originally devoted its
space to essays critical of the six-day creation position, but in recent years, it has
branched out, publishing articles that deny the legitimacy of applying Old Testament biblical standards in many other academic areas besides geology and biology.

7. Van Dahm writes: "This article did not deal with the basic issue of whether Old
Testament laws and even New Testament 'instructions' are binding on Christians — and others — in contemporary society. A recent treatment of this issue,
offering a definite 'no' answer I found persuasive is Walter J. Chantry's *God's Righteous Kingdom. . . ."* *JASA,* p. 35, footnote 44. Here we have it: the defenders of
power religion (statist planning) join hands with the defenders of escapist religion
(antinomian pietism) in their opposition to dominion religion (biblical law).

winists of the college classroom. ("Proof texting" apparently means citing a biblical passage which undercuts their position.) These men think that John Maynard Keynes' *General Theory* (which, in fact, they have never read, since practically no one ever has, so convoluted are its language and arguments) is the essence of permanent truth, on a par with Newton's *Principia* (which they also have never read). On the other hand, they regard the Old Testament as "the Word of God (emeritus)."

Perhaps the most notable example of this sort of thinking is the "Keynesian-Christian" economist, Professor (emeritus) Douglas Vickers. He has adopted Keynes' economic theories in the name of Jesus, but he has not adopted Keynes' economy of language. Thus, he does his best to refute my approach to economics with arguments such as this one: ". . . it is the economist's task so to understand the deeper determinants of economic conjectures and affairs that his policy prescriptions can be intelligently and properly shaped toward their proper ordering, or, where it is considered necessary, their correction and resolution. This should be done in such a way as to accord with the demands of both those deeper causal complexes now perceived in the light of God's word and purpose, and the requirements and basic desiderata of economic thought and administration."[8] This is what he substitutes for "Thus saith the Lord!" His book has yet to go into a second printing. I can understand why not.

These scholars regard the Old Testament as a kind of discarded first draft. Now that God has wisely seen fit to revise it (that is, now that He has completely replaced it), they argue, it is wrong to appeal to it as the basis for the construction of a Christian social order.[9] But the Christian Reconstructionists continue to appeal to all Old Testament laws that have not been explicitly revised by the New Testament. So the classroom scholars are outraged; they are incensed; they threaten to hold their breath until they turn blue if Reconstructionists keep writing books like this one. They have sounded the alarm. But nobody pays much attention to them. This enrages them even more. Their temper tantrums probably will get even worse. It is best to ignore them. They have bet on the wrong horse — the welfare State — and they resent anyone who tries to embarrass, let alone shoot, this aging horse.

---

8. Douglas Vickers, *Economics and Man: Prelude to a Christian Critique* (Nutley, New Jersey: Craig Press, 1976), p. 90.

9. See, for example, Vickers' remarks to this effect: *ibid.*, pp. 47-48.

The End of an Era

The fires of the Enlightenment are beginning to burn low. The civilization of the Enlightenment is losing confidence in its own principles. Perhaps even more important, *it is beginning to lose faith in the future.* The American historian-sociologist Robert Nisbet has put it well:

> It was belief in the sacred and the mythological that in the beginning of Western history made possible belief in and assimilation of ideas of time, history, development, and either progress or regress. Only on the basis of confidence in the existence of divine power was confidence possible with respect to design or pattern in the world and in the history of the world. . . .
>
> But it is absent now, whether ever to be recovered, we cannot know. And with the absence of the sense of sacredness of knowledge there is now to be seen in more and more areas absence of real respect for or confidence in knowledge — that is, the kind of knowledge that proceeds from reason and its intrinsic disciplines. From the Enlightenment on, an increasing number of people came to believe that reason and its works could maintain a momentum and could preserve their status in society with no influence save which they themselves generated. But the present age of the revolt against reason, of crusading irrationalism, of the almost exponential development and diffusion of the occult, and the constant spread of narcicissm and solipsism make evident enough how fallible were and are the secular foundations of modern thought. It is inconceivable that faith in either progress as a historical reality or in progress as a possibility can exist for long, to the degree that either concept does exist at the present moment, amid such alien and hostile intellectual forces.[10]

The leaders of this staggering humanist civilization have now adopted the strategy of every dying civilization which has ever lost the confidence of its citizens: they resort to the exercise of raw power. This was the strategy of the Roman Empire, and it failed.[11] This *substitution of power for ethics* is the essence of the satanic delusion. It is the essence of the power religion. It also is the essence of failure.

What will replace this phase of humanist civilization? Some version of the society which Solzhenitsyn has called the Gulag Ar-

---

10. Robert Nisbet, *History of the Idea of Progress* (New York: Basic Books, 1980), p. 355.

11. Charles Norris Cochrane, *Christianity and Classical Culture: A Study of Thought and Action from Augustus to Augustine* (New York: Oxford University Press, [1944] 1957).

chipelago? As a form of judgment, this is possible. God used Assyria and Babylon as rods of iron to bring Israel to repentance. Or will it be the steady grinding down of freedom by the West's massive bureaucracies? This was Max Weber's vision of the future of the West, and it is not a pretty picture.[12] It has also come progressively true since he wrote his warnings from 1905 to 1920. Or will it be a new society based on a religious revival? Nisbet has seen this as a real possibility: "Much more probable, I believe, is the appearance of yet another full-blown 'awakening,' even a major religious reformation. For some time now we have been witnessing what might properly be called the beginnings of such a transformation, beginnings which range from popular to scholarly, from eruptions of fundamentalism, pentecostalism—and, even within the Jewish, Roman Catholic and Protestant establishments, millennialism—all the way to what has to be regarded as a true efflorescence of formal theology."[13]

The time has come for a program of Christian reconstruction. Something new must replace humanism, from the bottom up, in every sphere of human existence. The dominion religion must replace the power religion. Humanism's world is collapsing, both intellectually and institutionally, and it will drag the compromised Christian academic world into the abyss with it. That is where they both belong. Weep not for their passing. And if you happen to spot some aspect of humanism which is beginning to wobble, take an appropriate action. Push it.

Liberation from the State

The liberation theologians keep appealing to the Book of Exodus as their very special book. Michael Walzer's study of Exodus calls this assertion into question. Walzer's earlier studies of the Puritan revolution established him as an authority in the field. His study of Exodus argues that this story has affected politics in the West, especially radical politics, for many centuries. But it is a story which does not fit the model used by liberation theologians, whose enemy is the free market social order. As he says, the Israelites "were not the victims of the market but of the state, the absolute monarchy of the pharaohs. Hence, Samuel's warning to the elders of Israel against

---

12. Gary North, "Max Weber: Rationalism, Irrationalism, and the Bureaucratic Cage," in North (ed.), *Foundations of Christian Scholarship: Essays in the Van Til Perspective* (Vallecito, California: Ross House, 1976).

13. Nisbet, *op. cit.,* p. 357.

choosing a king. . . . Egyptian bondage was the bondage of a people to the arbitrary power of the state."[14]

The misuse of the Exodus story by liberation theologians is another example of the misuse of the Bible generally to promote anti-biblical social, political, and economic views. This is why practical commentaries dealing with specific disciplines are needed. The Bible still commands great authority, and this public perception of the Bible's authority is increasing, especially regarding social issues. This willingness on the part of social critics to appeal to the Bible is itself a major break with the recent past, yet a return to a more distant past.

Prior to 1660, it was common for conservatives and radicals to appeal to the Bible to defend their visions of a righteous social order. Almost overnight, in 1660, this appeal to the Bible ended. Defenders of the free market appealed to logic or experience rather than "debatable" religious or moral views.[15] Socialists and reformers also dropped their appeal to the Bible after 1660, again, almost overnight. Shafarevich writes: "The development of socialist ideas did not cease, of course. On the contrary, in the seventeenth and eighteenth centuries, socialist writings literally flooded Europe. But these ideas were produced by different circumstances and by men of a different mentality. The preacher and the wandering Apostle gave way to a publicist and philosopher. Religious exaltation and references to revelation were replaced by appeals to reason. The literature of socialism acquired a purely secular and rationalistic character; new means of poularization were devised: works on this theme now frequently appear under the guise of voyages to unknown lands, interlarded with frivolous episodes."[16]

The Exodus was a time of liberation — liberation from the statist social order that had been created by adherents of the power religion. The spiritual heirs of those statist Egyptians are now coming before the spiritual heirs of the Israelites with a new claim: the need to be liberated from the institutions of the once-Christian West. They offer chains in the name of liberation, bureaucracy in the name of individual freedom, and central economic planning in the name of

---

14. Michael Walzer, *Exodus and Revolution* (New York: Basic Books, 1985), p. 30.

15. William Letwin, *The Origins of Scientific Economics* (Garden City, New York: Anchor, 1965), ch. 6.

16. Igor Shafarevich, *The Socialist Phenomenon* (New York: Harper & Row, [1975] 1980), pp. 80-81.

prosperity. They offer men a return to power religion in the name of the God of the Bible. What this commentary offers, in contrast, is a call for men to return to dominion religion — the religion of biblical orthodoxy.

How to Read This Book

There is an old line that asks: "How do you eat an elephant?" The answer: "One bite at a time." That rule should be applied to this book.

Yes, this is a fat book. Some of its chapters are lengthy, but they are broken down into convenient sections and subsections. The idea is not to memorize each chapter. The idea is to get a general sense of what happens in the field of economics when rival religions clash: *power religion* vs. *dominion religion*. If you want to follow up on any particular idea, footnotes are provided at no extra charge — and at the bottom of the page, too, so that you will not spend extra time flipping to the back of the book. Footnotes are there to help you, not to intimidate you.

Read the conclusions of each chapter before you read the chapter. Then skim over it rapidly. If it seems worth your time, reread it more carefully. You can read this book a chapter at a time, since it is a commentary. It deals with one or two verses at a time. The book develops its chain of arguments only insofar as the verses show a progression. I think they do reveal a progression, but not so rigorous a progression as you would find in a logic textbook, or even an economics textbook (Keynes' *General Theory* excluded, since it substitutes confusion for progression).[17]

Subsequent sections of this commentary on Exodus will cover the Ten Commandments and the biblical case laws that apply the principles of the Ten Commandments to society.[18]

---

17. One of the reasons why I am sure that his *General Theory* is a classic example of deliberate "disinformation" is that most of Keynes' other books are models of logic and clarity. But the *General Theory* is nearly unreadable. He was writing nonsense, and the book reflects it. For a good introduction to this classic example of jargon-filled nonsense, see Henry Hazlitt's book, *The Failure of the "New Economics"* (Princeton, New Jersey: Van Nostrand, 1959). Hazlitt never went to college, so he was not fooled by Keynes, something two generations of Ph.D.-holding power religionists cannot say for themselves. For more technical scholarly critiques, written quite early in response to Keynes by economists who were not power religionists, see Hazlitt (ed.), *The Critics of Keynesian Economics* (Van Nostrand, 1960).

18. See also James B. Jordan, *The Law of the Covenant: An Exposition of Exodus 21-23* (Tyler, Texas: Institute for Christian Economics, 1984).

INTRODUCTION

This book is about a clash between two religions, with believers in a third religion standing on the sidelines, waiting to see the outcome of the clash. The Bible presents it as the archetypal clash in history between these two religions. This confrontation has been going on since the garden of Eden. The first of the conflicting religions was power religion, the religion of Pharaoh, who was Satan's representative in the battle. The second was dominion religion, the religion of Moses, God's representative in this mighty battle. The testimony of the Book of Exodus is clear: first, *those who seek power apart from God are doomed to comprehensive, total defeat.* Second, those who seek God are called to exercise dominion, and they shall be victorious over the enemies of God. But this victory takes time. It is not achieved instantaneously. It is the product of long years of *self-discipline under God's authority.* The power religionists do not want to wait. Like Adam in his rebellion, sinners choose to dress themselves in the robes of authority, so that they can render instant autonomous judgment.[1] They do not want to subordinate themselves to God.

The third form of religion is what I call escapist religion. It is a religion which proclaims the inevitability of external defeat for the people of God. The defenders of temporal impotence thereby become the allies of temporal power. This religion was dominant in the lives of the Hebrew slaves. They became easy prey for the power religionists. But when the power manifested by dominion religion overcame the pagan power religion, they grudgingly followed the victors.

Before discussing the specifics of the clash between Moses and Pharaoh, it is necessary to survey briefly the first principles of these three religious outlooks.

---

1. Gary North, "Witnesses and Judges," *Biblical Economics Today,* VI (Aug./Sept. 1983), pp. 3-4.

1

1. *Power Religion*

This is a religious viewpoint which affirms that the most important goal for a man, group, or species, is the capture and maintenance of power. Power is seen as the chief attribute of God, or if the religion is officially atheistic, then the chief attribute of man. This perspective is a satanic perversion of God's command to man to exercise dominion over all the creation (Gen. 1:26-28).[2] It is the attempt to exercise dominion apart from covenantal subordination to the true Creator God.

What distinguishes biblical dominion religion from satanic power religion is *ethics*. Is the person who seeks power doing so for the glory of God, and for himself secondarily, and only to the extent that he is God's lawful and covenantally faithful representative? If so, he will act in terms of God's ethical standards and in terms of a profession of faith in the God of the Bible. The church has recognized this two-fold requirement historically, and has established a dual requirement for membership: profession of faith and a godly life.

In contrast, power religion is a religion of *autonomy*. It affirms that "My power and the might of mine hand hath gotten me this wealth" (Deut. 8:17). It seeks power or wealth in order to make credible this very claim.

Wealth and power are aspects of both religions. Wealth and power are covenantal manifestations of the success of rival religious views. This is why God warns His people not to believe that their autonomous actions gained them their blessings: "But thou shalt remember the LORD thy God: for it is he that giveth thee power to get wealth, that he may establish his covenant which he sware unto thy fathers, as it is this day" (Deut. 8:18). God's opponents also want visible confirmation of the validity of their covenant with a rival god, but God warns them that "the wealth of the sinner is laid up for the just" (Prov. 13:22b). The entry of the Hebrews into Canaan was supposed to remind them of this fact: the Canaanites had built homes and vineyards to no avail; their enemies, the Hebrews, inherited them (Josh. 24:13).

Those who believe in power religion have refused to see that long-term wealth in any society is the product of ethical conformity

---

2. Gary North, *The Dominion Covenant: Genesis,* vol. 1 of *An Economic Commentary on the Bible* (Tyler, Texas: Institute for Christian Economics, 1982).

to biblical law. They have sought the blessings of God's covenant while denying the validity and eternally binding ethical standards of that covenant. In short, they have confused the fruits of Christianity with the roots. They have attempted to chop away the roots but preserve the fruits.

2. *Escapist Religion*

This is the second great tradition of anti-Christian religion. Seeing that the exercise of autonomous power is a snare and a delusion, the proponents of escapist religion have sought to insulate themselves from the general culture—a culture maintained by power. They have fled the responsibilities of worldwide dominion, or even regional dominion, in the hope that God will release them from the requirements of the general dominion covenant.

The Christian version of the escapist religion is sometimes called "pietism," but its theological roots can be traced back to the ancient heresy of *mysticism*. Rather than proclaiming the requirement of *ethical union* with Jesus Christ, the perfect man, the mystic calls for *metaphysical union* with a monistic, unified god. In the early church, there were many types of mysticism, but the most feared rival religion which continually infiltrated the church was *gnosticism*. It proclaimed many doctrines, but the essence of gnostic faith was *radical personal individualism*—personal escape from matter—leading to *radical impersonal collectivism:* the abolition of human personality through absorption into the Godhead. It proclaimed retreat from the material realm and escape to a higher, purer, spiritual realm through various "Eastern" techniques of self-manipulation: asceticism, higher consciousness, and initiation into secret mysteries.

Gnosticism survives as a way of thinking and acting (or failing to act) even today, as Rushdoony has pointed out. The essence of this faith is its *antinomianism*. Gnostics despise biblical law. But their hatred for the law of God leads them to accept the laws of the State. "Gnosticism survives today in theosophy, Jewish Kabbalism, occultism, existentialism, masonry, and like faiths. Because Gnosticism made the individual, rather than a dualism of mind and matter, ultimate, it was essentially hostile to morality and law, requiring often that believers live beyond good and evil by denying the validity of all moral law. Gnostic groups which did not openly avow such doctrines affirmed an ethic of love as against law, negating law and morality in terms of the 'higher' law and morality of love. Their contempt of law and time manifested itself also by a willingness to comply with the state. . . . The usual attitude was one of contempt for the material world, which included the state, and an outward compliance and indifference. A philosophy calling for an escape from time is not likely to involve itself in the battles of time."[3]

Their denial of the continuing validity of biblical law has led them to deny the relevance of earthly time. By denying biblical law, they thereby foresake the chief tool of dominion — our means of using time to subdue the earth to the glory of God. The basic idea which undergirds escapist religion is the *denial of the dominion covenant.* The escapist religionists believe that the techniques of self-discipline, whether under God or apart from God (Buddhism), offer power over only limited areas of life. They attempt to conserve their power by focusing their ethical concern on progressively (regressively) narrower areas of personal responsibility. The "true believer" thinks that he will gain more control over himself and his narrow environment by restricting his self-imposed zones of responsibility. His concern is *self*, from start to finish; his attempt to escape from responsibilities beyond the narrow confines of self is a program for gaining power over self. It is a religion of works, of *self-salvation.* A man "humbles" himself — admits that there are limits to his power, and therefore limits to the range of his responsibilities — only to elevate self to a position of hypothetically God-like spirituality.

Escapist religion proclaims institutional peace — "peace at any price." Ezekiel responded to such an assertion in the name of God: ". . . they have seduced my people, saying, Peace; and there was no peace" (Ezk. 13:10a). Patrick Henry's inflammatory words in March of 1775 — "Peace, peace — but there is no peace"[4] — were taken from Ezekiel and also Jeremiah: "They have healed also the hurt of the daughter of my people slightly, saying, Peace, peace; when there is no peace" (Jer. 6:14). This rival religion proclaims peace because it has little interest in the systematic efforts that are always required to purify institutions as a prelude to social reconstruction.

---

3. Rousas John Rushdoony, *The One and the Many: Studies in the Philosophy of Order and Ultimacy* (Fairfax, Virginia: Thoburn Press, [1971] 1978), p. 129.

4. Norine Dickson Campbell, *Patrick Henry: Patriot and Statesman* (Old Greenwich, Connecticut: Devin-Adair, 1969), p. 130. The substance of Henry's famous St. John's Church speech, which mobilized the Virginia Assembly, was reconstructed by a later historian, William Wirt, but is generally considered representative. This was Henry's famous "Give me liberty or give me death" speech, one of the most famous speeches in U.S. history.

In short, escapist religion calls for flight from the world, and because man is in this world, it calls for *a flight from humanity.*[5] Its advocates may hide their real concern—the systematic abandonment of a world supposedly so corrupt that nothing can be done to overcome widespread cultural evil—by appealing to their moral responsibility of "sharing Christ to the world" or "building up the Church" rather than rebuilding civilization, but their ultimate concern is *personal flight from responsibility.* It is a revolt against maturity.[6]

3. *Dominion Religion*

This is the orthodox faith. It proclaims the sovereignty of God, the reliability of the historic creeds, the necessity of standing up for principle, and the requirement that faithful men take risks for God's sake. It proclaims that through the exercise of saving faith, and through ethical conformity to God's revealed law, regenerate men will increase the extent of their dominion over the earth. It is a religion of conquest—*conquest by grace through ethical action.* The goal is ethical conformity to God, but the results of this conformity involve dominion—over lawful subordinates, over ethical rebels, and over nature. This is the message of Deuteronomy 28:1-14. It is also the message of Jesus Christ, who walked perfectly in God's statutes and in God's Spirit, and who then was granted total power over all creation by the Father (Matt. 28:18). I am not speaking here of Christ's divine nature as the Second Person of the Trinity, who always had total power; I am speaking of His nature as perfect man, who *earned* total power through ethical conformity to God and through His death and resurrection.

Dominion religion recognizes the relationship between *righteousness* and *authority,* between covenantal faithfulness and covenantal blessings. Those who are faithful in little things are given more. This is the meaning of Christ's parable of the talents (Matt. 25:14-30). The process of dominion is a function of *progressive sanctification,* both personal-individual and institutional (family, church, business, school, civil government, etc.: Deut. 28:1-14).

---

5. R. J. Rushdoony, *The Flight from Humanity: A Study of the Effect of Neoplatonism on Christianity* (Fairfax, Virginia: Thoburn Press, [1973] 1978).

6. R. J. Rushdoony, *Revolt Against Maturity: A Biblical Psychology of Man* (Fairfax, Virginia: Thoburn Press, 1977).

Moses vs. Pharaoh

Pick up any commentary on the Book of Exodus. Read its account of the first fifteen chapters. You will find a lot of discussion of Hebrew vocabulary, Moses' theology, and the sovereignty of God's power. But what you will not find is a detailed discussion of Egypt. You will not find an analysis of the theology and culture of the society which placed the Hebrews under bondage. You will not find a discussion of the relationship between Egypt's theology and Egypt's economic and political institutions.

These are remarkable omissions. It is not that commentators have no knowledge about Egypt. Rather, it is that they have failed to understand the theological and political issues that were inherent in this confrontation. Sufficient information is available to construct at least an outline of Egyptian society. While Egyptology is a highly specialized and linguistically rigorous field of study, there are numerous scholarly summaries of the religion and social institutions of Egypt. I am no specialist in this field, and I have no immediate access to a large university library of books and manuscripts relating to Egypt, but interlibrary loans and normal intelligence are sufficient to "open the closed book" of at least the bare essentials of Egyptian thought and culture. The bare essentials are sufficient to enable anyone to draw some simple conclusions concerning the differences between the gods of Egypt and the God of the Israelites. Furthermore, it is not that difficult to make other comparisons: socialism vs. market freedom, bureaucracy vs. decentralized decision-making, the omniscient State vs. limited civil government, static society vs. future-oriented society, stagnation vs. growth. Yet the commentators, as far as I have been able to determine, have systematically refused to discuss such issues. They have been blind to the all-encompassing nature of the confrontation. To a great extent, this is because they have been blind to the implications of biblical religion for both social theory and institutions.

Chronology

There are other topics that need to be discussed. One of the most important is the problem of chronology. Commentaries can be found that do attempt to deal with this issue, but I have yet to find one which openly faces the overwhelming difficulties posed by the almost universal acceptance of the conventional chronology of Egypt. What readers are not told is that *Egyptians did not believe in chronology.* The historical records which modern (and even classical Greek) historians have used to reconstruct Egypt's chronology are woefully deficient. The Egyptians simply did not take seriously their own history. They did not believe in the importance of linear time. The records they left reflect their lack of concern. A century ago, historian George Rawlinson began his chapter on Egyptian chronology with this statement: "It is a patent fact, and one that is beginning to obtain general recognition, that the chronological element in early Egyptian history is in a state of almost hopeless obscurity."[7] He was incorrect, however, concerning the coming "general recognition" of the problem. Only the most scholarly and detailed monographs on Egypt bother to warn readers about the problem.

There are several kinds of chronological documents, including the actual monuments. "The chronological value of these various sources of information is, however, in every case slight. The great defect of these monuments is their incompleteness. The Egyptians had no era. They drew out no chronological schemes. They cared for nothing but to know how long each incarnate god, human or bovine, had condescended to tarry on the earth. They recorded carefully the length of the life of each Apis bull, and the length of the reign of each king; but they neglected to take note of the intervals between one Apis bull and another, and omitted to distinguish the sole reign of a monarch from his joint reign with others."[8]

Readers are also not informed of the fact that virtually all chronologies of the ancient Near East and pre-classical Greece are constructed on the assumption that the conventional chronology of Egypt is the legitimate standard. What modern scholars believe is the proper chronology of Egypt is then *imposed on the chonologies of all other civilizations of the ancient Near East,* including the biblical chronology of the Hebrews. Thus, when the Bible says explicitly that the Exodus took place 480 years before Solomon began to construct the temple (I Kings 6:1), historians interpret this information within the framework of the hypothetical Egyptian chronological scheme. When they even admit that the pharaohs of the supposed dynastic era of the fifteenth century before Christ were extremely powerful kings—men like Thutmose III—whose mummies still exist,[9] they

---

7. George Rawlinson, *A History of Egypt*, 2 vols. (New York: Alden, 1886), II, p. 1.
8. *Ibid.,* II, p. 2.
9. Photographs of the mummies of Thutmose III and Amenhotep II appear in Donovan Courville, *The Exodus Problem and Its Ramifications*, 2 vols. (Loma Linda, California: Challenge Books, 1971), I, p. 37.

are tempted to ignore these difficulties, or even to ignore the clear
teaching of the Bible. Many of them date the Exodus much later.
They allow a hypothetical chronology of Egypt to dictate their interpretation of Scripture. This is not the way that Christian scholarship
is supposed to be conducted.

In the early 1950's, Immanuel Velikovsky, a genius (or fraud, his
critics say) began to publish a series of studies that reconstructed
(among other things) the chronologies of the ancient world. Velikovsky began his reconstruction with a discussion of an ancient Egyptian document, long overlooked by historians, which contains references to a series of catastrophes that look remarkably similar to those
described in early chapters of the Book of Exodus.

Then, in 1971, an amateur historian named Donovan Courville
published a book which was based in part on Velikovsky's work, but
which went far beyond it. Courville's book has been systematically
ignored by Egyptologists and Christian scholars alike. I know of one
case where a seminary professor absolutely refused to discuss the
book with his students, either publicly or privately, when asked
about it. Why the hostility? Because Courville's book, like Velikovsky's books, offers a frontal assault on the reigning presuppositions of
historians regarding the reliability of Egyptian records and the
reliability of the conclusions based on them. In Courville's case, the
affront is worse: he is saying that Christian specialists in the field of
ancient history have accepted the testimony of humanist (Darwinian) scholars and humanist (Egyptian) records in preference to the
clear testimony of the Bible. Conservative scholars resent the implication that they have compromised their scholarship in order to seek
recognition from (or avoid confrontation with) the conventional,
dominant humanist academic community. Thus, I have seen no
commentary on the Book of Exodus which refers to (let alone promotes) either Velikovsky or Courville, nor do the standard Christian
encyclopedias.

This commentary is the exception. For this reason, it represents
a break with prevailing scholarship concerning the circumstances of
the Exodus. It may be incorrect, but it is incorrect in new
ways — ways that do not begin with the presupposition that conventional humanist historical scholarship is binding, or the presupposition that the biblical account of history is inferior to the Egyptian
record. My position is clear: it is better to make mistakes within an
intellectual framework which is governed by the presupposition of

the Bible's infallibility than it is to make mistakes that are governed by the presupposition that Darwinian scholarship is the eternal standard of truth.

Confrontation

The first fifteen chapters of the Book of Exodus deal with the confrontation between God and Egypt. This confrontation was comprehensive. It involved a dispute between two radically different worldviews. It involved a war between the God of the Hebrews and a false god called Pharaoh. Every aspect of civilization was at stake. It was not "merely" a war over theology as such. It was a war over *theology as life.* This commentary brings into the open several areas of confrontation that previously have not been discussed. These subordinate areas of confrontation were inescapably linked to the main confrontation between God and Pharaoh. Amazingly, the terms of even this primary confrontation are seldom discussed.

It is my contention that essentially the same confrontation has continued from the beginning, meaning from the garden of Eden. It has manifested itself in many ways, but the essential question never changes: *Who is God?* Secondarily, *what is the relationship between God and His creation?* The answers given by the rulers of Egypt were essentially the same answer proposed to man by Satan: "ye shall be as gods" (Gen. 3:5). Because the modern world has come to a similar theological conclusion — that, in the absence of any other God, man must be the only reliable candidate — the modern world has come to similar social and economic conclusions. The rise of totalitarian bureaucracies in the twentieth century can and should be discussed in relation to the rise of a humanistic variation of Egyptian theology. It is not that humanists have adopted Egypt's polytheism (though modern relativism sounds suspiciously like polytheism), but rather that they have, as Darwinians (or worse), adopted Egypt's theology of the *continuity of being,* with the State, as the most powerful representative of "collective mankind," serving as the primary agency of social organization.

The remaining chapters in the Book of Exodus describe the continuation of this same confrontation with Egypt. In this case, however, the departing slaves of the now-smashed Egyptian civilization replaced their former rulers as the defenders of the old order. God dealt with them in very similar ways, though with greater mercy, as a result of Moses' prayer on behalf of the integrity of God's name and

God's promises (Ex. 32:9-14; Num. 14:13-16).

It should not surprise us, therefore, that there are still many, many Christian defenders of that same old statist order in our wilderness wanderings (especially in the barren wastes of the college and seminary classroom) — slaves who have not recognized the freedom which God has offered to His people through the establishing of His revealed law-order. When men sit as slaves for too long at the table of the Satanists, hoping for a few crumbs (or academic degrees) to fall from their table, they find it difficult to imagine that *it is the enemies of God who are supposed to sit at the table of the righteous,* begging for scraps until the day of judgment provides them with no further opportunities for repentance (Matt. 15:22-28). Let us not forget that it was a Canaanite woman, not a ruler of Israel, who first articulated this principle of biblical government. Israel's leaders were sitting at the table of the Romans, begging. Some things haven't changed.

Conclusion

Three and a half millennia ago, Moses was commanded by God to confront the Pharaoh. The result was the Exodus, the archetype historical event in the life of Israel, the event to which the prophets appealed again and again in their confrontations with the rebellious Hebrews of their day. This same confrontation goes on in every era, and the contemporary prophet must be equally willing to confront the pharaohs of his day with the same theological distinctions: sovereign God or sovereign man, God's revelation or man's revelation, biblical society or the bureaucratic State, God's law or chaos. "Choose this day whom ye will serve." Serve God or perish.

POPULATION GROWTH:
TOOL OF DOMINION

And all the souls that came out of the loins of Jacob were seventy souls: for Joseph was in Egypt already. And Joseph died, and all his brethren, and all that generation. And the children of Israel were fruitful, and increased abundantly, and multiplied, and waxed exceeding mighty; and the land was filled with them (Ex. 1:5-7).

The words relating to growth are repeated in verse 7: fruitful, increased (teemed), multiplied, waxed (numerous), with exceeding strength, strongly, and filled — a seven-fold representation.[1] Bible-believing commentators have seldom focused much attention on these verses, possibly because they are so difficult to explain by means of their usual assumption, namely, that only 70 people originally descended into Egypt. How could it be that 70 people and their spouses multiplied to 600,000 men, plus women and children, by the time of the Exodus (Ex. 12:37)? A probable explanation is this one: the 70 were not the only source of the original population base. Presumably, they brought with them many *household servants who had been circumcised* and who were therefore counted as part of the covenant population. We do not know for certain how many of these circumcised household servants came, but it must have been in the thousands.

We should also bear in mind that "70" is a significant number in Scripture, in terms of age, chronology, and also in terms of numbering people. In Genesis 10, 70 peoples of mankind are listed, 14 from

---

1. U. Cassuto, *A Commentary on the Book of Exodus,* trans. Israel Abrahams (Jerusalem: Magnes Press, Hebrew University, [1951] 1974), p. 9. He says that the "seven expressions for increase are used in this verse, a number indicative of perfection. . . ."

Japheth, 30 from Ham, and 26 from Shem.[2] At the feast of tabernacles in the seventh month, beginning on the fifteenth day, the
priests were to begin a week of sacrifices. For seven days, a descending number of bullocks were to be sacrificed: 13, 12, 11, 10, 9, 8, and 7,
for a total of 70 bullocks. Then, on the eighth day (the beginning of
the next week), one final bullock was to be sacrificed (Num. 29:12-36).
Presumably, these were sacrifices for all the nations of the world, plus
Israel. There were 70 elders in Israel at the time of God's confirmation
of the covenant at Sinai (Ex. 24:1). God at one point took His Spirit
from Moses and gave it to the 70 elders (Num. 11:16). Also, when the
Israelites defeated Adoni-Bezek after the death of Joshua, he confessed
that he had slain 70 kings (Judges 1:7), presumably a number referring symbolically to the whole world. Seventy men were sent out by
Jesus to evangelize southern Israel (Luke 10:1, 17).[3] In Christ's day,
there were 70 members of the Sanhedrin, plus the President.[4] So the
number "70" meant for the Hebrews something like "a whole population," although this does not deny the validity of 70 as the number of
lineal heirs who came down into Egypt.

The growth of the Hebrew population has to be considered a remarkable expansion. How long did it take? This question has also
baffled Bible-believing commentators. When did the Exodus occur?
When did Jacob's family enter Egypt? Were the Israelites in Egypt a
full 430 years? Donovan Courville, the Seventh Day Adventist
scholar, has called this chronology question "the Exodus problem."[5]

---

2. Frederick Louis Godet, *Commentary on the Gospel of Luke,* 2 vols. (Grand Rapids,
Michigan: Zondervan, [1887]), II, p. 17. Godet discusses the problem of 70 vs. 72,
which occurs in this estimation, and also in the differing New Testament references
to the 70 or 72 sent out by Jesus (Luke 10:1).

3. Some manuscripts read 72. Godet argues that 70 is the correct reading: *idem.*

4. Alfred Edersheim, *The Life and Times of Jesus the Messiah,* 2 vols. (Grand Rapids, Michigan: Eerdmans, [1886]), II, p. 554. Cf. "Sanhedrim," in McClintock and
Strong, *Cyclopaedia of Biblical, Theological, and Ecclesiastical Literature* (New York: Harper & Bros., 1894), IX, p. 342.

5. Donovan A. Courville, *The Exodus Problem and Its Ramifications* (Loma Linda,
California: Challenge Books, 1971), 2 volumes. Courville's original insight concerning the need for a reconstruction of Egypt's chronology came from Immanuel
Velikovsky's study, *Ages in Chaos* (Garden City, New York: Doubleday, 1952), which
presents the case against the traditional chronologies of the ancient world. Velikovsky identified the Hyksos rulers ("shepherd kings") of Egypt as the invading Amelek-
ites. He argued that modern scholars have inserted a 500-700 year period into all the
histories of the ancient world (since all are based on Egypt's supposed chronology), a
period which must be eliminated. Velikovsky wrote that "we still do not know which
of the two histories, Egyptian or Israelite, must be readjusted" (p. 338). Courville's
book shows that it is modern scholarship's version of Egypt's chronology which is
defective, not the chronology of the Old Testament. See Appendix A: "The Reconstruction of Egypt's Chronology."

The Problem of Chronology

Exodus 12:40 reads as follows in the King James Version: "Now the sojourning of the children of Israel, who dwelt in Egypt, was four hundred and thirty years." *Fact number one:* a sojourn of 430 years. The Samaritan Pentateuch and the Septuagint (the Greek translation of the Old Testament dating from the second century B.C.) both say "Egypt and Canaan,"[6] rather than just "Egypt," which indicates the likely solution to the Exodus problem.

We can see the nature of the problem in Stephen's testimony, just prior to his martyrdom. It includes this statement: "And God spoke on this wise [in this way], That his seed should sojourn in a strange land; and that they should bring them into bondage, and entreat them evil four hundred years" (Acts 7:6). *Fact number two:* bondage of 400 years. This was also the period promised by God to Abraham: "Know of a surety that thy seed shall be a stranger in a land that is not their's, and shall serve them; and they shall afflict them four hundred years; And also that nation, whom they shall serve, will I judge: and afterward shall they come out with great substance" (Gen. 15:13-14). *Fact number three:* deliverance in the fourth generation. "But in the fourth generation they shall come hither again: for the iniquity of the Amorites is not yet full" (Gen. 15:16). Did God mean the fourth generation of captives? If the period of bondage was 430 years, how could only four generations have filled up the entire period assigned to them?

Paul provides additional crucial information: "Now to Abraham and his seed were the promises made. . . . And this I say, that the covenant, that was confirmed before of God in Christ, the law, which was four hundred and thirty years after, cannot disannul, that it should make the promise of none effect" (Gal. 3:16a, 17). *Fact number four:* 430 years from the covenant to the Exodus. This further complicates the problem: *the entire period, from Abraham to the Exodus, was 430 years* — a period which encompassed Isaac's life, Jacob's, Joseph in Egypt, the arrival of the brothers and their families, the years of prosperity and population growth in the land of Goshen in Egypt, Moses' birth, his departure at age 40, his 40 years in the wilderness, and the Exodus itself. Paul's language is unambiguous. What, then, are we to make of the other three accounts?

---

6. Note in the *New International Version* (Grand Rapids, Michigan: Zondervan, 1978), p. 83.

The Patriarchal Era: 215 Years

The best place to begin to unravel this problem is with the chronology of Abraham's family. We are told that he was called out of Haran when he was 75 years old (Gen. 12:4). Isaac was born 25 years later, when Abraham was a hundred (Gen. 21:5). Jacob and Esau were born 60 years later, when Isaac was 60 years old (Gen. 25:26). Finally, Jacob died at age 130 in Egypt (Gen. 47:9). Therefore, from Abraham's entrance into a foreign land until the Israelites' descent into Egypt, about 215 years elapsed (25 + 60 + 130). If we assume that the establishment of the covenant took place in the first year or so of Abraham's sojourn in Canaan, with 25 years in between the covenant (Gen. 15) and the birth of Isaac (Gen. 21), then we can begin to make sense of the data. God said that Abraham's heirs would be in *bondage* for *400* years, while Paul said it was *430* years from the *covenant to the Exodus.* If we subtract 25 from 430—from the covenant to the birth of Isaac, the promised son of the covenant line—we get 405 years. This is very close to the 400 years of the "affliction" promised in Genesis 15:13-14 and mentioned by Stephen in Acts 7:6.

We are now arguing about only five years, from the birth of Isaac to the period in which the captivity "in" Egypt—*under Egypt's domination*—began. We are told in Genesis 21 that it was only after Isaac was weaned that Ishmael mocked him—"laughing" in the Hebrew (vv. 8-9). This can be understood as the beginning of the period of Egyptian persecution, for Ishmael was half Egyptian.[7] It was the time of Isaac's youth, perhaps about age five. Abraham then expelled the Egyptian woman and her son, who travelled into the wilderness (21:14). Thus, it was not the bondage period in geographical Egypt that God had in mind, but the *entire period of pilgrimage,* during which they were afflicted by strangers.

Residence in Egypt: 215 Years

The culmination of this period of rootlessness, or life in foreign lands, was the final era of outright bondage in Egypt (Gen. 15:14). Courville's comments are appropriate, that

the period of affliction began back in the time of Abraham and not with the Descent. Actually, the affliction in Egypt did not begin with the Descent but

---

7. I am indebted to James Jordan for this insight. If it is incorrect, then we would have to adopt Courville's approach, namely, to argue that it seems legitimate to understand the 400 years of Gen. 15:13 as a rounding off of 405.

only with the rise of the king "who knew not Joseph." That the "sojourn" also began back in the time of Abraham is clear from the statement in Hebrews 11:9 which reads:

> By faith he [Abraham] sojourned in the land of promise, as in a strange country, dwelling in tabernacles with Isaac and Jacob, the heirs with him of the same promise.

Others of the ancients than Paul thus understood the 430-year sojourn. The translators of the Hebrew Scriptures into Greek have added a phrase to make clear the meaning of Exodus 12:40 as they understood it. The Septuagint reading of the verse is:

> The sojourning of the children and of their fathers, which they sojourned in the land of Canaan and in the land of Egypt. . . .

Josephus, as a Hebrew scholar of antiquity, thus understood the verse:

> They left Egypt in the month Xanthicus, on the fifteenth day of the lunar month; four hundred and thirty years after our forefather Abraham came into Canaan, but two hundred and fifteen years only after Jacob removed into Egypt.[8]

This citation from Courville's important study indicates that it was long ago understood that the 430 years of Exodus 12:40 must be interpreted in terms of *the entire pilgrimage experience, Abraham to Moses.* The reference to "the children of Israel" must be understood as *Hebrews in general,* not simply to those born of Jacob. It includes Abraham and Isaac. This means that Palestine was an Egyptian vassal region throughout the Patriarchal era of Exodus 12:40. It also helps to explain why Abraham journeyed to Egypt during the famine (Gen. 12:10). Egypt was the capital.

On the next page is Courville's chart of his proposed reconstructed chronology of Egypt and Israel.[9] Understand that Courville's book is almost unknown in Christian circles, and even less known in academic circles. His reconstructed chronology is not taken seriously by archeologists and historians, any more than Velikovsky's chronology in *Ages in Chaos* was (or is) taken seriously.

What Courville has accomplished is a brilliant reconstruction of Egypt's chronology in terms of the 215-215 division. He has pinpointed the famine as having begun 217 years before the Exodus,

---

8. *Ibid.,* I, p. 140. For Josephus' statement, see *Antiquities of the Jews,* Book II, ch. XV, sec. 2, in *Josephus: Complete Works,* William Whiston, translator (Grand Rapids, Michigan: Kregel, 1960), p. 62.

9. Taken from *The Journal of Christian Reconstruction,* II (Summer 1975), p. 145.

Correlation of Scriptural Incidents with Egyptian History
by the Traditional and Reconstructed Chronologies

Incident or Era	Traditional Background or Date	Reconstruction Background or Date
Noachian Flood	Not recognized as factual. The proper background for the immediate post-diluvian period is the Mesolithic period, dated *c.* 10,000 B.C. or earlier.	The Mesolithic background for the immediate post-diluvian period is accepted. Date *c.* 2300 B.C.
Dispersion from Babel	If recognized at all, the incident is set far back in the pre-dynastic.	Dated 27 years before the unification of Egypt under Mena. Date, *c.* 2125 B.C.
Abraham enters Canaan	Commonly set in early Dynasty XII dated *c.* 1900 B.C. Earlier dates are entertained.	Dated very soon after the beginning of Dynasty IV; 1875 B.C.
Famine of Joseph	No famine inscription datable to the era of Joseph as placed in the Hyksos period.	Equated with the famine inscription in the reign of Sesotris I of twelfth dynasty. Dated 1662 B.C.
Enslavement of Israel	Eighteenth dynasty theory of Exodus must recognize an early king of this dynasty as the pharaoh initiating the enslavement. This would be Amenhotep I or Thutmose I.	Enslavement initiated by Sesostris III of Dynasty XII. Date, *c.* 1560 B.C.
The Exodus	Eighteenth dynasty theory must recognize the position either at the end of the reign of Thutmose III or early in the reign of Amenhotep II. Date *c.* 1445 B.C.	The reconstruction places the Exodus at the end of the five year reign of Koncharis, second primary ruler of Dynasty XIII, but 26th in the Turin list. Date is 1446-1445 B.C.
Period of the Judges	Encompasses the period of Dynasty XVIII from Amenhotep III, all of XIX as currently composed, and the first half of XX. Dates: 1375-1050 B.C.	Falls in the Hyksos period, *c.* 1375-1050 B.C.
United Monarchy of Israel	Background is in Dynasties XX and XXI. Dates, 1050-930 B.C.	Background is in early Dynasty XVIII ending near the beginning of the sole reign of Thutmose III. Dates, 1050-930 B.C.
Sacking of Solomon's Temple	Shishak identified as Sheshonk I of Dynasty XXII. Date is 926 B.C. in fifth year of Rehoboam.	Shishak identified as Thutmose III of Dynasty XVIII. Date 926 B.C.
Fall of Israel to Assyria	Must be placed in the background of Dynasty XXIII to retain the established date 722-721 B.C.	Falls in the fifth year of Merneptah dated 721 B.C. Synchronism indicated by inscription of this year telling of catastrophe to Israel.
Fall of Judah to Babylon	In Dynasty XXVI. Date *c.* 606 B.C.	In Dynasty XXV. Date *c.* 606 B.C.

meaning in 1662 B.C.[10] He has provided evidence from Egyptian inscriptions of a famine in this era, and he has even identified the Pharaoh of this era, Sesostris I. He thinks that references to a vizier of Sesostris I, Mentuhotep, refer to Joseph.[11]

His thesis is simple, though complex in its demonstration: the king lists presented by the conventional sources — Manetho's, the Turin list, the Sothis list — are in error when they assume that each king's reign followed another. Actually, Courville demonstrates, many of these "kings" were not kings at all, but lower officials whose rule overlapped the reign of the true pharaohs. In short, the conventional histories of Egypt have overestimated the age of Egypt's kingdoms because they have relied on a *false assumption,* namely, that *the kings on the various lists did not frequently have overlapping reigns.* Thus, among other problems, Courville's reconstructed chronology solves the problem of the conventional dating of the origins of Egypt thousands of years prior to a Bible-based estimate of the date of the Noachian flood. In short, what Courville has sought to prove is that Christian scholars are still in bondage to Egypt. He offers them an intellectual Exodus. And like the slaves of Moses' day, they cry out against the proposed deliverance. They prefer to remain in bondage. The onions of Egypt — Ph.D. degrees, tenured teaching positions, and intellectual respectability among their heathen masters — still entice them.

---

10. Courville, *Exodus Problem,* I, p. 151.

11. *Ibid.,* I, p. 141. George Rawlinson has written of Mentuhotep: "This official, whose tombstone is among the treasures of the museum of Boulaq, appears to have held a rank in the kingdom second only to that of the king. He filled at one and the same time the offices of minister of justice, home secretary, chief commissioner of public works, director of public worship, and perhaps of foreign secretary and minister of war. [He cites Brugsch's *History of Egypt.*] 'When he arrived at the gate of the royal residence, all the other great personages who might be present bowed down before him, and did obeisance.' He was judge, financier, general, administrator, artist." George Rawlinson, *History of Ancient Egypt* (New York: John B. Alden, 1886), II, p. 83.

The fact that a tombstone exists does not necessarily mean that the bones of "Mentuhotep" were still under it when it was discovered. Joseph's bones were removed from Egypt and taken to Israel (Ex. 13:19). It is possible that the Hebrews decided to leave the tombstone behind as a reminder to their former taskmasters, and that the Egyptians, in the confusion of the Amalekite invasion, subsequently neglected to dispose of it. Later Egyptians may not have remembered who this official really was.

The possibility exists, of course, that Courville is incorrect concerning the Joseph-Mentuhotep identity.

Jacob's Heirs

Unquestionably, the growth of the Hebrew population was rapid. If the sons of Jacob, which included each family's circumcised bondservants, came down to Egypt 215 years before Moses led their heirs out of Egypt, then the Hebrews experienced long-term population growth unequaled in the records of man. Remember, however, that people lived longer in Joseph's era. Kohath, Moses' grandfather, lived for 133 years (Ex. 6:18). Levi, Kohath's father, died at age 137 (Ex. 6:16). Moses' brother Aaron died at age 123 (Num. 33:39). Moses died at age 120 (Deut. 34:7). Nevertheless, Moses acknowledged that in his day, normal life spans were down to about 70 years: "The days of our years are threescore and ten; and if by reason of strength they be fourscore years, yet is their strength labour and sorrow; for it is soon cut off, and we fly away" (Ps. 90:10). (Again, the number "70" appears, in this case to describe a whole lifetime, rather than a whole population.) Caleb boasted about his strength for a man of 85 (Josh. 14:10-11), indicating that in his generation life spans had shrunk.

These years of long life were reduced after the Exodus. Men seldom survived to age 130. (One exception: Jehoiada, the high priest, lived to 130: II Chron. 24:15.)[12] But if, during the years in Egypt, they begat children from an early age and continued to bear them until well into their eighties and nineties, as Jacob had done before them, then we can understand how such a tremendous expansion of numbers was possible. As I explain below, foreigners in large numbers covenanted themselves to Hebrew families. It is also possible that Hebrew men married Egyptian wives in the first century of prosperity, as Joseph had done (Gen. 41:45). This would have greatly expanded the number of children born into Hebrew families, since the Hebrew husbands would not have been limited exclusively to Hebrew women. A family of five boys and five girls could have become a family of 100 Hebrew grandchildren within a generation. Of course, not every family could have seen this happen, since some

---

12. Dr. Arthur C. Custance, a creationist scholar and medical physiologist, argues in *The Seed of the Woman* (Brockville, Ontario, Canada: Doorway, 1980) that there are fairly reliable records concerning several dozen long-lived individuals (over 110 years of age), including 32 age 150 or more, and one, Li Chang Yun, who died in China in 1933 at the startling age of 256. He had survived 23 wives (p. 481). "Those who saw him at age 200 testified that he did not appear much older than a man in his fifties."

Hebrew men would have had to marry Hebrew wives (along with Egyptian wives) in order for the daughters of all the families to have remained inside the covenant lines. On the other hand, Egyptian men might have converted to the faith, especially during the period of Israel's preeminence in Egypt (e.g., Lev. 24:10). Even apart from the assumption of multiple wives (some Egyptian), it is obvious that long lives, high birth rates, and low death rates could have produced a huge population within two centuries.

Household Servants

We should also understand that the 70 direct heirs of Jacob described in Exodus 1:5 were lineal heirs, "out of the loins of Jacob." *But the total number of households under each lineal heir would have been far larger.* Servants who were circumcised were part of the families, and they would have come down to Egypt with the direct lineal heirs. These servants would have participated in the blessings of Goshen, which was the best land in Egypt (Gen. 47:6). The Pharaoh of the famine gave his best land to Joseph's relatives, but this included their entire households. The size of the land indicates this: the land needed administration. Pharaoh even wanted to place his own cattle under the administration of "men of activity" among the households (Gen. 47:6b). He expected them to care for the best land of Egypt (Goshen), but this would have required more than 70 men and their immediate families.

Therefore, when the households of Israel went into bondage under a later Pharaoh, the descendants of the servants were counted as the covanantal heirs of Jacob.[13] They also went into bondage. When the Exodus from Egypt freed the Israelites, all those who had been part of the families of Jacob went free. The multitude that swarmed out of Egypt included *the heirs of the circumcised servants* of the 70 lineal heirs of Jacob.

How many people actually came down into Egypt during the famine? It could have been as many as 10,000. One estimate of Abraham's household is 3,000, given his 318 fighting men (Gen. 14:14).[14] We are not told how many servants were still under the ad-

---

13. See Numbers 1:4-18 and 7:2-11 for an indication that the *princes* of each tribe were the physical descendents of the twelve patriarchs. Cf. E. C. Wines, *The Hebrew Republic* (Uxbridge, Massachusetts: American Presbyterian Press, 1980), pp. 99-100. This was originally published in the late nineteenth century as Book II of the *Commentary on the Laws of the Ancient Hebrews.*

14. Folker Willesen, "The *Yalid* in Hebrew Society," *Studia Theologica,* XII (1958), p. 198.

ministration of Jacob. It is likely that most of Isaac's servant families
went with Esau rather than Jacob. But Jacob had recruited servants
during his stay with Laban (Gen. 32:16), although we do not know
how many. We do know that Pharaoh wanted his best land to be
taken care of by Jacob's family, and he would have recognized the
covenantal relationship between the lineal heirs and their servants.
The servants would have been responsible administrators because
they were under the authority of Jacob's heirs. Any relationship between the God of Jacob and his lineal heirs would have included the
household servants. Pharaoh, as a king, would have understood this
covenantal principle, especially since the theology of Egypt asserted
the divinity of the Pharaoh. All Egyptians were his servants; any
relationship between him and the gods of Egypt was therefore also a
relationship between the gods and the Egyptian people.[15] It seems
safe to conclude that the 70 households included non-lineal heirs.

Exponential Growth

We need to understand the remarkable aspects of compound
growth. If as few as 3,000 came into Egypt in Joseph's day, then the
rate of population growth over the next 215 years was 3.18% per annum in order to reach 2.5 million by the time of the Exodus. Had
this rate of increase been maintained after their settlement of Canaan, there would have been over 2 *billion* of them 215 years later,
not counting the "mixed multitude" (Ex. 12:38) that went with them
out of Egypt. Two hundred and seventy five years after the settlement of Canaan, there would have been 13.8 billion, roughly
equivalent to three times the world's population in 1980. In short,
they would have spread across the face of the earth.

If there were more than 3,000 people in the families of the
Israelites who came down to Egypt in Joseph's day, then the rate of
growth was under 3% per annum over the 215-year period in Egypt.
A lower rate of growth would have lengthened the time necessary to
reach 13.8 billion people, but the speed of increase would still have
been startling. If there were 10,000 who entered Egypt in Joseph's
day, then to reach 2.5 million people 215 years later, the annual rate
of increase would have been 2.6%. Had this "low" rate been main-

---

15. This covenantal relationship proved to be the undoing of the Egyptian people
at the time of the Exodus. Their Pharaoh's rebellion against God brought them low,
just as the obedience to God by the Pharaoh of Joseph's day brought them the external blessing of survival.

tained after their entry into Canaan (assuming no population growth during the 40 years in the wilderness and in five years of fighting to conquer Canaan), the Hebrews would have multiplied to 620 million people 215 years after settling the land, 2.9 billion in 275 years, 5.5 billion in 300 years, 10 billion in 325 years, and 13.8 billion in 335 years. But God told them that there would be no miscarriages or diseases if they obeyed His law, implying a more rapid rate of population growth than they had experienced in Egypt.

We get some idea of just what kind of growth was implied by a 2.6% annual increase when we consider that Solomon began building the temple 480 years after the Exodus (I Kings 6:1). Subtracting the 40 years in the wilderness and five years spent in conquering that part of Canaan which was on the far side of the Jordan River (Josh. 14:10),[16] we get 435 years after the settlement of Canaan. If 2.5 million Hebrews began to reproduce when the land was settled, and the rate of increase was 2.6% per annum, 435 years later there would have been 176 billion Hebrews. The land of Israel was about 7 million acres. The population density by Solomon's time would have been 15,143 Hebrews per acre. An acre is a square about 210 feet per side, or 44,000 square feet. Obviously, either the rate of population increase would have fallen well before Solomon's day, or else they would have spread across the face of the earth. Even with a nation of high-rise apartment houses, 176 billion Hebrews would not have squeezed into the land of Israel. More than this: a population of 176 billion Hebrews implies that the earth would have been filled well before Solomon's day. It therefore implies that the requirement of the dominion covenant relating to multiplying and filling the earth would long since have been fulfilled.

These numbers should lead us to question the whole scenario of compound growth of over 2.5% per annum for many centuries on end. Nothing like this has ever taken place in man's history. Only since the Industrial Revolution in the late eighteenth century has anything like it taken place in recorded history. We need to examine some of the statistical relationships before we can make valid conclusions concerning what happened in this 215-year period.

---

16. Actually, part of Canaan began to be conquered 38 years after the Exodus (Deut. 2:14). The first generation of Hebrews had all died by this time (Deut. 2:15-16). Seven years later, all of Canaan was under Israel's control, except for those pockets of resistance that never were conquered (Jud. 1:27-2:4).

The 2.5 Million Hebrews

The standard estimation of how many people left Egypt at the Exodus is 2-2.5 million Hebrews, not counting the "mixed multitudes." Why is this figure reasonable? The best answer relates to the number of Hebrews a generation later, after the deaths of all of the members of the adult Hebrews who fled, with only two exceptions: Joshua and Caleb.

The generation in the wilderness entered Canaan with approximately the same number of men who had left Egypt 40 years earlier. There were 600,000 men who left Egypt (Ex. 12:37), and one year later (Num. 1:1), there were 603,550 fighting men (Num. 1:46), plus 22,273 Levites (Num. 3:43). The number of adult males was only slowly increasing. When the second census was taken before they entered the land, 40 years later, the population of the tribes had decreased slightly, to 601,730 (Num 26:51), plus 23,000 Levites (Num. 26:62).

What this points to is population stagnation. More important, it points to at least two generations of stable reproduction: one male child and one female child per family. Why do I say this? Because populations that are growing experience the after-effects of prior high birth rates, even in later periods when the birth rate in the society falls below the bare minimum reproduction rate of 2.1 children per woman. This is what most Western industrial nations are facing today: birth rates below the reproduction rate. Nevertheless, the populations are still growing. The reason is that in previous periods, there were higher birth rates, and young women born up to 45 years earlier are still in the child-bearing ages. As these women marry and begin to have children, the upward curve of population continues to rise, although it is slowing down. Women may be having fewer children than their mothers did, but there are lots of women still within or entering the child-bearing ages. It takes decades of below-reproduction-rate births to begin to bring down the aggregate number of people in a society, as middle-aged women cease having children, and the very old members of society continue to die off.

What is abnormal at any time in history is for a population to remain stable for a full generation. A steady-state population is far more common on islands or in very small nations, where emigration is possible or where abortion or even infanticide is practiced as a means of population control. In the ancient world, steady-state populations may have been common because of high death rates for children, but that had not been the experience of the Hebrews during the years of rapid growth. Their population growth rate had been sufficiently high that the Pharaoh of the oppression issued his edict concerning infanticide.

Sometime in between this edict and the Exodus, the Hebrew population became a steady-state population. Thus, the fathers of the Exodus generation were succeeded by almost exactly the same number of sons. This points to the fact that their fathers had also reproduced at close to a steady-state level, since there was no "bulge" of women entering the child-bearing years — women who had been produced 20 years earlier by a higher fertility culture. Just about the same number of men "came on-stream" in the wilderness years, just barely replacing their dying fathers. This points to a figure of 2.5 million at the Exodus: 600,000 men, about 600,000 women, and 1.3 million children. The average Hebrew family was therefore the *replacement rate family* of about 2.1 children per family. (It is assumed that about 5% of the children — one in 21 — will not marry or at least will not bear children: ill health, mental or physical defects, infertility, or just an unwillingness or inability to marry.)

The stable population of the wilderness experience points to a total population of 2.5 million at the time of the Exodus. Only with high death rates in the wilderness could we imagine that significantly more than 2.5 million Hebrews departed. With the exception of the judgments against adult rebels, totalling about 40,000 (Num. 16:35, 49; 25:9), there are no records of high death rates for Israel during the wilderness years. We can safely conclude that the steady-state reproduction rate of the wilderness generation points back to approximately 2.5 million Hebrews involved in the Exodus.

If the Exodus generation averaged two children per family, this reveals a "mature" or zero-growth population in the generation prior to the Exodus. But since there were only four generations from the descent into Egypt and the conquest of Canaan (Gen. 15:16), and the generation of the Exodus was already into the steady-state growth phase, the growth to 2.5 million had to take place in the first two generations. There is simply no way that this could have been accomplished by biological reproduction alone.

If we examine the age distribution of a growing population, age group by age group, we find that the numbers get larger as the age group gets lower. Those under age 15 constitute the largest single segment of the population. While it was biologically possible for 3,000 Hebrews and their circumcised servants to have reached 2.5 million in 215 years (3.18% increase per annum), the departing Hebrews would have had very large families. There could not have been 600,000 adult males. There would have been fewer men and far more children in the total population of 2.5 million.

We now must make sense of the data. It is not conceivable, biologically or mentally, that the 3,000 or 10,000 people who came at the descent had multiplied to 600,000 adult males at the Exodus. Then where did the 2.5 million Hebrews come from? There is only one possible explanation: *from conversions.* The number of circumcised servants must have grown rapidly until the era of the oppression, at least 80 years before the Exodus. Thus, for about 135 years (215 – 80), the Hebrews *and their circumcised servants* experienced high birth and survival rates. The Pharaoh feared their fertility. But their fertility was not sufficient to explain the 600,000 males who departed at the Exodus. There must also have been foreigners who covenanted with the favored Hebrews who lived in the choice land of Goshen. They became Hebrews by circumcision.

We can now better understand Moses' words to the Hebrews: "The LORD did not set his love upon you, nor choose you, because ye were more in number than any people; for ye were the fewest of people" (Deut. 7:7). Their growth was due primarily to conversions to the faith. The external blessings of God enabled them to multiply, but especially to *multiply by conversion.* The majority of those who conquered Canaan were not the biological descendants of Abraham, but they were the *covenantal descendants.*

This has enormous implications for Judaism. The religious issue of "who is a Jew?" is not primarily the question of physical birth; the issue is the covenant. When Jesus warned the Pharisees that God could raise up descendants of Abraham from the stones (Matt. 3:9), he was speaking of vast conversions of gentiles. This was about to happen through the ministry of the church. The true heirs of Israel, Paul writes, are the spiritual heirs of Abraham, the *heirs of the promise of Abraham* (Rom. 9:7-8). But what must be recognized is that this had been true from the beginning. It was the promise, as transferred through the covenant, which was the essential mark of the Hebrew. The mark in the flesh only testified to this more important mark, which was spiritual and covenantal. Their numbers had not come from biological generation alone, but from the dominion process of *conversion and circumcision.* It was not biology which was fundamental, but *faith.*

The Uniqueness of Hebrew Fertility

We can begin to perceive the magnitude of the judgment against Egypt, which was probably also a steady-state population. Zero population growth was an aspect of their static religion and static social theory. In the ancient world, populations did not grow rapidly as they do in the modern world. Thus, the death of the firstborn male in a steady-state population was tantamount to the destruction of that population. Children normally died in their youth. It might take the birth of ten or more children to maintain a two-child legacy. Adam Smith, as late as 1776, remarked that it was common knowledge that poverty-stricken Highland Scot women would bear 20 children in their lifetimes, yet only two or fewer would actually grow to adulthood.[17] After the death of the firstborn Egyptian males, there was no assurance that there would be replacement male children who would reach adulthood and marry.

We know that the Egyptians were facing something uniquely threatening in the population growth of the Hebrews. It is understandable why the Egyptians had been terrified of the Hebrews. With such a growing population in servitude, it would not be long before their sheer numbers would have overpowered the Egyptian guards. Furthermore, chattel slaves are notoriously unproductive, and the Egyptians had to feed them. The vast bureaucratic projects that the pharaohs were building by means of chattel slave labor were by nature unproductive and resource-absorbing. How much longer beyond Moses' era would they have been able to feed and control the Hebrews? Their policy decision was the oppression.

The oppression shocked the Hebrews. The drowning of the male infants must have had cataclysmic psychological effects on all the Hebrews, and we can easily understand why few if any converts subsequently presented themselves for circumcision. This explains why, in their final 80 years in Egypt, the Hebrews (which meant all circumcised males and their families) experienced a steady-state population growth rate, that is, zero population growth. The dead males, coupled with the psychological effects, brought population stagnation overnight to the Hebrews.

---

17. Adam Smith, *The Wealth of Nations* (1776), Modern Library edition, p. 79.

Conclusion

The historically unprecedented growth of the Hebrew population in Egypt startled the Egyptians. It took 215 years for the 70 lineal heirs of Jacob *and their circumcised servants,* plus *circumcised converts attracted during the first 135 years in Egypt,* to grow to 600,000 men, plus women and children. This sign of God's grace was visible to all.

Rapid, long-term population growth in response to covenantal faithfulness is one of the promised blessings of biblical law. A potentially greater blessing waited for them in the land of Canaan: no miscarriages, long lives, reduced sickness (Ex. 20:12; 23:25-26). These blessings did not occur; the continuing ethical rebellion of the Hebrews led instead to population stagnation, a curse.

A growing population is a tool of dominion, as are all the blessings of God. The humanists' hostility to population growth in the final decades of the twentieth century is part of a growing suspicion of all forms of economic growth. Growth points to an eventual using up of finite resources, including living space. This, in turn, points either to the *end of growth* or the *end of time.* The thought of an end of time within a few centuries is not acceptable to humanists. Therefore, they have instead attacked the concept of linear growth, since growth — especially population growth — cannot be linear indefinitely in a finite universe.[18] (See Appendix B: "The Demographics of Decline.")

Until these attitudes are seen by large numbers of Christians for what they are — *aspects of paganism* — Christians will continue to labor under a modern version of Egyptian slavery. This slavery is both religious and intellectual. It cannot be limited to the spirit and the intellect, however; ideas do have social consequences. *Christians cannot legitimately expect to conquer the world for Jesus Christ in terms of the ideology of zero-growth humanism.* Such a philosophy should be handed over to the humanists as their very own "tool of subservience," the opposite of dominion. Even better would be *population decline for the God-haters.* They would simply fade away as an influence on earth.

---

18. This hostility to population growth compromised even Wilhelm Röpke's economic analysis. His fear of "mass society" overwhelmed his otherwise good sense. He never understood that it is not sheer numbers of people that create "mass society," but rather the rebellious ethical and religious assumptions of the population that create "mass society." Röpke's anti-population growth theme appears in several of his books, but especially in *International Order and Economic Integration* (Dortrecht, Holland: Reidel, 1959), Pt. II, ch. IV: "The International Population Problem."

This is the long-term implication of a birth rate below 2.1 children per woman. It is a birth rate below 2.1 children per woman which alone is fully consistent with the Bible's description of the God-hating ethical rebels: "all they that hate me love death" (Prov. 8:36b). It is this suicidal birth rate which presently prevails in all Western industrial nations. This is the population program which Pharaoh hoped to impose on his enemies, the Hebrews. He was not sufficiently stupid, or so utterly perverse, to have sought to impose it on his own people.

Pharaoh saw the necessity of protecting his nations resources from the prolific Israelites. Three and a half millennia later, fearful and defensive socialists have similar concerns. Bertrand Russell, the British socialist philosopher and mathematician, saw clearly the dilemma of socialism: to produce rising per capita wealth, low-productivity socialism requires zero population growth. Socialism also still requires the imposition of harsh penalties against rival populations that continue to grow, just as it did in ancient Egypt. "Socialism, especially international socialism, is only possible as a stable system if the population is stationary or nearly so. A slow increase might be coped with by improvements in agricultural methods, but a rapid increase must in the end reduce the whole population to penury, and would be almost certain to cause wars. In view of the fact that the population of France has become stationary, and the birth rate has declined enormously among other white nations, it may be hoped the the white population of the world will soon cease to increase. The Asiatic races will be longer, and the negroes still longer, before their birth-rate falls sufficiently to make their numbers stable without the help of war and pestilence. But it is to be hoped that the religious prejudices which have hitherto hampered the spread of birth control will die out, and that within (say) two hundred years the whole world will learn not to be unduly prolific. Until that happens, the benefits aimed at by socialism can only be partially realized, and the less prolific races will have to defend themselves against the more prolific by methods which are disgusting even if they are necessary. In the meantime, therefore, our socialistic aspirations have to be confined to the white races, perhaps with the inclusion of the Japanese and Chinese at no distant date."[19]

The more progressive modern socialist ideology appears, the more satanically backward it becomes. The spirit of Pharaoh still lives. The anti-dominion defensive spirit of modern socialism has its roots deep in the past, as well as deep in hell.

---

19. Bertrand Russell, *The Prospects of Industrial Civilization* (2nd ed.; London: George Allen & Unwin, 1959), p. 273. First edition: 1923. He did not change his views enough to warrant a revision of this passage.

2

IMPERIAL BUREAUCRACY

Now there arose up a new king over Egypt, which knew not Joseph. And he said unto his people, Behold, the people of the children of Israel are more and mightier than we: Come on, let us deal wisely [shrewdly] with them; lest they multiply, and it come to pass, that, when there falleth out any war, they join also unto our enemies, and fight against us, and so get them up out of the land. Therefore they did set over them taskmasters to afflict them with their burdens. And they built for Pharaoh treasure cities, Pithom and Raamses. But the more they afflicted them, the more they multiplied and grew. And they were grieved because of the children of Israel (Ex. 1:8-12).

Who was this new Pharaoh? Old Testament scholars are divided, but Donovan Courville's reconstruction of Egyptian chronology points to Sesostris III. A major transformation of the Egyptian system of rule was imposed by this Twelfth Dynasty Pharaoh. The political centralization of the pharaohs of the Pyramid Age had disintegrated. Egypt had become a feudal State. Courville writes: "During the period preceding Sesostris III, Egypt had existed as a feudal system, and historians speak of this period as the 'feudal age.' Under this arrangement, the territory of Egypt was divided into numerous local areas called nomes, over each of which was a prince or governor. He was not a servant of the Pharaoh and was permitted to rule undisturbed so long as he contributed his alloted quota to the king's treasury and perhaps to the army in case of need. . . . Under the reign of Sesostris III, this situation was changed. For the most part, these local princes were stripped of their power and stripped of their excessive possessions. For the first time in a hundred years or more, Egypt was now under the immediate and direct dictatorship of the pharaoh. . . . From this time on, we find no more of the tombs of these princes nor of the prolific inscriptions which they had previously left."[1]

A centralization of political power was accompanied by an extensive building program. Courville argues that this program had to have been accomplished by means of slave labor. Furthermore, "Unlike the structures of the huge building program in the Pyramid Age, and again unlike that which occurred later in the XVIIIth Dynasty, this building was of brick and not of stone."[2] This corresponds with the account in the Book of Exodus; the Hebrews used bricks to fulfill their assignments (Ex. 1:14). Another important historical correlation is this: the building programs of Sesostris III and his successor, Amenemhet III, were in the eastern Delta region, which included the land of Goshen, where the Hebrews lived. The cities of Pi-Raamses and Pi-Thom have been discovered in this region, but modern scholars have attributed the bulk of these ruins to Rameses II, a king of a much later date.[3] Courville argues also that the list of the Ramessides kings in the Sothis list correlates to the earlier line of kings,[4] which would explain why the land of Goshen was described as "the best in the land, in the land of Rameses" (Gen. 47:11).[5]

If Courville's identification of the Pharaoh of the oppression is incorrect, then what can we say with confidence? First, he did have an extensive military force at his disposal. He put into slavery a nation of formerly independent people. Second, he was financially capable

---

1. Donovan A. Courville, *The Exodus Problem and Its Ramifications* (Loma Linda, California: Challenge Books, 1971), I, pp. 146-47. Rawlinson commented on the career of Sesostris III (Usurtasen III): "At the head of disciplined troops he gained repeated victories over the half-armed and untrained races, in part negro, in part Ethiopic, of the south. By a continued merciless persecution, he so far intimidated them, that they were induced to submit to Egyptian supremacy, and to endure the loss of freedom and independence. As he understood the value of fortresses as a means of establishing a dominion, of riveting a detested yoke on a proud nation's neck, and of making revolt hopeless, if not impossible. He was also so far ambitious, so far desirous of posthumous fame, that he took care to have his deeds declared in words, and graven with an iron pen in the rock forever. But in this respect he merely followed the previous traditional practice of the Egyptian kings, while in his conquests he only a little exceeded the limits reached by more than one of his predecessors." George Rawlinson, *History of Ancient Egypt* (New York: John B. Alden, 1886), II, p. 86. This description certainly seems to fit the personality of the man who enslaved the Hebrews, though of course Rawlinson did not believe that Sesostris III was the Pharaoh of the oppression.

2. Courville, *ibid.*, I, p. 147.

3. *Ibid.*, I, p. 148.

4. *Ibid.*, I, p. 149; cf. p. 120.

5. *Ibid.*, I, pp. 24, 33, 45.

of building treasure cities. This would have required an extensive and well-developed taxation system. Third, he was ruthless, as his attempt to execute the Hebrew male infants indicates.

Egypt's Theology: The Continuity of Being

The religion of ancient Egypt, like all religious systems of the ancient Near East,[6] viewed history as a struggle between chaos and order. Our world had its origin in the primordial waters of the underworld, the Egyptians believed.[7] Atum, the original god, created two other gods (male and female), which in turn created two more, and these two created Osirus (male sun god) and Isis, who gave birth to Horus, the falcon god of the sky.[8] John A. Wilson concludes that chaos was not overcome by Re-Atum, the creator god, since the god of the underworld and the god of darkness continued to live, "but they continued in their proper places and not in universal and formless disorder."[9]

The Egyptians lacked a specific mythological account of the creation of man.[10] However, as Wilson makes clear, basic to Egyptian mythology was the concept of *continuity*. "To be sure," writes Wilson, "a man seems to be one thing, and the sky or a tree seems to be another. But to the ancient Egyptian such concepts had a protean and complementary nature. The sky might be thought of as a material vault above earth, or as a cow, or as a female. A tree might be a tree or the female who was the tree-goddess. Truth might be treated as an abstract concept, or as a goddess, or as a divine hero who once lived on earth. A god might be depicted as a man, or as a falcon, or as a falcon-headed man. . . . There was thus a continuing substance across the phenomena of the universe, whether organic,

---

6. Joseph Fontenrose, *Python: A Study of Delphic Myth and Its Origins* (Berkeley: University of California Press, 1959), pp. 218-19, 473.

7. John A. Wilson, "Egypt," in Henri Frankfort, *et al.*, *The Intellectual Adventure of Ancient Man: An Essay on Speculative Thought in the Ancient Near East* (University of Chicago Press, [1946] 1977), p. 45. Penguin Books published a version of this book called *Before Philosophy.*

8. Rudolph Anthes, "Mythology of Ancient Egypt," in Samuel Noah Kramer (ed.), *Mythologies of the Ancient World* (Garden City, New York: Doubleday Anchor, 1961), pp. 36-39. Anthes thinks that the cosmology of Heliopolis, which was only one of the religious centers of Egypt, and only one of the Egyptian cosmologies, was more concerned with establishing the divinity of the king than with the actual details of creation: p. 40.

9. Wilson, "Egypt," *op. cit.*, p. 53.

10. *Ibid.*, pp. 54-55.

inorganic, or abstract."[11] There was no absolute distinction between creator and creature; instead, there was a *continuity of being.*

The Divine Monarch

The doctrine of continuity of being has a tendency to become the doctrine of the divinization of man. Furthermore, the divinization of man has an equally distinct tendency to become a doctrine of the divine State, or the divine Church, or the divine Church-State. The State, as the most concentrated power in human affairs, becomes the mediating institution between the gods and evolving mankind. We can see this in the history of Egyptian kingship. Wilson's summary is to the point: "The king of Egypt was himself one of the gods and was the land's representative among the gods. Furthermore, he was the one official intermediary between the people and the gods, the one recognized priest of all the gods. Endowed with divinity, the pharaoh had the protean character of divinity; he could merge with his fellow-gods and could become any one of them. In part this was symbolic, the acting of a part in religious drama or the simile of praise. But the Egyptian did not distinguish between symbolism and participation; if he said that the king was Horus, he did not mean that the king was playing the part of Horus, he meant that the king *was* Horus, that the god was effectively present in the king's body during the particular activity in question."[12] The Pharaoh deputized priests to perform religious duties, just as he deputized bureaucratic functionaries to perform administrative duties, but State theory maintained that these deputies acted for him as the supreme incarnation of the gods. Egyptian theology was polytheistic, but it was also *monophysite:* ". . . many men and many gods, but all ultimately of one nature."[13]

To understand the enormous significance of the Hebrews' stay in Egypt, we have to understand the central position of the Pharaoh. Joseph's ability to interpret the king's dream, and then to administer the collection and distribution of grain, elevated the Pharaoh's position, reinforcing the traditional Egyptian State theology. Then, two centuries later, Moses smashed the very foundations of Egypt by smashing men's faith in their king's position as a divine figure. Again, citing Wilson: "The gods had sent him forth to tend

---

11. *Ibid.,* p. 62.
12. *Ibid.,* pp. 64-65.
13. *Ibid.,* p. 66.

mankind, but he was not of mankind. This is perhaps the most fitting picture of the good Egyptian ruler, that he was the herdsman for his people. . . . The herdsman is primarily the pastor, the 'feeder,' and a first responsibility of the state was to see that the people were fed. Thus the king of Egypt was the god who brought fertility to Egypt, produced the life-giving waters, and presented the gods with the sheaf of grain which symbolized abundant food. Indeed, an essential function of his kingship was that of a medicine man, whose magic insured good crops. In one of the ceremonials of kingship, the pharaoh encircled a field four times as a rite of conferring fertility upon the land."[14]

God blessed Sesostris I through Joseph. The arrogance of power led Sesostris III, his great-grandson, to enslave the heirs of Joseph.[15] Within a century, Egypt was in ruins, under the domination of foreign invaders, the Hyksos (Amalekites). In the light of all this, we can better appreciate God's words to the (probable) Pharaoh of the Exodus, Koncharis: "For now I will stretch out my hand, that I may smite thee and thy people with pestilence; and thou shalt be cut off from the earth. And in very deed for this cause have I raised thee up, for to shew in thee my power; and that my name may be declared throughout all the earth" (Ex. 9:15-16).

Slavery

The Pharaoh of the enslavement followed a pattern which had become familiar in the lives of the Hebrews. Like Laban in his dealings with Jacob, and Potiphar in his dealings with Joseph, the Pharaoh recognized the economic value of the Hebrews. At the same time, he resented certain concomitant aspects of Hebrew productivity, in this case, their fertility.[16] Yet he was unwilling to take the obvious defensive step, namely, to remove them from the land. He wanted to expropriate their productivity, to compel their service. It was not enough that they were in Egypt, bringing the land under dominion, filling the nation with productive workers. Their productiv-

---

14. *Ibid.,* pp. 78, 79-80.

15. Courville, *Exodus Problem,* I, p. 218.

16. "The terms *fecundity* and *fertility,* originally used synonymously, were differentiated from one another only gradually. In 1934 the Population Association of America officially endorsed the distinction between **fecundity,** the physiological ability to reproduce, and **fertility,** the realization of this potential, the actual birth performance as measured by the number of offspring." William Peterson, *Population* (2nd ed.; New York: Macmillan, 1969), p. 173.

ity was a threat to the Egyptian theocratic State. These foreigners did not serve Egyptian gods, nor did they acknowledge the divinity of the Pharaoh, the link between the gods and mankind. They were foreigners in Egypt, and they threatened to fill up the land, making the Egyptians a minority population in their own nation. How, then, could the Egyptian State appropriate their obvious productivity without surrendering sovereignty to a foreign people and a foreign God? The answer, so familiar in the history of the ancient world, was slavery.

It is a fact of economic life that people always want to buy goods and services on more favorable terms than are presently available. They want "more for less," in other words. The Egyptians wanted a better deal. They hoped to gain the economic benefits of a godly people's productivity by offering (commanding) terms of employment that were hostile to long-term productivity. They hoped to enslave the Hebrews, making it impossible for them to revolt, or to replace Egyptian sovereignty, or to flee. Yet they also expected these slaves to remain as productive as before. The Pharaoh of the Exodus even accused them of being lazy, and he burdened them with the task of gathering their own straw to manufacture bricks (Ex. 5:6-19). He wanted "more for less," or better stated, he wanted the *same output* for *reduced expenditures.* He hoped to pay less for his non-labor inputs and no more for labor inputs.

The Egyptians wanted the fruits of godly behavior and God's visible blessings without having to humble themselves before that God and His laws. *They believed that by capturing God's people, they could enslave God Himself.* By enslaving the Israelites, they believed that it was possible to bring the God of the Israelites under subjection. This was a common belief of the ancient world: when a nation defeated another nation in battle, or otherwise subdued it, the gods of the defeated nation were themselves defeated.[17] The Egyptians thought that they could trap the God of the Hebrews, as someone might ensnare a wild stallion, by capturing its "harem." They would use the Hebrews as living amulets or talismans — magical devices that could be manipulated in order to call forth powers of the gods. They understood that the Hebrews had a special relationship with a God who provided them with wealth and knowledge. They knew that it was better to enslave such a people (and such a God) than to destroy them.

---

17. Fustel de Coulanges, *The Ancient City: A Study on the Religion, Laws, and Institutions of Greece and Rome* (Garden City, New York: Doubleday Anchor, [1864] 1955), Bk. III, ch. 15.

The Pharaoh of Joseph's day acknowledged Joseph's access to accurate secret knowledge, and he honored him and his family, transferring the sovereignty of the State to Joseph. He placed his own ring on Joseph's hand, arrayed him in fine linen and gold, and placed him in the second chariot after his own (Gen. 41:42-43). That Pharaoh bowed to God's sovereignty and to God's dream-mediated Word, and his kingdom was blessed by God.

In contrast, the Pharaoh of the oppression wanted Jacob's heirs to produce on Egypt's terms, without the transfer of any of the king's sovereignty, but he expected to be able to control and even reduce that fertility, while appropriating the fruits of their labor. He was wrong; their fertility continued, and he was forced to attempt the murder of all the male infants in order to stop this Hebrew population explosion (Ex. 1:15-19). He, like the Pharaoh of the Exodus, found that he could not control God through His people. Laban had discovered the same thing in his dealings with Jacob.

God's plan was sovereign over Egyptian history, not the plans of the pharaohs. The Pharaoh of Joseph's day had recognized this, and Egypt had prospered because he was wise enough to transfer the symbols and prerogatives of State sovereignty to Joseph. His successors sought to reassert their self-proclaimed divine sovereignty over the Hebrews, and the Pharaoh of the Exodus saw Egypt's wealth and military power swallowed up.

The Bureaucratic Megamachine

It was not just the Hebrews who were enslaved. Sesostris III recentralized the Egyptian social and political order. He began to construct treasure cities, indicating that he had begun to use tax revenues in order to strengthen the visible sovereignty of the central government. Centuries earlier, pharaohs had used State revenues to construct the giant pyramids — monuments to a theology of death and resurrection for the Pharaoh (and later, of the nobility) — but the Pharaoh of the oppression settled for less grandiose displays of his immediate sovereignty.

By Joseph's day, the pharaohs no longer built pyramids. The total centralization of the Pyramid Age had disintegrated. Nevertheless, the theology of the continuity of being was still basic to Egyptian theology, and the lure of centralized power in the person of the Pharaoh was still ready to find its political expression. Although it is true that Joseph had bought all the land of Egypt, excepting only the land belonging to the priests (Gen. 47:20-22), in the name of the Pharaoh (Sesostris I), the visible and institutional manifestation of that implicit centralization (public works pyramids) did not take place until a century later. When Sesostris III abolished the prerogatives of the regional princes, simultaneously placing the Hebrews in bondage, he thereby asserted the sovereignty of *theocratic monophysitism*, with the Pharaoh as the link between heaven and earth. He formally reversed the special position of the Hebrews, which Sesostris I had acknowledged in return for special knowledge of the future — a special revelation which Joseph stated came from God (Gen. 41:16), thereby placing the Pharaoh under God's control. Joseph had announced, "What God is about to do he sheweth unto Pharaoh" (Gen. 41:28), making plain the true source of history and agricultural productivity. Sesostris III attempted to deny any sovereignty other than his own, and in a massive centralization of political power, he cancelled the special position of both the Hebrews and the regional princes.[18]

Pyramids and Power

The Pyramid Age had demonstrated the degree to which a political order could be bureaucratized. Max Weber, the influential German historian-sociologist, devoted the last fifteen years of his life to a series of studies on the West's tendency to rationalize and bureaucratize itself. In 1909, he wrote: "To this day there has never existed a bureaucracy which could compare with that of Egypt."[19] Lewis Mumford, who has specialized in the history of architecture, concluded that nothing short of total bureaucratization would have enabled Egypt to construct its pyramids. More than this: it required the creation of a social machine. Egypt became the first *megamachine,* to use Mumford's terminology.[20] Egyptian society had to be molded along the lines of a pyramid — a hierarchy, with the divine Pharaoh as the capstone.

The divinity of the king had to serve as the universal faith, given

18. Courville, *Exodus Problem,* I, p. 146.

19. "Max Weber on Bureaucratization" (1909); in J. P. Mayer, *Max Weber and German Politics: A Study in Political Sociology* (London: Faber and Faber, [1943] 1956), p. 127.

20. Lewis Mumford, "The First Megamachine," *Daedalus* (1966); reprinted in Mumford, *Interpretations and Forecasts: 1922-1972* (New York: Harcourt Brace Jovanovich, 1972), ch. 24. It is an oddity of history that an essay on the Egyptian pyramid society should appear in a journal named after Daedalus, the legendary figure of Greek mythology who built King Minos' famous labyrinth on Crete. He supposedly learned the secret of the labyrinth from the Egyptians. See Appendix C: "The Garden and the Labyrinth."

the magnitude of the undertaking. "This extension of magnitude in every direction, this raising of the ceiling of human effort, this subordination of individual aptitudes and interests to the mechanical job in hand, and this unification of a multitude of subordinates to a single end that derived from the divine power exercised by the king, in turn, by the success of the result, confirmed that power. For note: it was the king who uttered the original commands: it was the king who demanded absolute obedience and punished disobedience with torture, mutilation, or death: it was the king who alone had the god-like power of turning live men into dead mechanical objects: and finally it was the king who assembled the parts to form the machine and imposed a new discipline of mechanical organization, with the same regularity that moved the heavenly bodies on their undeviating course. No vegetation god, no fertility myth, could produce this kind of cold abstract order, this detachment of power from life. Only one empowered by the Sun God could remove all the hitherto respected norms or limits of human endeavor."[21]

The construction of the pyramids required a reliable organization of knowledge, both supernatural (priesthood) and technological (bureaucracy). The great Cheops (Khufu) pyramid contains at least 2,300,000 stone blocks, each weighing two and a half tons, on the average.[22] These stone blocks, if cut into cubes one foot on each side, would circle two-thirds of the earth's surface at the equator. Such a construction task could not have been carried out without a bureaucratic transmission belt. It would not have been possible to build the pyramids apart from a significant *depersonalization* of the people who made up this massive human machine.

Mumford has summarized the nature of this bureaucratic machine: "The removal of human dimensions and organic limits is indeed the chief boast of the authoritarian machine. Part of its productivity is due to the use of unstinted physical coercion to overcome human laziness or bodily fatigue. Occupational specialization was a necessary step in the assemblage of the human machine: only by intense specialization at every part of the process could the superhuman accuracy and perfection of the product have been achieved. . . . These human machines were by nature impersonal, if not deliberately dehumanized; they had to operate on a big scale

---

21. *Ibid.,* p. 263.
22. Charles F. Pfeiffer and Howard F. Vos, *The Wycliffe Historical Geography of Bible Lands* (Chicago: Moody Press, 1967), p. 69.

or they could not work at all; for no bureaucracy, however well organized, could govern a thousand little workshops, each with its own traditions, its own craft skills, its own willful personal pride and sense of responsibility. So the form of control imposed by kingship was confined to great collective enterprises."[23]

The Bureaucratization of Life

What kind of society emerges from an economic and political system which is determined to construct pyramids to glorify the eldest sons of a kingly line, and to glorify each one's transition from the god Horus to the god Osiris (at death)?[24] Such a bureaucratic society infringes upon the ability and responsibility of individuals to extend dominion across the earth. Such a *concentration of capital* in a single bureaucratic enterprise absorbs the resources that could otherwise be used to finance smaller, decentralized businesses. It also concentrates so much responsibility into the hands of a single monarch or bureaucratic regime that *an error on the part of the hierarchy can threaten the survival of the entire social order.* This is the kind of centralization, though on a less intense level, which brought down Egypt at the time of the Exodus. *Egypt lived or died in terms of one man's decisions:* Joseph's Pharaoh (life) vs. Moses' Pharaoh (death).

Another important danger of bureaucracy is its *lack of creativity.* "Now the important part about the functioning of a classic bureaucracy," Mumford writes, "is that it originates nothing: its function is to transmit, without alteration or deviation, the orders that come from above. No merely local information or human considerations may alter this inflexible transmission process — except by corruption. This administrative method ideally requires a studious repression of all the autonomous functions of the personality, and a readiness to perform the daily task with ritual exactitude. Not for the first time does such ritual exactitude enter into the process of work: indeed, it is highly unlikely that submission to colorless repetition would have been possible without the millennial discipline of religious ritual."[25] From top to bottom, in the massive Church-State of Egypt, ritual was dominant over ethics. *This kind of bureaucracy produces a static social order which eventually disintegrates from external pressures, or disintegrates*

---

23. Mumford, p. 265.
24. Wilson, "Egypt," p. 74; E. O. James, *The Ancient Gods* (London: Weidenfeld and Nicholson, 1960), p. 117.
25. Mumford, p. 266.

from its own weight and inability to generate productive resources. Both events took place in Egypt: an early disintegration into feudalism, and then a revival of centralization during what conventional historians call the Twelfth Dynasty (from Joseph to the fleeing of Moses), which was followed by national defeat immediately after the Exodus. Then, after a century or more under the Hyksos (Amalekites), Egypt experienced a brief rise of power under the Eighteenth Dynasty,[26] and then further decline.

Egypt could not throw off the static rule of the pharaohs, for the Egyptians remained faithful to their monophysite theology, the continuity of being. The only major change, late in Egyptian history, long after the Exodus, was an extension of the process of divinization to the common man, so that he, too, might become Osiris after his death, as the pharaohs had before him.[27] Egyptian culture was remarkably stable; it was the longest-lived of all the ancient kingdoms, but it was "life through institutional death." E. O. James is correct when he refers to Egypt's characteristic feature as the *cult of the dead,* one which assumed "gigantic proportions."[28] The pyramids are the most visible, most impressive, and most representative monuments to Egyptian religion and society. (The other major Egyptian design was the labyrinth, discussed in greater detail in Appendix C: "The Labyrinth and the Garden.")

The Cult of the Dead

The Egyptian cult of the dead was, in fact, a religion of *death and rebirth.* It was also a fertility cult. The voluminous and painstaking researches of E. A. Wallis Budge in the early years of the twentieth century have made this clear. "The central figure of the ancient Egyptian Religion was Osiris, and the chief fundamentals of his cult were the belief in his divinity, death, resurrection, and absolute control of the destinies of the bodies and souls of men. The central point

---

26. Velikovsky argues cogently that the Egyptian king Shishak, mentioned in II Chronicles 12:2-4, was Thutmose III of the Eighteenth Dynasty: Velikovsky, *Ages in Chaos* (Garden City, New York: Doubleday, 1952), pp. 152-55. The invasion of Israel by Shishak was in the fifth year of King Rehoboam, or about 925 B.C., according to Thiele's chronology: Edwin R. Thiele, *A Chronology of the Hebrew Kings* (Grand Rapids, Michigan: Zondervan, 1977), p. 75. This dating, of course, is over 500 years after the conventional dating of Thutmose III's dynasty, which is commonly placed in the early or mid-fifteenth century, B.C.

27. James, *Ancient Gods,* p. 61.

28. *Ibid.,* p. 57.

of each Osirian's Religion was his hope of resurrection in a transformed body and of immortality, which could only be realized by him through the death and resurrection of Osiris."[29]

Budge tried to reconstruct the basics of Egyptian religion without too extensive a reliance on the native Egyptian literature, since "we find that in no portion of it does there exist a text which is not associated with magic, that no text contains a connected statement of the purely religious beliefs which we know the Egyptians certainly possessed. . . ."[30] But magic was basic to Egyptian religion, as Moses' confrontation with the court magicians indicates. It will not do to attribute such "base characteristics" of Egyptian religion to later developments, as Budge did, and to link them with foreign gods.[31] The Egyptians believed in a *power religion,* in contrast to the ethics religion of the Hebrews.

The gods of the Egyptians remind us of the nature gods of the American Indians. Like the Amerindians, the Egyptians were polytheistic. Budge said in 1911 that Egyptologists knew then of at least three thousand different names of their gods. But he could not resist adding, as so many anthropologists add to their accounts of pagan polytheism, "the Egyptians believed in the existence of One Great God, self-produced, self-existent, almighty and eternal, Who created the 'gods,' the heavens and the sun, moon and stars in them, and the earth and everything on it, including man and beast, bird, fish, and reptile. They believed that he maintained in being everything which He had created, and that He was the support of the universe and the Lord of it all."[32] In short, the Egyptians supposedly believed in the same sort of distant, impotent god that late-nineteenth-century nominal Anglicans believed in, and this god was just about as important to the Egyptians in their daily lives as the Anglicans' god was to the English in 1900.

According to Budge, the Egyptians seldom even mentioned this god's name, "Neter." "No proof of any kind is forthcoming which shows that the Egyptians ever entirely forgot the existence of God, but they certainly seem to have believed that he had altogether ceased to interfere in human affairs, and was content to leave the destinies

---

29. E. A. Wallis Budge, "Preface," *Osiris: The Egyptian Religon of Resurrection* (New Hyde Park, New York: University Books, [1911] 1961), p. xi.

30. *Ibid.,* p. xiii.

31. *Ibid.,* p. xiv.

32. *Ibid.,* pp. xxvii-xxviii.

of men to the care of the gods' and spirits."[33] In short, Budge implies, they were all basically Deists when it came to formal theism, and polytheists when it came to ritual. But ritual was the heart and soul of Egyptian religion.

Ethics vs. ritual: here is the heart of the difference between the Egyptians' religion of death and resurrection and the Hebrews' religion of death and resurrection. Biblical religion places ethics above ritual. In the Book of Micah, we read: "Wherewith shall I come before the LORD, and bow myself before the high God? Shall I come before him with burnt offerings, with calves of a year old? Will the LORD be pleased with thousands of rams, or with ten thousands of rivers of oil? Shall I give my firstborn for my transgression, the fruit of my body for the sin of my soul? He hath shewed thee, O man, what is good; and what doth the LORD require of thee, but to do justly, and to love mercy, and to walk humbly with thy God?" (Micah 6:6-8). In contrast, consider Budge's summary of the Egyptians' concern over resurrection, and their attempt to achieve this exalted state through the manipulation of physical means. Theirs was a world filled with demons that could be controlled only by magic, especially word magic. They were obsessed with the physical signs of death. He writes of the dynastic-era Egyptians that they

attached supreme importance to the preservation and integrity of the dead body, and they adopted every means known to them to prevent its dismemberment and decay. They cleansed it and embalmed it with drugs, spices and balsams; they annointed it with aromatic oils and preservative fluids; they swathed it in hundreds of yards of linen bandages; and then they sealed it up in a coffin or sarcophagus, which they laid in a chamber hewn in the bowels of the mountain. All these things were done to protect the physical body against damp, dry rot and decay, and against the attacks of moth, beetles, worms and wild animals. But these were not the only enemies of the dead against which precautions had to be taken, for both the mummified body and the spiritual elements which had inhabited it upon earth had to be protected from a multitude of devils and fiends, and from the powers of darkness generally. These powers of evil had hideous and terrifying shapes and forms, and their haunts were well known, for they infested the region through which the road of the dead lay when passing from this world to the Kingdom of Osiris. The "great gods" were afraid of them, and were obliged to protect themselves by the use of spells and magical names, and words of power, which were composed and written down by

---

33. *Ibid.,* pp. xxviii-xxix.

Thoth. In fact it was believed in very early times in Egypt that Ra, the Sun-god, owed his continued existence to the possession of a secret name with which Thoth provided him. And each morning the rising sun was menaced by a fearful monster called Aapep which lay hidden under the place of sunrise waiting to swallow up the solar disc. It was impossible, even for the Sun-god, to destroy this "Great Devil," but by reciting each morning the powerful spell with which Thoth had provided him he was able to paralyze all Aapep's limbs and rise upon this world.[34]

Theologically, it was the Egyptians who were in bondage. It was they who needed deliverance: ethical, political, and social. Instead, they enslaved those people whose God could alone grant Egypt the deliverance which all men need, the God who had granted them preliminary manifestations of His power and mercy under Joseph.

Death and Resurrection: The Contrast

The significant point here is the difference between the biblical and pagan views of death and resurrection. The places of the dead did not become centers of religion or culture for the Hebrews, nor were these locations considered the dwelling places of spirits, human or otherwise. They were just the caves or burial places of those who would one day be resurrected, either to life or death (Dan. 12:1-3). Death and resurrection were central concerns of both pagan and biblical religion, but the heart of biblical religion is ethics, not ritual. As James Peters has remarked, the center of the tabernacle and the temple was the ark of the covenant, and inside this ark were the two copies of God's covenant with Israel, a covenant of ten "words" or commandments. It is this summary of God's laws of life, not the physical remains of death, which is primary in biblical religion.

The periodic celebrations of social renewal by the ancients — the chaos festivals — were their attempt to achieve metaphysical renewal. The very cosmos itself was to be reborn periodically through men's acts of ritual chaos. They believed in a *religion of revolution*. By ritually recreating the "time before time" — the time of the creation, meaning the advent of order out of disorder — pagans celebrated their concept of death and resurrection. In these festivals, of which the Caribbean's carnival and New Orleans' Mardi Gras are pale imitations, *regeneration comes from below* during a temporary cultural and rit-

---

34. E. A. Wallis Budge, "Preface," *The Book of the Dead* (New Hyde Park, New York: University Books, [1920] 1960), pp. xi-xii.

ual overthrow of all normal ethical and social standards.[35] They wanted *power from below.*[36] (A very similar theology has undergirded nineteenth-century and twentieth-century revolutionary movements of both the "right" and the "left.")[37]

These chaos festivals find no parallel in Israel. Instead, *Israel's social renewal was covenantal,* when the people gathered annually for the Passover and other festivals, and *judicial,* when they gathered every seventh year for a national abolition of debt (Deut. 15:1-4), the release of bondservants (Deut. 15:7-11), and the reading of the whole law to all people, including strangers (Deut. 31:10-13). It was *covenantal renewal,* not a ritual renewal of the cosmos, which was paramount. They did not celebrate the creation, which was solely the work of God; instead, they celebrated their deliverance from Egypt by the power of God, in which they had participated historically. They were to look *backward* toward a real historical event of ethical and national deliverance, so that they could look *forward* in confidence to the coming of the Messiah-deliverer, who in turn would make possible the ultimate deliverance, their resurrection from the dead, so graphically revealed to Ezekiel in the vision of the resurrection of the dry bones of Israel (Ezk. 37).[38]

The theme of life after death is basic to most religions, and certainly to Egyptian religion. But there was a radical distinction between the Egyptian view and the Bible's. Life after death — the resurrection — for the Egyptians, as for those ancient pagan societies that imitated the Egyptian cult of the dead, was seen as a metaphysical extension of this life. The doctrine of the *continuity of being from man to God* on this side of the grave implies that there will be a *continuity of existence* between man's life now and man's life in the resurrection.

---

35. Mircea Eliade, *Cosmos and History: The Myth of the Eternal Return* (New York: Harper Torchbook, 1959), surveys many aspects of this theology, the religion of revolution. Eliade is correct in linking Marxism and chaos festivals: p. 149. Cf. Gary North, *Marx's Religion of Revolution: The Doctrine of Creative Destruction* (Nutley, New Jersey: Craig Press, 1968), ch. 4: "The Cosmology of Chaos." A microfiche copy of this out-of-print book is available from the Institute for Christian Economics.

36. R. J. Rushdoony, "Power from Below," *The Journal of Christian Reconstruction,* I (Winter 1974).

37. James Billington, *Fire in the Minds of Men: Origins of the Revolutionary Faith* (New York: Basic Books, 1980).

38. Partial fulfilment of this vision took place immediately after Christ's resurrection from the dead: "And the graves were opened; and many bodies of the saints which slept arose, and came out of the graves after his resurrection, and went into the holy city, and appeared unto many" (Matt. 27:52-53).

Therefore, ethical regeneration was not seen as being necessary now in order to make possible participation in the life of the renewed world beyond the grave. In such religions, there is only one kind of final resurrection: resurrection unto life. If a man can evolve into God, either on this side of the grave, or in the shadows of death, or through successive reincarnations, then God cannot require man before death to meet ethical standards that are appropriate to man as the image of God—an image which never can become God because of the absolute Creator-creature distinction.

In other words, the cult of the dead rested on the assumption that the kind of being or existence which men now enjoy is the same sort of life that they will enjoy beyond the grave. This is why pagan tombs have their walls covered with paintings of hunters, or dancers, or people involved in sexual debauchery.[39] This is why Egyptian kings were buried with their gold and other valuables, including (sometimes) the bodies of their ritually executed wives.

The essence of such a religion is metaphysics, not a final judgment based on God's revealed ethics. There is no ethical transformation required of man, no regeneration of man by God's grace, this side of the grave. Ritual and magic—man's manipulation of the cosmos, man's manipulation of God—are substituted for ethics as the basis of the man's transition from this life through death to resurrection. Man's departed spirit must draw the labyrinth pattern to perfection, or utter the proper words to the guardian of the gate, or greet the guardian with the proper handshake. Man needs to be wearing the proper clothing or amulet at the time of death, or be buried according to tradition, or have the proper prayer prayed over him by the priest (just before death or soon thereafter), or have the ancient rites performed on schedule by the family's future priest-patriarchs down through the generations. Such practices testify to a religion's adherence to aspects of the satanic delusion.

The conflict between Moses and Pharaoh involved the clash between two radically different concepts of death and resurrection, of salvation and final judgment. One was overwhelmingly ritualistic and metaphysical; the other was distinctly ethical and judicial. One was linked to salvation through ritual chaos; the other was linked to regeneration through faith and adherence to revealed, fixed, ethical law. One deified man; the other did not. One venerated the dead;

---

39. The paintings on the walls of the "Palace of Minos" on Crete probably are tomb paintings.

the other did not. One was a fertility cult; the other was not. As Wunderlich remarks: "The idea of a link between veneration of the dead and a fertility cult runs counter to our modern ways of thinking. But there is a close connection, so close that we might almost speak of the cult of the dead as a form of fertility magic. . . . It is based on an ancient belief that the dead know the future. Ancestors are also responsible for providing for the continuation of the race."[40]

Such a view of the legitimacy of consulting the dead is utterly foreign to biblical religion. The one example in the Bible of a Hebrew leader consulting the dead was Saul's use of the witch of Endor — a "medium" with a familiar spirit (I Sam. 28:7) — who called up Samuel from the dead. This was in direct violation of Leviticus 19:31. God cut Saul off the very next day, as Samuel told him (I Sam. 28:19), thereby fulfilling the law's warning: "And the soul that turneth after such as have familiar spirits, and after wizards, to go a whoring after them, I will even set my face against that soul, and will cut him off from among his people" (Lev. 20:6). The use of the word "whoring" points to the fertility cult aspects of the cult of the dead.

Neither system could be reconciled with the other. There could be a temporary truce between them, but ultimately one or the other had to triumph. The confrontation between Moses and Pharaoh was to determine which system would surrender to, or be defeated by the other. God made it clear in advance to Pharaoh just which system would lose: "For now I will stretch out my hand, that I may smite thee and thy people with pestilence; and thou shalt be cut off from the earth. And in very deed for this cause have I raised thee up, for to show in thee my power; and that my name may be declared throughout all the earth" (Ex. 9:15-16).

A Digression on Greece

It is revealing that Wunderlich, whose intellectual reconstruction of the Egypt-influenced "palace" of Knossos — the Bronze Age, labyrinth-based mausoleum venerating the cult of the dead on the island of Crete — recognizes that only sterility and stagnation could result from the cult of the dead. But instead of looking to Christianity for an answer as to how the ancient world eventually escaped from this cult, he looks to the classical Greeks. He sees the classical Greeks as the inheritors of Knossos. It was they, he argues, who

---

40. Hans George Wunderlich, *The Secret of Crete* (New York: Macmillan, 1974), pp. 294-95, 295-96.

converted the rituals of death, including funeral plays, into a celebration of life. He asserts that this transformation was the origin of Western civilization.[41]

He fails to acknowledge just how oppressed Greek culture was by the fear of spirits, departed souls, and demons. He looks to Olympus for his explanation of the Greeks, rather than to the underground gods that dominated their lives.[42] He looks to a political religion, the Olympian gods and Olympian myths, rather than to demonology, which was the *real* religion of Greece.

Olympic mythology temporarily unified some of the city-states of Greece, and it bonded local families to particular city-states. Today it still unifies humanist historians and anthropologists. That fleeting century of Athenian democracy in the fifth century, B.C. continues to hypnotize Western scholars. It was a century of war and the reckless expansion of Athenian political power which ultimately led to the downfall of Athens (when their gold ran out) to Sparta, and later to the fall of Greece to the Macedonians. *Periclean Athens was a massive welfare State* in which the State built huge public works projects, organized public assistance, offered pensions to the disabled, subsidized bread purchases, established price controls on bread, imposed export controls, established free theater programs for the poor, and regulated corn merchants.[43] The "bread and circuses" political religion of Athens ended in an enforced inter-city alliance, war with Sparta, defeat, tyranny, and finally the loss to Macedon. That is the fate of all bread and circus religions.

Athens worshipped politics with all its being, on a scale barely understood by most historians. It was understood by Glotz:

Five hundred citizens were to sit in the Boule for a whole year. The heliasts, whose functions were originally confined to hearing appeals against awards made by the magistrates, were now to judge in first instance and without appeal the increasingly numerous cases in which citizens of Athens and the confederate towns were involved: they formed a body of six thousand

---

41. Wunderlich, ch. 25: "The Origin of Western Civilization."

42. Jane E. Harrison, *Prolegomena to the Study of Greek Religion* (3rd ed.; New York: Meridian, [1922] 1960); *Epilogomena to the Study of Greek Religion* (1921) and *Themis: A Study of the Social Origins of Greek Religion* (2nd ed., 1972), published in one volume by University Books, New Hyde Park, New York, 1962. See also John Cuthbert Lawson, *Modern Greek Folklore and Ancient Greek Religion* (New Hyde Park, New York: University Books, [1909] 1964).

43. G. Glotz, *The Greek City and Its Institutions* (New York: Barnes and Noble, [1929] 1969), pp. 131-32.

members of which half on an average were in session every working day. There were ten thousand officials within the country or outside, five hundred wardens of arsenals, etc. Thus public affairs did not merely demand the intermittent presence of all the citizens of the Assembly; they required besides the constant exertions of more than a third of them.[44]

Consider it: one-third of all the estimated 35,000 to 44,000 resident male citizens of Athens in the year 431 B.C. were in State service.[45] At least 20,000 were "eating public bread," meaning that they were either on the payroll or on the dole.[46] The legend of Pericles, the legend of Athenian democracy, and the legend of Olympus constitute the basis of the legend — a Renaissance legend — of the glory that was Athens and the greatness that was Greece. It is the most enduring of all Greek myths.

The Denial of Time

What kind of society was early dynastic Egypt, the Egypt of the Pyramid Age? Mumford's words ring true: "Bureaucratic regimentation was in fact part of the larger regimentation of life, introduced by this power-centered culture. Nothing emerges more clearly from the Pyramid texts themselves, with their wearisome repetitions of formulae, than a colossal capacity for enduring monotony: a capacity that anticipates the universal boredom achieved in our own day. Even the poetry of both early Egypt and Babylonia reveal this iterative hypnosis: the same words, in the same order, with no gain in meaning, repeated a dozen times — or a hundred times. This verbal compulsiveness is the psychical side of the systematic compulsion that brought the labor machine into existence. Only those who were sufficiently docile to endure this regimen at every stage from command to execution could become an effective unit in the human machine."[47] The culture denied linear time. It substituted endless repetition for progress, monotony for hope.

While the recentralization of power by the Pharaoh of the oppression did not revive the enormous capital outlays of the Pyramid Age, it did reflect more accurately than feudalism Egypt's theology of the continuity of being. It did establish slavery, and it did involve

---

44. *Ibid.*, p. 126.
45. Alfred E. Zimmern, *The Greek Commonwealth: Politics and Economics in Fifth-Century Athens* (Oxford: At the Clarendon Press, 1915), p. 172.
46. *Ibid.*, pp. 172-73.
47. Mumford, "Megamachine," p. 266.

the construction of State-worshipping public works projects. In the era of the oppression and the Exodus, Egypt's presuppositions concerning the true nature of God, man, and law were manifested in the new bureaucratization.

Here was a culture devoid of any concept of progress, a culture which ignored its own history, except insofar as it built monuments to the dead. It did not even have an accurate chronology of its own kings, as Courville's study demonstrates, a problem which Western historians have wrestled with for two thousand years. The Greeks paid more attention to Egypt's dynastic chronology than the later Egyptians did. Egypt was a society without a future, so it was not particularly concerned about its past. As Wilson writes, "For the Jews the future is normative. For the Egyptians, on the other hand, the past was normative; and no pharaoh could hope to achieve more than the establishment of the conditions as they were in the time of Re, in the beginning."[48] The State would, at best, be able to preserve the status quo. Static peace, not any fundamental alteration, was the ideal, despite the fact that certain kings — Sesostris III, Thutmose III — were able to expand the dynasty's limits at least as far as Asia Minor.

Order Out of Chaos

The Egyptians believed that the creation originated in chaos. Here is the reigning cosmological vision of all pagan thought, from Egypt to Darwin, from Babel to Marx: *order developed from chaos and is in perpetual tension with chaos.* Mircea Eliade's voluminous studies have surveyed this theme in dozens of pagan cosmologies, and Egypt was no exception. Rushdoony has summarized this theme in ancient religion: "True social order requires peace and communication with both chaos and deity, and society either moves downward into chaos or forward into deification. The significance of the Tower of Babel is thus apparent: it denied the discontinuity of God's being and asserted man's claim to a continuity of being with God and heaven. The Tower was the *gate* to God and *gate* of God, signifying that man's social order made possible an ascent of being into the divine order. The Egyptian pyramid set forth the same faith."[49] Egyptian culture was inescapably statist. "The one and the many were brought

---

48. Wilson, "Egypt," p. 26.

49. R. J. Rushdoony, *The One and the Many: Studies in the Philosophy of Order and Ultimacy* (Fairfax, Virginia: Thoburn Press, [1971] 1978), p. 40.

together in the person of the king. The Egyptian language had no word for 'state.' For them, the state was not one institution among many but rather the essence of the divine order for life and the means of communication between heaven, earth, and hell. Life therefore was totally and inescapably statist. In this perspective, anything resembling liberty and individuality in the contemporary sense was alien and impossible. . . . Deification was entry into the oneness of the divine order, and membership in the state in this life was similarly participation in the divine oneness manifested in the pharaoh and protection against the horror of chaos and meaningless particularity."[50] The product of such a theology was imperial bureaucracy.

The Pharaoh of Moses' day looked at the remarkable growth of the Hebrew population, even in the face of affliction, and he grew fearful. What if these people allied themselves to an invading army? How was it that they could multiply like this? What would stop their growth? This population growth, promised to Abraham four centuries before (Gen. 17:2), was a threat to all the plans of the Pharaoh —an uncontrolled factor in a human megamachine. Growth, in a static culture, represents a frightening challenge, something beyond the calculations of the planning agencies. Uncontrolled growth— growth outside the bureaucratic plan—is a destabilizing factor for planned economies. Pharaoh knew that it had to be thwarted. Yet he was powerless to call it to a halt.

Conclusion

Imperial bureaucracy is one of the two major political manifestations of the society of Satan.[51] The other is anarchism. Imperial bureaucracy is *a top-down system of central planning* which inescapably rests on the presupposition (stated or implied) that the planners are near-gods, that they have sufficient imagination and a God-like comprehensive knowledge to set forth their decrees, and that their words shall come to pass. Imperial bureaucracy is produced whenever men believe that at least some men—the central planning elite—are essentially divine, or what is the same thing, that they have no god above them to whom their subjects (slaves) can successfully appeal.

---

50. *Ibid.,* pp. 44-45.

51. The best account I have ever read on this subject is R. J. Rushdoony's 1964 essay, "The Society of Satan," reprinted in *Biblical Economics Today,* II (Oct./Nov. 1979). This is available on request from the Institute for Christian Economics, P. O. Box 8000, Tyler, Texas 75711.

The idea of imperial bureaucracy therefore rests on the idea of the continuity of being: *from God to the planning elite,* the representatives of the people (who may or may not be considered part of this continuity of being).

The Egyptian State created a bureaucracy so vast, so all-encompassing, that nothing in man's history rivaled it until the rise of the modern industrialized socialist commonwealths. The State enshrined the cult of the dead in a desperate attempt to achieve life beyond the grave.[52] Life was seen as static, something which possesses unchanging continuity with life after death, at least for the Pharaoh. This static culture was statist to the core.

When the Exodus came, it did not simply free an enslaved population from physical bondage. It freed them from a static, hopeless society that was doomed, even if economically successful for the kings and nobles, to endless boredom — a kind of living death. *The "living" death of the Pharaoh's mummy was mirrored in the living death of the society.* God delivered Israel from a society which was based on the theology of the divine State. No king in Israel ever claimed to be divine, for only God has that right of absolute sovereignty. The people of Israel, even under the worst of Israel's kings, were never again to live within the imperial bureaucracy of a centralized divine order, except when they were again in bondage to foreign rulers.

The freedom which God provided for them was comprehensive, and the heart of this freedom was religious: the denial of absolute sovereignty any place on earth except in God's "holy of holies" in His temple, the center of which was the ark which contained the summary of His law. There is sovereignty only in God's word, not in the secret labyrinth recesses of some dead man's pyramid.

---

52. In the Soviet Union, Lenin's tomb has become the national shrine. They keep his embalmed body in a glass case for the masses to visit. He is probably the best-dressed person in the USSR — all dressed up, with nowhere to go.

3

RIGOROUS WASTE

The Egyptians made the children of Israel to serve with rigour: And they made their lives bitter with hard bondage, in mortar, and in brick, and in all manner of service in the field: all their service, wherein they made them to serve, was with rigour (Ex. 1:13-14).

The Egyptians subjugated the Israelites. The language of this passage indicates a grinding servitude, for it lists a seven-fold subjection: serve, rigor, bondage, slavery, service, serve, and rigor.[1] Unquestionably, the Egyptians were able to extract extensive labor services out of these captives. This period of servitude may have lasted over a century; certainly, it lasted from Moses' birth until the Exodus, 80 years later. (Given the Old Testament's familiar 40-year period of servitude and "wilderness wandering," I believe that 80 years is more likely.) Therefore, we might be tempted to conclude that the Egyptians were the beneficiaries of the Hebrews' labor services. Yet in retrospect, the Egyptians (through the decisions of their sovereigns, the pharaohs) made a disastrous error in their estimate of costs and benefits. They overestimated the benefits of the Hebrews' productivity, and they underestimated the costs of enslaving them. As they learned after the Exodus, if Courville's reconstructed chronology is correct, a nation is defenseless without its army, and the invading Amalekites (Hyksos, identified by conventional historians as the shepherd kings) were able to conquer them. They lost their Hebrew labor force, and they became the servants

---

1. U. Cassuto, *A Commentary on the Book of Exodus,* trans. Israel Abrahams (Jerusalem: Magnes Press, Hebrew University, [1951] 1974), p. 12. The word for "slave labor" occurs five times, and the word "rigor" appears twice. A seven-fold emphasis appears also in verse 7, which lists seven aspects of Israel's population growth. If Cassuto is correct in his assertion that the number 7 is "indicative of perfection" (p. 9), then Egypt's oppression was perfectly horrible.

(slaves).[2]

It is difficult to understand how so valuable an economic resource as human labor might be wasted in a slave system, yet economics informs us that *excessive waste is characteristic of any slave economy which is not closely linked to a free market.* It is the institution of a competitive market which enables slave owners to assess the productivity of the slaves. The South's slave system of the United States prior to the Civil War (1861-65) appears to have been a profitable institutional arrangement for the slave-owning planters,[3] but they operated within a free market, and they produced cash crops, especially cotton, which were sold in worldwide markets. Slaves were sold at price-competitive auctions, and a resale market existed. The output of the slaves could be calculated rationally. Owners and renters (slaves were sometimes rented out) could make estimates of costs and benefits within the framework of a money economy which possessed a high degree of economic specialization.

The Egyptians used the Hebrews to construct treasure cities, or storehouse cities, made of brick. They also used them in the fields. However, we must recognize that treasure cities were huge public works projects built for the Pharaoh. They were statist enterprises, not market enterprises. Furthermore, there was almost certainly no open market for the bulk of these Hebrew slaves, as if all branches of the Egyptian government were competitively pitted in an open auction for their services. This is not to say that all the slaves were held by the State, but it is likely that the majority of them were. When the Pharaoh imposed the punishment that they gather their own straw for brick-making, he was acting as a political sovereign. The punishment made sense only as a political-theological-military decision, not as a profit-seeking economic measure (Ex. 5:5-7). Such

---

2. Immanuel Velikovsky, *Ages in Chaos* (Garden City, New York: Doubleday, 1952), ch. 2.

3. Alfred H. Conrad and John R. Meyer, "The Economics of Slavery in the Ante-Bellum South," *The Journal of Political Economy,* LXVI (April 1966); reprinted in Robert W. Fogel and Stanley L. Engerman (eds.), *The Reinterpretation of American Economic History* (New York: Harper & Row, 1971). Cf. Fogel and Engerman, "The Economics of Slavery," *ibid.,* and Yasukichi Yasuba, "The Profitability and Viability of Plantation Slavery in the United States," *The Economic Studies Quarterly,* XII (Sept. 1961), in *ibid.* For a general introduction to the question of the profitability of slavery in the American South, see Harold D. Woodman (ed.), *Slavery and the Southern Economy: Sources and Readings* (New York: Harcourt, Brace & World, 1966). The essays in this collection are older, written before the advent of the "new economic history," with its statistical techniques and econometric market models.

a restraint on productivity made sense only within the framework of a State-operated construction program in which the slaves were an instrument of State power.

The Pharaoh, in any case, was the owner of all Egypt (Gen. 47:20). He was the official source of meaning in the cosmos. He was responsible for allocating scarce economic resources for the benefit of the State. The estimation of the Pharaoh, not the estimations of acting buyers and sellers in free markets, was the standard of economic value. It was incumbent on the Pharaoh to make accurate cost-benefit estimates if the nation was to prosper. "The king," writes Frankfort, "is not only instrumental in producing the 'fat of the land'; he must also dispense it. Only then is there evidence that he functions effectively. His bounty proves that he disposes, as a king should dispose, of the earth and its produce. . . . But the king also keeps alive the hearts of all those subjects who do not directly partake of his bounty. For he exercises a never ending mysterious activity on the strength of which daily, hourly, nature and society are integrated."[4] The king was understood to direct the very forces of nature. It was the king, and only the king, whose judgments concerning economic production were sovereign.

Economic Calculation

When the Pharaoh enslaved the Hebrews, he made a cost-benefit analysis. He concluded that the risks in allowing them to remain free were too high (Ex. 1:10). He concluded that the risks of breaking Egypt's covenant with the Hebrews — and, by implication, with their God — were minimal. He decided that any loss of productivity on their part could be compensated for, assuming his taskmasters used whips and other coercive measures to compel their hard labor. In other words, he concluded that sheer force, and not the profit opportunities of a free market, was the best means of extracting valuable labor services from them. He forfeited the productivity of a profit-seeking people who willingly bore the costs of their own actions. He concluded that coercion was more efficient in extracting their services, despite the necessity of having to feed them, supervise them constantly, and continually pressure them to greater output. In short, he underestimated the productivity-engendering features of a

---

4. Henri Frankfort, *Kingship and the Gods: A Study of Ancient Near Eastern Religion as the Integration of Society & Nature* (University of Chicago Press, [1948] 1962), pp. 59-60.

free market, and he overestimated the benefits of coercion. When they left Egypt triumphantly, after God had reduced Egypt's economy by means of plagues and spoils, *the Egyptians learned just what kind of economic losses a nation can sustain as a result of kings' errors in cost-benefit analysis.*

The Hebrews worked very hard. Did this ensure their productivity? Can we conclude that hard work is efficient work? How do we measure or calculate efficient labor? How could the Egyptians have made such estimations? How did they know when they were getting "their money's worth" out of these slaves?

If we accepted the labor theory of value, we would have to conclude that no matter what they were assigned to achieve, their rigorous efforts *must* have produced profitable results. (This is a very good argument against the labor theory of value.) But how can anyone measure efficiency if there are no profits? A socialist economy has no profits and losses to compare. A divine monarch does not permit a free market in labor services once he enslaves a people. Slavery in Egypt in Moses' day meant hard labor in constructing treasure cities. Hard work led to waste on a massive scale. The slaves' efforts benefited the king, and *the Egyptians paid for their king's public works projects in many ways:* lost labor that the Hebrews might have provided the general population, lost raw materials that went into the projects, and the greatest cost of all, the growing wrath of God which would culminate in the destruction of the economy, the Pharaoh, and the army. The enslaving kings no doubt were satisfied with the transaction; the people, governed by a false theology, temporarily may have approved; but the end result was unmitigated destruction. The mere expenditure of human effort on State public works projects does not guarantee a return on the investment which is positive. *Without a free market, in which the competing bids of buyers and sellers of resources determine the allocation of scarce resources, there is no way for the State's officials to calculate economic value accurately.* They can only make estimates, but there is no self-correcting information system available to inform them of the accuracy or inaccuracy of their judgments.

Egypt had a theology which asserted the ability of the Pharaoh to make such judgments, which is precisely the theology a consistent socialist commonwealth *must* have if it is to be a valid substitute for a market economy. The integration of all economic plans can be furthered by the market, or it can theoretically be accomplished by an omniscient agency; in Egypt's case, this agency was supposedly the Pharaoh. "He was a lonely being, this god-king of Egypt," writes Wilson. "All by himself he stood between humans and gods. Texts and scenes emphasize his solitary responsibility. The temple scenes show him as the only priest in ceremonies with the gods. A hymn to a god states: 'There is no one else that knows thee except thy son, (the king), whom thou causest to understand thy plans and power.' It was the king who built temples and cities, who won battles, who made laws, who collected taxes, or who provided the bounty for the tombs of his nobles."[5] Egypt possessed the necessary theology for a consistent socialist commonwealth, but this theology was wrong, as the Egyptians learned in the year of the Exodus. The king did not possess omniscience; he did not know what the true costs of enslaving the Hebrews really were.

The pharaohs who constructed the mighty pyramids of the Old Kingdom had weakened the Egyptian economy drastically. Wilson has described these structures quite accurately: huge, noneconomic construction projects that were supposed to last for eternity, but which had to be followed by more of them in each generation.[6] The brick pyramids of the later pharaohs were not equally majestic, but their construction involved comparable problems. Were they cost-effective? Only the Pharaoh could decide, since there was no free market available for men to use as a means of evaluating the true costs involved. The Hebrews were forced to work *rigorously,* but this could not guarantee that they were working *efficiently.* The wit's definition of modern commercialism applies to the Pharaoh's pyramids and cities: something done magnificently which should not have been done at all. The Pharaoh, as a divinity, was supposed to know what ultimate value really is, but he was not divine, so he faced the inescapable economic problem that has baffled all central planners, namely, *the impossibility of making rational economic calculation in an economy without competitive free markets.* This is the problem described by Ludwig von Mises as the problem of economic calcula-

---

5. John A. Wilson, "Egypt," in Henri Frankfort, *et al., The Intellectual Adventure of Ancient Man: An Essay on Speculative Thought in the Ancient Near East* (University of Chicago Press, [1946] 1977), p. 77.

6. John A. Wilson, *The Burden of Egypt: An Interpretation of Ancient Egyptian Culture* (University of Chicago Press, [1951] 1967), p. 98.

tion in a socialist commonwealth.[7] *An economy without competitive markets is an economy without rational economic guidelines.* It is an economy which is "flying blind."

The central planner does not know what slave labor is really worth, for such labor commands no free market price. He does not know what the true cost of his capital equipment is, since there is no competitive market for capital goods. The Pharaoh, like any other socialist planner, could only guess. All he could do was to make *intuitive judgments* about what his cities were worth to him and what the actual costs of production really were. The larger the scope of the projects, and the larger the slave labor supply, the more difficult it was to make such intuitive estimates apart from fully competitive prices. But competitive pricing is precisely what socialist economic planning denies.

Socialism's Economic Miscalculation

Mises commented at some length on this problem of economic calculation in his book, *Socialism* (1922). "Let us try to imagine the position of a socialist community. There will be hundreds and thousands of establishments in which work is going on. A minority of these will produce goods ready for use. The majority will produce capital goods and semi-manufactures. All these establishments will be closely connected. Each commodity produced will pass through a whole series of such establishments before it is ready for consumption. Yet in the incessant press of all these processes the economic administration will have no real sense of direction. It will have no means of ascertaining whether a given piece of work is really necessary, whether labour and material are not being wasted in completing it. How would it discover which of two processes was the most satisfactory? At best, it could compare the quantity of ultimate products. But only rarely could it compare the expenditure incurred in their production. It would know exactly — or it would imagine it knew — what it wanted to produce. It ought therefore to set about ob-

---

7. Ludwig von Mises, "Economic Calculation in the Socialist Commonwealth," (1920), in F. A. Hayek (ed.), *Collectivist Economic Planning* (London: Routledge & Kegan Paul, [1935] 1963), ch. 3. Cf. Mises, *Socialism: An Economic and Sociological Analysis* (2nd ed.; New Haven, Connecticut: Yale University Press, [1922] 1951), Pt. II. This has been reprinted in both hardback and paperback editions in 1981 by Liberty Classics, Indianapolis, Indiana. See also Hayek, *Individualism and Economic Order* (University of Chicago Press, 1948), chaps. 7-9; T. J. B. Hoff, *Economic Calculation in the Socialist Society* (London: Hodge & Co. 1948); reprinted by Liberty Classics, 1981.

taining the desired results with the smallest possible expenditure. But to do this it would have to be able to make calculations. And such calculations must be calculations of value. They could not be merely 'technical,' they could not be calculations of the objective use-value of goods and services. . . . The economic administration may indeed know exactly what commodities are needed most urgently. But this is only half the problem. The other half, the valuation of the means of production, it cannot solve. It can ascertain the value of the totality of such instruments. That is obviously equal to the satisfactions they afford. If it calculates the loss that would be incurred by withdrawing them, it can also ascertain the value of single instruments of production. But it cannot assimilate them to a common price denominator, as can be done under a system of economic freedom and money prices."[8]

Mises was too generous here to his ideological opponents, the socialists. Unless the State is defined as the desires of one man — which is what the Pharaoh could claim — it is not possible for socialist planners to "know exactly what commodities are needed most urgently." They cannot possibly ascertain "the value of the totality of such instruments," precisely because no planning agency can ever estimate "the satisfactions they afford." The satisfactions afforded to a multitude of citizens by any single mix of consumer goods cannot possibly be known; they can only be guessed at. Furthermore, *there is no way for the socialist planners to judge the failure of their estimations, outside of massive revolution by the victimized consumers* — a contingency made less likely by the systematic repression by the police and military leaders of most socialist commonwealths. They know that they cannot possibly make such calculations accurately, and so they spend great quantities of sorely needed capital on the suppression of potentially violent consumer dissatisfaction.

Rothbard's summary of Mises' argument is illuminating: "In short, if there were no market for a product, and all of its exchanges were internal, there would be no way for a firm or for anyone else to determine a price for the good. A firm can estimate an implicit price when an external market exists; but when a market is absent, the good can have no price, whether implicit or explicit. Any figure could then be only an arbitrary symbol. Not being able to calculate a price, the firm could not rationally allocate factors and resources

---

8. Ludwig von Mises, *Socialism,* pp. 120-21.

from one stage to another."[9] In fact, Rothbard concludes, *a universal monopoly by one great corporation is theoretically impossible,* since a universal monopoly would have no market-determined array of prices to guide its production decisions. "As the area of incalculability increases, the degrees of irrationality, misallocation, loss, impoverishment, etc., become greater. Under *one* owner or *one* cartel for the whole productive system, there would be no possible areas of calculation at all, and therefore complete economic chaos would prevail."[10] Yet this kind of universal ownership was precisely what the pharaohs had attempted to create since Joseph's day. Only to the extent that a particular pharaoh would turn his back on his theoretical ownership of Egypt, and would allow independent buyers and sellers to produce for a free market in goods and services, could the Egyptian economy reverse its drift into economic chaos.

Lange's "Refutation" of Mises

There was an attempt by a Polish socialist economist of the 1930's, Oskar Lange, to refute Mises by arguing that socialist economies can use prices to allocate production rationally.[11] These would be hypothetical prices, established initially on a purely arbitrary basis by the central planners. If supplies cleared the markets, the price structure would be left unchanged. If not, prices would be changed until production did clear all markets.[12]

---

9. Murray N. Rothbard, *Man, Economy, and State* (New York: New York University Press, [1962] 1975), p. 547.

10. *Ibid.,* p. 548.

11. Lange wrote: "Socialists have certainly good reason to be grateful to Professor Mises, the great *advocatus diaboli* of their cause. For it was his powerful challenge that forced the socialists to recognize the importance of an adequate system of economic accounting to guide the allocation of resources in a socialist economy. Even more, it was chiefly due to Professor Mises' challenge that many socialists became aware of the very existence of such a problem. And although Professor Mises was not the first to raise it, and although not all socialists were as completely unaware of the problem as is frequently held, nevertheless, that, particularly on the European Continent (outside of Italy), the merit of having caused the socialists to approach this problem systematically belongs entirely to Professor Mises. Both as an expression of recognition for the great service rendered by him and as a memento of the prime importance of sound economic reasoning, a statue of Professor Mises ought to occupy an honorable place in the great hall of the Ministry of Socialization or of the Central Planning Board of the socialist state." Lange, in Oskar Lange and Fred M. Taylor, *On the Economic Theory of Socialism* (New York: McGraw-Hill, [1938] 1956), pp. 57-58.

12. *Ibid.,* pp. 70-98. For a refutation of Lange, see Hoff, *Economic Calculation in the Socialist Society, op. cit.*

This argument ignores many things, such as the possibility of any central planning agency's establishing an initial array of prices for millions of consumer goods and services, or even the basic raw materials and capital—human and physical—that would be needed to produce these goods. Second, if there is no private ownership, especially of capital goods, how could consumers enforce their preferences on the planners? So what if markets do not clear? So what if some firms do poorly? Since no one owns them, how can the central planners act as surrogates for consumers and persuade all managers to produce the proper number and quality of goods? Third, why would central planners want to enforce the preferences of consumers on managers? After all, we are speaking of self-conscious slave-holding societies. What is the Gulag Archipelago, with its millions of inmates, if not a system of slavery?

It is revealing that no socialist economic commonwealth has ever adopted Lange's hypothetical "solution" to the objections raised by Mises. What is even more revealing is that the myth of Lange's supposed "refutation" is still found in textbooks on comparative economic systems. Mises' 1920 essay and his book, *Socialism,* are never cited; only brief references are made to Lange's supposed answer.

Flying Blind

The socialists may believe that the systematic planning of specialized agencies will lead to a huge increase in productivity. They may believe that the co-ordination of all segments of a nation's economy can be achieved only by central planning. They may believe that men will work rigorously and therefore effectively only when compelled to do so in the name of the sovereign political order. What we learn from Israel's experience in bondage is the opposite. Men can serve the State rigorously, but *the centrally planned State is economically blind.* The State may indeed overcome the so-called "anarchy" of an unregulated free market, but this in no way assures the triumph of economic rationality. As Mises wrote in the early decades of the twentieth century: "Instead of the economy of 'anarchical' production, the senseless order of an irrational machine would be supreme. The wheels would go round, but to no effect."[13] Without the ability to calculate the value of any resource's contribution to the economy, and its economic burden on the economy as it is used up,

---

13. Mises, *Socialism,* p. 120.

the socialist central planning agency is "flying blind." Without a free market, especially a free market in capital goods, it is impossible for central planners to make any more than woefully uneducated guesses concerning economic costs and benefits. No economically rational prices exist to guide them in their task. The longer they do without a market economy, the less educated are their guesses.

A fine summary of the problem of economic calculation in a socialist commonwealth was provided by I. Borovitski, a disgruntled enterprise manager in the Soviet Union, in 1962. He complained in the newspaper, *Pravda* (Oct. 5, 1962): "The department of Gosplan [the Soviet central planning agency — G.N.] which drafts the production program for *Sovnarkhozy* [regional economic councils — G.N.] and enterprises is totally uninterested in costs and profits. Ask the senior official in the production program department in what factor it is cheaper to produce this or that commodity? He has no idea, and never even puts the question to himself. He is responsible only for the distribution of production tasks. Another department, not really concerned with the costs of production, decides on the plan for gross output. A third department or subdepartment, proceeding from the principle that costs must always decline and labor productivity increase, plans costs, wages fund and labor on the basis of past performance. Material allocations and components are planned by numerous other departments. Not a single department of Gosplan is responsible for the consistency of these plans."[14] And if such a department existed, it would still be helpless. It would possess no reliable information concerning competitive prices by which to estimate economic costs.

Oppression and Misallocated Resources

When the Pharaoh enslaved the Hebrews, he reduced the economic rationality of the Egyptian nation. When he and his successors began to use the labor of the Hebrews to construct treasure cities, they took another step in the direction of economic irrational-

---

14. Cited by Alec Nove, *The Soviet Economy: An Introduction* (rev. ed.; New York: Praeger, 1966), p. 207. Cf. Gary North, "The Crisis in Soviet Economic Planning," *Modern Age,* XIV (1969-70); reprinted in North, *An Introduction to Christian Economics* (Nutley, New Jersey: Craig Press, 1973), ch. 22. See also North, *Marx's Religion of Revolution: The Doctrine of Creative Destruction* (Nutley, New Jersey: Craig Press, 1968), Appendix B: "Soviet Economic Planning." A microfiche of this book is available from the Institute for Christian Economics. At some point, I hope to revise and reprint it.

ity and tyranny, for they were extracting these labor services from the consumer-oriented markets and redirecting them into statist projects. These projects were State monopolies; there was no way to calculate the benefits they conveyed to Egypt, except insofar as Egypt was defined as the State, and the State was equated with thé Pharaoh. This enormous transfer of productive wealth—human capital—from the market to the bureaucratic State benefited the pharaohs in the short run, but it made the Egyptian economy less productive and less rational economically. The value of the labor services of an individual Hebrew could easily be calculated on a free market; the value of the labor services of all Hebrews could not be calculated in the State's public works programs.

The Hebrews were forced to work rigorously. This was significant as a *means of oppression;* it was not necessarily significant as a testimony to the rationality of the Egyptian economy. By transferring their labor services to statist building projects, the Egyptian taskmasters reaffirmed the commitment of the State to its own deification at the expense of national per capita wealth. The State would collect its huge "tithe" on a permanent basis. Yet it could not guarantee that this "tithe" would be used efficiently. As the Egyptians learned in the year of the Exodus, there had been far better uses for Israel's labor than the construction of treasure cities and coerced work in the fields. The State could, for a time, extract labor from the Hebrews; it was unable to escape the inevitable costs. It was also unable to escape the necessity of making accurate cost-benefit analyses, despite the fact that the pharaohs believed that they had done so. The Hebrews worked rigorously, but at the time of the Exodus, Egypt learned how expensive this labor had been, and how wasteful the expenditure had been. The Pharaoh of the Exodus was no longer able to enjoy his treasure cities; he was at the bottom of the Red Sea, and the treasures were gone.

A drowned Pharaoh, it should be noted, renders questionable the simultaneous belief in two possibilities: 1) the conventional dating of the powerful Eighteenth Dynasty in the fifteenth century (whose pharaohs' mummies still exist); and 2) the dating of the Exodus in the fifteenth century. If you assume the former, you cannot easily hold to the latter. Yet virtually all Christian historians accept the fifteenth-century dating of the Eighteenth Dynasty. Thus, with the exception of amateur historian Courville, they have wound up arguing for both positions simultaneously, or worse, arguing for a later date for the Exodus. Such is the power of humanist scholarship in our day that well-meaning Christian scholars have surrendered themselves to the humanists.

Anyone who argues for a thirteenth-century date of the Exodus has sold out the case for biblical inerrency by denying the truth of I Kings 6:1. This is far more serious than making yourself look ridiculous by arguing for the doubtful proposition that the Exodus really did take place in the fifteenth century, but somehow it left no trace — not even a hint of a minor regional dislocation — in the records of the Eighteenth Dynasty, and furthermore, that the Pharaoh's body was somehow retrieved from the sea, mummified, and buried honorably.

It is the initial assumption which must be rejected — the fifteenth-century dating of the early Eighteenth Dynasty — because I Kings 6:1 makes it impossible to date the Exodus in any other century except the fifteenth. It was not some powerful early Eighteenth Dynasty Pharaoh, whose mummies have all survived, who died in the Red Sea. Some other Pharaoh, whose mummy did not survive, and who was a member of some other dynasty, was the Pharaoh of the Exodus. The Eighteenth Dynasty is therefore improperly dated by conventional historians, Christian and non-Christian. This is why we should take seriously Courville's reconstructed chronology, at least as a preliminary step for a thorough reconsideration of the chronology of the ancient Near East.

Conclusion

The pharaohs, claiming omniscience, abandoned the free market for labor — a market which offers men at least some means of evaluating economic value. They claimed omnipotence, yet the Pharaoh of the Exodus was totally vanquished. They extracted rigorous service from the Israelites, yet they had no way of knowing whether or not such service from the Israelites was a national benefit. They believed that slavery was a national benefit, yet one of them finally learned that it was a national disaster. The arrogance of a sovereign central planning system was shattered in the year of the Exodus. What several pharaohs had believed was rigorous service to the Egyptian State turned out to be rigorous waste on a scale undreamed of by the Pharaoh who first enslaved Israel. It was Egypt, finally, which paid the price for this waste.

The modern version of the pharaohs' economy, socialist economic planning, also rests on an implicit assumption of near-omniscience of the central planning agencies. Like the pharaohs, socialist planners are "flying blind." They cannot accurately calculate true costs and benefits because they do not have access to the information which is produced on a competitive free market. Centrally planned economies are wasteful, tyrannical, and ultimately self-destructive, just as the pharaohs' economy was. Socialist economic planning is an updated application of the religion of ancient Egypt.

4

ILLEGITIMATE STATE POWER

The king of Egypt spake to the Hebrew midwives, of which the name of the one was Shiphrah, and the name of the other Puah: And he said, When ye do the office of midwife to the Hebrew women, and see them upon the stools [birthstools]; if it be a son, then ye shall kill him: but if it be a daughter, then she shall live. But the midwives feared God, and did not as the king of Egypt commanded them, but saved the men children alive (Ex. 1:15-16).

The goal of every imperial bureaucracy is *control.* No factor in the economy is supposed to be left to chance. This includes the population factor. Since it is one of the most basic of all economic inputs, a central planning agency which would leave population growth to "chance"—the natural fertility rate of the population's sexual partners —would be abdicating its responsibilities. The Hebrews were therefore an "unknown quantity" economically. *The very presence of their growing numbers in the face of deliberate oppression was a denial of the sovereignty of the Egyptian bureaucracy.*

There was also a religious issue at stake. Here was a significant portion of the total population of Egypt which was clearly out of favor with the ruler. The Pharaoh was in theory a divine figure; his protection was given to his subjects in the name of the gods. (Egypt was extremely polytheistic.) Yet one of the primary symbols of blessing, population growth, was present to a startling extent among this foreign, enslaved people. The literal fulfillment of God's covenantal promise to Abraham (Gen. 17:2-6) before the eyes of the Egyptians was a standing testimony to the sovereignty of a God other than the gods of Egypt, a universal God whose power and authority were not limited to the original homeland of these displaced people. Here was a God who showed His presence among a defeated people, in stark contrast to the theory of pagan antiquity that gods are local in their sovereignty and are themselves defeated when their people are defeated by troops of another State. (See the disastrously erroneous but typical arguments of the king of Syria in this regard: I Ki. 20:23-25.) *The fertility of the Hebrew slaves was a visible contradiction of the theology of the imperial bureaucracy.* The Egyptians were determined to call a halt to the extraordinary population growth of their newly en-slaved Hebrew servants, and they were willing to resort to infan-ticide to achieve their ends.

The unprecedented population growth of the Hebrews served as a major threat to the sovereignty of the Pharaoh, who was the em-bodiment of the Egyptian State. They posed a potential military threat, since they might ally themselves to an invading foreign army (Ex. 1:9-10). They might succeed in displacing the Egyptians, since such population growth, if continued over several centuries, would fill up the land. Furthermore, the very presence of a growing popula-tion constituted an economic factor of great magnitude. How was such a factor to be incorporated into the State economic plan? How could they be controlled? How could the State supply them with basic necessities? How could the State be certain that their labor was being used in an efficient, productive fashion? How many imperial cities could the Pharaoh afford to build? How long would the resources of Egypt be absorbed by the Hebrews in their status as public works employees? The Egyptians made them work *rigorously* (Ex. 1:14), but this could not guarantee that their efforts would be *productive.*

The Lying Midwives

In response to the Hebrews' multiplication, Pharaoh called in two Hebrew midwives. He ordered them to kill all male infants born to the slave women. Two women acting alone would not have been able to kill more than a fraction of the male children born on any day; therefore, many commentators have concluded that these two midwives were the leaders of a midwives' guild. As representatives of the guild, they would have been required by Pharaoh to pass along the order to the other midwives.

The midwives refused to participate in these evil plans. They made a moral decision. They refused to obey the king, and they lied to him about the reason for their supposed inability to obey: "And the midwives said unto Pharaoh, Because the Hebrew women are not as the Egyptian women; for they are lively, and are delivered ere [before] the midwives come into them" (Ex. 1:19).

This passage has bothered far too many orthodox commentators. One person who could not accept the obvious — that God was pleased with their successful lie — was John Murray. His chapter on "The Sanctity of Truth" challenges their actions, just as it challenges Rahab's famous lie to the authorities of Jericho concerning the whereabouts of the Hebrew spies. "Let us grant, however, that the midwives did speak an untruth and that their reply was really false. There is still no warrant to conclude that the untruth is endorsed, far less that it is the untruth that is in view when we read, 'And God dealt well with the midwives' (Exodus I: 20). The midwives feared God in disobeying the king and it is because they feared God that the Lord blessed them (cf. verses 17, 21). It is not at all strange that their fear of God should have coexisted with moral infirmity. The case is simply that no warrant for untruth can be elicited from this instance any more than in the cases of Jacob and Rahab."[1]

I have commented elsewhere at some length on the legitimacy of Jacob's lie to Isaac.[2] I have also commented on the legitimacy of Rahab's lie to the Jericho authorities.[3] Many of the same arguments apply here. First, what else could the Hebrew midwives have done to save the lives of the children, except lie? Second, did Pharaoh deserve to be told the truth? Did the Nazis in World War II deserve to be told where Jews were being hidden? If those Dutchmen or Germans who hid Jews in their homes to protect them in World War II had been approached by the Nazis and asked if they had Jews hidden in their homes, knowing that all Christians are somehow morally bound to tell the truth at all times, no matter what, there would have been a lot of condemned Christians and captured Jews. Silence under such circumstances would have been regarded as an admission of guilt, and searches would have been conducted. Third, what is spying, other than a lie? (This is why the rules of Western warfare sanction the execution of spies during wartime, but men who are captured in foreign territory wearing their nation's uniform are supposed to be treated as prisoners of war.) Fourth, what is wartime

---

1. John Murray, *Principles of Conduct: Aspects of Biblical Ethics* (Grand Rapids, Michigan: Eerdmans, 1957), pp. 141-42.

2. Gary North, *The Dominion Covenant: Genesis* (Tyler, Texas: Institute for Christian Economics, 1982), ch. 19: "The Uses of Deception."

3. Gary North, "Appendix 5," in R. J. Rushdoony, *The Institutes of Biblical Law* (Nutley, New Jersey: Craig Press, 1973), pp. 838-42. Cf. Jim West, "Rahab's Justifiable Lie," *Christianity and Civilization,* 2 (Winter 1982-83).

camouflage, other than a lie?

This last question bothered Murray, a veteran of the First World War. When teaching a children's catechism class, he criticized the lie of Rebekah and Jacob to Isaac. Then he asked the class about camouflage. He denied that camouflage is a form of lying. It is only *concealment,* not deception, and concealment is legitimate under certain conditions. We are allowed to conceal something from someone "when that person has no right to know. . . ."[4] But that, of course, is the whole point. Did the authorities at Jericho have a "right to know," since they had been marked out by God for total destruction? Did Pharaoh have a "right to know," when he was seeking the destruction of God's people?

So desperate is Murray to maintain his position of the universal immorality of lying that he speculates about the possibility that the midwives' tale really might have been the partial truth. "We need not suppose that the midwives' reply to Pharaoh was altogether void of truth. There is good reason to believe that the Hebrew women often bore their children without aid of the midwives. We may therefore have an instance of partial truth and not total untruth, and partial truth relevant to the circumstances."[5] But he does not tell us *why* "there is good reason to believe that the Hebrew women often bore their children without the aid of midwives." If this was the case "often," then how did the midwives survive as a guild? This, in fact, is precisely the question Pharaoh should have asked them. He did not think to ask: "What have you midwives been doing all these years? Why is it that the Hebrew wives have only recently begun to deliver their babies so rapidly?" That he failed to ask them this question indicates that God had blinded him. That Prof. Murray also failed to ask this question indicates that his false presupposition blinded him.

The Pharaoh's decision was clearly ad hoc in nature. He immediately imposed a new policy of extermination: drowning, or at least abandonment (1:22). This new policy also obviously failed, since younger men participated in the Exodus — Joshua and his generation — and someone in Moses' generation must have fathered them. The extermination policy was clearly an interim measure, and it was unsuccessful. Whether the original Pharaoh's intent was the

---

4. *John Murray: A Memorial with Tributes* (Edinburgh: Banner of Truth, 1975), p. 46.

5. Murray, *Principles of Conduct,* p. 141.

ultimate extermination of the Hebrew slave population, or merely a short-run population control device, it failed.

Conclusion

The midwives lied directly to the Pharaoh. Given the preposterous nature of the tale, they lied baldly and shamelessly to him. And the Bible is very clear concerning God's opinion of such outright lying: "Therefore God dealt well with the midwives: and the people multiplied, and waxed very mighty. And it came to pass, because the midwives feared God, that he made them houses" (1:20-21).

By no bending of the Scriptures can legalistic commentators (whose names, sadly, are legion in our era) find the slightest trace of condemnation by God in the midwives' act of defiance against the constituted authority of Egypt. The State had spoken, and the midwives dealt with it in devious defiance. A biblical principle is hereby demonstrated. *The illegitimate laws of a civil government may be legitimately skirted when they come into direct conflict with a fundamental biblical principle.* (This principle was announced clearly by Peter in Acts 5:29: "We ought to obey God rather than men.")[6] In this case, the principle being upheld by the midwives was the morality of resisting the genocide of God's covenant people. Godly men must obey God, not the illegitimate demands of an apostate bureaucratic State.

Had the midwives been contemporary legalists, the infants would either have been slaughtered, or else the lying, "compromising" legalists would have had guilty consciences and no new houses. But the midwives were neither legalists nor moralists. They honored God's law in preference to the State's law. In doing so, they acknowledged *the absolute sovereignty of God,* as well as *the limits that God places on the authority of the State.*

(An interesting document relating to the historicity of Shiphrah, or at least someone bearing this name, is provided by a papyrus which is held by the Brooklyn Museum. It is a document from the Thirteenth Dynasty. It lists 90 slaves, 30 of whom had Northwest Semitic names. Shiphrah was one of these names. The conventional dating of this document is about the eighteenth century B.C. However, according to Courville's reconstructed chronology, the Thir-

---

6. For a symposium on the question of the right of Christian resistance against tyranny, see *Christianity and Civilization,* 2 (Winter 1982-83), published by the Geneva Divinity School, Tyler, Texas.

teenth Dynasty was the dynasty of the Exodus. Though the attempted execution of the Hebrew males took place at least 80 years before the Exodus, in the Twelfth Dynasty, Shiphrah could still have been alive in the new Pharaoh's household. At least, Shiphrah was a name that could have been used both in the era of the oppression and the Exodus. This lends further support to Courville's chronological reconstruction.)[7]

7. Donovan A. Courville, "A Biblical Reconstruction of Egypt's Early Chronology," *Journal of Christian Reconstruction,* II (Summer 1975), p. 152. On the papyrus, see Jack Finegan, *Light from the Ancient Past* (Princeton University Press, 1959), pp. 93-94; John J. Davis, *Moses and the Gods of Egypt* (Grand Rapids, Michigan: Baker Book House, 1972), pp. 49-50.

5

ENVY, RUMOR, AND BONDAGE

And it came to pass in those days, when Moses was grown, that he went out unto his brethren, and looked on their burdens: and he spied an Egyptian smiting an Hebrew, one of his brethren. And he looked this way and that way, and when he saw there was no man, he slew the Egyptian, and hid him in the sand. And when he went out the second day, behold, two men of the Hebrews strove together: and he said to him that did the wrong, Wherefore smitest thou thy fellow? And he said, Who made thee a prince and a judge over us? Intendest thou to kill me, as thou killedst the Egyptian? And Moses feared, and said, Surely this thing is known (Ex. 2:11-14).

This passage raises several difficult points of interpretation. First, was Moses a murderer? Second, why was he resented by the Hebrew who had initiated the wrong? Third, what was the motivating force behind the rumor? Fourth, what were the results when this rumor became widespread?

Was Moses a murderer? Biblically, a murderer is a person who fatally wounds another individual, and who has not received the sanction of legitimate civil or divine law for carrying out the violent act. "Thou shalt not kill" (Ex. 20:13) refers to the autonomous act of one individual against another. It does not refer to capital punishment by the civil government, since the law of God singles out crimes that must be punished by execution (cf. Ex. 22:18-20). Also, self-defense is a legitimate excuse; a biblical case law authorizes the slaying of a thief if he breaks in at night, when his intentions — theft, violence, or murder — cannot be readily known (Ex. 22:2-3). By implication, we can legitimately slay a life-threatening (or potentially life-threatening) attacker in defense of an innocent third party, just as Moses did. It is the *unsanctioned* slaying which constitutes murder. A man takes the law into his own hands; it has not been placed there by God or society. Murder is an act of self-proclaimed autonomous man against another man, created in God's image, who is entitled to protection by the law of God.

Moses was not sanctioned by Egyptian law to execute the Egyptian taskmaster. But this man had no biblically legitimate authority over the defenseless Hebrews. Their land had been stolen, and they had all been kidnapped — a capital offense (Ex. 21:16). He deserved death, as did all the taskmasters in Egypt. The New Testament affirms that Moses was a faithful man in the decision to stand with his fellow Hebrews and then in his flight from Egypt (Heb. 11:24-27).

Why did he do it? In part, because he made a miscalculation concerning the hearts of his brethren. "And seeing one of them suffer wrong, he defended him, and avenged him that was oppressed, and smote the Egyptian. For he supposed his brethren would have understood now that God by his hand would deliver them: but they understood not" (Acts 7:24-25). The Pharaoh sought to kill Moses, despite Moses' position in the Pharaoh's family, when he learned of Moses' act (Ex. 2:15).[1]

Moses was clearly the most highly placed Hebrew of his day. No other Hebrew resided in the king's household. No other Hebrew had access to the highest authorities in the land. No other Hebrew had grown up under the instruction of Egyptian tutors, possibly even to serve as a ruler in the State. If Moses' act was not murder, then we have to view him as a judge of Israel comparable to Samson, Deborah, Ehud, and other judges who defended Israel from conquering enemies.

Israel was a captive people. The Hebrews had been unlawfully thrown into slavery. The covenant between the Egyptian State of Joseph's day and the Hebrews had been broken by Egypt. They had become captives in a foreign land. Moses, who was used to the trappings of authority, witnessed a criminal act by an Egyptian against a Hebrew brother. Moses took action, thinking there were no

---

1. Donovan Courville speculates that the daughter of Pharaoh was Sebek-nefru-re, the daughter of Amenemhet III, and the last of the kings of Dynasty XII. He also speculates that she married Kha-nefer-re, the twenty-fourth king on the Turin papyrus. There is a legend that Chenephres (Greek transliteration) was the foster-father of Moses, but prior to Courville's chronological reconstruction, it was not believed possible, given this king's placement on the Turin papyrus. Courville, *The Exodus Problem and its Ramifications* (Loma Linda, California: Challenge Books, 1971), I, pp. 155-57.

witnesses. He brought judgment against a representative of the Pharaoh, who had enslaved the Hebrews illegitimately. He acted as a judge of Israel.

Immediately, the rumor spread. The man who had been defended by Moses must have spread the word. When Moses confronted two striving Hebrews, the guilty initiator of violence resisted Moses' intervention into the case. He challenged Moses' right to rule by threatening him. He reminded Moses of his own act, and by implication he threatened Moses with death, since the Egyptian authorities were ready to execute any slave who killed an Egyptian. Moses instantly recognized the threat, and he fled Egypt.

The guilty man who had been challenged by Moses did not want judgment by another Hebrew. He preferred to act immorally against a Hebrew brother, striking him if necessary, while remaining in bondage to the Egyptian State. He was ready to call the wrath of the Egyptians down upon Moses, who represented Israel's best hope and highest placed representative. He wanted to remain free to commit violence against another Hebrew, even if this freedom to act immorally would continue to cost him his opportunity to live as a free man. He preferred bondage under Egypt rather than the rule of biblical law. He preferred slavery under pagan law to freedom under biblical law. This was to be the continuing theme for many years: biblical law vs. slavish Israelites.

The speed with which the rumor spread astonished Moses, but he knew that it would be hopeless to call its further transmission to a halt. In only one day, the story had spread to one of the combatants, and possibly to both of them. Moses recognized his vulnerability. He was highly placed. He was not a slave. He was a Hebrew, yet he did not share the trials and tribulations of the Hebrews. If he could remain in his station as the adopted son of Pharaoh's daughter, he could escape the rigorous service which was the expected fate of the other Israelites. But he had already decided to cast his lot with the Israelites (Heb. 11:24), and so, as the rumor spread, he knew that he would be brought down, possibly even executed. The rumor spread, which is to say that *people actively spread the rumor.*

The Envy Factor

What would have been their motivation? If Moses was brought low, what possible benefit could this have brought the Israelites? Was it not a benefit to have a Hebrew in the house of the Pharaoh? It certainly was beneficial centuries later, when Esther was the wife of the Persian king. In fact, her high position saved the lives of her fellow Hebrews. Would it not have been a wise policy for every hearer of the rumor to caution the tale-bearer against spreading it further? Wouldn't such gossip threaten the one person in high places who might mitigate the burdens of their slavery? And if Moses tumbled from power, what Hebrew had anything to gain from his loss of influence and wealth?

The answer should be obvious: *no Hebrew would have been helped by Moses' fall.* Yet the rumor spread like wildfire, forcing him to flee. Someone must have told an Egyptian, who carried the story to Pharaoh. The joy of acting as a tale-bearer was too intense.[2] It was not covetousness which motivated them; it was *envy.* It was not the expectation of increased personal wealth as a result of Moses' fall, but rather an intense excitement from contemplating Moses' loss as such. It was Moses' very position that grated on the Israelites. It was his ability to escape their daily life style that angered them. *It was the sheer joy of seeing Moses brought low that helped to fan the flames of resentment and spread the rumor.*

Helmut Schoeck's study of envy brings out the tremendous social consequences of this universal sin. It is the root of socialism, he argues. We cannot understand socialism as strictly the product of covetousness (which Schoeck calls "jealousy"), that is, of the desire of one group of voters to legislate for themselves a portion of another group's assets. These voting patterns are also maintained by envy: the desire to destroy those who are perceived to be better off, better looking, more privileged, or whatever. Writes Schoeck: "It is anguish to perceive the prosperity and advantages of others. Envy is emphatically an act of perception. As we shall see, there are no objective criteria for what it is that stimulates envy. And herein lies the error of political egalitarians who believe that it is only necessary to eliminate once and for all certain inequalities from this world to produce a harmonious society of equals devoid of envy. Anyone who has a propensity for envy, who is driven by that emotion, will always manage to find enviable qualities or possessions in others to arouse envy. . . . One begrudges others their personal or material assets,

---

2. On the sociology of secrecy, see *The Sociology of Georg Simmel,* translated by Kurt H. Wolff (New York: Free Press, 1950), Pt. 4: "The Secret and the Secret Society." Simmel was an early twentieth-century sociologist.

being as a rule almost more intent on their destruction than on their acquisition. The professional thief is less tormented, less motivated by envy, than is the arsonist. Beneath the envious man's primarily destructive desire is the realization that in the long run it would be a very demanding responsibility were he to have the envied man's qualities or possessions, and that the best kind of world would be one in which neither he, the subject, nor the object of his envy would have them. For instance, an envy-oriented politician regards a lower national income *per capita* as more tolerable than one that is higher for all and includes a number of wealthy men."[3]

The Hebrews of Moses' day were envious, more arsonists than thieves, more hostile to his outward success than desirous of personally replacing him in his position of authority. *They were fleeing responsibility,* and they did not want to be judged by a man who would force them to adhere to God's revealed law, to stand up against their unlawful captors, and to take risks associated with full personal responsibility. They preferred to remain slaves and to delight in gossip against their perceived superiors.

Another point stressed by Schoeck is that envy is primarily a product of *social proximity.* The closer someone is to the successful person — not geographically, but socially — the more likely it is that envy will spring up. "Envy plays a negligible part where it is a question of restraining a prince, a head of state or a tycoon from absurd expenditure, but it plays an important part when one among almost equals has got out of step."[4] This was Moses' problem. He was socially and racially a Hebrew, but he had escaped the burdens of his people. The envy of the Hebrews was not directed against the Pharaoh or his vizier; it was directed against a Hebrew who was enjoying the external comforts of Pharaoh's household. The Pharaoh was seemingly beyond a downfall; he was the incarnate god, the State walking on earth. Moses, on the other hand, was uniquely vulnerable: a Hebrew in an Egyptian court, a judge who had executed an Egyptian, and a member of an enslaved race.

The slaves viewed Pharaoh as a legitimate monarch, although by God's standards, he had broken a covenant between Egypt and Israel. Moses was not seen as being a legitimate judge. "Who made thee a prince and a judge over us?" taunted the Hebrew offender.

---

3. Helmut Schoeck, *Envy: A Theory of Social Behavior* (New York: Harcourt Brace Jovanovich, [1966] 1970), p. 19.

4. *Ibid.,* p. 349.

Wasn't Moses trying to elevate himself over his own people? How dare he? He could be cut down to size! The Pharaoh had unassailable power; Moses had completely assailable power. Moses was envied; the Pharaoh was not. Social proximity was a threat to Moses. As a rich man among envious people, he was too close for comfort. He fled.

Modern democratic societies are especially threatened by envy, just as slaves within a slave society are. The similarity is this: men are officially alike within a democratic social order; so are slaves in a slave society. The official social proximity of the members of a democratic society makes envy far more likely than in a caste society or traditional-feudal society, with their supposedly innate class or status hierarchies. What is resented is not luxury as such, but *relative* luxury on the part of people who are regarded by the envious as being essentially on a par with them.[5] This is why it is futile and even dangerous to pursue political programs of coercive wealth redistribution in an age of envy. The closer society comes to the egalitarian goal, the more envious men will become.

Moses seemed to be "lording it over" the Hebrews. He *was* a lord, as the adopted son of the daughter of Pharaoh, but socially (racially) he was a Hebrew. He was close to them racially, and therefore he was vulnerable. He could be brought low — back down to the level of his fellow Hebrews — by the information they possessed. Even if it might mean his life, they were willing to spread the tale.

Moses was not a murderer; he was a *judge*. Yet he was forced by the murderous envy of the Hebrews to seek safety in a strange land, where he married (Ex. 2:21). He was not accepted as a judge by the Hebrews of his generation. He was like Joseph, whose envious brothers sold him into slavery. He, too, went to a strange land, and he also married the daughter of a foreign priest (Gen. 41:45). In both instances, the key role God gave to each — the delivery of his kinsman from a crisis — could be achieved only by *geographical separation* and *social separation*. Moses would return from Midian as an 80-year-old man whose old enemy, the Pharaoh, had died (Ex. 2:23). He had been forgotten by his brethren, who still groaned for deliverance. For a full generation, the Hebrews remained in bondage, while the one who might have delivered them, had it not been for their intense envy, lived in the wilderness. They paid dearly for their envy. And later, when they refused to forsake envy after the Exodus, they paid with another 40 years of sufferings.[6]

---

5. *Ibid.*, p. 220.
6. On envy in the wilderness, see Numbers 12 and 16.

Envy vs. Economic Growth

Another aspect of envy is its inhibiting effect on social and economic advance. The successful man who struggles to raise himself above the common denominator faces envy because of his success. Since those around him are socially close to him, every sign of success raises the threat of envy. It then becomes imperative to conceal the extent of one's success, to keep others from discovering one's plans for the future.[7] Those who would advance themselves will resort to deception. (The other alternative: moving away. This removes success symbols and successful role models and skills from the community.) Shared social goals in such circumstances must be of a sort that do not involve the kind of economic or social change which might elevate one man or a few families above the average. But elites induce economic change by testing new processes and new products. Only later, when the success of the venture has been proven, will capital be made available widely to finance an extension of its benefits to the masses.

Inequality is basic to human progress. Elites always are important in the development of new ideas, new products, and new technologies. The question is this: On what basis will the elites gain access to capital? By political power? By an ecclesiastical monopoly? Or by productivity that is valued by consumers, as demonstrated on the free market? But we cannot escape the process of innovation by elites. The key area of innovation is *knowledge.* Hayek comments:

The growth of knowledge is of such special importance because, while the material resources will always remain scarce and will have to be reserved for limited purposes, the uses of new knowledge (where we do not make them artificially scarce by patents of monopoly) are unrestricted. Knowledge, once achieved, becomes gratuitously available for the benefit of all. It is through this free gift of the knowledge acquired by the experiments of some members of society that general progress is made possible, that the achievements of those who have gone before facilitate the advance of those who follow. At any stage of this process there will always be many things we already know how to produce but which are still too expensive to provide for more than a few. . . . If we, in the wealthier countries, today can provide facilities and conveniences for most which not long ago would have been physically impossible to produce in such quantities, this is in large measure the direct consequence of the fact that they were first made for a

---

7. *Ibid.,* p. 50.

few. . . . A large part of the expenditure of the rich, though not intended for that end, thus serves to defray the cost of the experimentation with the new things that, as a result, can later be available for the poor. . . . The path of advance is greatly eased by the fact that it has been trodden before. It is because scouts have found the goal that the road can be built for the less lucky or less energetic. What today may seem extravagance or even waste, because it is enjoyed by the few and even undreamed of by the masses, is payment for the experimentation with a style of living that will eventually be made available to the many. The range of what will be tried and later developed, the fund of experience that will become available to all, is greatly extended by the unequal distribution of present benefits; and the rate of advance will be greatly increased if the first steps are taken long before the majority can profit from them. Many of the improvements would indeed never become a possibility for all if they had not long before been available to some. If all had to wait for better things until they could be provided for all, that day would in many instances never come. Even the poorest today owe their relative material well-being to the results of past inequality.[8]

Compulsory, State-enforced programs of wealth redistribution are inimical to the social and economic progress of civilization. So is envy.

Envy leads to a *present-oriented society*. This is a *lower-class society*, in Edward Banfield's definition.[9] Why should this present-orientation be the product of envy? Schoeck elaborates: "The future, the only field where the fruits of any development are to be reaped, lends itself to a co-operative approach, to exploitation by men able to exchange and co-ordinate their ideas, knowledge and desires. But this is conceivable only when fear of the other's envy, of his possible sabotage or malicious sorcery, has to some extent been overcome. No one can even begin to have rational aspirations for the future unless he has a realistic view of what the future may be; but no such prognosis can be made so long as each member of the group carefully

---

8. F. A. Hayek, *The Constitution of Liberty* (University of Chicago Press, 1960), pp. 43-44. Chapter 6 of Hayek's book, "The Common Sense of Progress," is invaluable.

9. Edward Banfield, *The Unheavenly City Revisited* (Boston: Little, Brown, 1973), pp. 53-54, 61-62. In the original book, *The Unheavenly City* (Little Brown, 1970), he included a more hard-hitting analysis of the lower-class, present-oriented individual: pp. 217-23. Writes Banfield in *Revisited:* "The implication that lower-class culture is pathological seems fully warranted both because of the relatively high incidence of mental illness in the lower class and also because human nature seems loathe to accept a style of life that is so radically present-oriented" (p. 63). He is incorrect on one point: it is not "human nature" as such which is loathe to accept present-oriented, lower-class culture. It is Christianity which finds it loathesome.

keeps hidden *his* view of the future. Nor can a view that is conducive to social and economic development be formed within a group until its individual members are able, in frank discussion, to compare, weigh and synchronize all their different pictures of the future. It is precisely this, however, which more than anything else is impeded by the ever-present fear that basically everyone, more especially our near neighbour, is potentially envious and that the best defence against him is to pretend complete indifference about the future."[10]

Envy vs. Deliverance

This analysis throws light on Moses' experience. How could he serve as a leader of his people, given their entrenched envy? How could he conspire with them to co-ordinate their efforts? He knew within 24 hours of his execution of the Egyptian that his position as a judge of Israel had been rejected by the Israelites. The best approach was immediate flight. He would wash his hands of them.

God refused to allow him to wash his hands of them. For decades, he was able to concentrate on his own affairs, independent of his brethren, developing his talents as a shepherd — skills that he would subsequently put to use during the final 40 years of his lifetime — but at last God called to him out of the burning bush. Moses resisted, but eventually he went back to Egypt. This time, he came as a stranger. This time, he came as an independent outsider from another land. This time, he was not easily envied, since few Hebrews could look upon him as a social equal who had somehow been elevated to a position of vulnerable authority. This time, he came with signs and wonders to demonstrate his position as a judge, one who came in the name of the God of Abraham, Isaac, and Jacob. This time, he would confront the Pharaoh directly, not intervene secretly to eliminate one Egyptian persecutor. This time, he would not be in a position to be ruined by the envy-motivated gossip of a slave population. This time, a God-inspired future-orientation would motivate him, and the Hebrew slaves followed out of awe, fear, and hope. This time, he came as God's agent, not as a social equal. This time, his continual victories over Pharaoh would demonstrate just who it was who had raised him up. This time, it was Pharaoh, not a Hebrew slave, who would ask him who he thought he was. No Hebrew in Egypt would again taunt him with the words,

---

10. Schoeck, *Envy,* p. 46.

"Who made thee a prince and a judge over us?" This time, they knew. This time, most important of all, they went free.

Conclusion

Moses was the victim of envy when the Hebrews of his youth refused to subordinate themselves to his rule, and when they spread the rumor of his execution of the Egyptian. He fled into the wilderness for 40 years, leaving his brethren in slavery for an additional 40 years. Gossip placed a whole generation in needless bondage. It was God's judgment on them.

The sin of envy strikes the sinner. It restricts his ability to co-operate with his fellow man. It rankles in his heart and can lead to slower or even zero economic growth. In the case of the Israelites, it led to an additional 40 years of bondage. The Hebrews preferred to live in bondage to a socially distant, cruel, self-proclaimed divine monarch than to subordinate themselves under a man of their own covenant. They preferred to be slaves than to be under God's representative, Moses. They preferred the delights of rumor-spreading to the delights and responsibilities of freedom. They preferred to tear down Moses from his pedestal rather than elevate themselves, under Moses' leadership, to freedom. They received what they wanted, another generation of servitude.

6

CUMULATIVE TRANSGRESSION AND RESTITUTION

And I will give this people favour in the sight of the Egyptians: and it shall come to pass, that, when ye go, ye shall not go empty: But every woman shall borrow [ask] of her neighbour, and of her that sojourneth in her house, jewels of silver, and jewels of gold, and raiment: and ye shall put them upon your sons, and upon your daughters; and ye shall spoil the Egyptians (Ex. 3:21-22).

This promise of God to Moses was explicitly and completely fulfilled at the time of the Exodus. Plague after plague had come upon the Egyptians, and they could stand no more after the final plague, the death of the firstborn child of every house. "And the Egyptians were urgent upon the people, that they might send them out of the land in haste; for they said, We be all dead men" (Ex. 12:33). In order to speed the Hebrews along their way out of the land, the Egyptians gave them what they requested: spoils. God's promise to Moses had not been a mere prophecy; it had been a command. "And the children of Israel did according to the word of Moses; and they borrowed of the Egyptians jewels of silver, and jewels of gold, and raiment" (Ex. 12:35). The Hebrew verb translated as "borrow" is the normal, everyday Hebrew word for "ask."[1] This was a form of *tribute,* like military spoils. The Israelites incurred no debt to repay. Both the Egyptians and the Israelites understood this.

The language of the Bible is peculiar here. First, the Israelites were told that they would find favor in the eyes of the Egyptians. This is an odd use of the word "favor." It did not signify love on the part of the Egyptians. Their favor was the product of extreme fear.

---

1. U. Cassuto, *A Commentary on the Book of Exodus* (Jerusalem: The Magnes Press, The Hebrew University, [1951] 1974), p. 44.

They feared the Israelites, for the God of these slaves was too powerful and dangerous. The Egyptians were not converted to this God;
they did not choose to worship Him. They chose instead to remove
His people from their midst, to put the fearful arm of God into a
different nation. They hoped to escape the earthly wrath of God by
encouraging the Israelites to leave as rapidly as possible, even
though the Israelites possessed the "borrowed" wealth. Pharaoh did
not even wait until morning to call Moses and Aaron before him
(12:31). The favor of the Egyptians was a fear-induced favor.

The second peculiarity of language is the use of the word
translated by the King James translators as "borrow." It clearly
means "ask," but here it *implies* "to extract under threat of violence."
It meant *tribute* — in this case, tribute to a *departing* army rather than
to an invading one. The Israelites had not tried to invade Egypt
militarily, but the Egyptians had *created* a hostile nation within the
boundaries of Egypt by having placed the Israelites in bondage.

Slavery

It is not clear just how long the Israelites had been in bondage.
By the year of the Exodus, they had been slaves for at least 80 years,
since Moses was born during the reign of the Pharaoh of the infanticide edict, and he led the nation out of Egypt when he was 80 (Ex.
7:7; he died at age 120 [Deut. 34:7], and Israel spent 40 years in the
wilderness [Num. 14:33-34]). Courville's reconstruction indicates
that the daughter of Pharaoh who brought up Moses was the
daughter of Amenemhet III, who succeeded Sesostris III.[2] Sesostris
III, concludes Courville, was the Pharaoh who first enslaved the
Israelites.[3] Therefore, the Israelites were in actual bondage for
perhaps a century, possibly one or two decades longer. I believe they
were in bondage for 80 years: two 40-year periods. It would depend
on the point of time in the reign of Sesostris III that he placed the
Israelites in bondage. If Courville's reconstruction is incorrect, or if
he has not accurately identified the proper kings of Egypt (assuming
his dating is basically correct, i.e., 1445 B.C. for the Exodus), then all
we can say in confidence is that the enslavement was at least 80
years. This conclusion rests on the additional assumption that the
Pharaoh of the enslavement was the same as the Pharaoh of the in-

---

2. Donovan Courville, *The Exodus Problem and Its Ramifications* (Loma Linda,
California: Challenge Books, 1971), I, p. 157.

3. *Ibid.,* I, pp. 147-48.

fanticide edict, and that the edict was made at the same time as the enslavement, and that Moses was born in that year. Since none of these correlations is mandatory, it is possible that the enslavement was longer than 80 years.

Slavery is a valid form of economic activity, according to the Bible, but only under very specific limitations. The maximum term of a brother's service is six years (Deut. 15:12). Even if a Hebrew were to sell himself to a foreigner, he retained the right of redemption, as did his relatives (Lev. 25:47-55). No Hebrew could be enslaved under any circumstances for more than 49 years, for all of them belonged to God (Lev. 25:54-55). The only perpetual slaves were those of the *conquered local tribes* of Canaan, and only *after* Israel had taken possession of her land, and also slaves purchased from caravaners (Lev. 25:44-46). The Hebrews had been given the land of Goshen, for Joseph had saved the lives of all Egyptians (Gen. 47:11). The Egyptians had stolen Israel's freedom. They had executed Hebrew children (Ex. 1). They had stolen generations of Hebrew labor. They had asserted illegitimate sovereignty over God's people. They had not set them free in the seventh year. In 1445 B.C., the bills came due.

Restitution

If Israel could be punished by God for ignoring His laws regulating slavery, it is not surprising that Egypt should be forced to offer restitution. The years in Egypt were to serve as a reminder to Israel of the horrors and injustice of unregulated slavery, the terrors of being a stranger. The experience was supposed to move them to justice (Ex. 22:21; 23:9; Deut. 10:17-19; 15:15). Jeremiah spared no words when Israel violated the laws regulating slavery. He promised them the sword, the pestilence, and the famine; he promised them captivity (Jer. 34:8-17). His words were fulfilled. They did not take the preferred form of escape. Neither did the Egyptians.

The Egyptians had sinned for several generations. God had spared their fathers, but in Moses' day, God extracted restitution from the sons. He visits the iniquity of the fathers upon later generations of those who hate Him (Ex. 20:5). Not that the sons are punished for their fathers' sins (Deut. 24:16); every man is to be put to death for his own sin. But the iniquities of fathers in a society tend to be the iniquities of the sons. There is historical continuity in life. Some of the fathers and grandfathers had escaped external, cultural judgment, and their sons continued in the same sin. But there came a time when the restitution came due. All the sabbatical years of release that had been ignored, and all the capital goods that had been required for them to give to the released slaves (Deut. 15:14), had to be paid, plus a penalty for theft (Lev. 6:5), by that final generation. They themselves went into bondage to the invading Amalekites (Hyksos, called the shepherd kings by conventional historians) for at least a century.[4] The glory of Egypt was removed.

If the sons are not to be punished for the sins of their fathers, why should the generation in the year of the Exodus have been required to bear such a heavy economic burden? The explanation which is most consistent with biblical law is the argument from the concept of familistic capital. The heirs of earlier generations of enslaving Egyptians had become the beneficiaries of the labor of earlier generations of Hebrews. The fathers and grandfathers had extracted labor from the Hebrews at below-market prices. Had below-market pricing not been in effect, they could have hired the Hebrews to construct the cities. However, *they wanted something for nothing:* rigorous labor without competitive wage rates. They had sunk their capital into monuments for the Egyptian State. They had escaped the taxation levels that would have been necessary to hire the services of the Hebrews, had there been a free market for labor services. Their heirs had become the beneficiaries of all the capital which had been retained within the families—capital that would have gone to the Pharaoh in the form of additional taxes to finance his self-glorifying public works projects.

Furthermore, we can conclude that such capital could have been invested in growth-producing activities. We have no idea what the compound rate of economic growth was in that era, but some growth in capital was possible. Therefore, the sons who saw their riches "borrowed" by the Hebrews were simply *returning the compounded capital that they and their ancestors had coercively extracted from the Hebrews.* The Hebrews had been forced to pay homage, in the form of taxes in kind (labor services, forfeited freedom), to the Egyptian State. Now the heirs of Joseph were collecting on past accounts which had finally

4. Siegfried J. Schwantes, *A Short History of the Ancient Near East* (Grand Rapids, Michigan: Baker Book House, 1965), p. 76. Other historians believe that the period of the Hyksos may have been two centuries. Courville believes that the Hyksos period was over four centuries: from the Exodus to Solomon. *The Exodus Problem,* I, pp. 124-25.

come due. They were collecting capital which lawfully belonged to them. *The Egyptians were simply paying restitution.* God had prospered the pharaohs by giving one of them a monopoly over the grain supplies in an era of famine. God's representative, Joseph, had provided the necessary agricultural forecast and the efficient administration of the program.[5] Then the heirs of the Pharaoh enslaved the Hebrews, who had been promised the land of Goshen as a permanent reward (Gen. 45:8-10; 47:6). The State, in the person of Pharaoh, had broken the covenant. That covenant was a civil covenant with God, since it had been established with His people. God, in the day of the Exodus, collected His lawful tribute. They had broken their treaty with His people, and as the Hebrews' lawful sovereign, He intervened to bring judgment upon the Egyptians.

There is no escape from the laws of God, either individually or socially. God held the Egyptians fully responsible for upholding their covenant with the Hebrews. The Egyptians had profited from Joseph's warning. They had also profited from the labor provided by generations of Hebrews. They were held fully responsible for decisions made by the pharaohs. They paid for their sins, and because of the additional capital possessed by the Egyptians of the Exodus period — as a direct result of the reduced taxes paid by their ancestors — they also paid for the sins of their fathers. After all, the Egyptians of the Exodus period were the beneficiaries of the sins of their fathers. They had been bound by the terms of their fathers' promise to Israel that the land of Goshen would belong to Israel, and they had broken this covenant.

The Egyptians paid more than jewels to the Hebrews. They paid their firstborn. God had told Moses that this would be the price extracted from them if they did not repent through their representative, the Pharaoh: "And thou shalt say unto Pharaoh, Thus saith the Lord, Israel is my son, even my firstborn. And I say unto thee, Let my son go, that he may serve me: and if thou refuse to let him go, behold, I will slay thy son, even thy firstborn" (Ex. 4:22-23). The Egyptians had enslaved God's firstborn. They had, in effect, *kidnapped* them. The penalty for kidnapping is death (Ex. 21:16). By refusing to allow the Israelites to go and sacrifice to their God, the Pharaoh was admitting that he was guilty of kidnapping, for he was

---

5. Gary North, *The Dominion Covenant: Genesis* (Tyler, Texas: Institute for Christian Economics, 1982), ch. 23: "The Entrepreneurial Function."

stating clearly that the people of Israel were his, when in fact they belonged to God. When the Egyptians made restitution, it was expensive beyond their wildest imaginations. The heirs (firstborn) of the slave-owners were slain.

Tribute

The Pharaoh, as a self-proclaimed divinity, was viewed as the only incarnate representative on earth of the Egyptian gods. It was the king who brought the crucially important annual flood of the Nile. Frankfort comments on this: "Even as late an author as Ammianus Marcellus [late 4th century, A.D. — G.N.] knew that the Egyptians ascribed plenty or famine to the quality of their king — not, in a modern sense, to his quality as an administrator, but to his effectiveness as an organ of integration, partaking of the divine and of the human and entrusted with making the mutual dependence of the two a source of 'laughter and wonder.' "[6] It was the king who, as a divine being, brought *moral order* to the whole world. Thus, when the Pharaoh of the famine established policies that assured Egypt's survival during seven years of famine, thereby reestablishing his ownership of all Egypt, his followers could interpret his acts as inspired. The Pharaoh could be understood as having reemphasized his own divinity, and the power of the Egyptian gods, before his people.

By enslaving the Hebrews, the later Pharaoh was elevating the gods of Egypt above the God of Joseph. The ancient world interpreted a military victory by one nation or city-state as the victory of its gods over the gods of the defeated people. Thus, by enslaving the Hebrews, the Pharaoh was announcing the sovereignty of Egypt's gods over Joseph's God. By bringing Egypt to its knees at the time of the Exodus, God was ritually announcing His sovereignty in the most graphic way possible. The Egyptians had lost their prosperity, their children, and now their jewelry. The gods of Egypt had been brought low. Only the outright destruction of Egypt's army, followed by an invasion and conquest by foreigners, could have made the picture any more graphic, and these events were shortly to follow. The Pharaoh-god would perish with his army.

The gods of Egypt paid tribute to the God of Israel. This tribute was paid by the representative of Egypt's gods, Pharaoh, as well as his

---

6. Henri Frankfort, *Kingship and the Gods: A Study of Ancient Near East Religion as the Integration of Society & Nature* (University of Chicago Press, [1948] 1962), p. 58.

subordinates, the nobles and wealthy people who had amassed great capital. It was paid to servants who represented the God of Israel. The humiliation in such a transaction is easily understood.

The Slave Wife

The Exodus can be seen from another perspective, that of a man who rejects his slave-wife. Exodus 11:1 has been translated in the King James Version as follows: "And the LORD said unto Moses, Yet will I bring one plague more upon Pharaoh, and upon Egypt; afterwards he will let you go hence: when he shall let you go, he shall surely thrust you out hence altogether." An alternative reading throws more light on the concluding clause: ". . . after that he will let you go hence; as one letteth go a slave-wife shall he surely expel you hence."[7]

Exodus 21 begins the detailed presentation of the laws of God, immediately after the presentation of the ten commandments, or general principles of God's law. What is significant about Exodus 21 is that *it begins with the laws applying to slavery, the social and economic condition from which God has just freed His people.* It was a topic which was eminently familiar to them.

Exodus 21:7-11 provides the laws dealing with the slave wife. If a man sold his daughter to be the wife of a master, with the purchase price going to the father rather than to the wife as her dowry, then she needed protection. The dowry was permanently forfeited by the husband if he unlawfully divorced her, or did not deal with her as a lawful wife. Rushdoony has commented on the function of the dowry: "The dowry was an important part of marriage. We meet it first in Jacob, who worked seven years for Laban to earn a dowry for Rachel (Gen. 29:18). The pay for this service belonged to the bride as her dowry, and Rachel and Leah could indignantly speak of themselves as having been 'sold' by their father, because he had withheld from them their dowry (Gen. 31:14, 15). It was the family capital; it represented the wife's security, in case of divorce where the husband was at fault."[8]

The girl who was sold to a master did not personally possess a

---

7. David Daube, *The Exodus Pattern in the Bible* (London: Faber & Faber, 1963), p. 56. He relies heavily on the work of Reuven Yaron's article in the *Revue Internationale des Droits de l'Antiquite,* 3rd Series, Vol. IV (1957), pp. 122ff.

8. R. J. Rushdoony, *The Institutes of Biblical Law* (Nutley, New Jersey: Craig Press, 1973), pp. 176-77.

dowry; it belonged to her father. She had the legal status of a *concubine,* a wife without a dowry. Biblical law nevertheless protected her. If the master decided not to marry her after all, he was required to allow her to be redeemed (bought back); he could not sell her into a foreign nation, "seeing he hath dealt deceitfully with her" (Ex. 21:8). "And if he have betrothed her unto his son, he shall deal with her after the manner of daughters. If he take him another wife; her food, her raiment, and her duty of marriage, shall he not diminish. And if he do not these three things unto her, then she shall go out free without money" (Ex. 21:9-11). In other words, her family, which had received payment for her, owed the master nothing under such circumstances. She did not have to be bought back.

Israel had not been treated justly in Egypt. Her Egyptian "husband" had not dealt with her as a lawful wife. She deserved her freedom, but the Egyptians had refused to let her go. Furthermore, Israel had never been a slave-wife. Joseph had increased Egypt's wealth, and Pharaoh had granted Israel the *land of Goshen.* The value of that good land, the best in Egypt (Gen. 47:11), had been transferred to Israel. *This was Israel's dowry.* Now Israel was being cast out, as if she were a slave-wife. A real wife is entitled to her dowry. Instead of a mortgage on the land of Goshen, which the Egyptians should have paid to Israel, the Israelites took the jewels (female adornment) of the Egyptians. Egypt could not legitimately treat Israel as a slave-wife, sending her out without her lawful dowry. The verse following God's revelation that Pharaoh would expel Israel as a slave-wife reads: "Speak now in the ears of the people, and let every man borrow of his neighbour, and every woman of her neighbour, jewels of silver, and jewels of gold" (Ex. 11:2).

Conclusion

Egypt could not escape the principle of restitution. Restitution extends to the cross. God required payment by His Son, Jesus Christ, to atone for the sins of mankind, both collectively (common grace) and individually.[9] This transaction should also be understood as the payment of a dowry, thereby making the church, Christ's bride, a lawful wife, not just a concubine. Egypt made restitution. Egypt offered her sacrifice, the firstborn, to God, since no Egyptian

---

9. Gary North, "Common Grace, Eschatology, and Biblical Law," *The Journal of Christian Reconstruction,* III (Winter 1976-77).

was willing to make restitution by the shedding of a lamb's blood, "for there was not a house where there was not one dead" (Ex. 12:30b). God required restitution for the years of servitude beyond the maximum permitted, six. In fact, Egypt even owed Israel for the first six years, since the six-year slave contract was a debt-slavery contract, and Israel had not been in debt to Egypt. Egypt had acted as though Israel had been a lawful captive in wartime, or a debtor to Egypt. Israel was neither. Furthermore, Egypt owed restitution for having kidnapped Israel. Egypt owed Israel for having treated Israel as less than a full wife, trying to expel her without returning her dowry, as though she had been a slave-wife. Egypt paid dearly for these acts of long-term lawlessness.

The cost of the pharaohs' brick pyramids and brick treasure cities turned out to be far higher than any Egyptian, especially the various pharaohs, had dared to calculate. Any intuitive cost-benefit analysis in the mind of a pharaoh—so many benefits, in time and eternity, from a new pyramid or city *versus* so many expenditures in feeding and controlling the Hebrew slaves—turned out to be catastrophically erroneous. The pharaohs drastically overestimated the benefits of their construction projects, and they underestimated the real costs of enslaving the Hebrews. The pharaohs had abandoned the most important pair of guidelines for making accurate cost-benefit analyses, namely, the *free market,* which establishes prices, and the *law of God,* which establishes God's justice. All the pharaohs, from the enslaving Pharaoh to the Pharaoh of the Exodus, ignored the principle of restitution in their dealings with the Israelites. When the final bills came due, ancient Egypt collapsed.

7

THE OPTIMUM PRODUCTION MIX

And Pharaoh said, Behold, the people of the land now are many, and ye make them rest from their burdens. And Pharaoh commanded the same day the taskmasters of the people, and their officers, saying, Ye shall no more give the people straw to make brick, as heretofore: let them go and gather straw for themselves (Ex. 5:5-7).

God, having witnessed the oppression of His people by the Egyptians for at least 80 years (Ex. 3:9), sent Moses and Aaron before the Pharaoh. God did not instruct Moses to ask for an immediate and permanent release of His people from bondage; Moses was only to request a time of religious sacrifice for them (Ex. 3:18; 5:1). However, given the theology of Egypt, this would have to be regarded by the Pharaoh as blasphemy. The Pharaoh was believed to be the sole divine-human link, the god Horus walking on earth, who would become Osiris at his death, and who was also the descendant of Re, the sun god. Frankfort has summarized this doctrine of divine kingship: "Egyptian kingship emerged at the end of the predynastic period. Of this the Egyptians were well aware; they recognized a first king of the first dynasty, Menes. Tradition named as his predecessors the 'semidivine spirits' who had succeeded rule by the gods. These in their turn had been preceded by the Creator, Re. Monarchical rule, then, was coeval with the universe; the Creator had assumed kingship over his creation from the first."[1]

Moses' request to allow the Israelites to sacrifice to a foreign God was an affront to this Pharaoh. This Thirteenth Dynasty king[2] — a weak dynasty — was not ready to admit the existence of any rival to

---

1. Henri Frankfort, *Kingship and the Gods: A Study of Ancient Near Eastern Religion as the Integration of Society & Nature* (University of Chicago Press, [1948] 1962), p. 15.

2. I am assuming the correctness of Donovan Courville's reconstructed chronology of Egypt.

his self-professed divine status. His answer was the answer of a supposed cosmological sovereign: "And Pharaoh said, Who is the LORD, that I should obey his voice to let Israel go? I know not the LORD, neither will I let Israel go" (Ex. 5:2). Like Nebuchadnezzar after him (Dan. 3:15), Pharaoh saw himself as the divine-human link, the capstone of a bureaucratic pyramid in a divine State, beyond which there could be no appeal. Also like Nebuchadnezzar, he was to be cut down in the midst of his kingdom. Pharaoh was so enraged at the request of Moses, that he decided to impose a punishment on the Israelites. He forbade the taskmasters to deliver straw to the Hebrews for the construction of bricks. Their work load would therefore increase, since the size of the bricks would remain the same, and presumably also the numerical quotas. "And the tale of the bricks, which they did make heretofore, ye shall lay upon them; ye shall not diminish ought thereof: for they be idle; therefore they cry, saying, Let us go and sacrifice to our God" (Ex. 5:8).[3]

This punishment was calculated to accomplish several ends. *First,* and perhaps most important, it was to discourage Moses and Aaron from challenging his authority as a divine master. If they did it again, their people would be injured even more. *Second,* it was an effective means of alienating the people from these two leaders. If, every time they came before Pharaoh in the name of their God, the two leaders would draw the wrath of Pharaoh upon the Israelites, the Israelites would presumably seek to disassociate themselves from the pair. They would bring pressure on them to cease and desist. This would tend to discourage all future leaders from rising up in the name of the slaves, or in the name of their God. The slaves, without leadership, would remain slaves. *Third,* the Pharaoh would be able to reduce the costs of construction of his cities. The output of the slaves would remain constant, but the State's input costs would be reduced. No longer would Egyptians be expected to supply the Israelites with straw. This labor service would henceforth come from the slaves. *Fourth,* the slave population would be scattered (Ex. 5:12), thereby reducing the potential military threat to Egypt.

---

3. Prof. A. S. Yahuda argued that the use of the Hebrew word for "tale" is so specific that it demonstates that Exodus was not written by some post-exilic priest. The "tale" was a specific measurement, not a numerical quantity. He points to the discovery of a tomb picture which shows a man measuring the bricks. The writer of Exodus was therefore familiar with this specific usage. Yahuda, *The Accuracy of the Bible* (New York: Dutton, 1935), pp. 76-77.

Pharaoh removed one of the crucial factors of production from the brick-making process. Yet he required that the daily output of bricks be maintained. His edict reduced the division of labor, since it forced the Hebrews to search out and collect straw, in addition to producing the bricks. *Specialization was reduced.* The edict required the same output despite a reduction in raw material costs. Given the inescapable reality of scarcity, the edict therefore required a compensating increase in *labor inputs* from the slaves. These would be *unpaid* labor inputs. Previously, the slaves had been allowed to concentrate on the task of producing bricks from the raw materials supplied by the Egyptian State. Now their time would be also expended in achieving an additional step in the production process. They would have to work longer hours, or work more intensively, or both, in order to produce the same quantity and size of bricks. Specialists in straw-gathering may have been recruited from within the Hebrew community and trained. They would have been removed from the normal work force, thereby increasing the labor burden on those who remained in close proximity to the construction projects. The edict by Pharaoh placed a great burden on the backs of an already heavily burdened slave population.

Reduced Efficiency

The punishment was fully consistent with the nature of the sin of the slaves, as perceived by Pharaoh. He said that they were idle, since they wanted time off to sacrifice to their God. Such a waste of time could not be tolerated. It was idleness to substitute the worship of God for brick production. "Let more work be laid upon the men, that they may labour therein; and let them not regard vain words" (Ex. 5:9).

Obviously, there was no day of rest for these slaves. It was a life of almost unending drudgery, one which provided little hope. The Hebrews were destined to spend their lives working on public works projects that honored a false god, the Egyptian Pharaoh, and by implication, the Egyptian State. Only the god of the State might be legitimately honored, and its service was a heavy yoke, one devoid of hope. The static empire of Egypt would, if the Pharaoh had his way, require the compulsory service of the Hebrews until the end of the world. For them, life would be a hell on earth. There would be no rest, no progress, and no escape.

The *scattering* of the slaves was also important to Pharaoh. Like

Christ, who told his enemies that anyone who does not gather with Him scatters abroad (Matt. 12:30), the Pharaoh also wanted his enemies scattered. He no doubt recognized, as had the Pharaoh of the enslavement, that the concentrated population of Hebrews in the land of Goshen constituted a potential military threat to Egypt (Ex. 1:10). The Hebrews were scattered by the king's edict (Ex. 5:12), for they were no longer the recipients of straw imported from outside Goshen. Obviously, in these massive building projects, the supplies of straw in the immediate vicinity would have been depleted rapidly. In all likelihood, the supplies had been depleted long before the edict of Pharaoh, since it would have been less expensive for the Egyptian suppliers to have collected the straw close to the construction sites, which were in the region around Goshen. The cost of transporting straw to the construction sites would continually rise, and the Pharaoh transferred this economic burden to the Hebrews. They would have to send more and more of their straw-gatherers out across the Nile valley in order to find this necessary factor of production.

Predictably, the better quality resource, straw, was depleted, and the Hebrews found it economically advantageous to substitute a less efficient — *technically* less efficient — resource: stubble (Ex. 5:12). The cost of locating and transporting straw grew too great; they had to use stubble, working harder to produce as high a quality of brick as before. This was *economically* more efficient, given the rising cost of using straw, even though the straw was more efficient technically. The Hebrews were forced to "cut corners" with stubble.

Pharaoh used the innate restraints of the land's productivity as a means of disciplining the Hebrews. This decision to misuse a fundamental law of economics — the God-imposed scarcity of nature — turned out to be a disastrous one for Egypt. This was a deliberate misuse of the phenomenon of scarcity. Instead of encouraging trade and economic specialization, which scarcity is intended to encourage — a curse which can become a blessing[4] — Pharaoh's edict reduced both trade and specialization. Instead of reducing the costs of production, Pharaoh's edict deliberately increased the costs of production, simply as a punishment. He was misusing God's laws of economics in order to humiliate His people and to keep them from worshipping the true God. For this, Pharaoh subsequently paid dearly, as did his people.

---

4. Gary North, *The Dominion Covenant: Genesis* (Tyler, Texas: Institute for Christian Economics, 1982), ch. 10: "Scarcity: Curse and Blessing."

The nature of the punishment testifies to Pharaoh's understanding of the issues involved: theological, political, and economic. He also grasped at least some of the implications of the law of the optimum mix of production factors. This law of the optimum production mix is a corollary to the law of diminishing returns. Perhaps it would be more accurate to say that the law of the *optimum production mix* is really another way of stating the *law of diminishing returns*.[5] The existence of the optimum factor mix is the conclusion we reach when we acknowledge the existence of the law of diminishing returns. What do economists mean when they speak of the law of diminishing returns?

Complementary Factors of Production

We note that when two or more complementary factors of production are combined in the production process, output per unit of resource input rises initially as we add the "sub-optimum" factor of production, and then output begins to fall after the formerly "sub-optimum" resource passes the point of optimality. This is an economic law which might better be described as *the law of variable proportions*.[6] One person, for example, cannot efficiently farm 800 acres, unless he has specialized equipment. Facing the task of farming 800 acres, he adds additional labor. He hires another man to help him work the land. By combining the labor of two workers, the worker-owner sees the value of his farm's total agricultural output increase by more than the cost of hiring the extra laborer. So he adds more laborers and/or equipment. Output value increases even faster than input costs increase, *initially*. But at some point, the law of diminishing returns (variable proportions) tells us, the increases in output value will begin to lag behind the increases in factor input costs. There will be too many workers on the fixed supply of 800 acres. They will get in each other's way, or spend too much time loafing, or fighting, or whatever. Output will actually decline if the owner adds still more laborers without buying or leasing more land. In other words, it will pay him to dismiss some workers. He will

5. Writes Murray Rothbard: "The *law of returns states that with the quantity of complementary factors held constant, there always exists some optimum amount of the varying factor.*" Rothbard, *Man, Economy, and State* (New York: New York University Press, [1962] 1975), p. 30.

6. Joseph Schumpeter, *History of Economic Analysis* (New York: Oxford University Press, 1954), p. 260.

either have to *dismiss workers* (the now excessive complementary production factor) or *add more land* (the now "sub-optimum" production factor) to the existing number of workers.

There is, in this agricultural example, *an optimum mix* (optimum proportions) of the complementary factors of production: more land or fewer workers. To produce a product at this optimum point minimizes waste and maximizes income. The existence of such an optimum point therefore pressures the resource owner to release one factor of production—in this case, labor—so that this scarce factor can be used in some other industry or on some other farm, thereby increasing total output and maximizing consumer satisfaction with a given quantity of resource inputs. The former resource renter is a beneficiary of this decision: he no longer needs to pay for the freed-up resource input. Other resource users also become beneficiaries, for a new source of the scarce resource has now been made available. The consumer is also a beneficiary: competition among producers will tend to reduce the cost of final output and will also eventually reduce the consumer price of the product.

We can examine this topic from another angle. If the law of diminishing returns were not true, then by taking a fixed supply of one factor of production and adding to it a complementary factor, eventually the proportion of the first (fixed) factor in the production mix would approach (though never quite reach) zero percent. After you reach the point of diminishing returns, the original (fixed) factor of production is increasingly "swamped" by the second (variable) factor. (Both factors are actually variable in practice; this is only an illustration.) To use an analogy from mathematics, the "swamped" factor of production is like a fraction with an increasingly large denominator, and therefore a decreasing value. One-to-two becomes one-to-three, and then downward to, say, one-to-five billion. One five billionth is obviously a lot smaller than one half. The value of the fraction approaches zero as a limit. By fixing the numerator and increasing the denominator, the "percentage contribution" of the numerator to the "value" of the fractional number is reduced.[7]

To return to the example of the 800-acre farm, as we add more and more men, we will eventually overwhelm the productivity of the resource factor which is in fixed supply, namely, land. *If* by adding

---

7. The analogy is imperfect because there are no "optimal" fractions. You never get increasing returns by adding to the denominator. The analogy applies only to the case where the optimum production mix has been passed.

men continually, without adding more land (the "swamped" fixed production factor), we could increase output forever, then land and labor in this example are not really complementary factors of production. They do not really "work together" in the production process, since we can endlessly increase the value of output by adding units of only a single factor. This is the same as saying that the *production factor* which we keep adding is, in fact, the *consumer product* we are producing. There really is no production process in this example; our *variable resource input* is, in fact, the *final output*.

Let us consider this argument from another angle: *subtracting* resources. If we could get an increase in the value of output by continually adding a variable resource, then we could also get a decrease in the cost of inputs without lowering the value of output simply by subtracting the previously "fixed" resource input. After all, why pay for a resource which really is not contributing anything of value to the production process? To use the subtraction example, assume that land is now the variable resource and labor is the fixed resource. (Maybe a labor union contract has made labor the fixed resource.) The value of output will not decline as we steadily reduce the land component of the production mix. But in such a situation, we really never had a production *mix;* the factors of production were not really complementary.

To summarize: if we can forever continue to increase the value of output by adding one factor of production, or (alternatively) if we can maintain the value of output by continually removing the other "complementary" factor, then there is no production process. There is no true combination of production factors. The factors are not really complementary.

We need not limit our discussion to land and labor. Land and water are equally good examples. If you take away all the water in agricultural production, you produce a fruitless desert. If you add water continually, you produce a lake. Neither is a farm. There is, in theory, *an economically optimum production mix,* in which the value of the water (cost of providing it) and the value of the land (cost of leasing or buying it) are combined to *maximize net income*—where one additional drop of water or one additional grain of dirt would reduce total net income if either were added (paid for) in the production process. Remember, we are talking about *income,* not technology as such. We are *not* talking about maximum numbers of goods, but about net income (revenues minus costs). We are, in short, discussing economics, not plant biology or engineering.

The law of diminishing returns (variable proportions) applies to every area of production, not just agriculture.[8] It is an aspect of the creation. It existed even before the Fall of man and God's curse of the ground.

Scarcity Before the Fall

Even in the garden, there were diminishing returns — if nothing else, in the fields of genetics, aesthetics, and technology. Adam had to work in the garden. He had to make it more productive. He had to combine factors of production in order to produce anything new. Perhaps he had to plant one species in one spot rather than another, for aesthetic effects. More likely, he would have begun to cross-breed within certain species to produce flowers or edible fruits that did not occur "naturally." We are not told. What we are told is that he had a responsibility to make the garden bloom. He needed to understand technology and aesthetics in order to produce a fruitful environment.

What about economics? Did Adam face an *economic* law (constraint) of variable proportions, rather than just technological and aesthetic constraints? I believe that he did. If we define *scarcity* as any good for which there is greater demand than supply at zero price, then Adam seems to have faced a world of scarcity. If nothing else, his time had to be allocated. If he had worked on one job, he could not simultaneously have worked on another. He would have faced the decision to invest time and natural resources in producing one capital good (tool of production). This would have been a true decision; he could not simultaneously have used these resources to produce a different sort of capital good. The very concept of an economic *production decision* implies an *optimum production mix*. Only if there was no scarcity (including a scarcity of time) before the Fall could Adam have escaped the constraints of an economically optimum production mix. Then the production constraint would have been exclusively technological, genetic, or aesthetic.

Knowledge

We need to focus on that most scarce of all resources, *knowledge*. Was Adam omniscient? The Bible teaches that God alone is omnis-

---

8. Schumpeter, *History,* p. 261. See also Gary North, *Genesis,* ch. 21: "The Law of Diminishing Returns."

cient. Omniscience is an incommunicable attribute of God. There is a special knowledge which belongs only to God: "The secret things belong unto the LORD our God: but those things which are revealed belong unto us and to our children forever, that we may do all the words of this law" (Deut. 29:29). Adam therefore faced limits on his knowledge. He had to learn. He faced a world which required *an educational process based on trial and error.* Eventually, there would have been children and descendants. He could not perfectly have known the mind of any other human being. Thus, he could not perfectly have known other people's wants, needs, and ability to pay in order to attain their goals. He would have needed a source of publicly available information (a price system) in order to learn about the kinds of economic demand other people placed on the available resources, including the demand for knowledge in its broadest sense, and the demand for time. He would have needed knowledge concerning just exactly what resources were available. His incentive to discover this would have been dependent on the economic demand for resources in the marketplace. Thus, the very concept of the incommunicable attribute of God's omniscience points to the inescapable concept of scarcity. Man has to give up something in order to gain certain kinds of knowledge.

The Fall of man came, in part, because man was unwilling to pay for a specific resource: righteous judgment. He refused to render righteous judgment on Satan when he heard the tempter's offer. Adam did not immediately judge Satan provisionally and then wait for God to return to render final judgment on the serpent. Adam did not wait for God to render this final judgment and invest him and his wife with the judge's robes of authority before he ate from the tree of the knowledge of good and evil. Adam therefore faced a scarce universe, even in the garden. He faced scarcity of good judgment and scarcity of time. He was unwilling to "pay the price," meaning the *judgment price* and the *time price.* He wanted instant gratification.[9] But he could not escape paying a price. The price he actually paid was a lot higher than he had estimated.[10] He therefore faced the restraint of scarcity.

---

9. Gary North, "Witnesses and Judges," *Biblical Economics Today,* VI (Aug./Sept. 1983), pp. 2-3.

10. North, *Genesis,* ch. 9: "Costs, Choices, and Tests."

Management and Specialization

The creation has built into it incentives for management. The very genetic structure of plants and animals makes management by man technologically productive. Men can master the art of breeding animals and plants, a subordinately creative skill which is analogous to God's original creative act. The genetic structure of man also makes management by man more productive, but not the kind of management possessed by the breeder. Man is not given that kind of authority over God's image. The genetic reality of mankind is that people are different in terms of their inborn capacities, despite being members of a single species. (In this respect, mankind reflects the Trinity, for God's three Persons have varying functions in relationship to the creation, despite being equal in essence and glory.) Men become more productive individually by co-operating with each other. The most important aspect of this social co-operation is ethical. The curse of the ground has made co-operation even more imperative, for the creation's original scarcity is accentuated by increasing costs as a result of the curse on both man and the ground.

The fact that in God's creation there are complementary factors of production implies that for any given output, there is a *structure of production*. The planner must actively *combine* factors of production. Complementary factors of production must be combined in terms of a *plan*. One plan meets the requirements of the planner better than all other possible plans. This plan is both *personal* and *objective*, because God's personal and objective plan undergirds all human planning, and gives meaning to all human planning. The existence of an omniscient God with a perfect plan is what makes possible human planning.[11] Thus, we must conclude that there is a law of diminishing economic returns, even without the curse; the curse has only increased the need to plan production carefully because of the effects of entropy. The importance of allocating resources is magnified in a cursed world, but there was still an allocation problem in the garden.

Epistemology and Optimum Production

We must recognize the reality of the economic implications of the fact of scarcity. If there were no optimum production mix, then Pharaoh's punishment would make no sense. It would have been no

---

11. *Ibid.*, ch. 4: "Economic Value: Objective and Subjective."

punishment at all. The Hebrews would have been able to manufacture just as many bricks as before with no additional inputs, including labor. But the punishment *was* a punishment, as the Hebrews complained to Moses. The Bible therefore draws our attention to economic theory at this point. There *is* an optimum production mix. There *is* a law of diminishing returns. We achieve greater output per unit of resource input by means of the division of labor and the consequent specialization of production. For any given process of production, *at any point in time,* the economist tells us that there is some *theoretically optimum mix of production factors.*

There is a major epistemological problem here: a "point in time" is a theoretically discrete unit of time which is in fact *immeasurable* and is therefore *outside of time.* A point in time is therefore *timeless.* It is analogous to a theoretically discrete point in a line which is also autonomous and immeasurable. A point in time is a theoretical (and indescribable) period in which human action is not possible—"no time for action"—and if human action is not possible, it becomes problematical (self-contradictory) to speak of such phenomena as market-clearing prices, knowledge, and responsibility. We are dealing here with innate contradictions or antinomies in all human thought, so at best we can only approach the idea of the optimum production mix, just as we can only approach the idea of economic equilibrium. If we lean too heavily on the weak reed of autonomous human logic, the reed collapses.

While men can never have perfect knowledge of this economically optimum production mix, either in theory or in practice, especially in a world of constant change (including technological change), they still must try to *approach* this optimum mix if they wish to minimize waste and maximize income. Biblical economics informs us that there is *an objective plan in the mind of God* which serves as a theoretical foundation for the assertion of the existence of this *economically* optimum mix. Maximum economic output (and therefore maximum income) requires specific *co-operation in terms of a plan.*

It must be understood, however, that approaching this optimum is not easy, even as a theoretical matter. What are the success indicators that enable planning agents to determine whether or not they are approaching the optimum production mix? The existence of *profit and loss indicators* in a competitive free market is the preliminary answer. Nevertheless, these indicators have built-in limits, both in practice and in theory. Modern economic theory is officially individualistic. But methodological individualism, if pursued to its logical conclusion, does not allow us to conclude anything about optimum aggregates. Once again, the problem of making interpersonal comparisons of subjective utility reappears to haunt the humanistic economist.

We cannot legitimately, as "neutral" humanistic economists, make interpersonal comparisons of subjective utility. This means that civil government cannot make such comparisons scientifically. "Since all costs and benefits are subjective, no government can accurately identify, much less establish, the optimum quantity of anything."[12] But neither can any other organization. According to the principles of methodological subjectivism, individuals can only make comparisons of the *subjectively interpreted results* of their own *subjectively constructed plans,* and even here, there is the epistemological problem of making *intertemporal* comparisons.[13] After all, I may have forgotten today what I really intended to achieve yesterday. Or my tastes may have changed in the meantime. Furthermore, the purchasing power of the monetary unit may have changed, yet I cannot measure the extent of this change without constructing an aggregate index number of prices, including the subjective importance or "weighted average" *for me* of each price change. I need permanent standards — ethical standards above all, but also aesthetic and economic standards — to make such comparisons over time. *I need an objective personal "index number" by which to measure economic change.* But by the logic of methodological individualism, there are no such fixed reference points, no unchanging standards. There are no objective standards by which I can formulate my subjective standards, nor can I measure economic changes over time. There are no such scientific measures.

In short, modern economic theory is incapable of discovering what this optimum production mix is, either in the case of a private firm or in the case of a society. The concept of "optimum" necessarily involves the use of aggregate value, including value aggregates that

---

12. Charles W. Baird, "The Philosophy and Ideology of Pollution Regulation," *Cato Journal,* II (Spring 1982), p. 303.

13. Ludwig Lachmann, *Capital, Expectations, and the Market Process: Essays on the Theory of the Market Economy* (Kansas City, Kansas: Sheed, Andrews & McMeel, 1977), pp. 83-85. Lachmann appeals to the epistemologically suspect "common experience" in a desperate and ill-fated attempt to refute Prof. G. L. S. Shackle's assertion that an individual cannot make intertemporal comparisons.

must be compared over time. But pure subjective value theory, if pressed to its logical conclusions, cannot deal with interpersonal value aggregates, nor is it possible for "scientific" economics to compare intrapersonal subjective utility over time. Thus, the more consistent economists have admitted that no one can scientifically determine the optimum quantity of anything.

This is why God's revelation of His permanent law structure is an imperative concept for the very existence of truly logical economics. Without such a permanent standard, simultaneously personal and objective, economics is logically impossible. In a subjective universe without an authoritative God who reveals Himself to man, who in turn is made in God's image and can therefore understand God's revelation to man, there can be no permanent objective standards that are relevant or meaningful for human action, including economics.

Other Things Never Remain Equal

One critic of the concept of the law of diminishing returns is Julian Simon. He argues that economists have erred in attempting to apply the concept in the case of mineral extraction. "The concept of diminishing returns applies to situations where one element is fixed in quantity—say, a given copper mine—and where the type of technology is also fixed. But neither of these factors apply to mineral extraction in the long run. New lodes are found, and new cost-cutting extraction technologies are developed. Therefore, whether the cost rises or falls in the long run depends on the extent to which advances in technology and new lode discoveries counteract the tendency toward increasing cost in the absence of the new developments. Historically, as we have seen, costs have consistently fallen rather than risen, and there is no empirical warrant for believing that this historical trend will reverse itself in the foreseeable future. Hence there is no 'law' of diminishing returns appropriate here."[14]

Simon also applies this interpretation of the law of diminishing returns to the field of population theory. He argues that classical economic theory followed Malthus and held that additional people would reduce the per capita share of fixed economic resources. "The more people using a stock of resources, the lower the income per person, if all else remains equal."[15] But new people coming into the

---

14. Julian Simon, *The Ultimate Resource* (Princeton, New Jersey: Princeton University Press, 1980), p. 53.

15. *Ibid.*, p. 257.

community have the effect of changing the responses of other people, especially their parents. Fathers start working harder, or longer hours, or both.[16] Parents become more future-oriented in many instances. They begin saving a larger proportion of their income. In short, the honeymoon is over when Junior arrives. "More mouths to feed" means more food to feed them in nations that are future-oriented and whose people possess what is known as the Protestant (or Puritan) work ethic.

These observations, however, must not be taken as refutations of the existence of the law of diminishing returns. On the contrary, such evidence points directly to the existence of such a law. If it is true, as it so often appears to be, that "necessity is the mother of invention," then from whence comes the perceived necessity? If additional mouths to feed call forth ever-greater exertion and creativity to feed them, how is it that these mouths produce the desirable stimulus? Isn't it because there was an optimum production mix under the old conditions that was disturbed by the new mouths? Isn't it because the new conditions changed the thinking of the former honeymooners, giving them new incentives to mature and become more responsible? Isn't it the very pressure of the optimum production mix which calls forth better efforts to find *new combinations of resources* (new plans) in response to *new economic conditions?*

The law of diminishing returns (optimum production mix) is an aspect of the creation which can, given the proper ethical and institutional circumstances, lead to human progress. Sinful men need to be pressured into greater self-discipline, more effective thinking, and better strategies of innovation. One of the means of calling forth these better efforts is scarcity. While the law of diminishing returns would have prevailed in the garden, the direct economic incentives to overcome scarcity in a cursed world augment this original aspect of the creation. Thus, it is unwise to de-emphasize the importance of this law of human action, as Simon appears to do. But the concept should not be misused, either. It should not lead men to conclude that the price of raw materials will necessarily rise if population grows. The concept should not be used to justify a zero population growth ideology.

What we should understand is that the existence of an optimum production mix is what lures entrepreneurs, inventors, and

---

16. *Ibid.,* p. 260.

economists to seek out better (less wasteful) ways to accomplish their goals in the midst of endless change. Discover this better way, *and then persuade the consumer to spend his money on your service or product* because you have, in fact, discovered this better way, and you, the producer, will prosper. So will the consumers. The existence of profits in a free market is the success indicator which reveals the better way, meaning a more optimal mix of scarce economic resources.

Success Indicators and Relevant Information

Men are supposed to co-operate. This is an ethical requirement, but it is also an economic imperative, if men wish to increase their per capita output. In almost all cases, the intervention of the State into the market reduces this co-operation, since such intervention thwarts the voluntary transfer of accurate, self-correcting economic information. State interference reduces the division of labor in most cases, although it can also lead to overspecialization when it encourages technical developments that are, from the point of view of the market, uneconomical.[17] To prevent both overspecialization and underspecialization, producers need the continual feedback of economic information provided by the market's pricing system. This means that they need private ownership, for without this, there can be no rational assessment of profit and loss, meaning no economic calculation. Without private ownership, it becomes difficult or im-

---

17. An example of such "forced" technological innovation is the development of capital-intensive, labor-saving equipment which has been adopted by producers because of the artificially high cost of hiring trade union laborers. The producers substitute expensive labor-saving equipment when the cost of labor gets too high. If the government had not granted to the trade union the right to keep employers from firing strikers and hiring replacements ("scabs") during a strike, the employers would have been able to hire laborers at a market price. The above-market price of unionized labor encourages employers to search for labor substitutes.

The mechanization of California fruit and vegetable farming accelerated after the "bracero" program, which allowed the growers to hire Mexican aliens to work in the fields, was made illegal in the 1960's. It was also at this time that the United Farm Workers, under Cesar Chavez, began to grow significantly. Laws against "illegal aliens" push up labor costs by restricting the supply of legal laborers; this encourages overinvestment in labor-substituting equipment — overinvestment compared to what economic freedom would have produced.

It is significant that Israel had no laws that discriminated against "strangers in the land." No laws against immigration or emigration exist in the Bible. A free market in labor services is established by biblical law. The "city on a hill" in the Bible has no barbed wire around it, to keep foreigners out or citizens in. It is the modern humanist societies that erect barbed wire barriers: the West to keep out "undesirables," and the East to keep in "desirables."

possible for future-predicting entrepreneurs to collect profits that are the residual of accurate forecasting.[18]

An enslaved population is unable to make full use of the information which is available to producers, for the source of the continual correcting of this information must come from a bureaucratic agency an agency which does not offer employee incentives comparable to employee incentives in a free market for the collection of *accurate and economically relevant* information, or incentives for affected institutions to respond appropriately to new information. If a society relies heavily on the output of an enslaved population, then its non-slave members are also unable to make the most efficient use of the available resources, for *the society's information-delivery system is made increasingly unreliable.* Neither the slaves nor the taskmasters know what scarce economic resources really should cost. Without a competitive market, the planners are flying blind. *Those who fly blind eventually crash.*

Conclusion

The Pharaoh decided to tighten the screws on the Israelites. In doing so, he reduced the freedom of a productive people to increase the per capita wealth of the Egyptian nation. He imposed new costs on them which could only reduce their productivity, either by reducing the division of labor or by grinding them into despair, both of which would ultimately waste Egyptian resources. He abandoned a free market in goods and services. He increased the authority of his bureaucratic State. He brought his judgment on the people of God, merely because their representatives asked for time off to worship God.

Because of Egypt's heavy reliance on the slave system, neither Pharaoh nor the nobles knew what the cost of any resource really was. The more rigorously he enslaved them, the less reliable was the economic knowledge available to the planners. The Pharaoh thereby proclaimed his faith in Egypt's theology: the sovereignty of the Pharaoh and the bureaucratic State which was incarnate in his own person. The result was the destruction of both the Egyptian State and his person.

---

18. North, *Genesis,* ch. 23: "The Entrepreneurial Function."

8

COVENANTAL JUDGMENT

Then the magicians said unto Pharaoh, This is the finger of God: and Pharaoh's heart was hardened, and he hearkened not unto them; as the LORD had said (Ex. 8:19).

The supernatural contest between the representatives of God and the magicians of Egypt escalated from the beginning. In the first confrontation, Aaron cast down the rod that God had presented to Moses. It became a serpent. The magicians matched this display of supernatural transformation, but then Aaron's serpent swallowed the serpents of the Egyptians. This presumably did not help the magicians to persuade Pharaoh that their magic was stronger than the supernatural power available to these two Hebrews (Ex. 7:10-12). The second display of power involved the Nile's water. Aaron stretched out the rod, and the waters of Egypt turned to blood. The magicians matched this supernatural act (Ex. 7:19-22). In this instance, their magic seemed comparable to Aaron's. However, this was no consolation to Pharaoh; now he had even more bloody water than he had before the contest. This same "victory" of Egyptian magic was matched in the coming of the frogs (Ex. 8:5-7). We can almost imagine Pharaoh's consternation, how he must have said to himself, "No, you idiots, not more frogs; *fewer* frogs! Show me how powerful you are by *removing* these frogs." His magicians were determined to prove their mastery of the black arts by matching Aaron, plague for plague, thereby *reinforcing God's judgment on Egypt.* But there is no indication that they brought additional blood and frogs to the land of Goshen, where the Hebrews lived. They simply multiplied the burdens of Egypt. The Egyptians were worse off as a result of the nation's magicians. The arrogance of the magicians had made things even less bearable.

It should be understood, however, that the first three plagues did affect Goshen: blood, frogs, and lice. Only with the fourth plague, flies (or insects), did God declare that Goshen would be spared (Ex. 8:22). As slaves, the Israelites were under the covenantal rule of the Egyptians, both for good (the economic benefits of living in an extensive empire) and evil. Like the animals who were cursed because of man's sin in the garden, or draftees in an army ruled by an incompetent Commander-in-Chief, so are the slaves of a rebellious culture. And in the case of the ethical condition of the Israelite slaves, their subsequent behavior indicated that they were not wholly innocent victims of a society whose first principles they should have utterly rejected. The leeks and onions of Egypt had their appeal in Goshen, too.

That God should bring frogs to curse Egypt as the second plague was fitting. The frog was an important fertility deity in Egypt. The frog-goddess Heqet at Abydos was pictured as sitting at the bier of Osiris, a god of death and rebirth. Frog amulets were popular as symbols of new life and new birth. "The 'matlametlo,' a great frog over five inches long, hides in the root of a bush as long as there is a drought, and when rain falls, it rushes out. It comes with the rain as the beetle with the rising of the Nile; both are symbolic of new life and growth."[1] Just as the Nile, Egypt's life-bringer, became the death-bringer, so did the frogs become a plague.

After the frogs came the third plague, when the dust of the ground became lice. Again, we can almost imagine Pharaoh's thoughts, as he stood scratching himself: "Look, I don't need any more proof of your mastery of magic. If you can't get rid of the lice, then just sit quietly. Who needs magical powers like yours at a time like this?" The magicians tried to match this event and failed (Ex. 8:18). At this point, they capitulated. If they could not make the nation even more miserable than it already was, if they were unable to louse up Egypt even more, then their opponent must be God. "This is the finger of God," they said, using the same term which Jesus used to describe the Spirit of God in casting out demons (Luke 11:20: "finger of God"; Matt. 12:28: "Spirit of God"). They recognized that they were dealing with supernatural power which was greater than their own, meaning a God who was more powerful than the gods of Egypt. By telling Pharaoh that the finger of God was the source of

---

1. Jane E. Harrison, "Introduction" to E. A. Wallis Budge, *Osiris* (New Hyde Park, New York: University Books, [1911] 1961), p. vii. The introduction actually first appeared as an essay in *The Spectator* (April 13, 1912), and was included in the 1961 edition.

the power facing him, they were advising him to capitulate. We are told that he hearkened not unto them, and that his heart was hardened. He understood what they meant, and he refused to listen.

Comparative Wealth

Then came seven other plagues: swarms of insects (the King James Version inserts the words "of flies" after swarms, but the Hebrew is not specific), the death of all the cattle of Egypt, pestilence, boils, hail, locusts, and darkness. In the final seven plagues, the Egyptians were afflicted, while the Israelites were not. Because of this protection, the Israelites were increasing their per capita wealth in comparison to the Egyptians. They were growing steadily richer — not just comparatively, but absolutely. How could this be? If the Israelites were not actually increasing the size of their herds, how could the plagues have increased their per capita wealth? Because demand for cattle in the marketplace was now focused on the only available local supply, and the Israelites possessed this local monopoly. The market value of their cattle rose, meaning that the exchange value of their cattle rose. Furthermore, their fields had not been struck by the hail, so their crops had survived. The kinds of wealth held by the Egyptians after the plagues — gold, jewels, etc. — always drop in value relative to survival goods during a major catastrophe. The "coin of the realm" during a famine is *food,* not pieces of metal or shining stones (Gen. 47:15-16).[2]. The Hebrews possessed food, and all the demand for food would have been concentrated on their possessions. They had what the Egyptians needed in order to survive. The market value of their assets increased.

The Problem of the Cattle

We face a difficult problem in explaining this economic event. The plague on the cattle of Egypt destroyed them all (Ex. 9:6). Then came the pestilence of the boils, which struck Egyptians, their other animals, and even the priests (Ex. 9:11). (Fortunately for the Egyptians, the magicians had by this time given up any attempts to match God's plagues, boil for boil.) Finally, Egypt was struck with a mighty hail. Some of the Egyptians believed Moses this time: "He that feared the word of the LORD among the servants of Pharaoh made

---

2. Gary North, *The Dominion Covenant: Genesis* (Tyler, Texas: Institute for Christian Economics, 1982), ch. 24: "The Misapplication of Intrinsic Value."

his servants and his cattle flee into the houses: And he that regarded not the word of the LORD left his servants and his cattle in the field" (Ex. 9:20-21). The problem: Where had they purchased these new herds of cattle?

They could either have bought or confiscated cattle from the Hebrews, since the Hebrews had not lost their cattle in the plague (Ex. 8:6). The Hebrews had cattle after the hail, since the hail did not strike Goshen (Ex. 9:26). It is also possible that cattle were imported from Canaan. We are not told. If the Egyptians bought cattle from the Hebrews, it meant that they were unwilling to confiscate the Hebrews' cattle. It would have been possible for them to have marched in and taken cattle out of Goshen. They did not confiscate all the cattle, nor did they buy all the cattle, since the Hebrews still had cattle when the hail began. Perhaps they never sought the Hebrews' cattle. We know that the Hebrews took large herds of cattle with them when they left Egypt (Ex. 12:38). This indicates that the Egyptians did not confiscate their cattle after the plague, and probably not after the hail. Conceivably, they did confiscate the cattle after the hail, and gave back the cattle at the time of the Exodus, but the Bible does not say that this happened.

When the hail stopped, the Israelites had all the cattle still alive in Egypt. Did the Egyptians buy from them? It is not easy to say. The Hebrews requested precious metals and jewels from the Egyptians at the time of the Exodus, which might be interpreted as a unique event, indicating that they had not owned any jewels before. Did the Egyptians buy their cattle from the Hebrews without paying in jewelry? We do not know. What we do know is that the Israelites had crops and cattle, the key resources, immediately following the hail. *The slaves were now rich.*

Of course, if the Israelites had been facing starvation, then their position would not have risen absolutely. They would have been better off than the Egyptians, but they would have had to consume their resources, making it impossible for them to have profited from their position of relatively greater wealth. But they were being protected by God; they were not going to starve. They might have traded their cattle and crops for the surplus gold and jewels of the Egyptians, had God decided to let them remain in Egypt. They would have collected the valuables of the Egyptians in exchange for their surplus food. However, God had even better plans; they would keep the food and *also* collect the jewels of the Egyptians. God's protection had already made them the beneficiaries of rising per capita wealth, even before they "borrowed" from their former masters. They had monopoly ownership of the crucial survival resources in a time of great shortages. They had what the Egyptians needed. Not only had their masters lost the necessities, they would shortly have to forfeit their luxuries, either in exchange for the Israelites' food or in restitution for the generations of bondage.

The Sovereign Who Failed

The Egyptians had been wiped out economically by the plagues. They had been ruined. Their ruler, who was theoretically divine, was stubborn and arrogant. He was the protector of Egypt, yet he had led Egypt into an economic disaster. He was the ruler of the Nile, and it had been turned to blood, killing the fish. Walter Brueggemann's comments on the significance of this judgment against the Nile are to the point: "We cannot grasp the trouble fully until we recall that the Nile River is not only a geographical referent. It is also an expression of the imperial power of fertility. It is administration of the Nile which permits the king to generate and guarantee life. The failure of the Nile and its life system means that the empire does not have in itself the power of life (cf. Ezek. 29:3). It is for this reason that the plague of the Nile is so crucial (Ex. 7:7-22). An assault on the Nile strikes at the heart of Pharaoh's claim to authority."[3]

Pharaoh was also the controller of the seasons, yet the nation's agricultural system had been disrupted by hail—hail in a land where it seldom rained! He was the shepherd of the nation's flocks, and the cattle had been struck with sickness and then with hail. Wilson writes, concerning the social function of the Pharaoh: "The herdsman is primarily the pastor, the 'feeder,' and a first responsibility of the state was to see that the people were fed. Thus the king of Egypt was the god who had brought fertility to Egypt, produced the life-giving waters, and presented the gods with the sheaf of grain which symbolized abundant food. Indeed, an essential function of his kingship was that of a medicine man, whose magic ensured good crops."[4] This Pharaoh had failed in every respect to measure up to

---

3. Walter Brueggemann, *Genesis* (Atlanta: John Knox Press, 1982), p. 327.
4. John A. Wilson, "Egypt," in Henri Frankfort, *et al., The Intellectual Adventure of Ancient Man* (University of Chicago Press, [1946] 1977), pp. 79-80.

the theological system of Egypt. God had hardened his heart, thereby increasing his innate stubbornness, in order to display the power of a true God. Speaking of the Pharaoh, God said: "And in very deed for this cause I raise thee up, for to shew in thee my power; and that my name may be declared throughout all the earth" (Ex. 9:16). God would demonstrate before other kings just how sovereign the Pharaoh really was.

Except possibly for a brief period under Joseph, the Egyptians had clung to their theology of the *continuity of being* for centuries. They had placed themselves under the sovereign power of a god, they believed. Their prosperity was guaranteed by a divine man, and their future life beyond the grave would be analogous to their life on earth: under the jurisdiction of the Pharaoh. Again, citing Wilson: "Since the central factor in this world was the divine nature of the king, who owned and controlled everything within Egypt, the next world would be based on the same absolute authority. Life after death, independent of the Pharaoh, would thus be out of the question for this early period."[5] Everything in Egypt took place under the supposed sovereignty of a king-god. What the Egyptians assented to when the pharaohs put the Israelites in bondage was this: a king-god on earth had lawful, sovereign power over the the representatives of the God of the Bible. No king reigns apart from a concept of legitimate rule, and the assent of the Egyptians to the decisions of their ruler brought them into conflict with the God of the Bible.

Covenants and Representative Government

There are covenants on earth. The Egyptians were under a covenant with their king. This covenant had been reaffirmed when they sold their lands to the Pharaoh of the famine (Gen. 47:20-26). They had entered into another covenant when that Pharaoh gave the land of Goshen to the family of Joseph (Gen. 47:1-6). This covenant was broken by a later Pharaoh, and the Egyptians were under his rule — by choice, by the prior sale of their lands, and by the theology of Egypt. His covenant was their covenant; the breaking of his covenant with the family of Joseph was also the breaking of their covenant with the family of Joseph. *Men are judged in social orders in terms of the decisions made by their legitimate covenantal rulers.*

This is an important concept. The Bible teaches the doctrine of

5. John A. Wilson, *The Burden of Egypt: An Interpretation of Ancient Egyptian Culture* (University of Chicago Press, [1951] 1967), p. 65.

representative government. This refers to all government, not just civil government. Representative government applies to churches, corporations, trusts, and families. Adam, our representative before God, sinned, and we are under a curse. This "federal headship" of Adam was based on a concept of representative government under a covenant. So was the "federal headship" of Pharaoh.

Pharaoh was the federal head of Egypt. Egypt's theology recognized this; he was seen as the divine-human link, the representative of the Egyptian gods. When the judgment of God began, it struck the Pharaoh's house first. His magicians' serpents were consumed by Aaron's. Then the escalation carried the conflict into the rivers and fields and homes of the whole land. Goshen was protected after the initial three plagues because God's people resided there, and because they were captives, not fully assenting citizens, of Egypt. Egyptians far removed from the seat of power were afflicted with the insects, pestilence, boils, and hail. They knew nothing of the conflict between Moses and the Pharaoh. They had never heard of Moses or Aaron. Yet their crops were destroyed, their waters turned to blood, their land filled with the stench of death. When they reclined on their beds or walked through their homes, the squishing of frogs was continual. Those Egyptians who had never personally owned, controlled, or punished a Hebrew slave were scratching lice day and night. Poor farmers, who lived on the edge of starvation, saw their milk cows die. What had they done to deserve this? They had believed in a false god. Now that this god was at last being brought under judgment by the true God, they became recipients of that judgment. Their self-proclaimed god had stood in terms of his sovereign kingdom and its prosperity to challenge God's own representatives. To demonstrate the true source of sovereignty, God smashed the Pharaoh and his kingdom, including his people.

Methodological Individualism

To imagine that the judgments of God, in time and on earth, are limited to personal, individualistic penalties, is to misread the Bible. If anything, the reverse is true, in time and on earth. *It is the collective judgment of God, like the collective blessings of God, which is set forth in the Bible.* God does not promise that every good man will prosper economically, or that every evil man will be brought low. What the Bible promises is that covenantally faithful *societies* will prosper in the long run, and that covenantally rebellious ones will be crushed eventually.

This brings up the question of methodological individualism. The Bible teaches *methodological covenantalism,* not methodological individualism. When we speak of "society," we have in mind an association of men which is under the law of God, and through which men and institutions are blessed or judged by God. A social covenant *does* exist, whether explicit or implicit in human documents or institutions. Thus, methodological covenantalism conflicts with the anarchism of the methodological individualist. Rothbard's libertarian view of society is not conformable to the story of God's judgment of the Egyptian masses. "We have talked at length of individual rights; but what, it may be asked, of the 'rights of society'? Don't they supersede the rights of the mere individual? The libertarian, however, is an individualist; he believes that one of the prime errors in social theory is to treat 'society' as if it were an actually existing entity. 'Society' is sometimes treated as a superior or quasi-divine figure with overriding 'rights' of its own; at other times as an existing evil which can be blamed for all the ills of the world. The individualist holds that only individuals exist, think, feel, choose, and act; and that 'society' is not a living entity but simply a label for a set of interacting individuals. Treating society as a thing that chooses and acts, then, serves to obscure the real forces at work."[6]

Rothbard rejects methodological holism (collectivism), which sees the evolution of society as a force independent of human will and human action. But methodological covenantalism is not methodological holism; it does not view society as a personal entity separate from men. It sees men as being *represented by others before God* in various institutional relationships. Men suffer and prosper not only by what they do as individuals, but also by the decisions of those in authority over them. It teaches that there are law-governed arrangements by which God deals with people — not impersonal natural law, or the law of karma (reincarnation), or evolutionary law, but God-ordained law. The biblical view categorically rejects the utilitarian view of law presented by classical liberals, e.g., Mises and Hayek.[7]

---

6. Murray N. Rothbard, *For a New Liberty: The Libertarian Manifesto* (rev. ed.; New York: Collier, 1978), p. 37.

7. For a critique of Hayek, see Appendix B, "The Evolutionists' Defense of the Market," in Gary North, *The Dominion Covenant: Genesis.*

Mises vs. the Covenant

Mises' rejection of this covenantal outlook, which he equates with holism, is characteristically uncompromising:

According to the doctrines of universalism, conceptual realism, holism, collectivism, and some representatives of Gestaltpsychologie, society is an entity living its own life, independent of and separate from the lives of the various individuals, acting on its own behalf and aiming at its own ends which are different from the ends sought by the individuals. Then, of course, an antagonism between the aims of society and those of its members can emerge. In order to safeguard the flowering and further development of society it becomes necessary to master the selfishness of the individuals and to compel them to sacrifice their egoistic designs to the benefit of society. At this point all these holistic doctrines are bound to abandon the secular methods of human science and logical reasoning and to shift to theological or metaphysical professions of faith. They must assume that Providence, through its prophets, apostles, and charismatic leaders, forces men who are constitutionally wicked, i.e., prone to pursue their own ends, to walk in the ways of righteousness which the Lord or *Weltgeist* or history wants them to walk.[8]

In other words, Mises rejects the epistemological significance of the fact that *God converts men*. Sometimes, these men become representative agents before God for other men whom God places under their jurisdiction, whether those represented approve of it or not (as in the case of the Israelites who wanted Moses and Aaron to go away and leave them alone). Mises rejects this explanation of human affairs.

"This is the philosophy," he continues, "which has characterized from time immemorial the creeds of primitive tribes. It has been an element in all religious teachings. Man is bound to comply with the law issued by a superhuman power and to obey the authorities which this power has entrusted with the enforcement of the law. The order created by this law, human society, is consequently the work of the Deity and not of man. If the Lord had not interfered and had not given enlightenment to erring mankind, society would not have come into existence. . . . The scientific theory as developed by the social philosophy of eighteenth-century rationalism and liberalism and by modern economics does not resort to any miraculous interference of superhuman powers. . . . Society is a product of human action, i.e., the human urge to remove uneasiness as far as

---

8. Ludwig von Mises, *Human Action* (3rd ed.; Chicago: Regnery, 1966), p. 145.

possible. In order to explain its becoming and its evolution it is not necessary to have recourse to a doctrine, certainly offensive to a truly religious mind, according to which the original creation was so defective that reiterated superhuman intervention is needed to prevent its failure."[9] In other words, "a truly religious mind" is the mind of an eighteenth-century Continental European deist, whose silent, distant God is sufficiently irrelevant to human affairs to satisfy a generous and broad-minded humanistic economist (assuming he is not a follower of Ayn Rand's atheistic "objectivism"—and few economists are).[10]

For Mises, a confirmed utilitarian, "Law and legality, the moral code and social institutions are no longer revered as unfathomable decrees of Heaven. They are of human origin, and the only yardstick that must be applied to them is that of expediency with regard to human welfare."[11] His methodological individualism is grounded in human expediency, which somehow (he cannot say how) is understood by all men, or at least all *reasonable* men who recognize the value of free market economics and economic growth. In short, economists—*true* economists, meaning defenders of the free market —"have repeatedly emphasized that they deal with socialism and interventionism from the point of view of the generally accepted values of Western civilization."[12] Even a methodological individualist sometimes finds collectives—"the values of Western civilization"—epistemologically indispensable. Sadly, Mises never admitted what should have been obvious, specifically, that he was dependent upon the epistemological holism which he officially and vociferously rejected.[13]

The idea of representative civil government was basic to nineteenth-century liberalism. The defenders of classical liberalism

---

9. *Ibid.*, pp. 145-47.

10. Rothbard once remarked concerning the Randians: "They hate God more than they hate the State." For a comprehensive critique of Rand's thought, see John Robbins, *Answer to Ayn Rand: A Critique of the Philosophy of Objectivism* (Washington, D. C.: Mt. Vernon Pub. Co., 1974), distributed by the Trinity Foundation, P.O. Box 169, Jefferson, Maryland 21755.

11. Mises, *Human Action*, p. 147.

12. Mises, *Theory and History: An Interpretation of Social and Economic Evolution* (New Rochelle, New York: Arlington House, 1969), p. 33. Published originally by Yale University Press in 1957.

13. Gary North, "Economics: From Reason to Intuition," in North (ed.), *Foundations of Christian Scholarship: Essays in the Van Til Perspective* (Vallecito, California: Ross House, 1976), pp. 87-96.

wanted limited civil government and a free market economy. But there are few strict defenders of the old faith today. Mises and Hayek have few followers. Their intellectual heirs are either Christians or outright anarchists. Neither group (a holistic noun) accepts the viewpoint of nineteenth-century classical liberalism.[14] Christians base their views on the Bible, and the anarchists want no civil government — certainly not one which is supported by compulsory taxation.

The empirical or "positive economics" of the Chicago School defends the limited-government viewpoint. These scholars do not appeal to hypothetically universal rights of man that are based on natural law. They explain economics strictly in terms of economic self-interest, and they use scientific tools of "empirical," value-free economic analysis, especially mathematics, which implies some sort of holism (economic aggregates). Mises categorically rejected such holism as a valid tool for understanding human action. Therefore, the old classical liberalism, with its strict commitment to methodological individualism, is today a shadow of its former moral self.

Conclusion

The Pharaoh's court magicians warned him. They told him that he was facing God almighty. He did not accept their evaluation, or at least he chose to challenge the God of Moses anyway. Did this protect the families of the magicians? Did they avoid the plagues? Did they escape the death of their firstborn? Not without the blood on the doorposts. Not without an outward covenantal sign indicating that they had placed themselves under the sovereignty of

---

14. It is one of the ironies of recent history that the two main groups that continue to read and quote Mises both reject his utilitarianism. The anarcho-capitalists, led by Rothbard, are defenders of natural law theory, and they explicitly reject utilitarianism as a legitimate foundation of social and economic theory: Rothbard, *For a New Liberty,* p. 16. They are anarchists, and Mises explicitly rejected anarchism. He even said that a military draft is sometimes legitimate: "He who in our age opposes armaments and conscription is, perhaps unbeknown to himself, an abettor of those aiming at the enslavement of all." *Human Action,* p. 282. The anarcho-capitalists seldom go into print against Mises by name, since they are self-professed followers of Mises and Austrian economic theory, but they have abandoned much of his epistemology (he was a self-conscious Kantian dualist, as well as a utilitarian) and his philosophy of limited (rather than zero) civil government. The other group that uses Mises' economic arguments is the Christian Reconstruction movement, whose members reject his humanism-agnosticism and his methodological individualism. There are virtually no strict followers of Mises — Kantians, utilitarians, non-anarchists — under 60 years of age who are still writing in the early 1980's.

God. They gave the king good advice, but he did not take it, and they did not escape.

When God brought judgment on Egypt, the seemingly innocent Egyptians were not spared. This was because there were no innocent Egyptians. They were all under the Pharaoh's covenant, they all operated in terms of his divinity, and they all felt the wrath of God, in time and on earth. They were doomed because he was doomed. He was their representative in a great confrontation with God, almost as the Philistines were represented by Goliath. The result was the same in each instance: death for the representative, and scattering and defeat for the represented.

Covenants cannot be avoided. Man cannot serve two masters; he serves only one (Matt. 6:24). The system of representative government has been with mankind since the beginning. Adam's heirs cannot escape the results of Adam's choice in the garden. He served as our representative head; his loss was our loss. The Pharaoh's loss was the Egyptian peasant's loss. Men do not stand alone, as independent, totally autonomous entities, facing a cosmos which is impersonal. Though covenant-breaking man would like to believe its conclusion, William Ernest Henley's late-nineteenth-century poem, *Invictus,* proclaimed a false doctrine of man's autonomy. Its concluding lines:

> It matters not how strait the gate,
> How charged with punishments the scroll,
> I am the master of my fate:
> I am the captain of my soul.

Henley is forgotten today, as is his poem, but the last two lines of this stanza are part of the English language, familiar to millions who have never heard of him. Its sentiments are basic to the twentieth century, in which more people have died as a result of disastrous decisions by national leaders than in any previous century, with the possible exception of Noah's generation, depending upon the size of that population.

9

ORIGINAL OWNERSHIP

And Moses said unto him [Pharaoh], As soon as I am gone out of the city, I will spread abroad my hands unto the LORD; and the thunder shall cease, neither shall there be any more hail; that thou mayest know how that the earth is the LORD's. But as for thee and thy servants, I know that ye will not yet fear the LORD God (Ex. 9:29-30).

This is not the first statement in Scripture concerning the ownership of the earth. Melchizedek blessed Abram, who was "of the most high God, possessor of heaven and earth" (Gen. 14:19b), and Abram used the same phrase, "possessor of heaven and earth" (Gen. 14:22b). In that instance, Abram refused to accept any gifts from the king of Sodom, lest the king should say, "I have made Abram rich" (Gen. 14:23b). God's total sovereignty over the earth required Abram to tithe, in this case to the priest Melchizedek (Gen. 14:20). He understood that God could legitimately extract His portion from Abram, the steward, even though Abram believed it would be wise to forego the gifts from the king of Sodom. God was to be honored, not Abram. God was to receive the tithe, not Abram. Yet Abram was rich, and he took care to keep the king of Sodom from receiving the credit. God was the source of Abram's wealth, not a pagan earthly king.

It was different in the case of Pharaoh. He *did* owe a payment to the Israelites. He had challenged Moses and Moses' God. He came before God under a curse. He and his people had enslaved God's people, had broken their covenant with the Israelites, and had burdened them with the requirement to make bricks without straw. Pharaoh had changed his mind repeatedly, breaking each successive promise to Moses concerning the Israelites. Egypt would pay restitution to the Israelites before the Exodus. It was not a question of making the Israelites rich. Pharaoh would receive no credit in this regard. The restitution payment was being extracted from the Egyptians by a series of external judgments. Abram refused Sodom's payment, while God demanded Egypt's. Egypt's payment was no gift.

Moses' message to Pharaoh was clear: *God owns the world.* He also controls its operations. Moses reminded Pharaoh of the source of his miseries. The land was in ruins. Egypt had been overtaken by a series of disasters. But Moses' point was that these had not been "natural" disasters. They had been supernatural disasters. To prove his point, he promised to pray to God, and God would then halt the hail and thunderstorms. The *proof* of God's ownership is *God's word.* He made the world, He made man, and He is sovereign over both man and the world. But to demonstrate His ownership before Pharaoh, God stopped the hail.

His word was sufficient proof. He did not need to verify His word before Pharaoh. Nevertheless, God provided the additional evidence. Yet Moses told Pharaoh that he would not fear God, despite the evidence. Pharaoh's heart was hardened. The evidence did not matter. If he would not listen to God's prophet, he would not assent to the evidence of his eyes. If God's word was insufficient, then the absence of hail would not be sufficient. He would still not fear God. In this sense, he resembled Satan, whom he represented.

Pharaoh never did believe the testimony of his eyes. Right up until the moment when the waters of the Red Sea closed over him, he refused to assent to the obvious. He raced into the arms of death, shouting his defiance against God, breaking his word, and taking the Egyptian State with him. He refused to believe God's word, so the testimony of his eyes meant nothing. His operating presupposition was that he, the Pharaoh, was god. God is not the being He claims to be, nor could such a being exist, Pharaoh presupposed. No sovereign, absolute being can lay claim to total control, and therefore original ownership of everything, he believed. He died for his beliefs.

God's claim *is* comprehensive. He possesses absolute property rights to every atom of the universe. He created it, and He owns it. He, unlike man, does not operate in terms of a definition of ownership which requires the right and ability of an owner to *disown* the property at his discretion.[1] His ownership is original; no other being

---

1. F. A. Harper writes: "The corollary of the right of ownership is the right of disownership. So if I cannot sell a thing, it is evident that I do not really own it." *Liberty: A Path to Its Recovery* (Irvington, New York: Foundation for Economic Education, 1949), p. 106.

is absolutely sovereign, so therefore no other being can claim original, uncontested rights to any aspect of the creation. No other being owns any economic asset which he did not receive from God. Therefore, no other being can bargain with God to buy any part of the creation. All property is held by means of a transfer of rights from God to the new owner. It is held in terms of a covenant. Men or demons can break their covenant with God, denying the terms of subordinate ownership, but they cannot thereby achieve their goal of final sovereignty. Whatever rights (legal immunities and protections) they possess to buy or sell property, or even to confiscate property, are derivative rights. *Absolute ownership is an incommunicable attribute of God.*

Ownership and Sovereignty

God's statement that He owns the earth is an announcement of His total sovereignty. It is therefore a denial of all of the claims of rebellious man against the plan of God. Jesus' parable of the vineyard owner who hired the laborers throughout the day elaborates on the implications of God's ownership. The land owner hires men all day long, at an identical agreed-upon wage, and at the end of the day, each man receives his wage, one penny. The ones who had labored all day complained: those who came late to work received the same wage for a shorter day's work. They ignored the fact that they had no guarantee when they signed on in the morning that the owner would offer anyone employment later in the day. Neither did those who could not find employment that morning. The complainers were ignoring the effects of *uncertainty* on contractual obligations.

The owner answers them with questions. First, hadn't they agreed to work for this wage (Matt. 20:13)? Second, "Is it not lawful for me to do what I will with mine own? Is thine eye evil, because I am good?" (20:15). Here is the doctrine of God's absolute sovereignty, but conveyed by Jesus in an economic parable that could be understood by His listeners. God has the right to do what He wants with the whole creation. He owns the earth, just as the owner of a field owns that field. He is sovereign over it. *This is one of the key passages in the New Testament which defends the ethical and legal legitimacy of private property.* If the owner in the parable did not have the right to do what he wanted with his own property, then the meaning of the parable is lost. An individual's personal, private ownership is analogous to God's personal, private ownership of the earth, including the souls of men. Private ownership, not State ownership, is the foundation of the parable. *To challenge the legitimacy of God's delegated sovereignty of private ownership of the means of production is to challenge the doctrine of the original sovereignty of God. Socialism is therefore an innately demonic and evil doctrine.* It is not surprising that the rise of socialism and statism in the West was also accompanied by the rise of philosophies hostile to the sovereignty of God.[2]

Pharaoh's Assertion

Pharaoh recognized the implications of this doctrine of God's absolute ownership, and he rejected it. He refused to humble himself before the God of the Israelites. He had no fear of this God, despite God's control over the forces of nature. He rejected the doctrine of God's sovereignty over the affairs of Egypt. He, as a legitimate god, according to Egyptian theology, possessed at least some degree of autonomous sovereignty. He was entitled to the lives and labors of these Hebrews. Any attempt by their God to impose non-negotiable demands on Egypt had to be resisted. To capitulate on this issue would have implied a moral obligation on Pharaoh's part to conform his economic decisions to the law of God. If God owns the whole earth, then each man is merely a steward of God's property, and is therefore morally obligated to administer the original owner's property according to His instructions. Pharaoh would have had to acknowledge his position as a subordinate ruler under God, a prince rather than a king. He would not do it.

As Moses had predicted, as soon as the hail and thunder ceased, Pharaoh and his servants resumed their resistance (Ex. 9:34).

Their theology acknowledged the possibility of the appearance of a powerful god to challenge Egypt. Any war between states in the ancient world was believed to involve the gods of both nations. The idea that God might own *part* of the world, or might legitimately

---

2. On the rise of revolutionary socialism and equally revolutionary nationalism —both philosophies of State sovereignty—as religious and extensively occult phenomena, see James Billington, *Fire in the Minds of Men: Origins of the Revolutionary Faith* (New York: Basic Books, 1980). I regard this as the single most significant work of historical scholarship to be published in the United States in the post-World War II era. (Solzhenitsyn's *Gulag Archipelago* is the most important work overall, in terms of its impact on the thinking of Western intellectuals, forcing them to confront the reality of Soviet civilization. It is not, strictly speaking, a work of historical scholarship, since it foregoes the historian's paraphernalia of footnotes and extensive documentation, although I regard the work as accurate historically. The author has subtitled this work, "An Experiment in Literary Investigation.")

have *some* claim on the Hebrews as a form of His personal property, could be accepted in theory by the Egyptians. What was repugnant to them was the idea that He owned everything, "lock, stock, and barrel," in the traditional English terminology. That left them no bargaining room.

The Hebrews belonged to God, the Egyptians belonged to God, and Egypt belonged to God. God's assault against Egypt was not a form of competition for temporary advantage, God against Pharaoh. His victory was not an instance of a temporarily sovereign invader who might be overcome later, when conditions changed. The *same event* — the withdrawal of visible judgment — was *interpreted differently* by Moses and Pharaoh. Pharaoh acted as though he believed that God's withdrawal of the plagues was a sign of His weakening, as if cosmic forces or the gods of Egypt had finally begun to repel this invader. He grew arrogant each time a plague ended. Moses had told him that the removal of the hail and thunder was proof of God's continuing sovereignty, proof that the forces of nature are not autonomous, but under the direct administration of God.

The Marxists' Dilemma

This incident points to a fundamental problem for economic theory, namely, the establishment of a point of originating (and therefore final) ownership. The modern socialist movement, especially Marxism, asserts that all ownership should be collective, and the tools of production should be lodged in the State. Marx's words in Part II of the *Communist Manifesto* (1848) do not explicitly establish State ownership, but they deny the rights of private ownership: "In this sense, the theory of the Communists may be summed up in the single sentence: Abolition of private property."[3] Again, "Capital is a collective product, and only by the united action of many members, nay, in the last resort, only by the united action of all members of society, can it be set in motion. Capital is, therefore, not a personal, it is a social power."[4] At the end of Part II, he argues that under pure communism, class antagonisms will disappear, and therefore the State, as an organ of repression used by the ruling class to suppress the lower classes, will finally disappear. "When, in the

---

3. Karl Marx and Frederick Engels, "Manifesto of the Communist Party" (1848), in Marx and Engels, *Selected Works,* 3 vols. (Moscow: Progress Publishers, [1969] 1977), I, p. 120.

4. *Ibid.,* I, p. 121.

course of development, class distinctions have disappeared, and all production has been concentrated in the hands of a vast association of the whole nation, the public power will lose its political character. Political power, properly so called, is merely the organised power of one class for oppressing another. . . . In place of the old bourgeois society, with its classes and class antagonisms, we shall have an association, in which the free development of each is the condition for the free development of all."[5] The "vast association" replaces the State. This may sound as though Marx was not really in favor of the State as the owner of the tools of production. But how will the "vast association of the whole nation" allocate scarce economic resources, unless either the State or free markets order the decisions of producers? Marx's comment in *The German Ideology* (1845) is of little use: "Modern universal intercourse can be controlled by individuals, therefore, only when controlled by all."[6] Murray Rothbard, an advocate of the zero-State economy, calls attention to this confusion in Marx's thinking: "Rejecting private property, especially capital, the Left Socialists were then trapped in an inner contradiction: if the State is to disappear after the Revolution (immediately for Bakunin, gradually 'withering' for Marx), then how is the 'collective' to run its property without becoming an enormous State itself in fact even if not in name? This was the contradiction which neither the Marxists nor the Bakuninists were ever able to resolve."[7]

The Anarchists' Dilemma

On the other hand, the libertarians, or anarcho-capitalists, argue that the *individual* is absolutely sovereign over property. Even the settlement of disputes over property rights is to be solved by private organizations. There must be no political authority — no agency possessing a legal monopoly of violence — to suppress private violence. There must be only profit-seeking law courts, meaning courts without the legal authority to issue a subpoena to compel anyone to testify,[8] plus voluntary arbitration organizations and in-

5. *Ibid.*, I, p. 127.
6. Karl Marx, *The German Ideology* (London: Lawrence & Wishart, [1845] 1965), p. 84.
7. Murray N. Rothbard, "Left and Right: The Prospects for Liberty," *Left and Right*, I (1965), p. 8. For a discussion of this problem in Marxism and socialism, see my book, *Marx's Religion of Revolution: The Doctrine of Creative Destruction* (Nutley, New Jersey: Craig Press, 1968), pp. 111-17. A microfiche of this out-of-print book is available from the Institute for Christian Economics.
8. Murray N. Rothbard, *For a New Liberty: The Libertarian Manifesto* (rev. ed.; New York: Collier, 1978). p. 87.

surance companies.[9]

This raises an important question: How would this mythical libertarian society be different from Marx's mythical association? Neither one is supposed to be a political body, yet both seem to have important attributes of lawful authority. Why wouldn't private enforcement associations evolve into local police forces? How would the "senior administrators" be restrained from becoming warlords? How would *For a New Liberty* avoid becoming Volume I of *For a New Tyranny,* should a warlord society ever be constructed on the original legal foundation of the privatization of violence? How would "purely defensive, profit-seeking" armies be restrained from tearing a libertarian society apart in their quest for even greater short-run profits than peaceful competition can provide? These questions have proven to be equally as unsolvable, even in theory, as the socialists' problem of allocating scarce economic resources apart from either the State or the free market.

Conclusion

Ultimate sovereignty over economic resources is possessed by God, who delegates to men certain responsibilities over property. Some of these rights are delegated to individuals, who co-operate voluntarily in exchange. Other rights are delegated to the civil government. Associations also possess limited sovereignty: churches, corporations, clubs, charitable associations, educational institutions, and so forth. The law of God recognizes the legitimacy of *limited sovereignty* in many forms of organization, but none of them is regarded as absolutely sovereign over all spheres of life, or even in any given sphere. Fathers may not legally murder infants; churches may not

9. Bruno Leoni, *Freedom and the Law* (Princeton: Van Nostrand, 1961). Reprinted by Liberty Classics, Indianapolis, Indiana. Rothbard's review of the book criticizes it for not going far enough: "While Leoni is vague and wavering on the structure that his courts would take, he at least indicates the possibility of privately competing judges and courts. . . . Similarly, while in some passages Leoni accepts the idea of a governmental supreme court which he admits becomes itself a quasi-legislature, he does call for the restoration of the ancient practice of *separation* of government from the judicial function. If for no other reason, Professor Leoni's work is extremely valuable for raising, in our State-bemused age, the possibility of a workable separation of the judicial function from the State apparatus." Rothbard, "On Freedom and the Law," *New Individualist Review,* I (Winter 1962), p. 38. This short-lived journal of the 1960's has also been reprinted in one volume by Liberty Classics. Rothbard goes into greater detail concerning his theory of a judicial system in a society without a civil government with the power to impose sanctions, in his book, *For a New Liberty,* pp. 227-34.

embezzle funds; civil governments may not confiscate private property without due process of law. God, however, can do anything He wants, as the experiences of both Pharaoh and Job indicate. *God's total control* is correlative to *God's absolute ownership.*

To unravel the complex intertwining of the various spheres, in order to obtain the proper idea of the limits on the sovereignty of any or all of them, we need to search out the terms and implications of biblical law. Without the concrete examples of Old Testament law, seen as morally binding throughout history, men are left without any reliable guide to balance competing claims of all the self-proclaimed sovereign owners, or even admittedly derivative owners, assuming no one knows which group is sovereign in any given instance. Those who reject the idea that biblical law governs property rights, and who also recognize the evil of attributing absolute sovereignty either to the civil government or the autonomous individual, have a distressing tendency to substitute platitudes for analysis. We hear phrases like, "We're neither socialists nor free market capitalists." Fine; then what are we? Medieval guild socialists? Keynesian interventionists? Social credit advocates? Henry Georgists? "Ordo" liberals (followers of Wilhelm Röpke)? Or can we discover basic biblical principles and case-law applications that offer us a framework of responsible, though subordinate, ownership? Can we discover biblical laws of stewardship? Pharaoh could not, or at least he did not, and the Egypt of his day perished.

10

TOTAL SACRIFICE, TOTAL SOVEREIGNTY

And Pharaoh called unto Moses, and said, Go ye, serve the LORD; only let your flocks and your herds be stayed: let your little ones also go with you (Ex. 10:24).

Pharaoh was a battered despot. His original inflexibility was becoming more pliant, at least on the surface. When Moses first came before Pharaoh to request a time for sacrifice to God, Pharaoh absolutely rejected his request (Ex. 5:2). He denied knowing the God whom Moses spoke about. He punished the Hebrews by withdrawing the State-supplied straw for their brick-making. He retained his self-confident prohibition through four plagues: the Nile's transformation into blood, the frogs (after which he temporarily capitulated), the lice, and the swarms of insects.

Pharaoh then called Moses and informed him that it would be all right if the Israelites sacrificed in the land of Egypt (Ex. 8:25). Moses rejected the offer with the argument that lawful sacrifice involved the sacrifice of an animal which was an abomination in the sight of the Egyptians (Ex. 8:26). This probably meant sheep, since the profession of shepherd was an abomination to the Egyptians (Gen. 46:34). So Pharaoh backed down some more: they could go into the wilderness, but not too far away (Ex. 8:28). He would not permit them to travel a full three days' journey, as Moses requested (Ex. 8:27). Pharaoh again reversed himself and refused to allow them to go (Ex. 8:32). Then came three more plagues: dying cattle, the boils, and the hail (Ex. 9).

At this point, Moses came and announced the imminence of another plague: locusts. Pharaoh's response to Moses and also to his own advisors was a compromise which was, in reality, the same old stubbornness. The New American Standard Bible's translation is far more clear than the King James:

And Pharaoh's servants said to him, "How long will this man be a snare to us? Let the men go, that they may serve the LORD their God. Do you not realize that Egypt is destroyed?" So Moses and Aaron were brought back to Pharaoh, and he said to them, "Go, serve the LORD your God! Who are the ones who are going?" And Moses said, "We shall go with our young and our old; with our sons and our daughters, with our flocks and our herds we will go, for we must hold a feast to the LORD." Then he said unto them, "Thus may the LORD be with you, if ever I let you and your little ones go! Take heed, for evil is in your mind" (Ex. 10:7-10).

God then brought the plague of locusts upon Egypt. Pharaoh repented, asked Moses to remove them, and then once again forbade them to depart. Next, God brought thick darkness upon Egypt. "And Pharaoh called unto Moses, and said, Go ye, serve the LORD; only let your flocks and your herds be stayed: let your little ones also go with you" (Ex. 10:24). Moses again rejected this compromise: "Our cattle also shall go with us; there shall not an hoof be left behind; for thereof must we take to serve the LORD our God, until we come thither" (Ex. 10:26). The next verse repeats the familiar theme: "But the LORD hardened Pharaoh's heart, and he would not let them go." Pharaoh then sent Moses and Aaron away permanently (Ex. 10:28).

What was in Pharaoh's mind? A probable explanation is this: Pharaoh wanted to tie the Hebrews to an anchor. At first, of course, he did not want them to travel anywhere or sacrifice to any other God. Then he was willing to have them travel a little distance, just out of sight of the Egyptian people (Ex. 8:28). This way, Egypt's army could put them under surveillance, and if they tried to escape, the army could easily get to them in time to pull them back. A three days' journey would have given them too great a head start. Moses was unwilling to capitulate. So Pharaoh and his counsellors came up with the idea of letting only the males go to sacrifice. Again, Moses was totally uncooperative. So Pharaoh counter-offered: "All right, how about this? All the people go, but not the animals. Leave your capital here." Unacceptable, said Moses.

Non-Negotiable Demands

What we see is a conflict between two very stubborn men. Pharaoh appeared to be the more "reasonable." After all, hadn't he retreated from his original prohibition? Hadn't he tried his best to work out a solution? True, it took two or three plagues each time to convince him to make a counter-offer to Moses, but he always seemed to repent. But Moses—what an ideologue! He refused to budge. He had to have it all. He kept making non-negotiable demands. All the people had to go. All the animals had to go. They had to go three days' journey away from Goshen. They had to be out of sight of the Egyptians. Moses, as God's representative, did not choose to work out a compromise. It was "all or nothing" with Moses: *all for the Israelites,* and, if Pharaoh remained obstinate, it was *nothing for the Egyptians.* Pharaoh's advisors saw this clearly: "Egypt is destroyed," they reminded Pharaoh. Little did they suspect just how destroyed Egypt would shortly become.

The Bible's account is equally uncompromising: it was Pharaoh, not Moses, who had his heart actively hardened by God. Yet Moses appears to be the uncompromising representative in this battle of the wills. Why should Moses seem so rigid to modern readers? The modern world, with its presupposition of relativism, has a tendency to regard compromise as an almost universal benefit. "You go along to get along," is an old saying in the United States Senate.[1] Speaker of the House of Representatives Sam Rayburn made it famous.[2] You compromise. You rise above your principles. You make a deal.

Moses stood with God. He asked for a few days to sacrifice to God—a *comprehensive sacrifice* which would have involved the whole of Israel: men, women, children, and animals. All of them would be separated from their earthly captors. All of them would be outside the direct sovereign control of the Egyptian State. In short, they would be utterly under the dominion of God, and visibly so.

They did not propose to escape. When Moses asked Pharaoh to "let my people go," he was not asking him to give up control of God's people. At least, Moses did not ask this directly. But when he came to a self-proclaimed god, the ruler of a supposedly divine State, there could be no question of what was implied by his request. He was asking the Pharaoh to revoke an area of his self-proclaimed total sovereignty in Egypt. He was asking the Pharaoh to announce that the continuity of being between him and the gods of Egypt was in fact not a divine continuity at all, that there is a God who is higher, and who commands the sacrifices of a slave population. *Moses was asking the Pharaoh to make a symbolic commitment to God.* The Pharaoh was to admit to everyone that he held power over the Israelites by permis-

1. William Safire, *Safire's Political Dictionary* (New York: Ballentine, 1978), p. 303.

2. Anthony Champagne, *Congressman Sam Rayburn* (New Brunswick, New Jersey: Rutgers University Press, 1984), p. 161.

sion from the God of Israel, and that this foreign God had the authority to compel Egypt to suspend all signs of its sovereignty over Israel for several days, perhaps a week. (The phrase, "three days' journey," may have meant a round-trip of three days, or three days out and three days back, although the latter seems more plausible: Ex. 5:3.) The Pharaoh had to put the Israelites on their "good behavior," relying on their sense of justice to return to bondage. To have done so would have meant abandoning his role as absolute sovereign.

What if he had agreed to Moses' request? The Israelites had not requested freedom. God had not instructed Moses to call for a permanent release from Egypt. God had told Moses that He intended to lead them out of Egypt on a permanent basis (Ex. 3:8), but He did not instruct Moses to demand their release. Moses was only to request a week or less of freedom. God promised: "And I am sure that the king of Egypt will not let you go, no, not by a mighty hand" (Ex. 3:19), or as the New English Bible puts it, "unless he is compelled." Why was God so certain? Because He intended to control Pharaoh's very decisions: ". . . and the LORD hardened Pharaoh's heart, so that he would not let the children of Israel go out of the land" (Ex. 11:10). God's active hardening of Pharaoh's heart was basic to His promise to deliver Israel permanently: "And I will harden Pharaoh's heart, and multiply my signs and my wonders in the land of Egypt. But Pharaoh shall not hearken unto you, that I may lay my hand upon Egypt, and bring forth mine armies, and my people the children of Israel, out of the land of Egypt by great judgments" (Ex. 7:3-4).

The Question of Sovereignty

God demands absolute commitment from all creatures. Pharaoh, who was believed by the Egyptians to be an absolute sovereign, only needed to proclaim his partial sovereignty in order to challenge God's claim of total sovereignty. All he needed to do was to retain a token sovereignty over Israel to make his claim valid. If the children stayed, or the wives stayed, or the animals stayed, then the Israelites were symbolically acknowledging the legitimate divine sovereignty of the Egyptian State. If they would sacrifice inside Egypt's borders, or at least not too far into the wilderness, then God's claim of total sovereignty would be successfully challenged. If the Pharaoh could extract even the tiniest token of symbolic sovereignty, then God's claim to the whole of the lives of all the Israelites would be invalidated. In other words, if the Pharaoh, as a self-proclaimed divinity, could extract a sign of his sovereignty from another self-proclaimed divinity, *then neither of them could claim full sovereignty.*

Pharaoh's strategy implicitly admitted that he was not fully sovereign. Full sovereignty had been his initial claim, but the plagues had beaten him down. By now, he was willing to accept *partial sovereignty,* for that would pull the God of the Israelites down to his level, or at least low enough to re-establish the theology of the continuity of being. He could acknowledge that the God of the Israelites was a powerful God, even more powerful than the Pharaoh, *at that point in time.* Both of them would then be gods, both striving to overcome the external world, both with limitations, both willing to deal with each other as sovereign beings possessing the same fundamental being. *This would preserve Egypt's theology of the continuity of being.* This would sanction the Pharaoh's position as the highest representative in Egypt of the gods. If Moses would compromise, as the authorized representative of his God, then the Pharaoh could achieve a theological victory in principle: the God of the Israelites would thereby cede him lawful authority, in time and on earth, as a full-fledged god, who possessed the right to demand and receive concessions from Israel's God. Had Moses capitulated, with God's acquiescence, Pharaoh would have successfully challenged God's claim of total sovereignty, His claim that He was the only God to whom Israel owed total obedience, and who therefore had the right to demand total sacrifice from His people, leaving no outward symbol of original, primary sovereignty over them for Pharaoh to display.

Implicit Statism

Pharaoh, at the end of his attempts to bargain with Moses and Moses' God, was hoping to extract at least *token control over the terms of Israel's sacrifice.* He wanted to retain at least one sign of his sovereignty over their worship. If God had capitulated to Pharaoh on this point, He would thereby have acknowledged Pharaoh's lawful authority to grant to the Israelites their right to worship. *The Egyptian State would then have become the earthly, institutional source of religious rights,* since God Himself had been compelled to accede to at least one of the terms Pharaoh had laid down. This would have made the State the final institutional authority on the question of the nature of legitimate worship. *The needs of the State would have become the criteria for external worship.* By extracting from God even the tiniest compromise, this self-proclaimed god of a divine State would have been sanctioned as the *final earthly authority concerning religion,* and also the *source of the rights of religion.* God would thereby have acknowledged the legitimacy of Egypt's prior claim of lawful authority over the religious affairs of the Israelites. God would thereby have acknowledged the right of the Pharaoh to retain at least token authority, which meant the right of the Pharaoh and his heirs to compete with God at any time in the future for total authority. The God of the Hebrews might eventually be compelled to give back to the State what the State had originally claimed.

Pharaoh had rejected Moses' initial request because he had believed that he possessed total authority. At each stage, he gave up something, but he never was willing to give up everything. He was willing to relinquish some of his authority temporarily, for as long as God brought the plagues. However, should God change His mind, or lose power, or forget the Israelites, then Pharaoh might be able to re-establish his claim of total sovereignty. Pharaoh viewed this contest as a sort of cosmological "tug of war," in which he retained lawful authority of at least one end of the rope. God might pull him close to the line temporarily, but one end was rightfully his. If God would simply acknowledge Pharaoh's right to his end by allowing him the right to set any of the terms of Hebrew sacrifice, then Pharaoh's case would not be completely destroyed. If he bided his time, the God of the Hebrews might go away, leaving Pharaoh with the whole rope.

If the State can establish a foothold — even a temporary toehold — of autonomous sovereignty, then it has established a lawful claim to as much sovereignty as it can gain through the imposition of raw power. God's claim to absolute, uncompromised sovereignty is successfully challenged by man whenever God is forced to surrender even token autonomous sovereignty to man. Only if God's sovereignty is absolute can God claim to be the sole source of meaning and power in the universe. It is fallen man's goal to share some of that sovereignty. It is also Satan's goal, even if man becomes, temporarily, the holder of any fraction of this original, autonomous sovereignty, for if Satan can demonstrate that *man* has any final (or original) sovereignty whatsoever, then God's claim of total sovereignty collapses, which is the very essence of Satan's challenge to God. Satan can collect from man whatever sovereignty man might snatch from God, given the fact of Satan's greater power; but he must first place man in the same continuity of being with God. This attempt is always futile, from Genesis to Revelation.

No Compromise

God refused to grant Pharaoh anything. He rejected the seemingly reasonable compromises offered to Him by this self-proclaimed god, this ruler of a supposedly divine State. God hardened the Pharaoh's heart, so that he might not capitulate and let the Israelites journey into the wilderness to sacrifice to God. Pharaoh is the great historical example in Scripture of Proverbs 21:1: "The king's heart is in the hand of the LORD, as the rivers of water: he turneth it whithersoever he will." Yet Pharaoh was totally responsible for his acts. In great wrath, he challenged God, and God killed the firstborn of Egypt. Then the Egyptians expelled the Israelites in great fear, allowing them not merely a week of freedom to sacrifice to God, but permanent freedom to sacrifice to God. The Egyptians fulfilled God's promise to Moses, that the whole nation of Israel would go free and claim the land of Canaan (Ex. 3:8). God gave them total victory, yet Moses had officially requested only, at most, a week's freedom to sacrifice. However, *this sacrifice was comprehensive:* every man, woman, child, and beast had to go three days' journey into the wilderness.

The Pharaoh, unwilling to acknowledge the validity of this claim upon the whole of Israel, because it would have denied absolute sovereignty on his part and on the part of the Egyptian State, resisted unto death. He could not allow Israel a week of freedom, a week of rest, a week in which no tokens of subservience to Egypt's gods would be adhered to by the Israelites. He realized that all the claims of absolute authority on the part of Egypt would be refuted by such a capitulation on his part. Therefore, he hardened his heart, hoping to preserve the theology of Egypt and the autonomous sovereignty of man. When the Israelites left triumphantly, he lashed out against them, in a suicidal attempt to destroy them or drag them back. God had not compromised with him; the all-or-nothing claim of God could not be sacrificed by some token acknowledgment of lawful Egyptian sovereignty.

Pharaoh recognized the nature of God's total rejection of his claims to divinity, the absolute denial of the continuity of being. God had cut away his claim to divinity in front of his people and the kings of the earth, just as He had promised (Ex. 9:16). Pharaoh preferred to risk his own death, the destruction of his army, and the captivity of Egypt, rather than submit meekly to the triumph of the Israelites. He bet and lost. As such, Pharaoh's experience is archetypal for all the societies of Satan. They all make the same bet; they all lose. The only exception in the Bible was the case of the Gibeonites. They tricked the Israelites into making a covenant with them. By becoming permanent slaves to the Hebrews, they thereby acknowledged the sovereignty of God (Josh. 9).

Conclusion

The State is not absolutely sovereign. There is no divine right of kings, irrespective of what they say or do. There was no way for Moses to deal with the Pharaoh on Egypt's terms without compromising the sovereignty of God. Moses refused to compromise.

The State is not the source of the right (duty) of religious worship; God is. The State may *acknowledge* the right (duty) of men to worship God by providing a legal code or bill of rights, but the State is not the source of this right. This right cannot be revoked unilaterally by State officials without bringing into play the *vengeance of God*. To acknowledge the permanent right (duty) of men to sacrifice to God is to acknowledge the comprehensive and absolute sovereignty of God — an original sovereignty, a final sovereignty, and a primary sovereignty, which is all one fundamental sovereignty. All human sovereignty is secondary; it is a derivative sovereignty. It is, above all, a completely accountable sovereignty, in terms of which every individual will be judged, and in terms of which every institution is also judged, in time and on earth (Deut. 8; 28).

11

SEPARATION AND DOMINION

But against any of the children of Israel shall not a dog move his tongue, against man or beast: that ye may know how the LORD doth put a difference between the Egyptians and Israel (Ex. 11:7).

God announced that there was a radical covenantal difference between the Hebrews and the Egyptians. This difference was about to be manifested in a sharp break historically: the Exodus. So great was this difference, that no dog would lick its lips (literal translation: sharpen its tongue) at the Hebrews upon their departure from Egypt. No dog would eat any Hebrew (as dogs later ate Jezebel, the result of God's special curse: II Kings 9:36). The Egyptians now respected them and their leader, Moses. "And the LORD gave the people favour in the land of Egypt, in the sight of the Egyptians. Moreover the man Moses was very great in the land of Egypt, in the sight of Pharaoh's servants, and in the sight of the people" (Ex. 11:3). The meaning was clear: the Hebrews would leave victorious, having seen their enemies so thoroughly defeated, that not one of them would raise a cry against them. No jeering crowds would force them to "run the gauntlet," throwing rocks or garbage at them as they departed. The Egyptians believed in the continuity of being, and Moses had vanquished the representative of Egypt's gods, who himself was believed to be divine. Were not the Hebrews linked to that victorious God, through Moses?

Consider the Exodus from the point of view of a citizen of Egypt or one of the Canaanitic nations. A slave population had successfully challenged the dominant political order of its day. Egypt's wealth and power, even in decline (if Courville's chronology of the dynasties is correct), were recognized throughout the ancient world. Yet Egypt could not bring these Hebrews into submission. The ancient world viewed a military defeat as a defeat for the gods of the vanquished

132

city-state. What a defeat for the gods of Egypt! A slave population had risen up, under the very noses of the Egyptians, and had smashed the political order. So complete was this victory, that the invading Hyksos (Amalekites) swept over Egypt without encountering military resistance. God had been so victorious over Egypt that His people did not even bother to remain in the land as conquerors. So contemptuous of Egypt were the Hebrews that they marched out, leaving the spoils of war to the Amalekites, who were being replaced in Canaan by the Hebrews.[1] Here was a God so great, that He did not even bother to subdue the land of Egypt. And now, the Canaanites knew, these people were coming for them. Is it any wonder that they trembled for a generation (Josh. 2:9-11)?

The division between Egypt and Israel was assured. The Hebrews could not be tricked back into submission. Egyptians would not be able to subdue them, as vanquished populations sometimes do, by intermarrying, nor would the Hebrews absorb Egyptian religion and culture by intermarrying. The religious and linguistic separation would be maintained permanently, since God was taking them out of Egypt and was preparing to displace the Canaanites. The Canaanites knew what was in store for them (Josh. 2:9-11). Israel took no prisoners (Josh. 6:21). Israel, if the people remained faithful to their God, would annihilate the Canaanites.

When the LORD thy God shall bring thee into the land whither thou goest to possess it, and hath cast out many nations before thee, the Hittites and the Girgashites, and the Amorites, and the Canaanites, and the Perizzites, and the Hivites, and the Jebusites, seven nations greater and mightier than thou; And when the LORD thy God shall deliver them before thee; thou shalt smite them, and utterly destroy them; thou shalt make no covenant with them, nor shew mercy unto them: Neither shalt thou make marriages with them; thy daughter thou shalt not give unto his son, nor his daughter shalt thou take unto thy son. For they will turn away thy son from following me, that they may serve other gods: so will the anger of the LORD be kindled against you, and destroy thee suddenly. But thus shall ye deal with them; ye shall destroy their altars, and break down their images, and cut down their groves, and burn their graven images with fire. For thou art an holy people unto the LORD thy God: the LORD thy God hath chosen thee to be a special people unto himself, above all people that are upon the face of the

---

1. Immanuel Velikovsky, *Ages in Chaos* (Garden City, New York: Doubleday, 1952), ch. 2.

earth (Deut. 7:1-6).[2]

There was a difference between the Egyptians and Israel. That difference was God. He had made a covenant with them. They had been a tiny nation; now they would be victorious. They had already been so victorious over Egypt that Egypt's dogs recognized it; they would not lick their chops at Israelites. Yet it had not been their strength which had led them to freedom. "The LORD did not set his love upon you, nor choose you, because ye were more in number than any people; for ye were the fewest of all people: But because the LORD loved you, and because he would keep the oath which he had sworn unto your fathers, hath the LORD brought you out with a mighty hand, and redeemed you out of the house of bondmen, from the hand of Pharaoh king of Egypt" (Deut. 7:7-8). It was God's choice, not theirs, to redeem them — to buy them back by destroying their enemies. It was God's choice when He had promised the land of Canaan to Abraham for his seed. It was God's choice when He had selected Moses as their leader. It was God's choice to harden Pharaoh's heart, so that he would not compromise and permit the Hebrews to go and sacrifice to their God. God had done it all, and God would continue to do it all, *if* they remained faithful to His covenant.

The covenant was a great dividing sword. It was the dividing line between Israel and Egypt. Israel received its blessings; Egypt received its curse. It was also the dividing line between Israel and the nations of Canaan. It separated Egypt from Israel, and it was to serve as a means of destruction in Canaan. God had separated Israel from Egypt geographically; He planned to separate Israel and the tribes of Canaan biologically: the Canaanites would all die. The Canaanites recognized this, according to Rahab (Josh. 2:9-11).

Among the Hebrews of Moses' day, only Joshua and Caleb recognized the commitment of God to give His people total victory, in time and in Canaan (Num. 14). (A similar incident took place a millennium and a half later, when the Jews and Romans had a stone rolled across Jesus' tomb, in order to keep His disciples from taking His body and claiming that His prophecy concerning His resurrec-

---

2. It should be obvious that pacifism as a moral philosophy has no support in the Bible. The same God who was incarnate in Jesus Christ ordered the Hebrews to annihilate the Canaanites. Any discussion by God-fearing people of the legitimacy of warfare from a biblical standpoint must begin with a consideration *and moral acceptance* of these verses.

tion had been fulfilled; meanwhile, the disciples scattered to the winds in self-imposed defeat.) The Hebrews of Moses' era did not recognize the inevitability of their impending victory. They had not recognized the nature of their victory over the Egyptians. They did not understand the nature of the God who had given them freedom, nor did they understand the nature of the ethical covenant which He had set before them. They had to serve Him continuously. They chose to serve other gods intermittently. They were supposed to exercise dominion continuously. They chose to exercise dominion intermittently. They were supposed to be victorious continuously. They were defeated intermittently.

The Covenant and Separation

The covenant is the means by which God separates His people from the world. It is supposed to be the means by which his people bring the world into conformity with biblical law. He shows grace to His people and gives them the tool of dominion, His law-order. This separation finally results in the *permanent separation* between God and His enemies, on the day of judgment. *Eternity is marked by this covenantal separation.*

God separated His people from the surrounding cultures in the Old Testament era. He separated Noah from the pre-flood world. He separated Abram from both Ur of the Chaldees and Haran. He separated Israel from Canaan during Israel's sojourn in Egypt. He separated Israel from Egypt's masses by putting them in Goshen. He separated Israel from Egypt completely at the time of the Exodus. All of these separations were essentially separations from pagan gods and pagan cultures. But separations *from* did not imply retreat and impotence. These separations were established by God in Israel's *history* in order to give God's people confidence concerning Israel's *future*. The covenantal *separation from* other nations established the possibility and the requirement of Israel's *dominion over* those nations. Israel wiped out most of the Canaanites, and Israel was supposed to wipe out, or drive out, all of them. *God had prepared for His people a new training ground, a type of paradise, a land flowing with milk and honey (covenant feast), which pointed back to the garden of Eden and forward to the new heavens and new earth.* This land had been cleared of wild beasts, except for relatively few of them (Ex. 23:28-29), and Israel's victory cleared the land of most of the wild cultures.[3] It was to have been a

---

3. Joshua 10:21 reads: "And all the people returned to the camp to Joshua at Mekkedah in peace: none moved his tongue against any of the children of Israel." Literally, this can be translated: "Not (he) sharpened (his) tongue against a man." It seems to refer back to Exodus 11:7, meaning that no Israelites died in battle.

theological, cultural, and political *clean sweep.* Israel was to take the land by force, and this land was to become the base of operations in a mighty conquest, fueled by a population explosion and compound economic growth, which was to have carried God's dominion across the face of the earth. To fulfill the terms of the dominion covenant, God's redeemed people must separate themselves ethically from Satan's unredeemed people.

The separation of God's people from ethical rebels is a permanent separation. Heaven does not eventually fuse with hell. The new heavens and the new earth do not eventually merge into the lake of fire. The residents of the new heavens and new earth rule eternally (Rev. 21; 22); the residents of the lake of fire are subjected to endless defeat (Rev. 20:14-15). The people of God are separated from the ethical rebels on a permanent basis after the final judgment, and this *final separation* brings with it *absolute dominion.* It is the final victory of God over Satan, and it involves the permanent dominion of man over the creation. The rebels are killed, for they suffer the second, permanent death (Rev. 20:14). *Covenantal separation therefore implies covenantal dominion.*

This necessary relationship was never meant to be postponed until the day of judgment. It is supposed to be progressively worked out, in time and on earth.[4] *God's separation* of Abram from his people, of Abraham's seed from the other nations, of Israel from Egypt, and of Israel from all the religious traditions of Canaan, all required *action by His covenanted people, in time and on earth.* Abram left Ur and Haran, and he circumcised Isaac. Similarly, Moses acted to challenge Pharaoh. Israel did not stay in Egypt. Israel did not wander in the wilderness forever. *Israel fought and won, in history, in terms of God's separating covenant, which is a dominion covenant.* These mighty acts of God were designed to convince Israel of the necessity of remaining true to the covenant. The prophets kept returning to these historical acts of God in the life of Israel, especially the delivery from Egypt (I Sam. 8:8; Isa. 11:16; Jer. 2:6; Hos. 13:4). So did Stephen in his sermon (Acts 7). *Men's separation from Satan and his works is to bring them dominion over Satan and his works:* in politics, economics, military affairs, art, medicine, science, and every other area of human action.

---

4. I use this phrase repeatedly in my writings. It refers to human history prior to the second coming of Christ at the final judgment, and therefore prior to the establishment of a sin-free world after the resurrection. It is easier to use the phrase than continually search for substitute phrases.

Ancient Humanism's Separation

Basic to many of the ancient cultures was the distinction between "the people," the group to which a citizen belonged, and "the others," or "barbarians," who were outside the covenantal membership. Egypt was no exception. Wilson comments: "In their feeling of special election and special providence, the Egyptians called themselves 'the people' in contrast to foreigners."[5] So deeply embedded in Greek and Roman thought was the division between peoples, that classical legal theory recognized no common law within the city.[6] "No one could become a citizen at Athens," writes Fustel de Coulanges, "if he was a citizen in another city; for it was a religious impossibility to be at the same time a member of two cities, as it also was to be a member of two families. One could not have two religions at the same time. . . . Neither at Rome nor at Athens could a foreigner be a proprietor. He could not marry; or, if he married, his marriage was not recognized, and his children were reputed illegitimate. He could not make a contract with a citizen; at any rate, the law did not recognize such a contract as valid. . . . The Roman law forbade him to inherit from a citizen, and even forbade a citizen to inherit from him. They pushed this principle so far, that if a foreigner obtained the rights of a citizen without his son, born before this event, obtaining the same favor, the son became a foreigner in regard to his father, and could not inherit from him. The distinction between citizen and foreigner was stronger than the natural tie between father and son."[7]

There was also the linguistic difference. The very term "barbarian" has its origins in Greek grammar. The Greeks spoke Greek, of course, while foreigners' languages all sounded like "bar bar"—incoherent, in other words. This, at least, is the standard explanation of the term, and it is repeated by the influential British historian of classical culture, H. D. F. Kitto, in the introduction to his book, *The Greeks* (1951). Both Kitto and C. M. Bowra argue that "barbarian" did not have a pejorative sense in Homer, but later the term came to mean inferior status.[8] Gilbert Murray, whose *Five Stages of*

---

5. John A. Wilson, *The Burden of Egypt: An Interpretation of Ancient Egyptian Culture* (University of Chicago Press, [1951] 1967), p. 112.

6. Fustel de Coulanges, *The Ancient City: A Study on the Religion, Laws, and Institutions of Greece and Rome* (Garden City, New York: Doubleday Anchor, [1864] 1955), Bk. III, ch. XI, pp. 192-93.

7. *Ibid.,* Bk. III, ch. XII, pp. 196-97.

8. H. D. F. Kitto, *The Greeks* (Baltimore, Maryland: Penguin, [1951] 1962), pp. 8-10; C. M. Bowra, *The Greek Experience* (New York: Mentor, [1957] 1964), p. 26.

Greek Religion (1925) is regarded as a classic, says that we can mark the origin of *classical* Greece with the advent of the cultural distinction between the Greek and the barbarian, when the Greek historian Herodotus could write that "the Hellenic race was marked off from the barbarian, as more intelligent and more emancipated from silly nonsense."[9] By the middle of the fifth century, B.C., the difference between Greek and barbarian, in the minds of the Greeks, was enormous.

We see the linguistic origin of the word "barbarian" in Paul's comments on tongues in the church. "Therefore if I know not the meaning of the voice, I shall be unto him that speaketh a barbarian, and he that speaketh shall be a barbarian unto me" (I Cor. 14:11). Again, in Romans 1:14: "I am debtor both to the Greeks, and to the Barbarians. . . ." Paul, however, did not distinguish between Greeks and barbarians in terms of their innate differences, but only in terms of linguistic differences.

The Ethical Disunity of Man

The unity of man, which was assumed and announced architecturally at the tower of Babel, had been shattered by God when He confounded their language and scattered them. God's restraint on the creation of a one-world State brought freedom to men — freedom to develop personally and culturally. Yet it also brought audible distinctions between men. These distinctions are more fundamental than race, for races can mix, leaving few if any traces of their genetic past, but linguistic distinctions, at least in literate cultures, resist alterations, and even when linguistic changes occur, the written records of the past draw men's thoughts and commitment back to a once-distinct past. It was no accident that the perceived international unity of the Roman Catholic Church was maintained for centuries by the Latin Mass, and it was also not accidental that the historically unprecedented disruptions within that church, which took place from the mid-1960's onward, were intimately related to the successful efforts of the church's religious liberals in abolishing the use of the Latin Mass.

Religious humanists sometimes have attacked this kind of division between men. Ludwig Feuerbach was one example. His book,

---

9. Gilbert Murray, *Five Stages of Greek Religion* (Garden City, New York: Doubleday Anchor, [1925] 1955), p. 38.

The Essence of Christianity (1841), created a sensation, and converted a whole generation of European intellectuals to atheism. Frederick Engels, Marxism's co-founder, remarked once that "One must himself have experienced the liberating effect of this book to get an idea of it. Enthusiasm was general; we all became at once Feuerbachians."[10] In this book, Feuerbach attacked Christianity's concept of saved and lost. Such a view of man separates men from other men. Yet man is a unified whole, a species being. In fact, Feuerbach said, God is really nothing more than man's own thoughts, projected into the religious consciousness of men. "God is the human being; but he presents himself to the religious consciousness as a distinct being."[11] The Christian denies that man is God, and this is unforgivable. Even worse, Christians say that some men will be saved by God, and others will not be saved. "To believe, is synonymous with goodness; not to believe, with wickedness. Faith, narrow and prejudiced, refers all unbelief to the moral disposition. In its view the unbeliever is an enemy to Christ out of obduracy, out of wickedness. Hence faith has fellowship with believers only; unbelievers it rejects. It is well-disposed towards believers, but ill-disposed towards unbelievers. *In faith there lies a malignant principle.*"[12]

Marx and Engels, his most famous converts, rejected Feuerbach's brand of non-divisive humanism. They saw the "illusion" of God as a product of a deliberate lie: a weapon used by capitalists to suppress the proletariat. The problem is class divisions; the solution is class warfare, with the proletariat finally emerging victorious over the bourgeoisie.[13] They called for unconditional surrender by the bourgeoisie; they called for all-out warfare. They predicted absolute victory. They saw that true victory over evil involves triumph, in time and on earth.[14] They saw that there must be a self-awareness on the part of the "vanguard" of history, the proletariat, concerning the irreconcilable differences between them and

---

10. Frederick Engels, "Ludwig Feuerbach and the End of Classical German Philosophy" (1888), in Karl Marx and Frederick Engels, *Selected Works,* 3 vols. (Moscow: Progress Publishers, [1969] 1977), III, p. 344.

11. Ludwig Feuerbach, *The Essence of Christianity,* trans. George Eliot (New York: Harper Torchbooks, [1841] 1957), p. 247.

12. *Ibid.,* p. 252. Emphasis in original.

13. Marx and Engels, "Manifesto of the Communist Party" (1848), in *Selected Works,* I, pp. 125-26.

14. Gary North, *Unconditional Surrender: God's Program for Victory* (2nd ed.; Tyler, Texas: Geneva Divinity School Press, 1983).

their class enemies, the bourgeoisie.[15] They substituted the forces of dialectical, materialistic history for the providence of God, thereby preserving *an eschatology of victory.*[16] They saw that there must be separation in order to achieve victory. To that extent, Marxism adheres to a humanistic variant of a fundamental doctrine of the Bible. It is one reason why the Marxists have been so successful in promoting their imitation gospel in the twentieth century.

Conclusion

It was Israel's continuing refusal to break with the theology and culture of Egypt as such which condemned that first generation to a life of wandering in the wilderness. It was not the covenantal separation from Egypt which resulted in Israel's wilderness journey. God did not bring Israel into the wilderness to die. This was the accusation of the rebels against Moses, time after time (Ex. 14:11-12; 16:3), so *they* all died in the wilderness. Their children, led by Joshua and Caleb — those two men who had understood the nature of God and His covenant — took possession of the land. It was *Satan's lie* that covenantal separation from "establishment civilization" — first from Egypt, and later from the remains of the Canaanitic cultures — meant historical defeat and impotence for Israel. This same lie has been one of the most important factors in Satan's success against the church in the twentieth century. Whenever this lie becomes the dominant opinion among God's covenanted people, they can expect to die in the wilderness, just as the complainers and defeatists of Moses' day also died in the wilderness.

Christians must also recognize that *the defeat of complainers and defeatists in one generation does not necessarily condemn the next generation to a similar defeat.* When men recognize the optimistic nature of God's separating covenant, and when they seek to work out the terms of God's law-order in their various spheres of influence and responsibility, they will discover the impotence of God's enemies, even as Joshua and 85-year-old Caleb discovered it. Their *separation by God*

---

15. "All previous historical movements were movements of minorities, or in the interests of minorities. The proletarian movement is the self-conscious, independent movement of the immense majority, in the interests of the immense majority. The proletariat, the lowest stratum of our present society, cannot stir, cannot raise itself up, without the whole superincumbent strata of official society being sprung into the air." *Communist Manifesto,* in *ibid.,* I, p. 118.

16. F. N. Lee, *Communist Eschatology: A Christian Philosophical Analysis of the Post-Capitalistic Views of Marx, Engels, and Lenin* (Nutley, New Jersey: Craig Press, 1974).

implies their *victory with God,* in eternity but also in history. Further-more, with respect to the enemies of God, their *separation from God* leads directly to their *defeat by God,* not only throughout eternity, but in time and on earth. Their eventual defeat by the people of God — those who honor the terms of God's separating covenant — in time and on earth is an earnest (down payment) of their coming eternal defeat. *Without biblical law, men become progressively impotent culturally.* [17]

When God separates His people from the world by means of His separating covenant, He provides them with the means of external victory, not simply their individualistic internal victory over per-sonal sin. As God progressively separates His people in terms of their conformity to His law, He thereby gives them their tool of do-minion. The dogs of Egypt had more understanding of this fact than did the fleeing slaves of Moses' day. The dogs of Egypt had a better understanding of the implications of God's covenantal partition than the twentieth century's hordes of self-proclaimed experts in biblical prophecy. The dogs of Egypt may have whetted their tongues, but if they ate anyone, it was dead Egyptians, not dead Hebrews.

---

17. Gary North, "Common Grace, Eschatology, and Biblical Law," *The Journal of Christian Reconstruction,* III (Winter 1976-77).

12

CONTINUITY AND REVOLUTION

And thus shall ye eat it; with your loins girded, your shoes on your feet, and your staff in your hand; and ye shall eat it in haste: it is the LORD's passover. For I will pass through the land of Egypt this night, and will smite all the firstborn in the land of Egypt, both man and beast; and against all the gods of Egypt I will execute judgment: I am the LORD (Ex. 12:11-12).

A social philosophy which does not contain an explicit concept of social change — or lack of social change — is incapable of producing the kinds of cultural transformations that are required by the dominion covenant. Without a belief in the possibility of progress, men are left without one of the fundamental motivating factors necessary to the building of (or maintaining of) a civilization.[1]

Is progress possible? If so, then what is the characteristic nature of social progress? Is it essentially a revolutionary process, or is it marked by slow, organic change? In short, is is *discontinuous* or *continuous?* Or is it some mixture of the two? Here is a fundamental issue which has divided social philosophers from the beginning. This question was the crucial philosophical dividing line between the revolutionaries of France in 1789 and the conservative doctrines of Edmund Burke.[2] Modern conservatism can be dated from the publication of Burke's *Reflections on the Revolution in France* (1790). Certainly, the question of continuity vs. revolution is the heart of the dispute between Marxism and all other non-revolutionary social philosophies.

---

1. See Robert A. Nisbet, *History of the Idea of Progress* (New York: Basic Books, 1980), especially the epilogue.

2. Russell Kirk, *The Conservative Mind: from Burke to Santayana* (Chicago: Regnery, 1953), ch. 2; Nisbet, *The Social Philosophers: Community and Conflict in Western Thought* (New York: Thomas Y. Crowell, 1973), pp. 265-80.

The Bible provides an answer to this most fundamental of social questions. The key factor is *ethics*. Whether a society experiences long-term progress, or catastrophic external judgments that produce discontinuous social change, depends on the ethical condition of those who compose the society, especially the religious and political leaders.

The Book of Exodus provides the archetype of all discontinuous social events, which is why the story of the Exodus initially appeals to revolutionaries, "liberation theologians," and other proponents of humanistic confrontations between "the exploited poor" and the "exploiting rich."[3] But the revelational ethical framework which the Bible sets forth gives little support for the dreams and schemes of social revolutionaries. To understand the biblical concept of social change, we must understand the theology of the Passover.

Promise and Deliverance

God promised to pass over those households which had blood sprinkled on the doorposts (Ex. 12:13). All other homes He would allow the destroyer (Ex. 12:23) to enter, bringing death to the firstborn male of both man and beast.[4] This was *the avenger of blood,* who was about to avenge the land of Egypt for the pollution caused by the murder of the Hebrew males at least 80 years before.[5] Any family which did not acknowledge its need for a sacrificial substitute would make its sacrifice with its firstborn son. There was no escape from this sacrifice; it was only a question of *which kind of firstborn sacrifice* a family would choose to offer to God: human or animal.

---

3. "The God of the Bible cares when people enslave and oppress others. At the Exodus he acted to end economic oppression and bring freedom to slaves. . . . The Exodus was certainly the decisive event in the creation of the chosen people. We distort the biblical interpretation of this momentous occasion unless we see that at this pivotal point, the Lord of the universe was at work correcting oppression and liberating the poor." Ronald J. Sider, *Rich Christians in an Age of Hunger: A Biblical Study* (Downers Grove, Illinois: Inter-Varsity Press, 1977), pp. 60-61.

4. This destroyer may have been an angel, possibly the angel of the Lord. Hebrews 11:28 personifies the destroying agent: "he that destroyed," in the King James Version; "the destroying one" in the Greek. James G. Murphy, *A Critical and Exegetical Commentary on the Book of Exodus* (Minneapolis, Minnesota: James Publications, [1868] 1976), p. 128.

5. The avenger of blood was the judge of all the inhabitants of Egypt, including the Hebrews and the mixed multitude. He was avenging the land at last for the murder of the Hebrew infant males, who had been drowned in the Nile (Ex. 1:22). The first judgment had been against the Nile, turning it into blood (Ex. 7:17-21). Now the death of the firstborn male children would cleanse the land of its pollution.

The Egyptians chose to cling to their faith in Pharaoh's divinity, in the hope that this final plague would not come upon them. Not one Egyptian family took its stand with the God of the Hebrews, "for there was not a house where there was not one dead" (Ex. 12:30b). Once again, the gods of Egypt failed them. God had executed judgment upon all the gods of Egypt, including the Pharaoh, the self-proclaimed divine-human link on earth. The Egyptians had seen the Pharaoh fail to protect the nation; plague after plague came upon them, yet they did not recognize the imminence and inescapability of this judgment. Egypt had seemed immune to foreign invasion and foreign domination; now the slaves of Egypt would alone be protected from judgment. Goshen, the home of God's people, would alone receive protection, but only because of the willingness of these people to recognize judgment and take steps to avoid it.[6]

The Hebrews had been in Egypt for at least two centuries. They had worked on the Pharaoh's monuments and cities for at least two generations. The Egyptians expected this slave population to remain subservient on a permanent basis. So did most of the members of that population. God's promise to Abraham had been forgotten. Even with Moses' words before them, and the Passover meal required of them, they did not really expect deliverance. "And they baked unleavened cakes of the dough which they had brought forth out of Egypt, for it was not leavened; because they were thrust out of Egypt, and could not tarry, neither had they prepared for themselves any victual" (Ex. 12:39). They had prepared no food for the journey. Why had they made no preparations for their imminent journey? The answer seems obvious: *they really did not expect God's overnight deliverance.* The Passover ceremony pointed to just such a deliverance, but they did not really believe it. They did what they were instructed by Moses and Aaron (Ex. 12:50), but no more. Their religion was a minimal religion, as their actions demonstrated repeatedly for the next 40 years.

---

6. It could be objected that God never did offer a way of escape to the Egyptians. There is no explicit evidence that God did tell them of the blood on the doorposts, but there is little doubt that Egypt's representatives by this time were monitoring everything the Hebrews did or said. They must have known. These people were not ignorant of God's law; they had been placed under the administration of Joseph two centuries before. Also, the confrontations between Moses and Pharaoh indicate that Pharaoh knew exactly the crimes Egypt had committed against the Hebrews. Finally, I would argue that the free offer of the gospel must not be denied: John Murray, "The Free Offer of the Gospel," in *Collected Writings of John Murray,* 4 vols. (Edinburgh: Banner of Truth Trust, 1982), IV, pp. 113-32.

After at least two centuries in Egypt, the Hebrews had grown accustomed to their environment. The envy of the Hebrews against Moses forty years earlier had kept them in bondage, for they had not been content to be judged by Moses. They had preferred to bring Moses low, even though this meant that their Egyptian rulers would remain dominant over them. They had been willing to remain slaves rather than risk standing up with the young Moses. When Moses returned to challenge Pharaoh, their sons complained bitterly to Moses that his troublemaking had brought new burdens upon them (Ex. 5:21). They preferred to trust the continuing tyranny of Egypt rather than trust the promise of God or His servants, Moses and Aaron. *They put their faith in the Egyptian State rather than God.* To that extent, they agreed with the religion of their captors. As Joshua warned their children, "Now therefore fear the LORD, and serve him in sincerity and in truth: and put away the gods which your fathers served on the other side of the flood, and in Egypt; and serve ye the LORD" (Josh. 24:14). (Notice the words, "in sincerity and in truth"; they are important for understanding the apostle Paul's references to unleavened bread, discussed below.)

The familiarity of present troubles makes men hesitate to seek risky improvements in their condition. The risks of change seem too high, and the benefits seem too few or too far removed. Men choose today's horrors in preference to tomorrow's unfamiliar problems, even if those problems will be accompanied with the personal freedom to deal with them. Responsibility is too great a burden for slaves. The slave becomes *passive toward his environment,* content to accept what the world brings, so long as he can avoid life's hard decisions. What keeps slaves in bondage, even when freedom is possible? *It is their willingness to put up with a harsh environment, so long as it is a familiar one which brings few opportunities for personal initiative (and therefore personal responsibility).* Joseph was in bondage, but he did not evade responsibility. Such a slave usually does not remain in bondage permanently, for he is not mentally a slave. The willingness of some men to bear the burdens of responsible choice eventually makes them too valuable, or too powerful, for their masters to keep in servitude. Fully responsible men are difficult to enslave.

The Hebrews preferred low-risk institutional continuity. They preferred a life of little or no personal responsibility. This was a great asset for their masters, who could then devote more of their resources to something other than the suppression of rebellion. Fewer taskmasters and guards were needed, for the prisoners were docile. Even after their deliverance, that generation continued to complain to Moses about the rigors and dangers of the wilderness, despite the fact that God provided them with manna, clothing that never wore out, and feet that did not swell or blister (Deut. 8:3-4; Neh. 9:21).

Unquestionably, institutional continuity under some conditions is a valid goal in life. We want marital continuity when we exchange vows with our mates. We want continuity in our legal system, so that when we drive at the posted speed limit, for example, we are not issued a traffic citation by a police officer who has autonomously and arbitrarily made up new rules. At the same time, most of us want our marriages to develop, since maturity is basic to a successful life. And if we find that the existing speed limit is no longer adequate to protect life and limb, then we want legal procedures for having the speed limit changed. Therefore, *institutional continuity is to be understood within a framework of potential change,* except changes in certain areas that are governed by God's revealed law. And even here, God reserves the right to make changes, or suspend external judgment. Perhaps the best example is God's retroactive suspension of His law which prohibited Passover to ritually unsanctified Hebrews. Because some members of the nation under Hezekiah had not been ritually purified when they ate the Passover,[7] Hezekiah prayed that they be forgiven. God healed them retroactively, thereby overlooking the written requirements of the law (II Chr. 30:17-20).[8] If we seek the continuity of the Medes and the Persians, where the king's word was absolutely inviolable, then we may face potential disasters, as Darius did when he was forced to sentence Daniel to the lions' den (Dan. 6:14). Life's conditions change, and men's survival and prosperity depend on quick and competent reactions to changed conditions. Static continuity — the complete predictability of a familiar and dependable future — is an illegitimate goal. It is the world of the prison. Or the grave.

---

7. The nature of this lack of purification is not stated.

8. The priests had begun to cleanse the temple in the first month of the first year of his reign, which was also Passover month. Passover had to be celebrated by the 14th day, but they did not complete the cleansing of the temple until the 16th (II Chr. 29:17). It was too late to celebrate Passover normally. But the second month was legitimate for travellers or people defiled by a dead body on the normal day of Passover: Numbers 9:9-11. Hezekiah called for the Passover to be celebrated the next month, but all of the people were still not purified.

Structure and Change

We are here dealing with the inescapable problem of *structure and change,* a variation of the traditional philosophical problem, the one (structure, unity) and the many (change, diverse conditions). We want predictable law and predictable environments, yet we do not want to be strangled by our laws or our environment. In every science, in every field of human thought, we face the problem of structure and change, of law and flux.[9]

In the field of historiography, for example, scholars tend to be divided into two camps: the revolutionists and the consensus historians.[10] One group sees man's history as a series of revolutions, or at least major conflicts. Karl Marx is perhaps the most prominent of the revolutionists (since he actually was a proponent of violent revolution). "Revolutions are the locomotives of history," he wrote.[11] Yet even revolutions take place within a *framework of continuity.* They do not totally destroy the past. The conservative American sociologist Robert Nisbet has articulated a theory of social change which opposes both social revolutionism and social evolutionism as valid explanations of "inevitable" historical development: "That things should continue in time, persist, hold stable, is not to be doubted. Given such persistence, changes, however far apart, however random, discrete, and disconnected they may be in themselves, are nonetheless given the semblance of a continuity by the persisting identity itself—by the persisting kinship system, social class, religion, or whatever it may be. But, as a moment's reflection tells us, there is no continuity of *change* here; only continuity in the sense of persistence, punctuated, however, by the changes which occur

---

9. I used a chemistry textbook in college called *Structure and Change,* by Gordon S. Christiansen and Paul Garrett (San Francisco: W. H. Freeman, 1960). The problem is basic to every academic discipline.

10. See, for example, *Conflict or Consensus in American History,* edited by Allen F. Davis and Harold D. Woodman (Boston: D. C. Heath, 1966). They write in the introduction: "Has there been real conflict in American history between classes, sections, and interest groups, or has the story of the American past been primarily one of general agreement or consensus? This theme, expressed either explicitly or implicitly, may be found in virtually all major interpretations of our country's past" (p. vii). Cf. James P. Young (ed.), *Consensus and Conflict: Readings in American Politics* (New York: Dodd, Mead, 1972).

11. Karl Marx, "The Class Struggles in France, 1848 to 1850" (1850); in Karl Marx and Frederick Engels, *Selected Works,* 3 vols. (Moscow: Progress Publishers, [1969] 1977), I, p. 277.

from time to time."[12] Without a *consensus* against which revolutionaries can rebel, all revolutions would become mere chaos, without meaning or direction.[13]

In contrast to the revolutionists, consensus historians are defenders of the idea of continuity. Wherever they look, they cannot find "true" revolutions: the industrial revolution really was too slow to be called a revolution, as was the agricultural revolution, the American Revolution, the French Revolution, and possibly even the Russian Revolution. Since every revolution retains elements from the past, it is possible to focus on the elements that remained stable, and then conclude that these so-called revolutions, in and of themselves, really do not change societies very much in the long run. "The more things change, the more things stay the same," says a French proverb. When is a revolution *really* a revolution?

Ethical Continuity

Pharaoh did not really grasp the revolutionary nature of the crisis he was facing. He believed in the continuity of being between his own nature and the power gods of Egypt. He therefore believed in the eternality of Egyptian power. These upstart Hebrews, he knew, could be brought to heel. Their God was not really a totally sovereign being. Their God was not really able to deliver them out of his hand.

To a great extent, the Hebrews slaves shared his view. They also did not believe that Moses was representing a sovereign God who would deliver them from bondage. Not even after the plagues on

---

12. Robert A. Nisbet, *Social Change and History: Aspects of the Western Theory of Development* (New York: Oxford University Press, 1969), pp. 288-89.

13. Gunther Stent, a molecular biologist, has commented on this problem with respect to artistic revolutions. They are eventually self-defeating, he argues. "As artistic evolution unfolds, the artist is being freed more and more from strict canons governing the method of working his medium of creative expression. The end result of this evolution has been that, finally, in our time, the artist's liberation has been almost total. However, the artist's accession to near-total freedom of expression now presents very great cognitive difficulties for the appreciation of his work: The absence of recognizable canons reduces his act of creation to near-randomness for the perceiver. In other words, artistic evolution along the one-way street to freedom embodies an element of self-limitation. The greater the freedom already attained and hence the closer the approach to the random of any artistic style for the percipient, the less possible for any successor style to seem significantly different from its predecessor." Stent, *The Coming of the Golden Age: A View of the End of Progress* (Garden City, New York: Natural History Press, published for the American Museum of Natural History, 1969), p. 98.

Egypt had brought their Egyptian masters low did they believe that their external conditions would change. *Institutional continuity* was still dominant in their thinking, for *ontological continuity between God and man* was still dominant in their thinking. They trusted more in the theocratic power of Egypt's gods than they did in the God of Moses. They believed that they would still remain slaves in Egypt, as their fathers had been. And if the gods of Egypt were what the Pharaoh claimed, then there could never be a radical break with the past.

The history of the patriarchs should have warned them against such a view of history. The creation was itself an incomparably radical break — a break into history, or better stated, the advent of history out of nothing. The creation of the species, the creation of Adam, and the creation of Eve were all radical breaks. Adam's rebellion was a break, and the signs of that break are with men still, since the creation labors under a curse (Gen. 3:17-18; Rom. 8:19-22). The flood in Noah's day was a startling break with the past — a clean sweep of unimaginable proportions. The scattering at Babel, the calling of Abraham, the destruction of Sodom and Gomorrah, and the famine of Joseph's day were all discontinuities in history.

On the one hand, *historical continuity is guaranteed by the transcendent plan (decree) of God over history,* unshakable in its permanence. Historical continuity is therefore *ethical continuity.* Men and societies are totally responsible before God, who sustains the entire creation and whose decree is inescapable. On the other hand, actual historical events are sometimes sharp breaks from the historical continuities that preceded the breaks.

What the Passover was meant to teach the Israelites was that God judges kings and commoners in terms of His law, and that the foundation of human freedom and human progress is ethical. Which divinity will men worship, God or some idolatrous representation of another god, either natural or supernatural? Which law-order will men attempt to conform to, God's or some idol's?[14] The continuity which relates covenantal faithfulness and institutional blessings (Deut. 8:18; 28:1-14) is contrasted with the institutional discontinuities produced by God's judgment against ethical rebellion (Deut. 8:19-20; 28:15-68). The archetypal event in Israel's history which was to reveal the relationship between faithfulness and institutional

---

14. Herbert Schlossberg, *Idols for Destruction: Christian Faith and Its Confrontation with American History* (Nashville, Tennessee: Thomas Nelson Sons, 1983).

continuity, and the relationship between ethical rebellion and in-stitutional discontinuity, was the Passover.

The Passover: Deliverance and Conquest

When Moses announced to his people that the God of Abraham, Isaac, and Jacob was about to lead them out of bondage, they would not believe it. They had lost their faith in God's providence, which necessarily involves a concept of cosmic personalism. God had given a promise to Abraham, their patriarch. That promise involved the unfolding of history. But the promised unfolding was not a garment without wrinkles. It was inevitable, but it involved visible alterations of historical patterns. The years spent in captivity were not nor-mative. The years spent under the gods of Egypt were not to become static standards for future events. God told them that He was about to shake the very foundations of Egypt. Just as He had promised, they were about to be led into the land of Canaan. The famine had driven the Hebrews into Egypt in Joseph's day; now God would lead them out.

They had to be *driven* out. The Egyptians implored them to leave on the night of the death of the firstborn. "And the Egyptians were urgent upon the people, that they might send them out of the land in haste; for they said, We be all dead men" (Ex. 12:33). These slaves might otherwise have remained in Egypt; indeed, they later begged Moses to allow them to return to Egypt (Num. 14:3). The plagues were brought to Egypt not merely to convince the Egyptian Pharaoh to allow the Hebrews to go and sacrifice for a week; they were not imposed merely to convince the Egyptians to let the Hebrews leave permanently. They were imposed as a means of *making it impossible for the Hebrews to stay right where they were, in a position of irresponsible subservience to foreign gods*. The plagues forced the Hebrews out of Egypt and into the wilderness.

The Passover was designed to impress upon the Hebrews of Moses' day, as well as all succeeding generations of Hebrews, the stark reality of *rapid historical change in a culture which comes under the visible judgment of God*. They were to eat unleavened bread. There was no time for the yeast to do its work: unleavened bread was the only kind allowed. Unleavened bread is quicker to bake. Everything about the Passover pointed to *haste:* the unleavened bread, the roasted lamb which was to be completely consumed by morning, and even the eating: "And thus shall ye eat it; with your loins girded, your shoes on your feet, and your staff in your hand; and ye shall eat it in haste: it is the LORD's passover" (Ex. 12:11). Everything in the Passover pointed to God's deliverance of His people from bondage—literally, an *overnight deliverance.* The lamb was consumed in one night. The people were to stand, staffs in their hand, shoes on their feet, ready to march. *Ready to march:* out of Ur, out of Haran, out of Sodom, out of Egypt, and into the Promised Land. God's people were to celebrate a feast as an army celebrates a victory, for their feast pointed to the coming victory—over Egypt, over Canaan, and especially over sin (Eph. 6:10-18). It was a *pre-victory feast,* celebrated before marching orders were officially given.

The Passover reminds all future generations of God's people of the *miraculous discontinuity of God's redemption.* God passed over the houses of the Hebrews, and the destroyer passed through the houses of His enemies, taking as a lawful sacrifice the firstborn. Then Israel passed through the Red Sea and finally through the Jordan River. Had they remained faithful to God, they would have passed through the wilderness in much less than 40 years. When God "passes through" a rebellious culture, judgment is at hand. The Hebrews became instruments of His judgment in Canaan.

Marching Orders

The Passover feast was to remind them of both life and death. It was to remind them of *the need for immediate marching at the command of God.* There was no time to waste. A shattering of Egypt's foundations was about to begin. The Israelites were being called out of Egypt. Yet this also meant one of two things: being *called into the wilderness* for the remainder of their lives, or being *called into Canaan.* Leaving meant *going.* Going where? The wilderness or the Promised Land? We can never leave without going; even our departure from the world demands that we travel to a final destination: the new heavens and new earth, or the lake of fire. (Heaven and hell are "holding areas" or "embarkation points," not permanent resting places: Rev. 20:12-14.) The Hebrews knew what leaving Egypt meant: *a radical break with their immediate past,* and all of its familiar aspects—a break which would inaugurate a new era of personal responsibility. Their complaints in the wilderness demonstrated that they preferred not to remain there, and their refusal to enter the land of Canaan immediately indicated that they chose not to go there, either.[15] They preferred "Canaan at zero price." They could not get God to agree on the price they were willing to pay. Yet God would not permit them to return to Egypt. It was Moses' pleading on their behalf that kept them from departing from this world immediately — the obvious alternative for this complaining nation (Ex. 32:9-14).

The Passover necessarily pointed to *conquest*. They could not leave Egypt without marching to war. The Passover pointed to a *new life,* and this new life requires *full personal responsibility before God*. It pointed to *dominion*. The land of Canaan had to be subdued if God's promise to Abraham was to be fulfilled. The Passover feast was to be eaten in haste, for God was about to mobilize an army, where only 70 lineal heirs and their households had come down into Egypt two centuries before. Egypt had served as a recruiting depot; the wilderness came to serve as boot camp; and the army, under Joshua, won the battle.

The Hebrews believed Moses enough to sprinkle the blood and eat the Passover feast. That is all God required of them in order to avoid making the costly sacrifice which the Egyptians paid. Yet the Hebrew slaves did not believe Moses beyond that minimal commitment. They did not believe they could escape through the Red Sea. They did not believe they would find food and water in the wilderness. They did not believe they could defeat the cities of Canaan. They did not truly believe that Egypt, with all its tyranny, was really that terrible. They believed only that God would take their firstborn if they refused to participate, and that was sufficient. Their children, whom they did not sacrifice to God's wrath, became the firstfruits in the wilderness; it was they who conquered Canaan. The firstborn sons were preserved by the ritual conformity of their parents — minimal covenantal faithfulness. The parents did not save anything else. Their faith extended this far, and no farther; that was also the limit of their blessing. God kept them alive in the wilderness for the sake of their children. The covenant blood line was preserved (Gen. 49:10), and the tribes were preserved. Their own skins were preserved, but only to rot after death in the wilderness they dreaded.

---

15. It could be argued that the Israelites simply feared to enter Canaan, but they did not specifically choose *not* to go in. This argument is misleading. The concept of choice necessarily involves selection among alternatives. It involves giving up one set of conditions in exchange for another set. The Israelites chose not to exchange the perceived safety of wandering in the wilderness for the perceived danger of confronting the people of Canaan in battle. In short, they chose not to enter Canaan.

God had called an army into battle which was not ready to fight. All it was ready to do was to save its firstborn and then leave, under the intense pressure of their former captors.

The Peace Treaty

The New Testament Passover is Christ (I Cor. 5:7). When Christ celebrated the Passover, He sat down with the disciples (Luke 22:14). They did not stand with staffs in their hands, ready to march out of Egypt and into Canaan. They had at last arrived; they could rest in confidence.[16] Christ's sacrifice transferred all power to Himself (Matt. 29:18). Those who drink His cup and eat His bread are *judges* and *ambassadors* (Eph. 6:20). "And I appoint unto you a kingdom, as my Father hath appointed unto me; That ye may eat and drink at my table in my kingdom, and sit on thrones judging the twelve tribes of Israel" (Luke 22:29-30). *The world has been conquered in principle:* "I have overcome the world" (John 16:33b).

God's judges carry His law to the defeated kingdoms of Satan, just as they carried His law to Israel in the years before the fall of Jerusalem in 70 A.D.[17] The new Israel, the Israel of God (Gal. 6:16), is to be judged by the law (Rom. 2:12); but as an army which in principle has already conquered, this new Israel must sit in judgment of the world. *The whole world is Canaan now, and Christ announced His victory over it.* As judges, in time and on earth, we are to make manifest

---

16. Alfred Edersheim, the late-nineteenth-century historian, reports that even before Christ's celebration of the Last Supper, the Hebrews had abandoned the original Passover requirement that they remain standing. "As the guests gathered around the Paschal table, they came no longer, as at the first celebration, with their 'loins girded,' with shoes on their feet, and a staff in their hand—that is, as travellers waiting to take their departure. On the contrary, they were arrayed in their best festive garments, joyous and at rest, as became children of a king. To express this idea the Rabbis also insisted that the Paschal Supper—or at least part of it—must be eaten in that recumbent position with which we are familiar from the New Testament. 'For,' say they, 'they use this leaning posture, as free men do, in memorial of their freedom.' And, again, 'Because it is the manner of slaves to eat standing, therefore now they eat sitting and leaning, in order to show that they have been delivered from bondage into freedom.' " Edersheim, *The Temple: Its Ministries and Services* (Grand Rapids, Michigan: Eerdmans, 1975), p. 234.

17. For a grim account of the fall of Jerusalem, see the primary source document written by Josephus, a Hebrew zealot who defected to the invading Roman army before defection became impossible. *Wars of the Jews,* Books V and VI, in Josephus, *Collected Works,* translated by William Whiston (Grand Rapids, Michigan: Kregel, [1960] 1977).

that victory by imposing the terms of the treaty of the great King.[18] *Armies stand,* for they must be ready to march. *Judges sit,* ready to dispense judgment. Christians are not warriors whose primary assignment is to physically destroy nations that are not yet ethically subdued; they are instead *ambassadors* — an army of ambassadors — who come before a defeated population to announce the terms of peace. But every peace treaty involves *surrender;* every peace treaty is imposed by a *victor.* The enemy's commander was defeated at Calvary; it is our task to convince his subordinates to lay down their weapons and sign the peace treaty.[19] The decisive battle was won at Calvary; the mopping-up operation is still going on (Rom. 16:20; I John 3:8).

New Testament Revisions

There has been a shift in assignments since the days of the Passover. The Hebrews were commanded to annihilate their Canaanitic enemies. God planned to make a clean sweep of the land of Canaan. He intended the total devastation of those nations. The Hebrews were to spare no one (Deut. 7:16-24). Dominion was to be by means of military might initially, and then by settling the land. While there was eventually to be evangelism, as the Book of Jonah indicates, the Hebrews were first to establish the kingdom in Israel on a firm basis, and then God's promised blessings were to bring a particular response on the part of Israel: *expansion.*

Since the resurrection, Christ has been planting His kingdom by means of *the sword of the gospel.* The word of God, we are told, is sharper than a two-edged sword (Heb. 4:12). We possess "the sword of the Spirit, which is the word of God" (Eph. 6:17). The prophecy of Isaiah is progressively coming true: "He shall smite the earth with the rod of his mouth, and with the breath of his lips shall he slay the wicked" (Isa. 11:4). Those who bring the message of Christ are *ethical soldiers;* their main task is to judge the world, subduing it by means of the Holy Spirit, but in terms of His law. The kingdom has been removed from genetic Israel and given to those who bring forth its fruits (Matt. 21:43). The fruits produced by righteous living manifest the kingdom. It is lawful living, in time and on earth,

---

18. The phrase is Meredith Kline's: *Treaty of the Great King: The Covenant Structure of Deuteronomy* (Grand Rapids, Michigan: Eerdmans, 1963).

19. Gary North, *Unconditional Surrender: God's Program for Victory* (2nd ed.; Tyler, Texas: Geneva Divinity School Press, 1983), pp. 64-65, 69-70, 111-13.

which verifies a man's claim to the kingdom (Matt. 7:16-20).

The entry into Canaan was a preliminary battle. God's title to the land was made manifest by the success of His people on the battlefield. He demonstrated His sovereignty for all to see, in Egypt and in Canaan. The victory over Satan at Calvary released *an army of judges* which began to spread the message of salvation throughout the world. These ambassadors rest in Christ's victory. They know the mortal blow has been delivered by Christ; Satan roars like a dying wild beast—dangerous to those in his path, but nonetheless vanquished.

We no longer celebrate the Passover standing up, as if we were a literal army about to receive marching orders. We have *already* received our marching orders; we are in fact on the march, as agents of a victorious commander, calling out the terms of surrender as judges. Men must sign the peace treaty now, *before* they meet the church's commander. We are the emissaries of a mighty commanding officer, who sends us to the enemy with an offer of peace, as required by biblical law (Deut. 20:10). To refuse to surrender means total defeat, eternal defeat.

The New Testament soldier is a *judge*. We are to establish a new civilization based on God's law. Rushdoony writes: "In brief, every law-order is a state of war against the enemies of that order, *and all law is a form of warfare.* Every law declares that certain offenders are enemies of the law-order and must be arrested. For limited offenses, there are limited penalties; for capital offenses, capital punishment. *Law is a state of war;* it is the organization of the powers of civil government to bring the enemies of the law-order to justice. The officers of the law are properly armed; in a godly state, they should be armed by the justice of the law as well as weapons of warfare, in order to defend society against its enemies. Friends of the law will therefore seek at all times to improve, strengthen, and confirm a godly law-order. Enemies of the law will accordingly be in continuing warfare against the law. . . . Men cannot seek co-existence with evil without thereby declaring war against God."[20] Christ's peace treaty involves surrender to Him, but the promise of victory, in this world, as well as in eternity. His law will triumph, for His kingdom has been established on the battlefield at Calvary.[21]

---

20. R. J. Rushdoony, *The Institutes of Biblical Law* (Nutley, New Jersey: Craig Press, 1973), pp. 93-94.

21. David Chilton, *Paradise Restored: A Biblical Theology of Dominion* (Tyler, Texas: Reconstruction Press, 1985); Roderick Campbell, *Israel and the New Covenant* (Tyler, Texas: Geneva Divinity School Press, [1954] 1982).

Continual Warfare

Paul wrote, concerning the internal warfare of regenerate men, "But I see another law in my members, warring against the law of my mind, and bringing me into captivity to the law of sin which is in my members" (Rom. 7:23). He also wrote: "For we wrestle not against flesh and blood, but against principalities, against powers, against the rulers of the darkness of this world, against spiritual wickedness in high places" (Eph. 6:12). Yet we also know that Christ, having spoiled principalities and powers, "made a shew of them openly, triumphing over them in it" (Col. 2:15b). So the chief battle is behind us. The mopping-up operation in our own hearts continues. Our weapon of personal self-dominion is the law of God. It is a lifetime battle against sin and its effects.

There is *continuity in our warfare* today — a step by step process of conquest. First of all, it is *internal ethical warfare:* "Whom shall he teach knowledge? And whom shall he make to understand doctrine? Them that are weaned from the milk, and drawn from the breasts. For precept must be upon precept, precept upon precept; line upon line, line upon line; here a little, and there a little" (Isa. 28:9-10). Second, it is *external cultural warfare:* "But the word of the LORD was unto them precept upon precept, precept upon precept; line upon line, line upon line; here a little, there a little; that they might go, and fall backward, and be broken, and snared, and taken" (Isa. 28:13). Line upon line, law upon law, institution by institution, nation by nation: the whole earth is subdued to the glory of God.

The Hebrews marched out of Egypt victorious. That victory had been won by a series of ten radically discontinuous events: blood, frogs, lice, swarms, cattle plague, boils, locusts, hail, darkness, and the death of Egypt's firstborn. Then they marched across the dry path cleared through the Red Sea. A generation later, their children, under Joshua, marched through a path in the Jordan River, and one by one, the cities of Canaan fell. Like the walls of Jericho, they all (or almost all) came tumbling down. God's miraculous delivery was to demonstrate His control over the realm of human history. The prophets reminded their listeners of this *radically discontinuous history* — a history marked by the miracles of God — when they came before them to call the people to repentance.

At the same time, *the Israelites were to rely increasingly on the regularities of biblical law.* The manna ceased when they crossed into

Canaan (Josh. 5:12). In Hebrews 9:4 we are told that the Ark of the Covenant contained the tables of the covenant, a pot containing manna, and Aaron's rod. These were manifestations of God's dealings with them, and they involved discontinuous events in Israel's history. But Aaron's rod no longer has power, and the manna has ceased. It is God's law-order, proclaimed on the tablets of stone, and empowered by the Spirit, which remains powerful.[22] It is the *continuity of God's law,* not the implements of God's previous miraculous discontinuities in history, which is the tool of dominion in New Testament times, and was the primary tool even in Old Testament times.

New Testament Revisions

We are not to celebrate the Passover in the way prescribed by Moses in Exodus 12. We are not to wait for the earthly appearance of the Messiah. He has already appeared. He has won His victory. The chief battle is long over. We are in the land of Canaan. We have crossed over the Jordan River. There are still cities to conquer, but the sharp discontinuities of the past are not to become our standards of conquest for today. It is the steady preaching of the gospel, the subduing of sin in each man, and the continuous extension of God's law over human culture, which constitutes the New Testament's program of conquest. That is why we can sit with Christ at His communion table, knowing that we will sit with him on thrones. *We are presently symbolically seated with Him on thrones of authority, even as the Hebrews were symbolically standing with Him, ready to march.* The difference is based on the historical position of the chief military victory, the cross. That victory is behind us, so we can take it for granted. The battle is now spiritual and cultural: subduing our spirits and our environment to the Lord, by means of His law.

The revolution *was.* We no longer look for a future radical discontinuity which will establish our earthly dominion. The next discontinuity is the coming of Christ in final judgment. This takes place *after* God's rule has been manifested, but prior to the final judgment. "Then cometh the end, when he shall have delivered up the kingdom to God, even the Father; when he shall have put down all rule and all authority and power. For he must reign, till he hath put all

---

22. Obviously, it is not the tablets of stone which are powerful, but the laws proclaimed on them. It is God's law, written in the hearts of His people (II Cor. 3:3; Heb. 8:10), which is the proper tool of dominion, both internal and external.

enemies under his feet. The last enemy that shall be destroyed is death" (I Cor. 15:24-26). Yet Christ's victory is in principle behind us: "For he hath put all things under his feet" (I Cor. 15:27a). Christ has all power right now (Matt. 28:18). *The great discontinuities of God's covenantal history are past:* His crucifixion, resurrection, and ascension. The arrival of His Spirit at Pentecost gave us our official papers as His ambassadors, our commissions as His judges. There are only two great discontinuities remaining: Satan's final rebellion (Rev. 20:7-8) and defeat (Rev. 20:9-10), and the final judgment (Rev. 20:12-15). (Some commentators might call these two discontinuities the last continuity, since they take place close together.) In between, there are the daily struggles between the two armies, the ebb and flow of the mopping-up operations, and the progressive extension of God's kingdom, in time and on earth.

It is a mistake, then, to expect what Israel was told to expect. It is a mistake to expect the delivery of our marching orders. It is a mistake to expect visible, direct, cataclysmic interventions of God on earth. Miracles still occur, but not the pillar of the cloud and the pillar of fire. God's law is still in force, but we no longer need to have its terms delivered to us on tablets of stone actually written by God. There are still spiritually Canaanitic cities to be conquered, but not by the blast of trumpets on our seventh day of marching around them. We *sit* at the Lord's victorious table. We no longer stand, staffs in hand. The lamb has been consumed already. We need not offer it again. The blood is on our doorposts. We need not sprinkle it on them again (Heb. 9). The *continuity of God's law,* not the discontinuities of God's military victories or miracles, is our standard.[23]

Unleavened and Leavened Bread

The unleavened bread which the Hebrews were commanded to use during the Passover feast (Ex. 12:15) was a symbol of the *impending discontinuity,* their deliverance from Egypt. They had to cook and eat in haste. It was not to symbolize affliction as such, for as Edersheim wrote in the late nineteenth century, "the bread of the Paschal night was not that of affliction because it was unleavened; it was unleavened because it had been that of affliction. For it had been

---

23. It is one of the major weaknesses of revivalism in general, and the twentieth-century Pentecostal movement in particular, that Christians have relied so heavily on miraculous manifestations of the power of God, rather than relying on the continuous power of the law of God as a tool of dominion.

Israel's 'affliction,' and a mark of their bondage and subjection to the Egyptians, to be driven forth in such 'haste' as not even to have time for leavening their bread. . . . The Passover, therefore, was not so much the remembrance of Israel's bondage as of Israel's deliverance from that bondage, and the bread which had originally been that of affliction, because that of haste, now became, as it were, the bread of a new state of existence. None of Egypt's leaven was to pervade it; nay, all the old leaven, which served as the symbol of corruption and of death, was to be wholly banished from their homes. They were to be 'a new lump,' as they were 'unleavened.' "[24]

They did not have time to allow the yeast of Egypt to leaven their bread. This symbolized God's *overnight* deliverance of His people from Egypt, another reason why the lamb was to be eaten in one night, with nothing left over (Ex. 12:10). *Here was the greatest discontinuity in Israel's history.* Here was the discontinuity which they were to teach to their children (Ex. 12:26-27).

Paul, as a Pharisee, was thoroughly familiar with the meaning of the Passover. He did not require us to eat unleavened bread, nor are the bitter herbs required. His own teacher, Gamaliel (Acts 22:3), taught the meaning of the lamb, bitter herbs, and unleavened bread, and his words have become authoritative in Jewish law: "Whoever does not explain three things in the Passover has not fulfilled the duty incumbent on him. These three things are: the Passover lamb, the unleavened bread, and the bitter herbs. *The Passover lamb* means that God passed over the blood-sprinkled place on the houses of our fathers in Egypt; *the unleavened bread* means that our fathers were delivered out of Egypt (in haste); and *the bitter herbs* mean that the Egyptians made bitter the lives of our fathers in Egypt."[25] Christians no longer eat bitter herbs, because Christ has delivered us from sin; the bitterness of Egypt is no longer to be part of our worship. It is the Lamb that was slain, not the deliverance from Egypt, which is our central celebration as Christians. *We are on the offensive now, carrying redeemed Canaan's leaven back into Egypt* (Isa. 19).

Leaven

The progress of Christ's kingdom is to be like the leavening of bread. "Another parable spake he unto them; The kingdom of heaven is like unto leaven, which a woman took, and hid in three

---

24. Edersheim, *The Temple,* pp. 249-50.
25. Gamaliel, cited by Edersheim, *ibid.,* p. 237.

measures of meal, till the whole was leavened" (Matt. 13:33). It must be understood from the first that *leaven is not as such a symbol of sin.* Yes, the leaven of Egypt was evil. The corrupting effects of Egyptian culture and Egyptian religion no doubt burdened the Israelites. They were to purge away all their leaven in the week before the Exodus (12:15). This meant that none of Egypt's leaven was to be carried into Canaan with them, to serve as the source of corruption in the promised land. It was *Egypt's* leaven which was perverse, but not leaven as such. The Hebrew term for leaven in Exodus 12:15, "put away leaven out of your houses," and in Exodus 12:19a, "Seven days shall there be no leaven found in your houses," is transliterated *se'or.* It was leavened dough, and a bit of it was retained in an unbaked form so that it could be used to "start" the next batch of dough. Leavened bread, the finished product, was also forbidden: none of the actual products of Egypt's leaven would go into Canaan. Neither the "starter" nor the finished product would leave Egypt with the Hebrews. Egypt's leaven stood for sin, but there can also be holy leaven. In fact, there *must* be holy leaven. Modern expositors who follow a dispensational-premillennial outline fail to recognize this distinction,[26] but the ancient Hebrews understood it quite well.

How do we know this? Because leavened bread was offered as the firstfruits of the Lord, meaning that leavened bread was the *best* of a family's productivity: "Ye shall bring out of your habitations two wave loaves of two tenth deals: they shall be of fine flour; they shall be baken with leaven; they are the firstfruits unto the LORD" (Lev. 23:17). Leaven is the *best* bread man has to offer, the bread he eats with pleasure. It is man's best grain offering to God. Leaven, in short, is a symbol of *growth, maturation, continuity,* and *prosperity.* But such leaven must be the *leaven of the promised land,* the *leaven of redeemed Canaan.* It must not be the leaven of Egypt.

It is important to understand the general peace offerings made by individual Israelites, as well as the nationally observed ritual of the firstfruits. The peace offerings of unleavened bread were also accompanied with unleavened cakes mingled with oil, and unleavened wafers anointed with oil (Lev. 7:12). The priests and offerer ate the peace-offering, which was a unique feature of the peace-offering. In this sense, concluded Andrew Jukes, this offering shows *communion:*

---

26. The standard view is that of the *Scofield Reference Bible* (New York: Oxford University Press, 1909): "Leaven, as a symbolic or typical substance, is always mentioned in the O.T. in an evil sense. . . ." Note 4, p. 1016: Matthew 13:33.

God, priest, and offerer.[27] Christ was our offering, yet He was the offerer; He was also the High Priest and God.[28] He was the firstfruits (I Cor. 15:23), from which the peace-offering had to be made.

Leavened dough could not be burned on the altar (Lev. 2:11). It had to be brought already baked, ready for eating. Leavened bread was offered as a *finished work,* the fully-risen product of the "starter." It was not to be burned on God's altar, not because it was "corrupted" or "sin-laden," but because it was a finished loaf.[29] Burning it would have ruined it. It was not the "corrupted" nature of leaven that kept it off God's fiery altar, for honey was also prohibited (Lev. 2:11). There was nothing corrupt about honey. Honey, like leavened bread, is a finished product, the product of labor, capital, and time.

Pentecost

It is extremely important to note that this compulsory offering of the firstfruits, which included the leavened bread offering, came on the day of Pentecost. The Greek word, "pentekostos," means fifty. The firstfruits offering was made on the fiftieth day after the sabbath day of the Passover week, the feast of unleavened bread (Lev. 23:15-16), or forty-nine days after the wave offering. On the day after the sabbath which fell during the Passover week, the priests brought a sheaf of grain offering and waved it before God. Then, forty-nine days of maturation later, came the baked bread of the day of Pentecost. At Passover, the people were required to use unleavened bread, the symbol of religious, cultural, and historical discontinuity. At Pentecost, they were required to offer leavened bread, the symbol of continuity and completion. At the Passover, Israel found its release from bondage. At Pentecost, they experienced full blessings.

---

27. Andrew Jukes, *The Law of the Offerings* (Grand Rapids, Michigan: Kregel, 1968), pp. 115-21. The book was first published in the late nineteenth century.

28. *Ibid.,* pp. 118-19.

29. I rarely disagree with the published conclusions of R. J. Rushdoony, but I think his assessment of the meaning of leaven is incorrect. He writes: "Leaven is taken by some as a symbol or type of sin; it is rather a symbol of corruptibility. . . . Man's obedience to the law is a leavened offering, clearly corruptible, yet when faithful and obedient to God's authority and order, a 'sacrifice' well-pleasing in His sight and assured of His reward." *Institutes of Biblical Law,* p. 83. I am arguing that leaven symbolizes neither sin nor corruptibility; leaven is a *symbol of the continuity of development,* meaning *maturation over time.* All of men's offerings are corruptible; focusing on leaven as a uniquely corruptible offering misses the point. Leaven as a symbol of continuity fits Rushdoony's postmillennial eschatology far better than leaven as a symbol of corruptibility.

Cassuto believes that the law was given to the Israelites seven weeks after the Exodus. Exodus 19:1 reads: "In the third month [new moon], when the children of Israel were gone forth out of the land of Egypt, the same day came they into the wilderness of Sinai." Cassuto comments: "The mention of the third new moon is not unintentional. Since the Exodus from Egypt, the last two weeks of Nissan and four weeks of Iyyar had passed, and we are now in the seventh week. Since seven was considered the number of perfection, seven days constituted, according to the customary conception of the ancient East, a given unit of time, while seven weeks formed a still higher unit; and just as after six days of labour the seventh day brought rest and the enjoyment of the results of that labour, so after six weeks of the travails of journeying, the seventh week brought a sense of exaltation and of drawing nearer to the word Divine. Although the Torah does not state the exact day on which the Revelation on Mount Sinai occurred, and only the later tradition connects the Festival of Weeks with the commemorative of the giving of the Torah, yet it is obvious that this tradition corresponds to what, if not expressly stated in Scripture, is at least alluded to therein by inference."[30]

The firstfruits offering the day following the sabbath of Passover week was marked by the wave offering of the sheaf of grain — the unbaked offering (Lev. 23:10-11). At Pentecost, or the Feast of Weeks, forty-nine days later, the wave offering was a pair of leavened loaves (Lev. 23:17). In the interim, the grain had been harvested, ground into flour, allowed to rise by means of yeast, and baked as a completed offering to God. This symbolism of discontinuity, followed by continuity, should be clear enough.

New Testament Symbolism

The same parallelism is present in the New Testament events: the Passover meal of Christ and the disciples, followed by His death and resurrection.[31] Then, forty-nine days after Christ's resurrection,

---

30. U. Cassuto, *A Commentary on the Book of Exodus,* translated by Israel Abrahams (Jerusalem: The Magnes Press, The Hebrew University, [1951] 1974), p. 224.

31. There are some difficult problems associated with the dating of Christ's Passover meal with the disciples. The most convincing presentation is Hoehner's: they met on Thursday night, Nissan 14, which was the Pharisees' practice. The Passover lamb was slain betwen 3-5 P.M. that afternoon by the Pharisees and Galileans. The Judean dating, used by the Sadducees, was different. They slew the lamb that year on Friday afternoon, since they dated Nissan 14 from Thursday

came the day of Pentecost. The break with the old covenant was established by Christ's death and resurrection, when He inaugurated a new era. He gave the Holy Spirit to His disciples on the day of resurrection (John 20:22). The manifestations of power of the Holy Spirit came seven weeks later, at Pentecost (Acts 2). The church, Christ's body (I Cor. 12:12-27), was established as a visible unity at Pentecost. "For we being many are one bread, and one body: for we are all partakers of that one bread" (I Cor. 10:17). Yet Christ equated His own body with bread (I Cor. 11:24). The New Testament parallels with Passover and Pentecost in the Old Testament should be obvious. *The coming of God's Spirit at Pentecost was God's presentation of the newly leavened loaf of the church* — a presentation to the Son (Dan. 7:13-14). The day of Pentecost in the New Testament was God's presentation of the *risen bread of the church,* which paralleled the *risen Lord Jesus* (an event which took place forty-nine days earlier), who is called "Christ the firstfruits" by Paul (I Cor. 15:23). Leaven is a product of *resurrection:* Christ's, the church's, and the day of judgment's. *The great discontinuity at Calvary has produced a new continuity: the civilization of the kingdom of God.*

Paul speaks of the leavened and unleavened bread. "Your glorying is not good. Know ye not that a little leaven leaveneth the whole lump? Purge out therefore the old leaven, that ye may be a new lump, as ye are unleavened. For even Christ our Passover is sacrificed for us. Therefore, let us keep the feast, not with old leaven, neither with the leaven of malice and wickedness; but with the unleavened [bread] of sincerity and truth" (I Cor. 5:6-8). Paul was contrasting the old leaven (evil) with unleavened (a new ethical beginning). (The King James translators added the word "bread.") He was speaking of Christ our Passover. In the Passover feast, unleavened bread was eaten, in order to purge away the leaven of Egypt, the leaven of sin. Christ, like the unleavened bread of the

---

evening. This explains why Jesus and the disciples ate their Passover meal the night before Jesus was crucified, and why the Jews did not enter the Praetorium when they took Jesus to Pilate, "lest they should be defiled; but that they might eat the Passover" (John 18:28b). This confrontation between Jesus and His accusers took place on Nissan 15, as reckoned by the Pharisees, and on Nissan 14, as reckoned by the Sadducees. Jesus died at about 3 in the afternoon, at precisely the time that the Judeans were slaying their Passover lamb, 24 hours after the Pharisees and Galileans had slain theirs. See Harold W. Hoehner, *Chronological Aspects of the Life of Christ* (Grand Rapids, Michigan: Zondervan, 1977), ch. 4, especially the chart on p. 89. Jesus died on Friday (sixthday) and arose on Sunday (firstday) morning.

Passover, represented a *discontinuous break* with normal historical development, a break with the maturation of the principle of evil. This is what unleavened bread always symbolized: *a new beginning, a break with the evil maturation principle (leaven) of the past.* This is what Joshua meant when he told the Israelites to serve God in sincerity and truth (Josh. 24:14). Evil leaven does not mature into a holy loaf; it must be purged out. It must be *replaced.* Replaced with what? A new, holy leaven.

Christ was quite specific about this. "How is it that ye do not understand that I spake it not to you concerning bread, that ye should beware of the leaven of the Pharisees and of the Sadducees? Then understood they how that he bade them not beware of the leaven of bread, but of the doctrine of the Pharisees and of the Sadducees" (Matt. 16:11-12). The *leavening process of unsound doctrine* leads to evil acts; it is the *maturation process of evil yeast.* It must be purged out from the beginning. Purge out the *old* leaven. This purging is ethical, intellectual, and theological. It means becoming a new creation (II Cor. 5:17). It means being born again, or born from above (John 3:3-8). *God replaces the old unethical leaven with a new, holy leaven.*

John Calvin recognized the ethical focus of Paul's words regarding leaven and unleavened. "Now, in the solemnity of this sacred feast we must abstain from *leaven,* as God commanded the fathers to abstain. But from what leaven? As the outward passover was to them a figure of the true *passover,* so its appendages were figures of the reality which we at this day possess. If, therefore, we would wish to feed on Christ's flesh and blood, let us bring to this feast *sincerity and truth.* Let these be our loaves of *unleavened bread.* Away with all *malice and wickedness,* for it is unlawful to mix up *leaven* with the *passover.* In fine, he declares that we shall be members of Christ only when we shall have renounced *malice* and deceit."[32] Calvin did not say that we must eat unleavened bread at the communion table. He said only that we must not bring malice and deceit in our hearts when we come to the Lord's Supper. It is *God's people* who must be *set apart as unleavened* — free from the religious *leaven of rebellion* against God and His law. This is the symbolism of discontinuity. It is the symbolism of Christ the Passover. But Christ is also the firstfruits, both unleavened (waving the sheaf) and leavened (waving the

32. John Calvin, *Commentary on the Epistles of Paul the Apostle to the Corinthians,* translated by John Pringle, Vol. I, which appears as Vol. XX of *Calvin's Commentaries* (Grand Rapids, Michigan: Baker Book House, 1979), p. 189.

loaves). The *discontinuity from sin* is supposed to lead to the *continuity of dominion* — ethical, ecclesiastical, social, political, and cultural.

The Process of Maturation

Leaven is not a symbol of sin. Leaven is a symbol of rising up, *the process of maturation.* But there must first be a discontinuous act of implanting the original leaven. Adam, yielding to Satan's temptation, brought forth the leaven of evil, and implanted it into man's history. Christ, the second Adam, removes the old Adamic leaven, implants His new leaven, and creates *a maturing kingdom which steadily replaces Satan's older leaven.* Immediately following the unleavened bread is the beginning of the new leavening process, the *rising up.* Israel was brought *up* out of Egypt (Ex. 17:3). On the third day, Christ *rose* from the dead. On the day of Christ's resurrection, many saints *rose* from the dead (Matt. 27:52-53). On the day of Pentecost, the Holy Spirit presented the *risen* (leavened) bread offering, the church. *The discontinuous event of redemption is supposed to be followed by the ethical leavening process, a rising up in victory, in time and on earth.* Christ does not simply remove the old leaven. He is not content with unleavened bread, the symbol of deliverance. *Christ produces the new leavened bread, the leavening process of victory.* It is not enough to escape from Egypt; Canaan must be conquered. It is not enough to remain in a spiritually unleavened condition, the condition of "not being leavened with evil." We must become fully leavened as God's individual saints and also as His gathered church. *Where this leaven is absent, there is no life, no growth, and no dominion.*

No Leaven on the Old Testament Altar

Neither leaven (yeast) nor the products of leaven (leavened loaves) could be placed on God's fiery altar during the Old Testament era (Lev. 2:11). We are not told specifically why not. We also are not told why honey was also prohibited. There are two possible explanations that seem to make sense of the prohibition.

1. *Full Development*

Leavened loaves and honey are finished, *fully developed products.* They are fully matured. No further development is possible. They are both the products of *time.* Neither is hastily produced. They symbolize the end of the maturation process, the fruits of thorough labor.

What was offered on God's altar in the Old Testament economy was that which had not had time to mature fully. The animals were yearling lambs (Num. 28:3, 9), young bulls (Num. 28:11), a young goat, or kid (Num. 28:15), and young pigeons (Lev. 1:14; 5:7). The day of atonement required young animals (Num. 29:1-5). These animals had not yet begun their work. The red heifer, which was used to make the ashes for the water of purification, had to be umblemished, three years old, and never yoked (Num. 19:2). The sacrifices required *an animal cut down in its prime,* with its productive life ahead of it. This animal forfeited both the joys and labors of the bulk of its adult life. Unquestionably, *this symbolism pointed to Jesus Christ, the lamb of God slain in the midst of His prime.* In time and on earth, He forfeited a life of dominion. He forfeited the joy of eating the fruits of His labor. He forfeited the leavened loaves and the honey. He forfeited the blessings of long life, despite His perfect keeping of the law of God. He forfeited all this, so that His people might receive these blessings. They are to exercise dominion, in time and on earth. They are to labor. They are to eat the firstfruits, symbolized by Pentecost. They are also to eat the honey and the baked leaven loaves.[33] They are to serve, in short, as *God's leaven,* "incorrupting" Satan's former kingdoms, causing the kingdom of God to rise up. They are given what Christ forfeited: *visible dominion,* in time and earth. God does not burn up the leaven before its time, before it has matured, before it is fit for communion's joyful eating. A leavened offering, like honey, is not burned on God's altar.

But what about Satan? Isn't Satan eventually burned? Aren't Satan's followers burned, as salted offerings? Haven't they been given time? This points to the removal of the devil's ability to continue to develop. He will be cut down in the midst of his rebellion

---

33. I know of no church which celebrates the communion meal with honey, yet many of them use leavened bread. This is inconsistent. The use of leaven points to the use of honey. The completed work of Christ's sacrifice is behind us historically. The completed offering of Christ at Calvary points both to the use of leaven (the formerly prohibited completed baked bread) and honey (the formerly prohibited completed sweetener). Honey ought to be substituted for the bitter herbs. The church has not been consistent with its symbolism; bitter herbs were never incorporated into the Christian Passover, yet honey has not replaced the Old Covenant's required herbs — an obvious lack of consistency. Passover was to be *tasted.* What was bitter is now sweet. The contrast has not been made visible symbolically. Deliverance has not been consistently symbolized. The taste of victory implied in honey's sweetness has not been a feature of the church's sacraments. When the church's eschatology changes to a more optimistic view of the role of the church in history, and its victory over creation is made progressively clearer, churches will then adopt the use of honey in the communion service.

against God's church (Rev. 20:9). *The very essence of leaven, its ability to spread through the dough, will be removed from Satan.* He will be like unleavened dough, fit only for burning, cut down in God's final discontinuous event, just as Pharaoh was cut down. The "leaven of Egypt" will be purged out, finally, at the end of time. It will be leaven which can no longer do its work. It is finally made useless, like savorless salt, fit only for being ground underfoot (Matt. 5:13). Satan's leaven is purged at the end of time when the leaven of God's finished loaf has fully matured. *Christ's leaven will have done its work.* The fire of the last day bakes this bread, for it is ready for the oven, but Satan's partial leaven is left on the altar forever, never fit for consumption, never fit for God's blessed communion feast. Satan's cultural leaven never fully rises, in time and on earth, since his leaven eventually is *replaced* by God's leaven.

2. *Living Sacrifices*

There may have been an additional reason for prohibiting leaven from God's altar. The leaven, until baked, was a living thing. No living thing was ever sacrificed on the altar. Animals were killed at the door of the tabernacle (Lev. 1:3). Then they were brought to the altar for burning. In the case of Satan and his followers, they will be placed in the lake of fire only after they have been slain (Rev. 20:14). This burning is referred to as the second death. No living being was to be burned on the altar, according to Old Testament law.

The one legitimate exception in history was Jesus Christ. As a perfect creation, a perfect human who had fulfilled the terms of the law, Christ was allowed to become a living sacrifice. God accepted this living sacrifice as a substitute. *No other living being was suitable.* All other beings are subject to death. Christ was not, yet He gave up His life for His friends (John 15:13). The sacrificial animals were cut down in the prime of life, but they all faced death eventually. Jesus Christ was cut down in the prime of life when, in terms of His perfect fulfilling of the law, He had not been faced with death.

Christ was a leavened offering — an *ethically* fully developed offering — on the symbolic altar, the cross. Christ was a living sacrifice, too. In neither case was He violating the laws of the offering. He was instead fulfilling them. The leaven offering (unbaked leavened loaves) and the final baked leavened loaves were not to be burned, but Christ, as a *living man,* and as a *fully developed perfect humanity,* did die on God's altar. Christ, being perfect, was God's own *leavened, liv-*

ing sacrifice to God's own holiness.

Christ was also a honey offering, thereby completing the symbolism. He is said to be the word of God (John 1:1), and the word of God is equated with honey (Ezk. 3:1-3; Rev. 10:9-10). "How sweet are thy words unto my taste! Yea, sweeter than honey to my mouth" (Ps. 119:103). The completeness of God's word, the completeness of Christ's work, and the completeness of honey as a sweetener come together in Christ's complete sacrifice on Calvary. His perfect honey was acceptable to God as a legitimate offering in this one instance in man's history. These three offerings, which had previously not been allowed on God's altar — leaven, living animals, and honey — completed and ended the Old Testament sacrifices. Only Christ, and not man's leavened imitations, or nature's (honey), was ethically fit for God's altar. His perfect offering was the culmination of the sacrificial system, as the Book of Hebrews teaches. It was His *ethical perfection* which was always the goal of the sacrificial system; the law's prohibition against the use of leaven and honey was there to keep imperfect men from claiming the perfection that only Christ legitimately can and did claim.

Christians are told to offer themselves as living sacrifices (Rom. 12:1). The sacrificial system is now straightforwardly *ethical*. The old sacrifices of rams and goats are over; Christ has replaced them, once and for all, as the true living sacrifice, the only living sacrifice suitable for God's altar. His last words were, "It is finished" (John 19:30). It was the end of the Old Covenant, the end of the sacrificial system, and the end of Christ's work, in time and on earth, in fulfilling the terms of the law. He would no longer appear before men, angels, or God as a man under the curse; the final discontinuity had come to Him as a suffering servant. *There could be no remaining potential ethical development for mankind, as a creature. Christ had fulfilled all of mankind's ethical potential, in time and on earth.* Ethically perfect humanity had been fully realized, in time and on earth. Christ was, in this sense, a *leavened offering*, for He was fully matured, ready for eating, the ultimate development of humanity. Christ, and Christ alone, could become a suitable *living* sacrifice, a living *blood* offering, as well as a legitimate *leavened* offering. None of Egypt's leaven was in Him.

What Christ is, man is told to become: not a member of the Trinity, but a perfect man. This is why the church is called His body (I Cor. 12:12-27). This is why it is called bread: "For we being many are one bread and one body: for we are all partakers of that one bread" (I Cor. 10:17). The *principle of maturation* has a goal: *full development.* Christ, the head of the church, has already attained this goal. The discontinuity is behind us. The lamb has been sacrificed. The fully developed, fully leavened bread, without a trace of Satan's leaven, has conquered our satanic foe, and has served as redeemed mankind's peace offering, and also as our thank offering. Christ was both *unleavened* (free from Satan's leaven) and *leavened* (fully developed perfect humanity); He was both our *discontinuity* (the definitive break from the sin principle) and our *continuity* (the full development of human perfection).

The Kingdom as Leaven

The kingdom of God is like leaven. Christianity is the yeast, and it has a leavening effect on pagan, satanic cultures around it. It permeates the whole of culture, causing it to rise. The bread which is produced by this leaven is the *preferred bread*. In ancient times — indeed, right up until the advent of late-nineteenth-century industrialism and modern agricultural methods — leavened bread was considered the staff of life, the symbol of God's sustaining hand. "Give us this day our daily bread," Christians have prayed for centuries, and they have eaten leavened bread at their tables. So did the ancient Hebrews. The kingdom of God is the force that produces the fine quality bread which all men seek. The symbolism should be obvious: *Christianity makes life a joy for godly men. It provides men with the very best.*

Leaven takes time to produce its product. It takes time for the leaven-laden dough to rise. *Leaven is a symbol of historical continuity, just as unleavened bread was Israel's symbol of historical discontinuity.* Men can wait for the yeast to do its work. God gives man time for the working of His spiritual leaven. Men may not understand exactly how the leaven works — how the spiritual power of God's kingdom spreads throughout their culture and makes it rise — but they can see and taste its effects. If we really push the analogy (pound it, even), we can point to the fact that dough is pounded down several times by the baker before the final baking, almost as God, through the agents of Satan in the world, pounds His kingdom in history. Nevertheless, the yeast does its marvelous work, *just so long as the fires of the oven are not lit prematurely.* If the full heat of the oven is applied to the dough before the yeast has done its work, both the yeast and the dough

perish in the flames. God waits to apply the final heat (II Pet.
3:9-10). First, His yeast — His church — must do its work, in time and
on earth. The kingdom of God (which includes the institutional
church, but is broader than the institutional church) must rise, having "incorrupted" the satanic dough of the kingdom of Satan with the
gospel of life, including the life-giving reconstruction of all the institutions of culture.

What a marvelous description of God's kingdom! Christians
work inside the cultural material available in any given culture,
seeking to refine it, permeate it, and make it into something fine.
They know they will be successful, just as yeast is eventually successful in the dough, if it is given sufficient time to do its work. This
is what God implicitly promises us in the analogy of the leaven:
enough time to accomplish our individual and collective assignments. He tells
us that His kingdom will produce the desirable bread of life. It will
take time. It may take several poundings, as God, through the
hostility of the world, kneads the yeast-filled dough of men's cultures.[34] But the end result is guaranteed. God does not intend to
burn His bread to a useless crisp by prematurely placing it in the
oven. He is a better baker than that.

The Symbolism of Communion

Christians should not eat unleavened bread *exclusively* at their
celebrations of the Lord's Supper. They should eat large chunks of
leavened bread, delighting in the flavor and its ability to fill them.
This is what God says His kingdom is like. *The leavened bread is a symbol of God's patience with us, a symbol of His restraint.* As Peter wrote,
concerning the fiery judgment to come at the last judgment, God is
not slack concerning his promise, "but is longsuffering to us-ward,
not willing that any should perish, but that all should come to repentance" (II Peter 3:9b). He delays the application of fire to the earth
(II Peter 3:10). As Christians celebrating the Lord's Supper, we look
toward the future, toward the effects of our labors, in time and on
earth. We are God's yeast, inevitably permeating the whole loaf, until the risen dough is ready for the final fire. *God does not intend to throw
the dough into the fire prematurely.* He does not intend to burn up the
work of His hands. He allows us to make our peace offering. Christ

---

34. I am using the analogy of pounding the dough to apply to historical circumstances. It is a suggestive analogy, not necessarily an inescapable implication of
the biblical text.

was the firstfruits offering (I Cor. 15:20), yet so are we, every man in his own order (I Cor. 15:23).

It could be argued that we should eat both unleavened and leavened bread at the communion table. The symbol of discontinuity may still be ritually legitimate: the decisive break with sin at the cross, when the lamb was slain. But a communion table with only unleavened bread conflicts with the symbolism of Christ's church (His body), which has the task of building His kingdom. "This is my body," He said (Matt. 26:26). But if the church is His body (I Cor. 12:12-14), then how can this body remain flat (unleavened) in history, if it is to replace Satan's evil leaven? Churches must strive to make the symbolism of the Lord's Supper clear to Christ's people, and unleavened flat bread, if eaten without leavened bread, conveys the symbolism of historical and cultural impotence.[35] To use both unleavened and leavened bread, unless the congregation has sophisticated instructors and members with a taste for biblical theology and biblical symbolism, is to risk confusion. If we eat one type of bread only, let it be leavened bread.

("Unleavened wine," meaning grape juice, never had a place in the symbolism of the Old Testament offerings. Contrary to the opinion of some commentators, *wine is fermented.* Jesus' metaphor of the wine and wineskins makes this clear: new wine breaks old wineskins [Matt. 9:17]. To break wineskins, it has to be fermenting. There is no ritual significance for grape juice in the New Testament. It is not a symbol of discontinuity, as unleavened bread is. It is not a biblical symbol at all. Grape juice may, however, be the symbol for the church which is most preferred by Satan, symbolizing the historical impotence of the church—a new wine which breaks nothing because it is not wine at all.)

Let us eat sitting down. Let us eat no bitter herbs. Instead, *let us spread our leavened bread with honey.* The basis of our victory is past; let us look forward with confidence. *Victory is sweet.* Let Satan's troops eat bitter herbs, not Christ's troops. The church has never eaten bit-

---

35. It is true that Jesus ate unleavened bread at the Last Supper. It is also true that He had not yet suffered and died, thereby fulfilling the ethical demands of the Old Testament's sacrificial system, and thereby also abolishing it for all time. He had also not yet risen from the dead. The day He rose from the dead, the historical and cultural impotence of ancient Israel was at last definitively broken, even as new wine breaks old wineskins. Pentecost pointed to this definitive break with the old covenant's defensive mentality and rituals.

ter herbs at the Lord's Supper.[36] Some Christians still insist on unleavened bread exclusively. Those who argue that the communion feast should be celebrated with unleavened bread point to I Corinthians 5, which I cited earlier, where Paul writes:

Your glorying is not good. Know ye not that a little leaven leaveneth the whole lump? Purge out therefore the old leaven, that ye may be a new lump, as ye are unleavened. For even Christ our passover is sacrificed for us. Therefore let us keep the feast, not with old leaven, neither with the leaven of malice and wickedness; but with the unleavened bread of sincerity and truth (I Cor. 5:6-8).

Several comments are in order. First, Paul was dealing with sin in the Corinthian church. When he speaks of purging out the old leaven, he is referring to a specific individual, a man who was practicing incest (I Cor. 5:1-5). Second, the word "bread" was added by the translators of the King James Version. It is not in Paul's text. Third, he tells us to celebrate the Lord's Table with the unleaven of sincerity and truth—a definitive, discontinuous break from Satan's insincerity and lies. This "unleaven" is the starting point of ethical and cultural maturation. It is the "old leaven" that is forbidden. This is the same imagery which was basic to the Passover. It was the old leaven of Egypt that was forbidden. Israel had to make a symbolic break with the religion and culture of Egypt before leaving Egypt for the land of Canaan. *Unleavened bread in this instance symbolized the discontinuity with sin that God's deliverance represents.* (I have already referred Calvin's comments on this passage. He did not use the passage to advocate the use of unleavened bread during communion. He used it to drive home the ethical implications of the communion feast.) The fourth comment is simply that Paul also refers to Christ as the firstfruits, and this involved a leavened offering. Paul held to both images. Thus, to insist on unleavened bread as alone symbolically valid for the communion table is to claim too much. To the extent that churches want the communion celebration to point forward to victory, leavened bread is far more preferable.

---

36. Why were the Israelites required to eat bitter herbs? To remind them of the horrors of cultural bondage to a foreign, anti-God power. The threat of another period of bondage was always before them. But from the day of Christ's resurrection, the old geographical and cultural wineskins were broken. The church is on the offensive internationally, for the ethical requirements of God have been met, in time and on earth. *Definitive ethical victory is behind us, once and for all.*

The Final Revolution

There will be another great discontinuity, in time and on earth. It will come on the heels of long years of continuity. This next revolution of prophetic significance is Satan's final attempt to throw off godly rule (Rev. 20:3). It will be grounded in *a continuity of despair.* Satan's despairing forces will vainly attempt to throw off the continuity of godly rule. It will be a perverse image of the Exodus. The Hebrews had experienced generations of ungodly servitude to the gods of Egypt, through the representative of the gods, the Pharaoh. They were pushed into rebellion after generations of despair. Neither they nor their Egyptian masters had expected this revolt to be successful. Satan's rebellion will come in much the same way, except that it will be *an active rebellion perversely directed against the visible manifestations of the benefits of godly rule.* Unlike the Hebrew rebellion, it will be cut short in rapid order (Rev. 20:9).

The forces of Satan will acknowledge as binding the terms of the peace treaty, but they will secretly resist them. They will organize their forces for the final rebellion. Their sins will be that much greater, for they will heap coals upon their heads by rebelling in the face of the visible blessings of God (Pr. 25:21-22; Rom. 12:20). It is our responsibility, as agents of the victorious commander, to dispense justice, thereby calling forth the external blessings that will condemn the rebels to their well-deserved punishment. The steady extension of godly rule will have its long-term effects, in time and on earth, and these effects will have implications throughout eternity: *training for dominion* by the saints, and *training for defeat* by the rebels.

We should not expect a great discontinuity in training for either camp. We should not expect endless external defeat for the spiritual army of a victorious commander, Jesus Christ, only to have victory handed over on a silver platter to troops that have proven themselves totally incompetent for thousands of years. We should also not expect to see endless victories for Satan, only to have victory snatched away from his troops in the final moments of the ancient contest. Our victory is past: Calvary. Their defeat is past: Calvary. *History is a progressive working out of the implications of that crucial discontinuity.* We should not expect to see the progressive historical defeat of the implicit victors, members of Christ's church, nor should we expect to see the progressive historical victory of the implicit losers.[37] What we

---

37. Gary North, "Common Grace, Eschatology, and Biblical Law," *The Journal of Christian Reconstruction,* III (Winter 1976-77).

should expect to see is the Satanists' equivalent of the Exodus: a desperate rebellion by a people who had experienced generations of rule by their enemies.[38]

Let the Satanists celebrate their communion standing up, staffs in hand. Those staffs were broken at Calvary. We are seated on the thrones of judgment in history, and we shall dispense continual justice, making their final revolt all the less justified, all the more culpable, and all the more unsuccessful. *The continuity of the word of God will bring external cultural victory, step by step.* "But the word of the LORD was unto them precept upon precept, precept upon precept; line upon line, line upon line; here a little, and there a little; that they might go, and fall backward, and be broken, and snared, and taken" (Isa. 28:13). The enemies of God cannot survive the steady onslaught of God's people, as the latter progressively fulfill the terms of the dominion covenant.[39]

Conclusion

The *Passover* points to a radical break with evil. The leaven of the world—sin, death, and corruption—is not to be the ethical foundation of God's kingdom. *Unleavened bread* symbolized this radical ethical discontinuity with Egypt and Egypt's gods and culture. Bitter herbs symbolized the grim reality of life under the dominion of Satan and his representatives. God called the Israelites to obey His law. Obedience to God's law was to become the foundation of a new civilization. At the feast of *Pentecost,* they were to celebrate the founding of this new civilization, and they were to use *leavened bread* in this ritual.

To accomplish the liberation of Israel from the bondage of sin, represented by Egyptian civilization, God destroyed Egypt. The avenger of blood gained vengeance for the blood-stained land on Passover night. A *radical historical discontinuity* was the event which drove the Israelites out of bondage and toward the land of Canaan. This, in turn, was designed to bring the *continuity of the maturation process.* Ethical conformity to God over time produces this *continuity of growth,* both personally and culturally.

The *ethical discontinuity of sin* brings the *historical discontinuity of God's judgment.* Adam learned this lesson when God expelled him

---

38. Gary North, *Unconditional Surrender,* pp. 200-1.
39. *Ibid.,* ch. 8.

from the garden; the people of Noah's day learned it; and so did Pharaoh, though only in his last minutes in a watery grave. God cuts off the leaven of sin in history, so that the leaven of righteousness can develop and become the dominant cultural force.

The biblical concept of social change is therefore grounded in the doctrines of creation, ethical rebellion, redemption, dominion, and final judgment. In short, the Bible teaches a doctrine of *linear time*. We are both pushed and pulled through time, and not by impersonal forces, but by a personal God. God's declared and inescapable future draws us through present history, but always by way of the past. What has gone before has its influence over us, but so also does all that is yet to come. The link between past and future is *responsible decision-making*, primarily by God and secondarily by men.

The Exodus was a discontinuous event, yet the covenantal life of Israel was to be renewed annually by a continuing series of Passover meals down through the ages. The great discontinuous event (for it is essentially one event) of the death and resurrection of Jesus Christ took place once and only once, yet the Communion meals that announce His definitive triumph over death and evil are to be continually celebrated by His people through the ages. In short, a definitive and completed past event — a discontinuity — is to be celebrated continuously through history, for it points to *a definitive final event in the future:* the final judgment. This next great discontinuity becomes the foundation of the great future continuity: the New Heavens and New Earth (Rev. 21, 22).

History is therefore equally influenced both by discontinuities and continuities, the "one great event" and the "many little events." History is simultaneously one and many. In this sense, history reflects the being of God, which is simultaneously one and many. But above all, *historical change is personal:* God proposes, God disposes, and men are fully responsible (Rom. 9:10-24).

In a world of cosmic personalism, the "great men" theory of history is valid. Great men do produce historical discontinuities that are crucial. But they make these changes within a framework of historical continuity. They become crucial as pivotal characters precisely because there is a broad historical milieu which is ready to be pivoted. The "great man" is nothing without the "little men," past and present, who have participated in the development of the historical setting that at last makes a radical break with the past.

The law of God is one important aspect of historical continuity.

It is man's tool of dominion, and the measure by which man is either blessed or judged. It speaks to men in all eras because man is still made in God's image in all eras. Thus, it true, as the French proverb says, that "the more things change, the more they stay the same." It is also true that as things stay the same — man's creaturehood, God's law — the more things are able to change.

The radical discontinuity in a person's individual life is *ethical:* from death unto life, from the old creature to the new creature, from condemnation to blessing, from rebellion to obedience, from covenant-breaking to covenant-keeping. Without this discontinuity, every man stands condemned by the original discontinuity of Adam's ethical rebellion. Adam inaugurated a continuity of death by his act of rebellion. The *continuity of spiritual death* will otherwise prevail in each person's life apart from the discontinuity of regeneration.

The discontinuity of regeneration has been the same discontinuity which has prevailed from the day of Adam's sin. It has created a rival continuity: *the continuity of life.* This continuity has many institutional forms, but the chief one is the church. The basis of this regenerational discontinuity has always been the grace of God, which in turn is made possible by the greatest of all discontinuities: the incarnation, death, and resurrection of Jesus Christ.

As this regenerational discontinuity takes place in more and more lives, the continuity of growth in the kingdom of God is revealed. In short, a series of radical ethical discontinuities in individual lives produces Christian *cultural* and *civilizational* continuity. Biblical revival is therefore radically different from revivalism. Revivalism promotes an emotional personal break from an existing social order, but not the transformation of that order. Biblical revival is a comprehensive, all-encompassing, civilization-transforming revival.[40] It comes by means of a series of rapid multiple ethical discontinuities — *personal* ethical discontinuities — that combine to create an historic *civilizational* discontinuity. Biblical revival lays the foundation of Christian *civilization's* continuity.[41] It lays the foundation, in short, of the visible manifestation of the dominion covenant.

---

40. Gary North, "The Pressing Need for Revival," *Christian Reconstruction,* VIII (Nov./Dec. 1984).

41. Gary North, "Comprehensive Redemption: A Theology of Social Action," *The Journal of Christian Reconstruction,* VIII (Summer 1981).

13

UNCONDITIONAL SURRENDER

And Pharaoh rose up in the night, he, and all his servants, and all the Egyptians; and there was a great cry in Egypt; for there was not a house where there was not one dead. And he called for Moses and Aaron by night, and said, Rise up, and get you forth from among my people, both ye and the children of Israel; and go, serve the LORD, as ye have said. Also take your flocks and your herds, as ye have said, and be gone; and bless me also (Ex. 12:30-32).

The Pharaoh and his people had been subjected to the final humiliation, they believed. They had suffered plague after plague, and their priests had been impotent to combat them. The Pharaoh himself, the great god of Egypt, had now lost his son, heir to divinity. The gods of Egypt had been decisively defeated by the God of Moses and Aaron. Surely their defeat was total. The Israelites had won.

The Israelites then took their belongings, packed them up, and made ready to depart. They collected the tribute of the Egyptians, who pressed them to leave. The tribute money was paid; restitution was made. The slaves were now officially free men. They had been returned to *bondage under God,* the basis of human freedom.

This capitulation on the part of Pharaoh was not to last long. His defeat was not yet total. He still had his life, his army, his chariots, and his authority. Egypt still had sovereignty over the land; possibly Egypt still maintained considerable sovereignty in Canaan, although Courville's dating of the Exodus, coupled with his reconstruction of the dynasties, indicates that the Pharaoh of the Exodus was much weaker than the Pharaoh of the late Twelfth Dynasty who had first enslaved the Hebrews. Pharaoh was once again about to reverse himself and seek a victory over the departing slaves, and this proved to be the final humiliation for him, and also for Egypt, which was defeated by the invading Hyksos (Amalekites) and subjugated for at least a century, and possibly four—about twice the duration of Israel's stay in Egypt.

Pharaoh knew precisely what his surrender implied. The gods of Egypt had been decisively defeated. Pharaoh had been driven to capitulate completely to the demands of Moses and Moses' God. This God had demanded that Pharaoh allow the whole nation of Israel to journey three days in order to sacrifice to Him. Now God had been able to extract His demands from Pharaoh. Pharaoh was implicitly admitting that the Egyptian theology was a myth, that there is no continuity of being between man and God, that there is a God so great and so powerful that He can extract His every demand from mighty Egypt, the center of the earth. Here was a God unlike any ever encountered by Pharaoh or his predecessors.

Pharaoh also understood what Egypt's sin against the Hebrews had been. They had enslaved Israel, breaking their treaty with Israel and Israel's God. They had treated Israel as a concubine, a slave wife. They had stolen Israel's dowry, the land of Goshen. There was restitution to pay. Pharaoh, however, did not want to pay all that he owed. He wanted one last admission on the part of the Hebrews that he was not really guilty. He wanted Moses to bless him.

How could this man have hoped for one moment that the God of Israel might bless him? How could he have imagined that God would regard him as anything but a lawless rebel? Was Pharaoh at last asking for mercy? Was he at last humbling himself before the God of the Israelites? Was his request for a blessing a sign of his repentance? The answer is unconditionally *no* to all these questions. What was Pharaoh really asking for? He was asking for *God's seal of approval* on his actions as a monarch, the master of Egypt. He was asking for God's sanction as a *lawful* former master of Israel. He was trying to justify his tyranny and his continual lying. He was trying to cover himself with the protecting law of God, but without humbling himself before that law. He was trying to get God to acknowledge publicly that Pharaoh's acts of charity—which were in fact tribute payments extracted by God's awesome power—entitled him to God's protection.

The Year of Release

The law of God respecting Hebrew slaves placed specific requirements on the Hebrew masters. Pharaoh must have understood the basic principle of lawful slave ownership. "And if thy brother, an

Hebrew man, or an Hebrew woman, be sold unto thee, and serve thee six years; then in the seventh year thou shalt let him go free from thee. And when thou sendest him out free from thee, thou shalt not let him go away empty. Thou shalt furnish him liberally out of thy flock, and out of thy floor, and out of thy winepress: of that wherewith the LORD thy God hath blessed thee thou shalt give unto him" (Deut. 15:12-14). It is revealing that the justification of this law was the bondage they had experienced in Egypt: "And thou shalt remember that thou wast a bondman in the land of Egypt, and the LORD thy God redeemed thee: therefore I command thee this thing today" (Deut. 15:15).

Pharaoh wanted to be recognized as a lawful master, for he was giving liberally of Egypt's wealth. Was he not treating the Hebrews honestly, as a brother might treat them? In fact, it was God's responsibility to bless him, for he was adhering to the law: "It shall not seem hard unto thee, when thou sendest him away free from thee: for he hath been worth a double hired servant to thee, in serving thee six years: and the LORD thy God shall bless thee in all that thou doest" (Deut. 15:18). The blessing, Pharaoh insisted. Where is the blessing?

Pharaoh the slavemaster, Pharaoh the kidnapper, Pharaoh the treaty-breaker, Pharaoh the slave-wife-divorcer, and Pharaoh the divine ruler was once again demanding to be recognized as a sovereign. He was arguing that he and his predecessors had possessed the right to violate all of the laws concerning lawful servitude, enslaving the Israelites unlawfully, just as surely as Potiphar threw Joseph into prison unlawfully. He had conducted himself lawfully, he implied, and now his payment to the Israelites testified, he wanted God to admit, to his position as a covenant-keeper. Facing a victorious slave population and their victorious God, Pharaoh wanted to be justified by works: his liberality in giving the Hebrews their seventh-year payment. This was not tribute. This was not restitution. This was not the restoration of the stolen dowry. This was simply lawful payment for lawful slaveowning, which had been conducted by a well-meaning brother in the faith. He wanted all the promised benefits of the law, the blessing in "all that thou doest," in return for this final payment to Israel. If he could get God's blessing, his payment would wipe the slate clean. God would be testifying to the legitimacy of Egypt's past rule over His people.

Pharaoh was not offering unconditional surrender to God. Once again, he was bargaining with God. This time, he used the law of God to try to justify his actions. Instead of flatly denying the right of Israel to sacrifice to God, or denying Israel the right to take along wives, or children, or cattle, he was now denying the legitimacy of any judicial case that God might bring against him as a rebellious, law-denying sovereign. He was asking God to sanction all of his past transgressions, including his unwillingness to grant the Hebrews the right to worship their God. But if these earlier transgressions were not really illegitimate, then God would have to sanction Pharaoh's original argument, namely, that he had been a lawful sovereign during the period of the subjugation. In fact, he was asking for God's sanction on the whole era of enslavement. He wanted his blessing; he was paying for it "fair and square." God *owed* him this blessing.

God did not grant him a blessing. What Pharaoh was paying was restitution, and he was paying it under extreme duress. He would gain no blessing from God; he would have no stamp of approval on his actions as a self-proclaimed divine monarch. He was not going to be able to buy his way out of judgment. He still had not recognized the nature of the God he was dealing with.

God warned Moses as they were leaving Egypt: "For Pharaoh will say of the children of Israel, They are entangled in the land, the wilderness hath shut them in. And I will harden Pharaoh's heart, that he shall follow after them; and I will be honoured upon Pharaoh, and upon all his host; that the Egyptians may know that I am the LORD. And they did so. And it was told the king of Egypt that the people fled: and the heart of Pharaoh and of his servants was turned against the people, and they said, Why have we done this, that we have let Israel go from serving us?" (Ex. 14:3-5).[1] It is clear that Pharaoh covenantally represented his subordinates well. The Egyptians were not innocent victims of a misguided leader who did not represent them ethically and spiritually. They advised him to pursue the fleeing Hebrews. They had not learned, and they had not humbled themselves before God for their generations of sinful dealing with the Israelites. They had not yet received God's final verdict on the assertion of Egypt's continuity-of-being theology. They had

---

1. The phrase, "entangled in the land," is expressive of the labyrinth concept which dominated Egyptian and ancient pagan thought. The Hebrews' wandering in the wilderness did become an entanglement—an ethical entanglement, rather than a physical entanglement. On the labyrinth, see Appendix C: "The Labyrinth and the Garden."

not yet surrendered unconditionally.

Dominion and Surrender: Unconditional but Progressive

God requires unconditional surrender from mankind. He does not offer terms of permanent peace on anything other than full, unconditional surrender.[2] God's dealings with the Egyptians and the Canaanites were about to demonstrate, for all the world to see, just how unconditional His terms of surrender are. Egypt faced at least a century of submission to foreign rulers, and most of the cities of Canaan faced absolute annihilation. The Canaanites understood this when Israel crossed the Red Sea, as Rahab told the spies (Josh. 2:9-11). Men must submit themselves to God as their lawful, absolute master, or else they perish. The terms of surrender are stated in His covenant of law: ethical perfection.[3] However, since no one except Jesus Christ is perfect before God, a sacrifice has been prepared, so that those relying on it might be justified by God and adopted back into God's family (Rom. 8:29-30; Eph. 1:4-5). The passage of His people out of bondage and through the Red Sea was symbolic of the salvation offered by God to His people. The failure of the Egyptians to prevent their escape testified to Canaan and to all the nations of the futility of challenging God by challenging God's people.

Dominion comes through adherence to the terms of God's covenant of peace. Pharaoh attempted to achieve dominion over Israel by defying God and denying the terms of unconditional surrender. He tried to buy

---

2. Gary North, *Unconditional Surrender: God's Program for Victory* (2nd ed.; Tyler, Texas: Geneva Divinity School Press, 1983).

3. It is misleading to redefine the Bible's definition of ethical perfection to mean simply spiritual maturity. Maturity implies ethical progress through time, and progress implies movement toward a fixed ethical standard. This standard is perfection. The perfection of the Bible is *definitive* as well as *progressive*. It is important to consider usage when we read that Noah was perfect (Gen. 6:9), or most notably of all, that Job was perfect and upright (Job. 1:1). The Bible does not teach perfectionism — that men can attain ethical perfection in time and on earth. But it does teach that Jesus Christ did attain ethical perfection in time and on earth. Christ's perfect conformity to the law of God, in time and on earth, is the foundation of the regenerate person's *definitive sanctification,* as well as his *progressive sanctification.* On this point, see North, *Unconditional Surrender,* pp. 43-47. Any discussion of perfection as either exclusively definitive or exclusively progressive is incomplete. On the heresy of perfectionism, see B. B. Warfield, *Perfectionism,* either the abridged one-volume version published by Presbyterian and Reformed (1954) or the two-volume set published originally by Oxford University Press in 1931, and reprinted in 1981 by Baker Book House, Grand Rapids, Michigan.

God's acceptance by offering tribute money to the Hebrews, but also by implying that this was nothing more than a lawful payment, voluntarily given to lawfully enslaved brothers. Pharaoh wanted God's blessing on Egypt's statist order, for he still believed that He was the divine-human link. Not so, God declared. There would be no blessing on the terms laid down by Pharaoh. Pharaoh once again failed to gain any sort of compromise from God. The God of Israel was implacable except to those who acknowledged His lawful authority as a true slave-master. When Israel later refused to acknowledge this from time to time, God gave them into the hands of other slave-masters, like the archetypal slave-masters of Egypt. Pharaoh could not obtain what Israel, God's own people, could never obtain: an admission from God of the legitimacy of partial surrender to His authority.

God's requirement of unconditional surrender is *ethical.* "And when Abram was ninety years old and nine, the LORD appeared to Abram, and said unto him, I am the Almighty God; walk before me, and be thou perfect" (Gen. 17:1). "Thou shalt be perfect with the LORD thy God" (Deut. 18:13). "Be ye therefore perfect, even as your Father which is in heaven is perfect" (Matt. 5:48). The standard of perfection is the standard met by Jesus Christ and imputed to His people by grace (Rom. 5:13-19). There can be no compromise here: perfection means *definitive perfection.*[4]

What about *progressive perfection,* or the process of spiritual maturation? God, by His grace, honors this process. The terms of the covenant are unquestionably *conditional:* if men do *this,* then God will give *that.* He honors the terms of His covenant, not because men have performed innately righteous acts perfectly, but because Jesus Christ did, and by seeking to imitate Christ, and Christ's perfect humanity (but not His divinity), men become the recipients of God's blessings, in time and on earth. Covenant-keeping men cannot command God's blessings in the way that a magician thinks he can command blessings from occult forces, namely, on the basis of some precisely performed ritual. God is not bound by some autonomous cosmic order to respond automatically to the requests of men, including covenant-keeping men. Whatever men receive from God is by God's grace, since fallen men cannot claim to be in absolute and unconditional subordination to God, that is, totally righteous. But

---

4. See footnote #3.

God's moral universe is orderly (common grace), so there are cause-and-effect relationships between righteousness (covenant-keeping) and prosperity. This orderliness is no less a matter of grace than God's imputation of Christ's perfect righteousness to His people. It is a world-ordering grace.

Terms of Surrender

God instructed Israel to destroy utterly the Canaanites (Deut. 7:16-24). It was failure on Israel's part that resulted in the failure of their mission (Jud. 1:21-36). They did not utterly destroy the cities of Canaan. Why was this total destruction required by God? Because God was establishing a new base of operations for Israel, one which was to have been unpolluted by foreign gods. Once established in the land, however, the Israelites were not to demand the unconditional and immediate surrender of every pagan nation. They were to offer *terms of peace*, which might involve perpetual servitude, to nations far away from Canaan (Deut. 20:10-15). Furthermore, Israel was not supposed to have a standing army, meaning a king who multiplies horses, which are too easily used in offensive military operations (Deut. 17:16). Conquest was by means of God's word, as Jonah the prophet was instructed to deliver to Nineveh. The "clean sweep" in Canaan was unique in Israel's history, and even here, the terms of God's unconditional surrender were not successfully imposed, for these terms required totally faithful servants. The imposition of the terms of unconditional surrender by God's people demanded *unconditional faithfulness* on their part. They failed.

Christ, however, was unconditionally faithful to God, and therefore He was able to impose these terms on Satan at the cross. *The extension of His terms of surrender is what the New Testament era is all about.* The steady encroaching on Satan's fallen kingdom is what the *preaching of the gospel* and the *establishment of Christian institutions,* governed by God's law, are intended to accomplish. God's terms are still unconditional; men must surrender totally to God, either before they die (or, in the case of the final generation, before Christ comes in judgment), or else after they die (or after Christ comes in judgment). Eventually, all mankind will surrender unconditionally. "Wherefore God also hath highly exalted him, and given him a name which is above every name, that at the name of Jesus every knee should bow, of things in heaven, and things in earth, and things under the earth; and that every tongue should confess that Jesus

Christ is Lord, to the glory of God the Father" (Phil. 2:9-11). In time and on earth, however, not every knee will bow, and among those who formally bow themselves before Christ, not every heart will bow. The principle of unconditional surrender is nonetheless valid even before the final judgment. It will not be *consummately* extended in history by fallen men, but as the followers of Christ progressively conform themselves to Christ's image, to a greater and greater extent, the preaching of the gospel and the construction of institutions based on the full application of biblical law will extend Christ's kingdom: *progressive* unconditional surrender, the working out in history of the *definitive* unconditional surrender of Jesus Christ to God the Father.

Pharaoh's Negotiations

It is part of Satan's imitation kingdom that he, too, requires unconditional surrender. He wants men to bow to him and worship him, which is what he demanded of Jesus in the wilderness (Matt. 4:9). Pharaoh seemed to compromise with Moses, but at no stage was he asking for anything less than unconditional surrender *from* God, for Pharaoh asked God to sanction the idea that Pharaoh had some trace of divinity in him, that he represented true divinity in the continuity of being between God and man. God refused to compromise, for anything less than total sovereignty on His part is a denial of who He is and what He is. Satan wants "just a speck" of sovereignty, so that he can successfully deny that God is who God says that He is. This is not unconditional surrender to God, for it requires that God deny Himself. In effect, it would be the unconditional surrender of God to Satan, for by having testified falsely concerning both Satan and Himself, God would thereby have sinned against Satan. He would have borne false witness concerning the nature of divinity and false witness against His maligned (not malignant) neighbor. False testimony concerning the nature of God is a capital offense. This challenge to the validity of God's self-testimony was the very heart of Satan's temptation of Adam and Eve: an assertion that God had testified falsely concerning God, man, and reality.[5]

After Pharaoh finally allowed the Hebrews to depart in total

---

5. Gary North, "Witnesses and Judges," *Biblical Economics Today,* VI (Aug./Sept. 1983). I intend to reprint this as Appendix E of *The Dominion Covenant: Genesis* when it goes into its second edition.

triumph, without maintaining a shred of original sovereignty for himself or the Egyptian State, he raced after the Hebrews in a rage. Why had he let them go? Didn't they know who he was? Didn't they know what Egypt was? Didn't they know that he represented man's divinity in this world? He would show them. He would bring them low. Every Hebrew knee would bow to him, for they had not allowed him even a trace of sovereignty. They had wanted him to surrender unconditionally to their God (and therefore to them, given the Egyptian theology of the continuity of being), although God allowed him to keep his kingdom. But it was the principle of the thing that concerned him. If they were going to demand unconditional surrender by him to their God in principle, then he was going to demand visible unconditional surrender from them once again. He was going to drag them back. They would not go free. They would not sacrifice to any God who would not acknowledge at least a degree of independent sovereignty to Pharaoh and his State. It would be a fight to the finish. It turned out to be just exactly that.

Pagan kingdoms implicitly want unconditional surrender from their enemies. Lawless men want the same. As men grow more arrogant, as they attempt to divorce themselves from the concept of lawful dominion under the restraints of God's law, they adopt policies of unconditional surrender, in time and on earth. They launch sneak attacks, in violation of Deuteronomy 20:10-15, as the Japanese did against the Russians in 1904 and as they did against the United States in December of 1941. Pagan governments demand unconditional surrender, as the Allies demanded from Germany, Italy, and Japan in the Second World War.[6] In short, they want "a fight to the finish," just as Pharaoh wanted when he pursued the Israelites into the Red Sea. They seek to be free of the restraints of God's law in order to impose a law-order which violates God's law.

Conclusion

Unconditional surrender is an inescapable concept: the question is, "Surrender to whom?" Will it be surrender to God, progressively through time, until the final day of judgment, when surrender will be absolute and unconditional? Or will it be surrender to Satan's kingdom, in time and on earth, through Satan's radical breaks in the

---

6. Ann Armstrong, *Unconditional Surrender* (Brunswick, New Jersey: Rutgers University Press, 1961).

continuities of history, the wars and conquests of his earthly kingdoms, all of which are at war with God's kingdom and His law? Satan wants a final break with history *in* history, a radical break with the sovereignty of God. He wants the abolition of history, for history testifies to his failure, in time, at the cross. He wants the unconditional surrender of time to revolutionary chaos or static timelessness, where the progressive, linear extension of God's kingdom will be overcome. Satan imitates God by demanding total, immediate, temporal surrender.

The argument favoring discontinuous breaks in history was valid when the static kingdoms of the ancient world faced the discontinuity represented by Israel. But now the church is bringing God's peace treaty to the nations. There are minor discontinuities, as nations rise and fall, but the next biblically significant discontinuity is Satan's final rebellion and Christ's return in judgment. At that point, unconditional surrender will be required. The kingdom will be delivered, in completed form, to the Father (I Cor. 15:24). The history of fallen, rebellious man will end. Until that time, it is the *continuity of God's progressive dominion,* through the preaching of the gospel and the construction of institutions imposing God's law, which is *the criterion of historical change.* It is the steady extension of Christ's kingdom, not the desperate discontinuities of Satan's kingdoms, with their treaties of *immediate* unconditional surrender, which is the basis of historical change.

There will be one final, all-out attempt by Satan to avoid total surrender. Then will come the return of Christ in full power and judgment. It will be the death knell of Satan's kingdom, in time, on earth, and in eternity (Rev. 20). All satanic imitations of this great discontinuity of God's final judgment will wind up as Pharaoh's attempted discontinuity in covenantal history wound up: buried in the depths of the sea. *Satan's theology is the religion of revolution, and it cannot survive the steady, implacable onslaught of God's theology of progressive dominion.* It is not the minor discontinuities of history that serve as our criteria of victory, but the steadiness of the word of God: "But the word of the LORD was unto them precept upon precept, precept upon precept; line upon line, line upon line; here a little, and there a little; that they might go, and fall backward, and be broken, and snared, and taken" (Isa. 28:13). God used discontinuities in history to smash the kingdoms of the ancient world: "I will overturn, overturn, overturn it: and it shall be no more, until he come whose right it is; and I will give it to him" (Ezk. 21:27). Give what? The diadem of power (Ezk. 21:26). God still overturns Satan's kingdoms, but by the steady expansion of the gospel age, the progressive dominion of God's law and God's people, in time and on earth. It is our task to lay the groundwork for a new kingdom, built on the foundation of God's law — which is to govern every human institution — by God's grace, which is applied to the heart of every Christian (Heb. 8:7-13). Christianity does not preach a religion of social revolution, but a religion of ethical regeneration, restitution, and repentance.

While Christianity preaches the tactics of social continuity during its "minority religion" phase — go the extra mile with your enemy, turn the other cheek — it nevertheless is a religion of social transformation. The Christian revolution takes place in the hearts and minds of men — the place where all revolutions begin. The opponents of Christianity recognize that Christianity is indeed a religion of total transformation. To them, the ethical discontinuity between the Old Adam and the New Adam represents a revolutionary doctrine. It threatens them with the destruction of their anti-Christian civilization.

The Roman emperors launched a series of bloody, though intermittent, persecutions against the early church because they recognized the all-or-nothing nature of the confrontation. It was either Christ or Caesar. The Roman State was quite willing to tolerate any religion which acknowledged the divinity (or genius) of the emperor. Christians refused. They paid a heavy price. But Rome paid a heavier price in the long run. So did Egypt.

14

THE RULE OF LAW

And when a stranger shall sojourn with thee, and will keep the passover to the LORD, let all his males be circumcised, and then let him come near and keep it; and he shall be as one that is born in the land: for no uncircumcised person shall eat thereof. One law shall be to him that is homeborn, and unto the stranger that sojourneth among you (Ex. 12:48-49).

The Passover was closed to outsiders who had not been circumcised. A man's slave, if he had been purchased with money and subsequently circumcised, had the obligation of participating in the Passover rites (Ex. 12:44). He had a place in the family and was under the sovereignty of God, through his master. The mark of subordination was in his flesh. In contrast, the foreigner and hired servant were excluded from the Passover, since they had not visibly (physiologically) humbled themselves before God, and were therefore not part of the covenant: "There shall no stranger eat thereof: But every man's servant that is bought for money, when thou hast circumcised him, then shall he eat thereof. A foreigner and an hired servant shall not eat thereof" (12:43b-45). No foreigner could eat leavened bread anywhere in Israel during Passover week (12:19). Any stranger who wished to participate in the Passover could do so, if he and all the males of his household were circumcised (12:48). This indicated his *subordination* to God and His *dominion* in the name of God over his own household. A circumcised stranger was to be treated as one born in the land, although it is unclear how he could ever have owned land permanently because of the redistribution back to the original family owners which was required at the Jubilee year (Lev. 25:10).

The rites of circumcision and Passover were simple enough. Biblical law in Israel was public. In fact, it had to be read in its en-

188

tirety every seventh year in front of the assembled nation:

And Moses wrote this law, and delivered it unto the priests the sons of Levi, which bare the ark of the covenant of the LORD, and unto all the elders of Israel. And Moses commanded them, saying, At the end of every seven years, in the solemnity of the year of release, in the feast of tabernacles, When all Israel is come to appear before the LORD thy God in the place which he shall choose, thou shalt read this law before all Israel in their hearing. Gather the people together, men, and women, and children, and thy stranger that is within thy gates, that they may hear, and that they may learn, and fear the LORD your God, and observe to do all the words of this law: And that their children, which have not known any thing, may hear, and learn to fear the LORD your God, as long as ye live in the land whither ye go over Jordan to possess it (Deut. 31:9-13).

The God of the Old Testament is the God of the New Testament. He is the Creator. As such, He owns the whole world. He commands respect from all men, and the terms of His law are binding on all men. The stranger within Israel's gates, no less than the priests, had to honor the law. There was no mystery about the law. While some things are known only to God (Deut. 29:29), these secret matters are as closed to the priests as to the stranger. Public law was in principle open to every resident in the land of Israel. The law had to be an open book for everyone to understand and observe, including the children of strangers (Deut. 31:13). The Hebrews were not to make a mistake concerning the universality of God's rule. He is not confined to one city, one nation, or one people. His rule is universal. So is His law, revealed to men in the Bible, which is the judicial manifestation of His sovereign rule.

Access to Citizenship

God's law for Israel did not permit every circumcised stranger to become a full citizen immediately upon being circumcised. There were exceptions. Certain nations had been especially evil in their treatment of Israel, indicating a cultural perverseness that might take several generations to overcome in the lives of family members. The strong bond of the family covenant was acknowledged. It had taken the death of Israel's Exodus generation to cleanse their families of the cultural legacy of Egypt; such a legacy remained a potential threat to Israel from newly circumcised pagans. Thus, it took three generations for circumcised Egyptians and Edomites (the heirs of

Esau) to become full citizens (Deut. 23:7-8). Second, it took ten generations for Ammonites and Moabites:

An Ammonite or Moabite shall not enter into the congregation of the LORD; even to their tenth generation shall they not enter into the congregation of the LORD for ever. Because they met you not with bread and with water in the way, when ye came forth out of Egypt; and because they hired against thee Balaam the son of Beor of Pethor of Mesopotamia, to curse thee (Deut. 23:3-4).[1]

The language here is incomplete. We need other passages to help us understand. Does it say that they could become citizens in the tenth generation or does it say that they are banned forever? Was "forever" understood to mean a nearly permanent ban against them — to the tenth generation — or was it in fact permanent?

We read in Nehemiah 13: "On that day they read in the book of Moses in the audience of the people; and therein was found written, that the Ammonite and the Moabite should not come into the congregation of God for ever; because they met not the children of Israel with bread and with water, but hired Balaam against them, that he should curse them: howbeit our God turned the curse into a blessing" (vv. 1-2). I believe that this use of "forever" was figurative; it meant ten generations. We are given an analogous prohibition in the case of bastardy. Bastards were also prevented from entering the congregation of the Lord to the tenth generation (Deut. 23:2). The most conspicuous example of the enforcement of this restriction is seen in the adultery of Judah and Tamar (Gen. 38), which produced Pharez and Zarah. They were bastards in terms of God's law. David was the tenth in the line of those born of Pharez.[2] He became king.

The Case of Ruth

Despite this prohibition against Moabites, Ruth became a respected member of the covenant, though not a full citizen; she was a woman of humility and faithfulness. She even became the great-grandmother of David and an ancestor of Jesus Christ (Matt. 1:5). The grace of God is our standard; full ethical conformity to God's

---

1. James Jordan points out that the sin of Sodom was inhospitableness (Gen. 18:1-8; 19:1-11). This was also the sin of Moab and Ammon, who came out of Sodom through their grandfather Lot (Gen. 19:20-38; Zeph. 2:8-9).

2. The generations were: Pharez, Hezron, Ram, Amminidab, Nahshon, Salmon, Boaz, Obed, Jesse, and David (Ruth 4:18-22).

covenant, through faith in God's grace (Hab. 2:4), overcomes the general restrictions against the greatest sinners. Ruth's covenant was secured in a three-fold manner: through her marriage to her first husband, a Hebrew; through her faithfulness to her mother-in-law, Naomi; and through her marriage to her second husband, Boaz. She was in subjection to him, as she had been in subjection to the other two. Her children were counted as Israelites, although not as members of the congregation, because of Boaz's position as an heir of Pharez.[3] But her great grandson — the third generation — became the king; therefore, any general prohibition on her heirs from serving as judges to the tenth generation was overcome by her marriage to Boaz.

It might be argued that Ruth is not an adequate example, since as a woman, she could never have exercised political or judicial office. Possibly; but the ban would have applied to her male heirs. Furthermore, it is instructive that this was a marriage between a politically restricted Moabite and an equally restricted heir of a bastard. It was part of the most important covenantal line in Israel — indeed, the most important in all history. It produced David, and it eventually produced Jesus (Matt. 1; Luke 3). Therefore, the crucial issue is ethics, not genetics. The covenant is fundamentally ethical; those under the ban were under it because of the transgressions of their forebears. But this ban could be overcome through righteousness over time. *Time is a means of testing covenantal faithfulness and external performance across generations.*

Neither genetics nor time was ever determinative in the covenant structure. The covenantal grafting in of the gentiles through faith in Christ alienated the Pharisees who failed to understand this fundamental principle of the covenant (Rom. 11). The administrative period of ethical testing — even ten generations — had its limits. "Forever" thus was figurative in the case of citizenship for Moabites and Ammonites.

Covenantal Citizenship

The concept of citizenship in the Old Testament was unquestionably covenantal. This is because God had established the nation

---

3. A member of the congregation could serve as a judge or elder. It is fitting that the restoration of this family, through God's grace, came with David, the most powerful ruler in Israel's history. This tends to support the idea that being cut off from the congregation did not mean religious excommunication — prohibiting participation in the rituals of Israel — but rather separation from rulership, meaning separation from dominion through service in the civil government.

by His sovereign act of grace, and had placed all the Israelites under the rule of His covenantal law-order. Covenants are always *restrictive;* they exclude even as they include. The civil covenant is also restrictive. Rushdoony comments on Israel's civil covenant: "God as the source of law established the covenant as the principle of citizenship. Only those within the covenant are citizens. The covenant is restrictive in terms of God's law; it is also restrictive in terms of a bar against membership, which appears specifically, naming certain kinds of groups of persons. This aspect of the law is usually overlooked, because it is embarrassing to modern man. It needs therefore especial attention. In Deuteronomy 23:1-2, eunuchs are barred from citizenship; bastards are banned through the tenth generation. Ammonites and Moabites were banned through the tenth generation, or they are totally excluded, depending on the reading of the text. Edomites and Egyptians were eligible for citizenship 'in their third generation'; the implication is that they are eligible after three generations of faith, after demonstrating for three generations that they believed in the covenant God and abided by His law. The throne being the ark in the tabernacle, and the tabernacle being also the central place of atonement, membership in the nation-civil and in the nation-ecclesiastical were one and the same."

There is therefore a covenantal relationship between the kind of god a society believes in and the kind of citizenship which the society creates. The foundation of both the theological covenant and citizenship is *faith.* "Citizenship rested on faith. Apostasy was treason. The believing alien had some kind of access to the sanctuary (II Chron. 6:32-33), at least for prayer, but this act did not give him citizenship. The alien[s]—Egyptian, Babylonian, Ethiopian, Philistine, Phoenician, and any others—could be citizens of the true or heavenly Zion, the city of God (Ps. 87), but the local Zion, Israel, was not to admit the banned groups except on God's terms. . . . Thus, it would appear from the evidence of the law that, *first,* a restrictive membership or citizenship was a part of the practice of Israel by law. . . . *Second,* the predominant fact in Israel was one law for all, irrespective of faith or national origin, that is, the absolute requirement of justice for all without respect of persons."[4] Non-citizens were protected by God's law. This meant *protection from citizens* who might use their possession of citizenship as a means of exploiting strangers. It there-

---

4. R. J. Rushdoony, *The Institutes of Biblical Law* (Nutley, New Jersey: Craig Press, 1973), pp. 99, 100.

fore meant *protection from oppression by the civil government.*

The legal protections ("rights") granted by biblical law to non-citizens were so comprehensive that it is difficult in retrospect to specify exactly what privileges citizens enjoyed that non-citizens did not. One possibility: not being members of any tribe, the non-citizens could not have served as judges. Foreigners were not automatically prohibited from serving in Israel's army, for David's officer, Uriah, was a Hittite, or at least his family background was Hittite (II Sam. 11:6). No privileges of citizenship are spelled out in the Old Testament that are explicitly restricted to Israelites, although there must have been such privileges, since Deuteronomy 23:3-8 provides a list of those nations whose members are prohibited from joining the "assembly" (civil, not ecclesiastical). A circumcised stranger could, however, participate in the Passover (Ex. 12:48). So it is not a simple matter to determine just what protections were not available to strangers.

Differing Applications

There were a few cases where the law was *applied* differently between strangers and Israelites. Two of these dealt with slavery. *First,* a stranger could become a *debt slave* as a result of some economic crisis. It was not legal for a Hebrew to make interest-bearing loans to a fellow Hebrew who was in need of a charitable loan. "Thou shalt not lend upon usury to thy brother; usury of money, usury of victuals, usury of any thing that is lent upon usury. Unto a stranger thou mayest lend upon usury; but unto thy brother thou shalt not lend upon usury" (Deut. 23:19-20a). It must be understood that this prohibition was against interest-bearing loans to the needy poor, not against loans for business endeavors in which the lender shared some of the risk: "If thou lend money to any of my people that is poor by thee, thou shalt not be to him as an usurer, neither shalt thou lay upon him usury" (Ex. 22:25). Strangers, however, were regarded as *slaves to foreign gods,* and therefore as *slaves to sin.* The Hebrew was allowed to charge them interest. The Hebrew also owed his tithes and offerings to God, including God's portion of any interest payments received, so the stranger in this way paid at least a portion of what he owed to God. *Second,* heathens could be purchased as *permanent slaves* (Lev. 25:44-46), or taken as captives in war (Num. 31:9; Deut. 21:10-14). The Gibeonites, by tricking the Israelites, became permanent servants to Israel (Josh. 9). A Hebrew bondservant went free in the jubilee year (Lev. 25:39-41). The stranger did not go free; he and his children remained in the Hebrew family as permanent capital assets (Lev. 25:45-46).

Third, strangers could worship foreign gods in the privacy of their households (though not publicly), but it was a capital offense for a Hebrew to do so (Deut. 13; 17:2-7). Apostasy—breaking the theological covenant—was a capital offense, but being unconverted wasn't. *Fourth,* strangers could legally eat the meat of beasts that died naturally; Hebrews couldn't (Deut. 14:21).

What could the purposes of the exceptions have been in the case of slavery? James Jordan's analysis is illuminating: "Why does the law differ in regard to the unbelievers? Is this *merely* to symbolize the difference between a covenant people and those outside it? Not so. As the earlier chapters of this monograph demonstrated, the psychology of the unregenerated man is radically different from that of the regenerate man at the most basic level. The unbeliever is by nature an anti-dominion man, and thus lazy and unproductive. He is suicidal as well, and a rebel against all authority. He is a murderer. The Bible is realistic about this, and makes slavery a provision for the unbeliever, both for his own protection and wellbeing, and for the protection of society. Additionally, the enslavement of the heathen is, as has been noted before, an excellent means of evangelization and acculturation. There is to be one law and one standard for the believer and unbeliever (Lev. 24:22); the differences in application of this one law are due to the differing psychological situations of the believer and the unbeliever."[5]

God requires one legal standard, for all men are held accountable to Him. His law specifies *differences in application,* and these differences must be respected. Nevertheless, the law did not give the Hebrew rulers the right to multiply exceptions to a straightforward application of the law. Debt and slavery were the main exceptions with respect to strangers in the land, plus the privileges and duties of citizenship, most notably (and possibly only) serving as a judge.

No Respect for Persons

Again and again in the books of the law, the warning and reminder is given by God concerning the rule of law for strangers: "I am the LORD your God, which brought you forth out of the land of

---

5. James Jordan, Slavery in Biblical Perspective (Master's Thesis, Westminster Theological Seminary, Philadelphia, 1980), pp. 95-96.

Egypt, to give you the land of Canaan, and to be your God" (Lev. 25:38). He redeemed (bought back) Israel from oppression; therefore, Israel is not to become an oppressor. "Thou shalt neither vex a stranger, nor oppress him: for ye were strangers in the land of Egypt" (Ex. 22:21; cf. 23:9; Lev. 19:33; and Deut. 10:19). The prophets also repeated this warning against oppressing strangers (Jer. 7:6-7; Zech. 7:10; Mal. 3:5).[6]

The rule of law is established unmistakably: "Ye shall not respect persons in judgment; but ye shall hear the small as well as the great; ye shall not be afraid of the face of man; for the judgment is God's: and the cause that is too hard for you, bring it unto me, and I will hear it" (Deut. 1:17). This was Moses' recapitulation of his decision to create a hierarchy of judges over Israel (Ex. 18). The judges must not respect persons, for they act as God's agents. God does not respect persons: "For the LORD your God is God of gods, and Lord of lords, a great God, a mighty, and a terrible [God], which regardeth not persons, nor taketh reward. He doth execute the judgment of the fatherless and widow, and loveth the stranger, in giving him food and raiment. Love ye therefore the stranger: for ye were strangers in the land of Egypt" (Deut. 10:17-19). *This is the biblical doctrine of judicial love: we are required to render honest judgment, and to bring the rule of law over all men, including the stranger.* The very next verse tells us why we must love all men in this way: "Thou shalt fear the LORD thy God; him shalt thou serve, and to him shalt thou cleave, and swear by his name" (Deut. 10:20). Those who love God, who cleave to His name,[7] and who swear (give a binding oath) by His name, are to love His law and apply it without prejudice of persons.

---

6. One of the continuing themes in the writings of "liberation theologians" is the evil of oppression. They always equate oppression with economic oppression, and economic oppression with free market capitalism. What is important to consider here is the implicitly statist nature of oppression: Israel was oppressed in Egypt precisely because the Egyptians did not honor God's law. Hebrews are to honor God's law and enforce it throughout the land. The State is to be restrained by biblical law. This makes it very difficult for anyone to gain oppressive powers over others; potential oppressors cannot gain the co-operation of public officials in applying the State's monopoly of violence against certain economic groups or organizations. When the civil government refuses to enforce God's law on all people, the result is oppression. *The whole of the law must be enforced in order to avoid oppression.* The liberation theologians are universally unwilling to recommend that the civil government enforce the whole of Old Testament law. Thus, they are advocates of oppressing institutions.

7. The Hebrew word translated here as "cleave"—*dawbak*—means "to join to" or "cling to," the same word used in Genesis 2:24: "cleave unto his wife." It refers to a covenant.

The *universality of God's law* implies the *universal responsibility of all men to obey His law.* Both principles are based on the idea of the *total sovereignty of God.* By establishing a unified law code for all residents of Israel, God thereby announced His kingdom. No one was exempt. It was not a person's participation in family rites, as in Greece and Rome, which opened the courts of law to him — courts to which strangers could therefore not appeal with hope of receiving justice. The principle of *justice for all* is based on the principle of *God's final judgment on all.* This was seen first within the geographical confines of Israel, and all nations were to stand in awe of the legal system built on the principle of justice for all (Deut. 4:5-8). The biblical principle is clear: *one God, one law-order.* Deny the universality of a single law-order, and you thereby deny a universal God. This is precisely what ancient paganism denied.

Pagan Citizenship

One God, one law-order: here is a principle that stood in stark contrast to the law structures of the ancient world. The pagan kingdoms of the ancient world made it exceedingly difficult for foreigners to gain citizenship, for this meant the right to participate in the religious rites of the city. *Religious exclusion meant political exclusion.* It also meant exclusion from courts of law. It meant, ultimately, *exclusion from justice.* Polytheistic societies recognized the biblical principle in its reverse form: *many gods, many law-orders.* They understood that they could have no legal standing in another city's courts, for the same reason that foreigners could possess no legal standing in theirs: they worshipped different gods.

Let us consider the "democratic" city-states of the classical world, since they represent the "best case" of ancient pagan politics. Fustel de Coulanges' book, *The Ancient City* (1864), remains the classic in the field. He wrote about the link between classical (Greek and Roman) religion and politics. Religion and politics were inseparably linked. Because classical religion was essentially initiatory and mystery-oriented, politics was equally based on secrecy and participation in closed rites. Unlike the closed rite of the Passover, however, classical religion and politics were closed rites based on blood lines, meaning family lines. "As law was a part of religion, it participated in the mysterious character of all this religion of the cities. The legal formulas, like those of religion, were kept secret. They were concealed from the stranger, and even from the plebeian. This was not because the patricians had calculated that they should possess a great power in the exclusive knowledge of the law, but because the law, by its origin and nature, long appeared to be a mystery, to which one could be initiated only after having first been initiated into the national worship and the domestic worship."[8]

This meant that residence in a city was not the same as citizenship. This is a universal distinction: residency vs. citizenship. But it is possible for residents to receive the protection of civil law. This was the case in Israel, the only example in the ancient world of a political order which granted comprehensive legal protection for religious aliens. Not so in classical civilization: "To live in a city did not make one subject to its laws and place him under their protection; one had to be a citizen. The law did not exist for the slave; no more did it exist for the stranger. . . . These provisions of ancient law were perfectly logical. Law was not born of the idea of justice, but of religion, and was not conceived as going beyond it. In order that there should be a legal relation between two men, it was necessary that there should already exist a religious relation; that is to say, that they should worship at the same hearth and have the same sacrifices. When this religious community did not exist, it did not seem that there could be any legal relation. Now, neither the stranger nor the slave had any part in the religion of the city. A foreigner and a citizen might live side by side during long years, without one's thinking of the possibility of a legal relation being established between them. Law was nothing more than one phase of religion. Where there was no common religion, there was no common law."[9] In short, *many gods, many law-orders.*

Fustel had a tendency to exaggerate the impact of family religion in later Greek culture, although its influence never died out. There were important modifications in Greek political religion, especially in Athens, from the sixth century before Christ until the conquest of Greece by Macedonia, late in the fourth century, B.C. Early in the sixth century, Solon revised the laws of Athens and began to encourage immigration.[10] Foreign craftsmen were promised citizen-

---

8. Numa Denis Fustel de Coulanges, *The Ancient City: A Study on the Religion, Laws, and Institutions of Greece and Rome* (Garden City, New York: Doubleday Anchor, [1864] 1955), Bk. III, ch. XI, p. 192.

9. *Ibid.,* pp. 192-93.

10. H. D. F. Kitto, *The Greeks* (Baltimore, Maryland: Penguin, [1951] 1962), p. 100.

ship if they came to dwell permanently in Athens. Alfred Zimmern saw this as an important innovation in ancient Greece, for "the states of the Greek world had not been trained by generations of competition to regard the foreigner as a unit of labour. They were in their nature select and exclusive corporations, rigidly subdivided into lesser and still selecter circles; and there was no place in them for outsiders. Solon's policy, therefore, marks the beginning of a far-reaching change of attitude. Henceforward newcomers are no longer to be despised, as in the old days, as 'cityless vagrants without hearth-fire or lands,' but welcomed as useful comrades and helpers in the work of the community. In other words, Athens was now willing to accept new blood on its merits, quite apart from questions of religion and nationality."[11] Better put, Athens found ways to enroll skilled foreign craftsmen onto the lists of the civic religion.

Nevertheless, Athens was unique, and even this uniqueness had limits. In the law of 451-450 B.C., Pericles, who is regarded as the consummate Athenian democrat by modern scholars, had a law passed which limited citizenship for outsiders to those whose parents were both Athenians, thereby closing citizenship to outsiders, including the sons of Athenian men with foreign-born mothers.[12] Glotz's statement is representative of the Greek city-states: "Within each city aliens had only very limited rights, even if their position were established not only by law but also by a treaty, and even if they were permanently domiciled in it as metics. These principles persisted to the end; but their severity was tempered, in international and public law alike, without, however, infringing on the sovereignty of the State."[13] Foreigners could become citizens, but the practice was always rare. Women, slaves, freedmen, and foreigners were not given the rights of citizenship. Greek political religion excluded them.

Dominion, Law, and Citizenship

Why the difference in access to citizenship between Israel and classical civilization? It was the difference between metaphysical and ethical religion, between ritual religion and judicial religion, be-

---

11. Alfred E. Zimmern, *The Greek Commonwealth: Politics and Economics in Fifth-Century Athens* (Oxford: At the Clarenden Press, 1915), p. 136.

12. G. Glotz, *The Greek City and its Institutions* (New York: Barnes & Noble, [1929] 1969), p. 270.

13. *Ibid.,* p. 263.

tween power religion and dominion religion. The difference is found in the differing conceptions of man that were proclaimed by the two religions. The biblical view of mankind is simultaneously universal and particular (both one and many). There is *unity:* all men are made in God's image, and all men (apart from grace) are ethical rebels, disinherited by their Father in heaven. There is also *disunity:* some men have been regenerated and put under *a new household covenant,* the household of faith, God's household. In contrast to pagan religion, the meaningful differentiation is not between those born in one geographical area versus those born in another. The differentiation is between birth in Adam's flesh versus moral rebirth by God's spirit. It is the "old birth" versus the "new birth" which ultimately divides men.

There is, on the one hand, a *divisive* aspect in biblical religion, as in every religion. It is the division between saved and lost, between covenant-keepers and covenant-breakers. In short, this division is ethical, not geographical. The new creation is equally ethical, not the product of civic rituals of chaos, or the family religion of placating dead ancestors. On the other hand, there is also a *universal* aspect of biblical religion, which in turn creates a universality of biblical civic order. The link between all men, saved and lost, is the fact that all men are made in God's image, and all men have been assigned the dominion covenant (Gen. 1:26-28). This, in turn, implies the *universality of God's law,* for God's law is the primary tool of dominion. Since all men are in rebellion against God, all men need the restraint which biblical law offers. Biblical law provides social and political order. Thus, the covenantal law structure of Israel is morally binding on all men. This law-order is essentially *ethical.* All men are to live righteously and exercise dominion; therefore, all men deserve the protection of biblical civil law.

Aliens in Israel were to see the beneficial effects of the law and report back to their own nations concerning the rule of righteousness in Israel—righteousness which was not confined to citizens only. Therefore, biblical civil law was and still is to be a means of *evangelism.*

Behold, I have taught you statutes and judgments, even as the Lord my God commanded me, that ye should do so in the land whither ye go to possess it. Keep therefore and do them; for this is your wisdom and your understanding in the sight of the nations, which shall hear all these statutes, and say, Surely this great nation is a wise and understanding people. For what nation is there so great, who hath God so nigh unto them, as the LORD our God is in all things that we call upon him for? And what nation is there so great, that hath statutes and judgments so righteous as all this law, which I set before you this day? (Deut. 4:5-8).

The Medieval City: Covenantal

Max Weber, the German historian-sociologist, devoted considerable space to a study of the differences between the oriental city and the medieval city, especially the city in Northern Europe. He accepted Fustel's analysis of the clan-based ancient city. The primary difference between the two cities was the basis of citizenship: *clan* vs. *oath*. The personal covenantal oath of the individual was the basis of access to citizenship in the medieval city. Jews were excluded from citizenship, not because they were members of an outside clan, but because they could not swear allegiance to Christianity's God. "The medieval city, after all, was still a cultic association. The city church, the city saint, participation of the burgher in the Lord's Supper, the official celebrations of the church holy days—all these are obvious features of the medieval city. But the *sib* [brotherhood—G.N.] had been deprived of all ritual significance by Christianity, for by its very nature the Christian congregation was a religious association of individual believers, not a ritual association of clans."[14]

The city became the focal point of the advent of industrialism, free trade, and the accumulation of financial resources. The Western city was instrumental in the coming of capitalism, meaning rational production and distribution which is monitored by means of rational (monetary) calculation methods. The city was originally a Christian institution, a corporation based on a common oath and common law-order. It was, in short, a *covenantal association* based on a *shared faith*. This corporate faith was not clan-based but oath-based.

The Foundation of Social Order

The foundation of all social order is God. It is not the State. It is not the will of the majority. It is not the king. It is not any human in-

---

14. Max Weber, *Economy and Society: An Outline of Interpretive Sociology*, edited by Guenther Roth and Claus Wittich (New York: Bedminster Press, 1968), p. 1247. This is the English-language version of Weber's never completed and posthumously published *Wirtschaft und Gesellschaft*, 4th edition (1956). He died in 1920. This section on the city also appears in Weber, *The City*, translated and edited by Don Martindale and Gertrude Neuwirth (New York: Free Press, 1958), pp. 102-3.

stitution. Biblical law provides us with the only reliable long-term program for the establishment of true social order.

God created the universe, created man, and made man in His image. He assigned to man the tasks of dominion. Man therefore was endowed by God with the ability to interpret and classify the creation. Adam named the animals of the garden (Gen. 2:20). After man's rebellion, God gave men verbal instructions, and in our day, we possess written instructions in His word. Man, in short, has access to an *integrating principle* which links God, man, human institutions, and the creation within one ethical order. Understand: this order is *ethical;* it is not ontological. We are not unified with God's being, nor is God an aspect of the creation. But we can achieve *ethical* union with God through Jesus Christ, who is both God and a perfect man, two natures in union but without mixture in one Person. The link between God and man, between time and eternity, is Jesus Christ, and only Jesus Christ.

Biblical Law, Biblical Order

We can say with confidence that *the enforcement of biblical law provides man with the social order he requires for efficient dominion.* This efficiency is present precisely because it is in harmony with the moral law. In other words, formal rationalism and substantive rationalism are in harmony under the terms of biblical law. We can attain *economic efficiency* at the same time that we attain *valid ethical ends.* We find in God's law the link between the *letter of the law* (formal rationalism) and the *spirit of the law* (substantive rationalism). We know that the common good of mankind is promoted by biblical law, not because we claim the ability to make interpersonal comparisons of subjective utility,[15] and not because we believe that the "general will" of man is expressed by majority vote,[16] but because we have faith in the reliability of God's law to integrate each man with other men and with man's environment. The law is *designed* to fit the creation, including man's institutions. The law did not evolve, nor did man evolve. We can have confidence in biblical law, not because it has been useful *up until now* in promoting the dominion of evolving man, but because it is established by God as the tool of dominion and the

---

15. Gary North, *The Dominion Covenant: Genesis* (Tyler, Texas: Institute for Christian Economics, 1982), ch. 4.

16. Robert A. Nisbet, *Tradition and Revolt: Historical and Sociological Essays* (New York: Random House, 1968), ch. 1: "Rousseau and the Political Community."

foundation of social peace.

This perspective relieves us of the philosophical contradictions of the humanistic concept of natural rights or human rights. It shifts sovereignty back to God and away from man, whether individual man or collective mankind. Natural rights theory, like its philosophical corollary, natural law theory, cannot give us *specifics* that are supposedly agreed upon by all rational investigators (see below: "Natural Law Theory vs. Biblical Law").

T. Robert Ingram has given us a cogent summary of the problem of natural rights theory. "The Texas Right to Life Committee has a bill to put before the State Legislature in an attempt to control unlimited abortions. But this bill seeks to control the unlawful killing of unborn children on the grounds that the state exists to protect their right to life. The abortionists say they are protecting the privacy of the mother and her right to kill her unborn infant if she wants to. Whose rights prevail? There is no solution in this unlawful principle of society and government rooted in the rights of persons. There is a simple and immediately effective solution in the common law. In the language of the church centuries ago it was simply declared, 'It is unlawful to kill a man, or that which will become a man.' Abortions are punished because they are wrong. Individual rights have nothing to do with it. The law declares in statute form what is wrong and to be punished—without respect of individuals."[17] We do not need to make assumptions about the comparative rights of mother vs. child. We do not need to attempt to make interpersonal comparisons of subjective utility, mother vs. child. We simply have to acknowledge the grim reality of all abortions, namely, that in every abortion, at least half the patients die. The mother may die, but the infant virtually always dies. It is murder, and it must be put to a stop, irrespective of hypothetical human rights, irrespective of the respective subjective utilities involved, murderous mother vs. unborn child.

God's Judgment of Collectives

What the humanist always neglects to consider is the response of God to continuing public moral evil which is not suppressed by governments, including the civil government. God brings visible judg-

---

17. T. Robert Ingram, "The Common Law and the Common Good," *The Journal of Christian Reconstruction*, II (Winter 1975-76), p. 38.

ment on evil societies (Deut. 28:15-68). The refusal to recognize this fact was (and is) a major weakness in all versions of eighteenth-century and nineteenth-century classical liberalism. The liberals look only at what men do *to* other men, ignoring what evil men do *in association with* other evil men. Hayek writes concerning "victimless crimes": "Since for a case to come before a judge a dispute must have arisen, and since judges are not normally concerned with relations of command and obedience, only such actions of individuals as affect other persons, or, as they are traditionally described, actions towards other persons . . . will give rise to the formulation of legal rules. . . . At the moment we want merely to point out that actions which are clearly not of this kind, such as what a person does alone within his four walls, or even the voluntary collaboration of several persons, in a manner which clearly cannot affect or harm others, can never become the subject of rules of conduct that will concern a judge."[18] Examples of "victimless crimes" are such "capitalist acts between consenting adults" as the sale and use of hard drugs, prostitution, homosexuality, and so forth.

Such acts are assumed by classical liberals and modern libertarians to be harmless to other people; they are matters "which clearly cannot affect or harm others." Hayek is honest enough to put in this qualifying sentence: "At least where it is not believed that the whole group may be punished by a supernatural power for the sins of individuals, there can arise no such rules from the limitation of conduct towards others, and therefore from the settlement of disputes."[19] The heart of the matter is here: there *is* a supernatural God who promises the destruction of societies that permit immoral, though voluntary, acts between consenting adults. If these acts are public, or if they are contracted in a public manner (soliciting, in other words), then they should be punishable by law.

The Bible says that strangers are under the law in a biblical commonwealth. The fact that they are strangers in no way exempts them from the requirements of the law. They are a part of the social order, so they must abide by the legal foundation of that order, biblical law. The strangers have to conform to God's law. Christians have unfortunately adopted variations of Greek and Roman concepts of natural law and natural rights in order to convince the humanists, pagans,

---

18. Hayek, *Law, Legislation and Liberty*, 3 vols., *Rules and Order* (University of Chicago Press, 1973), vol. 1, p. 101.
19. *Idem.*

and other "strangers within the gates" of the advantages and moral necessity of accepting biblical laws.[20] They long ago adopted the language of "right reason" and "human rights" to defend the common law, which was heavily influenced by biblical law. In adopting incompatible judicial doctrines, Christians relinquished their claim to the *only* law-order which is universally valid and universally binding: biblical law.

God's law-order cannot be successfully defended intellectually in terms of natural law, because no system can be defended successfully in terms of natural law. The strangers within the gates have the *work* of the law written on their hearts, but they actively and wilfully suppress this testimony (see below: "Natural Law Theory vs. Biblical Law"). They need the protection of biblical law, which has been revealed to us in God's word. God's people also need the protection of biblical law, to protect them from the evil deeds of others. Every man needs biblical law; and every man had better acknowledge his need for a substitutionary sacrifice because of his own transgression of at least some of the requirements of biblical law.

Self-Government

When biblical law is enforced without respect to persons, society is given the legal structure which favors economic development and external blessings. Men are told of their moral and legal responsibilities before God. *Self-government under God's law* is the *primary form of government* in every sphere of life: civil government, family government, church government, economic government. There is to be a means of settling disputes: an *appeals court* which enforces biblical law without respect of persons. There is an appeals court in the church (Matt. 18:15-20; I Cor. 6:1-10) and the civil government (Ex. 18:13-26). *No earthly government can possibly afford to police every aspect of human action.* No human court possesses sufficient economic resources to do so. Any court which would attempt this seeks to impose a top-down bureaucracy which is antithetical to personal initiative, personal responsibility, and economic development. Such a concept of government is the pyramid view, where the State is god, an omniscient directing agent staffed by automatons who simply carry out orders to the letter. The *pyramid society* is self-defeating; it is

---

20. Gary North, "The Intellectual Schizophrenia of the New Christian Right," *Christianity and Civilization,* No. 1 (1982). This is a publication of the Geneva Divinity School, in Tyler, Texas.

parasitic, uncreative, and stifling. It destroys self-government.

The biblical form of government is a system of *multiple sovereignties* ("authorities" we read in Romans 13:1), with *multiple hierarchies* (the appeals court structures), and with none universally sovereign over all other human institutions. This is a system of decentralized government, competing institutional sovereignties, and limited civil government. It is a system of government which rejects absolute human sovereignty. It recognizes the implicit total depravity of man — the definitive depravity of man apart from God's common or special grace — and therefore the explicit total depravity of any absolutely sovereign human institution — assuming that any institution could ever be free of God's restraints, which is not possible.

The basic and absolutely indispensable form of *social discipline* is *the preaching of the whole counsel of God.* The church must do this, the civil government must proclaim biblical civil law, and the fathers in all the families should proclaim it. *It is self-government under biblical law which is the primary means of attaining social order.* This does not deny the need for appeals courts, but it places such courts in their proper perspective. The individual has the greatest responsibility for conforming to God's law, since the individual must give an account of his actions, thoughts, and words on the day of judgment (Matt. 12:36; Rom. 14:12). God polices everything and judges everything. He provides perfect justice and perfect punishment. There is no escape. Since the punishment is individual (Luke 12:47-48), and the rewards are individual (I Cor. 3:11-15), the primary agent of earthly law enforcement is the individual. No one else has comparable knowledge of his own actions. No other earthly authority has comparable incentives to conform a man's actions to the standards presented in God's law. The *incentive system* described by God in His word makes it plain that *the most important agency of government is the individual.*

For the individual to exercise self-government as required by biblical law, he must be aware of the terms of the law. He must understand what his responsibilities are before God. This is why every human institution ought to proclaim biblical law as it applies to that particular institution. Men should be openly confronted with biblical law, from morning to night to morning, in every sphere of life, for each man is responsible to God, and in some cases to his fellow men, from morning to night to morning, in every sphere of life. *There is no neutral zone which is free from the requirements of God's law, no area of lawlessness.* There can be conformity to the law of God or rebellion against biblical law, but there can never be sheer lawlessness. The Bible speaks of "lawless" men, but it really means rebels against biblical law.

Multiple Hierarchies

The Protestants' most important contribution to the social theory of the West was their refinement of the Christian and medieval view of multiple sovereignties and therefore multiple hierarchies.[21] No man is an island. No man is solely responsible to any single institution, either. There is no divine right of kings, who owe allegiance only to God. There is no divine right of citizens, who owe allegiance only to God. There is no divine right of the free market. *There is no divine right of any earthly institution.* Each is under God; none is completely independent of all the others. This legal pluralism is one of the sources of Western liberty. But note: Western legal pluralism was not a self-conscious pluralism of law-orders ("polylegalism," which is implicitly polytheistic), but a pluralism of human institutional sovereignties under a single law-order, God's law. The absolute sovereignty of any human institution is denied by such a doctrine. It was canon law which broke decisively with any doctrine of the unitary State. As Rushdoony has noted:

To understand the implications of canon law, it is necessary to realize that ancient society was unitary, and it had a single, visible, human sovereignty. It was totalitarian in practice and in faith. A visible "divine" authority governed the whole of life and admitted the existence of no independent order. For the ancient state, the uncontrolled was the enemy, and the controlled was the subject. Neither man nor any of his activities and institutions possessed any free, uncontrolled, or independent domain wherein the state had no jurisdiction. The sovereignty of the state meant that man was the creature of the state and entirely its subject.

But Biblical faith asserted instead the sovereignty of God and the

---

21. On the multiplicity of legal jurisdictions in medieval legal theory after 1150, see Harold J. Berman, *Law and Revolution: The Formation of the Western Legal Tradition* (Cambridge, Massachusetts: Harvard University Press, 1983), Pt. II. Berman writes: "Perhaps the most distinctive characteristic of the Western legal tradition is the coexistence and competition within the same community of diverse jurisdictions and diverse legal systems. It is this plurality of jurisdictions and legal systems that makes the supremacy of law both necessary and possible. Legal pluralism originated in the differentiation of the ecclesiastical polity from secular polities. The church declared its freedom from secular control, its exclusive jurisdiction in some matters, and its concurrent jurisdiction in other matters" (p. 10).

ultimacy of His decree and law, so that man, the state, and every institution were under God and His law. Instead of the sovereign state providing the overall shelter for all things, the sovereign God is that over-lord, and all of man's institutions are directly under God and His word. Instead of a mediatorial state, Christ is man's mediator. The Bible provides a legal mandate for the institutions, and the state is made the ministry of justice, and the church the ministry of the word and the sacraments. The family is under God's law, as is agriculture, commerce, science, education, and all things else. Neither the church, nor the state, nor any other institution has a legitimate overall power of control. But the state in antiquity, and again today, has played the overall role of God, the sovereign over every realm and with basic and ultimate power over every realm. The state can permit or grant to its children or creatures certain privileges, but it cannot tolerate their denial of its sovereign authority. For the church therefore to issue canons placing Christians under the canons of Christ, under the laws of God, was a denial of the sovereignty of the state and of its canons. It was a shattering of the concept of the totalitarian unitary state.[22]

Harold Berman's brilliant and comprehensive history of medieval law has concluded much the same concerning the role of canon law, although he does not discuss the theological foundations and implications in the same detail as Rushdoony does. He sees clearly the importance of legal pluralism in the development of Western liberty. "The pluralism of Western law, which has both reflected and reinforced the pluralism of Western political and economic life, has been, or once was, a source of development, or growth — legal growth as well as political and economic growth. It also has been, or once was, a source of freedom. A serf might run to the town court for protection against his master. A vassal might run to the king's court for protection against his lord. A cleric might run to the ecclesiastical court for protection against the king."[23]

Let us consider an example of the legal operation of the principle of multiple sovereignties. A person is found to be an adulterer. This obviously has implications for *family government*. The authority structure of the family has been broken by the guilty individual. There are lawful ways of handling this problem, at the discretion of the injured party (Matt. 1:19). At the same time, adultery is a matter of *church government*. The church can bring discipline to the guilty party,

---

22. R. J. Rushdoony, *The Foundations of Social Order: Studies in the Creeds and Councils of the Early Church* (Fairfax, Virginia: Thoburn Press, [1969] 1978), pp. 132-33.
23. *Law and Revolution*, p. 10.

by excommunication if necessary. But the *civil government* is also involved. A civil contract has been broken. The civil government, upon complaint of the injured partner, or on the complaint of citizens who discovered the crime, must step in and bring justice (Lev. 20:10). The penalty for adultery is death. There are legal questions that must be dealt with, questions of evidence. Any decision by any of the governmental units will also have *economic implications:* the dowry, the custody of the children (if the State fails to execute the guilty party), and so forth.[24] Each of these sovereign agencies has limited but legitimate sovereignty. None is absolutely sovereign.

Moral Norms and Market Order

What I am describing is a *decentralized social order.* Even in the largest city, each man is to be under the rule of some local agencies of governments (plural). This brings to the forefront each man's personal responsibility before God. The law of God is able to provide the norms of righteousness in every sphere of life, since it provides the proper view of man, the responsible creature. We are not describing an autonomous social order, one in which there are no norms other than personal self-interest. Even the free market, which does function well in terms of personal self-interest among market participants, requires a moral foundation. Hayek has admitted this, but no economist has defended more eloquently the *necessity of moral norms*—norms beyond mere market profitability—than Wilhelm Röpke. This is why he is such an important economist.

The market system is based neither on violence nor on charity, Röpke argued, but it is never morally neutral. Without the bedrock of morality—essentially Christian morality—the free market cannot be sustained. Most remarkably, this economist even understood that the market is based on a *creed.* "It is certainly true that the competitive market system—the 'business economy'—keeps itself at an equal distance from both the ethically negative system of violence or ruse and the ethically positive one of altruism and charity. It reduces both to the common level of a mild standard of commercial good behaviour, but it would be a great mistake to think that that would make the market system an ethically neutral sphere. On the contrary, it is a highly sensitive artefact of occidental civilization, with

---

24. Gary North, *Unconditional Surrender: God's Program for Victory* (2nd ed.; Tyler, Texas: Geneva Divinity School Press, 1983), pp. 170-71.

all the latter's ingredients of Christian and pre-Christian morality and its secularized forms; and it should not be forgotten that the 'economic man' of the classics was really an English gentleman of the eighteenth or nineteenth century, whose normal code was fixed by the church and by tradition. In fact, the market economy is an economic system which cannot exist without a minimum of mutual trust, confidence in the stability of the legal-institutional framework of the economic process (including money), contractual loyalty, honesty, fair play, professional honour, and that pride which considers it beneath one to cheat, bribe, or misuse the authority of the state for one's own egoistic purposes. Above all, there must be a 'creed' in the most general sense of the term, a belief in a definite scale of ultimate values giving sense and purpose to the ordinary doings of all participating in the economic process, and, finally, at least a provisional understanding of the meaning and working of this economic process."[25]

The free market economy needs a *creed*—what Rushdoony has called the foundation of social order—in order to be maintained by any society. If that creed is not based on an ethical code which is in conformity to the one presented by the Bible, the free market social order cannot survive. God removes the prosperity of that culture by removing the *moral foundation of the market,* namely, men's *faith* in the legitimacy of the market process—a process which is sanctioned by orthodox Christian doctrine. Röpke warns: "Thus the market economy is living on certain psycho-moral reserves, which are taken for granted when everything is going well, and only reveal their supreme importance when they are giving out."[26] That these "capital reserves" of morality are running out in the late twentieth century is increasingly obvious, and it was obvious to Röpke when he wrote this book in the early 1940's.

Röpke makes another important point concerning the moral order undergirding the market. There is no doubt that the division of labor is basic to the market order, a point driven home graphically by Adam Smith in his deservedly famous story of the pin-makers with which he begins *Wealth of Nations.* But the division of labor is a fragile and therefore potentially dangerous feature of modern society. Each of us is dependent on one another's productivity. "We saw

---

25. Wilhelm Röpke, *International Economic Disintegration* (London: Hodge, [1942] 1950), pp. 68-69.
26. *Ibid.*, p. 69.

that an intensive economic intercourse, which involves a wide scale of division of labour and a high degree of mutual dependence of individuals, is possible only under a number of conditions, which all fall under the head of 'socio-political' integration. It is this latter which, in the last resort, sets the limits to the extent and degree of economic integration. There must be a framework of institutions and of a strong legal order, and behind them, there must be a generally observed and undisputed code of moral norms and principles of behaviour. In this way, it is possible to have a society in which all its members may feel sheltered in an atmosphere of mutual confidence, security, and continuity. Only in this way is it possible to reduce and make bearable the enormous risks involved in a high degree of dependence, which is inevitably connected with the division of labour. Every page of economic history proclaims the truth of this statement, which is, indeed, the ultimate principle explaining the rise and decay, the expansion and contraction of economic organization."[27] If this economic division of labor collapses, which is possible in a program of price and wage controls — which Röpke called repressed inflation[28] — the very survival of modern, industrialized populations is threatened.

Röpke saw what was coming: *statism*. Political centralization destroys the market. It destroys the whole concept of responsible personal self-government. "The wider the span of proletarianisation, the wilder become the cravings of the uprooted to be guaranteed social services and economic security by the state, the more do the few remaining in possession of a sense of responsibility despair, all the more stringently is the greater part of the national income claimed for and directed by the state; the more oppressive becomes the burden of taxation, a burden heavy enough already and one made all the worse through war, revolution, and public spending, and which will of course have to be extracted predominantly from the pockets of the middle classes. . . . There is no reason to foresee that this process is likely to stop, since this apparatus of insurance and social services is nothing other than a thirst-creating substitute for the anchor of property and can never lead to the real satisfaction of the needs of the unhappy victims of proletarianisation. The total burden will become ever more oppressive, the burden of taxation

---

27. *Ibid.*, p. 72.
28. Röpke, *Economics of the Free Society* (Chicago: Regnery, 1963), p. 104.

ever harder and more embittering, the apparatus ever more un-
wieldy, and the social bureaucracy ever more numerous. Any bits
coming to the individual out of the national hotch-pot will become
ever more subject to formulae, tickets, reportings on and off,
income-tax forms, etc.; the hair-spring of a sense of responsibility
cum self-respect which keeps the whole thing going will become ever
weaker, the whole economic process will function more and more
clumsily, its defects will increase and become ever more tiresome; all
in all enough to increase the individual's sense of insecurity and also
to put up his demands. The only possible end to all this would seem
to be complete catastrophe for nation and society, nor need we go
back for examples to the latter period of the Roman Empire."[29] He
wrote this in the late 1940's, before the process of bureaucratization
had fully accelerated. It was the same process Max Weber had seen
at the beginning of the twentieth century, except that Weber did not
even have the hope of economic collapse as a possible way to escape
what he called "the bureaucratic cage."

The Pyramid Society

By centralizing power, the modern State is recreating the *pyramid
society*, the top-down system of total control — or attempted total
control — that destroys the fabric of society. The *caretaker State* steadily
replaces the biblical concept of the *night-watchman State*. The most important form of government, responsible self-government under
God, is steadily eroded by a new concept of government, the messianic State. Social order also erodes. As the French Catholic social
philosopher, Lamennais, wrote in the early nineteenth century,
"Centralization induces apoplexy at the center and anemia at the ex-
tremities."[30] Nobody has ever put it more graphically than this.

The biblical social order is utterly hostile to the pyramid society. The
biblical social order is characterized by the following features. *First,*
it is made up of multiple institutional arrangements, each with its
own legitimate, limited, and derivative sovereignty under God's
universal law. *Second,* each institution possesses a hierarchical chain
of command, but these chains of command are essentially *appeals
courts* — "bottom-up" institutions — with the primary duty of responsi-

---

29. Röpke, *Civitas Humana: A Humane Order of Society* (London: Hodge, 1948), pp.
141-42.
30. Cited by Robert A. Nisbet, *The Sociological Tradition* (New York: Basic Books,
1966), p. 115.

ble action placed on people occupying the lower rungs of authority. *Third,* no single institution has absolute and final authority in any instance; appeal can be made to other sovereign agents of godly judgment. Since no society can attain perfection, there will be instances of injustice, but the social goal is harmony under biblical law, in terms of an orthodox creed. God will judge all men perfectly. The State need not seek perfect justice, nor should citizens be taxed at the astronomical rates necessary to sustain the quest for perfect justice.[31]

Hayek has made a point which must be taken seriously by those who seek to explain the relationship between Christianity and the advent of free enterprise capitalism in the West. "There is probably no single factor which has contributed more to the prosperity of the West than the relative certainty of the law which has prevailed here."[32] Sowell's comments are especially graphic: "Someone who is going to work for many years to have his own home wants some fairly rigid assurance that the house will in fact belong to him — that he cannot be dispossessed by someone who is physically stronger, better armed, or more ruthless, or who is deemed more 'worthy' by political authorities. Rigid assurances are needed that changing fashions, mores, and power relationships will not suddenly deprive him of his property, his children, or his life."[33] Hayek quite properly denies the validity of the quest for perfect certainty, since "complete certainty of the law is an ideal which we must try to approach but which we can never perfectly attain."[34] His anti-perfectionism regarding the rule of law is also in accord with the anti-perfectionism of Christian social thought in the West.[35] Christianity brought with it a conception of social order which made possible the economic development of the West.

Biblical Law and Capitalism

There is no doubt that *formal legal predictability* was a major factor in the rise of capitalism. By "capitalism," I mean a system of private

31. Macklin Fleming, *The Price of Perfect Justice* (New York: Basic Books, 1974). For an analysis of Fleming's critique of the modern criminal justice system, see my review of the book in *The Journal of Christian Reconstruction,* II (Winter 1975-76).

32. Hayek, *The Constitution of Liberty* (University of Chicago Press, 1960), p. 208.

33. Thomas Sowell, *Knowledge and Decisions* (New York: Basic Books, 1980), p. 32.

34. Hayek, *Constitution of Liberty,* p. 208.

35. Benjamin B. Warfield, *Perfectionism* (Philadelphia: Presbyterian & Reformed, 1958). This is an abridged version of Warfield's two-volume study, published by Oxford University Press in 1931, and reprinted by Baker Book House in 1981.

ownership, which involves the freedom of contract, freely fluctuating prices, and a money economy. I am not speaking of traditional political capitalism, such as the tax-farming capitalism of ancient Rome, or the court-oriented capitalism of Spain in the sixteenth century. This is the distinction used by Max Weber to delineate modern from ancient capitalism.

Weber made a very important observation concerning the relationship between Protestantism and market-oriented capitalism. He sharply distinguished market capitalism from "political capitalism," in which producers sell primarily to the State rather than to a competitive market. "The closest connection between ethical religion and rational economic development — particularly capitalism — was effected by all the forms of ascetic Protestantism and sectarianism in both Western and Eastern Europe, viz., Zwinglians, Calvinists, Baptists, Mennonites, Quakers, Methodists, and Pietists (both of the Reformed and, to a lesser degree, Lutheran varieties). . . . Indeed, generally speaking, the inclination to join an ethical, rational, congregational religion becomes more strongly marked the farther away one gets from those strata which have been the carriers of the type of capitalism which is primarily political in orientation. Since the time of Hammurabi political capitalism has existed wherever there has been tax farming, the profitable provisions of the state's political needs, war, piracy, large-scale usury, and colonization. The tendency toward affiliation with an ethical, rational, congregational religion is more apt to be found the closer one gets to those strata which have been the carriers of the modern rational enterprise, i.e., strata with middle-class economic characteristics. . . ."[36]

The idea of the *congregational unit,* where men worship God as equals before the law, where God is not a respecter of persons, where the law is read and understood by all members of the group, and where each man receives his calling to labor before God in a holy occupation, produces a mentality favoring *personal responsibility* and *production for a universal market.* Men's universal understanding of the civil law reduces the arbitrary decisions of the authorities, and this in turn reduces a major area of uncertainty. *This reduction in bureaucratic arbitrariness reduces production costs.* Fewer economic resources need to be set aside for bribes or court defense costs.

---

36. Weber, *Economy & Society,* pp. 479-80; *The Sociology of Religion,* translated by Ephraim Fischoff (Boston: Beacon Press, 1963), pp. 93-94.

Yet it is not simply the universality of the legal system which is important. Specific aspects of the legal system, such as the honoring of private contracts, the respect for private property, the non-discriminatory nature of the tax system, and the restriction of the civil government to the preservation of order, primarily by preserving public peace and preventing private fraud and coercion, have made it possible for capitalism to flourish. All of these aspects are basic to biblical law. Four such principles of biblical law come to mind. First, the concept of the *covenant* between God and man undergirds the right of private contract. Second, the *commandment against theft* is basic to the extension of the rights of private property. Third, the *tithe,* as a fixed percentage of a man's income, preserves the non-discriminatory nature of taxation. Fourth, the enforcement of *honest weights and measures* is indicative of the Bible's view of the civil government as essentially a restraining institution, not a positive, initiating force in economic development, and certainly not a coercive agency of wealth redistribution.

Hayek's summary of the principles of a liberal economic order reveals how closely nineteenth-century liberalism resembled the view of civil government held by the Protestant congregational churches in the United States, Holland, and Britain in the eighteenth century.[37] In short, *nineteenth-century liberalism is the humanists' version of "work out your salvation with fear and trembling."* When humanism's evangelists and social theorists finally persuaded men (especially leaders) to cease fearing God and trembling in His presence, the classical liberal economic order was doomed. Rather than killing God, classical liberalism killed itself.[38]

---

37. Hayek writes elsewhere (in language as convoluted as Weber's): "The extension of an order of peace beyond the small purpose-oriented organization became thus possible by the extension of purpose-independent ('formal') rules of just conduct to the relations with other men who did not pursue the same concrete ends or hold the same values except those abstract rules — rules which did not impose obligations for particular actions (which always presuppose a concrete end) but consisted solely in prohibitions from infringing the protected domain of each which these rules enable us to determine. Liberalism is therefore inseparable from the institution of private property which is the name we usually give to the material part of this protected individual domain." Hayek, "The Principles of a Liberal Social Order" (1966), in Hayek, *Studies in Philosophy, Politics and Economics* (University of Chicago Press, 1967), p. 165.

38. Gary North, *Dominion Covenant: Genesis,* Appendix A: "From Cosmic Purposelessness to Humanistic Sovereignty."

Whose Law Is Sovereign?

A few modern secular scholars still give lip-service to classical liberalism's idea of the rule of law. The advocates of classical liberalism in the nineteenth century, most notably the English economist and social theorist, John Stuart Mill,[39] and the constitutional scholar, A. V. Dicey,[40] believed in the idea of the rule of law. The problem which faced these legal theorists — a problem which they never overcame — was the problem of the *content* of the law. They frequently accepted the validity of *formal* rationalism, which meant that they wanted to establish formal "rules of the game" for all participants in society to observe. They wanted *legal predictability*. On the other hand, they could not agree on the *substantive* principles of law, meaning the ethical rules and regulations that ought to be imposed on all members of society. They saw the formal rationalism of law as the "universal," but substantive rationalism — ethics, in other words — resisted treatment by any universally agreed-upon human logic, since the existence of such a universal logic is perhaps the most outrageous myth of human autonomy. It has not existed since the Fall of man. The myth of intellectual or moral neutrality has finally died in the final third of the twentieth century, but it enjoyed a long life and a lingering terminal illness.

Max Weber, writing of substantive rationality or value-rationality, concluded: "There is an infinite number of possible value scales for this type of rationality, of which the socialist and communist standards constitute only one group. The latter, although by no means unambiguous in themselves, always involve elements of social justice and equality. Others are criteria of status distinctions, or of the capacity for power, especially of the war capacity, of a political unit; all these and many others are of potential 'substantive' significance."[41] What is important is that no system of purely formal philosophical inquiry can determine which of these substantive or ethical systems is valid or universal. More than this, Weber con-

---

39. Mill, *On Liberty* (1859).

40. A. V. Dicey, *An Introduction to the Study of the Law of the Constitution* (8th ed.; Indianapolis, Indiana: Liberty Classics, [1915] 1982). Cf. Richard Cosgrove, *The Rule of Law: Albert Venn Dicey, Victorian Jurist* (Chapel Hill: University of North Carolina Press, 1980).

41. *Economy & Society,* p. 86. A slightly different translation appears in Weber, *The Theory of Social and Economic Organization*, translated by Talcott Parsons (New York: The Free Press, 1947), pp. 185-86.

cluded: formal rationality (legal predictability) will always be in tension with substantive rationality (ethics). Humanist ethics are always pluralistic. There is no unifying set of ethical principles which will unify mankind's ethical vision; therefore, formal rationalism can never escape a dialectical tension with substantive rationalism.

Humanist scholars have singled out the operations of the free market as an example of this supposedly inescapable perpetual tension. The market is essentially a huge auction. Producers of goods and services sell to those who bid highest in terms of the monetary unit, irrespective of moral criteria, Weber said. Weber, as a liberal social democrat during his most productive years (1904-20), was willing to admit that formal rationality and substantive rationality did fit together quite well from the latter decades of the nineteenth century. "The reasons lie in the nature of the incentives which are set into motion by the type of economically oriented social action which alone is adequate to money calculations. But it nevertheless holds true under all circumstances that formal rationality itself does not tell us anything about real want satisfaction unless it is combined with an analysis of the distribution of income."[42]

This supposed tension between efficiency and ethics has made the free market, both in terms of practice and theory, vulnerable to ethical criticism, and the critics have been both the socialists and the conservative traditionalists, sometimes joining together in their lambasting of the market.[43] Why this two-sided ethical criticism of eco-

---

42. *Economy & Society,* p. 109; *Social & Economic Organization,* p. 212.

43. Gertrude Himmelfarb, *The Idea of Poverty: England in the Early Industrial Age* (New York: Knopf, 1984), ch. 8: "The Tory Opposition: Paternalism and Humanitarianism"; Robert A. Nisbet, *The Sociological Tradition* (New York: Basic Books, 1966), pp. 25-28. The best example of this is Engels' use of the famous Sadler Committee's (1832) criticisms of industrialism's abuses against children: *Condition of the Working Class in England in 1844* (1845). The Sadler Committee was headed by Michael Thomas Sadler, a Tory. On Sadler and the "high Tories," see Robert Blake, *The Conservative Party from Peel to Churchill* (New York: St. Martin's, 1970), pp. 21-25. See also E. P. Thompson, *The Making of the English Working Class* (New York: Vintage, 1963), pp. 342-43. It was the conservatives under Bismarck in Germany who brought in the first compulsory social welfare programs in the form of insurance schemes for workers, inaugurated in the early 1870's and expanded for almost two decades thereafter: accident insurance funded by employers (1871), sickness insurance (1883), old age insurance (1888): J. H. Clapham, *Economic Development of France and Germany, 1815-1914* (Cambridge: At the University Press, 1966), pp. 336-37. This, however, was done as part of an overall anti-socialist program, a means of defusing worker unrest. This anti-socialist program failed to achieve its

nomic freedom? Tyrrell's answer is incisive: both the socialist and the reactionary conservative share a *hatred for the present.* "Today's socialist is not greatly different, in truth, from the reactionary. The latter idealizes a past that never was. The former idealizes a future that never will be. Both have an unscotchable and irrational yearning to escape the present or to destroy it."[44] Equally incisive is Clarence Carson's observation that European conservatives and socialists share a common view of the State, that of a *substitute father.* The American tradition was originally very different. Not only did the Founding Fathers separate church from State at the Federal level, they also separated *parenthood* from State.[45]

"Ethical" Critiques of the Market

The standard—indeed, nearly inevitable—criticism of the free market which is made by socialist and reactionary critics is that while the free market provides us with inexpensive goods and services, it nonetheless caters to those who have money to spend. Originally, socialists claimed that socialist economic planning is more efficient than decentralized, individualistic market planning. From Marx to the Fabians in Britain, this was their belief. As late as 1949, a British promoter of socialist planning could write of the British experiment in nationalization of industry: "Here at last a practical test of two vast and so far unproven assumptions is taking place. The first is that a planned socialist system is economically more efficient than a private-enterprise system; the second is that within democratic socialist planning the individual can be given broader social justice, greater security, and more complete freedom than under capitalism."[46] By the 1970's, the proponents of democratic socialism had abandoned the first assumption as erroneous, or at the very least, still unproven. The socialist economies had all failed the test of efficiency in the post-War world. Socialist scholars have grudgingly

---

short-run objectives; the Social Democratic Party continued to grow. In 1890, when Bismarck proposed the desperation policy of abrogating the constitution, shrinking the franchise, and driving the Social Democrats out of existence, the new emperor, William II, threw Bismarck out of office: Geoffrey Barraclough, *The Origins of Modern Germany* (New York: Capricorn, [1946] 1963), pp. 426-27.

44. R. Emmett Tyrrell, Jr., *The Liberal Crack-Up* (New York: Simon & Schuster, 1984), p. 211.

45. Clarence B. Carson, *The World in the Grip of an Idea* (New Rochelle, New York: Arlington House, 1979), p. 289.

46. Francis Williams, *Socialist Britain* (New York: Viking, 1949), p. 5.

admitted over the years, free market economic incentives have led to a great outpouring of production, but, they say, this is not enough. They still assert that capitalism necessarily fails the second test, that of social justice. We have to see who gets the wealth. We have to see who is getting rich. We have to see if the needs of the people are being met. Ethics, not efficiency, must be our standard.

This humanistic appeal to ethics is illegitimate. The secular humanist logically cannot appeal to any universal ethical principle in order to criticize any economic outcome of market competition, precisely because *there is no universally agreed-upon humanistic ethical system*, and also because by the standards of rationalism, *we cannot legitimately make interpersonal comparisons of subjective utility.* We cannot legitimately, scientifically add up columns of costs and benefits for whole populations.[47] We cannot subtract the "psychological quantity" (if such a thing existed) lost by one person as the result of some market event from the "psychological addition" gained by another person. I cannot estimate just how much I have gained in an exchange, and then compare it with just how much one of my competitors forfeited by not bidding higher than I bid. Therefore, the attempt of the humanists, whether free market defenders, or economic interventionists, or communists, to make scientifically valid statements concerning the success or failure of *any* economic system to "deliver the goods" for the benefit of mankind, is an attempt which must inevitably fail as a scientific endeavor.[48] *On the basis of scientific economics, no possible comparison of subjective utilities can be made, one citizen to another.*

Any supposedly "scientific" evaluation between two rival economic systems is totally deceptive. The evaluator must make several assumptions beforehand about what criteria should be used for evaluating success or failure. Such assumptions are scientifically illegitimate. Why? First, there is no universal set of such standards. Second, if one person disagrees with the proposed standards, science or reason has no way to evaluate which criteria are correct. Third, even if we all agreed about these criteria, we could not be sure our assumptions are correct. Fourth, even if we could agree, and then also discover the truth of our agreed-upon standards, we lack the ability to evaluate the success or failure of any program or system, because we cannot tally up costs and benefits, disadvantages and ad-

---

47. Lionel Robbins, *An Essay on the Nature and Significance of Economic Science* (2nd ed.; New York: St. Martins, [1935]), p. 140.

48. Cf. North, *The Dominion Covenant: Genesis*, ch. 4.

vantages, losers and winners. Economists cannot make valid scientific interpersonal comparisons of subjective utility. This may not sound like a very important observation, but the problem of interpersonal comparisons of subjective utility has undermined the epistemology of every so-called science of economics or social welfare policy. To defend socialistic or free market programs of taxation, coercive wealth redistribution, free trade, or any other economic policy, economists must first scrap the whole structure of modern scientific economics, and then appeal to intuition or metaphysics as the basis of their proposed reforms.[49]

Humanistic Formal Law: A Vain Hope

The quest for a system of *neutral formal law* which also produces universally agreed-upon ethical benefits, and which does not limit the freedom of any of society's members, is a demonic quest. This is why the free market economists and legal theorists can never come to any agreement concerning the extent to which civil governments ought to interfere or refrain from interfering with the operations of the free market. They cannot agree upon the universally valid, or at least universally beneficial, formal legal rules. They certainly have not devised a theory of civil government which preserves the formal freedom of men to change their laws peacefully, yet which simultaneously guarantees full legal predictability to all market participants. This is one reason why nineteenth-century liberalism, which was democratic, decentralist, and free market-oriented, became twentieth-century liberalism, which is bureaucratic, centralist, and interventionist in economic policy. Nineteenth-century liberals wanted to defend political democracy as a means of preserving *peaceful transfers of political power,* yet they also wanted to preserve *legal predictability for market transactions.* As the philosophy of Western social philosophers (and then voters) shifted toward man-directing, bureaucracy-managing evolution, and away from man-responding, market-governed evolution,[50] the formal rules of political democracy allowed the advent of market-disrupting changes in the "economic

---

49. Gary North, "Economics: From Reason to Intuition," in North (ed.), *Foundations of Christian Scholarship: Essays in the Van Til Perspective* (Vallecito, California: Ross House, 1976). For a similar conclusion by radical economists, see Mark A. Lutz and Kenneth Lux, *The Challenge of Humanistic Economics* (Menlo Park, California: Benjamin/Cummings, 1979), pp. 67-69, 97-101.

50. Gary North, "From Cosmic Purposelessness to Humanistic Sovereignty," Appendix A in *The Dominion Covenant: Genesis.*

rules of the game." *The formal rules of political democracy overcame the formal rules of legal predictability and equality before the law.*

Legal Predictability and Judicial Sovereignty

What are some of the basic judicial aspects of a legal order which respects the rule of law? Joseph Raz lists eight convenient guidelines:

1. All laws should be prospective, open, and clear. One cannot be guided by a retroactive law that does not exist at the time of action.

2. Laws should be relatively stable.

3. The making of particular laws should be guided by open, stable, clear, and general rules.

4. The independence of the judiciary should be guaranteed.

5. The principles of justice must be observed — open and fair hearings, absence of bias.

6. The courts should have review powers over the implementation of the other principles.

7. The courts should be easily accessible.

8. The discretion of crime-preventing agencies should not be allowed to pervert the law.[51]

The emphasis is on legal predictability. However, Raz is overly confident in the courts as protectors of human freedom through the rule of law. What is to prevent the courts from exercising the same sorts of arbitrary rule that are characteristic of legislatures and executives? By establishing the civil court system as finally sovereign, a defender of the rule of law violates the biblical principle of multiple sovereignties. He lodges absolute final sovereignty in a human institution. Freedom can never survive long under such an absolutist system. We have already seen in the United States the creation of what lawyer Carrol Kilgore has called judicial tyranny,[52] and what Harvard law professor Raoul Berger has called government by judiciary.[53] As Berger concludes: "Let it not be said of us as Gibbon said of Rome: 'The *image* of a free constitution was preserved with decent

---

51. Joseph Raz, "The Rule of Law and Its Virtue," in Robert L. Cunningham (ed.), *Liberty and the Rule of Law* (College Station, Texas: Texas A&M University Press, 1979), pp. 7-11.

52. Carrol D. Kilgore, *Judicial Tyranny* (Nashville, Tennessee: Nelson, 1977).

53. Raoul Berger, *Government By Judiciary: The Transformation of the Fourteenth Amendment* (Cambridge, Massachusetts: Harvard University Press, 1977).

reverence. The Roman senate *appeared* to possess the sovereign authority, and devolved on the emperors all the executive powers of government.' Here no Senate devolved the policymaking powers on the Court; they are self-conferred only because the American people are unaware that there is a yawning gulf between judicial professions and practice."[54]

To preserve freedom, there must be constitutional provisions that reduce this grant of sovereignty to the courts. One such reduction specified in the U.S. Constitution is the ability of Congress to limit the jurisdiction of the Supreme Court. Congress can determine what sort of cases can be appealed to the Court: "In all Cases affecting Ambassadors, other public Ministers and Consuls, and those in which a State shall be Party, the supreme Court shall have original jurisdiction. In all the other Cases before mentioned, the supreme Court shall have appellate Jurisdiction, both as to Law and Fact, with such Exceptions, and under such Regulations as the Congress shall make" (Art. III, Sec. 2). Congress has the authority to limit the Court's jurisdiction — the "exceptions."[55] This has been an exceptional power in U.S. constitutional history, however, and only occasionally used.[56]

Another important limitation is the jury system. A jury has the ability to decide both the law and the facts in any case. A "not guilty" decision of a jury is irrevocable under the common law rule against

---

54. *Ibid.*, pp. 417-18.

55. The Court declared in *The Frances Wright* (1882): "[W]hile the appellate power of this court under the Constitution extends to all cases within the judicial power of the United States, actual jurisdiction under the power is confined within such limits as Congress sees fit to prescribe. . . . What those powers shall be, and to what extent they shall be exercised, are, and always have been, proper subjects of legislative control. Authority to limit the jurisdiction necessarily carries with it authority to limit the use of the jurisdiction. Not only may whole classes of cases be kept out of the jurisdiction altogether, but particular classes of questions may be subjected to reexamination and review, while others are not." Cited in Congressional Research Service, *The Constitution of the United States of America: Analysis and Interpretation,* Annotations of Cases Decided by the Supreme Court of the United States to June 29, 1972 (Washington, D.C.: Government Printing Office, 1973), pp. 752n-753n. Cf. H. Hart, "The Power of the Congress to Limit the Jurisdiction of the Federal Courts: An Exercise in Dialectic," *Harvard Law Review,* vol. 66 (1953), pp. 1362ff.

56. One example is *Ex Parte McCardle* (1869), where Congress removed the Court's jurisdiction over *habeus corpus* during Reconstruction. See Alfred H. Kelley and Winfred A. Harbison, *The American Constitution: Its Origins and Development* (rev. ed.; New York: Norton, 1955), pp. 479-80.

double jeopardy.[57] "The idea of the sovereign authority of the jury dates from the jury's earliest appearance. During the Middle Ages the English jury replaced a system that included trials by battle or ordeal, by which the judgment of Heaven was thought to be manifest. The jury system put the responsibility of judgment squarely upon the representatives of the community. Its sovereignty was emphasized by the familiar characterization of the jury as a 'barrier . . . between the liberties of the people, and the prerogative of the crown' [*Blackstone's Commentaries*, V, p. 349]. Its almost plenary authority was evident in its familiar power to determine the law as well as the facts. When nineteenth-century judges began giving instructions on the law, formally limiting the jury's function to resolving disputed facts, juries nevertheless continued to exercise control over the law in certain cases by their acknowledged power to return a general verdict of guilt or innocence or without stated reasons."[58]

Double jeopardy can and should be seen as an outgrowth of Christian legal procedure.[59] It represents an important barrier against the messianic expansion of central power. Local juries can always refuse to convict, which is what happened in the years prior to the American Revolution, especially in cases involving smuggling (violations of the British Empire's import restrictions in the colonies).[60] This created major enforcement problems for the British bureaucracy. From the very founding of the United States, trial by jury was one of the legal pillars of the republic.[61] That the Supreme Court in 1970 unilaterally decided that a six-man jury is adequate, thereby reversing 600 years of common law tradition, was no accident.[62] It was one more assertion of judicial sovereignty.

---

57. On double jeopardy, see Martin K. Friedlander, *Double Jeopardy* (Oxford: Clarendon Press, 1969); Jay A. Sigler, *Double Jeopardy: The Development of a Legal and Social Policy* (Ithaca, New York: Cornell University Press, 1969).

58. Dallin H. Oaks and Marvin S. Hill, *Carthage Conspiracy: The Trial of the Accused Assassins of Joseph Smith* (Urbana: University of Illinois Press, 1979), p. 211. Cf. Mark De Wolfe Howe, "Juries as Judges of Criminal Law," *Harvard Law Review*, vol. 52 (1939), pp. 582ff.; Harry Kalven and Hans Zeisel, *The American Jury* (New York: Little, Brown, 1966), pp. 227-36, 286-97.

59. Greg L. Bahnsen, "Double Jeopardy: A Case Study in the Influence of Christian Legislation," *The Journal of Christian Reconstruction*, II (Winter 1975-76).

60. Charles M. Andrews, *The Colonial Period in American History*, 4 vols. *England's Commercial and Colonial Policy*, vol. 4 (New Haven, Connecticut: Yale University Press, [1938] 1964), pp. 224-26.

61. Berger, *Government By Judiciary*, pp. 399-400.

62. *Ibid.*, ch. 22. The case was *Williams v. Florida* (1970).

A related restriction on judicial sovereignty is the pardoning power. The U.S. Constitution grants this power to the President with respect to all Federal crimes, except Impeachment (Art. II, Sec. 2). State constitutions very often grant this pardoning power to the governor. Like jury nullification, this power is only exercised on a case-by-case basis; the decisions do not become binding as precedents.

The biblical principle of multiple human sovereignties points to the necessity of creating checks and balances to all branches of civil government, including the judiciary. There should be no *unitary* institutional final court of earthly appeal for every conceivable kind of judicial dispute. For some sorts of cases, yes, by agreement among the other branches, but not for every type of case. Plural sovereignties in civil government are basic to the preservation of liberty. There must be no Pharaoh in Israel.

Law: Man's Discovery or Man's Creation?

The courts have become the law-makers of final appeal. They interpret the law, apply the law, define the law, and overturn the decisions of legislatures and executives. They have become sovereign in the West. They even make new laws retroactively. Legal scholar Gordon Tullock remarks that this writing of new law by the courts is "a bizarre characteristic of Anglo-Saxon law. . . ."[63] He goes on to state: "In general, laws should have only future effect, and individuals should not be punished for actions not contrary to the law at the time the actions occurred. The retroactive effect in our law comes from a fact that the judges in mythology were attempting rather to find out what the law actually was than to create new law; hence, when the Supreme Court ruled as to what the law was, this did not create a new rule—it simply made manifest what had already been true. I think this myth is not much longer believed. Unfortunately, the consequence of it—that is, retroactive effect of court decisions—is still with us."[64]

Tullock does not discuss the origin of this "myth" of judge-discovered law. The roots of this idea are Christian. Anglo-Saxon common law was originally based indirectly on Old Testament law.

---

63. Gordon Tullock, "Courts as Legislatures," in Cunningham (ed.), *Liberty and the Rule of Law*, p. 132.
64. *Ibid.*, p. 134.

Canon law mixed Roman law and Old Testament law extensively.[65] The language of the Old Testament, including Mosaic law, was used to support all the institutions of Christendom. From the very early stages of Anglo-Saxon law, there was a concept of a "higher law," a concept which governed the writing of the U.S. Constitution.[66] Judges and legislators were supposed to search the Bible, and then search the principles of "right reason," in order to find what God requires from the civil government. Rulers were not to make law; they were to discover *God-made* law — an eternally existing revealed law. This law was believed to be revealed in the Bible and also in the hearts of all men. Rulers were then to apply this law to specific circumstances. But this law was not to be applied retroactively, in the sense of punishing people who had never heard of such law. All men were to know the principles of the law because of their access to instruction in biblical law from priests and magistrates, and also from their own internal reflection based on "right reason."

Hayek's account of the origin of "judge-discovered law" indicates that the concept was originally Christian. It was a medieval idea, especially dominant in England. He states quite openly that "it might also be said that it was because England retained more of the common medieval ideal of the supremacy of law, which was destroyed elsewhere by the rise of absolutism, that she was able to initiate the modern growth of liberty."[67]

This medieval view, which was profoundly important as background for modern developments, though completely accepted perhaps only during the early Middle Ages, was that "the state cannot itself create or make law, and of course as little abolish or violate law, because this would mean to abolish justice itself, it would be absurd, a sin, a rebellion against God who alone creates law." For centuries it was recognized doctrine that kings or any other human authority could only declare or find the existing law, or modify abuses that had crept in, and not create law. Only gradually, during the later Middle Ages, did the conception of deliberate creation of new law — legislation as we know it — come to be accepted. In England, Parliament thus developed from what had been mainly a law-finding body to a law-creating one.[68]

---

65. Berman, *Law and Revolution,* p. 204.

66. Edwin S. Corwin, *The "Higher Law" Background of American Constitutional Law* (Ithaca, New York: Cornell University Press, 1955).

67. Hayek, *Constitution of Liberty,* p. 163.

68. *Idem.*

He might also have added that it was the American colonists' hostility to the assertion of unlimited Parliamentary sovereignty in making laws which was a major factor in the coming of the American Revolution.[69] They believed, especially after 1770, that the common law of England could make void certain acts of Parliament, a doctrine taken directly from the writings of the early seventeenth-century English jurist Sir Edward Coke [COOK], who had greater influence on this point in the thinking of colonial lawyers before the Revolution than the *Commentaries* of Blackstone, who was a defender of Parliamentary sovereignty.[70] The American ideal of the doctrine of judicial supremacy and constitutionalism was not invented by Chief Justice John Marshall.[71]

Hayek traces the origin of Western legal liberty to the struggles between Parliament and Crown in the Puritan revolution or British Civil War, and subsequently in the Glorious Revolution of 1688.[72] There was a concerted effort to secure the independence of judges. The debates from 1641 to 1660 focused on the prevention of arbitrary actions by the civil government. Hayek even notes the influence of Puritan Samuel Rutherford's defense of the rule of biblical law: "Throughout, the governing idea was that the law should be king or, as one of the polemical tracts of the period expressed it, *Lex, Rex.*"[73]

This faith in biblical law, and subsequently the faith in independent natural law and right reason, began to wane as a result of rationalism and secularism, especially after Darwin, for Darwin destroyed men's faith in nature, including morality "naturally" in harmony with the forces of nature.[74] Because there is no longer a doctrine of fixed and infallible revealed law to govern the courts, and no longer any faith in a universal "higher law," the courts have

---

69. Bernard Bailyn, *The Ideological Origins of the American Revolution* (Cambridge, Massachusetts: Belknap Press of Harvard University Press, 1967), ch. 5; Edmund S. Morgan and Helen S. Morgan, *The Stamp Act Crisis: Prologue to Revolution* (rev. ed.; New York: Collier, 1963); R. J. Rushdoony, *This Independent Republic: Studies in the Nature and Meaning of American History* (Fairfax, Virginia: Thoburn Press, [1964] 1978), ch. 4: "Sovereignty."

70. Randolph G. Adams, *Political Ideas of the American Revolution: Britannic-American Contributions to the Problem of Imperial Organization, 1765-1775* (2nd ed.; New York: Barnes & Noble, [1939] 1958), p. 141.

71. *Ibid.,* p. 142.

72. *Constitution*, p. 169.

73. *Idem.*

74. R. J. Rushdoony, *The Biblical Philosophy of History* (Nutley, New Jersey: Presbyterian & Reformed, 1969), p. 7.

become autonomous law-givers. "Unfortunately," writes Tullock, "although legislatures realized a long time ago that they were writing new law, the courts have only very, very gradually come to the realization that they are doing the same thing. Further, when they did realize sometime in the nineteenth century, that they were writing new law, they continued making their decisions retroactive. It is only in the past ten years that the U.S. Supreme Court has begun to act as if it realized it was making retroactive decisions. Up to that time, the Court had always acted as if any decision was the discovery of a preexisting law rather than the formulation of new law, although surely judges were aware of the hypocrisy of this position for a least a hundred years."[75]

Democracy vs. Bureaucracy

Thus, with the abandonment of faith in revealed law that is open to both judge and jury, citizen and legislature, humanistic civil law has become perverse. Judges instruct juries to decide only in terms of the facts, not the validity of the law, when in fact the juries unquestionably have the authority and the power to interpret and apply both. Legislatures write new legislation, but they cannot easily preserve their own sovereignty; bureaucracies "interpret" these laws and are nearly autonomous in applying the laws in whatever way they want, in the name of the legislatures. *Elitist law dominates.* No layman is supposed to be able to understand the law. He must become subservient to the experts. Democracy, which is supposedly the process of widening the franchise and widening the base of sovereignty, becomes progressively bureaucratic and elitist. Increasingly, elitist rule is governed by the principle of secrecy, or to reverse President Wilson's dictum, of "closed covenants secretly arrived at."

Weber has described the process well: "Every bureaucracy seeks to increase the superiority of the professionally informed by keeping their knowledge and intentions secret. Bureaucratic administration always tends to be an administration of 'secret sessions': in so far as it can, it hides knowledge and action from criticism. . . . Political parties do not proceed differently, in spite of all the ostensible publicity of all Catholic congresses and party conventions. With the increasing bureaucratization of party organizations, this secrecy will prevail

---

75. Tullock, "Courts as Legislatures," in Cunningham (ed.), *Liberty and the Rule of Law,* p. 135.

even more."[76] The triumph of secret societies and secret accommodations in twentieth-century politics, both domestic and international,[77] is a product of the West's waning faith in God's revealed, open, and universally binding law.

We have come full circle. We are back to the pagan concept of true citizenship, based on membership in a clan which possesses secret knowledge. The pagan clan of antiquity was a bloodline clan, mitigated only by adoption. Citizens possessed the secret knowledge of the sacred rites — including political rites — through initiation into ritual mysteries. There are only formal differences between the two forms of pagan initiation, ancient and modern. Today, access to membership in the clan is also based on a kind of initiation, namely, the possession of specialized academic degrees or a certificate granted to those who have passed specialized examinations.[78] All of this has been accomplished in the name of the new religion, democracy, the apotheosis of mankind, but it has led to a new servitude, a new bondage, and to governing by arbitrary rules rather than universal law. The rhetoric of democracy — the sovereignty of the people — has led directly to its antithesis, the sovereignty of elites over the people in the name of the people. Weber writes:

We must expressly recall at this point that the political concept of democracy, deduced from the 'equal rights' of the governed, includes these postulates: (1) prevention of the development of a closed status group of officials in the interest of a universal accessibility of office, and (2) minimization of the authority of officialdom in the interest of expanding the sphere of influence of 'public opinion' as far as practicable. Hence, wherever possible, political democracy strives to shorten the term of office by election and recall and by not binding the candidate to a special expertness. Thereby democracy inevitably comes into conflict with the bureaucratic tendencies which, by its fight against notable rule, democracy has produced. The generally loose term 'democratization' cannot be used here, in so far as it is understood to mean the minimization of the civil servants' ruling power in favor of the greatest possible 'direct' rule of the *demos,* which in practice means the respective party leaders of the *demos.* The most decisive thing here — indeed it is rather exclusively so — is the *leveling of the*

---

76. Max Weber, "Bureaucracy," in H. H. Gerth and C. Wright Mills (eds.), *From Max Weber: Essays in Sociology* (New York: Oxford University Press, 1946), p. 233. The same passage appears in *Economy & Society,* p. 992.

77. Carroll Quigley, *Tragedy and Hope: A History of the World in Our Time* (New York: Macmillan, 1966).

78. Weber, "Bureaucracy," pp. 240-44; *Economy & Society,* pp. 998-1001.

governed in opposition to the ruling and bureaucratically articulated group, which in its turn may occupy a quite autocratic position, both in fact and in form.[79]

Tullock wants something better. He wants a return to the "good old days" of simple, predictable laws. He knows that he is unlikely to get his wish. "A switch to a system in which the bulk of the law is a code and there is a central body which produces detailed glosses upon it, the whole thing being relatively short and compact, would reduce immense amounts of legal human capital to worthlessness. Thus, the lawyers have the combination of very strong feeling with which they have been indoctrinated, even stronger material grounds for wanting their present position to remain stable, and practically a monopoly of all decision-making posts in our present system. Under the circumstances, I doubt very much if my arguments here will have any political effect."[80] He blames the economic self-interest of the judicial elite for our plight, but the problem is far deeper. Our problem is the abandonment of Christianity and biblical law.

Hayek's Dilemma: "Social Justice"

F. A. Hayek, whose intellectual roots are in late-nineteenth-century liberalism, has produced a series of books dealing with formal law and market freedom. His most famous and influential book, *The Road to Serfdom* (1944), argued that economic intervention by the civil government would eventually destroy the institutions of political democracy, for the bureaucracies created by socialism would eventually concentrate decision-making powers in the hands of the central economic planners. Central economic planning, he argued, would have to result in central planning for everything, since all aspects of human life involve economic choices.

In his later book, *The Constitution of Liberty* (1960), Hayek argued for the rule of law. He proposed a system of law which would be universally understood, where the "rules of the game" would be known by all participants in advance, thereby reducing the arbitrariness and unpredictability of the bureaucrats. But he could not guarantee market predictability by means of universally applicable law, as his critics immediately reminded him. Civil law can be

---

79. *Ibid.,* p. 226; *Economy & Society,* p. 985.
80. Tullock, in Cunningham (ed.), *Liberty and the Rule of Law,* p. 144.

changed. The law system may be unfair from the very beginning, discriminating against those who become economically successful.

Hayek has devoted the remainder of his distinguished career to the problem of legal order. How can we insulate the institutions of political democracy from those elements in society that are opposed to formal liberty, formal rationalism, economic inequality, and legal predictability? How can we preserve a working relationship between formal rationalism and substantive rationalism? He has never come up with a generally acceptable answer—acceptable to free market defenders, let alone to envy-dominated socialists and Communist revolutionaries. We therefore need to examine his thinking in detail, for if he cannot successfully defend the humanistic ideal of the rule of law, then we should have much greater confidence in a defense of the Christian ideal of the rule of biblical law.

Hayek does not equate liberalism with formal legalism as such. He says that liberalism also requires specific content to formal rationality, namely, *constitutionally limited civil government.*[81] Coercion by the civil government must be restricted by constitutional and statute law. Only this will permit the establishment of what he calls the "spontaneous order," or (less felicitously but more revealingly) the "self-generating order" or "self-organizing structures."[82] He writes: "But if liberalism presupposes the enforcement of rules of just conduct and expects a desirable spontaneous order to form itself only if appropriate rules of just conduct are in fact observed, it also wants to restrict the *coercive* powers of government to the enforcement of such rules of just conduct, including at least one prescribing a positive duty, namely, the rule requiring citizens to contribute according to uniform principles not only to the cost of enforcing those rules but also to the costs of the non-coercive service functions of government which we shall presently consider."[83]

Hayek introduces the concept of "non-coercive service functions of government." At this point, he makes at least *formal peace with the welfare State,* and therefore with its system of tax-financed social security. He goes on: "Liberalism is therefore the same as the demand for the rule of law in the classical sense of the term according

---

81. Hayek, *Law, Legislation and Liberty,* III, *The Political Order of a Free People* (University of Chicago Press, 1979).

82. *Ibid.,* p xii.

83. F. A. Hayek, "The Principles of a Liberal Social Order" (1966); reprinted in Hayek, *Studies in Philosophy, Politics and Economics* (University of Chicago Press, 1967), p. 165.

to which the coercive functions of government are strictly limited to the enforcement of uniform rules of law, meaning uniform rules of just conduct towards one's fellows."[84] But what if these "uniform rules" discriminate against a particular economic group? The graduated income tax is one example. There are thousands of others, since virtually all of the modern welfare State's legislation is economically discriminatory.

The Preservation of Social Order: Market or State?

Hayek is caught in a dilemma. He wants a social order which actually preserves order. He wants a society which is rational, both formally and substantively. On the one hand, he wants legal predictability (formal rationalism). He wants *equality before the law*. The problem is, market competition produces economic winners and losers. "From the fact that people are very different it follows that, if we treat them equally, the result must be inequality in their actual position, and that the only way to place them in an equal position would be to treat them differently. Equality before the law and material equality are therefore not only different but are in conflict with each other; and we can achieve either the one or the other, but not both at the same time. The equality before the law which freedom requires leads to material inequality."[85] *The losers can and do use democratic politics to redistribute the winnings in the name of social justice.* He then observes, with considerable historical justification, "More than by anything else the market order has been distorted by efforts to protect groups from a decline from their former position; and when government interference is demanded in the name of 'social justice' this now means, more often than not, the demand for the protection of the existing relative position of some group. 'Social justice' has thus become little more than a demand for the protection of vested interests and the creation of new privilege. . . ."[86]

On the other hand, he also wants the civil government to provide a *safety net,* so that the social order of capitalism can be insulated against revolutionary shocks. He thinks civil government can reduce social disorder by violating his earlier principle of "unequal results from equality before the law." He wants a *minimum welfare State:* "The reasonable solution of these problems in a free society would seem to

---

84. *Studies,* p. 165.
85. Hayek, *Constitution of Liberty,* p. 87.
86. Hayek, *Studies,* p. 173.

be that, while the state provides only a uniform minimum for all who are unable to maintain themselves and endeavors to reduce cyclical unemployment as much as possible by an appropriate monetary policy, any further provision required for the maintenance of the accustomed standard should be left to competitive and voluntary efforts."[87] Which of Hayek's two irreconcilable arguments are we to believe?

Hayek is stuck. Volume two of *Law, Legislation and Liberty* is titled, *The Mirage of Social Justice*. He proclaims the idea of one law for all men. He proclaims the benefits of general rules that are written without any attention to the specific individual results of such rules.[88] As a defender of methodological individualism, he attacks the very concept of social justice. Such a concept presupposes a hierarchy of collective ends. But we cannot as "scientific economists" speak of the "value to society" of any economic good or service.[89] We can only speak of a service's value to individually acting men or to an organization. Society is not an organization; it is a spontaneous order. Civil government is an organization; society is not. "And, though the order of society will be affected by actions of government, so long as it remains a spontaneous order, the particular results of the social process cannot be just or unjust."[90] Thus, it is illegitimate to speak of social justice. Such a concept is anthropomorphic and immature.[91] Society cannot act for a single purpose.[92] To whom can we appeal if we believe that the outcome of spontaneous and therefore unplanned market forces is somehow unjust? There is no answer.[93] The concept of social justice has meaning only in a command society.[94] The term itself has become an implement of demagoguery.[95]

Having said all this, he nevertheless calls for a State-imposed redistribution of wealth in the name of preserving social order. Yet he opposes socialism and democratic economic interventionism because such coercion is destructive of morality.[96] And then, as if to

---

87. Hayek, *Constitution*, p. 302.
88. *The Mirage of Social Justice,* ch. 7: "General Welfare and Particular Purposes."
89. *Ibid.,* p. 75.
90. *Ibid.,* p. 32.
91. *Ibid.,* pp. 62-63.
92. *Ibid.,* p. 64.
93. *Ibid.,* p. 69.
94. *Idem.*
95. *Ibid.,* p. 97.
96. *The Political Order of a Free People,* pp. 170-71.

confuse everyone (including himself), he denies any belief in absolute morality.

Moral Relativism

He rejects the idea of transcendent law, whether "natural" or "personal," for he is a defender of autonomous man and autonomous spontaneous social evolution. "The evolutionary approach to law (and all other social institutions) which is here defended has thus as little to do with the rationalist theories of natural law as with legal positivism. It rejects both the interpretation of law as the construct of a super-natural force and its interpretation as the deliberate construct of any human mind."[97] There is no overarching morality which governs society. "There can, therefore, be no absolute system of morals independent of the kind of social order in which a person lives. . . ."[98] He even goes so far as to argue that if a Westerner discovers a dying, elderly Eskimo who has been put into the snow to die by his people, according to Eskimo customs, he should leave him in the snow to die. It would be "morally wrong" to do otherwise, unless the outsider is personally willing to support him in non-Eskimo society forever.[99]

Hayek's moral relativism cannot sustain a vision of society without adopting pure anarchism, yet he cannot seem to bring himself to adopt anarchism, the logical outcome of full-blown methodological individualism. He still wants the civil government to provide everyone — presumably even that aged Eskimo — with a safety net. "There is no reason why in a free society government should not assure to all protection against severe deprivation in the form of an assured minimum income, or a floor below which nobody need descend." Why does he say this? Because he wants to defend *collective self-interest!* Because he wants to defend *morality!* "To enter into such an insurance against extreme misfortune may well be in the interest of all; or it may be felt to be a clear moral duty of all to assist, within the organized community, those who cannot help themselves." We are back to two previously forbidden justifications of social justice: collective self-interest and moral duty. "So long as such a uniform minimum income is provided outside the market to all those who,

97. *The Mirage of Social Justice,* p. 60.
98. *Ibid.,* p. 27.
99. *Idem.*

for any reason, are unable to earn in the market an adequate maintenance, this need not lead to a restriction of freedom, or conflict with the Rule of Law."[100] Question: *How is the civil government going to extract the economic resources needed to provide this safety net without interfering with the spontaneous order of the anarchistic free market order?*

A Self-Contradictory System

He is trapped in a logical and moral dilemma. The State must use coercion to obtain the "safety net" money. But such taxation is innately immoral, according to Hayek, the anarchist. It also threatens the existence of the spontaneous order.

The predominant view today appears to be that we should avail ourselves in the main of the ordering forces of the market, indeed must in a great measure do so, but should 'correct' its results where they are flagrantly unjust. [This, in fact, is precisely what Hayek himself has argued in the passages I have just cited — G.N.] Yet so long as the earnings of particular individuals or groups are not determined by the decision of some agency, no particular distribution of incomes can be meaningfully described as more just than another. If we want to make it substantively just, we can do so only by replacing the whole spontaneous order by an organization in which the share of each is fixed by some central authority. In other words, 'corrections' of the distribution brought about in a spontaneous process by particular acts of interference can never be just in the sense of satisfying a rule equally applicable to all. Every single act of this kind will give rise to demands by others to be treated on the same principle; and these demands can be satisfied only if all incomes are thus allocated.[101]

Here is Hayek, the all-or-nothing anarchist, holding forth bravely and decisively against Hayek, the defender of safety-net social justice. He refuses to give an inch to the demands of the special-interest groups who would destroy the free market, intervention by intervention, tax by tax, safety net by safety net. But in not giving an inch here, he cannot logically give an inch anywhere else. Yet he does. So his methodological walls come tumbling down, brick by brick, inch by inch.

The extent to which Hayek's thinking is not just muddled, but self-contradictory, testifies to the innate antinomies of humanist social thought. He has a great mind. He has had sixty years to

---

100. *Ibid.,* p. 87.
101. *Ibid.,* p. 142.

develop his ideas. He has been incomparably diligent in mastering the scholarly literature relating to these questions. And he has brought forth a heavily footnoted, self-defeating trilogy, the capstone of his life's work. The third volume is devoted to a classic piece of what he has called "constructivist" rationalism: an historically untested restructuring of the legislative, judicial and executive branches of civil government, complete with a "model constitution" (chapter 17). Here is "Benthamism" at its utopian worst—the same Benthamism which Hayek has battled against throughout his long career.[102] In the second volume, he proclaims forthrightly: ". . . we can always only tinker with parts of a given whole but never entirely redesign it."[103] In the third, he proposes a total redesigning of every nation's entire institutional system of civil government.

Who Decides?

We are back to the age-old problem: The rule of *which* law-order? The rule of *how much* civil government? Hayek, in seeking for formal rules of civil government—rules that will be applied to all citizens, irrespective of social or economic position—finds that the humanistic logic of free market economics cannot be reconciled fully with the humanistic logic of social and political stability. We are back to Weber's dichotomy between formal rationalism and substantive rationalism. The ethics of society supposedly demands that the civil government intervene in exactly the way that Hayek says is *most dangerous to freedom,* namely, *to preserve the economic position of a specific special-interest group.* How can this protection be denied to all other special-interest groups that possess sufficient political power to rewrite the legislation? This is Hayek's problem, and he devoted the second half of his illustrious academic career to a study of *how to insulate a liberal free market society from the effects of the liberal democratic political order.* Human logic did not give him his answer. There are too many logics, too many ethical views, and no way to make interpersonal comparisons of subjective utility.

Twentieth-century liberal democracy has eroded market freedom. Hayek's eloquent defense of freedom in terms of evolutionary law and evolutionary morality has not retarded this erosion; if anything, it has accelerated it. As J. R. Lucas has commented con-

---

102. *Ibid.,* pp. 19-20.
103. *Ibid.,* p. 25.

cerning Hayek's defense, "he comes perilously close to a position of moral indifferentism and makes a great virtue of the market's unconcern with moral merit. But this is, I shall argue, to expose free institutions quite gratuitously to the moral censure of moral men. The reason why the West has become increasingly critical of its economic arrangements is not that it has failed to deliver the goods—on the contrary, it has been spectacularly successful in doing that—but that the *theory* of them has failed to accord with our moral sentiments about society and has sometimes affronted our sense of justice."[104]

Natural Law Theory vs. Biblical Law

In the history of Christian social theory, there has been continuing confusion concerning the relationship between biblical law and Greek and Roman natural law theory. Before drawing this chapter to a close, we need to review what the Bible says about law. Christian social theory has been compromised again and again in the past because of errors in thinking about revealed law and the various aspects of this revelation.

The biblical doctrine of the universality of God's law is not the same as the concept of natural law, a theory developed especially by Greek and Roman philosophers, which passed into Western history through the writings of medieval church scholars.[105] Natural law is based on the idea of man's universal reason. The minds of men supposedly have in common the powers of reasoning, thereby implying the existence of a universal human mind, and the logic of this universal mind could, if respected, bring all men everywhere to acknowledge identical fundamental principles of law.

Aristotle's analytic distinction between particular laws and general laws is an excellent example of natural law philosophy. It rests on a concept of *human unity,* implying shared viewpoints. "Now there are two kinds of laws, particular and general. By particular laws I mean those established by each people in reference to themselves, which again are divided into written and unwritten; by general laws I mean those based upon nature. In fact, there is a general idea of just and unjust in accordance with nature, as all men in manner divine, even if there is neither communication nor agree-

---

104. J. R. Lucas, "Liberty, Morality, and Justice," in Cunningham (ed.), *Liberty and the Rule of Law,* p. 150.

105. Archie P. Jones, "Natural Law and Christian Resistance to Tyranny," *Christianity and Civilization,* 2 (1983).

ment between them."[106] Such a conception of natural law rests on
the assumption of a universal human logic, the universal applicability in history of that logic, and the universal recognition of this logic
and its universal applicability by all reasonable men. It assumes, in
short, the *neutrality* of human thought.

The Myth of Neutrality

The Bible explicitly denies any such neutrality. Men are divided
into saved and lost, keepers of God's covenant and breakers of God's
covenant. There is no agreement between the two positions. There
is such a thing as the *work* of the law of God which is written in
every human heart — not the law itself, which is a special gift of God
to His people (Heb. 8:8-11), but the work of the law (Rom. 2:14-15).
Nevertheless, this law serves only to condemn men, for they will not
abide by its provisions: "For there is no respect of persons with God.
For as many as have sinned without law shall also perish without
law: and as many as have sinned in the law shall be judged by the
law" (Rom. 2:11-12). Human reason, unaided by God's revelation —
untwisted by God's grace — cannot be expected to devise a universal
law code based on any presumed universal human logic. What
mankind's universal reason *can* be expected to do is to *rebel* against
God and His law. Ethical rebels are not logically faithful to God.

Biblical law had to be read to everyone in Israel at least once
every seven years (Deut. 31:10-13). God presumed that men would
not understand His law unless they heard it (Deut. 31:13). Every
resident of the land had to listen to this law. If the whole of biblical
law had been ingrained into the consciences of all men from the beginning of time, or if the terms of the law, including the law's explicit
penalties, were always available to all men through the exercise of
man's universal reason, then the law would not have required the
priests to read the Mosaic law before the congregation of Israel every
seventh year.

In our day, why should Christians who have biblical law written
in their heart (Heb. 8:9-11) still have to listen to the public teaching
of this law? Because the implantation of biblical law at the time of a
person's regeneration is *definitive*, not *progressive*, and certainly not
final. Biblical law is implanted in the believer, but the old sin nature

---

106. Aristotle, *Rhetoric*, I, 1373b; from *The Art of Rhetoric*, trans. John Henry
Freese (Cambridge, Massachusetts: Harvard University Press, 1926).

still wars against the law (Rom. 7). Thus, Christians also as sinners tend to hold back the truths of the law in unrighteousness (Rom. 1:18). Nevertheless, the definitive implanting of biblical law in the hearts of the regenerate — a definitive event leading progressively through study and application to our final understanding of the law — is different from the work of the law which is in the heart of the unbeliever. What the unbeliever has in his heart is *definitive rebellion,* in Adam. As he progressively works out the implications of his faith, he loses sight of the work of the law. He works out progressively what is *definitively inherited* by him, namely, *ethical rebellion.*

The popularity of natural law concepts has been very great throughout the history of the church. By importing Greek and Roman concepts of natural law into church law, medieval theologians unknowingly mixed together two rival systems of thought. The Greek and Roman concept of natural law rested on the presupposition of *man's autonomy.* It rested on the presupposition of *neutrality* in human thought. The Bible recognizes the common heritage of the image of God in man, but it sees this image as twisted and perverse in rebellious man. Thus, the universality of men's perception of certain aspects of biblical law is a *universality of condemnation.* The Bible requires that we build the kingdom of God in terms of a different universality, the universality of *the binding nature of biblical law.* It is the *whole of God's law* which is binding on individual men and corporate associations, not simply this or that dimly perceived, and improperly interpreted, aspect of God's law.

The Work of the Law

Romans 2:14-15 reads: "For when the Gentiles, which have not the law of God, do by nature the things contained in the law, these, having not the law, are a law unto themselves: which shew the work of the law written in their hearts, their conscience also bearing witness, and their thoughts the meanwhile accusing or else excusing one another." John Murray's extensive commentary on these verses is important in understanding what they do not mean, as well as what they do mean. Murray writes:

"By nature" is contrasted with what is derived from external sources and refers to that which is engraven on our natural constitution. What is done "by nature" is done by native instinct or propension, by spontaneous impulse as distinguished from what is induced by forces extraneous to ourselves. The things done by nature are said to be "the things of the law." It is to be observed that the apostle does not say that they do or fulfil the law and he must have intentionally refrained from such an expression. "The things of the law" must mean certain things which the law prescribes and refer to those things practiced by pagans which are stipulated in the law, such as the pursuit of lawful vocations, the procreation of offspring, filial and natural affection, the care of the poor and sick, and numerous other natural virtues which are required by the law. In doing these things "by nature" they "are the law unto themselves." This expression should not be understood in the sense of popular current use when we say that a man is a law to himself. It means almost the opposite, that they themselves, by reason of what is implanted in their nature, confront themselves with the law of God. They themselves reveal the law of God to themselves — their persons is the medium of revelation. . . . Hence with respect to those without specifically revealed law three things are true: (1) the law of God confronts them and registers itself in their consciousness by reason of what they natively and constitutionally are; (2) they do things which this law prescribes; (3) this doing is not by extraneous constraint but by natural impulse.[107]

It is not a different law which confronts them in their heart, Murray says; it is not a rival law to the law delivered to God's people through Moses. At the same time, "Paul does not say that the law is written upon their hearts. He refrains from this form of statement apparently for the same reason as in verse 14 he had said that the Gentiles 'do the things of the law' and not that they did or fulfilled the law. Such expressions as 'fulfilling the law' and 'the law written upon the heart' are reserved for a state of heart and mind and will far beyond that predicated of unbelieving Gentiles."[108] So the *work* of the law, or the *things* of the law, written in their hearts, is comprehensive enough to *condemn* them, but it is not the transforming reworking of the heart which the Bible refers to as regeneration.

There is no dominion apart from the categories of biblical law. All men are called to subdue the earth, and even rebellious men are sufficiently restrained by their own nature, in time and on earth, so that they might exercise dominion. God promised to drive the Canaanites out of the land slowly, so that the land might not revert to wilderness (Ex. 23:28-29). Better unregenerate man in control of Canaan than the wild beasts, God said. The unregenerate are given

---

107. John Murray, *The Epistle to the Romans*, 2 vols. (Grand Rapids, Michigan: Eerdmans, 1964), I, pp. 73-74. A later edition in one volume replaced the two-volume edition.

108. *Ibid.*, I, pp. 74-75.

a restraining knowledge of the law, so that they might exercise dominion. When we find a culture which is in almost total rebellion against the work of the law, we find almost total impotence. The African tribe, the Ik, serve as an example of almost total rebellion against God's law: envious, vicious, unwilling to nurture children after age three, a tribe of thieves, the Ik face extinction. They have almost lost the ability to exercise sufficient dominion to keep themselves alive.[109] Men cannot build societies by means of "natural" law.

Perhaps the clearest statement of the progressive separation of the righteous from the unrighteous over time was made by a character in C. S. Lewis' magnificent novel, *That Hideous Strength*. The character, Prof. Dimble, describes the effects of the development over time of both the Christian and non-Christian views. As time goes on, they become more and more self-consistent, and therefore less and less compatible. "If you dip into any college, or school, or parish, or family — anything you like — at a given point in its history, you always find that there was a time before that point when there was more elbow room, and contrasts weren't quite as sharp; and that there's going to be a time after that point when there is even less room for indecision, and choices are even more momentous. Good is always getting better, and bad is always getting worse: the possibilities of even apparent neutrality are always diminishing. The whole thing is sorting itself out all the time, coming to a point, getting sharper and harder."[110] The farther in time we get from the garden of Eden, or from Noah's flood, or from the crucifixion, the less that rebellious men will acknowledge or adhere to the testimony of the work of the law written on their hearts. To appeal to natural law is to lean on a weak reed.

The Collapse of Natural Law Theory

In the latter decades of the twentieth century, the West has experienced the long-term effects of a revolution which was begun in the Enlightenment, and which became institutionally inescapable with the outbreak of World War I. A crisis of confidence has appeared in the West which has undermined the West's confidence in its own legal institutions. Harold Berman's account of this erosion is masterful:

---

109. Colin Turnbull, *The Mountain People* (New York: Simon & Schuster, 1973).
110. C. S. Lewis, *That Hideous Strength: A Modern Fairy-Tale for Grown-Ups* (New York: Macmillan, [1946] 1965), p. 283.

That the Western legal tradition, like Western civilization as a whole, is undergoing in the twentieth century a crisis greater than it has ever known before is not something that can be proved scientifically. It is something that is known, ultimately, by intuition. I can only testify, so to speak, that I sense that we are in the midst of an unprecedented crisis of legal values and of legal thought, in which our entire legal tradition is being challenged — not only the so-called liberal concepts of the past few hundred years, but the very structure of Western legality, which dates from the eleventh and twelfth centuries.

The crisis is being generated both from within Western experience and from without. From within, social and economic and political transformations of unprecedented magnitude have put a tremendous strain upon traditional legal institutions, legal values, and legal concepts in virtually all countries of the West. Yet in the past there have been periods of revolutionary upheaval which have also threatened to destroy basic elements of the Western legal tradition, and that tradition has nevertheless survived. What is new today is the challenge to the legal tradition as a whole, and not merely to particular elements or aspects of it; and this is manifested above all in the confrontation with non-Western civilizations and non-Western philosophies. In the past, Western man has confidently carried his law with him throughout the world. The world today, however, is suspicious — more suspicious than ever before — of Western "legalism." Eastern and Southern Man offer other alternatives. The West itself has come to doubt the universal validity of its traditional vision of law, especially its validity for non-Western cultures. Law that used to seem "natural" seems only "Western." And many are saying that it is obsolete even for the West.[111]

The acids of the West's own humanism and relativism have eroded the foundations of Western legality, which has been one of the chief pillars of Western civilization. If all cultures are equally valid, then their legal traditions are also equally valid as aspects of these competing cultures. Therefore, Hayek recommends that we refuse to save that dying elderly Eskimo who has been left to perish in the snow by his peers. Is it any wonder, then, that Hayek's eloquent plea for a nineteenth-century version of the rule of law has failed to gain the commitment of scholars and social philosophers in the twentieth? His own twentieth-century relativism (implicit in nineteenth-century relativism) has eroded his economic and legal prescriptions. Is it any wonder that his logical defense of the free market economy, which rests on the legal foundation of plural legal sovereignties, limited civil government, and equality before the law, has lost its ap-

---

111. Berman, *Law and Revolution*, pp. 33-34.

peal in this age of democratic centralism?

Men seek a sovereignty greater than themselves, a sovereignty which can guarantee meaning to their lives and success in their many ventures. If God is not the source of law, and law is not universally valid because it is revealed, biblical law, then only a hypothetical universal power State remains to give man the sovereignty he seeks. If this also fails, then nothing remains to assure mankind that his works have meaning in time and on earth. Then the escapist religion leaves mankind with its only hope: mystical self-transcendance and flight from mundane reality.

The failure of natural law doctrine was assured when men at last ceased to equate natural law with biblical law. When natural law was at last recognized as "natural" rather than revealed, autonomous rather than created, then it gained its universality only to the extent that mankind is seen as a true universal. But with the rise of relativism as an epistemological principle, the hoped-for unity of man collapsed. Now only power remains, not natural law. Now only the rise of a new source of unity, the world State, can guarantee man's legal order the unity it requires to maintain its claim to "naturalness." Natural law thereby ceases being natural. A universal law can only be *imposed* by the power State. To summarize: natural law theory abandoned reliance on the revealed law of the God of the Bible in order to assert its autonomy and universality, only to lose both its autonomy and naturalness (self-attesting universal validity) to the new sovereignty of the power State.

The Primacy of Faith

Because different men and different nations are always in various stages of active rebellion against God—the active *restraining* of the truth of God which testifies to them in their own natures—we cannot hope to gain agreement about universal principles of law. It is not reason which opens the precepts of the law to rebellious men. They already have such precepts. Their consciences testify to them of the truth, but they restrain the truth, holding it back in unrighteousness (Rom. 1:18).[112] To believe that reason will reveal to men the universal principles of God's dominion covenant (which is also His treaty of unconditional surrender), is *to believe that reason is untainted by the Fall of man.* But reason has been as twisted by that ethical rebellion as

---

112. On this active suppression of the truth, see John Murray, *Romans,* I, pp. 36-37.

surely as any other aspect of man's personality. To believe in natural law is to believe in natural reason; to believe in natural reason, or "reason rightly understood," is to believe in the *primacy of the intellect*.[113] The Bible does not teach the primacy of the intellect; it teaches the *primacy of faith*.

When men say that "the Bible is not in contradiction to scientific truth," they generally mean that the Bible is not in opposition to the discoveries of the autonomous human intellect. This statement is absolutely false, if such a conclusion is intended. The Bible is absolutely *opposed* to such universally proclaimed "scientific truths" as evolution of one species into another through natural selection, or the eternality of matter-energy, or the doctrine of uniformitarian change. What a consistent Christian must maintain is this: "The Bible is the foundation for human reason, and no conclusion of the human mind which is in opposition to revealed truth in the Bible is scientifically valid." The truths of science, if they are to be accepted, must be in conformity to biblical revelation. There are not two truths — "natural science" and biblical revelation — but rather one truth: science *in conformity to* biblical revelation. And what is true of natural science — the man-interpreted regularities of the observed universe — must also be true of man's speculation in other areas of life.

We dare not say that "natural law" and biblical revelation are the same because the truths of human jurisprudence are "naturally" in conformity to biblical revelation. We must say, on the contrary, that the truths of human jurisprudence, insofar as they are true, are true *in spite of* man's twisted, rebellious, "natural" reason. This is why the Bible required that Israel assemble once every seven years to listen to the reading of the law of God.

Conclusion

The doctrine of the rule of law is distinctly biblical in origin. A law-order which is universally binding on all men is an idea which had its origins in biblical religion. The same God who judges all men

---

113. The rationalist apologetic methodology of "old Princeton" Seminary is representative of this error. Benjamin B. Warfield wrote of "irrational faith, that is, a faith without grounds in right reason." Warfield, "Introduction to Francis R. Beattie's *Apologetics*" (1903); reprinted in John E. Meeter (ed.), *Selected Shorter Writings of Benjamin B. Warfield — II* (Nutley, New Jersey: Presbyterian & Reformed, 1973), p. 98. He implicitly contrasted such a faith with Christianity, which apparently is a faith which *is* grounded in "right reason." The problem, of course, is that nobody agrees about the content or standards of "right reason."

also puts all men under the terms of biblical law. The God who made Adam also made all men responsible to Him through Adam. Thus, when the Hebrews placed foreign residents under both the restraints of biblical law and the benefits of biblical law, they made a fundamental break with paganism. Natural law theory, which was later paganism's attempt to appropriate the universalism of biblical law, was adopted by the West through the influence of church canon law and other remnants of Hebrew law.

Some fundamental aspects of the rule of law are these:

1. A common set of moral requirements
2. Public proclamation of the law
3. Universal application of these standards
4. Equality before the law (no respecting of persons)

In short, the law is to be *predictible and universal.* Civil law as it applies to citizens in their daily activities is to be sufficiently simple so that the vast majority of men can understand its general principles and its specific applications (case laws). This is not to deny that specialized applications of biblical law principles are never going to be complex. But those who work in specialized areas of society are to be aware of these specialized applications. It may be that a "jury of one's peers," or at least a portion of the jury's membership, should be composed of people selected randomly from a group of specialists in the particular sphere or calling of the litigants. The crucial issue is *legal predictability,* not the technicalities of the law. In short, men are to have reasonable expectations concerning the decisions of judges and juries in specific legal conflicts. Most important, *men must have confidence in the integrity of the law itself,* and not just the institutional agencies of law enforcement, for without confidence in the law itself, men will not believe that their day-by-day adherence to the law is related directly to external benefits, both individual and social. They will lose the major incentive of *self-government under law.*

Without the rule of law, capitalism could never have developed. It developed in the West precisely because Christianity was the religion of the West. As Christianity's influence has waned, especially in the last hundred years, capitalism has been challenged by increasingly hostile socialist critics. *Formal legal predictability,* the bedrock of a free market social order, has been abandoned by the intellectuals and the voters. The predictable "rules of the game" that govern capitalism are no longer respected by expansionist civil governments that are propelled by the politics of envy.

J. R. Lucas has commented on the relationship between atheism and State-worship: "In an age in which many people find it hard to believe in God, there is a strong tendency to worship the state — or society — as a God-substitute and to refer all our demands and duties to it alone, and then the demand for distributive justice will manifest totalitarian tendencies. The mistake lies in thinking too much of the state, not in seeking justice in our dealings with our fellow man."[114] As men's faith in God and His revealed word has declined along the greased skids of human autonomy — from Roman law to canon law, to scholastic natural law, to Deism's natural law, and then to the positive law of the State — the State has become increasingly dominant.

The pluralism of the law is the great threat to Western society. What was plural in the Western legal tradition was not the law-order itself, but rather the *legal order* — the institutions and spheres of application of a *universal law-order.* It was not the law-order which was plural, but the enforcement mechanisms in the various social and institutional spheres. What is today destroying the Western legal tradition is the pluralism of religious humanism — *a pluralism of law-orders.* This points to a pluralism of gods, or rather the absence of any one God as Creator and Guarantor of a single law-order. Men now seek to create a new unified law-order which will testify to a new god. This new god is the same old god of the satanic temptation: the power State, the highest and most powerful representative of the sovereign god of humanism, collective mankind.

The rise of arbitrary government, with its punitive legislation against economic profits, now threatens the West with a return to pagan barbarism. This was the lesson of the Hebrews in Egypt. It has also become the lesson of twentieth-century administrative law, administered by bureaucracies. We must take seriously the warning of Harold Berman regarding the collapse of faith in Western legality.

The crisis of the Western legal tradition is not merely a crisis in legal philosophy but also a crisis in law itself. Legal philosophers have always debated, and presumably always will debate, whether law is founded in reason and morality or whether it is only the will of the political ruler. It is not necessary to resolve that debate in order to conclude that as a matter of historical fact the legal systems of all the nations that are heirs to the

---

114. Lucas, "Liberty, Morality, and Justice," in Cunningham (ed.), *Liberty and the Rule of Law,* p. 148.

Western legal tradition have been rooted in certain beliefs or postulates: that is, the legal systems themselves have presupposed the validity of those beliefs. Today those beliefs or postulates—such as the structural integrity of the law, its ongoingness, its religious roots, its transcendent qualities—are rapidly disappearing, not only from the minds of philosophers, not only from the minds of lawmakers, judges, lawyers, law teachers, and other members of the legal profession, but from the consciousness of the vast majority of citizens, the people as a whole; and more than that, they are disappearing from the law itself. The law is becoming more fragmented, more subjective, geared more to expediency and less to morality, concerned more with immediate consequences and less with consistency and continuity. Thus the historical soil of the Western legal tradition is being washed away in the twentieth century, and the tradition itself is threatened with collapse.

The breakdown of the Western legal tradition springs only in part from the socialist revolutions that were inaugurated in Russia in October 1917 and that have gradually spread throughout the West (and throughout other parts of the world as well), albeit often in relatively mild forms. It springs only in part from massive state intervention in the economy of the nation (the welfare state), and only in part from the massive bureaucratization of social and economic life through huge centralized corporate entities (the corporate state). It springs much more from the crisis of Western civilization itself, commencing in 1914 with the outbreak of World War I. This was more than an economic and technological revolution, more even than a political revolution. If it had not been, Western society would be able to adapt its legal institutions to meet the new demands placed upon them, as it has done in revolutionary situations in the past. Western society would be able to accommodate socialism—of whatever variety—within its legal tradition. But the disintegration of the very foundations of that tradition cannot be accommodated; and the greatest challenge to those foundations is the massive loss of confidence in the West itself, as a civilization, a community, and in the legal tradition which for nine centuries has helped to sustain it.[115]

The age-old debate among legal scholars which he mentions— whether reason and morality are the source of law, or the ruler—is answered by the Bible. God is the Ruler and therefore the source of both reason and morality. Both morality and the law-order are harmonious and self-reinforcing, because they are both created by God and under God. Because men as philosophers, moralists, and political rulers are in the image of God, their thoughts and acts reflect the

---

115. Berman, *Law and Revolution,* pp. 39-40.

God who made them. They may deviate from His thoughts and
laws, for they are in various degrees ethical rebels, but man's law-
order can never wholly escape God's ultimate standards. God is absolutely sovereign; reason, morality, and kings are only derivatively
sovereign.

We must also respond to the crisis of Western law with the
answers that Berman is unwilling to call for: the restoration of Christianity as the foundation of Western religion, the restoration of this
religion as the foundation of morality and reason, and the establishment of biblical law — and not the restoration of natural law theory —
as the foundation of social order. Nothing else will revive the West. A
true religious revival — a *comprehensive revival* which restructures every
human institution in terms of biblical law — alone can establish the
West's foundations of long-term social and legal order. A true revival
alone can re-establish the long-term institutional foundations of the
free market economy.

15

THE FIRSTBORN OFFERING

The LORD spake unto Moses, saying, Sanctify unto me all the firstborn, whatsoever openeth the womb among the children of Israel, both of man and of beast: it is mine (Ex. 13:1-2).

God owns all things (Ps. 24:1). Nevertheless, He set apart ritually the firstborn males of Israel. It was a symbol to the people of Israel of the sovereignty of God. Each family had to regard the precious firstborn as God's property. "For all of the firstborn of the children of Israel are mine, both man and beast: on the day that I smote every firstborn in the land of Egypt I sanctified them for myself" (Num. 8:17). God set them apart—sanctified them—as His special possession.

The symbolism of the firstborn is important in the Bible. Adam was God's created firstborn son (Luke 3:38), and Adam was created to serve God as God's assistant in charge of the earth. Adam's rebellion called forth God's grace in sending Jesus Christ, the second Adam (I Cor. 15:45). Jesus Christ was more than a created firstborn Son; He was the only begotten Son of God, the second Person of the Trinity (John 1:14, 18; Acts 13:33). This only begotten Son was set aside by God as a living, literal sacrifice to God—the *second sacrifice* that forever removed the first sacrifices (Heb. 10:9)—so that God's people might not taste the *second death* (Rev. 20:14-15).

The sacrifices of the Old Testament looked forward to Christ's final sacrifice. The owner of the pregnant beast could not profit from the potential productivity of the first male offspring. "All the firstling males that come of thy herd and of thy flock thou shalt sanctify unto the LORD thy God: thou shalt do no work with the firstling of thy bullock, nor shear the firstling of thy sheep" (Deut. 15:19). The animal belonged to God. To use a modern phrase, "God took His cut (percentage) off the top." He received an immediate payment; the owner had to wait until the birth of the second male to reap his profit.

"The firstborn of thy sons shalt thou give unto me. Likewise shalt thou do with thine oxen, and with thy sheep: seven days it shall be with his dam; on the eighth day thou shalt give it me" (Ex. 22:29b-30). The firstborn male animal was separated from its mother and was eventually sacrificed in Jerusalem; the newborn son was circumcised (Lev. 12:3). In the case of all sons, circumcision was required, but the eighth day was significant. It marked the sign of God's wrath on all male flesh, the result of Adam's rebellion. It pointed to man's rebellion against God on the seventh day, God's day of rest, and testified to the need of restoration—a *new week* in which man might reconstruct a fallen order, under God. When man struck out on his own, as a self-professed autonomous being, inaugurating "man's week," God cut him off from the garden and from the tree of life. We are not specifically told in the Bible that Adam rebelled on the seventh day of creation, but it seems likely. That day was to have been a day of communion with God, a day which established Adam's covenantal commitment and religious perspective.

There is an apparent problem with the thesis of a seventh-day rebellion. Israel's bloody sacrifice of circumcision was performed on the eighth day. Also, the separation of firstborn male animals from their mothers in preparation for their slaughter (or their redemption) took place on the eighth day. The sorrow of the mothers on the eighth day seems to parallel the sorrow of women in childbirth (Gen. 3:16). (Female mammals suffer similar travails when giving birth, though the Bible does not record a specific curse on them by God.) Problem: If the judgment on Eve came on the seventh day because of her sin on that day, why was the eighth day the day of sorrow for mothers in Israel? Don't the eighth-day sacrifices point to an eighth-day rebellion—the day after the first sabbath? I deal with this problem below ("Christ, the Firstfruits").

The Economic Cost of Sacrifice

In the case of sacrificial animals (ox, sheep, goat), redemption was forbidden (Num. 18:17), so the loss of the firstborn male animal was irrevocable. It was a total loss for both its mother and the human owner. It symbolized the total extent of God's wrath against sin. The animal was forever lost; so was the time it had taken to breed the mother and care for her during her pregnancy. By sacrificing the firstborn male animals, the Israelites were admitting that they and all that they possessed were under the threat of judgment, and that only by conforming to the terms of God's covenant could they escape God's total cutting off of man and his works. Man's covenantal rebellion brings, apart from God's grace, permanent destruction. Egypt learned this on the night of the Passover meal.

Even an animal which was not allowed on God's altar had to die or obtain a substitute. "And every firstling of an ass thou shalt redeem with a lamb; and if thou wilt not redeem it, then thou shalt break his neck: and all the firstborn of man among thy children shalt thou redeem" (Ex. 13:13; cf. Num. 18:15-17). Just because a profitable donkey could not be sacrificed on the altar, the Israelites were not entitled to make use of it free of charge, as if it were not the Lord's. Either it died away from the altar or a lamb died before the altar. If the lamb was perceived by its owner to be of greater value, then he was allowed to execute the donkey. He could not reap the income available from a firstborn male without sacrificing something of comparable value. He did have some discretion, however. If donkeys were in high demand, and sheep were in relatively low demand, or vice versa, he had his choice. The Bible does not teach a doctrine of fixed or intrinsic market value. It does not teach that a donkey's market price is always equal to a lamb's during the first week of its life. The possibility of wide variations in market prices between the two firstborn animals was always present. The owner made his choice. The animals were symbolically equivalent, but not equal in market value.

It should be obvious, however, that *permanent large price discrepancies would have been unlikely.* If one or the other firstborn animal was highly valued, men would have begun to slay the other, which would have reduced the supply of the less valuable species. An increased supply of lambs in relation to donkeys, because men were choosing to break the necks of donkeys, would have tended to increase the price of donkeys relative to lambs. Owners would then have had an economic incentive to spare some donkeys and slay more lambs. Each species had a built-in economic protection from excessive losses.

The priests received the burnt offerings. Since they lived in Jerusalem, the animals set aside (removed from their dams) had to be brought to Jerusalem (Deut. 12:6). This indicates that on the eighth day the sacrificial animal was not immediately sacrificed by the father in the household, but set apart—*sanctified,* in other words—for God. Then, when the family journeyed to Jerusalem for the Passover or other visits, the animal, or its substitute, or its payment was taken. In the meantime, it could not be used for profit (Deut. 15:19). The formal or symbolic separation from the mother took place on the eighth day; to keep it alive, it would have been necessary to let it continue to nurse. This was the case in the dedication of Samuel by Hannah (I Sam. 1:11, 22-23). Perhaps the family devised some mechanical means to feed the newborn animals during the waiting period between the separation and the sacrifice or the redemption.

The firstborn male in each family had to be redeemed by means of a payment to the priests. The family had to pay five shekels (Num. 18:16). This was done one month after the birth of the child. The same payment could be made to save the life of an unclean beast (Num. 18:15). Possibly only the donkey had to be redeemed by means of a lamb; other unclean animals were purchased with money from death, although it may have been that all animals were redeemed with lambs.[1] The firstborn of cows, sheep, and goats had to die (Num. 18:17).

The language of the firstborn indicates that the firstborn son of every Hebrew family had to be dedicated to God for service. God made the following arrangement: "Take the Levites instead of all the firstborn among the children of Israel, and the cattle of the Levites instead of their cattle; and the Levites shall be mine: I am the LORD" (Num. 3:45). Families then made payment to the Aaronical priesthood instead of dedicating their own firstborn sons (Num. 3:48, 51). At the time of the segregation of the Levitical priesthood, each family with a firstborn son made this initial payment (Num. 3:46-47). From that time on, the payment for firstborn sons went to Aaron's house.

Egypt had chosen not to substitute the blood offering required by God to serve as a substitute payment. The firstborn sons of Egypt died. There is no escape from this required sacrifice. This is the only foundation of human history after the rebellion of Adam. God shows mercy to the sons of Adam for the sake of Christ's sacrifice as God's firstborn, the high priest, the one set apart by God to become the firstborn offering.

---

1. James Jordan suggests that all unclean beasts were "redeemed" by lambs, while humans were redeemed with silver. He cites I Peter 1:18-19: "Forasmuch as ye know that ye were not redeemed with corruptible things, as silver and gold, from your vain conversation received by tradition from your fathers; but with the precious blood of Christ, as of a lamb without blemish and without spot."

Christ, the Firstfruits

Jesus rose from the dead on the day after the Passover sabbath. It was the first day of the week (Luke 24:1). This day was also the day of the firstfruits offering, the day the lamb of the firstfruits was to be sacrificed (Lev. 23:12). Paul refers to "Christ the firstfruits" (I Cor. 15:23). I argued in the first edition of *The Dominion Covenant: Genesis* that this firstfruits offering was made on the eighth day (the day after the seventh day), and it covered the sin of Adam, who probably rebelled on the eighth day after God began His work of creation, meaning the day after the sabbath.[2] I have been persuaded by James Jordan that this explanation needs modification. Adam probably rebelled on the first full day of life, the sabbath. God covered him with the skins of animals on that day, which meant that blood was shed.

What about the shedding of blood of the Hebrew male in circumcision on the eighth day (Lev. 12:3), and the separation of the firstborn male from its mother on the eighth day (Ex. 22:30)? Why was this required on the eighth day, if the symbolic ethical covering (animal skins) had been provided by God in the garden on the seventh day, assuming that Jordan is correct concerning Adam's seventh-day rebellion? Jordan argues that the eighth-day rites pointed to the need for *a new creation,* a coming *ethical transformation* which would inaugurate a new kingdom and a new dominion. Adam's sin had polluted the sabbath. It had polluted the first day of man's week, a day which is supposed to prepare us for six days of service in the kingdom. This was the day on which he was to have received his marching orders in preparation for his work week. What mankind needed after Adam's rebellion was a new day, a cleansed day, for a new beginning.

"Christ the firstfruits" was resurrected on the eighth day (the day following the sabbath) *to inaugurate the new week of redeemed humanity,* beginning with a new day of rest. This was the long-expected culmination of the rites of circumcision and firstborn sacrifice, the necessary substitute payment for the sin of Adam, but timed so as to point to a new creation. Christ's resurrection proved that His sacrifice on the cross was sufficient to atone for men's sins, so the Old Testament's annual sacrifices, the circumcisions, and the firstborn

---

2. Gary North, *The Dominion Covenant: Genesis* (Tyler, Texas: Institute for Christian Economics, 1982), pp. 69-72.

sacrifices are no longer necessary (Heb. 7:26-28).

The Book of Nehemiah explicitly links together the firstfruits of the ground, the trees, the dough, the wine, and the firstborn of sons and animals (Neh. 10:35-37). *Christ can be seen as both the firstfruits and firstborn offerings.* He is the firstborn and only begotten Son of God. His resurrection proves that firstborn sons no longer need to die, that firstborn animals no longer need to be sacrificed, and that firstborn sons no longer need to be circumcised the eighth day. "For in Jesus Christ neither circumcision availeth any thing, nor uncircumcision; but faith which worketh by love" (Gal. 5:6). Christ's victory on the eighth day has overcome the need for sacrifices on the eighth day.

Christ's sacrifice transfers capital back to man. No longer are men required to sacrifice the firstborn animals of their flocks. No longer must they journey to Jerusalem to present their sacrificial animals. No longer are the "mothers in Israel" saddened on the eighth day by the loss of their firstborn males (animals) or the marring of their sons' flesh. No longer are fathers required to pay five shekels upon the birth of the first son. *Family capital is thereby increased by Christ's sacrifice.* Men paid token prices to a holy God in Old Testament times, only because God honored the incomparably costly future sacrifice of His Son. Now, even those token payments have been abrogated. Redeemed men keep their lives and their capital, for God's Son lost both His life and His capital at the cross. Not even a cloak to cover His nakedness was held back by Christ (Matt. 27:35). It cost Christ every earthly possession, including His modesty. His people are the immediate beneficiaries, for they retain a greater portion of their capital than they did before the cross. Our dominion tasks are made less onerous, and our celebrations become that much more splendid, as a result of this New Testament transfer of capital back to His people. The resurrection lightened the financial burdens of His people, forever. The restraints imposed on the outworking of the dominion covenant in the Old Testament have been removed with the coming of the Holy Spirit and the establishment of a new covenant. A righteous culture is now possible. Like the child/slave who matures into an adult (Gal. 4), we no longer suffer the dominical restraints of the ceremonial aspects of the law.

Conclusion

Christ's death and resurrection in principle erased our guilt and our obligation to offer blood sacrifices. It healed the rebellious hearts of God's adopted sons, allowing them to participate in redeemed man's week, which *begins with man's rest* because Christ's sacrifice is now behind us chronologically. Thus the Lord's day has been moved to the eighth day, so that the first day of man's week is, *as it was in the garden,* a day of rest. Redeemed men announce their dependence on God by beginning their work week with rest, a statement of their complete dependence on God's grace and blessings — a ritual declaration of their having abandoned autonomous man's week, which allows no cost-free rest for man. Christians announce their reliance on the work of the second Adam, Jesus Christ, thereby renouncing their reliance on their own efforts, as sons of the first Adam. God restores their capital to them by reducing their former obligation to pay in blood on the eighth day. We rest now, and we have increased wealth to show for it. Let the fathers rejoice, and let all mothers rejoice, too. The blood no longer flows in the new covenant Israel.

16

THE PSYCHOLOGY OF SLAVERY

Is not this the word that we did tell thee in Egypt, saying, Let us alone, that we may serve the Egyptians? For it had been better for us to serve the Egyptians, than that we should die in the wilderness (Ex. 14:12).

The day of the Lord had come to Israel, the long-awaited day of release from bondage. God had manifested His power in a series of mighty acts, culminating in the death of the firstborn of Egypt. If ever there was going to be a day of release, this was it. Remaining in bondage for "a better day to flee, a more opportune moment to escape" would have been preposterous. Pharaoh's will to resist their departure had been temporarily overcome. The Egyptians had encouraged their rapid departure. God had opened the way of escape to them, and the Egyptians had literally pushed them out of the land, paying them to depart.

All the same, neither Pharaoh nor the Israelites had escaped from their basic outlooks. Pharaoh had temporarily capitulated to the demands of Moses. The Israelites had temporarily taken heart at God's mighty acts, and they had even dared to demand restitution (spoils) from their Egyptian captors. But Pharaoh was a self-proclaimed divine monarch, theoretically sovereign over all Egypt, and the Hebrews had been his slaves. The Hebrews were convinced that their position as servants in the land was permanent. They had been slaves in body, and their responses to Moses, time after time, were the responses of people who were also slaves in their souls. Pharaoh soon became convinced that he had made a mistake in allowing them to leave (Ex. 14:5), and the Hebrews soon became convinced that they had made a mistake in listening to Moses and leaving. The Hebrews could not forget the earthly power of their former master; they seemed unable to acknowledge the awesome power of their new master, Jehovah. Their cry went up to Moses:

better to have served as earthly slaves in Egypt than to bear the visible risks and burdens of freedom under God. Neither the Hebrews nor Pharaoh wanted to admit that God does not call His people to be perpetual slaves in body, and that they are never to become slaves of men in spirit. Neither Pharaoh nor the Hebrews could admit that "where the Spirit of the Lord is, there is liberty" (II Cor. 3:17b).

The Bible contrasts two sorts of servitude: slavery to the earthly life and its sinful perspectives, on the one hand, and slavery to God, whose "yoke is easy" and whose "burden is light" (Matt. 11:30), on the other. Slaves unto life or slaves unto death: *men cannot escape from subordination.* The lure of Satan is to convince men that they can achieve freedom from all subordination by asserting their own autonomy and sovereignty—in short, to be as God. The result is temporal ethical subordination to Satan, and eternal judgmental subordination to God. When God's hand is lowered in judgment on a civilization, ethical subordination to Satan also means destruction, in time and on earth.

God recognized the weakness of these newly freed slaves. When it came time for them to depart from Egypt, He led them east to the Red Sea. Had they gone in a northeast direction, they would have had to pass through the land of the Philistines, although geographically speaking, it would have been a shorter route into Canaan. But God recognized their weakness; they were not ready for a direct military confrontation (Ex. 13:17-18). They might have returned to Egypt had they been challenged from the front. They were being driven from the rear, at first by the Egyptians who implored them to depart, and then by the attacking army of Pharaoh.

This pressure from the rear was accompanied by God's pillar of fire and cloud in front of them (Ex. 13:21-22). They looked forward toward the manifestation of God which preceded them, despite the fact that their major motivation was rearward. If they were to *flee,* they had to *march forward,* and they became used to following God's theophany, the fire and the cloud. Psychologically, they were still slaves of Egypt, always tempted to look backward at their former home and former masters, but because they had been ejected, they were forced to pay attention to the leadership of God. Psychologically speaking, they were marching *out* of Egypt more than they were marching *toward* Canaan. *But the discipline of marching was basic to their training,* a means of transforming their vision and motivation. (Marching is a universally recognized means of training military recruits.) The King James Version says that they went up "harnessed" out of the land of Egypt, but a better translation is provided by the Berkeley Version: "In martial order the Israelites went up out of the land of Egypt" (Ex. 13:18b). Cassuto translates it: "in orderly array."[1] James Jordan comments: "When Israel marched out of Egypt, she marched five in a rank. The term translated 'battle array' in Exodus 13:18 actually means 'five in a rank' (cf. also Josh. 1:14; 4:12; Jud. 7:11; Num. 32:17)."[2] God was treating them as recruits are treated in basic training: marching them in an orderly fashion, under the leadership of a drill instructor. They were to learn the art of war through the discipline of enforced marching, visible leadership, and a carefully staged "obstacle course." That obstacle course was the Red Sea. Later, their obstacle course was the wilderness.

Three Types of Slavery

Earthly slavery, as manifested clearly in the history of the Exodus, involves at least three factors: slavery to *food,* slavery to the *past,* and slavery to the *present.* The Hebrews cursed Moses, for he had served them as a deliverer. He had enabled them to cast off the chains of bondage. They looked to the uncertainty that lay before them (the Red Sea) and the chariots behind them, and they wailed. They had lost what they regarded as external security in Egypt, a welfare State existence, and they resented Moses' leadership. They had no confidence in God and God's promised future. Looking resolutely over their shoulders, they stumbled at the very border of freedom, the Red Sea. Fearing death in freedom, this generation died in the wilderness. Better to serve in Egypt than die in the desert, they proclaimed. God then proved to all but Caleb and Joshua, who never believed in this slave slogan, that it was much better to die in the wilderness than to serve in Egypt. Best of all, God showed the next generation, was the conquest of Canaan. But the Israelites of Moses' day could not see that far into the future; they saw only the past and the present—a present bounded, they believed, by Pharaoh's army and the Red Sea. What they saw as the end of their lives was in fact only an obstacle course.

Slaves to food. Once they had been delivered from their Egyptian enemies, they were determined to keep their heads riveted to the

---

1. U. Cassuto, *A Commentary on the Book of Exodus,* trans. Israel Abrahams (Jerusalem: Magnes Press, Hebrew University, [1951] 1974), pp. 156-57.
2. James Jordan, *The Geneva Papers,* No. 25 (Feb. 1984), [p. 3].

rear anyway. They were stiffnecked indeed. No longer able to hear the rumble of Egyptian chariots, they were deafened by the rumbling of their stomachs. Better to have died in Egypt, they complained, "when we did eat bread to the full," than to die in the wilderness (Ex. 16:3). They had short memories about their former condition. So the Lord gave them manna. "Not good enough," came the cries. "We need meat. In Egypt, we had garlic and onions and leeks and melons. Mere manna, even if accompanied by liberty, can hardly compare." So God gave them meat for a month — so much, He promised them, that it would come out of their nostrils, and they would loathe it (Num. 11:4-6, 18-21).

Their problem was not protein deficiency. Their problem was a theological deficiency. Their god was their belly (Phil. 3:19). Their stiff necks did not permit them to look up to the heavens and rejoice in the source of their manna.

The fact that man needs food in order to live indicates that he is a creature. Ascetic fasting, designed to "free" the individual from his "dependence" on food, is simply one more example of man's blasphemous move to transcend his creaturehood.[3] Food and drink, in Scripture, from Eden to the New Jerusalem, signify man's dependence on God, the Source of all life. Thus, the mere fact that Israel needed food, and that they asked Moses and God for it, was not sinful in itself, and might otherwise have been an act of faith. What is clear, however, is that they did not see food as a gift of God, and its lack as a token of God's displeasure; rather, they saw food as a thing in itself. Their affections were placed preeminently on the creature, not the Creator. Satisfaction of physical hunger was more important to them than the obtaining of spiritual and eternal life from the life-giver. Repeatedly God withheld food from them. Repeatedly they did not ask for food in faith. Repeatedly they complained against God and Moses, and expressed a preference for Egypt. They never got the message.

---

3. Several examples of mystics who live virtually without food are offered in Paramhansa Yogananda's popular book, *The Autobiography of a Yogi* (Los Angeles: Self-Realization Fellowship, [1946] 1971). The most impressive is the case of Roman Catholic mystic and stigmatic Therese Neumann of Konnersreuth: pp. 367-75. Yogananda cites other books about her: *Therese Neumann: A Stigmatist of Our Day* and *Further Chronicles of Therese Neumann,* by Friederich Ritter von Lama, and A. P. Schimberg's *The Story of Therese Neumann,* all published by the Bruce Publishing Co. of Milwaukee, Wisconsin; cf. Johannes Steiner, *Therese Neumann* (Staten Island, New York: Alba House).

Manna was a special kind of food. It was provided for them supernaturally. It was scheduled to appear predictably. It was also exceedingly plain — *the kind of food which is provided to an army in the field.* In World War II, the all-to-familiar canned C-rations became the objects of scorn and jokes, just so long as they were delivered on time. The U.S. Army was the best-fed army in history up to that time, but the boring food, especially the canned food that was the common fare when men were in the battlefield, was resented by the troops, unless a crisis occurred which cut them off from new supplies.[4] Israel resented manna, for the Israelites did not see themselves as an army on a battlefield. Their memories of special occasional meals in Egypt chased away their memories of bondage. They had developed a taste for slavery, literally.

Slaves to the past. How could they have forgotten the grinding bondage of their former state? Could they learn nothing from history? In a word, no. Historiography is an intellectual reconstruction which man attempts, and he hopes that his reconstruction resembles the actual events of the past. But being an intellectual reconstruction, it is dependent upon a philosophical foundation for accurate interpretation. The events of history teach nothing to those who are blind to God's sovereignty over these events. Or more accurately, their interpretation teaches something that is inaccurate.[5]

The Israelites told Moses that death in Egypt would have been preferable to the responsibilities of godly liberty. The pain of dying would have been over by now, they complained. Wouldn't the graves of Egypt have been preferable (Ex. 14:11)? They faced the responsibilities of life, and they grumbled. They were blinded by a false vision of the past. They preferred to live in terms of historical fantasy rather than face the realities of life. They preferred to remember their bondage in Egypt as a golden age by comparison, thereby trading the opportunities of the present for the imaginary comforts of the past. Is it any wonder that God imposed upon them the ritual observance of the Passover? Mouthing words that they did not really understand, the fathers of that generation transmitted a true vision of the past to their children. The mandatory bitter herbs were educational.

---

4. The U.S. soldier was also the most heavily laden foot soldier in history: 84 pounds of equipment. William Manchester, *The Glory and the Dream* (Boston: Little, Brown, 1974), p. 281.

5. C. Gregg Singer, "The Problem of Historical Interpretation," in Gary North (ed.), *Foundations of Christian Scholarship: Essays in the Van Til Perspective* (Vallecito, California: Ross House Books, 1976), ch. 4.

Slaves to the present. The laws of the Old Testament recognized the existence of psychological slavery. Restrictions were placed on the administration of that institution. The case laws of the Old Testament begin with the laws of slavery (Ex. 21). Slavery was never intended to be normative for the people of God. Debtors who sold themselves into slavery went free in the seventh (sabbatical) year (Deut. 15:2). Criminals who went into slavery to pay off the restitution payment owed to the victim could be kept in slavery until the debt was finally paid,[6] but criminal acts were not considered normative for Israel. It took a special vow, marked by a hole punched in the slave's ear, to place a man in voluntary lifetime slavery (Ex. 21:5-6). The biblical injunction regarding slavery is seen in Paul's assertion that a godly man should accept an offer of freedom from his master (I Cor. 7:21-22). The exercise of *godly dominion* under God is made more effective by *widespread personal freedom*.

There is little doubt that the affairs of this life are burdensome. If getting out of life's burdens were the essence of human life, then death would be preferable to life. Paul recognized this fact even more clearly than the murmuring Hebrews did. Yet he made it clear that the present responsibilities of godly service were more important than his desire to depart from the body to be with Christ (Phil. 1:22-26). As a free man, Paul saw the burdens of the present as an opportunity. He was to serve God as an instrument for the extension of God's kingdom. He did not think it proper to escape prematurely from this earthly service in order to enjoy heaven's rest.

Slaves to the Future

The Bible tells us that we are to be *slaves to the future.* Life, despite its petty burdens, is a resource. Free men are not chained to life; they are *users* of it. Servants of a sovereign God are to be free men, and free men use life as a means of attaining *long-run victory*, both personally and covenantally, in the final day, and also in time and on earth. Life is like a high-powered rifle which is painful to fire because of the recoil. In the hands of God's servant, life has a specific purpose. It is an instrument of victory. However painful it may be to fire, the godly man knows that it is much more painful for those on the "receiving end." Better to suffer the pain of a recoiling rifle than

---

6. James Jordan, Slavery in Biblical Perspective (Master's Thesis, Westminster Theological Seminary, 1980), p. 80

its projectile. Our task is to aim the weapon and pull the trigger. God will heal our bruised shoulders just as surely as he will guide the bullets to their predestined targets.

To the victors go the spoils. The Hebrews of Moses' day should have learned this on the night of the Exodus. Joshua and Caleb learned this lesson well. Their contemporaries were overtaken in the wilderness by death, the event they had feared most, for their fear of the present had blinded their vision of the spoils of Canaan which lay ahead.

It is this future-orientation that marks the free man's perspective. He makes decisions in terms of the future, has confidence in the future, and can happily sacrifice present income for increased income in the future. As a responsible agent in God's kingdom, the redeemed man is motivated more by future successes than by present enjoyments. The uncertainties of life are less of a threat to him than the certainties of the welfare State and slavery. To remain in bondage to Satan, whose destruction in the future is sure, is to remain earth-bound, and ultimately present-bound psychologically. A future-oriented man or culture is operating in terms of a perspective which is innately biblical, for it is Satan's goal to squander his assets in the present, given his inevitable defeat in the future. It is Satan who revels in the present, dreaming of his triumphs in the past. He shudders at his prospects for the future.

Joseph's bondage was external, not mental. The same was true of the three young Hebrews in the court of Nebuchadnezzar. Daniel was a captive, but he continued to wind up in positions of authority. Again and again, *external bondage became a training ground for external victory,* precisely because the bondage was merely external rather than psychological. Psychological bondage, a reflection of spiritual bondage to sin, is a more powerful form of bondage than physical bondage.

Conclusion

The Hebrews of Moses' day had become slaves psychologically because they had become slaves to sin and slaves to a false religion, the escapist religion. Having abandoned hope in the future, they clung mentally to the past. They hoped continually to return to the bondage of the past in order to escape the burdens of the present. Joshua and Caleb also resented the burdens of the present, but their focus was the promised victory in Canaan. Their chief burden in the present was the past-orientation of their fellow Hebrews. They had to wait for God to leave that generation in the dust of the wilderness before they could begin to organize the victory of the future. They had learned the lesson of the Red Sea. They had no desire to hear God's words again, the words He had spoken to Moses: "And the LORD said unto Moses, Wherefore criest thou unto me? Speak unto the children of Israel, that they go forward" (Ex. 14:15). But their contemporaries never learned that lesson, even after the army of their former masters had perished in the waters. As psychological slaves, they resisted unto the end God's call for them to go forward. The best they could manage was wandering around in a 40-year circle.

We need to recognize the extraordinary power of the psychology of slavery. For at least 80 years, the Hebrews in Egypt had been in physical bondage. When Moses returned from the wilderness, they did not want his deliverance. They did not want God's deliverance. They much preferred life in Egyptian slavery, despite its hardships. Their commitment to sin and slavery was to last an additional 40 years after the Exodus. So powerful is the psychology of slavery, which is a manifestation of the escapist religion, that it took 120 years, at the very least, to stamp it out in Israel. They were bondservants to a false religion — escapist religion — and also bondservants to sin, bondservants to the Egyptians, and bondservants to fear. They had adopted certain aspects of Egyptian religion and culture — the longing for leeks and onions and golden calves[7] — and their separation from these false gods was not purged out by the first Passover or the 39 that followed. The leaven of Egypt was still with them until the day that all but two of them died in the wilderness.

There is an alliance between power religion and escapist religion. The *psychology of tyranny* is the other side of the ethically rebellious coin of the *psychology of slavery*, just as sadism is the other side of masochism. Bullies need victims. The power religionists and the escapist religionists need each other.

---

7. Michael Walzer, *Exodus and Revolution* (New York: Basic Books, 1985), pp. 56-57.

17

THE METAPHOR OF GROWTH: ETHICS

Thou shalt bring them in, and plant them in the mountain of thine in-heritance, in the place, O LORD, which thou hast made for thee to dwell in, in the Sanctuary, O LORD, which thy hands have established (Ex. 15:17).

The sociologist-historian Robert Nisbet has written: "There has never been a time in Western thought when the image of social change has not been predominantly biological in nature."[1] Even his use of the English-language phrase, "in nature," is revealing of the influence of the metaphor; he means, as we all do, "in form" or "in essence," or "fundamentally," but we all frequently substitute the phrase "in nature." The power of the metaphor of nature is very great, intellectually and linguistically.

There is no doubt that the Bible uses the language of biological process in order to communicate certain truths concerning the affairs of mankind. Such terms as "planting," "grass," and "seed" are fairly common. The Bible unquestionably describes the processes of social change in the language of biological growth and decay. Nevertheless, the Bible does not teach that mankind is a reflection of nature, or that the affairs of man are reflections of nature's processes. The reverse is the case. Man is the archetype of nature, not the other way around. *It is nature's processes which are analogous to man's.*

Man's mortality does appear to be analogous to the processes of a *cursed* earth, of growth and decay, and his certain aspects of man's institutions also resemble living and dying biological organisms. But

---

1. Robert A. Nisbet, *Prejudices: A Philosophical Dictionary* (Cambridge, Massachussets: Harvard University Press, 1982), p. 274.

the essence of man is not his mortality; the essence of man is his position as God's agent of dominion over creation, a creature made in God's image. Man's rebellion led to the curse of nature, for nature is subordinate to man. Nature is afflicted with the process of growth and decay as a result of man's ethical rebellion. Both man and nature were cursed by God in response to this ethical rebellion. Therefore, what we ought to conclude is that man's *mortality* is analogous to the processes of nature, not because nature is normative, but because man is.

Social Sanctification

The Bible affirms the existence of social change which advances ideally from *spiritual immaturity to spiritual maturity*. This process is inescapably *ethical*. The Bible sets forth ethical standards in the law of God, and the extent to which people approach these standards in their daily activities determines their moral progress. Spiritual maturity is imputed to man at the time of regeneration,[2] but working out one's salvation with fear and trembling (Phil. 2:12b), in time and on earth, is the basis of a man's progressive sanctification.[3] Progressive sanctification cannot lead to perfection on this side of the grave.

What is true for the individual is also true for a society. Adherence to biblical law brings beneficial developments throughout the society's institutions; conversely, departure from adherence to the law brings God's historic judgment and social contraction. The external blessings are removed by God. Thus, it is not a case of social "birth, growth, senility, death, and decay," but rather grace

---

2. *The Collected Writings of John Murray*, 4 vols. (Edinburgh: Banner of Truth, 1977), II, ch. 21: "Definitive Sanctification." Speaking of the antithesis between moral regeneration and moral bondage, Murray writes: "There is no possibility of toning down the antithesis; it appears all along the line of the varying aspects from which life and action are to be viewed. In respect of every criterion by which moral and spiritual life is to be assessed, there is absolute differentiation. This means that there is a decisive and definitive breach with the power and service of sin in the case of every one who has come under the control of the provisions of grace" (p. 280). In short, progressive sanctification in the life of an individual begins with *definitive* sanctification.

3. Gary North, *Unconditional Surrender: God's Program for Victory* (2nd ed.; Tyler, Texas: Geneva Divinity School Press, 1983), pp. 43-47. See also John Murray, *Collected Writings*, II, ch. 23: "Progressive Sanctification."

(external blessings), covenantal faithfulness, added blessings in response to faithfulness, temptation, and then, if Satan's temptation is successful, covenantal rebellion, followed by God's judgment (Deut. 8 and 28).

Thus, there can be no greater contrast between true religion and false religion as it applies to social theory than the distinction between the metaphor of biological growth and the metaphor of spiritual growth from immaturity to maturity. What takes place in man's social institutions is a reflection of the society's adherence or rejection of the terms of the covenant — a covenant which is expressly *ethical* and *judicial*. This is one of the most important underlying theses of this commentary and those volumes that are scheduled to follow.

Nevertheless, we do find that the language of agriculture is used by the biblical writers to describe spiritual and institutional development. Paul wrote to the Corinthian church: "I have planted, and Apollos watered; but God gave the increase" (I Cor. 3:6). We need to understand the differences between the Bible's use of such biological language and the seemingly similar use of such terms by pagan social theorists.

Planting

"Thou shalt bring them in, and plant them in the mountain of thine inheritance, in the place, O LORD, which thou hast made for thee to dwell in, in the Sanctuary, O LORD, which thy hands have established" (Ex. 15:17). The translators of the King James Version capitalized "Sanctuary," which seems to imply that Moses was speaking of the Temple. Psalm 78:53-54 provides evidence that "sanctuary" should not be capitalized, since it refers in this case to *the land of Israel* itself: "And he led them on safely, so that they feared not: but the sea overwhelmed their enemies. And he brought them to the border of his sanctuary, even to this mountain, which his right hand had purchased." The Berkeley version translates verse 54: "He brought them to His holy domain, to the mountain which His right hand had gained." The passage refers, then, to a *special land* in which God's people would dwell with Him. God intended to plant His people in this land.

The metaphor of planting is a familiar one in the Bible. It is related to the metaphor of growth which was understood by ancient pagan cultures. While the Hebrew metaphor was similar in language to those pagan metaphors of agricultural prosperity, there were important differences in usage. These differences stemmed from the differing conceptions of the creation.

The Hebrews believed that God created the universe out of nothing. God's sovereignty in the fiat act of creation therefore guarantees His total sovereignty over the affairs of history. The doctrine of creation out of nothing implies the doctrine of God's providence. History is *linear*—creation, Fall, redemption (incarnation, crucifixion, resurrection), partial restoration, final judgment, total restoration—and it is totally *personal*. The Fall of man was seen as being ethical, an act of man's will in defiance of God. This Fall was not understood as a product of some flaw in nature, for nature had been created good. The Fall of man resulted in the judgment by God of both man and his environment, but the cause was man's ethical rebellion. Ethical restoration, which involves personal repentance and adherence to God's covenant, was promised by God. The original peace of nature will return (Isa. 11:6-9). Restoration therefore meant to the Hebrews the eventual victory of God in time and on earth. The New Testament's vision is the same (Rom. 8:18-23).

Pagan cosmologies did not share this view of creation. God was not seen as the Creator who brought the creation out of nothing. Matter, whether in the form of raw chaos, or water, or a cosmic egg, was seen as co-eternal with "god." This god's victory over chaos at the time of "creation" (the emergence of "ordered being")—the "original time"[4]—was viewed as a continuous process. God cannot guarantee the outcome of the struggle between order and chaos. He cannot guarantee the outcome because he himself is finite. Historical change is neither linear nor absolutely personal; it is inherently

---

4. The subject of pagan man's concept of "original time," the time of the creation, is treated in most of the books by Mircea Eliade, but especially in *Cosmos and History: The Myth of the Eternal Return* (New York: Harper Torchbooks, 1959), and in *The Sacred and the Profane: The Nature of Religion* (New York: Harper Torchbooks, [1957] 1961), ch. 2: "Sacred Time and Myths." Pagan men in primitive cultures have long believed that they can participate in this original time through special rituals, especially chaos festivals. It is significant that neither Judaism nor Christianity celebrates the creation ritually, nor does it appear in their religious calendars. The creation is understood as exclusively the work of God.

cyclical. The Fall of man was not primarily ethical, but metaphysical. A flaw in nature was involved. Man is now imprisoned in the bondage of time. Covenant-breaking man's goal is therefore *self-transcendence through the overcoming of time* — its abolition, generally through ritual chaos. Out of chaos came time, structure, and order; out of the progressive bondage of order will come a new chaos, which will then renew law-burdened order.[5] The two are eternal equals in many pagan cosmologies.

This *dialectical tension between chaos and order* is reflected in the natural processes of *growth and decay.* Eternal repetition swallows up historical development and historical meaning. The seasons of nature therefore become normative, both culturally and religiously. The importance of fertility rituals to ancient paganism was based on a particular view of the origin of being. It was a view not shared by the Hebrews.

Grass and Seed

In contrast to the normative processes of nature, which pagan cosmologies proclaimed, stood the Hebrew metaphor *grass.* David used grass to illustrate the universal extension of God's kingdom: ". . . they of the city shall flourish like grass of the earth" (Ps. 72:16b). Yet in other passages, the wicked are compared to another aspect of grass, something to be cut down (Ps. 37:2, 28). Man's transitoriness, in contrast to God's eternal word, is compared to withering grass (Isa. 40:6-8; cf. I Pet. 1:24-25). The uses of the metaphor of grass are *ethical* in intent.

Another metaphor of growth can be found in the Hebrews' metaphor of the *seed.* The generations of man are described as seed (Gen. 9:9; 13:16, etc.). Both cultural progress and cultural decline, being functions of man's ethical response to God's law rather than the products of forces in nature, are also characterized by the metaphor of growth and decay. The language of agriculture is used to describe both *cultural destruction* (Jer. 7:20; 8:13; Ezk. 17:1-10) and *cultural restoration* (Ezk. 17:23-24; Jer. 17:7-8). Cultural destruction

---

5. In addition to Eliade's books that deal with this theme, see Roger Caillois, *Man and the Sacred* (New York: Free Press, 1959). On man's attempt to achieve self-transcendence through the abolition of "normal" or "profane" time, see Gary North, *None Dare Call It Witchcraft* (New Rochelle, New York: Arlington House, 1976), ch. 9.

and cultural restoration are God's responses to the ethical decisions of whole nations or populations.

The New Testament uses the metaphor of the seed in several passages. The parable of the sower focuses on the effects of the various environments on four seeds that are scattered (Matt. 13:3-8). Another parable using the sower focuses on two different kinds of seeds that are planted by two rival sowers in the same field, the parable of the wheat and tares (Matt. 13:24-30). Obviously, these agricultural metaphors are only metaphors. They are used in varying ways to drive home spiritual points. They point to time's role in the process of maturation.

Paul used the metaphor of domestic agriculture to make his case for the restoration and victory of the kingdom of God. He used the metaphor of the wild olive branch which is grafted into the root. His goal was to describe the relationship historically between the Jews and the gentiles. The regrafting in of the elect Jews at the end of the era of the gentiles is seen by Paul as the foundation of external reconstruction and victory — the basis of Paul's eschatological optimism (Rom. 11:17-27). His usage of the metaphor makes it plain that *the whole process is unnatural.* God, as the plant domesticator, does not graft the domesticated branch into the wild root, which is the traditional agricultural practice. He grafts the wild olive branch (gentiles) into the original root (covenant Israel).[6] Not the process of growth and decay, but the *calculated, purposeful intervention* of the active tree grafter, is Paul's point. Natural or even traditional practices are not normative. *God's sovereignty is normative.*

Classical Culture and Cycles

The possibility of external progress was set before the Hebrew nation very early. This promise involved the possibility of *long-term economic development* as the product of *long-term covenantal faithfulness to God's laws.* Pagan cultures, including the Greeks and the Romans, took the cyclical processes of nature as normative, and never were able to develop a progressive philosophy of time.[7] They were unable

---

6. John Murray, *The Epistle to the Romans* (Grand Rapids, Michigan: Eerdmans, 1965), II, pp. 84-90.

7. Ludwig Edelstein argues in his posthumously published book, *The Idea of Progress in Classical Antiquity* (Baltimore, Maryland: John Hopkins Press, 1967), that the Greeks and Romans did not all believe in cyclical time, and that some of the prominent philosophers did believe that some linear progress is possible indefinitely. His

to believe in the possibility of long-term, cumulative social and economic progress.[8] To believe in such a possibility, they would have had to abandon their commitment to the twin doctrines of cycles and impersonal fate.[9]

In the debate over whether classical civilization was or was not committed to the ultimate pessimism of cycles, this much should be understood: the historians have not been able to produce evidence of a confident commitment to the idea of *inescapable* progress, or a doctrine of ultimate victory by man over nature. Nisbet's book, *History of the Idea of Progress,* presents worthy examples of fragments from classical authors that proclaimed *some* progress by man over the ages, and the possibility of continuing progress—if not for mankind in general, then at least for the beneficiaries of classical culture.[10] But to maintain that the classical world did not adopt almost completely the idea of historical cycles makes it very difficult to explain the Renaissance's rejection of linear history. Nisbet himself has written: "From Augustine down to the modern world, with the exception

---

evidence is weak, however. He has to admit that Plato and Aristotle held to a cyclical view of time, and that rampant skepticism throughout later Greek culture militated against a widespread belief in progress. There is no question that neither the Greeks nor the Romans had any concept of time that is exclusively linear—beginning, meaningful time, and final judgment—or that is necessarily progressive, meaning beneficial to mankind, in the long run. Greek and Roman society maintained the annual chaos festivals until the very end, which Edelstein fails to mention. This points to the cultural and religious commitment of classical civilization to a cyclical view of time. On the cyclical views of Greek science, see Stanley Jaki, *The Road of Science and the Ways to God* (University of Chicago Press, 1978), ch. 2.

8. I am here taking exception with Robert Nisbet's excellent book, *History of the Idea of Progress* (New York: Basic Books, 1980), ch. 1. He follows Edelstein, W. K. C. Guthrie, M. I. Findlay, and his own teacher, Frederick Teggert, in arguing that there were philosophers in Greece and Rome who held out the possibility of cumulative increases in men's knowledge, technological improvements, and even moral improvement over time. He rejects the thesis that classical thought was dominated by a notion of cyclical time, as argued by John Baillie, F. M. Cornford, W. R. Inge, R. G. Collingwood, and J. B. Bury, Nisbet's intellectual enemy in this debate. He sees the myth of Prometheus, the god who gave mankind fire, as the archetypal example of human advancement: pp. 17-18.

9. On the collapse of the ancient world's philosophical base, which led to the collapse of classical civilization, see Charles Norris Cochrane, *Christianity and Classical Culture: A Study in Thought and Action from Augustus to Augustine* (New York: Oxford University Press, [1944] 1957).

10. Cochrane points to the Roman poet Vergil as one who believed Rome might break out of the familiar cycle of growth and decay, to become eternal Rome. The Empire's universality might lead to a permanence that other empires had failed to achieve. *Ibid.*, pp. 68-73.

of the Renaissance, when cyclical conceptions of history crowded out the linear scheme inherent in the idea of progress, these ideas have been powerful in impact, adhered to by some of the greatest minds in Western history."[11] But the Renaissance was a self-conscious revival of pagan antiquity. How was it, then, that Renaissance scholars so completely misinterpreted the conception of non-cyclical history which Nisbet thinks was held by Greek and Roman thinkers? It is easier to believe—and much easier to demonstrate through the primary source documents of classical culture—that Renaissance scholars knew their religious forefathers well.

What no one has yet produced is any evidence that classical culture possessed any concept of *dominion,* in time and on earth, comparable to that held by the Old Testament authors and New Testament writers. The idea that an exclusive group of people was under the special care of an omnipotent God, and that this God had covenanted with them, guaranteeing comprehensive victory, on earth and in heaven, to His people, simply was absent in classical authors. They had no such view of God's sovereignty. Furthermore, according to Cochrane, "for classical idealism, the very possibility of growth is restricted to individuals; communal or social development in the sense envisaged by modern liberalism is completely beyond its horizon."[12] The end was faith in the superman, the divine Caesar, an idea with its roots in Greek thought,[13] as the figure who could bring permanence to Rome, the long-sought Pax Romana. At best, Rome might not capitulate "to the Great God *Whirl,* the terror of the 'political' mind."[14] Only *luck,* in its war with inexorable fate and inevitable chance, had made possible the advent of Caesar Augustus.[15]

Thus, the Hebrews and Christians held to a concept of development which was unique in the ancient world. They believed that progress is inevitable if and when men conform themselves covenantally to the God of the Bible.

---

11. Nisbet, *Prejudices,* pp. 239-40.

12. Cochrane, p. 103. Cochrane writes of Livy: "It is hardly necessary to comment upon the intense conservatism implied in such a view of human life. It betrays an utter lack of faith in the goodness of any possible 'world to come' and invites men to conform to established models. . . . One result of this is to engender a fear and hatred of social change, regardless of its character and potentiality; and, with Livy, this manifests itself in a disposition to condemn as pernicious every tendency to innovation." *Ibid.,* p. 104.

13. *Ibid.,* pp. 110-11.

14. *Ibid.,* p. 103. See especially Cochrane's analysis of the crisis of the third century, A.D.: ch. 4.

15. *Ibid.,* p. 160.

The Concept of Economic Growth

Redeemed man's hope is in continual internal and external progress, including economic growth (Deut. 8:6-9). The promise is ultimate external victory (Isa. 66:22). Even the normal processes of
nature will be overcome by the healing power of God's grace, as
hostile animals will find peace with each other (Isa. 65:25). The kind
of progress which the Bible denies is the progress hoped for by the
drunkard, a concept of progress which is autonomous: "Come ye, say
they, I will fetch wine, and we will fill ourselves with strong drink; and
tomorrow shall be as this day, and much more abundant" (Isa. 56:12).
This kind of progress cannot be sustained. God judges it.

Economic growth is always under severe restraints. Compound
growth rates of 5% per annum cannot continue for centuries.[16] But
it is valid to expect continual blessings in response to continued
faithfulness to God's laws. Economic growth is not an autonomous
process that can be engineered into a society. It is the product of a
world-and-life view that can be adopted by a society.

But there is an additional problem for humanist economics. The
Christian economist believes that the mind of God is comprehensive
and normative. God can make plans and evaluate economic growth,
and man, who is made in God's image, can also make plans and
evaluate aggregate growth, though not perfectly.[17] The blessings of
God that appear in the form of increased numbers of cattle or other
assets are meaningful because of the plan of God. He imputes value
to certain material objects, and therefore when individuals increase
their holdings of them, they are indeed better off than before.

The subjectivist economist has no consistent way to be sure that
economic growth is a blessing. Some economists, such as E. J.
Mishan, positively reject the idea that economic growth is beneficial.
But the problem is deeper than simply evaluating the costs and
benefits of growth. Is the metaphor of growth even applicable to the
economy, given the presuppositions of subjectivism?

Ludwig Lachmann recommends that economists abandon the
whole concept. He does speak of "economic progress," which he

---

16. Gary North, "The Theology of the Exponential Curve," *The Freeman* (May
1970); reprinted in *An Introduction to Christian Economics* (Nutley, New Jersey: Craig
Press, 1973), ch. 8.

17. Gary North, *The Dominion Covenant: Genesis* (Tyler, Texas: Institute for Christian Economics, 1982), pp. 59-65.

defines as "an increase in real income per head."[18] Yet even this is illegitimate. How can we divide "heads" into "real income," since we cannot even define "real income" without resorting to aggregates, index numbers, and similar anti-subjectivist concepts. But even if subjectivist economists could define such concepts, Lachmann's warning should make them hesitate. No model of a uniformly expanding or growing economy is valid. "This model embodies the notion of 'growth,' of progress at a known and *expected* rate. Its significance for the real world, however, is doubtful. Already the metaphor 'growth' is singularly inappropriate to the real world, as it suggests a process during which the harmony of proportions remains undisturbed."[19] But how can we be sure that there is harmony? he asks. Sometimes capital is malinvested—just before a depression, for example. Some capital is reduced in value by economic change; other capital assets appreciate. How can we "tally up" these changes in the value of capital? Only if there is harmony—a fitting together of personal plans into a coherent whole—can we use the metaphor of growth. But the radical subjectivist does not believe in any such harmonious aggregate. Economic aggregates are mythical in a world of consistent subjectivism. We cannot make interpersonal comparisons of subjective utility, or interpersonal comparisons of subjective plans, given the tenets of subjective economics. There is no plan of God in their system to provide the necessary unity and coherence. Thus, the metaphor of growth is misleading, Lachmann says. Growth of a tree or plant is orderly. It is governed by a genetic code. An economy has no similar regulative principle, the subjectivist has to say (if he is consistent).

The Christian can legitimately use the metaphor of growth, precisely because he believes in the sovereignty of God. While his explanation of the origins of growth should be based on ethics rather than the mind of man or some other creaturely source, he can use this universal metaphor to make sense of the world. "More is better," *if* it is the product of righteousness, and *if* it does not become a snare and a delusion.

Long-term economic growth is normative. The cyclical pattern of growth and decay, progress and regress, being hostile to the idea of the ethical covenant between God and man, is not the standard

---

18. Ludwig Lachmann, *Capital and Its Structure* (Kansas City, Kansas: Sheed Andrews and McMeel, [1956] 1977), p. 17.

19. *Idem.*

for a godly culture. The possibility of economic, social, military, and agricultural collapse always faces a covenantally faithful people—a warning of what will inevitably happen should they rebel against the terms of God's covenant (Deut. 28:15-68). Nevertheless, the cyclical pattern of prosperity and depression, which denies the possibility of perpetual expansion, is normative only for covenantally rebellious cultures. God nowhere says that all societies will conform historically to the cyclical pattern. *Covenantal dominion is expansionist.*

Economic growth is the inescapable product of the extension of God's kingdom. That the Protestant Reformation, and especially Puritan Calvinism, produced historically unprecedented economic growth, is not a random correlation.[20] Because nature is under the curse, and therefore limited, such compound growth cannot be an eternal process. Such expansion therefore points to an *end of time,* the end of the limits of our curse-induced scarcity. Such growth therefore points to a *coming judgment,* a cessation of the processes of the cursed earth. Paganism's attempt to substitute endless cycles of growth and decay is an ancient ploy to blind men to the reality of final judgment. The modern version of this ancient philosophy is the "zero growth" philosophy.[21] By abandoning the pagan use of the metaphor of growth—a metaphor which of necessity includes decay—and replacing it with a biblical version which relates ethical conformity to God's law with external dominion and expansion, godly men remind ungodly men of the coming judgment. Growth will end when time does; growth clearly cannot go on forever.

---

20. On this point, see Max Weber's classic study, *The Protestant Ethic and the Spirit of Capitalism* (New York: Scribner's, [1904-05] 1958). For a defense of Weber against those who have criticized his thesis, see Gary North, "The 'Protestant Ethic' Hypothesis," *The Journal of Christian Reconstruction,* III (Summer 1976). For documentation concerning the applicability of Weber's hypothesis in American colonial Puritanism, see my three essays on Puritan economic thought and practice in New England, 1630-1720, in *The Journal of Christian Reconstruction,* vol. V, no. 2; vol. VI, nos. 1, 2.

21. The most widely read example of this zero-growth philosophy is Meadows, *et al.*, *The Limits to Growth* (New York: Universe Books, 1972). The book is subtitled: A Report for the Club of Rome on the Predicament of Mankind. It was a kind of "media event" in the early 1970's. It is seldom quoted in the 1980's. Another example of this sort of analysis is *Entropy: A New World View,* by Jeremy Rifkin and Ted Howard (New York: Bantam New Age Book, 1980). The most forceful defense of zero economic growth is E. J. Mishan's book, *The Economic Growth Debate: An Assessment* (London: George Allen & Unwin, 1977).

Conclusion

God will plant his people in the mountain of His inheritance, which will be the whole earth. This is the ultimate use of the metaphor of growth in the Bible. The individual blades of grass will wither and die, but the grass itself—the fields of grass—will spread. The earth will become the promised garden. "The wilderness and the solitary place shall be glad for them; and the desert shall rejoice, and blossom as the rose" (Isa. 35:1). "For as the earth bringeth forth her bud, and as the garden causeth the things that are sown in it to spring forth; so the LORD God will cause righteousness and praise to spring forth before all the nations" (Isa. 61:11).

18

MANNA, PREDICTABILITY, AND DOMINION

Then said the LORD unto Moses, Behold, I will rain bread from heaven for you; and the people shall go out and gather a certain rate every day, that I may prove them, whether they will walk in my law, or no. And it shall come to pass, that on the sixth day they shall prepare that which they bring in; and it shall be twice as much as they gather daily (Ex. 16:4-5).

As former slaves in Egypt, the Hebrews had become accustomed to certain features of slave life. *First,* they had been assigned *regular tasks* by their masters. For the most part, these tasks had involved minimal creativity. The imperial bureaucracy had not been geared to local autonomy and individual responsibility of its slaves. The bureaucratic structure had to be predictable, from top to bottom. Deviations from the central plan had to be minimized. *Second,* they had been supplied with *tools and raw materials.* This had increased their productivity, since it had increased the division of labor. Capital investments had come from the State. Only as a form of punishment did the Pharaoh of Moses' day impose the requirement that they produce bricks without straw (Ex. 5:18). This reduced the division of labor within the slave community, which thereby increased the efforts of the slave population to produce the same quantity of bricks. Their productivity was therefore dependent on the continuing support of a bureaucratic State.

Third, they had been supplied with *food.* This food had been supplied to them on a regular, predictable basis. Some of this food they produced on their own. They owned cattle (Ex. 9:4), sheep (Ex. 12:3), and crops. We presume that they grew crops, since the hail and fire consumed crops in Egypt, but not in Goshen, where the Hebrews resided (Ex. 9:25-26). Despite their own food supplies, they were nonetheless dependent, as all Egyptians were, on the State, for the State owned all the land, except that owned by the

274

priests (Gen. 47:20-22). Furthermore, the predictable waters of the Nile, which were controlled by the State through irrigation projects and canals, made possible agricultural production in Egypt.[1] We can surmise that whenever the slaves were engaged on building projects located away from Goshen, the taskmasters must have maintained discipline by controlling access to food supplies. Controlling men's access to food is a traditional means of control in slave societies.

In short, the Hebrews experienced the *static world of slavery*. It was a society that did not systematically reward individual initiative and creativity. It was a society dominated by the decisions of senior officials. The Hebrew slave society was dependent on the representatives of foreign gods. A man's calling was established by the State. Egypt was governed by the annual cycle of the Nile, which in turn was understood to be under the control of a divine monarch, whose daily ritual observances determined even the rising of the sun. It was a culture which had no doctrine of progress, which built huge public works projects, and which concentrated its attention on death.

God had called them out of this static world. Their response was predictable for slaves: longing for the past. They lodged their bitter complaints against God, although indirectly (Ex. 16:8). Moses took the brunt of the criticism. They resented the inhospitable world of the wilderness. Their familiar surroundings were gone. The wilderness was a sparse land. No taskmasters supplied them with instructions, tools, raw materials, and food. Constant wandering denied them access to a fixed piece of land. Their new environment was filled with *risks*. New skills were needed to survive; self-reliance and self-confidence had to be built up over time. Again and again, the Hebrews complained that God had brought them out of slavery in order to kill them (Ex. 14:11; 16:3; 17:3). They had *no self-confidence* because they had *no confidence in the God who had delivered them*.

This slave population was not equipped psychologically to assume the heavy responsibilities of godly reconstruction. They lacked two primary requirements of successful reconstruction: 1) *optimism* concerning the future; and 2) a concept of revealed, reliable *law*. To subdue the earth, they needed a doctrine of law under God's sovereign authority, and the world under God's law. Law is a tool of social reconstruction which involves a progressive reduction in soci-

---

1. Karl Wittfogel, *Oriental Despotism: A Comparative Study of Total Power* (New Haven, Connecticut: Yale University Press, 1957), discusses several ancient civilizations that were tyrannies based on the centralized control of water by the State.

ety's reliance upon miracles. Simultaneously, the more predictable fruits of adherence to biblical law elevates to normality the benefits of the miraculous, such as abundance, health, long life, and the absence of disasters. Adherence to the law requires an increase of maturity on the part of those laboring to rebuild, yet it is itself the source of this spiritual maturity. Since the existence of a revealed law-order and the visible external results of the imposition of this law-order have to be understood as a sign of God's presence and ultimate sovereignty, man's need for miraculous intervention—"signs" —is reduced. As slaves, the Hebrews clung to the signs of God's presence, requiring endless miracles by God to protect them. Even with the pillar of fire by night and the cloud by day, they were not satisfied. They kept crying, in effect, "What has God done for us lately?"

Manna vs. the Slave Psychology

Manna was necessary to break this psychology of slavery. It filled the bellies of the first generation, but for the younger generation, the manna served as a means of transforming their minds. First, they received their *daily bread*. It was simple, tasty, and predictable to the point of monotony. Second, its appearance in the midst of a wilderness involved a *daily miracle*—a phenomenon not normally available to nomads. Their new taskmaster, God, supplied their needs as a display of His sovereignty over them. Furthermore, a weekly miracle was added: a double portion on the sixth day, and nothing on the seventh. The manna, which would rot if kept overnight on the other five days, was preserved for the sabbath meal (Ex. 16:17-26). The Hebrews could not store up large portions of manna, since it would rot within 24 hours. They had to rely totally on God, even as they had been forced to rely on Egypt's bureaucracy, Egypt's irrigation, and Egypt's gods.

Modern "critical" biblical scholarship is intensely hostile to such a view of manna. It is the element of the miraculous that appalls modern scholars. They want the regularities of biblical law, but without God, and certainly without God's alteration of the familiar regularities of nature. A typical statement from the world of secular scholarship is found in F. S. Bodenheimer's 1947 article on manna: "In Exodus 16 and Numbers 11 we find reports of manna in the desert. Some believe that this manna was similar to bread and that it was furnished in quantities large enough to feed a whole people.

Others regard it as a natural phenomenon which contributed to the diet of the Israelites in the desert. Only the latter view permits analysis and discussion. Since biblical history often is confirmed by archeology, why not confirm the reports of manna by existing natural phenomena?"[2] He concludes that the manna was really excretions of two species of insects, one found in the mountains and the other in the lowlands. Predictably, when the biblical account provides information that conflicts with his naturalistic explanation, he concludes that the biblical account is "a late and mistaken interpolation."[3] He prefers to "prove" modern naturalism by rewriting the Bible. He apparently wants us to believe that these insects were instinctive sabbatarians: excreting double portions on the day before the sabbath, and refraining from eating or excreting on the sabbath.

For forty years the manna came, and the younger generation could not have failed to appreciate its implications. They began to become confident in the *lawful administration* of Israel's sovereign monarch. The covenantal relationship between them and their new king — psychologically a new king, in their experience — was reaffirmed each morning. A totally supernatural, yet totally regular event reconfirmed the covenant daily. The daily provision of the manna taught the younger generation that God is *faithful.* At the same time, the prohibition against gathering it on the seventh day, and the double portion on the sixth, taught them that God is *holy.* A special day of rest was set apart for the people of Israel, even as God had set them apart from Egypt in a display of His sovereign grace. Violations of the prohibition against gathering food on the sabbath were viewed by God as symbolic violations of His law in general: "And the LORD said unto Moses, How long refuse ye to keep my commandments and my laws?" (Ex. 16:28).

The confidence of the younger generation in the whole of the law was built upon the observed regularities of the provision and administration of this seemingly innocuous substance. These were *supernatural regularities* that were not available to other wanderers in the wilderness. They needed faith in God's ability to overcome the normal regularities of wilderness ecology — an ecology which could not sustain two to three million wanderers — as well as faith in the

---

2. F. S. Bodenheimer, "The Manna of Sinai," *The Biblical Archaeologist,* X (Feb. 1947); reprinted in G. Ernest Wright and David Noel Freedman (eds.), *The Biblical Archaeologist Reader* (Garden City, New York: Doubleday Anchor, 1961), p. 76.

3. *Ibid.,* p. 79.

predictability of His providence. Manna provided a daily and weekly testimony to God's sovereign power: *providential regularity* within a framework of *ecological abnormality.* The curse of the ground was overcome daily, which pointed to the Author of that curse, and the power He possesses to deliver His people ethically and economically from the effects of that curse. A God who can be relied upon to overcome the laws of biology and ecology on a daily basis can also be relied upon to honor His covenantal promises to provide external blessings for those who honor His law-order.

A remnant of the wilderness experience of manna was provided by God in the land of Israel by guaranteeing a triple harvest in the year preceding that sabbatical year which preceded the jubilee year (Lev. 25:21). There is no subsequent reference to the occurrence of this miraculous triple crop, probably because the Hebrews in the pre-exilic period did not honor the sabbath year principle, which is why God sent them into exile (II Chron. 36:20-21). After their return to Israel they did honor the sabbatical year, according to a non-canonical source (I Maccabees 6:49), but there is no mention of the jubilee year or to its triple harvest. It seems likely that the manna experience was the background for Christ's multiplying of the loaves in "a desert place" (Matt. 14:15-20), which was part of a ministry which He announced in terms of the jubilee year (Luke 4:18-19).

Biblical Law and Conquest

This younger generation was being prepared to conquer Canaan. They had to learn two things about biblical law. First, biblical law is *personal.* Second, it is regular enough to be *predictable.* They also learned that self-discipline and faithfulness are necessary for survival, since violations of the sabbath requirements had brought criticism from God (Ex. 16:28). They learned of the *continuity* of biblical law over *time* (four decades) and over *geography* (wandering). God's provision of the manna created a *psychology of godly dominion.* Humble before God, and totally dependent upon His care, they could become totally confident in the face of human enemies. They expected to find a tight relationship between God's commands and God's blessings. They learned humility before God and confidence before the creation. "And he humbled thee, and suffered thee to hunger, and fed thee with manna, which thou knewest not, neither did thy fathers know; that he might make thee know that man doth not live by bread only, but by every word that proceedeth out of the mouth of the LORD doth man live" (Deut. 8:3).

The manna became a symbol of God's covenant with Israel. "And Moses said unto Aaron, Take a pot, and put an omer full of manna therein, and lay it up before the LORD, to be kept for your generations. As the LORD commanded Moses, so Aaron laid it up before the Testimony, to be kept" (Ex. 16:33-34). The New Testament informs us that the Ark of the Covenant contained the two tables of the law, Aaron's rod, and the golden pot that held the manna (Heb. 9:4). The manna came for forty years, until the people crossed over the Jordan into Canaan. They kept the Passover that day, and they ate of the old corn of the land. "And the manna ceased on the morrow after they had eaten of the old corn of the land; neither had the children of Israel manna any more; but they did eat of the fruit of the land of Canaan that year" (Josh. 5:12). A new generation crossed over Jordan. On the day they crossed over, God "rolled away the reproach of Egypt" from the nation (Josh. 5:9). They began the process of taking possession of their heritage. They no longer needed the daily bread of manna. Hard fighting, hard work, and hard-headed commitment to biblical law were to replace the manna. *Their faith in the welfare State regularity of static Egypt had at last been abolished; the true welfare civilization of advancing dominion could now begin.* The regularity of law replaced the regularity of daily miracles. Responsibility under God's predictable law replaced the predictability of manna, just as predictable manna had replaced the predictability of Egyptian slavery.

Slavery is a reproach to God's people. They are to exercise dominion under God, not be dominated by servants of foreign gods. *But to escape slavery, men must switch allegiances. They must make a covenant with the God of freedom.* That first generation made their covenant, but they barely believed in its God or its terms. They were still mental slaves. They still clung to the supposed benefits of the bureaucratic welfare State. They still hesitated to exercise dominion. God pulled them out of Egypt's welfare State, but He did not pull the welfare State mentality out of them. The forty years of wandering slowly pulled the next generation away from the mental chains that bound their fathers.

There was welfare in the wilderness, but no welfare State. No bureaucracy supplied their daily bread. God was visibly the source of their welfare. This welfare, they learned, was predictable. They could rely on it, which meant that they could rely on Him. They did not need to trust in some bureaucracy for their existence. They could rest in God. And because they could rest in God, visibly, one day each week, they learned that they could rest in God on the battlefield and in the work place. Each family gathered its own manna daily (Ex. 16:16). There was precisely enough for every individual, since God, not man, was the central planner (Ex. 16:18). Once they began to rely on God's mercy as the source of their prosperity, and on biblical law, which was their tool of dominion, they could abandon the religion of their fathers, *the religion of bureaucratic welfarism.* Each man could then attend to his own affairs in confidence, even as each man had gathered up his own manna. Each man knew that he was under the direct sovereignty of God, and that his own economic prosperity was not metaphysically dependent on the State and the State's bureaucratic planning. Their fathers had never fully grasped this principle, and their fathers had perished in the wilderness.

They would no longer long for Egypt. The sons would not be burdened by memories of a welfare State existence — unreliable memories — where they supposedly had eaten "bread to the full" (Ex. 16:3). The children would no longer pine away for the food of bondage, "the cucumbers, and the melons, and the leeks, and the onions, and the garlick" (Num. 11:5). Instead, they chose the bread of diligence, the fruits of victory.

Conclusion

If there has been any universal religion in the second half of the twentieth century, it has been the religion of the bureaucratic welfare State. Not since the days of Egypt, said Max Weber in the first decade of the twentieth century, have we seen a bureaucracy like the ones we are constructing, nation by nation.[4] And, he might have pointed out half a century later, not since the days of Egypt have we seen tax burdens like those which are universal today. In fact, neither the system of universal bureaucracy nor the system of confiscatory taxation in Egypt came anywhere near the systems the modern statist priests have imposed on their populations — populations that groan under the burdens, but who cry for more benefits, higher tax burdens on the rich, more coercive wealth redistribution,

---

4. "Max Weber on Bureaucratization in 1909," Appendix I in J. P. Meyer, *Max Weber and German Politics: A Study in Political Sociology* (London: Faber & Faber, [1943] 1956).

and more government programs to protect them. And if God should manifest His grace, and deliver them from bondage, we could expect the older generation to murmur against God, and tell their children about the safety in bondage and the onions of Egypt. After all, we even have Christian apologists for the present welfare State who cry out for more State programs, more redistribution, and the universalization of the welfare State system, all in the name of Jesus.[5] When the State-educated slaves come before their people to extol the benefits of the bureaucratic slave system, we can expect the slaves and their State-promoting "trusties" — the twentieth century's Christian version of the black overseers of nineteenth-century American Negro slavery — to complain against any Moses who calls them out of bondage and into responsible freedom.

---

5. Ronald J. Sider, *Rich Christians in an Age of Hunger: A Biblical Study* (Downers Grove, Illinois: Inter-Varsity Press, 1977). This book had gone into its sixth printing by 1979, after only two years on the market. Its influence was very great in educated American evangelical circles. Sider writes for the neo-evangelical community, but he is widely accepted in conservative Presbyterian circles, especially on seminary campuses. It makes me wonder about the possibility of writing a best-seller called *Guilt Made Easy for Evangelicals*. For a critique of Sider's thesis, see David Chilton, *Productive Christians in An Age of Guilt-Manipulators* (3rd ed.; Tyler, Texas: Institute for Christian Economics, 1985).

19

IMPERFECT JUSTICE

Moreover thou shalt provide out of all the people able men, such as fear God, men of truth, hating covetousness; and place such over them, to be rulers of thousands, and rulers of hundreds, rulers of fifties, and rulers of tens: And let them judge the people at all seasons: and it shall be, that every great matter they shall bring unto thee, but every small matter they shall judge: so shall it be easier for thyself, and they shall bear the burden with thee (Ex. 18:21-22).

The Bible is not a perfectionist document. While it lays down a standard of human perfection (Gen. 17:1; I Ki. 8:61; Matt. 5:48) — a standard met only by Jesus Christ (Matt. 3:17; Rom 3:23; II Cor. 5:21) — it nonetheless acknowledges in its very law code that the administration of even a perfect law system designed by God must be understood as fallible, limited, and tainted with sin. As this passage amply demonstrates, the Bible is hostile to the humanists' quest for perfect justice on earth.

Under Moses' direct rule, God's revelation was instantly available in any given case. Yet there was insufficient time available for Moses to hear every case of legal dispute in the land. Perfect justice was limited by time and space. Men had to come to Moses' tent and stand in (presumably) long lines (Ex. 18:14). The quest for perfect earthly justice from God through His servant Moses was eating up countless man-hours. Not only was Moses' time limited, but so was the time of those who stood in lines.

Jethro warned Moses that the people, as well as Moses himself, were wearing away (v. 18). He recommended the creation of a judicial hierarchy, thereby taking advantage of the principle of the division of labor. Moses could reserve time to hear the cases that were too difficult for his subordinates — "every great matter" (v. 22) — and in doing so, would redeem his allotted time more wisely by exercising leadership in areas of Hebrew life other than the court-room. Furthermore, this system would permit more rapid resolutions of disputes. Justice was to be dispensed continually — "at all seasons" — and speedily.

God gave no explicit revelation to Moses concerning the establishment of a court of appeals. It was an *ad hoc* decision based on informed common sense. Jethro, who was a priest of Midian (v. 1), must have been familiar with the problems of dispensing divine justice. He could see how large the nation of Israel was. Acknowledging the validity of the principle of scarcity — in this case, *the scarcity of time* — Jethro came to an obvious conclusion. This conclusion involved the acceptance of man's limitations. Even in this historically unique circumstance of men's access to perfect justice, it was preferable in the vast majority of cases to obtain speedy human justice rather than delayed divine justice. Human justice was at least available to everyone, while Moses' judgments were allocated by means of lining up. No one could be sure that his case would even be considered.

The scarcity of time demanded a judicial division of labor. The division of labor allows men to overcome many of the restrictions imposed by scarcity in every area of life. In this case, the judge's office was broken down into many offices, with specialists at each level (one in every ten judges) who could take appeals.

The criteria for admission into the position of judge were moral rather than technical or educational. Uncovetous men (bribe-resistant), fearful of God, with reputations of truthfulness, were the preferred judges (v. 21). Ability was also important, but moral qualities were emphasized.

Consider the available judges. They had grown up as slaves. The whole generation, except for Joshua and Caleb, possessed slave mentalities. Nevertheless, their rule was preferable in most cases to a system which offered perfect justice in individual cases, but which had to ration the number of cases. Conclusion: *regular* and *predictable* justice provided by *responsible amateurs* is better than perfect justice provided on a sporadic or "first in line" basis. The burden of dispensing justice had to be shared (v. 22). This was required in order to permit the people to endure, going their way in peace (v. 23).

The Right of Appeal

The right of appeal was limited to "great matters." Cases involving fundamental principle, and those that would be likely to have important repercussions throughout the society, were the ones that were to be sent up the judicial chain of appeals. In order to limit the number of cases being sent to Moses for a final decision, the judges at each level must have had the right to refuse to reconsider the verdict of a lower court. If the judge did not believe that the decision of the lower court was in error, and if the higher court decided that the case was of relatively little importance as a precedent for society at large, the case was settled. Access to Moses' supreme court was restricted to great cases, and this required screening by the lower courts. Jethro understood that the limitations on Moses' time were paralyzing the justice system. Obviously, if every case considered by the lower courts eventually wound up in front of Moses, the hierarchy of courts would have provided no respite for Moses. The screening feature of the court system was fundamental to its success. This meant that the majority of litigants had to content themselves with something less than perfect justice.

Jethro understood that *endless litigation threatens the survival of the system of justice.* Losers in a case clearly have an incentive to appeal, if the possibility of overturning the decision of the lower court judge offers hope. So there has to be restraint on the part of higher court judges to refrain from constant overturning of lower court decisions. Furthermore, a society composed of people who always are going to court against each other will suffer from clogged courts and delayed justice. A society, in short, which is not governed by *self-restrained people,* and which does not provide other means of settling disputes besides the civil government—church courts, arbitration panels, mediation boards, industry-wide courts, and so forth—will find itself paralyzed.

Macklin Fleming is a justice of the California Court of Appeal. His book, *The Price of Perfect Justice* (1974), documents the increasing paralysis of the legal system in the United States. It is this quest for earthly perfection that has been the legal system's undoing. "The fuel that powers the modern legal engine is the ideal of perfectability — the concept that with the expenditure of sufficient time, patience, energy, and money it is possible eventually to achieve perfect justice in all legal process. For the past twenty years this ideal has dominated legal thought, and the ideal has been widely translated into legal action. Yet a look at almost any specific area of the judicial process will disclose that the noble ideal has consistently spawned results that can only be described as pandemoniac. For example, in criminal prosecutions we find as long as five months spent in the selection of a jury; the same murder charge tried five different times; the same issues of search and seizure reviewed over and over again, conceivably as many as twenty-six different times; prosecutions pending a decade or more; accusations routinely sidestepped by an accused who makes the legal machinery the target instead of his own conduct."[1]

Where have modern secular humanistic courts failed? Fleming cites Lord Macaulay's rule: the government that attempts more than it ought ends up doing less that it should. Human law has its limits. Human courts have their limits. "The law cannot be both infinitely just and infinitely merciful; nor can it achieve both perfect form and perfect substance. These limitations were well understood in the past. But today's dominant legal theorists, impatient with selective goals, with limited objectives, and with human fallibility, have embarked on a quest for perfection in all aspects of the social order, and, in particular, perfection in legal procedure."[2]

The requirements of legal perfection, Fleming says, involve the following hypothetical conditions: totally impartial and competent tribunals, unlimited time for the defense, total factuality, total familiarity with the law, the abolition of procedural error, and the denial of the use of disreputable informants, despite the fact, as he notes, that "the strongest protection against organized thievery lies in the fact that thieves sell each other out."[3] Costless justice theory has adopted the slogan, "Better to free a hundred guilty men than to convict a single innocent man." But what about the costs to future victims of the hundred guilty men? The legal perfectionists refuse to count the costs of their hypothetical universe.[4]

The goal of *correct procedure* as the *only* goal worth attaining is steadily eroding both the concept of moral justice and the crucially important deterrent, a speedy punishment. Everything is to be sacrificed on the altar of technical precision. "In this way the ideal of justice is transformed into an ideal of correct procedure."[5] But the ideal is impossible to achieve perfectly, and by sacrificing all other goals, the cost has become astronomical. The incredible complexity

---

1. Macklin Fleming, *The Price of Perfect Justice* (New York: Basic Books, 1974), p. 3.
2. *Ibid.*, p. 4.
3. *Ibid.*, p. 5.
4. *Ibid.*, p. 6.
5. *Ibid.*, p. 9.

of perfect procedures has led to a revival of judge-made law — judicial arbitrariness — since judges have been able to pick and choose from the morass of conflicting decisions. Almost total legislative power has therefore been transferred to the courts. And, as Fleming argues, the courts are not efficient in creating law. They have no staffs, little time, too many cases, and too theoretical a knowledge of the law. "Partisans are quick to furnish whatever literature will promote their cause, and a cottage industry has grown up in the preparation of the sociological brief. . . ."[6]

The whole system procrastinates: judges, defense lawyers, prosecutors, appeals courts, even the stenographic corps.[7] Speedy justice is no longer a reality. Prisoners appeal constantly to federal courts on the basis of *habeus corpus:* illegal detention because of an unconstitutional act on the part of someone, anyone. In 1940, 89 prisoners convicted in state courts made such an appeal. In 1970, the figure was 12,000.[8] Thus, concludes Fleming: "The consequence of this expansion of federal power over state criminal procedure through the creation of fiat prohibitions and rigidly ritualistic rules has been to elevate formalism to constitutional right, to complicate every significant phase of criminal procedure to the point where in some instances the system of criminal law has difficulty functioning and in others it turns loose persons who are patently guilty."[9]

Salvation by Law

The quest for perfect justice leads inevitably to *arbitrary jurisprudence* and *public lawlessness.* Joseph in Pharaoh's jail, Daniel in the lions' den, and Jesus on the cross all testify to the imperfections in human courts of law. Nevertheless, godly men can live with imperfect justice, just as they live with imperfections in all other spheres of human life, because they know that perfect justice *does* exist and will be made manifest on the day of judgment. Life is too short to demand perfect justice on earth; better by far to have speedy justice handed down by godly amateurs than the clogged courts of messianic humanism. We need not wring our hands in despair because men's courts, in time and on earth, fail to meet the standards of perfection which will reign supreme in God's court. We are

6. *Ibid.,* p. 120.
7. *Ibid.,* p. 71.
8. *Ibid.,* p. 27.
9. *Ibid.,* p. 97. Cf. Raymond Posner, *The Federal Courts* (Cambridge, Massachusetts: Harvard University Press, 1985).

not saved either by the perfect spirit of the law or the perfect letter of the law. We are surely not saved by imperfect imitations of the spirit and letter of the law. We are not saved by law.

Salvation by law is an ancient heresy, and it leads to the triumph of statist theology. Christianity is in total opposition to this doctrine. As Rushdoony writes: "The reality of man apart from Christ is guilt and masochism. And guilt and masochism involve an unshakable inner slavery which governs the total life of the non-Christian. The politics of the anti-Christian will thus inescapably be *the politics of guilt*. In the politics of guilt, man is perpetually drained in his social energy and cultural activity by his over-riding sense of guilt and his masochistic activity. He will progessively demand of the state a redemptive role. What he cannot do personally, i.e., to save himself, he demands that the state do for him, so that the state, as man enlarged, becomes the human savior of man. The politics of guilt, therefore, is not directed, as the Christian politics of liberty, to the creation of godly justice and order, but to the creation of a redeeming order, a saving state."[10] Christian jurisprudence cannot adopt a doctrine of the saving State and remain orthodox. The adoption of just such a concept of the State in the twentieth century testifies to the extent to which the modern world has abandoned Christian orthodoxy.

Jamming the System

One of the most important aspects of any legal order is the willingness of the citizens of a society to exercise self-restraint. This means that men must emphasize self-government, as well as gain access to court systems that serve as alternatives to civil government. This was a basic feature of the Western legal tradition after the mid-twelfth century, although since World War I, the rise of socialistic administrative States has begun to undermine this tradition.[11]

Self-government is not a zero-price resource. The emphasis in the Bible on training up children in the details of biblical law must be understood as a requirement of citizens to provide "social overhead capital"—respect for law and therefore self-restraint—for civilization. Another aspect of the public's respect for civil law is the

---

10. R. J. Rushdoony, *Politics of Guilt and Pity* (Fairfax, Virginia: Thoburn Press, [1970] 1978), p. 9.

11. Harold J. Berman, *Law and Revolution: The Formation of the Western Legal Tradition* (Cambridge, Massachusetts: Harvard University Press, 1983), Pt. II.

self-restraint of government officials in not burdening the society with a massive, incomprehensible structure of administrative law. When civil law reaches into every aspect of the daily lives of men, the State loses a very important *subsidy* from the public, namely, men's willingness to submit voluntarily to the civil law. Any legal structure is vulnerable to the foot-dragging of the public. If men refuse to submit to regulations that cannot be enforced, one by one, by the legal system, then that system will be destroyed. Court-jamming will paralyze it. This is a familiar phenomenon in the United States in the final decades of the twentieth century.

It is possible to bring down any legal system simply by taking advantage of every legal avenue of delay. Any administrative system has procedural rules; by following these rules so closely that action on the part of the authorities becomes hopelessly bogged down in red tape (procedural details), the protestors can paralyze the system. Too many laws can produce lawlessness. The courts can no longer enforce their will on the citizens. At the same time, administrative agencies can destroy individual citizens, knowing that citizens must wait too long to receive justice in the courts. The result is a combination of anarchy and tyranny — the antinomian legacy.

Bukovsky's Protests

This possibility of bureaucratic paralysis is characteristic of all administrative systems, even a centralized tyranny such as the Soviet Union. A classic example is the case of the Soviet dissident of the 1960's and early 1970's, Vladimir Bukovsky. Bukovsky spent well over a decade in the Soviet gulag concentration camp system. He was arrested and sentenced in spite of specific civil rights protections provided by the Soviet Constitution — a document which has never been respected by the Soviet bureaucracy. But once in prison, he learned to make life miserable for the director of his camp. He learned that written complaints had to be responded to officially within a month. This administrative rule governing the camps was for "Western consumption," but it was nevertheless a rule. Any camp administrator who failed to honor it risked the possibility of punishment, should a superior (or ambitious subordinate) decide to pressure him for any reason. In short, any failure to "do it by the book" could be used against him later on.

Bukovsky became an assembly-line producer of official protests. By the end of his career as a "zek," he had taught hundreds of other inmates to follow his lead. By following certain procedures that were specified by the complaint system, Bukovsky's protesting army began to disrupt the whole Soviet bureaucracy. His camp clogged the entire system with protests—hundreds of them per day. He estimates that eventually the number of formal complaints exceeded 75,000. To achieve such a phenomenal output, the protestors had to adopt the division of labor. Bukovsky describes the process: "At the height of our war, each of us wrote from ten to thirty complaints a day. Composing thirty complaints in one day is not easy, so we usually divided up the subjects among ourselves and each man wrote on his own subject before handing it around for copying by all the others. If there are five men in a cell and each man takes six subjects, each of them has the chance to write thirty complaints while composing only six himself."[12] The complaints were addressed to prominent individuals and organizations: the deputies of the Supreme Soviet, the regional directors, astronauts, actors, generals, admirals, the secretaries of the Central Committee, shepherds, sportsmen, and so forth. "In the Soviet Union, all well-known individuals are state functionaries."[13]

Each complaint had to be responded to. The camp administrators grew frantic. They threatened punishments, and often imposed them, but it did no good; the ocean of protests grew. Bukovsky's description is incomparable:

The next thing that happens is that the prison office, inundated with complaints, is unable to dispatch them within the three-day deadline. For overrunning the deadline they are bound to be reprimanded and to lose any bonuses they might have won. When our war was at its hottest the prison governor summoned every last employee to help out at the office with this work—librarians, bookkeepers, censors, political instructors, security officers. And it went even further. All the students at the next-door Ministry of the Interior training college were pressed into helping out as well.

All answers to and dispatches of complaints have to be registered in a special book, and strict attention has to be paid to observing the correct deadlines. Since complaints follow a complex route and have to be registered every step of the way, they spawn dossiers and records of their own. In the end they all land in one of two places: the local prosecutor's

---

12. Vladimir Bukovsky, *To Build a Castle: My Life As a Dissident* (New York: Viking, 1979), p. 37.
13. *Idem.*

office or the local department of the Interior Ministry. These offices can't keep up with the flood either and also break their deadlines, for which they too are reprimanded and lose their bonuses. The bureaucratic machine is thus obliged to work at full stretch, and you transfer the paper avalanche from one office to another, sowing panic in the ranks of the enemy. Bureaucrats are bureaucrats, always at loggerheads with one another, and often enough your complaints become weapons in internecine wars between bureaucrat and bureaucrat, department and department. This goes on for months and months, until, at last, the most powerful factor of all in Soviet life enters the fray — statistics.[14]

As the 75,000 complaints became part of the statistical record, the statistical record of the prison camp and the regional camps was spoiled. All bureaucrats suffered. There went the prizes, pennants, and other benefits. "The workers start seething with discontent, there is panic in the regional Party headquarters, and a senior commission of inquiry is dispatched to the prison."[15] The commission then discovered a mass of shortcomings with the work of the prison's administration, although the commission would seldom aid specific prisoners. The prisoners knew this in advance. But the flood of protests continued for two years. "The entire bureaucratic system of the Soviet Union found itself drawn into this war. There was virtually no government department or institution, no region or republic, from which we weren't getting answers. Eventually we had even drawn the criminal cons into our game, and the complaints disease began to spread throughout the prison — in which there were twelve hundred men altogether. I think that if the business had continued a little longer and involved everyone in the prison, the Soviet bureaucratic machine would have simply ground to a halt: all Soviet institutions would have had to stop work and busy themselves with writing replies to us."[16]

Finally, in 1977, they capitulated to several specific demands of the prisoners to improve the conditions of the camps. The governor of the prison was removed and pensioned off.[17] Their ability to inflict death-producing punishments did them little good, once the prisoners learned of the Achilles' heel of the bureaucracy: paperwork. The leaders of the Soviet Union could bear it no longer: they deported Bukovsky.

---

14. *Ibid.*, pp. 37-38.
15. *Ibid.*, pp. 38-39.
16. *Ibid.*, p. 40.
17. *Idem.*

Subsequently, according to one Soviet defector, the Soviets have had to scrap the Constitution once again (unofficially, of course) in the area of protection of free speech.[18] Dissidents are again subjected to long-term incarceration in psychiatric hospitals, as they were before Bukovsky and other dissidents organized their protesting techniques, both insisde and outside the Gulag.[19] What this probably means is that international public opinion no longer is focused on the dissidents. As Bukovsky notes, "they wrote a Constitution with a plethora of rights and freedoms that they simply couldn't afford to grant, rightly supposing that nobody would be reckless enough to insist on them being observed."[20] Nevertheless, when internal dissidents and external observers have put the pressure of formal paperwork on the ruling elite, they have sometimes capitulated.

Centralization and the Declining Respect for Law

Economist Milton Friedman has suggested that the respect for law that prevails in capitalist societies is closely related to the absence of comprehensive, detailed administrative regulations. The British experience of the nineteenth century provides Friedman with a case study of the public's response to civil law.

In the early nineteenth century, British citizens were notorious law-breakers. They were a nation of smugglers, ready to offer bribes, ready to take advantage of every inefficiency in the law-enforcement system. Very little could be accomplished through legal channels. Friedman says that one of the reasons why Jeremy Bentham and the Utilitarians were hostile to civil government and adopted laissez-faire doctrines in the early nineteenth century was because they recognized that civil government was completely inefficient. "The government was corrupt and inefficient. It was clearly oppressive. It was something that had to be gotten out of the way as a first step to reform. The fundamental philosophy of the Utilitarians, or any philosophy that puts its emphasis on some kind of a sum of utilities, however loose may be the expression, does not lead to *laisser-faire* in principle. It leads to whatever kind of organiza-

---

18. He appeared on the Cable News Network in February, 1984.

19. On the use of mental hospitals as substitute prisons, see Zhores Medvedev and Roy Medvedev, *A Question of Madness: Repression by Psychiatry in the Soviet Union* (New York: Random House, 1971); Sidney Bloch and Peter Reddaway, *Psychiatric Terror: How Soviet Psychiatry Is Used to Suppress Dissent* (New York: Basic Books, 1977).

20. Bukovsky, p. 239.

tion of economic activity is thought to produce results which are regarded as good in the sense of adding to the sum total of utilities. I
think the major reason why the Utilitarians tended to be in favor of
laisser-faire was the obvious fact that government was incompetent to
perform any of the tasks they wanted to see performed."[21] (Friedman's assertion that Utilitarianism was not philosophically attached
to the free market social order is borne out by the fact that many
British Utilitarians in the late nineteenth century were ready to advocate government regulation in order to produce "the greatest good
for the greatest number"—a reversal of the conclusions of the early
Utilitarians, but not a reversal of their pragmatic philosophy.)[22]

Friedman then goes on to make some extremely important observations concerning what he calls *the capital stock of people's willingness to
obey the law*. First, there must be an increase in people's respect for
civil law through a reduction of the number of burdensome regulations. Second, there is an increase in the number of such laws, since
politicians and bureaucrats begin to take advantage of the citizens'
willingness to co-operate with the State. This, in turn, reduces the
ability of the State planners to achieve their publicly announced
goals. There are therefore *limits to centralization*.

Whatever the reason for its appeal, the adoption of *laisser-faire* had some
important consequences. Once *laisser-faire* was adopted, the economic incentive for corruption was largely removed. After all, if governmental
officials had no favors to grant, there was no need to bribe them. And if
there was nothing to be gained from government, it could hardly be a
source of corruption. Moreover, the laws that were left were for the most
part—and again, I am oversimplifying and exaggerating—laws that were
widely accepted as proper and desirable; laws against theft, robbery,
murder, etc. This is in sharp contrast to a situation in which the legislative
structure designates as crimes what people individually do not regard as
crimes or makes it illegal for people to do what seems to them the sensible
thing. The latter situation tends to reduce respect for the law. One of the
unintended and indirect effects of *laisser-faire* was thus to establish a climate
in Britain of a much greater degree of obedience and respect for the law
than had existed earlier. Probably there were other forces at work in this

---

21. Milton Friedman, "Is a Free Society Stable?" *New Individualist Review*, II
(Summer 1962); reprinted in one volume by the Liberty Press, Indianapolis, Indiana, 1981, p. 245.

22. Ellen Frankel Paul, *Moral Revolution and Economic Science: The Demise of
Laissez-Faire in Nineteenth-Century British Political Philosophy* (Westport, Connecticut:
Greenwood Press, 1979).

development, but I believe that the establishment of *laisser-faire* laid the groundwork for a reform in the civil service in the latter part of the century — the establishment of a civil service chosen on the basis of examinations and merit of professional competence. You could get that kind of development because the incentives to seek such places for purposes of exerting "improper" influence were greatly reduced when government had few favors to confer.

In these ways, the development of *laisser-faire* laid the groundwork for a widespread respect for the law, on the one hand, and a relatively incorrupt, honest, and efficient civil service on the other, both of which are essential preconditions for the operation of a collectivist society. In order for a collectivist society to operate, the people must obey the laws and there must be a civil service that can and will carry out the laws. The success of capitalism established these preconditions for a movement in the direction of much greater state intervention.

The process I have described obviously runs both ways. A movement in the direction of a collectivist society involves increased governmental intervention into the daily lives of people and the conversion into crimes of actions that are regarded by the ordinary person as entirely proper. These tend in turn to undermine respect for the law and to give incentives to corrupt state officials. There can, I think, be little doubt that this process has begun in Britain and has gone a substantial distance. Although respect for the law may still be greater than it is here [the United States], most observers would agree that respect for the law in Britain has gone down decidedly in the course of the last twenty or thirty years, certainly since the war [World War II], as a result of the kind of laws people have been asked to obey. . . .

The erosion of the capital stock of willingness to obey the law reduces the capacity of a society to run a centralized state, to move away from freedom. This effect on law obedience is thus one that is reversible and runs in both directions. . . .

This seems to me an important point. Once the government embarks on intervention into and regulation of private activities, this establishes an incentive for large numbers of individuals to use their ingenuity to find ways to get around the government regulations. One result is that there appears to be a lot more regulation than there really is. Another is that the time and energy of government officials is increasingly taken up with the need to plug the holes in the regulations that the citizens are finding, creating, and exploiting. From this point of view, Parkinson's law about the growth of bureaucracy without a corresponding growth of output may be a favorable feature for the maintenance of a free society. An efficient governmental organization and not an inefficient one is almost surely the greater threat to a free society. One of the virtues of a free society is precisely that the market tends to be a more efficient organizing principle than centralized direction. Centralized direction in this way is always having to fight something of a losing battle.[23]

Conclusion

What we can and should strive for is to conform our human law codes to the explicit requirements of the Ten Commandments and the case-law applications of biblical law. The answer to our legal crisis is not to be found in the hypothetical perfection of formal law, nor can it be found in the hypothetical perfection of substantive (ethical) justice. Judges will make errors, but these errors can be minimized by placing them within the framework of biblical law. Before God gave the nation of Israel a comprehensive system of law, Jethro gave Israel a comprehensive system of decentralized courts. By admitting the impossibility of the goal for earthly perfect justice, Moses made possible the reign of imperfectly applied revealed law — perfect in principle, but inevitably flawed in application. The messianic goal of a perfect law-order, in time and on earth, was denied to Moses and his successors.

One of the most obvious failures of the modern administrative civil government system is its quest for perfect justice and perfect control over the details of economic life. The implicit assertion of omniscience on the part of the central planners is economically fatal. The result of such an assertion is an increase of regulations, increased confusion among both rulers and ruled, and a growing disrespect for civil law. The productivity of the West cannot be maintained in the face of such an exponential build-up of central power. It is only because the laws are not consistent, nor universally enforced or obeyed, that the modern messianic State has survived. The price of perfect human justice is too high to be achieved by the efforts of men.

---

23. Friedman, pp. 245-47.

CONCLUSION

When Moses and the Israelites looked behind them from the eastern shore of the Red Sea and saw the army of Egypt overwhelmed by the water, they saw the judgment of God on the power religion and its institutional manifestation, the power State. They had been involved in an historic confrontation analogous to the original confrontation between Satan and God. They had been given visible evidence of the inescapable outcome of this confrontation between these two rival religions: in heaven, in the garden, at the cross, and at the final judgment. The power religion does not have the power to defeat a holy God and His holy people, whenever they conform themselves to the terms of His covenant. Seeking power, the power religionists lose it—in time, on earth, and in eternity.

Nevertheless, the victory of God's people, while assured, is not visibly manifested in every confrontation. Herbert Schlossberg is correct: "The Bible can be interpreted as a string of God's triumphs disguised as disasters."[1] As he says, "We need a theological interpretation of disaster, one that recognizes that God acts in such events as captivities, defeats, and crucifixions."[2] It often seems as though the power religionists—the seekers of gnostic salvation, the elite central planners—have all power. They don't. "Never ask the enlightened ones about their track record, which is a series of disguised disasters. . . ."[3] Most of Christianity's victories have been disguised in the past, and so have most of Satan's disasters.

The Hebrews' experience in Egypt testified to a truth summarized by Schlossberg: "When loyalty to God disappears, there is no longer a barrier to an omnicompetent state."[4] But the self-professed

---

1. Herbert Schlossberg, *Idols for Destruction: Christian Faith and Its Confrontation with American Society* (Nashville, Tennessee: Thomas Nelson, 1983), p. 304.

2. *Idem.*

3. *Ibid.,* p. 195.

4. *Ibid.,* p. 229.

omnicompetent State isn't omnicompetent; it is progressively incompetent, as Egypt's experience reveals. Such a State is simply the chief institutional manifestation of covenant-breaking man's attempt to imitate, and then usurp, the omnipotence of God. But omnipotence is an incommunicable attribute of God. Therefore, the only possible source of man's long-term but limited power is biblical ethics. Adherence to biblical law, by grace through faith, is the only means of fulfilling the terms of the dominion covenant.

Thus, there is no need for Christians to become adherents of the escapist religion in order to avoid becoming adherents of the power religion. The dominion religion is God's alternative. "We do not pretend that the fate of the world is in our hands. That way lies madness, being a burden that no human being can bear. Yet, we are not condemned to resignation and quietism, still less to despair. We are not the lords of history and do not control its outcome, but we have assurance that there is a lord of history and he controls its outcome."[5]

I cite Schlossberg repeatedly because it is his book, more than any other in my lifetime, which has best stated the theological case against the power religion. (Solzhenitsyn's *Gulag Archipelago* has best stated the historical case.) The idols of covenant-breaking man — history, humanity, mammon, nature, power, and religion — again and again reappear in the civilizations built by self-professed autonomous man. All idols, he asserts, are either idols of history or idols of nature.[6] Covenant-breaking man asserts his authority over both nature and history, but because man is a creature, mankind is thereby captured, for mankind is, in the humanist view, both a product of history and a product of nature. By seeking power over both, covenant-breaking people place themselves in bondage to the self-professed masters of the mysteries. By asserting that "man must take control of man," the humanist thereby implicitly asserts that "some men should take control over all the others." By seeking to exercise dominion apart from God, ethical rebels thereby deny their own creaturehood and therefore their status as humans.[7]

Egypt is the archetype of covenant-breaking society. It proclaimed divinity for its leader, the sole link between the gods and mankind. It sought escape from the rigors of nature (drought and famine) and

---

5. *Ibid.*, p. 304.
6. *Ibid.*, p. 11.
7. C. S. Lewis, *The Abolition of Man* (New York: Macmillan, 1947).

the rigors of history (change). The goal was static power — power over nature, over the netherworld, and over scarcity. But such a static state of existence can be achieved only in death. Thus, the monuments of Egypt were monuments of death: the pyramids, the tombs, and the labyrinths. Their quest for power, meaning freedom from the God-cursed changes in life, led to their cult of the dead. The Egyptians hoped for resurrection, but theirs was a resurrection based on magical manipulation, not a resurrection based on biblical ethics.

Pharaoh manifested this cult of the dead in his attempt to murder the Hebrew males. He could not stand the pressures of social change, particularly the social changes forced upon Egypt by the high birth rates of the Hebrews. He launched a program of genocide. In this respect, he was only marginally different from the humanitarians of the twentieth century. As Schlossberg says:

> It is no coincidence that humanitarian policy has reached the zenith of its influence at a time when death propaganda is so much in evidence. The arguments in favor of abortion, infanticide, and euthanasia reveal that the humanitarian ethic wishes to restrict the right to live and expand the right to die — and to kill. Humanism is a philosophy of death. It embraces death, wishes a good death, speaks of the horrible burdens of living for the baby who is less than perfect, for the sick person in pain. It is intolerable to live, cruel to be forced to live, but blessed to die. It is unfair to have to care for the helpless, and therefore merciful to kill. Those who wish to go on living, it seems, are guilty and ungrateful wretches dissipating the energies of "loved ones" who have better uses for the estate than paying medical bills.[8]

God confronted the Egyptian religion of death by calling into question its assertion of power. He dealt with the Pharaoh, his priests, and his people in terms of their religious presuppositions. He demonstrated publicly for all the world to see that the power religion of Egypt was a fraud. Pharaoh had no choice in the matter. God decided to make a spectacle out of him and out of Egypt. "And in very deed for this cause have I raised thee up, for to show in thee my power; and that my name may be declared throughout all the earth" (Ex. 9:16).

The Hebrews had this example behind them. They were to remind themselves and their children of the implications of the power religion. This was the educational function of the Passover. It was an

---

8. Schlossberg, p. 82.

institutional testimony to the futility of seeking power apart from biblical law. It is therefore futile to seek to fulfill the terms of the dominion covenant apart from God. It is equally futile to attempt to escape from the burdens of this covenant. Such an escape leads directly to historical impotence and slavery under some temporarily successful group of power religionists. Better to be Moses herding sheep in Midian than anywhere in Egypt, either as a Hebrew or as a Pharaoh. Better yet to be Moses confronting Pharaoh. Even better, to be Moses on the far side of the Red Sea watching Pharaoh drown. Better yet, to be in the Promised Land, with a copy of God's law in your possession. But best of all, to be at work in the wilderness, progressively converting it into a garden by means of hard work, in terms of the biblical law which is in your heart, and also in the hearts of all your neighbors (Ezk. 36:26-29; Jer. 31:31-34; Heb. 8:10-11).

APPENDIX A

THE RECONSTRUCTION OF EGYPT'S CHRONOLOGY

And it came to pass in the four hundred and eightieth year after the children of Israel were come out of the land of Egypt, in the fourth year of Solomon's reign over Israel, in the month of Zif, which is the second month, that he began to build the house of the LORD *(I Kings 6:1).*

There are some minor disagreements concerning the date of the beginning of the construction of the Temple. Graetz's *History of the Jews* states that Solomon's reign began around 1015 B.C.[1] Graetz believed that Solomon began construction of the Temple "immediately after his succession to the throne,"[2] and that it was completed and consecrated in 1007 B.C.[3] Alfred Edersheim, the late-nineteenth-century Christian convert from Judaism, dates the beginning of construction as 1012 B.C.[4] Another late-nineteenth-century Christian commentator believed that construction began in 1010 B.C.[5]

Conservative Bible commentators in the late twentieth century have revised these dates downward by about forty-five years. This revision appears to be the result of the Edwin Thiele's chronological studies of the later Hebrew kings, beginning with Rehoboam and Jeroboam, whose reigns he dates from 931.[6] Solomon's reign lasted

---

1. Heinrich Graetz, *History of the Jews,* 6 vols. (Philadelphia: Jewish Publication Society of America, 1891), I, p. 156.

2. *Ibid.,* p. 162.

3. *Ibid.,* p. 166.

4. Alfred Edersheim, *Bible History, Old Testament,* 7 vols. (Grand Rapids, Michigan: Eerdmans, [1890]), III, p. 10: chart based on Keil's calculations.

5. "Temple," in John McClintock and James Strong (eds.), *Cyclopaedia of Biblical, Theological, and Ecclesiastical Literature,* 12 vols. (New York: Harper & Bros., 1894), X, p. 250.

6. Edwin R. Thiele, *The Mysterious Numbers of the Hebrew Kings* (rev. ed.; Grand Rapids, Michigan: Eerdmans, 1965). Cf. Thiele, *A Chronology of the Hebrew Kings* (Grand Rapids, Michigan: Zondervan, 1977).

40 years (I Ki. 11:42). Thus, Solomon came to the throne around 971 B.C.[7] He therefore began construction of the temple around 967/66, B.C. the fourth year of his reign.[8]

The date of the Exodus therefore must be set within the narrow framework of about 1500 B.C. to 1440 B.C., according to I Kings 6:1. There is no escape from this biblically, unless the chronology of the later Hebrew kings is somehow shortened through more accurate research. Such research has not been provided by anyone, nor is it likely to appear. Nevertheless, the mid-fifteenth century dating of the Exodus is frequently rejected by conservative Bible scholars. Why? Because they key their dating of the Exodus to the known (and exceptionally vague) historical records of Egypt. Why do they do this? Because secular scholars do, and the Christians have followed their lead.

Conservatives and Compromise

A representative summary of the dating problem is found in the *International Standard Bible Encyclopedia* (1982): "The date of the Exodus is one of the most debated topics in OT studies because of the ambiguous nature of the evidence. Although the biblical texts seem to require a date in the middle of the 15th cent. B.C., archeological evidence seems to point to a date in the 13th cent. B.C."[9] The author, W. H. Shea, then goes on for eight two-column, small-print pages summarizing bits and pieces of conventional Egyptian chronology and archaeology. He wants to hold to the fifteenth-century dating, but his defense is weakened because of his presuppositions concerning methodology. His methodology is based on comparative chronology and comparative archaeology. This, we are supposed to believe, is the objective, neutral scholarship we need in order to make sense out of the Bible.

He affirms that the mid-fifteenth century is "the only date given for it in the Bible." But consider his reliance upon the category of pragmatism in defending the conservative view: "While it is possible that these [biblical] data could have been corrupted in transmission,

---

7. Merrill F. Unger, *Unger's Bible Handbook* (Chicago, Illinois: Moody Press, 1967), p. 12.

8. Cf. Merrill C. Tenney (ed.), *The Zondervan Pictorial Encyclopedia of the Bible,* 5 vols. (Grand Rapids, Michigan: Zondervan, 1975), V, p. 627.

9. "Exodus, Date of the," *International Standard Bible Encyclopedia,* 4 vols. (Grand Rapids, Michigan: Eerdmans, 1982), II, p. 230.

the most reasonable approach to them is to examine in more detail the historical context in which they [the data] date the Exodus. This biblical date for the Exodus has a reciprocal relationship with the events described in Exodus as related to Egyptian history. A pragmatic approach to this date suggests a period of Egyptian history that should be examined for a possible relationship to the biblical Exodus, and considerable agreement of the evidence from Egyptian and biblical sources pointing to that period supports the accuracy of the chronological datum (480 years) from which that search started."[10] He does his best to show why a mid-fifteenth century date is viable, but he does not begin with the premise that this *must* be the case, irrespective of modern interpretations of the Egyptian evidence. He appeals to pragmatism instead.

Roland Harrison, one of the *ISBE's* associate editors, elsewhere argues for a thirteenth-century dating. Harrison's study is based on a survey of the conclusions of the secular archaeologists, who debate endlessly about the proper dating of the various Bronze Ages (Early, Middle, and Late), a humanistic classification system which is based entirely on nineteenth-century evolutionary social theory.[11] He mentions the fact that early in the twentieth century, Bible scholars accepted a late-thirteenth-century date for the Exodus. In the 1920's and 1930's, excavations in Palestine, especially Jericho, convinced several archaeologists that the traditional mid-fifteenth century dating is correct. But he is not convinced: "The question cannot be settled simply by an appeal to the book of Kings in the light of an arbitrary dating for the fall of Jericho."[12] Notice his subtle shift in argumentation: he tries to overcome the explicit teaching of I Kings 6:1 by means of a brief reference to doubts concerning the reliability of certain archeological excavations conducted early in the twentieth century. But I Kings 6:1 does not mention the fall of Jericho; it does specifically mention the Exodus. Harrison's argument is muddled. His recommended chronology specifically rejects the testimony of I Kings 6:1. Yet this is all done in the name of Jesus. Such is the fate of ostensibly Christian scholarship which arbitrarily abandons a so-called "simple appeal" to the explicit testimony of the Bible. It is

---

10. *Ibid.,* p. 237.

11. On this point, see R. A. McNeal, "The Legacy of Arthur Evans," *California Studies in Classical Antiquity,* VI (1973), pp. 206-20.

12. R. K. Harrison, *Introduction to the Old Testament* (Grand Rapids, Michigan: Eerdmans, 1969), p. 175.

one more sign of just how much in "bondage to Egypt" twentieth-century Christian scholars have become.

The conservative *New Bible Dictionary* (1962) does not even mention the possibility of a mid-fifteenth-century date.[13] The author refuses to comment on the explicit chronological framework of I Kings 6:1 in relation to the Exodus as such. He tries to confuse the issue by bringing up the problem of possible overlapping judgeships in order to shorten the period of the judges. It is significant, however, that the author argues that the "problem" of the "long" reign of the Hebrew judges can be solved by an appeal to overlapping reigns. "In Near Eastern works involving chronology, it is important to realize that ancient scribes did not draw up synchronistic lists as is done today. They simply listed each series of rulers and reigns separately, in succession on the papyrus or tablet. Synchronisms were to be derived from special historiographical works, not the king-lists or narratives serving other purposes. An excellent example of this is the Turin Papyrus of Kings from Egypt. It lists at great length all five Dynasties, XIII to XVII, in successive groups, totalling originally over 150 rulers and their reigns accounting for at least 450 years. However, it is known from other sources that all five Dynasties, the 150-odd rulers and 450-odd regnal years alike, must all fit inside the 234 years from *c.* 1786 B.C. to *c.* 1552 B.C.: rarely less than two series, and sometimes three series, of rulers are known to have reigned contemporaneously."[14] This theory of *overlapping dynasties,* as we shall see, is the best solution to "the Exodus problem" of the 480 years of I Kings 6:1, which is the real problem, not the so-called "judges problem." This theory provides a solution the overall problem of Egyptian chronology.

The Problem of Egyptian Chronology

A century ago, historian George Rawlinson began his chapter on Egyptian chronology with this statement: "It is a patent fact, and one that is beginning to obtain general recognition, that the chronological element in early Egyptian history is in a state of almost hopeless obscurity."[15] There are several kinds of chronological

---

13. *The New Bible Dictionary* (2nd ed.; Wheaton, Illinois: Tyndale House, 1982), pp. 191-92.

14. *Ibid.,* p. 192.

15. George Rawlinson, *A History of Egypt,* 2 vols. (New York: Alden, 1886), II, p. 1.

documents, including the actual monuments. "The chronological value of these various sources of information is, however, in every case slight. The great defect of these monuments is their incompleteness. The Egyptians had no era. They drew out no chronological schemes. They cared for nothing but to know how long each incarnate god, human or bovine, had condescended to tarry on the earth. They recorded carefully the length of the life of each Apis bull, and the length of the reign of each king; but they neglected to take note of the intervals between one Apis bull and another, and omitted to distinguish the sole reign of a monarch from his joint reign with others."[16]

Incredibly, it is the chronology of Egypt which has been used to "key" the chronologies of the other ancient empires, including pre-Homeric Greece. Art historian Lewis Greenberg sounded a warning about this in a 1973 essay: "As far back as 1897 Tsountas[17] warned scholars not to ignore 'the unsettled state of Egyptian chronology' when enlisting the aid of Egyptology in dating Mycenaean products. And as recently as 1960 Cook[18] again reminded students of Greek pottery of the difficulties concerning the establishment of relative and absolute chronologies and their 'reconciliation.' Unfortunately, the Egyptian chronology is nowhere near as solid as the architectural wonders which are its hallmark. As a matter of fact, our knowledge of Egyptian events is extensively based upon the disjointed reports of Classical authors, damaged and incomplete written records, and chance records of astronomical phenomena. Even the latter factor has been questioned."[19] Velikovsky cited the 1921 statement of O. G. S. Crawford[20] that "A system of relative chronology can be established by excavation in any country that has been long inhabited, but it is left hanging in the air until linked up with Egypt, whether directly or indirectly through a third region."[21] Scholars have used a supposedly reliable Egyptian chronology based on inconclusive Egyptian sources as a means of criticizing the Bible's account of the Exodus and conquest of Canaan.

---

16. *Ibid.,* II, p. 2.
17. C. Tsountas and J. I. Manatt, *The Mycenaean Age* (1897), p. 317n.
18. R. M. Cook, *Greek Painted Pottery* (1960), pp. 261-70.
19. Lewis M. Greenberg, "The Lion Gate at Mycenae," *Pensée*, III (Winter 1973), pp. 26-27.
20. Crawford, *Man and His Past* (1921), p. 72.
21. Immanuel Velikovsky, "Astronomy and Chronology," *Pensée,* III (Spring-Summer 1973), p. 38. This was reprinted in *Peoples of the Sea* (Garden City, New York: Doubleday, 1977), p. 205.

Velikovsky's Controversial Reconstruction[22]

In 1952, the brilliant and controversial Jewish scholar, Immanuel Velikovsky, published *Ages in Chaos,* the first volume of a projected series.[23] The later volumes in the series were delayed for a quarter of a century.[24] *Ages in Chaos* offered startling evidence that the accepted chronology of the ancient world is deeply flawed. Specifically, there is a 500-700 year "gap" in conventional chronologies which actually should not be there. Because of the centrality of Egyptian chronology, he argues, this gap therefore exists in the other chronologies of the ancient Near East and classical civilization. He labored long and hard to prove his case, and his researches are awesome. His reconstructed chronology has been verified (though not in the eyes of conventional historians and archaeologists) by several of his followers.[25]

The Velikovsky Affair

It is not appropriate to deal with the whole of Velikovsky's works in this appendix. His *Worlds in Collision* (1950) created universal outrage among astronomers. So outraged were certain astronomers at Harvard University that they put great pressure on Macmillan, the publisher, to drop the book, despite its best-selling status. This campaign began before the book had been published, and before any of the critics had read it.[26] Refuse to suppress it, they threatened, and Harvard University's astronomy department will not offer manuscripts to Macmillan's textbook publishing division. Macmillan eventually capitulated and gave the publishing rights of this best-selling book to Doubleday, a company which had no textbook publishing division.

The book eventually went out of print in the United States and

---

22. "My work is first a reconstruction, not a theory. . . ." Immanuel Velikovsky, "My Challenge to Conventional Views in Science," *Pensée,* IV (Spring 1974), p. 10.

23. The whole series was to be called *Ages in Chaos,* with the first volume titled, *From the Exodus to King Akhnaton.* The book became so well known as *Ages in Chaos* that the real title never caught on.

24. Velikovsky, *Peoples of the Sea; Ramses II and His Time* (Garden City, New York: Doubleday, 1978). These books officially are part of the *Ages in Chaos* series. But as I said in the previous footnote, the general series' title, *Ages in Chaos,* became too closely associated with the title of the first volume, *From the Exodus to King Akhnaton,* a title which nobody except Velikovsky has ever bothered to use.

25. Cf. Israel M. Isaacson, "Applying the Revised Chronology," *Pensée,* IV (Fall 1974); Lewis M. Greenberg, "The Lion's Gate at Mycenae," *ibid.,* III (Winter 1973).

26. David Stove, "The Scientific Mafia," *Pensée,* II (May 1972), p. 6.

remained unavailable until the mid-1960's, when the counter-culture's revolution overturned most of the established tenets of every social science and several natural sciences — the era in which the myth of neutrality died on university campuses throughout the world.[27] It was republished and once again became a popular book, and a short-lived semi-scholarly periodical, *Pensée,* was begun in the early 1970's to explore his theories in relation to several academic disciplines, and courses in two dozen colleges that relied on some aspects of his research were being taught in 1973, although the colleges were not major universities.[28] A scholarly journal, *Kronos,* is now devoted to studies of the chronology of the ancient world in the light of Velikovsky's thesis. But in the early 1950's, outright lies were spread about *Worlds in Collision,* and they were repeated in major book reviews. It was a classic case of academic suppression.[29] Harlow Shapley, the Harvard astronomer who helped launch the anti-Velikovsky campaign, was still sending out letters in the late 1960's that referred to him a "fraud" and a "charlatan."[30]

"The Shapleyist proscription of Velikovsky and his revolutionary astronomical concepts," Horace Kallen writes, "extended to all who, even though doubting or questioning the concepts, did take them seriously. One such was Gordon Atwater, fellow of the Royal Astronomical Society, curator of the Planetarium, and chairman of the department of astronomy at New York's Museum of Natural History, who had read the manuscript for Macmillan. Although Atwater was skeptical of many of Velikovsky's findings, and doubted that Venus could have been ejected from Jupiter, he took the records of world-wide catastrophes in historical times to be evidential. He was dismissed from both his positions with the Museum the night before *This Week* published his review of *Worlds in Collision,* in which he urged open-mindedness toward the book. James Putnam, for 25 years with Macmillan and the editor who made the contract with Velikovsky, was immediately dismissed from that establishment."[31] Yet the book had

---

27. Gary North, "The Epistemological Crisis of American Universities," in North (ed.), *Foundations of Christian Scholarship: Essays in the Van Til Perspective* (Vallecito, California: Ross House, 1976).

28. A list of these courses appears in *Pensée,* III (Winter 1973), pp. 37-38.

29. Alfred de Grazia (ed.), *The Velikovsky Affair* (New Hyde Park, New York: University Books, 1966). No major publisher would touch this scholarly analysis of the Velikovsky thesis and the protest it produced.

30. Horace Kallen, "Shapley, Velikovsky and the Scientific Spirit," *Pensée,* II (May 1973), p. 36. Reprinted in *Velikovsky Reconsidered* (New York: Warner, 1977), p. 53.

31. *Ibid.,* p. 40; *Velikovsky Reconsidered,* pp. 62-63.

attained number-one standing on the best-seller list nationally.

I should state at this point that I do not "believe in Velikovsky." I think we need to consider his chronological reconstruction, but I do not take seriously his astronomical explanations—or Whiston's, for that matter—of such Bible events as the parting of the Red Sea (near-collision with Venus), the manna (hydrocarbons floating down from Venus), or the halting of both sun and moon in Joshua's day (another near-collision with Venus). While there may have been astronomical events of unusual magnitude at the time—though the Bible is silent concerning them—they do not *explain* the events. The quest for naturalistic explanations here seems futile, although not necessarily illegitimate. Velikovsky has not shown how Venus could have raised the sea, kept the waters high and the walkway dry for hours (Ex. 14:21), and then allowed the split "mountains" of water to crash down just in time to drown the Egyptians. (The evidence from mythology and literature that Velikovsky presents to buttress his case that Venus is a recent addition to the solar system seems plausible to me, but my competence to judge the scientific astronomical matters involved in such a hypothesis is non-existent.) Nevertheless, I regard Velikovsky as one of the most powerful scholars of this or any century, a man whose thorough command of diverse sources in half a dozen arcane scientific and linguistic disciplines bordered on genius or the occult. He is not to be ignored or dismissed lightly.

The Need for Reconstruction

Ages in Chaos never received the attention that *Worlds in Collision* did. It is a less comprehensive theory, limited primarily to chronology and the documentary records relating to chronology. He begins with a summary of the obvious: the Exodus cannot easily be placed in the dynasty of any Pharaoh whose accepted chronology matches the chronology of I Kings 6:1. The Eighteenth Dynasty, which by conventional dating occurred in the fifteenth century B.C., included pharaohs who were very powerful. The documentary record of their reigns provides no evidence of any successful rebellion of slaves. Scholars have long recognized this problem.

If this date cannot be accepted, then what about the period in between the Eighteenth and Nineteenth Dynasties? No good, says Velikovsky. "Stress has also been laid on the fact that Palestine was under Egyptian rule as late as the disturbances of -1358 [1358 B.C.—G.N.], which put an end to the reign of Akhnaton. [Quoting

Sir W. M. Flinders Petrie:] 'Joshua did not find any such Egyptian hold during his conquest.' . . . No reference has been found that could be interpreted as even hinting at an exodus during the interregnum between the Eighteenth and Nineteenth Dynasties, and only the fact that the situation was such as to make an exodus possible favors this hypothesis."[32]

The next theory reduces the age of the Exodus further: it has for its cornerstone a stele of Merneptah, in which this king of the Nineteenth Dynasty says that Palestine "is a widow" and that "the seed of Israel is destroyed." This is regarded as the earliest mention of Israel in an Egyptian document. Merneptah did not perish in the sea, nor did he suffer a debacle; he obviously inflicted a defeat on Israel and ravaged Palestine. The circumstances do not correspond with the pronounced tradition of Israel, but since it is the first mention of Israel, Merneptah is regarded by many as the Pharaoh of the Exodus (about -1220), and Ramses II, his predecessor, as the Pharaoh of the Oppression. Other scholars, however, consider the mention of Israel in Palestine in the days of Merneptah not as a corroboration, but as a refutation of the theory that Merneptah was the Pharaoh of the Exodus. They argue that if he found Israel already in Palestine, he could not have been the Pharaoh of the Exodus.

A further obstacle to placing the Exodus in the reign of Merneptah has also been emphasized. If he really was the Pharaoh of the Exodus, then the Israelites must have entered Palestine at least a generation later, about -1190 to -1180; on this theory there remains only a century for the events of Judges.[33]

Velikovsky then quotes from W. F. Albright, who in turn had been cited by Petrie: "Under any chronological system which can reasonably be advanced, the date of Israel's invasion and settlement falls within the period (1500-1100 before the present era) when the country was ruled by Egypt as an essential portion of its Syrian Empire." Then Velikovsky asks some key questions. "But if this is so, how could the Israelites have left Egypt, and, having left Egypt, how could they have entered Palestine? Moreover, why do the books of Joshua and Judges, which cover four hundred years, ignore the rule of Egypt and, indeed, fail to mention Egypt at all?"[34]

These are obvious questions, but few conservative Bible com-

---

32. Immanuel Velikovsky, *Ages in Chaos* (Garden City, New York: Doubleday, 1952), p. 8.

33. *Ibid.*, p. 9.

34. *Ibid.*, p. 11.

mentators, with only a few major exceptions, have even hinted to their readers that such questions exist, let alone have solutions. They have remained silent because they have no answers. In fact, Velikovsky himself never did come up with a final position. When did the Exodus take place? Velikovsky was never sure. What he *was* sure of was that either the chronology of Egypt was incorrect, or that the biblical account is flawed. He concluded his book with this summary: ". . . we still do not know which of the two histories, Egyptian or Israelite, must be readjusted. At the same time we observed how the histories of other ancient countries and peoples accord with either the Israelite or the Egyptian chronology; and how the histories of Cyprus, Mycenae, and Crete, in correlating with one side or the other, create confusion in archaeology and chronology."[35]

The Ipuwer Papyrus

If an event as discontinuous and comprehensive as the Exodus took place, then we might expect to find references to it in Egyptian history. The absence of such a document need not automatically be assumed to be evidence against the Exodus, for documents that old rarely survive, and we can also imagine that any document testifying to such a defeat of Egypt's gods would be destroyed by subsequent Egyptians. But such a document does exist. It is called the Ipuwer papyrus, also known as *The Admonitions of an Egyptian Slave,* the title selected by Alan Gardiner for his 1909 translation. It had been acquired by the Leiden Museum of the Netherlands in 1828, and it was translated and studied in the late nineteenth century. This ancient Egyptian document records a series of catastrophes that befell Egypt. Velikovsky offers fourteen pages of parallel references between this document and the account of the judgments in the Book of Exodus. There are some remarkable parallels, including the most startling, a reference to the Nile: "The river is blood" (Papyrus 2:10).[36]

The Ipuwer document goes on to say: "Nay, but gold and lapiz lazuli, silver and turquoise . . . are hung around the necks of slave-girls. But noble ladies walk through the land, and mistresses of houses say: 'Would that we had something we might eat.' "[37] I am

---

35. *Ibid.,* p. 338.

36. *Ibid.,* p. 26.

37. Cited by Henri Frankfort, *Ancient Egyptian Religion* (New York: Harper Torchbook, [1948] 1961), p. 85. Ipuwer's poem is reproduced by Adolph Erman, *The Literature of the Ancient Egyptians,* translated by A. M. Blackman (New York: Dutton, 1927), pp. 94ff.

strongly inclined to agree with Courville and Velikovsky: this document was the product of the Exodus. But even if it wasn't, it presents a picture of the shock to the Egyptian mind that such an event must have produced.[38] The gods of Egypt had been laid low; the order of the universe, which had been guaranteed by Pharaoh, had been overturned.

This document is one of the most important pieces of evidence used by Velikovsky in his reconstruction of Egyptian chronology. It offers evidence of a major discontinuity in the static order of Egypt, a break which deeply affected the writer.[39] Here is a side-by-side comparison produced by Velikovsky in 1973:[40]

SOME PARALLEL TEXTS

Exodus 7:21 . . . there was blood throughout all the land of Egypt.

Papyrus 2:5-6 Plague is throughout the land. Blood is everywhere.

Exodus 7:20 . . . all the waters that were in the river were turned to blood.

Papyrus 2:10 The river is blood.

Exodus 7:24 And all the Egyptians digged round about the river for water to drink; for they could not drink of the water of the river.

Papyrus 2:10 Men shrank from tasting — human beings, and thirst after water.

Exodus 7:21 . . . and the river stank.

Papyrus 3:10-13 That is our water! That is our happiness! What shall we do in respect thereof? All is ruin!

Exodus 9:25 . . . and the hail smote every herb of the field, and brake every tree of the field.

Papyrus 4:14 Trees are destroyed.
Papyrus 6:1 No fruit nor herbs are found . . .

Exodus 9:23-24 . . . the fire ran along the ground . . . there was hail, and fire mingled with the hail, very grievous.

Papyrus 2:10 Forsooth, gates, columns and walls are consumed by fire.

---

38. The focus of the poem is "the world turned upside down," in effect. The sage complains that slaves and poor people who formerly had nothing are now rich, while the formerly rich are now poor. The slave girls do not appear to have left the nation in a massive exodus. They remain in the land, with the jewels. If this poem is a product of the Hyksos invasion, it indicates that some wealth was still left to the upper-class Egyptians, since they must have had items of value that were later confiscated by poorer people.

39. *Ages in Chaos*, pp. 22-39.

40. Velikovsky, "A Reply to Stiebing," *Pensée*, IV (Winter 1973-74), p. 39.

Exodus 7:21 And the fish that was in the river died.

Exodus 10:15 . . . there remained not any green thing in the trees, or in the herbs of the fields, through all the land of Egypt.

Exodus 9:3 . . . the hand of the Lord is upon thy cattle which is in the field . . . there shall be a very grievous murrain.

Exodus 9:19 . . . gather thy cattle, and all that thou hast in the field. **Exodus 9:21** And he that regarded not the word of the Lord left his servants and his cattle in the field.

Exodus 10:22 . . . and there was a thick darkness in all the land of Egypt.

Exodus 12:29 And it came to pass, that at midnight the Lord smote all the firstborn in the land of Egypt, from the firstborn of Pharoah that sat on his throne unto the firstborn of the captive that was in the dungeon.

Exodus 12:30 . . . there was not a house where there was not one dead.

Exodus 12:30 . . . there was a great cry in Egypt.

Exodus 13:21 . . . by day in a pillar of a cloud, to lead them the way; and by night in a pillar of fire, to give them light; to go by day and night.

From the King James Version

Papyrus 10:3-6 Lower Egypt weeps . . . The entire palace is without revenues. To it belong (by right) wheat and barley, geese and fish.

Papyrus 6:3 Forsooth, grain has perished on every side.
Papyrus 5:12 Forsooth, that has perished which yesterday was seen. The land is left over to its weariness like the cutting of flax.

Papyrus 5:5 All animals, their hearts weep. Cattle moan . . .

Papyrus 9:2-3 Behold, cattle are left to stray, and there is none to gather them together. Each man fetches for himself those that are branded with his name.

Papyrus 9:11 The land is not light . . .

Papyrus 5:3; 5:6 Forsooth, the children of princes are dashed against the walls.
Papyrus 6:12 Forsooth, the children of princes are cast out in the streets.

Papyrus 2:13 He who places his brother in the ground is everywhere.

Papyrus 3:14 It is groaning that is throughout the land, mingled with lamentations.

Papyrus 7:1 Behold, the fire has mounted up on high. Its burning goes forth against the enemies of the land.

From A. Gardiner's translation of the Leiden Papyrus. He did not observe the similarities.

When was the Ipuwer document written? The Egyptologists disagree. Some historians believe that it was written in the period between the Old and the Middle Kingdoms, while Gardiner believed, as Velikovsky also believed, that it was a document from the Hyksos era, at the end of the Middle Kingdom, meaning at the end of the Thirteenth Dynasty.[41] Non-"Velikovskyite" John Van Seeters agrees.[42] Both eras were transitional eras marked by great disruptions.

Is it proper here to use the word "both"? The conventional chronologies of Egypt assume the existence of two great periods of political and economic chaos in Egypt's early history, one immediately following the Sixth Dynasty, supposedly beginning about 2150 B.C. (late Early Bronze Age) and lasting for perhaps a century,[43] and the second period, called the Hyksos period, beginning at the end of the Thirteenth Dynasty (or possibly the Fourteenth), also lasting for at least a century, 1670-1570 B.C.[44] Courville believes that these two chaotic periods were actually the *same period,* the era of Amalekite domination which immediately followed the Exodus, i.e., after 1445 B.C. Problem: he estimates the Hyksos rule as lasting 430 years, from the Exodus almost to the reign of Solomon.[45] This is a very long estimate.

Could there have been an earlier period of political catastrophe? Could Courville's telescoping of two sets of records into one era be incorrect? We know that the pyramid-building age ended before Moses' day, and probably before Joseph's day. There had been a period of feudalism prior to Sesostris III, who Courville believes was the Pharaoh of the oppression. It is easy to imagine some sort of national political disruption which had broken the power of the pyramid pharaohs. Why not two catastrophic periods? The main reason why not: the Early Bronze Age identification of the Ipuwer Papyrus. This seems to be the period of the Exodus.

Another major problem for Courville's thesis is that Ipuwer, who lived in the Sixth Dynasty, addressed his lament to Pepi II. Courville

---

41. Velikovsky, *Ages in Chaos,* pp. 49-50.

42. John Van Seeters, "A Date for the 'Admonitions,' " *The Journal of Egyptian Archaeology,* L (1964), pp. 13-23. Predictably, he omits any reference to Velikovsky. Cf. *Pensée,* III (Winter 1973), pp. 36-37.

43. Siegfried J. Schwantes, *A Short History of the Ancient Near East* (Grand Rapids, Michigan: Baker Book House, 1965), p. 67.

44. *Ibid.,* p. 76. Some Egyptologists believe this era lasted two centuries or more.

45. Donovan Courville, *The Exodus Problem and Its Ramifications,* 2 vols. (Loma Linda, California: Challenge Books, 1971), I, p. 124.

argues that the Sixth Dynasty, the Twelfth Dynasty, and the Thirteenth Dynasty all overlapped, because the kings associated with these "dynasties" often were not pharaohs, but were only officials. Thus, we really should not think of these parallel groupings as dynasties. Courville argues that Pepi II was the last significant king of the Sixth Dynasty, whose personal reign was remarkably long and therefore had to stretch into the era of the Hyksos.[46] He has to conclude this because conventional historians believe that the evidence from Manetho and the Turin Papyrus indicates that Pepi II reigned from age six to age 100, making him the longest-lived ruler in Egyptian history.[47] If the Sixth Dynasty overlapped the Twelfth and Thirteenth Dynasties, then Pepi II's reign must have extended into the Hyksos era, since Ipuwer addressed his poem or lament to Pepi II. Therefore, Courville has to conclude that this king, the son of a very powerful ruler whose monuments are found all over Egypt,[48] was not the Pharaoh of the Exodus, or even a Pharaoh at all. This is a major problem with Courville's reconstruction. Could this powerful man have been a subordinate ruler during the reign of a weak Pharaoh, Koncharis, whose reign ended in the Red Sea? This is another reason why I am not yet fully convinced by Courville's arguments. There may be some other way to unscramble the contradictions of Egyptian chronology. Nevertheless, there is much to be said for his thesis, despite some important problems. Courville's thesis is the place where any self-consciously Christian (i.e., anti-evolutionary) Egyptologist should begin his investigations.

Courville's Reconstruction: Overlapping Reigns

Courville is not a well-organized writer. His two-volume work, *The Exodus Problem and Its Ramifications,* is exasperating. Its index is atrocious, its footnotes are difficult to master, it does not stick to a clear-cut chronological development from the front of the book to the rear, it makes continual references to obscure documents, and it never really summarizes the thesis. As editor of *The Journal of Christian Reconstruction,* I asked him to produce a summary essay of his thesis for the journal. He submitted an initial manuscript which was barely more organized than his book, but he graciously consented to

---

46. *Ibid.,* I, p. 225.
47. James Henry Breasted, *A History of the Ancient Egyptians* (New York: Scribner's, 1908), pp. 127-28.
48. *Ibid.,* p. 119.

rewrite it to my specifications, and the result was a good introduction to his research.

The Conservatives' Dilemma

The Exodus, he points out, is the first event in Egyptian history for which there is a chronologically detailed parallel in Hebrew history.[49] Because of the similarity of names, the Rameses of Exodus 1:11 was linked initially to Rameses II, listed by the pre-Christian Egyptian historian Manetho. This later Rameses was part of the Nineteenth Dynasty of Egypt, which is now conventionally dated 1350-1200 B.C. Rameses II has been assigned dates as late as 1292-1226.[50] Either date makes the reign of Ramses II too late a date for the Exodus, according to I Kings 6:1. Courville dates his reign centuries later yet.

Many conservative scholars therefore switched to the early Eighteenth Dynasty kings. But these were powerful kings, and their tombs and mummies still exist. Furthermore, no king named Rameses is known to be of this dynasty. The kings of this dynasty reigned in Thebes, far south of the Delta region. The Delta region is believed to be the area of the ruins of Pithom and Pi-Rameses, of which Exodus speaks, and the Israelites were enslaved near the king's palace (Ex. 1:15-16). The Pharaoh was close by during all the plagues, indicating that the Delta was his full-time residence area.[51]

Both the 18th and 19th dynasty settings suffer from the discovery of the mummies of the pharaohs nominated as the pharaoh of the Exodus. It is thus necessary to either deny the death of the Exodus pharaoh in the Red Sea debacle, which view is contradictory to Psalms 136:15, or to assume that the body was recovered and returned to Egypt for burial. This latter explanation is contradictory to Exodus 15:5. Since the king, above all others in the army, would certainly wear armor, he would be among the first to find his final resting place at the bottom of the sea.

Even more traumatic to the 18th dynasty placement of the Exodus is the failure of the Egyptian inscriptions even to suggest that there was any significant crisis in Egypt at this time. The power and prosperity to which Egypt was elevated in the reign of Thutmose III continued unabated into the reign of Amenhotep II. The attempts to defend this placement of the

---

49. Donovan A. Courville, "A Biblical Reconstruction of Egypt's Chronology," *Journal of Christian Reconstruction*, II (Summer 1975), p. 131.

50. *Ibid.*, p. 132.

51. *Ibid.*, p. 133.

Exodus have overlooked one important factor—a factor which, standing alone, is adequate to negate this theory as far as meriting serious consideration. This is the well-recognized fact that it would have required far less than the situation described in Scripture to have resulted in a rapid and easy rebellion on the part of the tribute-paying peoples. There would certainly have resulted a complete loss of any empire that Egypt may have controlled at the time.

The empire of Thutmose III extended to the widest limits in all of Egyptian history. All the evidence points to the total absence of any such crisis at the death of Thutmose III. . . .[52]

The opponents of an infallible Bible have recognized these problems, and they have forced baffled conservative commentators to reduce the significance of the Exodus to an event "of more manageable proportions."[53] In short, conservative Christian historians have been forced by their own chronological presuppositions to retreat from the Exodus as an event of God's massive judgment—an event which God Himself said would be a warning and a testimony to the whole world (Ex. 9:16). Courville cites E. Eric Peet: ". . . if the numbers of the [Hebrew] emigrants were nearly 2,000,000, which is a legitimate deduction from Ex. 12:37, the movement was one which would have shaken Egypt to its very foundations, and which, even if it had failed to be recorded in one of the numerous monuments which have survived in Egypt, would at any rate have left some unmistakable impression in Egyptian history."[54]

Though Courville does not use the following analogy, it is clear to me that the conservative defenders of the Bible are as trapped in the chains of Egyptian chronology as the Israelites were trapped by Pharaoh's taskmasters. They, too, are afraid to depart from Egypt, with its leeks, onions, and tenured teaching positions, for the wilderness of an unknown chronology seems too great for them.

Courville is the closest thing to a Moses of biblical chronology that this generation has seen. Another Seventh Day Adventist, Edwin Thiele, did superb work in reconstructing the chronology of the later Hebrew kings, but the more difficult deliverance is the deliverance from the chronological empire of Egypt. Rather than making Israel's history the reference point for the chronologies of the ancient world, humanist scholars have clung to the unquestionably

---

52. *Ibid.*, pp. 133-34.
53. *Ibid.*, p. 135.
54. *Idem.* Peet, *Egypt and the Old Testament* (1924), pp. 105-6.

defective chronology of Egypt, a society which rejected the very idea of linear time and meaning for history. They will not subject themselves to the authority of God or His Bible; they prefer the bondage of Egypt. So do most Christian scholars, who are fearful of alienating their methodological masters. But Courville, a retired Ph.D. in chemistry, had nothing to lose. He and Velikovsky, like Moses and Aaron, marched into the camp of the enemy to challenge the priests of this generation. Courville was armed initially only with the "rod" of I Kings 6:1, but it has repeatedly swallowed the chronological snakes of the new Egyptian magicians.

The Basis of His Reconstruction

Courville's two-volume reconstruction is incredibly detailed, and it would be beneficial for scholars to study it carefully. But for this appendix, it is only necessary to reprint his two tables that compare the conventional chronology of the dynasties, which are *assumed* to be consecutive, with his reconstruction which argues that documents that describe Egyptian history describe overlapping reigns and overlapping dynasties. Whole segments of Egyptian history are "counted twice," in other words. The conventional numbering of the dynasties is therefore meaningless, though he retains the conventional numbers for the purpose of making chronological comparisons.

Notice, for example (see the following two pages), that Dynasty XIX was short-lived and was a mere offshoot of Dynasty XVIII. It ended before Dynasty XVIII did. We are now back to the observation made by the contributor to the *New Bible Dictionary:* "In Near Eastern works involving chronology, it is important to realize that ancient scribes did not draw up synchronistic lists as is done today. They simply listed each series of rulers and reigns separately, in succession on the papyrus or tablet. Synchronisms were to be derived from special historiographical works, not the king-lists or narratives serving other purposes. An excellent example of this is the Turin Papyrus of Kings from Egypt. It lists at great length all five Dynasties XIII to XVII in successive groups, totalling originally over 150 rulers and their reigns accounting for at least 450 years. However, it is known from other sources that all five Dynasties, the 150-odd rulers and 450-odd regnal years alike, must all fit inside the 234 years from *c.* 1786 to *c.* 1552 B.C.: rarely less than two series, and sometimes three series, of rulers are known to have reigned contem-

Table I
EGYPTIAN CHRONOLOGY
Traditional

Dynasties by number	Dates and Notes	
I		There are no dates of general agreement. Dates are assigned by individual scholars as each sees best. Some continue to recognize beginnings from 3400 B.C., others from 2850-2800 B.C. The period for the first eleven dynasties ends with the year 1991 B.C., regarded as astronomically fixed.
XI		
XII	1991-1788	
XIII	1788-1688	
XV with XVI + XIV	1688-1588	XV and XVI are Hyksos dynasties. XIV is a native line under the Hyksos.
XVII	1588-?	
XVIII	1580-1350	
XIX	1350-1200	
XX	1200-1090	
XXI	1090-950	
XXII	950-750	
XXIII	750-718	
XXIV	718-712	
XXV	712-663	
XXV	663-525	

(reprinted from *The Journal of Christian Reconstruction, op. cit.* pp. 140-41.)

Table I
EGYPTIAN CHRONOLOGY
Reconstruction

Dynasties by number	Dates and Notes	
I	*c.* 2125-1880	III is parallel to late I starting about one century later than I.
IV	*c.* 1880-1780	First half of II is parallel with IV.
V	*c.* 1780-1640	Last half of II is parallel with V.
XII	1692-1480	II and V extend briefly into the era of XII. VI is parallel with XII but starts about 75 years later and extends about 75 years past the end of XII. XIII is composed of subrulers and officials under XII.
XVI	1445-1028	XVI is Hyksos, ruling parallel with XV, also Hyksos. XIV, VII to X were local dynasties ruling by permission of the Hyksos. XVII was composed of the kings during the war of liberation.
XVIII	1028-700	The dates are for the recomposed XVIII. XIX is but a brief offshoot from XVIII dated 840-790 B.C. XXIII is a line of usurper kings ruling locally, 776-730 B.C. XX overlaps late XVIII as recomposed and was fragmented after the rule of Rameses III.
XXI	710-?	The fragmented rule of XX was in competition with XXI, composed itself of a dual line of High Priests ruling from Thebes, the other at Tanis. Dynasty XXI soon took over the fragments of XX. XXII was Assyrian and competed for control with XXIV, XXV and early XXVI.
XXVI	663-525	XXIII to XXVI retain the dates as traditionally held.

poraneously."[55]

Courville claims that his reconstruction provides solutions to over one hundred chronological problems that now bedevil conservative Old Testament scholars.[56] "By the reconstruction, the Exodus incident is set at the point of the Hyksos invasion of Egypt. This setting explains the enigmatic statement of Josephus[57] to the effect that the Hyksos were able to take over Egypt without a battle. Egypt had been beaten to her knees by the disasters resulting from the plagues. The slaves were gone, the army was gone, the king was gone, and there was not even an heir apparent to take over the control."[58]

Courville offers a comprehensive comparison of the conventional dates of Old Testament history and his reconstructed chronology. It should be used as a guide to both his book and the work of Velikovsky.

One of the more convincing arguments used by Courville to defend his thesis of a single period of political disintegration relates the destruction of Canaan to the chronology of Egypt. The archaeology of Canaan indicates a universal transformation of the various city-states in the *late Early Bronze* period, or about the twenty-first century, B.C., according to conventional chronology. This conventional chronology is erroneously dated, Courville argues; the date of the Early Bronze age should be placed in the mid-fifteenth century, B.C. He discusses this in chapter VI of Volume I. There is a correspondence, Courville argues, of archaeological evidence: the end of the Old Kingdom, and therefore the beginning of the "first" period of disruption, came in *this same late Early Bronze age,* according to conventional chronologies of Egypt. Therefore, he concludes, the period after the Exodus is *the sole period of disruption.*

I have already mentioned a difficulty with this argument. The pharaohs of what scholars have called the Sixth Dynasty, especially Pepi I, were powerful kings, according to Egyptian archaeological evidence. Courville has to argue that these Sixth Dynasty kings were actually subordinate officials under the rule of what scholars have called the Twelfth Dynasty pharaohs—Sesostris I, Sesostris III, Amenemhet III, etc.—and he also argues that the Thirteenth Dynasty parallelled the Twelfth. In fact, he argues that the Sixth Dynasty kings actually survived as subordinate rulers under the

---

55. *New Bible Dictionary, op. cit.,* p. 192.
56. "Biblical Reconstruction," p. 143.
57. Josephus, *Against Apion,* Bk. I, paragraph 14.
58. Courville, "Biblical Reconstruction," p. 144.

Amalekites (Hyksos).[59] That such powerful kings were subordinates who survived the fall of two dynasties, and even the fall of Egypt, is difficult to imagine. We need generations of well-trained Egyptologists and Palestine archaeologists to examine these issues, but without operating *a priori* in terms of the conventional chronologies, and without the evolutionary assumptions that undergird the "Bronze Age-Iron Age" classification system.

The Invasion of Canaan

Stan Vaninger has written a follow-up on Courville's reconstruction. He surveys the evidence, as of 1980, concerning Canaanite archaeology. The dating of numerous "digs"—the holes in the ground that constitute the humanist world's favorite refutations of biblical history—points to a tremendous disruption in the late Early Bronze Age. In city after city, there are signs of burning and destruction, indicating an invasion of the region by a militarily powerful outside army.

The conventional dating of this period is 2300 to 2200 B.C. Thus, the scholars continue to point to this disruption as having taken place at least seven centuries before the earliest date possible for the Exodus. Furthermore, there is no archaeological evidence of any disruption in the fifteenth century through the thirteenth century, B.C., the conventional dates of the Exodus. Thus, the scholars have concluded, the events described in the Book of Joshua as being a momentous victory for the Hebrews are obviously exaggerated. The invasion was a slow process, with the Hebrews being steadily assimilated by the existing Canaanite cultures. This story is given for Jericho, Ai, and Gilgal.[60] Archaeologist Kathleen Kenyon, who did the major work on Jericho, summarizes the evidence: "The final end of the Early Bronze Age civilization came with catastrophic completeness. The last of the Early Bronze Age walls of Jericho was built in a hurry, using old and broken bricks, and was probably not completed when it was destroyed by fire . . . all the finds show that there was an absolute break, and that a new people took the place of the earlier inhabitants. Every town in Palestine that has so far been investigated shows this same break."[61]

---

59. Courville, I, pp. 225-26.
60. Stan F. Vaninger, "Historical Revisionism: Archaeology and the Conquest of Canaan," *The Journal of Christian Reconstruction,* VII (Summer 1980), pp. 123-24, 128.
61. Kenyon, *Archaeology in the Holy Land* (New York: Praeger, 1960), p. 134; cited by Vaninger, *ibid.,* p. 120. He refers to similar statements by G. Ernest Wright and William Dever: p. 120n.

Even more revealing is a 1983 article in the conventional quasi-scholarly journal, *Biblical Archaeology Review:* "The Mysterious MBI [Early Middle Bronze Age] People." This period is dated by the author from 2200 B.C. to 2000 B.C. Who were these people? The author, Rudolph Cohen, speculates: "I would suggest that they were a people who migrated slowly, from the south or southwest, into the Central Negev of Palestine. I would further suggest that the dim, historical memory of their journey powerfully influenced the Biblical author who described Israel's entry into Canaan. In fact, these MBI people may be the Israelites whose famous journey from Egypt to Canaan is called the Exodus."[62]

It is interesting, however, to note that this migratory drift, as I have reconstructed it, bears a striking similarity to that of the Israelites' flight from Egypt to the Promised Land, as recorded in the Book of Exodus. . . . The establishment of the MBI settlements directly over the ruins of the EBII-EBIII sites in the Central Negev is consistent with the tradition that the Israelites dwelled in the area previously inhabited by their Amalekite foes (Deuteronomy 25:17-19). The northeastward migration of the MBI population into Transjordan has parallels in the Biblical recollection that the Israelites remained in Moab before crossing the Jordan River and laying siege to Jericho (Deuteronomy 3:29). In this connection, it is interesting to note that Early Bronze Age Jericho was destroyed by a violent conflagration, and the site was thinly reoccupied by MBI newcomers, who were apparently unaccustomed to urban dwellings.

In the central and northern parts of Israel, the EBIII urban culture flourished. The MBI invaders in the south overwhelmed this urban Canaanite civilization and destroyed their cities but thereafter persisted in a semi-nomadic way of life. This bears a striking similarity to the tradition of Joshua's devastating campaign against the Canaanite centers in central Palestine and his ban on rebuilding some of them (e.g., Joshua 8:28). Both Jericho and Ai were fortified cities at the end of the Early Bronze Age. According to the Biblical account, they were both destroyed by the Israelites; God specifically instructed that these cities should not be rebuilt. Interestingly enough, after the EBIII destruction of Jericho and Ai, both cities lay in ruins for hundreds of years.[63]

He states that scholars agree that the pottery and other aspects of their culture differ significantly from what went before. These new

---

62. Rudolph Cohen, "The Mysterious MBI People," *Biblical Archaeology Review,* IX (July/August 1983), p. 16.

63. *Ibid.,* p. 28.

people were not primarily urban, as their predecessors and followers (2000 to 1550 B.C.) were. It was W. F. Albright, the author reminds us, who concluded that the pottery of these people resembled more closely the Middle Bronze Age people who followed them than the pottery of those who preceded them.[64]

This is not surprising to those who understand that these MBI people were the invading Israelites, and the MBII people were their more urban descendants. What the conventional scholars refuse to acknowledge is that the solution to these enigmas is found in the reconstructed chronology of Velikovsky and Courville. The conventional chronology has inserted an extra seven centuries into the record. What took place in the fifteenth century before Christ in Egypt and Canaan took place in the late Early Bronze Age (EBIII) era or early Middle Bronze (MBI).

All Cohen can do is to appeal to the memory of these MBI people in the mind of the writer of the biblical account. "The migration of the MBI population from the southwest and their conquest of the Early Bronze civilization evidently made a very deep impression, and the memory of these events was preserved from one generation to the next. The late Yohanon Aharoni made a similar suggestion when he noted that the Biblical tradition concerning the destruction of the two Canaanite cities Arad and Horma could not be placed, archaeologically speaking, in the Late Bronze/Early Iron Age (there were no cities there then) — although this is the period to which the arrival of the Hebrews is normally ascribed — but had remarkable parallels in MBII, when these two strategic outposts in the Beer-Sheva basin guarded the country's southern approaches. (Aharoni identified Biblical Arad with MBII Tel Malhata and Horma with MBII Tel Masos.) He maintained that the recollection of these two important sites was perpetuated among the local populace and appeared in the Biblical saga of the conquest. The similarity between the course of the MBI migration and the route of the Exodus seems too close to be coincidental, and a comparable process may have operated here. The Late Bronze Age (1550-1200 B.C.) — the period usually associated with the Israelites' flight from Egypt — is archaeologically unattested in the Kadesh-Barnea area (as elsewhere in the Central Negev, for that matter), but MBI remains abound and seem to provide a concrete background for the traditions of settlement."[65]

---

64. *Ibid.,* p. 18.
65. *Ibid.,* p. 29.

Egypt and Crete

We must understand how modern archaeologists operate, and the extent to which they are tied to Egypt's chronology by way of Darwin. I have discussed the origin of the labyrinth design in Chapter 2 and in Appendix C. The link between Egypt's labyrinth and Crete's is recognized by informed archaeologists. Sir Arthur Evans excavated the "palace" of Minos from about 1902 to 1930. He was an evolutionist. He used the evolutionary speculations of anthropologists Edward Tylor and Lewis Morgan (as did Frederich Engels) to provide a stage theory of historic development. Both of these scholars became prominent in the 1870's. This stage theory — savagery, barbarism, and civilization — was first developed in the early nineteenth century by Swedish scholar Sven Nilsson, who wrote in the 1830's.[66] But where did Nilsson get the idea? From Danish scholar Christian Thomson.[67] Thomson came up with the idea of the division of ages by construction materials — stone, bronze, and iron. In 1816, he had been given the difficult task of sorting out huge quantities of artifacts possessed by the Royal Commission for the Preservation and Collection of Antiquities. This collection was jumbled together. What came first? He thought about it for three years, and then came up with the Stone Age, Bronze Age, Iron Age classification. There were few references to iron implements, he knew, prior to 800 B.C. Copper and bronze were mentioned much earlier. So the bronze age must have come later. Common sense told him that the stone age was earliest of all. The first scholars outside Denmark who accepted this classification scheme were the Swedes and Germans. At mid-century, the British scholars refused to accept it. A decade later, after Darwin's *Origin of Species,* the idea spread rapidly.[68]

Evans used this assumption of cultural evolution — from primitive to complex, from Bronze Age to Iron Age, from savagery to civilization — to explain the "palace." McNeal is forthright: ". . . I have said, in effect, that he went out to the hill of Knossos with certain ideas in his head, and that he excavated the site in the light of his previous intellectual commitments. In other words, the objects as they came out of the ground were compelled (by force if necessary!) to fit Evans' prior ideas."[69]

---

66. R. A. McNeal, "The Legacy of Arthur Evans," *California Studies in Classical Antiquity,* VI (1973), p. 207.
67. *Ibid.,* p. 208.
68. Barry Fell, *Saga America* (New York: Times Books, 1974), pp. 29-30, 43-44.
69. McNeal, p. 209.

By now Evans had made two very important assumptions, first that the civilization of the Cretan Bronze Age was a discreet [typo: he means discrete — G.N.] entity, and second that it could be considered in terms of youth, maturity, and old-age. Thus far little has been said about the artifacts, and one may wonder whether they have not become lost in the metaphorical shuffle. The point is, that Evans fitted the artifacts to his particular organic model of reality, and the way in which he did so was perfectly ingenious. Faced with the necessity of forging a link between the guiding abstraction and the artifacts which could be apprehended empirically, he wove into his synthesis another set of ideas, this time concerned with the nature of Minoan art. Evans looked at the artifacts and divided them into three classes corresponding to the tripartite scheme which he already had in mind. . . . In this way Evans connected the biological metaphor with the archaeological artifacts which he pulled from the ground. The result was a sequence, a relative chronology.[70]

He then divided the types of pottery into a scheme: Stone Age; Minoan: Early Minoan, Middle Minoan, Late Minoan; and Iron Age. He did the same with art. As he excavated, the stratigraphic evidence was lost.[71] McNeal refuses to say that this was deliberate, or that Evans falsified the record. Others have cast doubt on his handling of the evidence and his creativity in reconstructing the "palace," especially the paintings.[72] As McNeal says of the early archaeologists, "In their rush to construct elaborate evolutionary sequences, they tended to forget the strata. Or, to put the matter another way, there was a regrettable habit of interpreting the strata in terms of sequences previously constructed on solely evolutionary criteria."[73]

This practice probably arose from the mistaken idea, already noted, that pottery types could be stacked end-to-end like railroad cars. We know now that pottery does not go in and out of existence in just this way. A new style does not necessarily begin where another leaves off. Evans thought that only one style marked a given period. But quite apart from the existence of gradual transitions between different styles, we find totally different types in simultaneous use. Since potters are both conservative and progressive, old styles can be retained long after new ones are in vogue. There is thus a definite danger of refining the relative sequence too much and of marking off stages where no stages ever existed.[74]

---

70. *Ibid.,* pp. 216-17.
71. *Ibid.,* p. 218.
72. Hans Georg Wunderlich, *The Secret of Crete* (New York: Macmillan, 1974), pp. 79-82.
73. McNeal, p. 219.
74. *Idem.*

Cottrell, however, praises Evans for his attention to pottery and the finely drawn divisions he makes between styles.[75] In this regard, something else needs to be noted: *the dominance of the presumed chronology of Egypt.* Cottrell writes of this achievement, and he uses italics to emphasize the point: "Evans's achievement was to mark off the *three great periods of Minoan civilization which could be correlated with the three great periods of Egyptian civilization* — the Old Kingdom, the Middle Empire and the New Empire."[76] He immediately cites Evans' own *Palace of Minos* to show that Evans recognized that this was precisely what he had "proven."

Here is the great irony. Evans did not recognize that the "palace" was not a palace, but was a labyrinth structure for the Cretan cult of the dead. Refusing to recognize that the mummy-preserving air vents were not "indoor plumbing outlets," and maintaining that sarcophagi were "bathtubs," he then argued that this "high technology" civilization was unique, with no previous origins in Greek culture, and one which disappeared almost overnight. After all, no subsequent civilization possessed such high technology. He offered several possible explanations for the disappearance of this unique civilization, such as an earthquake, but geologist Wunderlich shows that the geological evidence indicates that this explanation is highly unlikely, and so are his other explanations.[77]

Evans tried for decades to decipher the "Minoan" language, and failed because he refused to see that it was related closely to Greek. He literally invented a civilization, "Minoan," where no independent civilization ever existed. In short, Evans didn't have any idea of what he was doing. And then, just to make things complete, he imported the erroneous three-kingdom Egyptian classification scheme used by modern Egyptologists to explain Egyptian history, and thereby helped to "prove" his three-stage theory of "Minoan" history. Such is the fate of those who adopt a cultural version of the paradigm of evolution.

Conclusion

The testimony of the Bible is clear: 480 years before Solomon began to construct the temple, Moses led the Hebrews out of Egypt. The archaeological evidence points to a late Early Bronze Age/

---

75. Leonard Cottrell, *The Bull of Minos* (New York: Rinehart, 1958), pp. 138-39.
76. *Ibid.,* p. 139.
77. Wunderlich, *Secret of Crete,* ch. 11.

Middle Bronze Age conquest of Canaan by a people who invaded from the southwest. The problem for conventional archaeologists and historians is that their dating of the Bronze Age places the archaeological evidence much earlier than fifteenth-century Egypt and therefore fifteenth-century Mediterranean civilization (which is keyed to Egypt).

The Bible is correct; the conventional scholars are incorrect. They have used the flawed chronological reconstruction of Egypt's history to govern their dating of the metallic ages. They have refused to go to the Bible for their chronological keying device. Instead, they use a mistaken chronology keyed to Egypt. It is therefore time for Christian scholars to abandon Egypt at last, and to head for the promised land, even if they must wander in the academic wilderness for a generation or two.

Appendix B

THE DEMOGRAPHICS OF DECLINE

Thou shalt be blessed above all people: there shall not be male or female barren among you, or among your cattle (Deut. 7:14).

What we need to understand is that *population stagnation,* prior to the fulfilling of the dominion covenant, is a *curse.* The curse aspect of population stagnation is recognized in almost all societies except the modern humanistic West. As British economist P. T. Bauer points out, the word "barren" is universally recognized as unfavorable.[1] Population stagnation is a restriction on the ability of men to fulfill the terms of the dominion covenant. Christians should not accept the reigning presuppositions of the humanist intellectuals regarding the supposed evils of rapid population growth. If the society in which such growth is taking place is God-fearing and biblical law-honoring, population growth is a sign of God's favor and should be regarded as *confirmation of God's covenant.* It is a blessing.

In contrast to the biblical view of population growth is the message of a fund-raising letter sent out by the lobbying organization, Zero Population Growth, and signed by biologist Paul Ehrlich, author of the best-selling book, *The Population Bomb.* His letter blames the social evils of our era on population growth. "To name just a few of these dilemmas: food shortages, polluted air, oil shortages, depleted energy supplies, lowered standards of education, escalating crime rates, excessive bureaucracy, economic instability, housing shortages, and inadequate health care. There is one basic condition that contributes to *all* these predicaments. It's this: We're overpopulated."[2]

---

1. P. T. Bauer, *Equality, the Third World and Economic Delusion* (Cambridge, Massachusetts: Harvard University Press, 1981), p. 62.

2. Cited in *Review of the News* (August 15, 1979), p. 29. The response by *Review* is correct: the growing threat to the West is population stagnation.

326

The assumption of Western intellectuals concerning demographics is that population growth threatens per capita income. "More mouths to feed" means more starvation. But this assumption is not correct. It is not the number of mouths to feed which is significant economically; rather, it is the *productivity* available to feed those mouths. This has been a continuing theme in Bauer's books. He writes: "Rapid population growth has not been an obstacle to sustained economic advance either in the Third World or in the West. Between the 1890s and 1930s the sparsely populated area of Malaysia, with hamlets and fishing villages, was transformed into a country with large cities, extensive agricultural and mining operations and extensive commerce. The population rose from about one and a half to about six million; the number of Malays increased from about one to about two and a half million. The much larger population had much higher material standards and lived longer than the small population of the 1890s. Since the 1950s rapid population increase in densely-populated Hong Kong and Singapore has been accompanied by large increases in real income and wages. The population of the Western world has more than quadrupled since the middle of the eighteenth century. Real income per head is estimated to have increased by a factor of five or more. Most of the increase in incomes took place when population increased as fast as, or faster than, in the contemporary less developed world."[3]

Bauer's focus is on character, attitudes, and institutional arrangements, not natural (physical) resources. How else can we explain the spectacular increase in per capita income which has been experienced in Hong Kong (at least prior to the fear that the Communist Chinese would not renew their lease with the British crown colony in 1999)? "The number of people who can live in any area at the specified standard of living is not determined by the extent of land or of other physical resources available there. It depends very largely on the personal qualities, social institutions and mores and political arrangements of the population, on the state of technology and on external market conditions for imports and exports."[4]

Thus, the guilt felt by the West's intellectuals concerning population growth in the Third World is valid, but not because "we" taught the Third World about modern medicine and other life-saving

---

3. P. T. Bauer, *Equality*, p. 43.
4. *Ibid.*, p. 50.

technologies. Unquestionably, we did send them key life-saving technologies. Which technologies? I am not referring here to DDT and other pesticides, important as these may be in extending life expectancy by killing disease-bearing insects (at least until the insect species produce pesticide-resistant progeny).[5] I have in mind the two greatest life-extending technologies that the West has exported to the Third World, the wire-mesh window and door screen (post-1860's) and the elementary public health measure, the separation of latrines from close proximity to community water supplies, a practice known since Alexander the Great,[6] and one which was required (though without a biological explanation) of the Hebrews, at least with respect to battlefield conditions (Deut. 23:12-13). These technologies should not be the basis of guilt among Western intellectuals. The intellectuals should feel guilty only because they — Western educators, politicians, missionaries, and propagandists — have persuaded Third World leaders that socialism and economic interventionism are the most productive, or at least the most moral, of all forms of social and economic organization. It is socialism, with its denial of personal responsibility — at least the personal responsibility of the poor — which has threatened the per capita wealth of underdeveloped nations, not population growth as such.

The Ultimate Resources

The ultimate resources for man are God's four gifts: *land, life, law,* and *time.* These were God's gifts in the garden, to which regeneration has been added as a gift in the post-Fall world. "All the commandments which I command thee this day shall ye observe to do, that ye may live, and multiply, and go in and possess the land which the LORD sware unto your fathers" (Deut. 8:1). It could not be any clearer. "But thou shalt remember the LORD thy God: for it is he that giveth thee power to get wealth, that he may establish his cove-

---

5. The "defeat" of malaria-carrying mosquitos by DDT in the mid-twentieth century was apparently only a temporary tactical victory. The disease has bounced back since the late 1960's. It requires a full-time campaign to control the mosquitos. Governments are not always willing to finance such campaigns, especially in Third World nations. Julian Simon argues that the one remedy that may be able to work is high human population density, which reduces the habitat for the mosquitos. Simon, *The Ultimate Resource* (Princeton, New Jersey: Princeton University Press, 1981), p. 253.

6. Peter Drucker, *Management: Tasks, Responsibilities, Practices* (New York: Harper, 1974), p. 330.

nant which he sware unto thy fathers, as it is this day" (Deut. 8:18). God's covenant establishes the possibility of *positive feedback,* or what is also called *compound growth.*

Population growth is specifically stated to be a covenantal blessing. To deny this is to deny God's word. There can be no compromise here. Therefore, we should expect to find evidence that population growth is, *in the long run,* accompanied by other economic benefits. Contrary to the assertion of the rebellious former slaves of the wilderness era (Ex. 14:11-12; 17:1-3; Num. 20:3-4), God does not bring His people out into the wilderness to kill them. Contrary to the handwringing of ethically rebellious slaves of our day, God does not multiply the seed of righteous mankind in order to bring a population catastrophe upon them.

Simon's Thesis

Professor Julian Simon of the University of Illinois has written a devastating book, published by Princeton University Press in 1981, called *The Ultimate Resource.* What is this resource? Human creativity. Simon examined the statistical and theoretical evidence of the various "doomsday books" published around the world, but especially in the United States, after 1964. He found all of them to be misleading prophecies: the coming famine, the coming pollution catastrophe (dead seas, dead lakes, cancer-producing air), the population explosion, the coming extinction of natural resources (especially "non-renewable" resources), the energy crisis, and the economic collapse.

What is the evidence? That food is getting cheaper, and has been for centuries under capitalism. That "non-renewable" resources aren't non-renewable, except fossil energy, which is only one among several energy sources, and even here, there is an ample supply for centuries. That economic catastrophes do happen, but in the modern world they are almost always the product of government planning and mismanagement. That an increasing population, if coupled with capitalist institutions, has invariably brought with it economic advance and an increasing per capita income within two generations and often within one generation. The problem, he says, is not that Western populations are increasing, but rather that *Westerners are not reproducing themselves.* Birth rates in many Western nations are below the reproduction rate of 2.1 children per woman. What the bulk of the historical evidence points to is that shrinking populations bring with them economic stagnation and declining per capita income.

Here is the main thesis of the book: "It is your mind that matters economically, as much or more than your mouth or hands. In the long run, the most important economic effect of population size and growth is the contribution of additional people to our stock of useful knowledge. And this contribution is large enough in the long run to overcome all the costs of population growth. This is a strong statement, but the evidence for it seems very strong."[7] The evidence *is* very strong—far stronger than anything the zero population growth propagandists have been able to muster. "More mouths" means, eventually, a larger population base from which minds will emerge. *More minds mean more creativity,* despite the short-run limitation which hypnotizes the doom-sayers: "more births mean more mouths to feed" and therefore supposedly also mean reduced per capita investment, leading to low or zero economic growth.

This latter approach is illustrated by the booklet published by the World Bank, an international organization which gives confiscated tax dollars and borrowed money to Third World nations: "There may historically have been countries which could have been considered under-populated, in terms of the economy's ability to make effective use of its natural resources. Perhaps the United States was in this position at some point in the past. However, instances when the addition of more people to the labor force led to increases in labor productivity and income per head must have been few in the past and are virtually nonexistent today."[8] The words "may," "perhaps," and "must have been" indicate how little evidence the

---

7. *The Ultimate Resource,* p. 196. It is this thesis which led Warren Brookes to write *The Economy in Mind,* published in 1982 by Universe Books, which a decade before had published *Limits to Growth.* Both Simon's book and Brookes' book have been highly recommended by Franky Schaeffer: *Bad News for Modern Man: An Agenda for Christian Activism* (Westchester, Illinois: Crossway Books, 1984), pp. 116, 120. The problem is this: Brookes is a kind of "higher consciousness" or "New Age" philosopher who sees man's creativity as limitless. He sees wealth as essentially metaphysical rather than essentially ethical. From this perspective, it is knowledge which saves man, not regeneration. This is the theology of *gnosticism.* It should not be surprising that he agrees with New Age guru Buckminster Fuller, who wrote that the important factor is the "metaphysical component of wealth." This New Age (and "old age" Emersonian) aspect of his thought does not come out in his book, but it does in his 1984 lecture to students at Hillsdale College, reprinted in *Imprimis* (April 1984), a publication of the college. On the New Age philsophy, see my book, *None Dare Call It Witchcraft* (New Rochelle, New York: Arlington House, 1976), ch. 9: "Escape from Creaturehood," and Constance Cumbey, *The Hidden Dangers of the Rainbow* (Shreveport, Louisiana: Huntington House, 1983).

8. *Population Planning: Sector Working Paper* (March 1972), p. 17.

author has for any of his conclusions.

Overstating His Case

On occasion, Simon needlessly overstates his case for economic growth. For instance, he argues that progress has been made in controlling "point sources" of water pollution, such as municipal and industrial sewage and chemical waste.[9] This is true, but it is the *nonpoint* sources of water pollution, especially agricultural — topsoil runoff, animal urea runoff — that are the biggest problem. Here there has been little progress.[10] But his main point is correct: that with freedom, future-orientation, and capital to finance human creativity, there probably will be economic growth and increases in per capita output (and therefore income).

Does this mean that there are no limits to growth? He argues that there are in principle none. This is clearly incorrect. The post-Fall world is under a curse. We know there are limits to growth because there are prices. At zero price, there is more *demand for* than *supply of* a scarce economic resource, meaning virtually all resources. To argue for a zero-limits world is to argue for a zero-price world. This is the eschatological argument of the Communists and "radical" political economists.[11] Simon knows this. Yet his language often points to a zero-price world which has been the dream of revolutionary communist visionaries for millennia.

Sometimes Simon guards his language. At other times he doesn't. For example, in his conclusion, he writes that "there are no meaningful limits to the continuation of this process," meaning a rising standard of living.[12] He rejects the use of the word "finite" because of the misconceptions associated with it. For instance, "finite" is not meaningful because "we cannot say with any practical surety where the bounds of a relevant resource system lie, or even if there are any bounds."[13] He is correct: we cannot *say* where the bounds lie. He is also incorrect: we *can* say that all resources are bounded. This is why we must *pay* to gain access to them.

---

9. Simon, p. 133.

10. Jerome W. Milliman, "Can Water Pollution Policy Be Efficient?" *Cato Journal*, II (Spring 1982), p. 190.

11. "The Unorthodox Ideas of Radical Economists Win a Wider Hearing," *Wall Street Journal* (Feb. 11, 1972); cf. *Business Week* (March 18, 1972), pp. 72, 74.

12. *Resource*, p. 345.

13. *Ibid.*, p. 48.

The Irreplaceable Resource: Time

Simon is a humanist—a very smart humanist—who is seeking to escape the curse-induced limits to growth. *He is attempting to escape the logic of all growth, for it points to a coming judgment and the end of time.* A one per cent per year expansion of today's human population will produce over 80 trillion people in a thousand years. There are, in short, limits to growth. There is finitude. We are not God; we are limited creatures. Our creativity is the creativity of creatures, a kind of "re-creativity."

The Bible says that the primary limit in the post-Fall world is *time:* a final judgment is coming. Simon categorically and foolishly denies this. Speaking of the increase of total resources over time — the product of superior insight, better technology, and capital accumulation—he writes: "But, you ask, how long can this go on? Surely it can't go on forever, can it? In fact there is no logical or physical reason why the process cannot do just that, go on forever."[14] In this sense, Simon is "whistling past the graveyard"—the entropy-bound cosmic graveyard. The process cannot go on forever, or anything like forever. The universe is bounded. Furthermore, this earth is bounded, and even 1% per annum growth in the world's population will press against these limits within a few generations. Eventually, population growth will end, thereby fulfilling one aspect of the dominion covenant. Other forms of growth will also end.

We have to recognize that Simon's book is an intellectual over-reaction. Nevertheless, his arguments are correct *within the God-imposed and (humanly speaking) indefinite limitations of the creation.* We do not live in an infinite environment, but we do live in an *indefinitely limited* environment. It is not infinite, but its boundaries cannot be known by a government committee. There are limits on men's creativity, but men do not know where these limits are. God does know, and therefore it is incorrect to deny the limitations of finitude. On the other hand, a State bureaucracy does not know, and therefore it is misleading (and State-enhancing) to speak of the need for limiting growth by political action.

Biblical Ethics vs. Stagnation

The answer, then, is to allow men's creativity to flow, and to allow profit-seeking investors to seek out previously undetected op-

---

14. *Ibid.*, p. 217.

portunities. It is this fusion of inventive genius and private capital accumulation and investment which is basic to the institutional framework of the growth process. But most important of all is the ethical framework, which in turn is the source of the institutional framework. Christian economic and social analysis must postulate a relatively close relationship in history between *ethics* and *economic performance*. First, there is a relationship between external righteousness and external blessings. This includes population growth. Second, we must never forget the relationship between *rebellion* and *stagnation* or even "negative income," as the economists like to put it, i.e., between evil acts and falling per capita income for a society. What we should argue, contrary to Simon, is that there are several "ultimate resources": 1) God's gift of life in the creation; 2) His gift to the creation of an assistant made in His image, man, who is subordinately creative (Simon's "ultimate resource"); 3) His gift of land (natural resources) — the creation itself; 4) His gift of time; 5) His gift of law; and 6) His gift of regeneration and sanctification to fallen humanity.

Simon's thesis, therefore, is flawed by his humanism. Nevertheless, his thesis is not nearly so flawed as his humanist opponents' theory, that is, that compound economic growth is not the proper standard, but is instead some sort of cosmic hubris on the part of man, his defiance of the laws of an entropic cosmos.[15] They assume that finitude is primary rather than ethics, that entropy is the fundamental reality rather than regeneration, sanctification, and blessing. His opponents assume that capitalism is evil because it provides the legal framework for long-term economic growth, and thereby encourages such growth. Capitalism does precisely that, of course, but the Christian response should be that this is one of the reasons why capitalism is a God-ordained and *God-required* form of economic organization. It is not capitalism which is innately evil, but rather the zero-growth ideology.

The Legacy of Malthus

Some have termed the fear of population growth "neo-Malthusianism."[16] Thomas Malthus, a late-eighteenth-century

---

15. Jeremy Rifkin, *Entropy: A New World View* (New York: Bantam, 1980).

16. For example, B. Bruce-Briggs, "Against the Neo-Malthusians," *Commentary* (July 1974).

cleric, amateur demographer, and economist,[17] wrote his enormously influential book, *An Essay on the Principle of Population,* in 1798.
In it, he made a series of dire analyses and prophecies concerning
overpopulation and looming food shortages—prophecies that he
revised downward in later editions of his book.[18] Unfortunately, his
nineteenth-century followers ignored his later revisions.[19]

The most famous—and erroneous—of Malthus' observations is
this: the means of subsistence increases arithmetically ("1, 2, 3, 4,
5. . . ."), while all species have a tendency to increase geometrically
("2, 4, 8, 16, 32. . . .").[20] There is no evidence for the existence of
these numerical relationships.[21] Most important, we cannot
measure a *fixed* "tendency"—and tendencies were all that he ever
claimed for his theory[22]—to geometrical expansion of population in
that crucial species, humanity. Malthus' theory was refuted in the industrial West by three developments: 1) contraceptive technologies;
2) even earlier, by the very means of restraint he recommended, late
marriages; and 3) the rise of scientific agriculture, by which
mankind multiplied food even faster than man multiplied himself.
Malthus began to recognize this in later editions of his book. He
wrote in the final chapter of the last edition: "From a review of the
state of society in former periods compared with the present, I
should certainly say that the evils resulting from the principle of
population have rather diminished than increased, even under the
disadvantage of an almost total ignorance of the real cause. And if
we can indulge the hope that this ignorance will be gradually
dissipated, it does not seem unreasonable to expect that they will be
still further diminished."[23] It should also be understood that he was
utterly opposed to abortion, contraceptive technologies, and other
"mechanical" means of reducing the birth rate. In this sense,
twentieth-century "neo-Malthusians" have recommended policies

---

17. In 1804, he became the very first person to hold a chair in political economy,
at the newly founded East India College. He filled this post until his death in 1834.
William Petersen, *Population* (2nd ed.; New York: Macmillan, 1969), p. 142.

18. Gertrude Himmelfarb, *The Idea of Poverty: England in the Early Industrial Age*
(New York: Knopf, 1984), pp. 113-22.

19. *Ibid.,* pp. 122-32.

20. See Petersen, *Population,* p. 149.

21. Himmelfarb, p. 127.

22. Antony Flew, "Introduction," Thomas Malthus, *An Essay on the Principle of
Population* (New York: Penguin, [1970] 1982), pp. 19-21.

23. Cited in Warren S. Thompson, *Population Problems* (3rd ed.; New York:
McGraw-Hill, 1942), p. 29.

totally at odds with his.[24]

The influence of Malthus in discussions of population theory has been enormous. Independently, both Darwin and A. R. Wallace came to their theory of "evolution through natural selection" by reading Malthus' insight that populations are constantly pressing against the means of subsistence.[25] In economics, with the exception of Marx,[26] the Malthusian perspective led to the "dismal science" (as Carlyle called it). Classical economic theory of the first half of the nineteenth century was firmly grounded on the so-called "iron law of wages," a corollary to the law of diminishing returns — the belief that the most productive land would be put into production first, and that the demand for food created by an increasing population would be satisfied only at greater and greater cost, as less and less productive land was brought into production.[27] This was Ricardo's intellectual legacy, built on Malthus' earlier population theory.

Readers should be aware that really scientific studies of population came only in the late nineteenth century.[28] The topic was almost never mentioned in English-language history textbooks until after World War II, if then, and really not until the mid-1950's.[29] The scientific study of historical population trends is equally recent. The French have been the pioneers here, yet the discipline of historical demography began no earlier than the early 1950's.[30]

Since the period after 1960, the neo-Malthusians have dominated the popular press and media. This, too, shall pass. Public opinion concerning the appropriate population growth rate, like the growth

---

24. Petersen, pp. 150-52.

25. Charles Darwin and Alfred Russel Wallace, *The Journal of the Linnean Society* (1858); reprinted in Philip Appleman (ed.), *Darwin: A Norton Critical Edition* (New York: Norton, 1970), p. 83; Wallace, "Note on the passages of Malthus's 'Principles of Population' which suggested the idea of natural selection to Darwin and myself," *The Darwin and Wallace Celebration held on Thursday, 1 July 1908 by the Linnean Society of London* (London, 1908), pp. 111-18, cited by Sir Gavin de Beer, *ibid.*, p. 71n. See also Wallace's reminiscences at age 75 in *The Wonderful Century;* cited by Arnold C. Brackman, *A Delicate Arrangement: The Strange Case of Charles Darwin and Alfred Russel Wallace* (New York: Times Books, 1980), p. 199. For extracts of the writings of both Darwin and Wallace concerning Malthus' impact on their thinking, see Flew, *op. cit.,* pp. 49-51.

26. See Flew's extracts from Marx and Engels, *op. cit.,* pp. 51-52.

27. E. P. Hutchinson, *The Population Debate: The Development of Conflicting Theories up to 1800* (Boston: Houghton Mifflin, 1967), esp. p. 395.

28. David Landes, "The Treatment of Population in History Textbooks," *Daedalus* (Spring 1968), p. 364. This issue was titled, *Historical Population Studies.*

29. *Ibid.,* pp. 372-78.

30. Louis Henry, "Historical Demography," *ibid.,* pp. 390-91.

rate itself, changes often, and it changes fast. So do opinions concerning optimum family size. Ideas have consequences, however, and the zero population growth rhetoric has had and continues to have serious consequences for the economy of the industrial West and its future. A radically anti-biblical ideology has been adopted by millions of citizens and, from what the evidence indicates, also by a significant percentage of Christian intellectuals and leaders. There is no organization in the United States specifically devoted to persuading people that it is generally beneficial to increase the rate of population growth and the birth rate. In contrast, there are dozens of well-funded organizations that are anti-natalists. There may come a day when the anti-growth promoters will become even more consistent and call for euthanasia—the execution of the "unfit." Some indications of this exist now, such as the words of pro-abortionist biologist Garrett Hardin:

Pascal wrote: "There is nothing more real than death, nor more terrible."

To me, there is nothing more false than this statement of Pascal's.

Who's right, him or me? Undoubtedly, that's a bad question. We are different. There is probably no possibility of bringing two such minds into agreement.

The political problem is one of coexistence. Let those who fear death reject abortion and all forms of euthanasia—*for themselves and possibly for the loved ones they control.*

Let those who do not fear death act otherwise *in their own lives.* . . .

With an embryo, it's *all promise and no memories.*

With the senile, it's *all memories and no promise.*

Someday, we should be able to find a course of action with respect to the senile that will be acceptable to all non-Pascalians. For the present, I think we are clear only on abortion.[31]

So far, pro-euthanasia organizations in the United States are not yet openly funded by taxes, the way that the zero population growth "family planning" organizations are. This could easily change.

Vegetarian Redemption

The popularity of Ronald Sider's tract, *Rich Christians in an Age of Hunger* (1977), points to the deterioration of evangelical theology in

---

31. Garrett Hardin, *Mandatory Motherhood: The True Meaning of "Right to Life"* (Boston: Beacon Press, 1974), pp. 84-85.

the latter decades of the twentieth century. Sider's book adopts the reigning "Malthusianism" and proclaims it in the name of Jesus.

I discuss the book at some length here, but not because it is important as a work of scholarship. On the contrary, there is nothing scholarly about it. David Chilton has disposed of it, line by line.[32] The important fact is its popularity; it has been a very effective piece of poorly documented propaganda. It has become a kind of "Bible" for "concerned" Christians and especially college-age Christians. It has gone through numerous reprints since its publication in 1977. Its wide acceptance indicates just how intellectually defenseless evangelical Christians have become, especially to charges of "exploitation" and "insensitivity." This Eastern Baptist Theological Seminary professor is one of the most sought-after speakers on the seminary circuit. He has even debated the nuclear freeze issue with fundamentalist celebrity Jerry Falwell on Cable News Network (CNN).[33] He is, in short, a Big Name Theologian.

The book calls for a new "food policy." (In the twentieth century, whenever you read the word "policy," you should mentally substitute the words "political program.") North America is criticized for having produced food in abundance. This agricultural productivity is discussed as if it were some sort of crime against humanity. And criminals must make restitution. North Americans eat lots of food. Third World residents sometimes starve. The connection is obvious to Sider. Anyone should be able to see this. In effect, *North Americans are cannibals.* We are eating our global neighbors, taking food right out of their mouths, consuming them in a carniverous orgy of protein consumption. Writes Sider: "The U.S. Department of Agriculture reports that when the total life of the animal is considered, each pound of edible beef represents seven pounds of grain. That means that in addition to all the grass, hay and other food involved, it also took seven pounds of grain to produce a typical pound of beef purchased in the supermarket. Fortunately, the conversion rates for chicken and pork are lower: two or three to one for chicken and three or four to one for pork. Beef is the cadillac of meat products. Should we move to compacts?"[34]

---

32. *Productive Christians in an Age of Guilt-Manipulators* (3rd ed.; Tyler, Texas: Institute for Christian Economics, 1985).

33. This debate appeared on the Sandy Freeman Show. Miss Freeman is probably the most thoughtful and effective interviewer on American television. For a critique of Sider and others on the nuclear disarmament issue, see Franky Schaeffer, *Bad News for Modern Man,* ch. 3: "Peace Now!"

34. Sider, *Rich Christians* (1977), p. 43; (1984), pp. 34-35.

The Psalmist wrote: "For every beast of the forest is mine, and the cattle upon a thousand hills" (Ps. 50:10). Apparently, Sider wants us to substitute more humane, more "truly biblical" words for this verse: "For every chicken of the forest is mine, and the soybeans upon seven thousand hills." What is in fact a sign of God's blessing upon efficiency, hard work, thrift, and technological innovation — agricultural productivity — is seen by Sider as one more piece of evidence proving the corruption of the West. We are not just pigs — or worse, "Cadillac cattle" — we are *monopolists*. Yes, monopolists. Why? Because we are so productive. You see, we grow all this food, and then we export it, and exporting it means selling it, and that means . . . *exploitation!*

North America, Lester Brown informs us, has virtually "monopolistic control of the world's exportable grain supplies." The percentage of all international grain exports controlled by the United States and Canada is higher than the percentage of oil exports controlled by the OPEC countries. Before World War 2 all major geographic areas except Western Europe grew more grain than they needed. Today every major geographic region except North America must import grain. Furthermore, it is estimated that by 1985, the annual grain shortage will reach 85 to 120 million tons. This means there simply will not be enough grain for 400 to 600 million people.[35]

Let us examine this string of assertions. First, he speaks of "North America's" control of grain and compares it with OPEC's control of oil. This is nonsense. It is not "North America" which grows the grain; it is farmers who live there, and who sell into international grain markets. The OPEC (Organization of Petroleum Exporting Countries) monopolies are all based on State control of oil sales. They exist as monopolies because State ownership is the reigning ideology in the Third World.

Second, before World War II, many Third World nations did indeed grow their own grain. This was before the ideology of socialism was brought back to the Third World by nationalistic intellectuals who had been educated in the "best" Western universities.[36] This was

---

35. *Ibid.*, p. 214. In the 1984 edition, he has dropped the section beginning with "Before World War 2 . . ." (p. 211). Another prophecy gone astray? Then drop it!

36. Paul Johnson, *Modern Times: The World from the Twenties to the Eighties* (New York: Harper & Row, 1983), ch. 14: "The Bandung Generation." Malcolm Muggridge has best described this phenomenon: "When independence was achieved [in 1947 — G.N.], however, and Nehru became the first Indian Prime Minister, it was editorials he had read in progressive publications like the *New Statesman* and the

before colonial rule had been replaced by the tribal tyrannies of Africa and the socialist tyrannies of India, Ceylon (Sri Lanka), and other Third World nations. Unfortunately, it was in the 1930's that colonial administrators began to be dominated by men of "progressive" views who were hostile to market forces. They left an intellectual and institutional legacy to the future leaders of the new Third World nations which was to lead to widespread socialism and therefore widespread poverty.[37]

Prior to World War II, private property rights in agriculture had not yet been abolished "in the name of the people" in Third World societies. This was the era before Third World governments used State export monopolies to extract taxes from farmers by paying them below-market prices for their agricultural products.[38] The creation of these State export monopolies was another disastrous legacy of the colonial period, since it was shortly after the outbreak of the War that the British government, beginning in November of 1939, created the cocoa cartel which henceforth bought all of British West Africa's cocoa.[39] In short, it was only after home-grown socialist regimes began to spring up from the "liberated" political and tribal soil that home-grown grain stopped springing up. The "white man's burden"—bureaucracy—has now become the black man's burden, too. Everyone, regardless of race, color, or national origin, is supposed to carry several bureaucrats on his back.

Third, the great purchaser of grain on international markets is the Soviet Union. This is because socialist agriculture produces shortages regularly and famines occasionally, rather than producing

---

Manchester Guardian which provided the basis for his domestic and foreign policy. By a weird accident of history, some four hundred million Asians were thus harnessed to the confused thoughts and fluctuating loyalties of old-style English Leftists like Kingsley Martin, Harold Laski and Pethick-Lawrence. What on its home ground was regarded as being, at best, an acceptable irritant, to be pushed aside the moment a government of the Left took office, became in India the only evident alternative to the Thoughts of Chairman Mao." Muggridge, *Chronicles of Wasted Time: Chronicle I: The Green Stick* (New York: Morrow, 1973), p. 112.

37. P. T. Bauer, *Reality and Rhetoric: Studies in the Economics of Development* (Cambridge, Massachusetts: Harvard University Press, 1984), p. 94.

38. P. T. Bauer, *Dissent on Development: Studies and Debates in Development Economics* (Cambridge, Massachusetts: Harvard University Press, 1972), p. 405. See this entire chapter: "The Operation and Consequences of the State Export Monopolies of West Africa," ch. 12.

39. *Reality and Rhetoric*, p. 96.

grain surpluses for export.[40] The Soviet Union is the nation, by the way, which Dr. Sider proposes that we surrender to unilaterally if it becomes necessary after we have unilaterally disarmed ourselves of both nuclear and conventional weapons, which he believes is a moral imperative. He admits that the USSR might invade, but we will meet the invaders with what he calls a "nonviolent blitzkrieg."[41]

The landing would be peaceful. No American artillery would fire; no jets would strafe. Instead of American soldiers crouching behind tanks and pointing guns at them, the invaders would see tens of thousands of unarmed people carrying signs with messages in the invader's language: Go Home! We Won't Harm You; Don't Shoot—We Are Your Brothers and Sisters; Your Life Is Precious; You Are a Child of God.

Like the Czechs, Hungarians and East Germans during the Russian invasion of those countries, Americans would climb up on tanks and try to talk to soldiers: "Why have you come? Why are you invading a peaceful nation that is not threatening you?" Loudspeakers would explain that the troops are welcome as tourists but will be opposed as invaders.

Demonstrators would hand out leaflets in the invaders' language, countering the propaganda they had been fed about the reasons for the invasion. The leaflet would explain that the invaders will not be harmed, but Americans will suffer and die rather than give up their democratic way of life.[42]

But what if some Americans should attempt to resist this invasion forcefully? "If members of the crowd were not able to keep discipline and started to threaten the soldiers, special U.S. Peace-keeping Teams would move in nonviolently to restrain the persons who were losing control."[43] The result of such a "nonviolent blitzkrieg" is rather obvious: so much for the dead and imprisoned Americans' "democratic way of life." So much for democracy. If democracy (or any political system) isn't worth fighting for at any time, under any cir-

---

40. Naum Jasny, *The Socialized Agriculture of the USSR* (Stanford, California: Stanford University Press, 1949); Nancy Nimitz, "Agriculture Under Khrushchev: The Lean Years," *Problems of Communism,* XIV (May-June 1965); reprinted in Morris Bornstein and Daniel R. Fusfeld (eds.), *The Soviet Economy: A Book of Readings* (rev. ed.; Homewood, Illinois: Irwin, 1966); Lazar Volin, *A Century of Russian Agriculture: From Alexander II to Khrushchev* (Cambridge, Massachusetts: Harvard University Press, 1970).

41. Ronald J. Sider and Richard K. Taylor, *Nuclear Holocaust and Christian Hope: A Book for Christian Peacemakers* (Downers Grove, Illinois: InterVarsity Press, 1982), p. 274. You should notice who published this theological monstrosity.

42. *Ibid.,* p. 275.

43. *Idem.*

cumstances, then it will not survivé. A political system which cannot defend itself militarily cannot survive the competition. North America would fall to the Soviet Union. That would certainly end North America's supposed monopoly of grain exports. It would then raise that fateful question: "Comrade, where will you buy your grain after you have conquered us?"

Fourth, the famine prophesied by Dr. Sider has yet to come. No wonder he dropped all references to this coming famine in the 1984 edition of *Rich Christians* (p. 215). It would come, however, if socialist agriculture were to be imposed on North America and Australia.

Fifth, it should also be pointed out that the U.S. (meaning consumers who live in the United States) is a major *importer* of food. This has been true for many decades.[44] In 1965, the U.S. Department of Agriculture estimated that the U.S. was the number-two importer of food, after Britain.[45] Grain farmers in the U.S. do indeed export a large amount of wheat, corn, and soybeans, but other agricultural products, including vegetables, fruits, and cattle, are imported.

The export of grain from North America is a matter of what economists call *comparative advantage in trade*. Consumers in the United States buy those items that foreign farmers can produce more efficiently (less wastefully) and therefore sell less expensively than American farmers can, and American farmers export whatever goods foreign consumers are willing to buy by "outbidding" domestic American consumers. Whether importing or exporting, *the high bid wins,* in agriculture as in anything else. This is the economic basis of the so-called "North American monopoly" of agricultural exports. American farmers sell foreign consumers what they want to buy at low prices. The shame of it!

Sixth, the "sacred cows" of India also eat a lot of grain. They, too, eat seven times their protein value in grain — Prof. Sider's seven-to-one bogeyman. But nobody eats them. Estimates of the number of such cows in India range between 175 million to over 200 million. They eat enough grain to feed 1.2 billion people. "This means that India produced enough food [around 1970], so that if you moved the cows out, you could move everybody in from the Continents of Antarctica, Australia, Africa and Europe. You could also move in

---

44. Dan Van Gorder, *Ill Fares the Land* (Belmont, Massachusetts: Western Islands, 1966).

45. *Foreign Agriculture* (March 15, 1966), p. 6.

everybody from most of the other nations in the world. Then all these people could eat better than the people of India eat today."[46]

Seventh, India's rats also eat. Rats and cows together consume half of India's agricultural output.[47] It would take a train 3,000 miles long to haul all the grain eaten by rats in India each year.[48] Rats in other nations are also big eaters. In one year, rats in the Philippines consumed over half the corn and 90% of the rice crop.[49] Is this the fault of the "monopolistic" West?

What is Dr. Sider's solution to the "problem" of the North American "monopoly"? "A new food policy *now* is one way to avoid such a dangerous situation. The constantly growing demand for food must stop—or at least slow down dramatically. That means reduced affluence in the rich nations and population control everywhere."[50]

Here we have a marvelous program which could easily produce an international food crisis. *First,* forced redistribution of wealth—in this case, food—by State bureaucrats in the West. This will help bankrupt Third World farmers, who will face competition in grain sales from their own socialistic bureaucracies, which are in need of subsidies from the West. Simultaneously, this will reduce economic incentives to produce food in the free nations of the West. *Second,* he proposes population stagnation, which, as Simon and other economists have shown (e.g., Colin Clark), tends to reduce economic output per capita over several decades.

Thus, the "moral insights" of liberation theology threaten the West's high per capita output, which is itself the product of the Protestant work ethic, coupled with biblical principles of private ownership, stewardship, and responsibility. Such insights also threaten the per capita income of all those Third World nations that trade with the West. As Prof. Bauer notes, "Famines occur in Third World countries largely isolated from the West. So far from condemning Third World people to death, Western contacts have been behind the large increase in life expectation in the Third World, so often deplored as the population explosion by the same critics."[51]

---

46. Robert L. Sassone, *Handbook on Population* (2nd ed.; Author, 1972), p. 53.

47. Robert M. Bleiberg, "Down a Rathole," *Barron's* (Aug. 11, 1975), p. 7.

48. The estimate of Dr. Max Milner of the Massachusetts Institute of Technology. "Over 40% of the World's Food Is Lost to Pests," *Washington Post* (March 6, 1977).

49. *Idem.*

50. *Rich Christians,* p. 214. Absent in 1984 edition.

51. Bauer, *Equality,* p. 68.

The guilt-manipulators have spotted their marks—soft-hearted and soft-headed Christian intellectuals who have become political "soft touches"—and they are merciless in their pursuit of their intended victims. If they should be successful in their ideological efforts, millions of Third World victims will join the ranks of the dead and dying—today's victims of an earlier "benevolent" colonial socialism. The international division of labor will collapse, along with per capita output, as it has in the Soviet bloc. And it will all be done in the name of Jesus and Christian justice. I am reminded of James Billington's remark concerning the French Revolution: "Most of the conspirators shared this belief in Christ as a *sans-culotte* at heart if not a prophet of revolution. The strength of the red curates within the social revolutionary camp intensified the need to keep Christian ideas from weakening revolutionary dedication."[52]

The Legalization of Abortion[53]

"Population explosion" is a pejorative phrase in the late twentieth century. Another variant is "people pollution." There will come a day when historians and social commentators will look back in disbelief and disgust at the billions of tax dollars that were granted to public and private propaganda agencies after 1965 to "spread the word" about the supposed evils that "inevitably" result from the growth of population.[54] In industrial nations that are facing literal extinction in the long run because the birth rate of their citizens is below the replacement rate of at least 2.1 children per woman, intellectuals are advocating abortion, mass education programs favoring contraception, and similar restraints on births. As of 1975, nations that no longer had fertility rates above the replacement rate included West Germany, Denmark, Austria, Belgium, France, Holland, Norway, Sweden, Switzerland, Great Britain, and the United States.[55] These

---

52. James Billington, *Fire in the Minds of Men: Origins of the Revolutionary Faith* (New York: Basic Books, 1980), p. 76.

53. For a survey of the history of abortion, from 2050 B.C. (conventional dating), see Part 2 of the essay by Eugene Quay, "Justifiable Abortion—Medical and Legal Foundations," *Georgetown Law Review*, XLIX (Spring 1961).

54. From 1965 through 1976, governments had spent the equivalent of a billion and a quarter dollars to promote worldwide programs of population reduction. Well over $850 million of this came from the taxpayers of the United States. An additional quarter of a billion had been spent by the Ford Foundation and the Rockefeller Foundation for this same goal. See Simon, *The Ultimate Resource*, p. 292.

55. "People Shortage," *Wall Street Journal* (Aug. 23, 1979), chart: "West European Fertility Rates." The peak in the fertility rate in the U.S. was 3.7, in 1957. By 1975, it

nations have also erected immigration barriers against newcomers who might at least be able to increase the size of the national populations sufficiently to maintain them in the long run.

In 1973, about a decade after the "population dilemma" propaganda began,[56] the Supreme Court of the United States overturned all state laws that outlawed "abortion on demand" in the *Roe v. Wade* decision. Within a few years, between a million and a million and a half now-legal abortions were being performed in the United States. Pro-abortionists offer a counter-argument: that there were as many as a million illegal abortions in 1960.[57] Another estimate of the combined legal and illegal abortions in the U.S. in 1972, a year before *Roe v. Wade,* is 1.25 million.[58] A less radical estimate is 587,000 abortions in 1972.[59] The number, obviously, was high. But the number of abortions increased after *Roe v. Wade.* The *Roe v. Wade* decision, however, has led not only to a vast number of abortions but also to a mobilization of Christians and conservatives in opposition.[60] By 1976, the number of legal abortions performed by physicians in the United States exceeded the number of tonsillectomies as the most

---

had fallen to 1.8. See *Population Estimates and Projections: Estimates of the Population of the United States and Components of Change: 1930-1975,* Series P-25, No. 632 (July 1976), p. 2; published by the U.S. Department of Commerce, Bureau of the Census.

56. Philip M. Hauser, *The Population Dilemma* (Englewood Cliffs, New Jersey: Prentice-Hall, 1963), copyright by the American Assembly, for whom it was compiled. Trustees of the Assembly included former President Dwight Eisenhower, former Federal Reserve Board Chairman (under President Roosevelt) Mariner S. Eccles, W. Averill Harriman, and Henry M. Wriston (later president of the second-largest bank holding company in the U.S., Citicorp).

57. Garrett Hardin, *Mandatory Motherhood*, p. 11.

58. Helen Dudar, "Abortion for the Asking," *Saturday Review* (April 1973), p. 34. The "teaser" copy which introduces the article reads: "It's still not the same as having a tooth pulled, yet few tears are shed."

59. "Another Storm Brewing Over Abortion," *U.S. News and World Report* (July 24, 1978).

60. Cf. Franky Schaeffer, *A Time for Anger: The Myth of Neutrality* (Westchester, Illinois: Crossway Books, 1982), ch. 6. The success of Francis Schaeffer's *A Christian Manifesto* (Crossway, 1980) and the moderate success of Franky Schaeffer's anti-abortion movie and his father's book, co-authored by Dr. C. Everett Koop, both bearing the title, *What Ever Happened to the Human Race?* (Old Tappan, New Jersey: Revell, 1976), led to the appointment in 1981 of Dr. Koop as Surgeon General of the United States. This symbolic appointment demonstrated that the Christians had attained at least some degree of influence in national politics by means of this topic. It was the only major appointment during President Reagan's first term that the Christians received. An anti-abortion book bearing President Reagan's name, *Abortion and the Conscience of the Nation,* was released in early 1984, a Presidential election year, by Thomas Nelson Sons, a religious publisher.

frequently performed surgical procedure.[61] The number of abortions performed annually finally peaked (possibly only briefly) in 1982.

The speed of the transformation of people's thinking was remarkable. In the early 1960's, the American public favored the right of a woman to elect to have an abortion if the unborn baby was known to be "defective." Still, only ten percent approved of abortion on demand simply on request of the woman.[62] By 1972, a Gallup Poll showed that 65% of Protestants and 56% of Roman Catholics answered "yes" to this question: "Do you agree that the decision to have an abortion should be made solely by a woman and her physician?"[63]

A grim reminder of the judgment which may be in store for today's aborting societies is the fact that Germany was the first modern Western nation to maintain a policy of mass abortions. This campaign to legalize abortion began prior to the coming to power of the Nazis, but it was under the Nazis that a full-scale policy of legalized abortion began. The parallels between Nazi Germany's disrespect for life and the West's disregard for the unborn are chronicled by William Brennan in two books, neither of which is pleasant to read.[64]

Abortion in the Soviet Union

It is also interesting that in 1965 — precisely the same time that the "population explosion" propaganda began in the West — a debate began on this topic within the Soviet Union. The official Soviet Marxist line had been that there could never be overpopulation in a Marxist nation. It was the West which worried about overpopulation because of the inability of capitalism to produce sufficient food and consumer goods. Soviet Premier Khrushchev had stated the "hard line" in a 1955 speech: "The more people we have, the stronger our country will be. Bourgeois ideologists have invented many cannibalistic theories, including the theory of overpopulation. They think about how to reduce the birth rate and the growth of popula-

---

61. Sullivan, Tietze, and Dryfoos, "Legal Abortion in the United States, 1975-76," *Family Planning* (May/June 1977), p. 116; cited by William Brennan, *Medical Holocausts* (New York: Nordland, 1980), I, p. 322.

62. Hardin, *Mandatory Motherhood*, p. 71.

63. *Ibid.*, p. 7.

64. Brennan, *Medical Holocausts, op. cit.*, and *The Abortion Holocaust: Today's Final Solution* (St. Louis, Missouri: Landmark Press, 1983).

tion. Matters are different among us, comrades. If we were to add 100,000,000 to our 200,000,000, it would be too few."[65]

Nevertheless, in that same year, a decree legalized both contraceptives and abortions. The official excuse was the large number of illegal abortions[66] — a favorite excuse in Western nations, too. The "hard line" prevailed, however, until Khrushchev's removal in 1964. In 1964, there was not a single demographic research institute in the USSR; two had been shut down. As late as 1970, whatever population research that was being conducted was done in separate departments of other kinds of institutions.[67] In short, the Soviet line, following Marx's lead,[68] was anti-Malthus. They did not worry about overpopulation.

In the 1920's and the early 1930's, the Party line had favored free love and was distinctly anti-family. This was a fulfillment of Engels' observation: "It is a curious fact that in every large revolutionary movement the question of 'free love' comes to the foreground."[69] The predominant view was that sexual life was supposed to be outside the regulation of the Party[70] — the only major activity which was still regarded as legitimately autonomous from political control. Easy divorce and free abortions were the rule after 1926.[71] There were widespread abortions in the early 1930's.[72] This policy was reversed by law in 1936. At the same time, public money began to be offered for births.[73] The mid-1930's therefore saw a dramatic reversal in

---

65. Speech to settlers departing to the "virgin lands," as translated in *Current Digest of the Soviet Press,* VII (Feb. 16, 1955), p. 12; cited in Philip R. Pryde, *Conservation in the Soviet Union* (Cambridge: At the University Press, 1972), p. 167.

66. Norton T. Dodge, *Women in the Soviet Economy: Their Role in Economic, Scientific, and Technical Development* (Baltimore, Maryland: Johns Hopkins Press, 1966), p. 24.

67. Pryde, p. 167.

68. *Marx and Engels on the Population Bomb,* edited by Ronald L. Meek (Berkeley, California: Ramparts Press, 1971). It is interesting that the original title of the 1953 edition was the more prosaic *Marx and Engels on Malthus* (New York: International Publishers). International Publishers is an exclusively Marxist publishing house, while Ramparts was a "new left" magazine and publishing house, which went out of existence in the 1970's. But the phrase "population bomb," made famous by Stanford biologist Paul Ehrlich, was too good for a profit-seeking radical publishing house to pass up.

69. Cited by Igor Shafarevich, *The Socialist Phenomenon* (New York: Harper & Row, [1975] 1980), p. 33.

70. H. Kent Geiger, *The Family in Soviet Russia* (Cambridge, Massachusetts: Harvard University Press, 1968), p. 61.

71. *Idem.*

72. Dodge, *Women in the Soviet Economy,* p. 9.

73. *Ibid.,* p. 23.

Soviet law toward the family, including a 1934 law against homosexuality.[74] The anti-abortion law remained on the books until 1955.

Between 1955 and 1965, the total number of legal and illegal abortions increased by a factor of four, according to published Soviet estimates.[75] A debate over the theory of overpopulation began in the USSR in 1965 and 1966, which indicated a weakening of the older "hard line" position.[76] A national network of abortion clinics was in operation by the mid-1970's which offered cheap abortions at a price of around $7 each.[77] Some 8 million abortions were being performed annually by this time.[78] Abortion became the major form of Soviet population control, three to one over contraception.[79]

The rulers of the Soviet Union now face the demographic and political problem of a stagnant "white Russian" (European) population which confronts a growing Muslim and Central Asian Soviet population. "Soviet demographers expected the 1970 census to produce a figure of over 250 million, with a projection of 350 million by the end of the century. In fact the 1970 total fell 10 million short and the 1979 figure produced only 262,436,000, meaning a population of not much over 300 million in 2000 A.D.. What the 1970 census revealed for the first time was a dual birth-rate: low in Slavic and Baltic Russia, high in the eastern USSR, Central Asia and the Caucasus. In the 1960s alone the Muslim population leapt from 24 to 35 million, adding another 14 million in the 1970s, giving a total of about 50 million by the beginning of the 1980s. By this point it was clear that at the turn of the century Central Asia and Caucasia would contribute about 100 million, that is a third, of the total. Even by 1979, the 137 million Great Russians, a markedly ageing population compared to the non-Slavs, felt demographically on the defensive."[80] God will not be mocked!

Abortion Worldwide

The extent of abortion worldwide is, from a biblical standpoint, horrendously large. A U.S. government publication cites estimates

74. Geiger, *Family*, p. 94.
75. Gail Warshofsky Lapidus, *Women in Soviet Society: Equality, Development, and Social Change* (Berkeley: University of California Press, 1978), p. 299, note 25.
76. Pryde, pp. 167-68.
77. "Sexual Revolution in Soviet [sic] Straining Strict Morality," *New York Times* (Sept. 25, 1977).
78. Lapidus, p. 299.
79. *Idem.*, note 25.
80. Paul Johnson, *Modern Times*, p. 711-12.

that by the late 1970's, about 55 million abortions, legal and illegal, were taking place annually, with half of these in the less developed nations. The United States is at the low end of the scale. "In the United States, the 1978 abortion rate as reported by the Center for Disease Control was 23 per 1,000 women of reproductive age. New estimates of induced abortion in China place that country's rate at 25 in 1978. Eastern bloc countries have very high rates. In the U.S.S.R., there were 180 abortions per 1,000 women of reproductive age in 1970, the latest year for which data are available. There were 88 abortions per 1,000 women of reproductive age in Romania and 68 per 1,000 for the same group in Bulgaria (1979). The latest data from Japan (1975) show an equivalent rate of 84 per 1,000."[81]

Japan, which legalized abortions early, in 1947, has some 12,000 licensed abortionists. Almost 600,000 abortions were performed annually, as of the early 1980's. One out of every three Japanese women in the 25 to 40 age group has had an abortion, reports one Japanese feminist organization. Temples are selling statues and rituals to families seeking atonement for the guilt produced by the abortions, and the popularity of these rituals is rising.[82]

China has put tremendous pressure on women to have abortions. Infant girls are being killed upon birth by parents who want sons, a fact confirmed by Premier Zhao Ziyang in his remarks critical of the practice in late 1982. But what else would he expect? The new Chinese population law restricts families to one child, and rural Chinese want a son if that is the only child they will be allowed to bring up. Childless couples are required to obtain a "birth quota" in advance. Very heavy fines are levied on violators.[83] The State, being a monopoly employer, can enforce its will on recalcitrants, and does.[84] Newborn third children were being killed in some hospitals, reports indicated in the early 1980's.[85] (The social effects a genera-

---

81. *World Population and Fertility Planning Technologies: The Next 20 Years* (Washington, D.C.: Office of Technology Assessment, 1982), p. 63.

82. Urban Lehner, "Japanese Ceremonies Show Private Doubts Over Use of Abortion," *Wall Street Journal* (Jan. 6, 1983).

83. Steven W. Mosher, "Why Are Baby Girls Being Killed in China?" *Wall Street Journal* (July 25, 1983).

84. Steven W. Mosher, *Broken Earth: The Rural Chinese* (New York: The Free Press, 1983), ch. 9. Mosher was dismissed from the Ph.D. program in anthropolgy at Stanford University not long after the Chinese government protested Mosher's reporting of the fact that in some rural districts in the late 1970's, Chinese were administering forced abortions. See the editorial in the *Wall Street Journal* (July 25, 1983).

85. Michael Vink, "Abortion and Birth Control in Canton, China," *Wall Street Journal* (Nov. 30, 1981).

tion later will threaten the very fabric of Chinese culture: there will be a scarcity of young women eligible for marriage.)

Romania, virtually alone among nations, saw the light in the late 1970's and outlawed abortions. This policy was reaffirmed in 1984. Romanian leaders fear the effects of a declining population. They have shown greater wisdom than Western intellectuals.

The old argument that illegal abortions are risky to mothers is over-blown. In the 1958-62 period, fewer than 375 women in the U.S. died each year as a result of both illegal and spontaneous (non-induced) abortions. By 1972, it was under 100.[86] Some pro-abortionists knew this all along. Mary S. Calderone wrote in 1960 that in 1957 "there were only 260 deaths in the whole country attributed to abortions of any kind."[87] But the lure of the "backstreet butchers" argument has always proven strong. It was used repeatedly in Germany during the Weimar years, and it bore its evil fruit under the Nazis.[88] Besides, why shouldn't murderers be subject to a little risk? The fact is this: in over 99% of all abortions, half the people involved die. The unborn half.

"Christian" Abortion

Given the inroads of humanistic thought into the Christian in-tellectual community, it should not be startling to learn that late-twentieth-century Christian intellectuals and physicians are propos-ing a program of reduced birth rates—yes, even including abortion, though not yet infanticide.[89] Psychiatrist M. O. Vincent offers this assessment: ". . . the foetus has great and developing value, but it is less than a human being. It will be sacrificed only for weighty reasons."[90] As a psychiatrist—a man of science, you understand—he gets to "weigh" these reasons: "I find it hard to know how to 'weigh' these reasons, but weigh them I must."[91] Ah, the responsibilities of

---

86. *World Population and Fertility Planning Technologies,* p. 64, Figure 7.

87. Mary S. Calderone, "Illegal Abortion as a Public Health Problem," *American Journal of Public Health,* 50 (July 1960); cited in Brennan, *The Abortion Holocaust,* p. 13.

88. Brennan, *ibid.,* pp. 10-11.

89. See, for example, several of the essays in the abominable book, *Birth Control and the Christian,* edited by Walter O. Spitzer and Carlyle L. Saylor (Wheaton, Il-linois: Tyndale House, 1969). This was a symposium held by the Christian Medical Society and *Christianity Today.* On *Christianity Today's* co-sponsorship, see Graham A. D. Scott, "Abortion and the Incarnation," *Journal of the Evangelical Theological Society,* XVII (Winter 1974), p. 30.

90. "Psychiatric Indications for Therapeutic Abortion and Sterilization," in *Birth Control and the Christian,* p. 213.

91. *Idem.*

becoming a "weigher" on a set of cosmic scales of value that God forbids men to use.[92] "To abort or not to abort, that is the question": for men in rebellion against God.

It is the responsibility of Christians to study the effects of population growth, we are informed by a professor of sociology who teaches in a state university.[93] You see, population growth creates "complications for the collectivity."[94] (Isn't scientific language wonderful?) For example, juvenile delinquency is apparently one result of unwanted children.[95] Furthermore, the government now provides welfare services (an ungodly coercive redistribution of wealth, which our sociologist fails to mention), so that today "billions of tax dollars are spent in an attempt to cope with the results of over-population. . . ."[96] (If you detect a bit of racism and middle-class resentment here, you are probably not alone.) He refers to only one remaining hold-out in the ideological war against over-population: the Black Power movement of the late 1960's. The Black Power advocates believed that this zero population growth philosophy is, in the sociologist's words, "the imposition of white middle-class standards on the black community, the white desire to limit the number of 'us beautiful blacks,' and the desire of whites to use birth control as an easy way to solve the basic problems of society."[97] I can only comment: the blacks he describes here possess more common sense (and better tools of sociological analysis) than a lot of professors of sociology who teach in state universities.

Evangelical Ethics, 1984

In the appropriate year of 1984, reminiscent of George Orwell's title, came the equally appropriately titled book, *Brave New People*, by a New Zealand professor of anatomy and medical ethicist, D. Gareth Jones, Ph.D. He claims he is a Christian. His book was published by Inter-Varsity Press, which also claims to be Christian. The book is a very clever defense of the ethical legitimacy of "therapeutic" abortion.

---

92. This is not a "battlefield" decision on whether to allow a man to die; this is a decision to intervene actively and stop a living person's normal developmental process.

93. Donald H. Bouma, "The Population Explosion: World and Local Imperatives," *ibid.*, pp. 329-39.

94. *Ibid.*, p. 330.

95. *Ibid.*, p. 337.

96. *Ibid.*, p. 335.

97. *Ibid.*, p. 339.

After spending six chapters discussing the admittedly difficult ethical issues relating to genetic manipulation, the author then introduces his chapter on the not at all difficult moral issue of abortion, the execution of the legally innocent. I call this the "confuse, then corrupt" technique. It has been used successfully by theologically liberal "higher critics" of the Bible for a century and a half. He warns us that "there are no slick answers,"[98] which is the typical approach of the morally confused (or morally perverse) but self-proclaimed "honest Christian" who is about to abandon the clear teachings of the Bible.

He wants Christian parents to make "a responsible decision."[99] This decision is, of course, "weighty."[100] (We are back to those cosmic scales that pro-abortionists insist we must use in making immoral decisions.) Naturally, "The issues are much more complex than is generally imagined."[101] (Be prepared: when Ph.D.-holding Christian "ethicists" start warning you about "complex moral questions," you are about to be told that you can safely violate the Bible's clear teachings.) He asks that all-too-familiar question: "*When* does the fetus *become* a person?"[102] When you call an unborn infant a "fetus," you have already prejudiced the case. You have begun to answer the question. The answer, predictably, is that honest people just can't agree on the answer to this question, so let's use the alternatives to the Bible that "logic" provides.

No Absolutes

He cites the Roman Catholic Church's absolute prohibition against abortion. "The major attraction of the Roman Catholic position for Christians is its high view of human life. It has the strengths of all absolute positions and it places the unborn directly in God's will. In practice, however, issues are often not so simple, and while we may wish to believe that abortion is always morally wrong, dilemmas abound."[103] In short, moral decisions are sometimes costly, and certain "ethicists" recommend not paying the price.

---

98. D. Gareth Jones, *Brave New People: Ethical Issues at the Commencement of Life* (Downers Grove, Illinois: Inter-Varsity Press, 1984), p. 7.

99. *Ibid.,* p. 157.

100. *Idem.*

101. *Ibid.,* p. 158.

102. *Ibid.,* p. 162.

103. *Ibid.,* p. 167.

In a remarkable abandonment of both logic and morality, he then accuses the Roman Catholic position of irresponsibility. He summarizes the implications of the position: "A fetus, once conceived, has the right to develop; this is an expression of natural forces and is a duty allotted to the mother by nature. Taken to its logical conclusion, this leaves no room for human responsibility. Instead, the erratic and impersonal forces of the natural environment are allowed sway. I do not consider this accords with the biblical emphasis on the responsibility God has bestowed upon mankind to control our environment."[104]

Raising the issue of natural law theory at this point in his argument is a verbal smoke screen, a cheap debate trick. By misdirecting the attention of his readers to a false issue, "impersonal natural law," he would have them overlook the obvious issue, namely, *the prohibition against murder in biblical law.* Jones spends page after page in Chapter 1 to demonstrate that the Bible teaches that all created reality is intensely personal, because God, the Creator, is personal. He denies any impersonality in the universe. "The world God has made is intrinsically personal."[105] Then he uses a weakness in Roman Catholic epistemology — natural law theory, which *is* ultimately impersonal — to undermine a great strength in Roman Catholic ethics: the defense of human life.

He argues, incredibly, that by teaching people never to abort the unborn, the Roman Catholic Church has removed the question of abortion from the realm of ethics. On the contrary, the Church has reaffirmed the ethical decision. It is not a question of "to abort or not to abort under which complex, difficult, dilemma-filled situations?" It is a question of "to abort or not to abort, under *any* situation?" The Church has quite properly called abominable the position defended by D. Gareth Jones, Ph.D., and he feels the heat.

He says that "Abortion for therapeutic reasons demands a serious response by those professing to follow Christ."[106] Indeed, it does. The serious response is: "Don't." The serious reason is: "God says not to."

The "Potential for Personhood"

He says that "each fetus is a human life, representing a potential for personhood from very early in its development. From this early

---

104. *Idem.*
105. *Ibid.,* p. 20.
106. *Ibid.,* p. 183.

stage it is a potential person, and from about eight weeks onwards has a recognizable individuality as manifested by its circulation and brain activity. It is well on the road to full personhood, and for most practical purposes may be considered to be a person. Nevertheless, I do not wish to draw a line between when a fetus *is not a person* and when a fetus *is a person*. Throughout the whole of its development the fetus is potentially an actual person, and deserves the respect and treatment due to a being with this sort of potential."[107] This is medical *ethics?* This is a call to responsible decision-making?

If Mary, a virgin who found herself pregnant, had decided to "take the easy way out" and had aborted her "fetus" in, say, the third month of her pregnancy, would she have eliminated a true Person? Or just a potential Person? Dr. D. Gareth Jones offers no principle that would give us a clear indication. Instead, he offers language that would have confused her, had she not understood the ethics of the Bible.

He goes on, and it gets worse. "A fetus is part of a more extensive continuum, the end-result of which is the emergence of an individual human being manifesting, under normal circumstances, the myriad facets that go to make up full personhood. The processes of this continuum, however, do not begin at conception; neither do they end at birth."[108] The *continuum:* here is a key idea in the biological speculations of D. Gareth Jones. First, "A new-born baby is a very incomplete human person . . ."[109] Second, "A corollary of the continuum-potentiality argument is that there is no developmental point at which a line can be drawn between expendable and non-expendable fetuses, that is, between non-personal and personal fetuses. It may be preferable to carry out abortions early rather than later during gestation, but that is a biomedical and not an ethical decision."[110] Not an ethical decision? Strictly a biomedical decision? You mean a strictly *technological* decision? This is precisely what he means. The official justification of this monstrous book is that it brings Christian ethics to bear on biomedical technology, but the end result is the imposition of the satanic ethics of abortion on the consciences of Christians in the name of autonomous biomedical technology.

But what about the unstated third but obvious point? What

---

107. *Ibid.,* p. 174.
108. *Idem.*
109. *Ibid.,* p. 175.
110. *Ibid.* pp. 175-76.

about a definitional "continuum" for personhood which does not "end at birth," to quote Dr. Jones? In short, *what about euthanasia*, "mercy killing"? Is this, too, strictly a biomedical decision? Dr. Jones is not about to say . . . not in 1984. Maybe in 1994. And you know what his answer will have to be, if he remains consistent to his stated presuppositions in this book. It will no doubt be a "difficult" answer, based as it is on "complex" issues. But when he gives his answer, pray that no civil government accepts it, and also pray that you are not 85 years old and no longer fully competent mentally or economically.

The arguments he offers in support of a family's decision to abort a child can be used equally well by a family looking for excuses to murder a senile adult. The person is unable to learn. He is unable to take care of himself. He may create terrible psychological burdens for other family members. In short, caring for him is costly, and there is no economic payoff at the end of the road. Such a person is the economic and psychological equivalent of a highly retarded child. He is, in terms of Dr. Jones' analysis, *an expendable elderly fetus*. Kill him. But don't do it thoughtlessly, of course. Do it in responsible Christian love. Also, it should be done only after considerable reflection and the "weighing" of costs and benefits. And don't put your finger on either side of the cosmic scales. That would be cheating. You know what God says about false weights and balances. We need to honor God's ethical principles, after all, however vague they may be. So say the abortionists.

The Quality of Life

He includes a section, "Possible grounds for therapeutic abortion." Biomedically possible, yes. Morally possible, no. But this is not what he concludes. What about the mental health of the mother? Maybe. He is not quite sure. This is "a difficult realm."[111] "These are not easy issues, and I do not believe there are easy answers to them."[112] "Fetal preservation is generally the course of choice in Christian terms. . . ."[113] *Generally.* Meaning, in short, not always. Maybe in 95 percent of the cases.[114] Or 93 percent. Or 82 percent.

---

111. *Ibid.*, p. 177.

112. *Ibid.*, p. 178.

113. *Idem.*

114. This is what one-time conservative neo-evangelical scholar Carl Henry said of Jones: "This is essentially an anti-abortion book. Ninety-five percent of all abortions would be considered immoral by D. Gareth Jones." *Christianity Today* (Sept. 21, 1984), p. 63. But Jones has never given any such concrete figure, nor does his vague

He is just not certain.

Then what are the grounds of decision-making? By what measure do we "weigh" the issue of abortion? Not the Bible. Not God's inscripturated word. No, the key issue is that slickest of slick slogans of the late 1960's: *the quality of life.* He tells us this at the beginning of the book. "Biology is power over the living world, and biomedicine is power over human nature. There are numerous consequences of this, and they are already the subject of daily decision-making. These decisions revolve around one crucial issue, namely, the quality of life we demand for the populations of technologically-advanced societies and for individuals within those societies. All other issues, whether at the commencement of life or at the end of life, revolve around this critical fulcrum."[115] Therefore, "In making the decision, a balance needs to be attained between the pursuit of biological quality and the potential that a deformed child within a family holds out for that family to be humanized and to grow as a loving, human unit."[116] In short, *more loving through chemical abortion.* Or to reverse a 1960's advertising slogan of the Monsanto Chemical Company, "Better Dying Through Chemistry." As Jones concludes: "Unfortunately some families cannot cope with such a challenge, and a compromise must be reluctantly adopted, namely, termination of the pregnancy."[117]

Such is the quality of life when it is not defined by the Bible, in terms of the ethics of the Bible. Such is the aesthetics of the self-professed autonomous man.

Humanism's Ethics of Sentimentality

The compromise *must* be adopted, the ethicist tells us, just so long as the decision is made *reluctantly.* This is the ethics of sentimentality, as Schlossberg has called it. "If good and evil are purely a matter of sentiment, then no action can be judged, since sentiments remain opaque to outside certification. Only the motives counts, not the action. In this way sentiment, not reason or law, is determinative of right and wrong."[118] Schlossberg has identified the source of the

---

ethical system allow such specificity. Henry actually had endorsed this book prior to publication. Known as a Christian conservative, Henry's continual hostility to the legitimacy of biblical law in New Testament times has finally led him into the pit of confusion and compromise with evil.

115. Jones, p. 10.
116. *Ibid.,* p. 179.
117. *Idem.*
118. Herbert Schlossberg, *Idols for Destruction: Christian Faith and Its Confrontation With American Society* (Nashville, Tennessee: Thomas Nelson Sons, 1983), p. 44.

ethics of sentiment in our day: *humanism*. "Humanism thrives on sentimentality because few religions are more dishonest in their doctrinal expressions. Unable to withstand dispassionate analysis, which would reveal its lack of foundation, it stresses feeling rather than thought. That is what makes sentimentality so vicious."[119]

The incomparable hypocrisy of D. Gareth Jones, Ph.D, is found in the closing paragraph of this chapter: "Decisions relating to the handicapped should always be difficult and will prove too onerous for some to bear. This is the knife-edge along which we walk. But as we do we should be encouraged by the prophecy of Isaiah that, ultimately, 'then will the eyes of the blind be opened and the ears of the deaf unstopped. Then will the lame leap like a deer, and the tongue of the dumb shout for joy' (Isaiah 35:5-6)."[120] *Not if their parents aborted them, they won't.*

Jones says, "There is no slick solution."[121] Oh, but there is. The slickest of all is the saline solution. It is this solution which burns the unborn to death. But the heat of such solutions is nothing compared to the heat which awaits the biomedical practitioners of abortion and their morally corrupt apologists. Also, the publishers of their tracts.

We can understand Franky Schaeffer's outrage at Inter-Varsity Press. He went on Pat Robertson's *700 Club* television show in the summer of 1984 and called attention to what should be obvious, namely, that it was the income from his father's books which created the economic base of Inter-Varsity Press in the late 1960's, and now they are using that capital base to spew out books like Ron Sider's *Rich Christians in an Age of Hunger* and *Brave New People*.

I agree entirely with his response to all the gibberish about complex moral issues. "The real issue is simple. *What do we do now?* It is a choice, not between competing slogans and word games, right or left, but between godlessness and godliness. Between inhumanity and humanity. Between life and death. Between Joseph Fletcher[122] and Jesus. Between the dignity of the individual (whether handicapped, unwanted, born or unborn) and death as a 'liberal' solution for social problems such as poverty, race, and medical costs. Between a sanctity

---

119. *Ibid.*, p. 46.
120. Jones, p. 184.
121. *Ibid.*, p. 169.
122. Joseph Fletcher, *Situation Ethics: The New Morality* (Philadelphia: Westminster Press, 1966).

of life ethic and the bestial gaggle of ethicists, judges, and doctors who cry for the blood of the innocent, all in the name of economics and 'compassion,' not to mention convenience. Between freedom and prosperity, or subservience, slavery, and the ever-expanding power of the welfare state."[123]

Of course, no Christian ethicist or Christian physician publicly advocates infanticide. Not yet. Christian physicians will not promote infanticide until the humanist medical profession has accepted the practice for at least five years, and even then not unless the net income per execution is significantly higher than performing an abortion in, say, the third trimester of pregnancy. After all, these are men of conscience — not as ethical as the Pharaoh of the enslavement, who at least would not have deliberately executed Egyptian infants as he did the Hebrew infants, but good enough in their own eyes.[124]

It is gratifying that the Board of Inter-Varsity Christian Fellowship overturned the decision of the editor of Inter-Varsity Press to publish the book. They pulled this book off the market in September of 1984. They did so reluctantly, under tremendous pressure and the threat of loss of financial support. Their public relations man said, "We did not publish, nor did Dr. Jones write, the book with the intention of supporting abortion in any way. However, the book is being perceived by the Christian public that way."[125] Nonsense; they capitulated to pressures that came because Dr. Jones' book demonstrates every sign of being precisely what it was perceived to be: a tract written in defense of therapeutic abortion. The fact that a book such as *Brave New People* was published in the name of Jesus testifies to the theological degeneracy of influential segments of the so-called "neo-evangelical" movement in the final decades of the twentieth century. Only financial pressure from prin-

---

123. Franky Schaeffer, *Bad News for Modern Man: An Agenda for Christian Activism* (Westchester, Illinois: Crossway Books, 1984), p. 84.

124. I have included this somewhat lengthy discussion of Christian abortion as part of a consideration of the Exodus because theology must be applied to historical situations, and commentators dare not ignore the theological issues of their eras. Those reading this chapter in a hundred or a thousand years will not, I trust, be facing anything so preposterous and morally corrupt as Christian abortionism. But in the late twentieth century, it is a problem — one which points to either a coming revival or a coming judgment, or both. God will spew these people out of His mouth, just as He did with the church at Laodicea (Rev. 3:16). He will throw out the baby-killers with the bathwater of humanism.

125. *Christianity Today* (Sept. 21, 1984), p. 63.

cipled Christians and controversy in the media brought the change. As U.S. Senator Everett Dirksen put it, "When I feel the heat, I see the light." The destroyers much prefer darkness because their deeds are evil (John 3:19). (Sadly, Eerdmans republished it in 1985.)

Unholy Crusades

A standard cliché used against the idea of Christian civilization is this: "What would you do, inaugurate another series of holy crusades?" This sort of comment implicitly assumes that religious warfare is uniquely the product of Christianity, and it also assumes that the crusades characterized Christian medieval civilization. Both assumptions are false.

First, the term "crusade" was never used in the era in which the four major ones took place, 1096-1204. It is a modern term. "People at that time spoke of the road to Jerusalem, the voyage, the journey, the pilgrimage."[126] Second, a crusade was perceived as a defensive war against an expansionist Islamic empire.[127] Third, the wars were supposed to be battles between professional armies. Except for the outrageous sack of Constantinople, in the fourth crusade of 1204,[128] common people were not deliberately chosen as victims. Remember, the feudal order in Europe was essentially military, and a code of military honor governed warfare. It was considered dishonorable for a soldier to battle against peasants or commoners — a violation of the separation of status groups. Finally, the armies were tiny, and so were the ships that carried them. Green's summary brings things into perspective: "It would be impossible to talk of a nation in arms in the Middle Ages. Most wars were fought by small armies, costly for those who equipped them, but lacking in the total effort which typifies modern warfare. Kings who started wars had no wish to exterminate or unduly spoil their adversary; they wanted to bring the issue to a successful negotiated conclusion. Wars were rarely national in any modern sense of the word, but conflicts over rights and honour. . . . Moreover the numbers involved were small. The Viking raiders (each of whose ships can hardly have carried more than

---

126. Regine Pernoud, *The Crusades* (New York: Capricorn, 1964), p. 13.

127. *Ibid.*, pp. 15-17.

128. The crusaders had only raised half of their expected troups, so they could pay only two-thirds of their transportation bills to the Venetians, who demanded payment. Finally, they sacked Constantinople to get the needed funds. R. W. Southern, *The Making of the Middle Ages* (New Haven, Connnecticut: Yale University Press, 1953), p. 58.

thirty-five warriors) can rarely have had more than 1,000 men at their disposal. When William of Normandy invaded England in 1066 he cannot have had many more than 5,000 men. . . . The Normans who conquered Sicily started their venture in 1061 with some 160 knights and never in any subsequent campaign appear to have had more than 700 at their disposal."[129]

In sharp contrast to the crusades—four limited, brief medieval battles, three of which were battles between small professional armies, Christian and Muslim—the twentieth century has become the century of mass executions of civilian populations by the civil governments established by God to enforce His law (Rom. 13:1-7). Modern warfare has become total, sparing almost no one and few institutions. In World War II, more civilians were killed than combatants.[130] The saturation bombing of civilians was standard operating policy by the Germans and the Allies, culminating in the senseless bombing of Dresden, a German city with no military targets, in the spring of 1945, where at least 135,000 civilians, and possibly a quarter million, perished in huge fire storms that were created when almost 2,000 bombers dropped 650,000 incendiary bombs on the defenseless city.[131] "Air raids involving the indiscriminate killing of enormous numbers of civilians were the current step in the natural evolution of the art of war. The very concept of the civilian hardly remained valid. The traditional distinction between men setting forth to risk their lives and those who stayed behind out of range of death disappeared in the first half of the twentieth century."[132] Yet there is little evidence that such indiscriminate area bombing contributed significantly to the defeat of Germany.[133]

The military defense strategy adopted by the United States government during the Kennedy Administration, "mutual assured destruction" (MAD), involves the threat of massive nuclear retaliation as the only defensive posture—in effect, holding the Soviet Union's civilians captive to our missiles (aimed at urban targets), and allowing the Soviet Union to hold our civilians captive by doing

---

129. V. H. H. Green, *Medieval Civilization in Western Europe* (New York: St. Martins, 1971), p. 238.

130. Carroll Quigley, *Tragedy and Hope: A History of the World in Our Time* (New York: Macmillan, 1966), p. 661.

131. David Irving, *The Bombing of Dresden* (London: William Kimber Co., 1963); cf. ALexander McKee, *Dresden 1945: The Devil's Tinderbox* (New York: Dutton, 1984).

132. Peter Calvocoressi and Guy Wint, *Total War: Causes and Courses of the Second World War* (New York: Penguin, [1972] 1981), p. 489.

133. *Ibid.*, p. 508.

the same thing with their missiles. The Soviets have wisely adopted the more traditional approach: targeting military targets, especially our missile silos, as the chosen objectives of a nuclear first strike.[134]

But warfare was not the only source of civilian deaths in this century. Domestic wars against civilian populations have been launched repeatedly by national governments established to defend their people from injustice. The Nazi concentration camps are well known, but they are only one example among many.

The numbers of man-caused deaths in the twentieth century are so huge as to defy calculation. Gil Elliot has settled on a total of 110 million, through 1969. He admits that it could be as "low" as 80 million, but as high as 150 million.[135] China is the great unknown.

To set such a figure against the scale of violence in previous times involves the difficulties of comparing like periods and of allowing for population increase. However, every attempt to do so shows the twentieth century to be incomparably the more violent period.

It is possible — in my view, certain — that in a future perspective this explosion of human lives will be seen as the significant 'history' of our period. Yet the events which have accumulated to form this history — millions upon millions of individual violent deaths — are often recorded in the historical footnotes or in quickly read and rather meaningless statistics. Many written histories don't even mention them, although dealing in detail with the events that led up to and followed them.[136]

Let me cite an example from his book. It is so obscure that it does not even appear in the book's index. He simply lists it in a chapter on minor conflicts. It is the Chaco War. Have you ever heard of it? Of course not. Neither had I. It was a war between Paraguay and Bolivia that took place between 1928 and 1935. The number of

---

134. One vociferous opponent of MAD is retired U.S. Army General Albion Knight, who is also an ordained Episcopalian minister. He writes: ". . . we have supported the Soviet march to military superiority by the strategic doctrine called Mutual Assured Destruction (MAD) whereby, should the Soviet Union attack, we would respond by destroying a percentage of the Soviet population. The doctrine requires us to strike cities and avoid military strategic weapon systems, while intentionally leaving our own people unprotected from a Soviet bomber or missile attack. The success of the strategy depends on the Soviet Union taking the same approach so as to make us mutually vulnerable. Thus, according to MAD, few weapons, especially defense weapons, are needed." Predictably, he points out, the Soviets reject the whole concept. *The Defense of America: From Assured Destruction to Assured Survival* (Houston, Texas: Texas Policy Institute, 1983), pp. 5-6. For a critique of MAD and a recommendation for the substitution of a true defensive strategy, see Gen. Daniel Graham, *High Frontier: A Strategy for National Survival* (New York: TOR Books, 1983).

135. Gil Elliot, *Twentieth Century Book of the Dead* (New York: Scribner's, 1972), p. 1.

136. *Idem.*

deaths in that war was 500,000.[137] That matched the death toll of the Greco-Turkish War of 1919-22, which was going on at the same time as the Russo-Polish war of 1919-21, which claimed 200,000 lives. The Mexican revolution of 1910-20—the first successful socialist revolution in modern times—took 2 million lives.[138] These were all minor wars in the twentieth century, seldom mentioned in textbooks. On page 155 of his book appears the most horrifying statistical chart ever published (I say this without fear of contradiction), "The Death Process":

	Individual Identity			
	MEN	MEN with some WOMEN, say 10%	MEN, WOMEN & CHILDREN	TOTAL
Millions of deaths				
CAMP PRIVATION				20
Enclosed ghetto			1	1
Prisoner-of-war camp	4.5			4.5
Concentration camp		2	0.5	2.5
Labour camp		12		12
CITY PRIVATION				16
Unenclosed ghetto			1	1
Siege			1	1
Occupation			6	6
Civil dislocation			8	8
DIFFUSE PRIVATION				26.5
Transit			1.5	1.5
Combat	1			1
Economic blockade			2	2
Man-made famine			5	5
Scorched earth			5	5
War dislocation			12	12
HARDWARE				47.5
Big guns	18			18
Small arms—formal execution	4			4
Small arms—massacre	1	1	4	6
Small arms—combat	14			14
Mixed—demographic		3		3
Aerial bombs			1	1
CHEMICALS—GAS			1.5	1.5
TOTALS:				
MEN	42	16	19	77
WOMEN		2	21	23
CHILDREN			10	10
	42	18	50	110

137. *Ibid.*, p. 99.
138. *Ibid.*, p. 98.

What we must understand is that it was only with the political triumph of modern humanism that systematic mass murder began in earnest in human history. When God became irrelevant in the minds of the world's leaders, the carnage accelerated rapidly. This is humanism's chief legacy to the world. It is a fulfillment of God's warning, "all they that hate me love death" (Prov. 8:36b).

The French Revolution

The first modern example of a systematic program of depopulation imposed by a civil government on its own people is the case of the French Revolution. It stands as revolutionary humanism's "preferred model" for our own bloody century: from 1789 to 1795, especially in the final three years. The Reign of Terror was part of a wartime measure to eliminate all enemies of the Revolution. It was also an outcome of the satanic religion of revolution, of regeneration through bloodshed and social chaos. At the end, it was scheduled by Robespierre to become a systematic program of depopulation.

Nesta Webster, in her detailed and deliberately ignored study of the revolution,[139] discusses this program. She cites the reports and memoirs of several of Robespierre's associates. Robespierre, we must remind ourselves, was the head of the famous Committee on Public Safety, which can also be translated "Committee on Public Salvation" [salut].[140] Courtois' report was seized at Robespierre's house after the latter's downfall in July of 1794. The report said: "These men, in order to bring us to the happiness of Sparta, wished to annihilate twelve or fifteen millions of the French people. . . ."[141] The population of France at that time was 25 million. A similar story came from Beaulieu, who claimed that a former associate of Robespierre, the Marquis d'Antonelle, told him of Robespierre's theory while the two of them were in prison. "He thought, like the greater number of the revolutionary clubs, that, in order to institute the republic on the ruins of the monarchy, it was necessary to exter-

---

139. Conventional historian Crane Brinton gives us one of the few references to Mrs. Webster when he contemptuously dismisses her (without mentioning any of her detailed histories of the period) as "frightened Tories like Mrs. Nesta Webster. . . ." Brinton, *The Anatomy of Revolution* (New York: Vintage, [1938] 1952), p. 56.

140. Robert A. Nisbet, *The Sociological Tradition* (New York: Basic Books, 1966), p. 34.

141. Nesta H. Webster, *The French Revolution: A Study in Democracy* (London: Constable, 1919), p. 424.

minate all those who preferred the latter form of government, and that the former could only become democratic by the destruction of luxury and riches, which form the support of royalty; that equality would never be anything but a chimera as long as men did not all enjoy approximately equal properties; and finally, that such an order of things could never be established until a third of the population had been suppressed. . . ."[142]

The most impressive testimony came from Gracchus Babeuf, the communist revolutionary who became a model for Karl Marx.[143] Babeuf and his disciple Buonarroti were the great promoters of the religion of revolution. "May everything return to chaos," Babeuf wrote in his *Plebeian Manifesto,* "and out of chaos may there emerge a new and regenerated world."[144] In 1795, Babeuf gave this account of Robespierre's depopulation scheme in his tract, "Sur le Systeme de la Depopulation, ou La Vie et les Crimes de Carrier": "Maximilien [Robespierre] and his council had calculated that a real regeneration of France could only be operated by means of a new distribution of territory and of the men who occupied it. . . . He thought that . . . depopulation was indispensable, because the calculation had been made that the French population was in excess of the resources of the soil and of the requirements of useful industry, that is to say, that, with us, men jostled each other too much for each to be able to live at ease; that hands were too numerous for the execution of all works of essential utility. . . ."[145]

Nesta Webster's analysis of the reasons lying behind the socialists' call for systematic depopulation, written in 1919, is as relevant today — the era of the population hysteria — as it was when she wrote it: "But could a nation of 25,000,000 be thus transformed? To the regenerators of France it seemed extremely doubtful; already the country was rent with dissentions, and any scheme for universal contentment seemed impossible of attainment. Moreover, the plan of dividing things up into equal shares presented an insuperable difficulty, for it became evident that amongst a population of this size there was not enough money, not enough property, not enough

---

142. *Ibid.,* pp. 424-25.
143. Karl Marx and Frederick Engels, "Manifesto of the Communist Party" (1848), in Marx and Engels, *Selected Works,* 3 vols. (Moscow: Progress Publishers, [1969] 1977), I, p. 134. Cf. George Lichtheim, *Marxism: An Historical and Critical Study* (New York: Praeger, 1963), pp. 61, 89.
144. Cited in Billington, *Fire in the Minds of Men,* p. 75.
145. Cited in Webster, p. 425.

employment, not even at this moment enough bread to go around; no one would be satisfied with his share, and instead of universal contentment, universal dissatisfaction would result. What was to be done? The population was too large for the scheme of the leaders to be carried out successfully, therefore either the scheme must be abandoned or *the population must be diminished.*"[146]

An odd aspect of the French Revolution was that it was officially "pro-marriage" (and therefore presumably pro-natalist) at the same time that the guillotine was in full force. This was also true for Stalin's Russia in the late 1930's, when a pro-marriage reformation of the Soviet law code was passed while he was executing millions, either deliberately or indirectly by putting them into slave labor camps. The French Revolutionary Assembly passed a head tax on unmarried persons over thirty years old. There was even a national celebration to honor husbands and wives.[147] The Nazi policies of the 1930's imitated this same schizophrenia: pro-family tax policies and subsidies for births, yet death-producing slave labor camps for millions.

The Armenian Genocide

The next major example of a deliberate policy of population extermination is the Turkish persecution of the Armenians. It came in two waves, in 1895-96 and two decades later in 1915-16. Mass murders were conducted in the first period, and again in 1909 under the so-called Young Turks. In the final wave, the number of victims was at least 800,000 and possibly as high as two million.[148] In this case, the victims were long-term residents of the Ottoman Empire, but were considered religious foreigners. Even the familiar "ian" and "yan" endings of the surnames of Armenians are emblems of their servitude; the Turks gave these name endings to Armenians in order to identify this "foreign population."[149]

---

146. *Ibid.*, pp. 423-24.

147. William Petersen, *Population,* p. 148.

148. Dickran H. Boyajian, *Armenia: The Case for a Forgotten Genocide* (Westwood, New Jersey: Educational Books, 1972), p. 1.

149. This was told to me by my father-in-law, R. J. Rushdoony, whose own family had resided in the far north of Armenia, close to the Russian border, and had escaped the required name change. His family escaped to Russia in the 1915 persecution, and since his father had British pounds, he was able to buy his way to Archangel and from there to New York City. Rushdoony was born in New York shortly after their arrival.

The Soviet Union

The Soviet Union did not use the excuse of "foreign populations" residing in the Soviet empire. The recurring Soviet depopulations were ideologically motivated. The first instances of serious food shortages took place during the First World War. But these were minor compared to the results of the forced collectivization of agriculture, first in the "war communism" phase of the early 1918-22,[150] and second in the early 1930's. The program of forced starvation of small landowners (the "kulaks") in the late 1920's and early 1930's led to resistance by the peasants, and Stalin's response was to starve them into compliance. Historian Paul Johnson quite properly refers to this as Stalin's "collossal exercise in social engineering, the destruction of the independent Russian peasantry."[151] We do not know how many peasants were executed—or as Stalin said, "liquidated"[152]—during the 1928-31 period, but Stalin once remarked to Churchill that ten million peasants had been "dealt with."[153] The general estimate is: one-third in concentration camps, one-third murdered, and one-third forcibly transported into Siberia or central Asia. Most of the large-scale violence took place over a few months, from the end of 1929 through early 1930.[154] In 1929, only about 4% of all peasant households were in collective or state farms. In 1930, this had risen to about a quarter of the peasant population. A year later, it was 53%. By 1937, it was 93%.[155]

The peasants, in response, burned their crops and ate their horses and cattle, rather than place this property in the collective farms and state farms. Stalin later admitted that in 1929, the Soviet Union had 34 million horses; only 16.6 million were left in 1934—a loss of 18 million. They also lost 30 million cattle (45% of the total), as well as nearly 100 million sheep and goats, two-thirds of the total.[156] Writes Robert Conquest: "The famine can be blamed quite

---

150. Lazar Volin, *A Century of Russian Agriculture*, ch. 7.

151. Paul Johnson, *Modern Times*, p. 267.

152. *Ibid.*, p. 269. This was the first time that Stalin used the term. It would not be the last.

153. *Ibid.*, p. 271. The reference appears in Vol. 8 of Churchill's *Second World War* (1964), p. 78.

154. *Idem.*

155. Volin, *A Century of Russian Agriculture*, p. 211.

156. Isaac Deutcher, *Stalin: A Political Biography* (New York: Vintage, [1949] 1960), p. 325. He cites Stalin's *Problems of Leninism* (Moscow, 1945), p. 480.

flatly on Stalin. The crop in 1932 was about 12 percent below average. This was far from being famine level. But procurements of food from the peasantry were up by 44 percent. The result was, and could not have been other than, large-scale starvation. It is perhaps the only case in history of a purely man-made famine. It is also the only major famine whose very existence was ignored or denied by the governmental authorities, and even to a large degree successfully concealed from world opinion."[157] (The one report on the famine by a foreign journalist was Malcolm Muggridge's, which appeared in the *Manchester Guardian* in three installments in March, 1933. He was the only journalist who had been in the famine areas without official supervision. The reaction in Britain to his articles was hostile.)[158] Volin's estimate of famine-produced deaths is five million.[159]

So desperate was Stalin for foreign currency that he began a series of sales of art treasures, including a famous one to capitalist Andrew Mellon in 1930-31; for $6.5 million, Mellon bought twenty-one paintings that became the basis of the Washington National Gallery.[160]

Johnson's explanation concerning Stalin's economic motivation is to the point: "There was no theoretical basis in Marxism, or anything else, for what Stalin now did. But it had a certain monstrous logic. There is no point of stability in a state which is socializing itself. It must go either forward or back. If it does not go forward, the power of the market system, which expresses certain basic human instincts of barter and accumulation, is such that it will always reassert itself, and capitalism will make its reappearance. Then the embryo socialist state will collapse. If socialism is to go forward, it must push ahead with large-scale industrialization. That means surplus food for the workers; and surplus food to export to raise money for capital investment. In short the peasants must pay the price for socialist progress. And since they are unwilling to pay this price voluntarily, force must be used, in ever-growing quantities, until their will is broken and they deliver what is required of them. That is the bitter logic of socialist power which Stalin grasped in the 1920s: there was no stable point of rest between a return to capitalism and the use of unlimited force."[161]

---

157. Robert Conquest, *The Great Terror: Stalin's Purges of the Thirties* (rev. ed.; New York: Collier, 1973), p. 45.
158. Malcolm Muggridge, *The Green Stick*, pp. 257-58.
159. Volin, *Century*, p. 233-34.
160. Johnson, *Modern Times*, p. 269.
161. *Ibid.*, p. 268.

Despite the repeated connection between socialism and genocide, this urge to mass destruction is more than mere economics. Stalin's purge of up to a million Communist Party members in the late 1930's indicates that some other motive is involved.[162] The Soviet dissident, Sakharov, says that between 1936 and 1939, over 1.2 million Party members went into the camps, and only 50,000 regained their freedom.[163] Total arrests of all citizens in 1938 were probably over 7 million, possibly in the 9 million range.[164] This was in addition to the 5 million already in the camps, and this did not include actual criminals.[165] For twenty years of Stalin's reign, 1930-50, at least *20 million* people died in the camps or were executed, and this figure is probably too low; it may have been 30 million dead.[166] The chapter title of Isaac Deutcher's account of the period is hyperbolic, but more accurate than he really believed: "The Gods are Athirst."[167]

Asian Communism

This readiness to execute millions for the sake of Communist doctrine has been repeated: in Communist China under Mao and in Cambodia in the 1970's. The Chinese death rate is a mystery. In the first phase (1949-51), as many as 15 million may have died, or as few as a million.[168] In the second phase, the period of the "Great Leap Forward" (late 1950's), we simply cannot know for certain. Mosher cites evidence that in 1960 alone, the number of famine-related deaths may have been as high as 30 million, or as low as 11 million.[169] In the third phase, the "Cultural Revolution" of the 1966-68, the Red Guards murdered at least 400,000 people.[170] As for Cambodia, a fifth of the Cambodian population, about 1.2 million people, died during the initial Communist take-over, from April of 1975 until early 1977.[171]

---

162. Robert Conquest provides various estimates that 500,000 to 1,000,000 people were executed: *The Great Terror*, pp. 702, 713. For a profound literary account of the purges, see the novel by Arthur Koestler, *Darkness at Noon*.

163. Conquest, p. 713.

164. *Ibid.,* p. 702.

165. *Ibid.,* p. 708.

166. *Ibid.,* p. 710.

167. Deutcher, *Stalin*, ch. 9.

168. Paul Johnson, *Modern Times*, p. 548.

169. Mosher, *Broken Earth*, p. 264.

170. Johnson, *Modern Times*, p. 558.

171. *Ibid.,* p. 657. This is the estimate of John Barron and Anthony Paul, *Murder of a Gentle Land* (New York: Reader's Digest Press, 1977), p. 206. This book provides many anecdotal accounts of the ruthless murders and torturings that went on in 1975 and 1976 in Cambodia.

This has been the application of the biblical truth that all those who hate God love death (Pr. 8:36b). It is the satanic hatred of the image of God in man which leads the most consistent satanic commonwealths to depopulate their own populations. Revolutionary socialism and genocide are linked by common theological doctrines, *the religion of revolution* and the *hatred of God's image in man*. The economic issues are relevant to genocide — the "fixed pie" doctrine of wealth and the growing number of "eaters" — but not primary.

Conclusion

The continuing propaganda against population growth is part of a comprehensive program of humanistic social regeneration. The image of God, mankind, is seen as a threat to ethically rebellious men. Population growth is therefore a threat to humanism. First, in a finite universe, such population growth points to the limits of time: a final judgment. Second, in a centrally planned economy, any uncontrolled resource is a threat to the overall economic plan. This creates problems — uncertainty — for the planners. Third, in an economy characterized by zero economic growth or declining output — which socialist economies tend to be — a growing population puts pressure on the total number of available economic resources. This leads to political problems.

Nevertheless, the economic arguments are secondary. The primary argument is theological. Satan hates mankind. Those who hate God love death. The war against God ultimately involves the death of God's image, mankind. Modern humanism, as it has grown more consistent with its own satanic presuppositions, has adopted as an ideal the philosophy of zero population growth and even population decline. Humanism hates God more than it loves man. Its population ideal is spoken of in the Bible as God's curse.

APPENDIX C

THE LABYRINTH AND THE GARDEN

For Pharaoh will say of the children of Israel, They are entangled in the land, the wilderness hath shut them in (Ex. 14:3).

The Labyrinth in Egypt

The pyramids are one architectural legacy of the death-obsessed religion of Egypt. Another less well known legacy is the labyrinth. The word is derived from the Greek word, *labrys,* the word for the two-headed axe, the design found throughout "Knossos," the massive structure excavated by Sir Arthur Evans on the Island of Crete. S. H. Hooke's study of the history and meaning of the labyrinth traces the origin of this almost universal symbol; it began in Egypt. Specifically, the labyrinth design was used for the plans of palaces, but more importantly, for royal tombs and mortuary temples.[1] The sign appears on mortuary jars and other containers that are found in the tombs.[2] "The plan of the Old Kingdom seal-sign is also to be found in the pottery 'soul-houses' from the cemeteries at Rifeh of the 9th and 10th dynasties. Some of these 'soul-houses' show a staircase leading to a floor above the tomb-chamber, where there is a throne. These 'soul-houses' indicate that there was an 'abode' above the tomb-chamber, to which the king mounted when he rose from his ritual death."[3]

It is also highly significant that the Egyptian labyrinths were related to the bull, as was the famous "palace" of Knossos on Crete. It represented the king-god, and was brought into the sanctuary on

---

1. S. H. Hooke (ed.), *The Labyrinth: Further Studies in the Relation between Myth and Ritual in the Ancient World* (London: SPCK, 1935), p. 4. It is significant that Sir Arthur Evans, who dug up and misinterpreted the "palace" of Knossos on Crete, believed that the labyrinth was "the palace sign." *Idem.* Evans wrote this in *The Palace of Minos,* vol. I, p. 359.

2. *Idem.*

3. *Ibid.,* p. 5.

ritual occasions and slain there.[4] Ritual sacrifice and dancing were connected to the bull-god in the Osirian religion, as was also the case in the legend of Crete's King Minos, the deadly Minotaur ("Minos-bull"), and the sacrifices by Minos of the Athenian youths (the legend of Theseus, Ariadne, and Daedalus).[5] Similar links between dancing and labyrinths also exist in Cornwall, England and also in Scandinavia and Northern Russia.[6] It is a dance of death and resurrection.[7]

Hooke points out that it was very early in the Egyptian dynasties, in the second dynasty, that the kings began to protect their burial places. This had not been true earlier. "Some of these chambers contained the bodies of those who accompanied the king to the after-life, his women and his body-guard who were killed and buried at the time of the royal funeral."[8] The tomb of King Perabsen of the second dynasty was surrounded by a passage, a new feature, according to Flinders Petrie, who excavated it.[9] But as Hooke says, there seems to have been no social or military reason for hiding the bodies of the kings.[10] The pyramids were an extension of this desire to protect the bodies of the monarchs.

The motivation was religious and ritualistic, not defensive. Hooke writes: "While pyramid and temple must be considered as one complex building, the internal construction of the pyramid became elaborate and labyrinthine in character. Nevertheless, the labyrinth name became attached to the temple, and it seems probable that the greater importance of the temple as the place of ritual, associated with Osiris, Amon or Re, as the case might be, would account for this. In the pyramid, and later in the rock-cut tombs, the body of the king was sealed up in his sarcophagus, and the entrances were blocked up and concealed. Nothing more happened there. But in the adjoining temple everything necessary for his welfare in the after-life was attended to. The plan and construction of the oldest known temple of Osiris at Abydos is interesting, therefore, in connection with the original meaning of the Labyrinth. Especially as [citing Budge] 'it is probable that there was a small temple of Osiris

---

4. *Ibid.*, pp. 7, 22-24.

5. *Ibid.*, pp. 24-27.

6. Hans Georg Wunderlich, *The Secret of Crete* (New York: Macmillan, 1974), p. 289.

7. Robert Graves, *The White Goddess: A Historical Grammar of Poetic Myth* (rev. ed.; New York: Farrar, Straus and Giroux, 1966), pp. 329-30.

8. Hooke, *op. cit.*, p. 11.

9. *Ibid.*, p. 12.

10. *Ibid.*, p. 13.

attached to every great temple in Egypt, and there is good reason to think that such temples of Osiris were better and more regularly served by the priests than the larger temples.' "[11]

Both Herodotus and Strabo described a huge Egyptian labyrinth at Hawara. It was a two-storied structure, with 1,500 rooms above and 1,500 below. It was excavated in 1888 by Sir Flinders Petrie.[12] Wunderlich writes: "The purpose of the costly pyramids and mortuary temples involved in the worship of the dead pharaoh was to propitiate Osiris, to win favor of the god of vegetation. The fifteen hundred burial vaults and dwellings for the dead in the labyrinth [on the bottom or underground floor—G.N.] were meant for provincial sovereigns, princes of the blood and similar highly placed personages of the Twelfth Dynasty of the Middle Kingdom. [This would have been the era of the pharaohs from Joseph to Moses' youth, according to Courville.—G.N.] The labyrinth, therefore, was not a mortuary *temple* in the strict sense of the word. By that is meant, in Egypt, a structure for the cult of the dead but not a burial place."[13]

The "Palace" of Knossos

Wunderlich traces the interrelationships between Egypt and Knossos, the so-called "palace" of the legendary King Minos, on the island of Crete. This relationship was recognized by the Roman historian Pliny, whose *Natural History* (XXXVI, 13) says that Daedalus, the designer of the labyrinth at Crete, took the design from Egypt.[14] The palace of Minos, which was so lavishly described—a better word might be "invented"—and partially reconstructed by the British archaeologist Sir Arthur Evans during the first three decades of the twentieth century, was in fact a giant tomb, not a palace. It was never intended to be inhabited by the living. Its soft gypsum floors that can be scratched by a fingernail, its huge and unmovable *pithoi* (urns), its dark labyrinthine hallways, its lack of any protecting wall, its distance from agriculturally productive land, its "bathtubs" without drain pipes (sarcophagi), and "indoor plumbing" without drain pipes (circulating vents for mummies) all point to a vast cult of the dead, not the residence of the king. The supposedly happy and free-

---

11. *Ibid.*, pp. 14-15.
12. Joseph Campbell, *The Masks of God: Primitive Mythology* (rev. ed.; New York: Penguin, [1969] 1978), p. 70.
13. Wunderlich, *Secret of Crete*, p. 248.
14. Hooke, p. 17.

spirited people who were called the Minoans by Evans were figments of his vivid imagination. The Minoans were an integral part of the Bronze Age culture — a demonic, fearful, death-obsessed culture.

These "Minoans" mummified their dead, as the Egyptians did, for similar theological reasons, at least with respect to the dead person's passage through the underworld.[15] As Wunderlich shows, they had trading relations with the Egyptians, who called them the Keftiu.[16] The link with Egypt is testified to by the Egyptian-style clothing of men pictured on the walls of the "palace," as well as by drawings of these "Minoan" people in a tomb in Egypt. Evans dug up an Egyptian statue in the "palace" which was made in the era of Egypt's Twelfth Dynasty.[17] Conversely, Egyptian ruins contain examples of pottery that look like the "Minoan" pottery.[18] (On Evans' misuse of the evidence to make it fit an evolutionary model, see Appendix A: "The Reconstruction of Egypt's Chronology," under the subhead, "Egypt and Crete.")

Beyond Crete

The labyrinth is an extremely important symbol. It appears in most of the ancient cultures in one form or another. Sir Arthur Evans discovered numerous coins on Crete that had the Minotaur and labyrinth designs on them.[19] These coins were not contemporaneous with the construction of Knossos, of course; coins began to appear about the sixth century, B.C. Hooke reports that examples of labyrinth designs appear constantly on seals from Asia Minor, Palestine, and Mesopotamia.[20] Archaeologists have discovered labyrinths drawn in rocks in Britain and Scandinavia. Hooke recognized this as the probable product of trade between the Mediterranean and the Baltic region.[21] But what Hooke did not know is that the Knossos labyrinth and Minotaur designs have been discovered in pre-Columbus North America and South America.

In rock formations in Oraibi, New Mexico and Cuenca, Ecuador, the labyrinth pattern of Knossos appears. The Minotaur — half

---

15. Wunderlich, ch. 21: "A Visit in the Underworld."

16. *Ibid.,* pp. 148, 174-80.

17. Leonard Cottrell, *The Bull of Minos* (New York: Rinehart & Co., 1958), pp. 136-37.

18. *Ibid.,* p. 138.

19. Hooke, pp. 9-10.

20. *Ibid.,* p. 10.

21. *Ibid.,* p. 41.

bull, half man—is the other famous Cretan design which is closely related to the labyrinth. It has also been found in Texas petroglyphs.[22] The explanation of how they got there is the same: *trade.* Barry Fell, whose books constitute a true intellectual revolution, argues convincingly that these rock carvings are reproductions of coins that were in circulation in North and South America several centuries before Christ.[23] This, of course, points to a system of worldwide trade—trade which Fell's *Bronze Age America* proves was going on in the second millennium B.C., and probably early in the second millennium.[24]

James Peters, whose work on the symbolism of architecture has not yet been published, believes that the labyrinth is related symbolically to the garden of Eden, which had the four rivers flowing out of it. This is reasonable. It would be a walled or square design surrounding lines resembling a river or rivers. (The wall must have been open only at one place, at the east gate, where God placed the angels: Gen. 3:24.) The later Greek key-pattern of the labyrinth, called a meander,[25] is related linguistically to a river in Phrigia, *maiandros,* noted for its winding path.[26] The English word "meander" is applied to both rivers and labyrinthian passages.[27]

Pagan versions of the labyrinth imagery include the swastika or twisted cross. Some scholars (along with their native informers) relate the swastika to the tree of life.[28] But in the Mediterranean world of the Bronze Age, the labyrinth was associated with death. Wunderlich comments: ". . . a labyrinth is not a necropolis. By necropolises we mean *cities* of the dead in which the dead are placed singly or together in dwellings or tombs. Necropolises may be attached to labyrinths. But a labyrinth has, in addition to its primary function of serving as a residence for the dead, quite a few additional functions: it is the spiritual center of the surrounding settlements; a religious site; an assembly point; an arena, an archive and scriptorium; a place of judgment, execution and sacrifice; and so on. The great courts and subsidiary buildings serve these purposes, as well as

---

22. Barry Fell, *Saga America* (New York: Times Books, 1974), pp. 104-5.
23. *Ibid.,* pp. 113-14.
24. Barry Fell, *Bronze Age America* (Boston: Little, Brown, 1982).
25. Hooke, p. 7.
26. *Oxford English Dictionary:* "miander."
27. *Idem.*
28. Clyde Keller, "Tree of Life and Labyrinth," *The Epigraphic Society: Occasional Publications,* V (1978), Pt. 2.

the prime purpose of holding impressive funeral ceremonies, which were accompanied by religious dramas and competitive games complete with music, dancing and banquets. In antiquity the usual meaning of a labyrinth as a structure in which the dead rested in the underground rooms was well understood."[29]

Gnostic Salvation

Joseph Campbell relates another tale of the labyrinth from the Melanesian island of Malekula. As the soul approaches the way of the dead to the Land of the Dead, having crossed the waters of death, the guardian of the underworld meets him. This guardian is female. She has drawn a labyrinth design in the ground in front of the entrance. As the soul approaches, she erases half the design. "The voyager must restore the design perfectly if he is to pass through it to the Land of the Dead. Those who fail, the threshold guardian eats. One may understand how very important it must have been, then, to learn the secret of the labyrinth before death; and why the teaching of the secret of immortality is the chief concern of the religious ceremonials of Malekula."[30] The way of salvation is therefore the way of *secret knowledge.* This is the essence of the heresy of gnosticism: salvation by initiation, meaning salvation by secret knowledge. It is the perpetual alternative to salvation by grace through faith.

Campbell is heavily influenced by the psychological and symbolic theories of C. G. Jung. His assessment of the meaning of the labyrinth is suggestive but not definitive. Nevertheless, the connections that he makes are important. "In archaic art, the labyrinth — home of the child-consuming Minotaur — was represented in the figure of a spiral. The spiral also appears spontaneously in certain stages of meditation, as well as to people going to sleep under ether. It is a prominent device, furthermore, at the silent ceremonies within the dark passages of the ancient Irish kingly burial mound of New Grange. These facts suggest that a constellation of images denoting the plunge and dissolution of consciousness in the darkness of non-being must have been employed intentionally, from an early date, to represent the analogy of threshold rites to the mystery of the

---

29. Wunderlich, p. 249.

30. Campbell, *Primitive Mythology,* p. 69. Cf. Mircea Eliade, *Rites and Symbols of Initiation: The Mysteries of Birth and Rebirth* (New York: Harper Torchbook, [1958] 1965), p. 62.

entry of the child into the womb for birth. . . . It is obvious that the idea of death-and-rebirth, rebirth through ritual and with a fresh organization of profoundly impressed sign stimuli, is an extremely ancient one in the history of culture. . . ."[31]

The Garden

We know that the garden of Eden was placed eastward in Eden (Gen. 2:8). When God closed its entrance by placing the cherubim and the flaming sword, they were stationed at the east of the garden (Gen. 3:24). This means that the garden itself must have been an enclosed space. Its walls protected it from those who would enter it on any terms except those established by God. Man was not to gain access to the tree of life by breaking into the closed space (Gen. 3:22, 24). From the day of man's expulsion, the only way to the tree of life is through ethical conformity to God's standards. The standard is perfection. Regeneration, not the scaling of physical or symbolic walls, is the foundation of eternal life.

The walled enclosure is therefore a significant design — one of the most significant in man's history. Pagan cultures again and again return to it. They invest it with many meanings. The heart of the pagan version, the labyrinth, is a closed space in which a winding pathway is dominant. Men who do not know the secret of the pathway are trapped, condemned to wander helplessly. Only by knowing the way out (or in) through the entrance can man attain his eternal goal. The walls, however, cannot be scaled by man.

Egypt as Garden-Labyrinth

Egypt was a symbol of the garden. In Abraham's day, it was the place that was spared during the famine (Gen. 12:10). Abraham journeyed to Egypt, but then went back up into Canaan. This was a *symbolic resurrection*. This was true again in Joseph's day: descent into a "garden," which became a labyrinth or wilderness, and then escape. Jacob wanted his body to be taken up out of Egypt after his death, and buried in the cave in Canaan in which his fathers were buried (Gen. 49:29-32). Joseph wanted his bones dug up and reburied in the promised land (Gen. 50:25). Again, this points to resurrection. So does Joseph's experience in Potiphar's house (the "garden") and his experience in prison ("wilderness-labyrinth"), a

---

31. *Ibid.,* pp. 65-66.

walled, enclosed space, from which he was delivered by God into a position of authority.

Goshen was the best of Egypt, and it was given to Israel by Joseph's Pharaoh (Gen. 47:6). Goshen was a garden. It was partially protected from the plagues of Egypt, at least plagues seven through ten (Ex. 8:22-24; 9:6, 26; 10:23; 12). Goshen was to have served as an Edenic training ground for Israel, a kind of headquarters for dominion. But by Moses' day, the hearts of the Israelites had been captured by the gods of Egypt, and therefore their bodies had been placed in bondage to the rulers of Egypt. The golden calf in the wilderness testified to their Egyptian faith. They fell once again, just as their father Adam had fallen in his garden environment. The Edenic training ground of Goshen became a wilderness training ground. The Bible's message is clear: a good environment does not necessarily produce good men. Men are not saved by manipulating their environment.

Egypt was not seen as a garden by the Egyptians. A garden is a preliminary training ground for redeemed man's dominion in a future-oriented world. This was not the world believed in by the Egyptians. They believed in a static and magical world. Egypt was understood as a labyrinth by Pharaoh. As the children of Israel were escaping, Pharaoh said to his subordinates, "They are entangled in the land, the wilderness hath shut them in" (Ex. 14:3). The barrier of the Red Sea was considered to be impenetrable. Egypt was an "enclosed space." The only visible outlet passed through the land of the Phillistines. But God warned Moses not to go by that route, for it might have meant a battle, and the Israelites were not ready for a fight. They might have returned to Egypt (Ex. 13:17). Thus, it appeared to Pharaoh that the Israelites were trapped, "entangled in the land."

What Pharaoh did not expect was that God would penetrate the labyrinth's walls. He could knock down the walls of any labyrinth, or create a passageway through the Red Sea. This was also to be His strategy with the Jordan River and the city of Jericho a generation later. It was not necessary for the Israelites to go through the gates of the city or around the river. God's answer was a direct assault on the barrier.

The people were led by God's glory-cloud. When the Egyptian army approached, the cloud went behind them. This cloud then served as a barrier to the Egyptians (Ex. 14:19-20), a source of darkness for the Egyptians and a source of light for the Israelites (v. 20). Like the flaming sword of the garden, the flaming glory cloud served as an unpassable barrier to the enemies of God. God created a protective enclosed space for His people. The tabernacle and the temple later symbolized this same sort of enclosed space. But at the heart of this enclosed space is *ethics*. In the case of the tabernacle and temple, the center was the holy of holies, in which the tablets of the law resided.

The last instance we have in the Bible concerning Egypt as a place of refuge prior to a "resurrection unto dominion" is the case of the parents of Jesus. They obeyed the angel which told them to go down into Egypt (Matt. 2:13-14). This was done to fulfill a messianic prophecy (Hosea 11:1), "Out of Egypt have I called my son" (Matt. 2:15b). After Herod's death, they returned to Israel (Matt. 2:20-21).[32] Herod, the "guardian" at the "gate" of Israel, was no longer a threat.

The Guardian

Men who would have sought to enter Eden's garden needed to bypass the angelic guardians. Similarly, in the Melanesian legend of the labyrinth, the supernatural female guardian serves as the destroyer of anyone who does not know the secret of the labyrinth. But what the Bible teaches is that access through the protected gate is not based on secret knowledge; it is based rather on one's covenantal relationship with the God who assigned the angelic guardians to their place.

Jacob, upon returning from the wilderness experience of labor under Laban, faced a barrier, the Jordan River (Gen. 32:10), and a guardian, his brother Esau. He wrestled all night with a theophany of God who renamed him and gave him a blessing (32:24-29). Moses, upon returning to Egypt with an uncircumcised son named Gershom (from a Hebrew root meaning "driven out"),[33] faced the guardian of the border, an angel, and he was not permitted to pass through until Zipporah circumcised Gershom (Ex. 4:24-26).[34] In

---

32. That they should have traveled to Egypt is not surprising. A thriving colony of Jews had lived in Alexandria since the days of Alexander the Great, who had attracted them by promising them the same legal rights that Greeks possessed. They prospered and helped the city to become a major commercial center. Henri Daniel-Rops, *Israel and the Ancient World* (New York: Image, 1964), p. 349.

33. *Strong's Exhaustive Concordance,* Hebrew and Chaldee Dictionary, p. 28, #1644.

34. For a detailed treatment of this deeply symbolic event, see my essay, "The Marriage Supper of the Lamb," *Christianity and Civilization,* 4 (1985).

another Old Testament judicial arrangement, the fugitive from the *ga'al* (kinsman-redeemer/avenger of blood) who fled to the safety of the enclosed space of a city of refuge had to wait until the death of the high priest before he could safely return home, for the *ga'al* was the guardian of the route of escape and could lawfully slay him if he passed through the gates of the city (Num. 35:12-28).

Resurrection

The garden is a sabbath resting place, a place of refreshment. From the garden men are to march forward in victory. The garden is the symbol or archetype of paradise. The labyrinth, on the other hand, is the archetype of hell, and was so understood by the ancients. It is a place from which men need to escape. Escape from the labyrinth is *resurrection*. Thus, the pagan rituals associated with the labyrinth are rituals of death and resurrection.

The night before His death, Jesus went into a garden. Gethsemane was His place of prayer to God. He told His disciples to continue to watch with Him (Matt. 26:38), to watch and pray (v. 41). He instructed them three times, but the disciples fell asleep each time. They were not ready to defend the garden from invaders. Then the garden was invaded by the authorities, led by Judas, Satan's man. Satan had invaded the garden once again. Jesus was then expelled from the garden, as if He had committed the sin of Adam. He was brought before the judges, as Adam had been brought before God the judge. He was executed, suffering death as God had promised to Adam. Then came the resurrection. Death and resurrection, given the sin of Adam, is inescapably linked to the garden in biblical imagery and biblical history. The question is: Will it be resurrection unto life or resurrection unto the second death (Rev. 20:14)?

Heaven and hell are temporary locations, just as the garden was. They serve as embarkation points. After the resurrection, the heaven-dwellers are returned to the new earth, while the hell-dwellers are dumped into the lake of fire (Rev. 20:14-15). Thus, physical resurrection at the day of judgment is not the basis of escape from the labyrinth. There is no escape after physical death. The only escape is the covenantal-ethical decision made in time and on earth.

Barriers

In one sense, *the barriers to escape or entry are broken by Christ*. The veil of the temple was torn at the death of Christ (Matt. 27:51). The stone barrier placed over His tomb by the authorities was rolled away (Matt. 28:2). Christ spoke of the impending fulfilment and removal of the old covenant's ceremonial barriers with the gentile world when He announced that new wine cannot be contained in old containers (Matt. 9:17). Israel would no longer serve as a geographical recapitulation of the garden, for sin had turned it into a gnostic labyrinth. Schlossberg remarks:

> Combining social purpose with expertise sets the stage for a gnosticism in which only the special few have the key to the secrets of the universe. This is not something that can simply be learned from books, although the cognoscenti are almost invariably well-educated. They must also have the requisite "social purpose," for the knowledge required to run society cannot simply be communicated rationally. They are like the Pharisees who taught that God gave Moses not only a written law but also an oral one, handed down through the generations to only the privileged few. This was the key to the power of the Pharisees: they had the knowledge to unlock the meaning of the Pentateuch, to be the recipients of wisdom had by no others. Not possessing esoteric knowledge, the masses have no choice but to turn their lives over to the elite to be managed. Never ask the enlightened ones about their track record, which is a series of disguised disasters; just accept on faith that they have the secret to life.[35]

The labyrinthine rules and teachings of Talmudic Judaism had made Israel into a place of death rather than life, a labyrinth rather than a garden. The goal was now to escape the labyrinth. The Christians were warned about 40 years in advance by Jesus not to trust in the walls of Jerusalem when the Roman army encompassed the city, but rather to flee to the hills (Luke 21:20-24). It would mean death to remain, and resurrection to escape. Josephus' account of what happened in A.D. 69-70 offers the horrible evidence of the truth of Christ's predictions concerning Jerusalem. Israel remained a 40-year wilderness experience for the early Jewish-Christian church, one from which they were delivered (forced out) just before the fall of Jerusalem. On the other hand, *there will always be enclosed sacred space.* The consummated church is described as a walled city (Rev. 21:10-21). Its gates are always open, however (v. 25). There will be no night there, no darkness (v. 25). Today, the church is also a place of refuge, a protected space. We journey weekly to eat with God and

---

35. Herbert Schlossberg, *Idols for Destruction: Christian Faith and Its Confrontation with American Society* (Nashville, Tennessee: Thomas Nelson, 1983), p. 195.

be refreshed — what Adam was supposed to have done in the garden. But it is still a dominion training ground, which it does not seem to be in the era after the resurrection. It is a place which points to the resurrection of many in the future, for it points backward to the resurrection of Jesus Christ.

Wilderness

Moses' career was a three-stage encounter with the labyrinth and the wilderness. For 40 years, he lived in Egypt, which had become a labyrinth for the Israelites. He fled, for he knew his life was doomed in Egypt (Ex. 2:15). For 40 years, he lived as a shepherd in the wilderness. There, in the "backside of the desert," God confronted him at Mount Horeb (Ex. 3:1). He was drawn out of that wilderness back into Egypt. Then he spent 40 years in a new wilderness, having been driven out of Egypt.

In each case, the number 40 was associated with a wilderness experience. In each case, this experience involved training. Noah's world had become a labyrinth, a spiritual wilderness, a place fit for judgment. The death of Noah's world was accomplished by 40 days of rain (Gen. 7:17), but he escaped in a massive enclosed space — a garden experience, where he cared for the animals. The army of Israel was stymied for 40 days on the battlefield by the Philistines under Goliath (I Sam. 17:16). Elijah fled into the wilderness (I Ki. 19:4), and journeyed 40 days until he reached Mount Horeb (v. 8), where he lodged in a cave (v. 16), an enclosed space. Jesus also spent 40 days in the wilderness, in preparation for His ministry (Matt. 4:1-2).

Moses' forty years in the wilderness of the Exodus points to the wilderness as both a labyrinth and a garden. For the older generation, it was a wilderness. They would all die there, except Joshua and Caleb. For the young, it was more of a garden, with the manna and springs refreshing them daily. It was a place of wandering for the older Israelites — a labyrinth from which there was to be no escape — and a place of training for the young. The way out was through the barrier, the Jordan River (Josh. 3:14-17). At Gilgal, they were circumcised (Josh. 5:2-4), they celebrated the passover (5:10), and on that day the manna ceased (5:12). The wilderness was no longer their garden; the land of Canaan was, if they would remain faithful and conquer it militarily in the name of the Lord. The way through the garden was direct confrontation, city by city, culture by culture, cutting each off, one by one. It was not a labyrinth for them, not a place of wandering and indirect excursions. The pathway was direct.

Broken Walls and Death

When the Israelites fled Egypt, Egypt died. When they fled the wilderness, the manna ceased, and the wilderness returned to its condition as a place of death. When the Israelites attacked the walled cities of Jericho and Ai, these cities died. The whole culture of Canaan died to the extent that the Israelites remained faithful and conquered the people of the land. But when Israel grew rebellious, various civilizations penetrated their walls (the Book of Judges), and finally Assyria and Babylon completed the process. There was no escape, God through His prophets warned them, no safe way out of the land except through Babylon — to the east. The east was the place of judgment. There would be no escape back into Egypt, Jeremiah warned (Jer. 42:19). Those who disbelieved him perished in Egypt when God delivered the Egyptians into the hands of Nebuchadnezzar (Jer. 44:30; 46).

God closed the Old Covenant era with the fall of Jerusalem. Israel had become spiritual Babylon.[36] Israel had brought Babylon back into the land through the Babylonian Talmud and other eastern practices. The destruction of Israel by Rome was the final judgment on geographic Israel. The Israelites were scattered in all directions. Israel would never again serve as a garden place. God's garden place today is the church, and only the church. What seems to be a garden place in our era — modern Israel — is a technological imitation of the garden, not the spiritual place prophesied of old.

The End of Old Israel

When men rebel against God, they are driven out of the garden. This happened to Adam. It happened to the Israelites when they fled from Egypt. It happened to them again with the invasions of Assyria and Babylon. Finally, it took place under Rome's dominion in 70 A.D. Biblically, we see that when the dragon invades the garden and men subordinate themselves to him ethically and covenantally, he captures them. The only hope of deliverance is ethical deliverance,

---

36. David Chilton, *Paradise Restored: A Biblical Theology of Dominion* (Tyler, Texas: Reconstruction Press, 1985), ch. 21.

but in Old Testament times, this meant geographical deliverance. Revelation 12 discusses the fate of ethnic Israel, the "woman" who brought forth the man child who became the deliverer.

> And she brought forth a man child, who was to rule all nations with a rod of iron: and her child was caught up into God, and to his throne. And the woman fled into the wilderness, where she hath a place prepared of God, that they should feed her there a thousand two hundred and three-score days. . . . And when the dragon saw that he was cast unto the earth, he persecuted the woman which brought forth the man child. And to the woman were given two wings of a great eagle, that she might fly into the wilderness, into her place, where she is nourished for a time, and times, and half a time, from the face of the serpent. . . . And the dragon was wroth with the woman, and went to make war with the remnant of her seed, which keep the commandments of God, and have the testimony of Jesus Christ (Rev. 12:5-6, 13-14, 17).

It is difficult to view the woman as the Christian church in history, since the dragon makes war against her seed when he cannot touch her. It could conceivably refer to the Jewish-Christian church in Israel during the transitional era from Pentecost to the fall of Jerusalem, with the "seed" referring to gentile Christians, who were persecuted in other parts of the Roman Empire. Garden Israel therefore became a wilderness for the Jewish-Christian church. But the wilderness is a place of *temporary residence,* a training ground during a period in which dominion is restricted for the sake of the *ethically immature.* The problem with identifying the "woman" with the Jewish-Christian church is that this church was not historically impotent. Peter and the apostles had been visited by the Holy Spirit in power. That transitional era church was the headquarters for worldwide evangelism. These are not the activities of a wilderness experience. It therefore seems more likely that the "woman" is ethnic Israel. Ethnic Israel will be regrafted into the olive tree of true faith when the era of the gentiles comes to an end (Rom. 11:11-17, 23-32).[37] Thus, ethnic Israel is presently in the wilderness — outside the framework of dominion history during the era of the gentiles.

Labyrinth vs. Garden

For the pagan, the labyrinth was forbidden space. It was to be dealt with through secret initiation and metaphysical manipulation.

---

37. John Murray, *The Epistle to the Romans,* 2 vols. (Grand Rapids, Michigan: Eerdmans, 1965), II, pp. 75-103.

It represented the nether world, or hell. For the God-fearing man, the garden is the product of ethics, a future goal toward which faithful people labor, first, by self-discipline under biblical law, and second, by external dominion through the imposition of biblical law over every area of life. The garden is a symbol, not of something foreboding, but of a future paradise. It is heaven on earth, or the new heavens and new earth.

For the pagan, the labyrinth was marked by its intricate passageways, its endless dead ends, and its enforced wandering. For the God-fearing man, the space within the walls of the enclosed garden is open space. One can go directly to the tree of life, which is in the center of the garden — which is also a city, the new Jerusalem. The garden is the place of righteousness, the place of obedience. "And he shewed me a pure river of water of life, clear as crystal, proceeding out of the throne of God and of the lamb. In the midst of the street of it, and on either side of the river, was there the tree of life, which bare twelve manner of fruits, and yielded her fruit every month: and the leaves of the trees were for the healing of the nations. And there shall be no more curse: but the throne of God and of the lamb shall be in it; and his servants shall serve him" (Rev. 22:1-3).

Adam had the power to have gone straight to the tree of life in the garden of Eden. He did not. He allowed his wife to sidetrack him ethically. Pagans view this detour as essentially a lack of knowledge. Salvation, they believe, is through knowledge, especially secret knowledge. This is the gnostic heresy. Thus, the labyrinth is essentially mysterious, not ethical. For paganism, if a man knows the magic words, "open sesame," the closed doors will open. The labyrinth is a place of riddles.

The Sphinx

The Sphinx, which is found in Egypt (half lion, half man) and Greece (half lion, half woman), is also associated with riddles in Greek mythology, for it was the Sphinx which asked Oedipus the famous riddle of the creature with four legs in the morning (man, who crawls as an infant), two legs in the afternoon (man, who walks as an adult), and three legs in the evening (man, who uses a cane in old age). The Sphinx was a guardian. The Sphinx challenged travellers to Thebes and asked them this riddle. Anyone who failed to answer the riddle was throttled and consumed by the Sphinx. Oedipus answered it, delivered Thebes from its clutches, and was made king.[38] The Sphinx in Greek legend is representative of pagan underground demons in general. Jane Harrison comments: "Two special features characterize the Sphinx: she was a Harpy carrying off men to destruction, an incarnate plague; she was the soothsayer with the evil habit of asking riddles as well as answering them. Both functions, though seemingly alien, were characteristic of underworld bogeys; the myth-making mind put them together and wove out of the two the tale of the unanswered riddle and the consequent deathly pest."[39] The Sphinx was also a tomb-haunter.[40]

Immanuel Velikovsky has identified the historical source of this Greek legend: the Pharaoh Akhnaton. It was not Greece's Thebes that was the original location of these legends; 'it was Egypt's Thebes. There is strong evidence that Akhnaton committed incest with his mother, Queen Tiy. Furthermore, this queen was associated with the first appearance of a female sphinx. Akhnaton had two sons, Velikovsky speculates, just as Oedipus had. One son, the famous King Tut (Tutankhamen), was buried with great splendor, just at Eteocles was in the Greek legend. The other son, Smenkhkare, was buried ignominiously, just as Polynices was (by his sister Antigone). The uncle of these two sons, Ay, the brother of Queen Tiy, then made himself Pharaoh, just as Creon, the brother of Jocasta, made himself king of Thebes.[41]

This is not some crackpot theory. There is no doubt that Akhnaton was incestuous. C. D. Darlington, the geneticist, has accepted Velikovsky's basic outline.[42] So has the distinguished historian, Cyrus Gordon, who calls the book a *tour de force*.[43] Three anatomists, using a microseriological method, demonstrated that both Smenkhkare and Tutankhamen belonged to the same rare blood group.[44] This increases the likelihood that these two were brothers, as Velikovsky suggested. The two mummies also had very similar skull structures, two of the anatomists, Harrison and Abdalla, have reported.[45]

38. Robert Graves, *The Greek Myths,* 2 vols. (Baltimore, Maryland: Penguin, 1955), II, p. 10, Sect. 105.*e.*

39. Jane Harrison, *Prolegomena to the Study of Greek Religion* (New York: Meridian, [1903] 1960), p. 207.

40. *Ibid.,* p. 211.

41. Velikovsky, *Oedipus and Akhnaton: Myth and History* (Garden City, New York: Doubleday, 1960).

42. C. D. Darlington, *The Evolution of Man and Society* (New York: Simon & Schuster, 1969), pp. 118-20.

43. Cyrus Gordon, "Oedipus and Akhnaton," *Pensée,* II (Fall 1972), p. 30.

44. *Nature,* Vol. 224 (Oct. 25, 1969), p. 325.

45. *Antiquity,* Vol. 46 (February 1972), p. 10.

Akhnaton, the Innovator

Recent scholarship on Akhnaton (who was originally named Amenhotep IV [Amenophis IV]) has begun to abandon the pre-Velikovsky humanist adoration of the "king who invented monotheism." Today, we read in utter amazement the turn-of-the-century assessment of Akhnaton by the otherwise judicious scholar, James Breasted: "In such contemplations he gradually developed ideals and purposes which make him the most remarkable of all the Pharaohs, and the first *individual* in human history."[46] The first individual in history? It gets worse: ". . . he is alike the first prophet and the first wise-man of history."[47]

Such obvious nonsense could not go unchallenged forever, and hasn't. Donald Redford's *Akhenaten: The Heretic King* (1984) is a hostile account. This worshipper of the sun disc was a failure. His experiment in monotheism was rejected by his successors, who defaced his monuments. He regards Akhnaton as a totalitarian.[48]

Redford does not stress the king's incestuous relationship with his mother, Tiy; instead, he hints at his incestuous relationship with his daughter, Meretaten, who was married to Smenkhkare.[49] If Smenkhkare was Akhnaton's son, then the genetic line, already visibly weakened in Akhnaton,[50] must have been jeopardised to a remarkable extent. Akhnaten's wife Nefertiti—this is in addition to his mother Tiy, who was never acknowledged to be his consort—because of the famous bust of her which is housed in the Berlin Museum,[51] is

---

46. James Henry Breasted, *A History of the Ancient Egyptians* (New York: Charles Scribner's Sons, [1905] 1908), p. 265.

47. *Ibid.*, p. 277.

48. Donald B. Redford, *Akhenaten: The Heretic King* (Princeton University Press, 1984), p. 235.

49. *Ibid.*, p. 188.

50. *Ibid.*, pp. 57-58.

51. The story of how it got there is a classic tale of bureaucracy and bureaucracy-overcoming. After Napoleon's invasion of Egypt in 1798, the French controlled all archeological exploration in Egypt. This monopoly was retained after 1904 as a result of a British-French agreement. (Thomas Hoving, *Tutankhamun: The Untold Story* [New York: Simon & Schuster Touchstone Book, 1978], pp. 24-25.) All antiquities exported from Egypt had to be approved by the Egyptian Department of Antiquities. In the 1930's, the Germans filled a room with four decades of uncatalogued junk: broken pottery, fragments, and molds of no value. They had never reported anything of significance in this collection. "Hidden" amongst tables full of junk was the head of Nefertiti, which the Germans must have known was a true treasure. Then they informed the director of the Antiquities Department that they intended to send it all back to Berlin. No important find had ever been announced in 40 years, so he sent a young subordinate to inspect the collection for anything of value. The young man did not spot the bust, and Berlin Museum got this treasure. The Egyptians have complained, but to no avail. (Velikovsky, *Oedipus and Akhnaton*, pp. 76-77.)

more familiar to most people than he is, although her prominence appears to have been great only during the first five years of his reign, when he had not yet declared his monotheism or moved his capital from Thebes to what is now called Tell-el-Amarna (Akhetaten).[52] (It turns out that as an infant, she had been wet-nursed by the wife of Ay,[53] who was the brother ["Creon," argues Velikovsky] of Queen Tiy.[54] Nefertiti was not the wife of King Tut, contrary to popular opinion.) Redford also acknowledges that Smenkhkare and Tutankhamen were brothers, but not that they were sons of Akhnaton.[55]

Akhnaton was narcissistic. Despite the destruction of his monuments by his successors, we still have more clay and stone bas-reliefs of Akhnaton and his family than we possess of the kings and queens of England, from William the Conqueror (1066) to Queen Elizabeth II. Many of the carvings are so detailed anatomically that they can be described as exhibitionistic — unique in Egyptian history.[56]

Akhnaton, Tutankhamen, and Smenkhkare were late eighteenth-dynasty monarchs. They followed Thutmose III by at least a century. What Velikovsky's reconstruction indicates is that Thutmose III was the Pharaoh Shishak, who invaded Israel in the reign of Rehoboam, the son of Solomon.[57] This was in the fifth year of Rehoboam's reign (II Chron. 12:2). Rehoboam came to the throne around 930 B.C.[58] Thus, Akhnaton, the great-great-grandson of Thutmose III,[59] ruled sometime in the late ninth or early eighth century, B.C., not in the mid-fourteenth century B.C., as the conventional histories insist.[60] In short, this Egyptian "inventor of monotheism" may even have been a contemporary of the prophet Isaiah, at least in the prophet's youth. So much for Breasted's "first prophet" theory.

Breasted's laudatory account of Akhnaton also includes the sculpture of the era. The king's artists were instructed to make the

52. Redford, pp. 78-79.

53. *Ibid.*, p. 151.

54. *Ibid.*, p. 207.

55. *Ibid.*, p. 192.

56. Velikovsky, *Oedipus and Akhnaton*, p. 78.

57. Velikovsky, *Ages in Chaos* (Garden City, New York: Doubleday, 1952), ch. 4.

58. Edwin R. Thiele, *A Chronology of the Hebrew Kings* (Grand Rapids, Michigan: Zondervan, 1977), pp. 21, 75.

59. Redford, *Akhenaten*, geneological chart, p. 13.

60. Christiane Desroches-Noblecourt, *Tutankhamen* (Boston: New York Graphic Society, [1963] 1978), p. 105.

king appear lifelike, he surmises (correctly, I would guess). "The modelling of the human figure at this time was so plastic that at the first glance one is sometimes in doubt whether he has before him a product of the Greek age."[61] We are supposed to conclude that in art, as in theology, Akhnaton was also a great innovator. Breasted missed the obvious: the sculptures appear Greek-like because they *were* contemporaneous with early Greece (Mycenae). Writing of the city of Akhetaton, Velikovsky notes: "Since it was inhabited for only about fifteen years, archaeologists have not had the tedious and often difficult task, encountered in other places, of separating various levels of occupation. Heaps of imported ceramics were found in Akhet-Aton; these came from Mycenae on the Greek mainland, or at least they were of the same manufacture as those found in Mycenae. Archaeologists dubbed a street in Akhet-Aton 'Greek Street' because of the abundance of this ware. On the basis of it, the age of King Akhnaton is established as synchronous with the Mycenaean Age in Greece. . . ."[62]

Conclusion

Egyptian culture was the dominant influence in the ancient Near East, well into the era of classical Greece. The cult of the dead, mummification (Crete), polytheism, labyrinths, and ultimately, the divinization of man: all were Egyptian legacies. All were based on the idea that man is saved, not by ethical regeneration, but by the manipulation of his own environment.

For the theology of the garden, it is not the knowledge of riddles which saves a person, but rather the knowledge of the Lord. It is covenantal faithfulness which determines access to the garden and the tree of life, not initiatory knowledge. It is *ethics,* not knowledge, which is central.

The labyrinth is the satanic imitation of the garden. It was a place of terror, a place of confusion. Success in escaping the labyrinth depended on one's initiatory knowledge of its secret passageways. In other words, it was an emblem of *metaphysical religion,* in contrast to the Bible's *ethical and judicial religion.* It was a magical device which promised to give the initiate power over the under-

---

61. Breasted, p. 279.
62. Velikovsky, *Oedipus and Akhnaton,* pp. 75-76.

world through magical manipulation. It was more a charm or talis-
man than a real place in which men might dwell. It was Egyptian to
the core.

SCRIPTURE INDEX

OLD TESTAMENT

(Boldface entries indicate a passage has been quoted or discussed at length)

389

NEW TESTAMENT

INDEX

(key pages are marked in bold)

WHAT IS THE ICE?

by Gary North, President, ICE

The Institute for Christian Economics is a non-profit, tax-exempt educational organization which is devoted to research and publishing in the field of Christian ethics. The perspective of those associated with the ICE is straightforwardly conservative and pro-free market. The ICE is dedicated to the proposition that biblical ethics requires full personal responsibility, and this responsible human action flourishes most productively within a framework of limited government, political decentralization, and minimum interference with the economy by the civil government.

For well over half a century, the loudest voices favoring Christian social action have been outspokenly pro-government intervention. Anyone needing proof of this statement needs to read Dr. Gregg Singer's comprehensive study, *The Unholy Alliance* (Arlington House Books, 1975), the definitive history of the National Council of Churches. An important policy statement from the National Council's General Board in 1967 called for *comprehensive economic planning*. The ICE was established in order to *challenge* statements like the following:

Accompanying this growing diversity in the structures of national life has been a growing recognition of the importance of competent planning within and among all resource sectors of the society: education, economic development, land use, social health services, the family system and congregational life. It is not generally recognized that an effective approach to problem solving requires a comprehensive planning process and coordination in the development of all these resource areas.

The *silence* from the conservative denominations in response to such policy proposals has been deafening. Not that conservative church members agree with such nonsense; they don't. But the conservative denominations and associations have remained silent because they have convinced themselves that *any* policy statement of any sort regarding social and economic life is *always* illegitimate. In short, there is no such thing as a correct, valid policy statement that a church or denomination can make. *The results of this opinion have been universally devastating.* The popular press assumes that the radicals who do speak out in the name of Christ are representative of the membership (or at least the press goes along with the illusion). The public is convinced that to speak out on social matters in the name of Christ is to be radical. *Christians are losing by default.*

The ICE is convinced that conservative Christians must devote resources to create alternative proposals. There is an old rule of political life which argues that "You can't beat something with nothing." We agree. It is not enough to adopt a whining negativism whenever someone or some group comes up with another nutty economic program. We need a comprehensive alternative.

Society or State

Society is broader than politics. The State is not a substitute for society. *Society encompasses all social institutions:* church, State, family, economy, kinship groups, voluntary clubs and associations, schools, and non-profit educational organizations (such as ICE). Can we say that there are no standards of righteousness—justice—for these social institutions? Are they lawless? The Bible says no. We do not live in a lawless universe. But this does not mean that the State is the source of all law. On the contrary, God, not the imitation god of the State, is the source.

Christianity is innately decentralist. *From the beginning, orthodox Christians have denied the divinity of the State.* This is why the Caesars of Rome had them persecuted and executed. They denied the operating presupposition of the ancient world, namely, the legitimacy of a divine rule or a divine State.

It is true that modern liberalism has eroded Christian orthodoxy. There are literally thousands of supposedly evangelical pastors who have been compromised by the liberalism of the universities and seminaries they attended. The popularity, for example, of Prof. Ronald Sider's *Rich Christians in an Age of Hunger,* co-published by Inter-Varsity Press (evangelical Protestant) and the Paulist Press (liberal Roman Catholic), is indicative of the crisis today. It has sold like hotcakes, and it calls for mandatory wealth redistribution by the

State on a massive scale. Yet he is a professor at a Baptist seminary.

The ICE rejects the theology of the total State. This is why we countered the book by Sider when we published David Chilton's *Productive Christians in an Age of Guilt-Manipulators* (3rd edition, 1985). Chilton's book shows that the Bible is the foundation of our economic freedom, and that the call for compulsory wealth transfers and higher taxes on the rich is simply *baptized socialism.* Socialism is anti-Christian to the core.

What we find is that laymen in evangelical churches tend to be more conservative theologically and politically than their pastors. But this conservatism is a kind of *instinctive conservatism.* It is *not* self-consciously grounded in the Bible. So the laymen are unprepared to counter the sermons and Sunday School materials that bombard them week after week.

It is ICE's contention that *the only way to turn the tide in this nation is to capture the minds of the evangelical community,* which numbers in the tens of millions. We have to convince the liberal-leaning evangelicals of the biblical nature of the free market system. And we have to convince the conservative evangelicals of the same thing, in order to get them into the social and intellectual battles of our day.

In other words, *retreat is not biblical,* any more than socialism is.

By What Standard?

We have to ask ourselves this question: *"By what standard?"* By what standard do we evaluate the claims of the socialists and interventionists? By what standard do we evaluate the claims of the secular free market economists who reject socialism? By what standard are we to construct intellectual alternatives to the humanism of our day? And by what standard do we criticize the social institutions of our era?

If we say that the standard is "reason," we have a problem: Whose reason? If the economists cannot agree with each other, how do we decide who is correct? Why hasn't reason produced agreement after centuries of debate? We need an alternative.

It is the Bible. The ICE is dedicated to the defense of the Bible's reliability. But don't we face the same problem? Why don't Christians agree about what the Bible says concerning economics?

One of the main reasons why they do not agree is that the question of biblical economics has not been taken seriously. Christian scholars have ignored economic theory for generations. This is why the ICE devotes so much time, money, and effort to studying what the Bible teaches about economic affairs.

There will always be some disagreements, since men are not perfect, and their minds are imperfect. But when men agree about the basic issue of the starting point of the debate, they have a far better opportunity to discuss and learn than if they offer only "reason, rightly understood" as their standard.

Services

The ICE exists in order to serve Christians and other people who are vitally interested in finding moral solutions to the economic crisis of our day. The organization is a *support ministry* to other Christian ministries. It is non-sectarian, non-denominational, and dedicated to the proposition that a moral economy is a truly practical, productive economy.

The ICE produces several newsletters. These are aimed at intelligent laymen, church officers, and pastors. The reports are non-technical in nature. Included in our publication schedule are these monthly and bi-monthly publications:

> **Biblical Economics Today** (6 times a year)
> **Christian Reconstruction** (6 times a year)
> **Tentmakers** (6 times a year)

Biblical Economics Today is a four-page report that covers economic theory from a specifically Christian point of view. It also deals with questions of economic policy. **Christian Reconstruction** is more action-oriented, but it also covers various aspects of Christian social theory. **Tentmakers** is aimed specifically at church officers, seminarians, and other people who are responsible for handling church funds.

The purpose of the ICE is to relate biblical ethics to Christian activities in the field of economics. To cite the title of Francis Schaeffer's book, "How should we then live?" How should we apply biblical wisdom in the field of economics to our lives, our culture, our civil government, and our businesses and callings?

If God calls men to responsible decision-making, then He must have *standards of righteousness* that guide men in their decision-making. It is the work of the ICE to discover, illuminate, explain, and suggest applications of these guidelines in the field of economics.

We publish the results of our findings in the newsletters.

The ICE sends out the newsletters free of charge. Anyone can sign up for six months to receive them. This gives the reader the opportunity of seeing "what we're up to." At the end of six months, he or she can renew for another six months.

Donors receive a one-year subscription. This reduces the extra trouble associated with sending out renewal notices, and it also means less trouble for the subscriber.

There are also donors who pledge to pay $10 a month. They are members of the ICE's *"Reconstruction Committee."* They help to provide a predictable stream of income which finances the day-to-day operations of the ICE. Then the donations from others can finance special projects, such as the publication of a new book.

The basic service that ICE offers is education. We are presenting ideas and approaches to Christian ethical behavior that few other organizations even suspect are major problem areas. *The Christian world has for too long acted as though we were not responsible citizens on earth,* as well as citizens of heaven. ("For our conversation [citizenship] is in heaven" [Philippians 3:20a].) *We must be godly stewards of all our assets,* which includes our lives, minds, and skills.

Because economics affects every sphere of life, the ICE's reports and surveys are relevant to all areas of life. Because *scarcity affects every area,* the whole world needs to be governed by biblical requirements for *honest stewardship* of the earth's resources. The various publications are wide-ranging, since the effects of the curse of the ground (Genesis 3:17-19) are wide-ranging.

What the ICE offers the readers and supporters is an introduction to a world of responsibility that few Christians have recognized. This limits our audience, since most people think they have too many responsibilities already. But if more people understood the Bible's solutions to economic problems, they would have more capital available to take greater responsibility — and prosper from it.

Finances

There ain't no such thing as a free lunch (TANSTAAFL). *Someone has to pay for those six-month renewable free subscriptions.* Existing donors are, in effect, supporting a kind of intellectual missionary organization. Except for the newsletters sent to ministers and teachers, we "clean" the mailing lists each year: less waste.

We cannot expect to raise money by emotional appeals. We have no photographs of starving children, no orphanages in Asia. We generate ideas. *There is always a very limited market for ideas, which is why some of them have to be subsidized by people who understand the power of ideas — a limited group, to be sure.* John Maynard Keynes, the most influential economist of this century (which speaks poorly of this century), spoke the truth in the final paragraph of his *General Theory of Employment, Interest, and Money* (1936):

> . . . the ideas of economists and political philosophers, both when they are right and when they are wrong, are more powerful than is commonly understood. Indeed, the world is ruled by little else. Practical men, who believe themselves to be quite exempt from any intellectual influences, are usually the slaves of some defunct economist. Madmen in authority, who hear voices in the air, are distilling their frenzy from some academic scribbler of a few years back. I am sure that the power of vested interests is vastly exaggerated compared with the gradual encroachment of ideas. Not, indeed, immediately, but after a certain interval; for in the field of economic and political philosophy there are not many who are influenced by new theories after they are twenty-five or thirty years of age, so that the ideas which civil servants and politicians and even agitators apply to current events are not likely to be the newest. But, soon or late, it is ideas, not vested interests, which are dangerous for good or evil.

Do you believe this? If so, then the program of long-term education which the ICE has created should be of considerable interest to you. What we need are people with a *vested interest in ideas,* a *commitment to principle* rather than class position.

There will be few short-term, visible successes for the ICE's program. There will be new and interesting books. There will be a constant stream of newsletters. There will be educational audio and video tapes. But the world is not likely to beat a path to ICE's door, as long as today's policies of high taxes and statism have not yet produced a catastrophe. We are investing in the future, for the far side of humanism's economic failure. *This is a long-term investment in intellectual capital.* Contact us at: **ICE, Box 8000, Tyler, TX 75711.**

Dr. Gary North
Institute for Christian Economics
P.O. Box 8000
Tyler, TX 75711

Dear Dr. North:

I read about your organization in your book, *Moses and Pharaoh*. I understand that you publish several newsletters that are sent out for six months free of charge. I would be interested in receiving them:

☐ *Biblical Economics Today*
   Tentmakers
   Christian Reconstruction
   and *Preface*

Please send any other information you have concerning your program.

_____
name

_____
address

_____
city, state, zip

☐ Enclosed is a tax-deductible donation to help meet expenses.

Analyzing Collapse

The AUC History of Ancient Egypt

Edited by Aidan Dodson and Salima Ikram

Volume Two

Analyzing Collapse
The Rise and Fall of the Old Kingdom

Miroslav Bárta

The American University in Cairo Press
Cairo New York

First published in 2019 by
The American University in Cairo Press
113 Sharia Kasr el Aini, Cairo, Egypt
200 Park Ave., Suite 1700, New York, NY 10166

Dar el Kutub No. 26095/16
ISBN 978 977 416 838 3

Dar el Kutub Cataloging-in-Publication Data

Bárta, Miroslav
    Analyzing Collapse: The Rise and Fall of the Old Kingdom /
Miroslav Bárta.—Cairo: The American University in Cairo Press, 2019.
    p.   cm.
    ISBN: 978 977 416 838 3
    1- Egypt — History — Old Kingdom, ca. 2686–ca. 2181 B.C.
    932.013

1 2 3 4 5   23 22 21 20 19

Designed by Jon W. Stoy
Printed in The United States of America

Contents

Preface

I first came to Egypt in 1991 as an undergraduate student of Egyptology and prehistoric archaeology at Charles University in Prague. The fall of that year was my first excavation in Abusir, a rural site among the pyramid fields, but one of the principal sites of the Old Kingdom period. It proved to be crucial for my future career in many ways.

There I experienced the thrill of observing how monuments, built millennia ago and now fallen into oblivion, were reappearing from the sands of the desert. Such discoveries challenged my imagination and my ability to piece together small fragments of evidence to build a picture of the past. Step by step, as the days passed, the ancient Egyptian world was becoming more and more tangible. Destinies of individual officials were gaining more concrete contours. Their fates started to fill in the outlines of the world they lived in and which they helped to shape. Individual lives of long-forgotten Egyptian officials of both high and lower standing, together with the general characteristics of the Old Kingdom society, were merging together; the micro- and macro-worlds started to form a unified and tightly interwoven whole. It took me quite a long time to reach this level of perception, and I have no doubt that to arrive at a complete state of knowledge and understanding of such a complex society is utterly impossible. This book is an attempt to offer my present perspective on one of several important periods of ancient Egyptian history—one of the first complex civilizations in the history of this planet. This book is a kind of interim testimony to the development of that society.

But ambitious as this sounds, there is yet another aspect of this pursuit that I wish to share: individual archaeological discoveries represent an indispensable micro-world from which a general picture of historical processes several centuries long may be reconstructed. Ancient Egyptian evidence may be viewed from the *longue durée* perspective. This is an approach formulated by the French School of Annals; it refers to the study of history through mapping and analyzing evidence for specific historical processes over long periods of time, combined with individual historical events and with a strong multidisciplinary component.[1] Only this specific approach of addressing historical issues by means of multidisciplinary research may have significant relevance for comparative studies with other known civilizations. Certainly, each civilization attested on this planet was or is specific and there are no algorithms that could compare them on a unified basis. Equally, there is no way our past can predict our future. Still, past civilizations were shaped and maintained by people like us, people with minds like ours, who were faced with many phenomena we know from our own contemporary world. It is above all the inner dynamics of any given society which offers many points for comparison: rising complexity; growing and proliferating bureaucracy; the role of the state and its eventual erosion; the role of nepotistic structures and interest groups in controlling energy resources and competing with the declining state structures for power and dominance; the importance of the elites and what happens when they fail to perform their duties.[2] These are just a few phenomena which can be encountered in any given civilization, in any age or location.[3] In the same manner, the ways in which any civilization adapts to a changing environment constitute yet another universal phenomenon which has been intensively studied.[4] All these aspects combined indicate why it is that archaeology sometimes appears to be political. This results from a simple observation, namely that archaeology addresses most of the issues and processes (some of the most important of which are mentioned above) which are present in our own modern world. In fact, multidisciplinary study of the past has become an increasingly strategic discipline, and the analysis of history of *longue durée* combined with a detailed analysis of

Fig. 0.1. Visual metaphor of modern study of history. Tiled windows in the cathedral in Rheims by Marc Chagall. In order to create such impressive windows, each of the colored tiles must be carefully produced; each on its own would be meaningless. To understand any civilization one must do the same—combine single events and *longue durée* analysis. (M. Bárta)

individual historical events, with their environmental background and dynamism, is beginning to claim more space in research and is receiving increasing attention from science as such.[5] The same is true of the comparative study of civilizations.[6] Last but not least, since Joseph Tainter's pioneering and still influential study of collapses in different societies and civilizations, it is considered productive to study the mechanisms of crises in which archaeology and history play a dominant role.[7]

Therefore, my focus throughout the book will be the following seven rules, which appear to form the essence of every civilization of which we have knowledge, and which can be distilled from comparative study of complex civilizations and *longue durée* history.

Law One

Every civilization is defined in space and time. It has geographical borders and temporal limits. Archaeology and history are the disciplines that analyze the emergence, rise, apogee, crisis, eventual collapse (understood as a sudden and deep loss of complexity), and the transformations leading to their new evolution. The making and unraveling of any civilization is a procedure that emphasizes the idea of time and process in combination with human agency.

Law Two

Every civilization develops by means of a punctuated equilibria mechanism, according to which major changes happen in a non-linear, leap-like manner when the multiplier effect is present.[8] Once periods of stasis separating individual leap periods become shorter or disappear completely, one expects a major system's transformation, most often a sudden and steep loss of complexity (metaphorically called 'collapse').

Law Three

Every civilization uses a language that is universally understood by its members (its lingua franca, typically English in our Western world) and a commonly accepted system of values and symbols. Every civilization has major centers characterized by a concentration of population, monumental architecture, a writing system (in most cases), sophisticated systems of communication, systems for storing and sharing knowledge, a hierarchically shaped society, arts, and a division of labor. It also has the ability to redistribute main sources of energy—in other words, it has elites who are able to establish and maintain the so-called social contract and allow the majority of the population to share in the profits generated by the system, which is controlled by a minority with decisive power.

Law Four

If the prevalent tendency within the civilization favors consumption of energy over producing it and investing it in a further increase of complexity, there is a declining energy return on investment (EROI). It means that a coefficient gained from the amount of energy delivered by a specific energy resource (such as water, sun, atom, gas, or coal) divided by the amount of energy necessary to be used in order to obtain that energy resource is becoming less and less significant, and therefore less economically profitable. As a consequence, the original level of complexity cannot be sustained or expanded. Eventually, in leaps rather than gradually, the system will lose its existing complexity and implode. This is what is traditionally and inaccurately called a 'collapse.'

Law Five

Individual components of a given civilization proliferate and perish through inner mechanisms inherent in the society (changing bureaucracy, quality of institutions, role of the elites and technologies, ideology and religion, mandatory expenses, social system, and so on), and through the ability of the civilization to adapt to external factors such as environmental change. These are the internal and external determinants that shape the dynamics of any given civilization. They are in permanent interaction, in cycles of varying length.

Law Six

The so-called Heraclitus Principle has a major impact on all civilizations: the factors that promote the rise of civilizations are, more often than not, identical with those that usher in their collapse. Thus if we want to understand the precise nature and causes of the collapse, we must study not only the final stage of the system but its very incipient stage, where the roots of the future crisis usually lie.

Fig. 0.2. Visual metaphor of a collapse. Impressive sarcophagus chest left behind in a corridor in the sacred animal cemetery of Serapeum, Saqqara, Egypt, Ptolemaic period. The sarcophagus, which was to contain the body of the sacred Apis bull, never reached its final destination. The works, the faith, the legitimacy of the painstaking work ceased literally overnight; all workers and officials participating in this process walked away on a single day. This is what is typically called a collapse—sudden loss of complexity, lack of economic means, lost legitimacy, and erosion of commonly shared values compromising the social contract. (M. Bárta)

Law Seven

A civilization disappears at the moment when its system of values, symbols, and communication tools disappears, and when the elites lose their ability to maintain the social contract. Yet the collapse does not necessary imply extinction. In most cases, a civilization that has consumed its potential gives way to a new one, usually carried on by the same or a slightly modified genetic substrate of the original population. Collapse in this context is a positive phenomenon, as it removes dysfunctional parts of the system.

All the features in the above seven laws play a role throughout the following chapters, and I leave it to readers to judge their effect and relevance. The study of civilizations in the manner indicated above may in fact turn into strategic directions of research in the years to come. These laws are capable of describing long historical processes from the incipient stage of a civilization through its rise, apogee, decline, collapse, transformation, and reemergence.[9] Ancient Egypt underwent this cycle at least three times. The study of the rise and fall of the era of the Old Kingdom pyramid builders in multidisciplinary perspective is just a limited part of the large mosaic of human history, but it may prove to be valuable as a description and evaluation of a complex society from its rise to its demise over several centuries, and provide an analysis of its internal and external dynamics.

I would like to thank all my friends and colleagues who read first versions of this text and contributed immensely to its completion—Salima Ikram, Aidan Dodson, and Guy Middleton. I am grateful to Miroslav Verner, Jiří Melzer, and Vivienne G. Callender for many valuable comments, criticisms, and insightful remarks during the process of the work on the manuscript. I also want to thank all my colleagues in the Czech Institute of Egyptology, without whom I would not have been able to complete the necessary research for this book. The American University in Cairo Press provided an excellent environment for the finalization of the manuscript. I owe a lot to just a few persons, and they know who they are.

The work on this book was accomplished within the framework of the Charles University Progress project Q11: "Complexity and Resilience: Ancient Egyptian Civilization in Multidisciplinary and Multicultural Perspective."

The present book and research builds on the Czech publication which appeared in 2016 under the title *Příběh Civilizace. Vzestup a pád doby stavitelů pyramid* (Academia).

Chronological Table
(based largely on Hornung, Krauss, and Warburton 2006: 490–98)

Early Dynastic Period	c. 2900–2592$^{±25}$ BC
First Dynasty Narmer, Hor-Aha, Djer, Djet, Den, Anedjib, Semerkhet, Qaa	c. 2900–2730$^{±25}$ BC
Second Dynasty Hetepsekhemwy, Raneb, Ninetjer, Peribsen, Sekhemib, Sened, Khasekhemwy	c. 2730–2590$^{±25}$ BC
Old Kingdom	c. 2592–2120$^{±25}$ BC
Third Dynasty Netjerykhet Djoser, Sekhemkhet, Khaba, Nebka, Huni	c. 2592–2544$^{±25}$ BC
Fourth Dynasty Sneferu, Khufu, Djedefre, Khafre, Menkaure, Shepseskaf	c. 2543–2436$^{±25}$ BC
Fifth Dynasty Userkaf, Sahure, Neferirkare Kakai, Raneferef, Shepseskare Isi, Niuserre Ini, Menkauhor, Djedkare Isesi, Unas	c. 2435–2306^{+25} BC
Sixth Dynasty Teti, Userkare, Pepy I Meryre, Nemtyemsaf Merenre I, Pepy II Neferkare, Nemtyemsaf Merenre II, Neitiqerti (Nitokris)	c. 2305–2118^{+25} BC
Eighth Dynasty attested kings such as Neferkaure, Neferkauhor, Neferirkare	c. 2150–2118$^{±25}$ BC
First Intermediate Period	c. 2118–1980$^{±25}$ BC
Ninth and Tenth Dynasties Herakleopolitan rulers, some with the name Akhtoy	c. 2118–1980$^{±25}$ BC
Middle Kingdom	c. 1980$^{±16}$–1760 BC
Eleventh Dynasty	c. 2080–1940$^{±16}$ BC
Twelfth Dynasty	1939^{+16}–1760 BC
Second Intermediate Period	1759–c. 1539 BC
New Kingdom	c. 1539–1077 BC
Third Intermediate Period	c. 1076–723 BC
Late Period	c. 722–332 BC
Greek Rulers	332–305 BC
Ptolemaic Period	305–30 BC
Roman Period	30 BC—AD 395

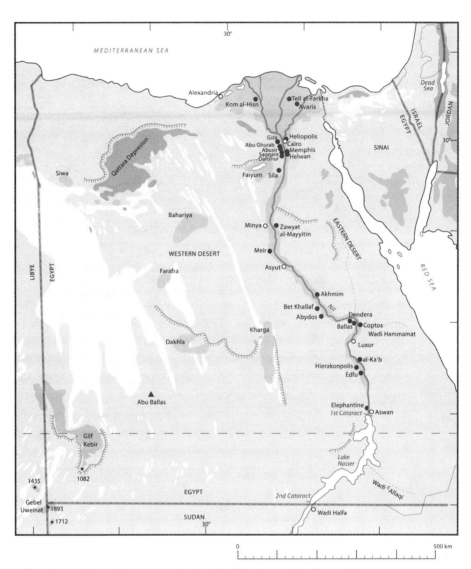

Map. Ancient Egypt. Source: compiled by J. Malátková, Czech Institute of Egyptology

1 Opening Up the Path: How Complex Societies Rise and Fail

> Civilizations are dynamic; they rise and fall; they divide and merge. And, as any student of history knows, civilizations disappear and are buried in the sands of time.[1]

THIS STUDY IS DEVOTED to the anatomy of the emergence, rise, and decline of the first ancient Egyptian state—the Old Kingdom, which lasted from the twenty-seventh through the twenty-second centuries BC. During this period, the foundations of ancient Egyptian civilization, which survived for millennia, were laid, elaborated, and refined. Egypt was a gift of the desert and of a global environmental change (the desiccation of the Sahara), but also, to a much greater degree, as the ancient Greek historian Herodotus wrote, a gift of the Nile, whose annual flood cycle provided the Egyptians with an enormous amount of energy that supported the emergence, sustenance, and growth of their civilization. Agriculture in the Nile Valley was an extraordinarily high-return activity. The accumulation of wealth that it generated led to the rise of a complex hierarchical society with a powerful elite class, which enabled the construction of costly state projects imbued with symbolic power.

This society's internal dynamics, combined with climatic cycles and the characteristics of the Nile's flow, defined many features of ancient Egyptian civilization, from the way in which it operated to the principles

1

of its continuity and longevity. Ancient Egypt shows that a civilization can last as long as its founding ideas are kept alive. The Old Kingdom has been chosen as the core theme of this book because it was during this period that the main pillars were formed which would support ancient Egyptian civilization for the next two millennia.

The reader will certainly remember the sometimes dull history lessons at school, when past cultures and civilizations were presented as long lists of buildings, kings, dynasties, and officially relevant dates. Symbols were often used to represent thousands of years of human development, such as, for Egypt, Khufu's pyramid at Giza or Tutankhamun's tomb in the Valley of the Kings, or for Mesopotamia, the Code of Hammurabi or the royal cemetery of Ur.

Naturally, ancient Egyptian civilization offers much more than that. Human history is a long and continuous journey reflecting the endless curiosity of the human mind, a path that is exemplified in the history of Egypt. This chapter will attempt to examine in some detail the way states (as major building blocks of a mature civilization), including ancient Egypt of the Old Kingdom, emerge, develop, and eventually fail. It will address many ways these processes are made manifest, explore the internal and external factors that influence long-term developmental trends, and examine whether, and to what degree, such processes may be continuous or marked ('punctuated') by sharp and sudden breaks. It will be demonstrated that the era of the pyramid builders is fascinating not just for its birth and rise but also for how and why it failed.

What Is Civilization?

At the end of the nineteenth century it was a relatively common belief that the difference between civilization and earlier stages of human social organization, represented by bands or tribes, was the ability to write.[2]

As we now know from early Mesopotamia and the Bronze Age Aegean, script originated as a means to record accounting details such as the place of origin and quantity of various commodities.[3] Only later did writing develop into a form that could be used to record speech and abstract ideological concepts. Moreover, certain early civilizations (in the Mexican highlands, Peru, West Africa) developed a complex hierarchical society and civilization despite not using script.[4] Thus, writing alone is not the key to understanding the nature and origins of civilization, although it plays a major role.

The Australian archaeologist Vere Gordon Childe (1892–1957) sought to understand civilizations by identifying their characteristics.[5] He produced a list of ten major traits:

1. Large urban centers;
2. Craftsmen, merchants, clerks, and priests living on the surplus provided by farmers;
3. Primary producers submitting their surplus to a deity or king;
4. Monumental architecture;
5. A ruling class exempted from manual labor;
6. A system for recording information;
7. Exact sciences for practical purposes;
8. Monumental art;
9. Regular import of different materials—luxury goods as well as raw materials for production; and
10. Specialized craftsmen controlled politically and economically by secular or religious officials.

Of course there are exceptions to every rule, and it pays to be wary of didactic generalization. In his monumental *A Study of History*, the historian Arnold Toynbee (1889–1975) emphasizes that every civilization is singular and that development is always specific in many ways and different every time.[6]

A modern analysis of civilizations would thus query whether Childe's individual traits are really universal. Nonetheless, more than sixty years later his reasoning still seems correct in principle.[7] Indeed, many modern studies dealing with early civilizations have focused on the very traits he identified, while adding to them at the same time. There are, for instance, broader discussions of the roles played by conflicts and armies, the institution of royalty, the family and kinship ties, and law in the development of civilizations, together with ideology and the role of an elite headed by the monarch.

Bruce Trigger, in his monumental opus *Understanding Early Civilizations*, argues convincingly against relying on lists to understand as

Fig. 1.1. Pyramids in Giza. These incredible monuments not only embody the ability and potential of the Egyptian Old Kingdom; they also manifest one of the pillars of Egyptian ideology and religion. (M. Bárta)

complex a system as a civilization. Yet he falls into the same habit when he attempts to characterize civilizations on the basis of social, economic, and political institutions.[8] And although recent research is dominated by arguments that favor multidisciplinary approaches to defining the 'essence' of a civilization, it seems that one cannot avoid at least some reliance on tentative lists of essential traits, however relative and prone to modifications such lists may be. The argument favoring multidisciplinary approaches for defining an 'essence' of a civilization, however, seems to dominate the recent research on the subject which is, nevertheless, not free of bias and one-sided statements.[9]

The development of a civilization and its attendant socioeconomic complexity requires an interaction among most of these essential traits, which influence one another in a multiplier effect, as defined by Colin Renfrew.[10] Without this, even if we have cities sprawling over hundreds of hectares in front of our eyes, it is very difficult to speak about civilization as such if there is no sign of social stratification, such as diversified architecture, socially specific artifacts, stratified settlements, religious centers, significant long-distance trade, or specialized production. The recently much-discussed towns of the Cucuteni–Trypillian culture in Ukraine, which thrived between 5200 and 3500 BC, may serve as a typical example of an entity with very low complexity.[11]

It is appropriate now to look at traits commonly displayed by the ancient Egyptian civilization. The following attributes characterize ancient riverine civilizations in general, and have been applied to ancient Egypt in particular.[12]

- It was territorial and maintained its borders;
- At the time of unification, it was strong enough to be able to invest profits into the specialization of labor and into expansion, which led to further rapid social differentiation and specialization;
- It had an advanced system of written communication that enabled the gathering, storing, and sharing of information throughout the state (the Egyptian script began to develop well before the unification of the country);[13]
- At its origins it had a hierarchical social structure consisting of four principal social strata (typical model: king, courtiers, local power representatives, majority population);
- It was characterized by partial urbanism (existence of towns and large residential agglomerations) and was able to provide for and organize the settlement of new territories under its jurisdiction and control;
- It had an advanced material culture displaying a considerable degree of standardization and homogeneity;
- It operated on commonly recognized norms of behavior;
- It engaged in long-distance trade to import otherwise inaccessible raw materials, which enabled the elites to demonstrate their privileged status;
- It had an elaborate state ideology and religious system that defended the status quo established during the fourth-millennium Naqada II, if not earlier, which depended on ideology, theology, and divine intent, all formulated to emphasize first the chieftain's, and later the king's, exclusive relationship with the gods;[14]

- It had a developed court culture, which identified power through symbols and religion, as exemplified by monumental architecture and art;
- It implemented projects, especially in monumental architecture, which served on the one hand to justify the existence and privileged status of the monarch and ruling class and, on the other, as a way for the ruling class to share and redistribute a part of its wealth among the lower classes, thus committing most of the population to participate in, develop, defend, and preserve the established system;
- It was able to exercise power and oversight within its entire territory, as shown by many texts, the iconography of the period, and the administrative titles of administrators;
- It deployed judicial institutions and a legal system to settle disputes, which helped to reduce the chaos that unavoidably accompanies the growth of state complexity;
- It was able to wage war beyond the borders of its own territory.[15]

For the archaeologist Colin Renfrew, a civilization is a recurring group of artifacts of a particular kind, a unique way that a specific group of people have adapted within defined temporal and geographic boundaries. According to Samuel Huntington, a civilization is characterized by its specific identity.[16] But while the features that characterize different civilizations may vary, each includes most of the features listed above. This may prove helpful in understanding the similarities. Civilization is thus necessarily a polythetic entity.[17]

Compared to ancient Egypt, the (city or regional) states of the Near East developed quite differently during the fourth and third millennia BC.[18] Drawing on archaeological research about communities east of the fertile floodplain of the Tigris and Euphrates (the Susian Plain), American archaeologists Henry T. Wright and Gregory H. Johnson produced a theoretical concept of the state, distinguishing between a complex society organized at state level and less complex structural units, such as chiefdoms.[19] Their reasoning started from the basic observation that Egypt, like the region along the lower course of the Tigris and Euphrates, preserved archaeological material providing evidence of significant settlement hierarchy. There were usually several—at least three—tiers of settlements (for instance center, minor center, and village). They concluded from a separate analysis of seal impressions and other administrative evidence that these could only constitute a state, as commonly understood, when the leader or chief (later king) had mediators (later members of the court and 'ministerial' officials) by his side to transfer decisions to the next (third or possibly even further) tier(s).[20]

Linked to this development was another essential characteristic of the state: the ability to collect and keep information with the help of a system of writing. This information served as the basis for decision-making controlled by the elites, which enabled decisions to be implemented in a unified way. At its inception, script gave unrivaled advantage: it recorded data and provided any reader with the same data in an unaltered, objective form, exactly as it had been recorded. This model suggests that societies in the Nile Valley, southern Mesopotamia, and southwestern Iran had reached the state phase of development as early as the end of the fourth millennium BC.[21]

The Genesis of a State and the Social Contract

The genesis of the state has fascinated scholars both ancient and modern. For example, Aristotle (384–322 BC) considered the existence of the Greek-type *polis* to be natural and automatic, assuming that a state naturally results from the self-organizing principle of an increasingly complex society.[22]

As our understanding of the human past has grown, however, so has our awareness that the situation today is more complex in some regards, especially as the birth of a state is the outcome of many phenomena and their various combinations.[23]

An approach not too distant from Aristotle's can be found in early modern philosophy. Thomas Hobbes (1588–1679) was, in his 1651 book *Leviathan*, one of the first modern writers to deal with the idea of the genesis of the state. Hobbes believed that a state is formed due to man's need to protect himself against imminent war. That is why he creates the state ('commonwealth') and enters a 'social contract' under which he surrenders his individual freedoms and power for the benefit of the higher entity. This process is not, however, fully automatic or voluntary; coercion plays a significant role.[24]

In principle, Hobbes distinguishes three forms of state: monarchy, if power is in the hands of one individual; aristocracy, if power is held by an assembly composed of a restricted group of people; and democracy, if decision-making processes are approved by all citizens.

Similar ideas were developed by John Locke (1632–1704) in his *Second Treatise of Government* (1690). According to Locke, the state is formed to ensure peace and security and human rights, including individual property rights: the state is an arbiter duty-bound to ensure that the property of its individual members is protected.

These schools of thought were taken up freely in the eighteenth century by the French philosopher Jean-Jacques Rousseau (1712–78) in *Du contrat social, ou Principes du droit politique*, first published in Amsterdam in 1762. Rousseau held the view that a state emerges as the result of the conclusion of a social contract when "each of us puts his person and all his power in common under the supreme direction of the general will; and in a body we receive each member as an indivisible part of the whole."[25] Although this implies a voluntary act, there is a coercive element to this theory, too, as Rousseau asserts that "whoever refuses to obey the general will shall be compelled to do so by the whole body. This means nothing less than that he will be forced to be free."[26]

In a similar vein, at the beginning of the twentieth century, the German sociologist Max Weber (1864–1920) defined the state as a human community that claims a monopoly on the legitimate use of physical force within a given territory.[27]

Unfortunately, all these views and theories have one thing in common: they reflect an abstract idea of the formation of a state rather than addressing the process through which a state emerges in real life. This may be due, at least in part, to the fact that in the seventeenth and eighteenth centuries not much was known about the history of civilizations. Since then, exhilarating advances in archaeology and cultural anthropology, especially in the twentieth century, have produced vital physical evidence about the development of past cultures. This has initiated a new wave of research into the origin of states and shed new light on the origins of complex states.

As our understanding of the human past has grown, however, so too has our awareness that the birth of a state is the outcome of many

Fig. 1.2. Catal Hüyük, Turkey (7500–5700 BC). One of the earliest cities in the world, with a population of up to 10,000. (reconstruction by P .Vavrečka)

phenomena in various combinations.[28] Current theories of the origin of the state can be roughly divided into two groups (albeit with fuzzy, overlapping boundaries): the first posits that a state is formed by voluntary unification of lower units, in a quasi-Aristotelian way; the second, that states are primarily coerced into being.

Childe theorized that the origins of the state were natural or noncoercive: that the introduction of agriculture and settled communities led to overproduction, which allowed segments of the population to specialize, as they were no longer needed for agriculture. This gave rise to a common need for such settled communities to come together and create larger and larger coalitions. Contemporary archaeological evidence shows that in the Near East this consolidation began as early as the fourth millennium BC in the form of the above-mentioned city-states, which were true centers of learning and crafts, as well as being the foci of the elite of that era.[29] On a general level, one might object that this is a grossly generalizing theory that does not take into account either the geography or the specific circumstances under which states originated, not to mention the fact that in many parts of the world, settled farming populations are known to have existed that never developed any

Fig. 1.3. Taxation of the whole territory of the Egyptian state was one of the principal prerequisites to build and maintain a highly complex society. Tomb of Mereruka, Saqqara, early Sixth Dynasty. (M. Bárta)

discernible system of government.[30] However, the evidence from Egypt and the Near East is rather convincing in this respect.

Karl Wittfogel (1896–1988), in his 1957 study, *Oriental Despotism: A Comparative Study of Total Power*, offered a different perspective based on the development of early civilizations in Mexico, China, Egypt, and Mesopotamia. Wittfogel argued that the basic impulse for the rise of all these civilizations was the need to organize labor in a large territory to implement the grand construction projects required to support agriculture in large river basins.

Wittfogel's theory was applied to Egypt several decades later by Karl Butzer (1934–2016), in his 1976 study *Early Hydraulic Civilization in Egypt: A Study in Cultural Ecology*, and by the German Egyptologist Wolfgang Schenkel, in his *Bewässerungsrevolution im Alten Ägypten* (1978).

It is evident today that while the origins of the Egyptian state really may have been linked to the need to deal with the annual flooding of the Nile, other cases (such as Mesopotamia) are not so clear-cut. And even as far as ancient Egypt is concerned, there is good reason to ask whether it was necessary to build irrigation projects of *such* size, for instance canals capable of distributing water over a wider territory than that affected directly by the Nile flood.

A more recent theory, proposed by Yale professor James C. Scott, is that early states could be established due to the new possibility of effective taxation that was enabled by developed agriculture, as grain taxation, collection, and redistribution were the most suitable means along which economies of the early agrarian states could be organized.[31]

War and Civilizations

In the present book there will be frequent references to the birth of the unified Egyptian state around the beginning of the third millennium BC. This has often been ascribed to wars waged by Upper Egyptian elites against their northern neighbors in line with the theories of the Enlightenment philosophers discussed above.[32] Like these earlier thinkers, the British sociologist Herbert Spencer (1820–1903), whose intellectual sources included the evolutionists Charles Darwin (1809–82) and Thomas Huxley (1825–95), also regarded the threat of war as the prime factor motivating the formation of states.[33]

In recent times, war or conflict has been a common focus of contemporary American economists and political scientists such as Douglass C. North, John Joseph Wallis, and Barry R. Weingast.[34] In many ways their work follows on from the ideas of the Enlightenment philosophers. Although their primary interests are the development of modern states and the modern phenomenon of war, they also deal with the effects of war and conflict on the development of populations since the agricultural revolution. They link their basic argument—which is not so different from Childe's—to the beginnings of agriculture: farming permitted the establishment of settled communities; unlike human groupings in earlier periods, these farming communities experienced rapid population growth, which naturally increased the potential for conflict over land, property, and influence.[35]

Roy A. Rappaport (1926–97), drawing on his research in Papua New Guinea, argued that even linear population growth can result in the exponential growth of the potential for conflict; he called it the "irritation coefficient."[36] While a nomadic group may have up to twenty-five members, a clan may have some two hundred and a tribe up to a thousand: social systems exceeding a thousand members are generally held to constitute chiefdoms. Comparative studies have looked at such groups in the real world, and they too regard war, or the growing threat of conflict, as being both directly dependent on population growth and the primary motivating factor in the formation of a state capable of exercising an exclusive monopoly on violence in its territory.[37]

It can thus be proposed that war, or the threat thereof, and the need to organize labor for large construction (and—yes!—irrigation) projects, which a small community would be unable to implement on its own, have been part of major driving forces behind the emergence of states. These factors will not have been exclusive causes, but their formative impact is beyond doubt.

Environmental and Social Circumscription Theories

The American anthropologist Robert Carneiro studied the diversity of the forms into which states develop, and in 1970 proposed an elaborate theory of the origin of the state. He noted that states have originated in diverse regions lying at different distances from the Equator, different heights above sea level, with different qualities of soil, temperatures, total rainfall, and many other variables. But he also observed that among all these variables, the states that developed in Mexico, Peru, Egypt, and the Middle East had one thing in common: the amount of land available for farming was constrained by sea, desert, or mountains. Carneiro refers to this feature as "environmental circumscription."

Carneiro developed his theory with a comparative analysis of two populations: agricultural communities in the Amazon lowlands and in the coastal lowlands of Peru. In the Amazon lowlands, the amount of agricultural land is almost limitless. Individual farming communities are dispersed over a large area; the distance between them is usually some fifteen to twenty-five kilometers. There were wars here, of course, but these were waged to demonstrate individual heroism, acquire women, or take personal revenge.[38] They were not primarily wars over land or property. Whenever a village was defeated, its inhabitants simply fled to another part of the forest to establish another settlement. Since there was a seemingly endless supply of agricultural land, there was no reason to forge military coalitions or organized, hierarchical units to defend or attack.

In contrast, agricultural land was the alpha and the omega of development for villages that had sprung up in the eighty or so valleys on the northern coast of Peru, which were constrained by the ocean, mountains, and desert. The settlement of these valleys expanded with the rising number of people living in the villages. Once a village population reached some three hundred people, some were dispatched to build a new village. The size of the individual villages thus remained fairly constant.[39] Once the valleys were settled, the pressure on land use increased.

Fig. I.4. Monte Albán. One of the driving forces of the early states was wars. Monte Albán rulers managed to unify the whole territory of Oaxaca and thus increased their available resources. Zapotec civilization, Oaxaca valley, Mexico. (M. Bárta)

This led to existing land being cultivated more intensely or to new arable land being acquired by building terraces on steep slopes, although the latter required much more energy and resulted in a declining EROI (Energy Return On Investment, or the amount of energy that must be expended compared to the amount of usable energy that it creates).[40] Eventually these technical options were exhausted and economic stress led to aggression against neighbors. Such wars had serious consequences for the defeated communities, but they were the unavoidable result of the scarcity of available land combined with the practical impossibility of escape because of the desert, mountain, or sea barrier. This was the mechanism by which a strictly hierarchical society emerged, grew over time to encompass larger territories controlled by individual chiefs, and eventually developed into kingdoms—as happened, for instance, with the Inca Empire and its predecessors, like the Moche culture.[41] It was a process that led naturally to deep social stratification, the rise of a small and powerful elite, larger groups of professional clerks and craftsmen with some privileges, and finally, large groups of farmers and war captives with no privileges at all.

The theory that states emerge as a result of external environmental stress is paralleled by a theory of "social circumscription," a concept introduced by Napoleon Chagnon (b. 1938) based on populations in Amazonia, and particularly on the Yanomamo tribe.[42] A tribe of some ten thousand members, the Yanomamo live in the rainforest where there is an abundance of arable land. Nevertheless, as Chagnon notes, the individual villages of this tribe are not spread out evenly over the area: they are mainly concentrated in a clearly defined center, and settlements on the periphery are sparse. As a result, the villages in the center are larger in both size and population than those on the edges, closer to one another, and their leaders are stronger and wield more authority. Social tension in the center is much greater and, besides environmental stress, there is also deeper social stratification, with communities growing stronger internally because of continuous social pressure on space, authority, power, and carrying capacity.

Some Factors to Add

Alongside war and expansion and the construction of large-scale projects and monuments, the basic framework for the genesis of the early state included an ideology leading to the formation of an elite headed by a king or ruler of some sort, the need for trade—especially long-distance trade for the purpose of acquiring (among other things) prestigious artifacts and raw materials—and technological innovation.

Another key characteristic of the early state is a central government with the ability to maintain law and order, if necessary by force. This includes the ability largely to prevent internal conflicts and the division of the population into a governing minority and governed majority.

Last but not least, the state's basic function is to create a surplus, which is needed to keep the state running, to support the state ideology, and to redistribute some economic potential and wealth for the benefit of most of the population, and thus maintain a kind of simple social contract—at least, this was the case of early states, such as Egypt or the city-states of

Fig. 1.5. Army of Nubian soldiers. Famous models from the tomb of Mesehti, Asyut, First Intermediate Period. (M. Bárta)

the Near East. Recent cross-cultural comparative study by Richard E. Blanton and Lane F. Fargher goes further and indicates that state formation (and evolution) results from strategic behavior by rational and self-interested actors from both the political elite and the majority that is outside the state's official administrative structure which are—in the case of archaic states—mainly peasants. The result is that building collective polities can provide mutual benefits to all bodies involved.[43]

It must be stressed that when we talk about central government in relation to early states, we are not necessarily referring to the same degree of centralization and verticality as in the modern state. The most realistic model of ancient Egypt in the third millennium BC appears to consist of a relatively powerful center or capital (Memphis) capable of exercising local rule over the country's most significant local settlements, which overlapped with the most economically productive and strategically important regions.[44] There can be no doubt, however, that this center was able to concentrate and redistribute the large economic flows without which it would be difficult to imagine the construction of pyramid complexes and other projects, or the sustenance of a large priestly class (see chapters 6 and 7). Centralization as it is understood today—implying detailed control of the institutions and processes all over the state's territory—probably did not exist in Old Kingdom Egypt. It is more likely that organically evolving agglomerations emerged, where the power elite and the central institutions were concentrated. True, there was a major center in Memphis, but it coexisted with smaller centers across the country which were semi-independent. Everyday aspects of governance, including services in temples of local gods, and often carried out by traditional local families, blended in these towns with elements of presentation of royal power and ideology often personified by an official dispatched on the order of the king.[45] All this, of course, took place within environmental and geographical constraints.[46]

There is a danger in comparing civilizations and cultures thousands of kilometers and centuries apart. A separate temporal and spatial analysis of the social development of any given polity must be carried out and the processes that characterize it identified, described, and understood. Only then can an attempt be made to generalize the results.[47]

Huntington and Annual Rings

External factors other than war and geography may also have played a role in state formation. We will focus especially on one 'superfactor'—the changes of climate over time.

The quest to understand the climate and its relevance for the human population is not new. A *Hymn to the Nile* (also known as the *Hymn to Hapi*) dating to the New Kingdom (sixteenth to eleventh centuries BC) is clear proof that the Egyptians, too, were very much aware of how important this mighty natural source of water, energy, and transport was for them:

    Adoration of Hapi:
    Hail to you, Hapi,
    Sprung from earth,

Come to nourish Egypt! . . .
Who floods the fields that Re has made,
To nourish all who thirst;
Lets drink the waterless desert,
His dew descending from the sky . . . .
When he floods, earth rejoices,
Every belly jubilates,
Every jawbone takes on laughter,
Every tooth is bared.
Food provider, bounty maker,
Who creates all that is good!
Lord of awe, sweetly fragrant,
Gracious when he comes.
Who makes herbage for the herds,
Gives sacrifice for every god . . . .
He fills the stores,
Makes bulge the barns,
Gives bounty to the poor.[48]

Mesopotamian literature also contains unique descriptions of climatic oscillations, which were thought to indicate divine displeasure with the human race. There is no lack of lively descriptions of consecutive years of crop failure and there can be no doubt that these descriptions are based in reality.[49]

Ibn Khaldun (1332–1406), a medieval author, in *The Muqaddimah: An Introduction to History*, addresses climate change and its effect on human populations in the harsh desert environment and the rich mountainous regions of the Maghreb (modern Morocco). According to Ibn Khaldun, the different geographical and climatic zones had a fundamental impact on the history of individual ethnic groups.[50] This was a precursor to the views of the French philosopher Charles Louis de Montesquieu (1689–1755), who believed the natural environment (among other things) shaped the nature and character of a specific society and determined whether it would be aggressive, peaceful, settled, nomadic, or agricultural. On that basis he concluded that a single political order could not apply to all societies.[51]

Fig. 1.6. Nile River. All early complex civilizations came into being in close proximity to major rivers. (M. Bárta)

One of the first modern works to deal with the supposedly causal relationship between climate change and civilization's development was the work of the American geographer Ellsworth Huntington (1876–1947), professor of geography at Yale. He observed that past waves of desiccation resulted in large migrations and also ultimately led to the collapse of the Roman Empire.[52] He was one of the first to measure and analyze, in 1911 and 1912, the annual rings of the Californian *Sequoiadendron giganteum* and draw a curve of climate fluctuations (dry and humid phases) between 1300 BC and AD 1900 on the basis of long-term rates of wood increment. He then drew a similar curve for western Asia, and by comparing the two, concluded that climate trends were global.[53]

There is a connection (probably unintended) between his work and that of Bedřich Hrozný (1879–1952), the renowned Czech archaeologist and linguist who deciphered Hittite, and in 1940 published a work titled *O nejstarším stěhování národů a o problému civilisace proto-indické* (On the migration of nations and issues of the Proto-Indian civilization) where he points to the desiccation of vast steppe regions in Asia as the main cause triggering the migration of nations.

Another scholar to argue that climate and history were linked was the American meteorologist Hurd C. Willett (1903–92). In studying the Holocene climate, he concluded that it was possible to identify approximately 1,850-year-long cycles characterized by a tendency toward warming or cooling.[54] Willet was among the first—at least of those known to the author—to deal with the concept of regular climatic cycles during the Holocene. He was soon followed by Rhys Carpenter (1889–1980), professor of classical archaeology at Bryn Mawr College, whose 1966 work *Discontinuity in Greek Civilization* is one of the first published historical studies focusing on the relationship between man and changing climatic conditions.

Bond and Climate Change

There has been further work since then on Holocene climate change, especially by Gerard Bond and his team,[55] who have found evidence that significant climate change occurred over a short period of time in a whole series of "events." Bond dated these to 9100, 8300, 7400, 6100, 3900, 2200, and 800 BC and AD 550, with a periodical incidence rate of approximately 1,470 years.[56] Thus, climatic oscillations during the Holocene occurred at approximately 1,500-year intervals. Each oscillation consisted of a gradual cooling and then a sharp drop in temperatures, followed by a cold period at the end of which temperatures rose steeply.[57]

In the ancient Egyptian context, a notable period is the one that dates roughly from 3000 BC to 2000 BC, the period of the second-largest Holocene change and tentatively equivalent to the Old Kingdom. This was a period of slow cooling that followed the climatic optimum in the early Holocene between 6200 BC and 3000 BC. Around 2500 BC there was an evident change in the trend—from the warmer and drier Sub-Boreal to a cooler and more humid Sub-Atlantic climate.[58]

Details of the second event are unknown, except that it was slower and culminated around 2200 BC.[59] This may have been the product of four different and mutually independent factors. The first to be mentioned is usually the radical cooling of the North Atlantic region. The second possible factor was the start of a 1,500-year-long oscillation period, and

Fig. 1.7. Climate change and fluctuations of the Holocene era. Climate has always had a significant impact on the character of civilizations and cultures. A protracted spell of droughts made the Anasazi culture disappear within several years at the end of the thirteenth century. Cliff palace, Mesa Verde, Colorado. (M. Bárta)

the third was a major El Niño–Southern Oscillation (ENSO) effect. The last could be the reaction of the atmosphere and vegetation to smaller orbital oscillations of the Earth.[60]

Collapses and the History of Ancient Egypt

This book is concerned mainly with the search for and description, evaluation, and interpretation of the processes leading to the birth, rise, and finally fall of the Egyptian Old Kingdom. Having evaluated some general aspects of the birth of civilizations, we must now discuss—in a necessarily limited manner—some general features associated with the famous and often misunderstood phenomenon of 'collapse.'[61]

Collapse has frequently been represented by an archetypal myth, most often in the form of a deluge or other large-scale natural event that annihilates a culture. Evidence of this myth and its different variants appears independently in many civilizations and cultures around the world, including ancient Egypt and the Middle East, early China, and Australia.[62] The common denominator of all these myths is a gigantic disaster that occurs in a relatively short space of time. The descriptions in the narrative usually have an ethical subtext: the collapse is a divine and deserved punishment. It typically represents a divide between the old and a new age.

Such myths are described in detail in, for instance, ancient Egyptian literature and Near Eastern texts.[63] They usually have a moralizing core: unless an individual abides by a certain ethical code and behaves in accordance with the order of things mediated by the gods, just retribution will follow. We can, of course, only speculate about the historical and political contexts in which these myths arose, but it would be difficult not to imagine that one of the reasons must have been the authors' desire to seek meaning in the development of their society and find hope for renewal after a crisis, with its attendant decline in living standards, quality of governance, and technology, crafts, art, and trade. Like the examples here, collapse will be presented throughout this book as a transformation, a fundamental change, an intrinsic part of the development of society, and a means of regeneration and restoration once the system becomes largely defunct and unsatisfactory to the parties entering into the social contract.

One of the oldest descriptions of collapse and doom is found in the third millennium BC Sumerian *Epic of Gilgamesh*. Longer versions have been recorded in an old Babylonian composition, where the god Enki comes to Atrahases and tells him that the gods intend to flood the world to punish humans for their sins, and orders him to build an ark to save his family and other living creatures.[64]

The Bible contains a similar description. Here, for forty days the flood waters kept rising to destroy every living thing (Genesis 7:17–19, 24), after which new life began. This flood came as a punishment for the inappropriate behavior of people on earth and for their arrogance. The biblical account is almost identical to the Mesopotamian version.

Another famous text of collapse and doom is Plato's rendition of the tale of the mythical Atlantis, as preserved in the *Timaeus* and *Critias* dialogues. Plato (427–347 BC) describes the mythical continent of Atlantis as a model, ideal state in which, at first, people lived in harmony with the will of the gods. Later, however, they turned away from this order and began to desire more wealth and power, which ultimately led to their doom.

Ancient Egyptian literature also contains a myth about the destruction of humanity for plotting against the Egyptian gods, though the versions currently known have been dated much later than the Old Kingdom. The obdurate god Re orders Sekhmet, the goddess of war and destruction, to destroy humanity. But he relents in time and the human race is saved.

> It happened [in the time of the majesty of] Re, the self-created, after he had become king of men and gods together: Mankind plotted against him, while his majesty has grown old, his bones being silver, his flesh gold, and his hair true lapis-lazuli. . . .
> They (i.e., the gods) said to his majesty: Let your Eye go and smite them for you, those schemers of evil. No Eye is more able to smite them for you. May it go down as Hathor.
> The goddess returned after slaying mankind in the desert, and the majesty of this god said: Welcome in peace, Hathor. Eye who did what I came for! Said the goddess: As you live for me, I have overpowered mankind, and it was balm to my heart. Said the majesty of Re: I shall power over them as king by diminishing them.[65]

These are the myths from ancient times as preserved through contemporary texts. But how did they come about and what did they mean to the people who actually listened to them? Did such disasters always mark an end, or can we consider them to be an inherent part of the historical process? And what options do archaeologists, historians, or environmental scientists have to study such disasters in the context of ancient Egypt, with the benefit of its written texts, religion, and complex social and state organization?

Ancient Egyptian history is said to have lasted for three thousand years. During that period, several empires emerged, peaked, and expired: the Old, Middle, and New Kingdoms, separated by intermediate periods (interregnums, which modern research shows were rife with local conflicts). The end of this development occurred in what is called the Late Period, which followed the New Kingdom. The final phase of Egyptian pharaonic rule was marked by two Persian conquests, in 525 and 343 BC, and Egypt's independence ended when the country was conquered for the third time by Alexander of Macedon in 332 BC. It was under Ptolemaic rule from 323 until 30 BC (Ptolemy was one of Alexander's successors who seized Egypt after his death), when it came under Roman domination. And yet, the language and religion lived on—albeit with many changes and modifications—practically until the fourth/fifth century AD.

While the individual kingdoms are characterized by economic, political, and intellectual expansion and the remarkable achievements of the human mind, the intermediate periods are less distinguished and bear clear signs of decline in the complexity of ancient Egyptian society. One interpretation might be that these were times of collapse, but they can also—and indeed preferably—be seen as a considerable simplification of the complexity of the system.

Nevertheless, the result is the same: a period of decline in the standard of living, of arts, crafts, and literature, and also a diminished ability by the state to carry out key tasks, which, in Egypt, involved defending the country's borders, building temples, collecting taxes, exercising the sovereign power of the king, and operating the redistributive system that was core to the economy and which provided the king and the ruling elite with legitimacy and superior status.[66] The central state apparatus fades out everywhere, the country disintegrates into smaller territorial units, and poverty spreads. All this is reflected on a general level, with only few exceptions, in the poor quality of grave goods found in cemeteries; there is evident leveling of the vertical structure of society.

A number of theories have been advanced to explain this decline, and in the next chapters, the following theses will be weighed:

- The Old Kingdom collapsed suddenly because of an internal coup or sudden 'revolution';
- The Old Kingdom collapsed due to a long-term, internal social, symbolic, and economic crisis of the state;
- The Old Kingdom collapsed quickly because of an invasion;
- The Old Kingdom collapsed due to the long-term effects of external factors, such as deteriorating climatic conditions and low Nile flooding;
- The Old Kingdom did not collapse at all; it is an illusion.[67]

We must also bear in mind that there may not be any single cause for a society's collapse, and that it is more likely to be a combination of various phenomena and long- and short-term trends working together. The next chapters will show how heterogenous and complicated was the process of non-linear evolution of ancient Egyptian society and how a number of phenomena played a role at different stages of development.

2 The River Nile and Egyptian History

CLIMATE AND CLIMATE CHANGE have had an omnipresent role in human development. Water and moisture can turn a desert into paradise; their absence can do the opposite. There is no life without water, and sooner or later people and societies start moving away from places where it is scarce. Ancient Egypt was no exception. Cultures and civilizations emerged in the Nile Valley because of the long-term drought of the Western and Eastern Deserts, and the Old Kingdom came to an end partly because of long-term aridification.[1]

The collapse of the Old Kingdom and other important entities in the Near East and elsewhere began at the same time: about 2200 BC.[2] The following pages will look at the climate change that took place in Egypt during the third millennium BC, focusing in particular on the main features of the period preceding that date.

Two extreme opinions seem to dominate the current debate around environmental change around 2200 BC.[3] The first is that there is no indication of climate change at that time. The second makes use of significant proxy data and defends the conclusion that many societies collapsed around this time due to a major deterioration in the climate.[4]

Nile Floods and the Palermo Stone

In Egypt, the main source of information on climate change is evidence about the rise and fall of the Nile. This phenomenon was, and in fact still is, the alpha and the omega of life in the valley. Nile flood levels were meticulously recorded until the completion of the Aswan High Dam in the 1960s, as the yearly measurement was of paramount importance in the Egyptian cyclical calendar.[5]

The earliest such data come from the early third millennium BC and are preserved on the Palermo Stone, and to a lesser extent on what is commonly called the South Saqqara stone.[6] The Palermo Stone was once part of a much larger monument that recorded the main events in each year of Egypt's existence as a unified country, from the advent of the first king of the First Dynasty to some time in the first half of the Fifth Dynasty, some six centuries later. It also listed the Predynastic rulers of (at least) Lower Egypt. The overall composition survives in seven fragments (not all of which necessarily come from the same original monument), but a substantial portion of the stone is lost.[7]

On its front side the Palermo Stone preserves a significant portion of the Royal Annals of the Old Kingdom. The space is divided into six horizontal registers inscribed with hieroglyphic texts running from right to left. The top register contains a list of Predynastic rulers of Lower Egypt. The following registers contain the names of the kings of unified Egypt, of the First to Fourth Dynasties. The second register starts with significant events in the last years of the rule of a First Dynasty king, probably Hor-Aha or Narmer, but the name is damaged. The details of Fifth Dynasty kings are on the back. Entries on the surviving fragments end with the reign of King Neferirkare, the third king of the Fifth Dynasty. In addition to the names of kings and the heights of yearly floods, the text includes the names of other members of the royal family, including the mothers of kings, who played a significant role in ancient Egyptian history, especially in matters of succession. Unfortunately, due to the way in which it is broken, it is not certain whether the record ended with King Neferirkare or continued for one or more later rulers.

The registers also record major events that occurred during each king's reign: the celebration of religious feasts, tax collection, the erection of statues in honor of different deities, building projects (often

Fig. 2.1. The Palermo Stone. (Photo courtesy Museo Archeologico Regionale di Palermo A. Salinas; photo M. Osman)

relating to the construction of royal palaces as major seats of the 'government'), military campaigns and the resulting booty, and details of the gifts (including land) that the king gave to individual temples, and, most important, the height of the Nile floods.

This was a phenomenon of extraordinary importance. The Nile flood season, *akhet* in the Egyptian calendar, marked a period of decreased agricultural activity—as the land was under water—when it became possible to transport heavy cargo by water across longer distances and into locations high above the normal level of the river. This was important especially in the transportation of large stone blocks from quarries as far south as Aswan—the origin of red granite, the most expensive building material in the Old Kingdom in terms of acquisition costs—to construction sites throughout Egypt, including the pyramid complexes of the kings.

Most revealing in this respect are the unique papyri discovered by the French archaeologist Pierre Tallet in Wadi al-Jarff on the coast of the Red Sea. They describe the transport of Tura limestone blocks (Tura was a major quarry for limestone for the Giza pyramids across the Nile) and date to the year 26 or 27 of King Khufu, which is the highest attested date for the reign of this ruler. This transport took place between July and November when the waters of the Nile were at their highest and the overland hauling of heavy cargo could be minimized.[8] One text preserved on the papyrus roll (papyrus B, Section B I) describes the daily routine of moving the stones by boat across the river during the inundation season:

> [Day 25]: [Inspector Merer spends the day with his phyle [h]au[ling]? st[ones in Tura South]; spends the night at Tura South [Day 26]: Inspector Merer casts o. with his phyle from Tura [South], loaded with stone, for Akhet-Khufu; spends the night at She-Khufu. Day 27: sets sail from She-Khufu, sails towards Akhet-Khufu, loaded with stone, spends the night at Akhet-Khufu. Day 28: casts o. from Akhet-Khufu in the morning; sails upriver <towards> Tura South. Day 29: Inspector Merer spends the day with his phyle hauling stones in Tura South; spends the night at Tura South. Day 30: Inspector Merer spends the day with his phyle hauling stones in Tura South; spends the night at Tura South.[9]

The height of the Nile flood was also a factor in the precise calculation of taxes from different types of fields across the country. Accurate measurement of the height of the flood was thus an inevitable part of the advance calculation of the tax yield from agriculture. An appropriate (neither too high nor too low) annual Nile flood was essential for the year's crops and thus for the output of the agriculture-based economy of the ancient Egyptians. Both too-low and too-high floods led to poor harvests and had a direct bearing on the state's economy.

Records of seventy-two floods—that is, seventy-two years of the Nile's history—are preserved on the Palermo Stone for the period from the First Dynasty until the middle of the Fifth Dynasty, specifically for the period from Djer to Neferirkare. This represents roughly 550 years, meaning that we have less than 13 percent of the expected number of records for the entire period. These are very limited data from which to conduct a detailed analysis of trends, but they do provide enough information to make basic observations.

Of the floods for which records survive, the largest number is concentrated during the First Dynasty: thirty-four entries altogether. The Second Dynasty has thirteen entries, and the Third Dynasty has fourteen. In contrast, only six have been preserved for the Fourth Dynasty and only five for the Fifth (from the reigns of Userkaf, Sahure, and Neferirkare). If the Palermo Stone did indeed contain data for every regnal year of every ruler, there would originally have been several hundred records. Within individual dynasties, the data are once again concentrated in the reigns of just a few kings: flood heights are documented for twelve different years during Djer's rule, thirteen during what has been estimated as Anedjib's rule, and the same for Ninetjer. As for the Old Kingdom, five entries have been preserved from what is estimated to be Djoser's reign, four from Sneferu's, and two from Khufu's.

The spread of the heights of individual floods is significant. The lowest are documented during the rule of King Ninetjer, only 0.52 meters (or exactly one cubit), and Anedjib, 1.04 meters. This latter is the third-lowest Nile flood for which we have records and is 0.5 meters higher than the documented lowest. The highest flood levels occurred during the reign of Anedjib, 4.22 and 3.55 meters, and Djer, 3.15 and 3.20 meters. There is no doubt that both the lowest and the highest floods had a devastating impact on the state's economy in those years.

It is interesting that records available from the time of King Anedjib testify to both extremely high and extremely low floods: the difference is more than three meters. The average inundation, judging from the entries preserved on the Palermo Stone, was approximately 2.04 meters. These data offer a clear view of the importance of floods to the ancient Egyptians and of the fact that the flooding was not just a monotonous annual event, but one that was anxiously awaited by everyone in Egypt.

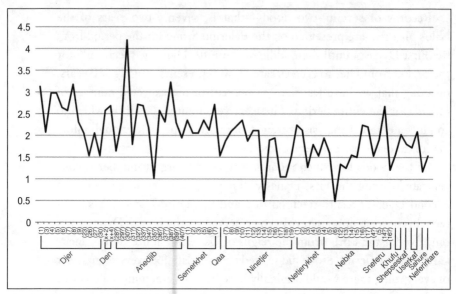

Fig. 2.2. Chart showing heights of the Nile floods as recorded on Palermo Stone. (compilation M. Bárta)

Although the Palermo Stone has been known since the mid-nineteenth century, it was not until the 1970s that the American Egyptologist Barbara Bell identified its great potential for the systematic evaluation of individual entries relating to the Nile floods.[10] Her study was followed and developed by Fekri Hassan in the 1980s.[11]

Interpreting details of the height of Nile floods has been difficult mainly because we do not know how or where the measurements recorded on the Palermo Stone were taken. But it is evident that this feature was measured continuously for several centuries and the acquired data systematically preserved.

One possibility, mentioned by Prince Omar Toussoun (1872–1944), a prominent member of the Egyptian royal family renowned for his scientific papers on the Nile and the Coptic monasteries in Wadi Natrun, is that these measurements were taken with a portable Nilometer, which during the periods between floods was kept in the temple of Apis (Toussoun refers to him as "Serapis") at Memphis. There is a report dating from the Greco-Roman period that describes a portable Nilometer, but it is possible that such a tool existed two thousand years earlier.[12]

The measured heights of the Nile floods would have changed over time owing to the deposit of sediments during the rise and retreat of flood waters, which resulted in an estimated accrual of Nile alluvium of ten centimeters over a single century. The change over a thousand years would be up to one meter, even considering that the process was non-linear and its rate may have varied along the Nile Valley. It is known, for example, that sedimentation rates in the Memphite region are much greater than, for instance, at Aswan, the area of the First Cataract of the Nile.[13]

The second possibility is that the floods were recorded with fixed Nilometers, familiar from many places in Egypt, including several temple complexes. These consist of a descending ramp or staircase leading down to the water table. The fluctuating height of the water level was read off a scale located on the side wall of this structure, within which the water rose during the flood. Nilometers of this kind are best known from temples such as Edfu, Kom Ombo, and Elephantine, although these are dated to much later periods than the one that concerns us here.

Comparing the details on the Palermo Stone with data from the famous medieval Nilometer still standing on Roda Island in modern Cairo shows that the ancient data record realistic differences between minimum and maximum floods. This suggests that the flood pattern has not changed much over the millennia. The same applies to the Nile oscillations, which at first glance may appear to be very large. For example, measurements of the water level from the Roda Nilometer for 1871 to 1902 vary from under 17.6 meters in 1877 and 1899 to 21.4 meters in 1874 (measurements above sea level). The 3.8-meter difference corresponds with similar evidence from the Palermo Stone.[14]

Four very high flood levels are recorded during the rule of three First Dynasty kings: Djer—3.15 and 3.20 meters; Den—2.60 meters; Anedjib—4.22 meters. Flood levels recorded during the Second Dynasty were much lower.[15] The average height of Nile floods during the First Dynasty was 2.32 meters, which means that the four identified above were very high even for that period. Entries for later dynasties show much lower averages: 1.64 meters during the Second Dynasty, 1.67 in the Third, 1.85 in the Fourth, and 1.69 during the Fifth. Thus, while the average height of flood levels during the Second and Third Dynasties remained practically the same, in the First Dynasty the floods were 0.70 meters higher.

Fig. 2.3. Example of the Egyptian Nilometer, though from a much later period, on the island of Elephantine, Aswan. Meticulous recording of the annual flood was the foundation of Egyptian economic life. (M. Bárta)

Macklin et al. in their 2015 study gathered all the data available (accumulated over the last twelve thousand years) for the history of the Nile during the Holocene.[16] They identified six major phases in the development of the Nile during this period, each of which signified a substantial and abrupt change in its flood regime and had a profound impact on the populations inhabiting the Nile Valley. The first phase is dated to the 6400 to 5800 BC interval, which roughly corresponds with the beginning of the desiccation of the Sahara. The second was the period culminating around 4500 BC, characterized by a major drop in temperatures and significantly declining water levels in Lake Tana and Lake Victoria. Significantly lower flow rates were recorded in the Nile Delta area, and fluvial (river) sedimentation was compensated by marine sedimentation. A large drop in the water levels of the lakes in Faiyum province has been documented for the period from 3700 to 3450 BC. The most important phase in the periods described by Macklin and his research team was the third, from 2800 to 2450 BC, when the flow rate of the Nile again declined steadily.[17] It was no doubt this trend that led to the diachronic settlement drift on Elephantine Island during the third millennium BC (see below).

As a matter of interest, the next period of lower flow rates, lower flood heights, and cooling started around 1600 BC. More recent stages of deteriorating hydroclimatic conditions occur between 1100 and 900 BC and, finally, between AD 1450 and 1650. It is also worth mentioning that available data show that from AD 200 to 500 the flow rate of the Nile increased, which is an interesting contrast to the decline of the Roman Empire during the same period, or to the documented wave of depopulation of settlements in some Egyptian oases at the beginning of the fifth century. This should be sufficient to demonstrate that the Nile has always played a dominating role in human history in northeast Africa. The 'temper' and the tendency of the river toward low or high floods was a crucial factor for the cultures of antiquity that depended on its omnipotent forces.

Small Houses on the Island

One of the sites where the variability of Nile floods over the third millennium BC can be studied in some detail is the region of the First Cataract, Elephantine Island in particular, where the main regional settlement was situated at that time. It functioned as a border town guarding the southern frontier, where Egypt proper ended and Nubia began.[18] According to ancient Egyptian tradition, it was at the First Cataract, in a cavern under the island of Bigeh, that the Nile had its source. An image illustrating this is found in the Ptolemaic temple at Philae.

Elephantine Island was formed by the joining of two separate islands that had been continuously settled since the very beginning of the unified ancient Egyptian state. Long-term German excavations have helped clarify the very close interconnection between the settlement of the island and the Nile floods, which were here an essential and limiting factor and physical constraint. Some of the observations made during this research complement what we already know about the development of the natural environment and Nile floods in the third millennium.

During the First Dynasty, the new settlement on Elephantine Island does not descend below 96 m above sea level (ASL) and even the foundations of its fort remain consistently above this line. The extensive network of settlement structures is supplemented during the Second Dynasty by a system of fortifications for the expanding settlement, but at a somewhat lower height, 94 to 94.5 m ASL (which suggests that the height of the Nile between floods may have been some 92 to 92.5 m ASL). During the Old Kingdom, a continuous descent of the settlement to increasingly lower levels can be observed. During the Fourth and Fifth Dynasties, the settlement was located below 94 meters ASL, and in one case the plastered floor of a house lies below 93.55 m ASL. The lowest settlement is recorded toward the end of the Old Kingdom, during the Sixth Dynasty: it lay at only 90.8 to 91.3 m ASL, which is clear evidence that the usual level of the Nile was particularly low in those years. One cannot fail to note that the difference in the heights of settlement levels between the beginning of the unified state and the end of the Old Kingdom was a striking five meters.

An interesting development was the return of higher floods at the end of the Old Kingdom and during the First Intermediate Period, as evidenced by the building of large stone walls that served as a platform on which the floors of lighter structures could be lifted as high as 92.7 m ASL. Analysis of the accumulated layers has proved, however, that even this floor level was flooded several times by the swollen river despite being above the height of the average floods.

The floor was subsequently raised by another 40 cm, to a height of 93.1 m ASL. At this level, the settlement buildings no longer show any trace of inundation. During the last construction phase, but still before the beginning of the Middle Kingdom, the residential level was raised one last time, to 93.7 m ASL; here, too, there are no traces of flood damage.[19] Archaeological data thus indicate that the island settlement changed dramatically over time, depending on the height of the Nile when a given phase was founded. The pattern of these changes corresponds, of course, with the common long-term trend in the height of the yearly Nile floods.

As we have seen, evidence from Elephantine Island and the Palermo Stone points to more or less constant average flood levels during the

Fig. 2.4. Elephantine settlement drift throughout the Old Kingdom provides ample evidence for the fluctuation of the annual Nile floods and their diminishing impact toward the end of the Old Kingdom. (M. Bárta)

Third to Fifth Dynasties. This brings us back to the question of how and where the height of flood levels was measured. In the Memphite region this may have been done by measuring the height of the water surface above the inundated area of the floodplain, possibly using a static measuring gauge built at a designated site. If point zero on the scale indicated a fixed height in the surrounding terrain (the Nile alluvium), the flood water level could then have been measured from this point. Since the average height of flood levels during the Third to Fifth Dynasties was practically constant, we can infer that there was no considerable increase in the amount of alluvium over this period (approximately 350 years). If that was the case, it follows that the absolute height of flood levels would have decreased over time.

And in fact even though the Palermo Stone data are incomplete, the figures do indicate a trend of decreasing flood levels between the Early Dynastic Period and the latter part of the Old Kingdom. This is supported by the evidence of floor levels on Elephantine and the study by Macklin et al., which clearly point to progressively lower Nile floods during the Old Kingdom era.[20]

The Abusir Beetles

The picture of the climatic context of the Old Kingdom has been supplemented in an interesting way by finds made at the Czech archaeological mission in Abusir. A mummification deposit dating to the period of the rule of Pepy I toward the end of the Sixth Dynasty was discovered in the burial complex of Judge Inti. It contained mostly ceramics and bandages that had been used to mummify a member of the judge's family, then ritually buried in a side shaft. One of the bowls in the set was covered by a residue of resin—a material commonly applied to desiccated corpses—and some beetles were stuck in it. They were identified as *Poecilus pharaoh*, a common insect living in desert zones with high salinity, which can neither migrate nor change its very specific ecological niche.[21] The beetles imprisoned in the hot aromatic resin therefore suggest two things: first, the strip of land adjacent to the Nile Valley had turned from savannah to desert; second, the wrapping and bandaging and perhaps some other elements of the mummification process did not take place near the Nile or some other water source, but in the desert, maybe in the immediate vicinity of the tomb.

The last stone in the mosaic is an observation made by geologists working on a Polish expedition in nearby Saqqara. To the west of King Djoser's pyramid complex there is a large burial ground dating to the end of the Old Kingdom. This was naturally exposed to many post-deposition factors, including massive strata of shifted material carried by a strong, rapid stream of water that contained layers of mud. Specific analyses have shown that these layers were deposited by flash floods running down from the Western Desert plateau (which by then already had a very low water absorption capacity) after torrential rains. Similar strata were also found in Abusir in Old Kingdom burial chambers, which had been robbed and left open. The authors suggest that the extreme rains at the end of the Old Kingdom were caused by the North Atlantic Oscillation.[22]

History Repeating Itself?

Having discussed the way environment limited the development of complexity in the ancient Egyptian state, we can now turn our attention to the cyclical nature of history, including the creation, rise, and fall of civilizations.

The work of the medieval Arab scholar Ibn Khaldun and his theory of the cyclical restoration of ruling Islamic dynasties is one of the earliest, most significant and inspiring contributions in this context. Ibn Khaldun postulates that societal change is the result of a gradual process. He discusses this theory in great detail in his *Muqaddimah*, which contains introductory reflections to the seven volumes of his *Book of Lessons*. The latter deals with the history of all the countries, regions, and nations that came into contact with the Islamic world. The part of the *Muqaddimah* that is probably most relevant to the idea that history is cyclical concerns the natural life span of ruling dynasties. Indeed, Ibn Khaldun comes very close to modern concepts of cyclicity, as encountered in recent research.

Ibn Khaldun's theory was based on his finding that a dynasty seldom lasts more than three generations, each of which lasts approximately forty years. After this period of roughly one hundred to 120 years there is a hiatus, which leads on to a new form of government. The description of this mechanism is based on the characteristics of mainly Arab 'Bedouin' dynasties:

> The first generation retains the desert qualities, desert toughness, and desert savagery. (Its members are used to) privation and to sharing their glory (with each other); they are brave and rapacious. Therefore, the strength of group feeling continues to be preserved among them. They are sharp and greatly feared. People submit to them.
>
> Under the influence of royal authority and a life of ease, the second generation changes from the desert attitude to sedentary culture, from privation to luxury and plenty, from a state in which everybody shared in the glory to one in which one man claims all the glory for himself while the others are too lazy to strive for (glory), and from proud superiority to humble subservience. Thus, the vigour of group feeling is broken to some extent. People become used to lowliness and obedience. But many of (the old virtues)

remain in them, because they had had direct personal contact with the first generation and its conditions, and had observed with their own eyes its prowess and striving for glory and its intention to protect and defend (itself). They cannot give all of it up at once, although a good deal of it may go. They live in hope that the conditions that existed in the first generation may come back, or they live under the illusion that those conditions still exist.

The third generation, then, has (completely) forgotten the period of desert life and toughness, as if it had never existed. They have lost (the taste for) the sweetness of fame and (for) group feeling, because they are dominated by force. Luxury reaches its peak among them, because they are so much given to a life of prosperity and ease. They become dependent on the dynasty and are like women and children who need to be defended (by someone else). Group feeling disappears completely. People forget to protect and defend themselves and to press their claims. With their emblems, apparel, horseback riding, and (fighting) skill, they deceive people and give them the wrong impression. For the most part, they are more cowardly than women upon their backs. When someone comes and demands something from them, they cannot repel him. The ruler, then, has need of other, brave people for his support. He takes many clients and followers. They help the dynasty to some degree, until God permits it to be destroyed, and it goes with everything it stands for.

As one can see, we have there three generations. In the course of these three generations, the dynasty grows senile and is worn out. Therefore, it is in the fourth generation that (ancestral) prestige is destroyed.[23]

This is, of course, a text that is several centuries old and refers to nomadic tribes that settled and established local dynasties based on blood relationship and family ties. But it can be used as a kind of intellectual stepping-stone to other historical concepts and reflections on history, and the *Muqaddimah* is valid even today, especially read broadly, in the way it describes cycles that demarcate the rise and fall of distinct social entities, whether dynasties or entire cultures, societies, and civilizations.

Later in the *Muqaddimah* Ibn Khaldun discusses the inner meaning of change, when a spent dynasty is replaced by another. This does not, to him, necessarily mean doom; it is rather the kind of regenerating, "self-renewing" mechanism that is often associated with the collapse of a social system—that is, with the moment when a system has either spent itself internally or been crippled by external factors and needs to be restructured from the beginning. The system does not cease to exist. It changes, and its transformation requires a period of relatively low complexity, an interval during which it will have few resources to expend on growth.

Vico, Marx, Spengler, and Toynbee

Ibn Khaldun's notion that civilization developed in cycles was elaborated by a succession of authors, including Giambattista Vico (1668–1744), who theorized that civilization developed in three stages: divine, heroic, and human. Oswald Spengler (1880–1936) and Arnold Toynbee were among the leading twentieth-century proponents of the theory. Karl Marx (1818–83), by contrast, was an advocate of linear development.

Marx needs no special introduction. The founder of the philosophy known as 'historical materialism' based his political tracts (in *Capital*, first English edition 1887) on the premise that the purpose of history was to move ever forward in a linear way driven by confrontation between social classes.[24] This was supposed to culminate in a struggle between the capitalists and the exploited working class, which would lead to communism—a society where all people were equal. Marx never specified how communism would develop. Sometimes his contemporaries compared him to Charles Darwin. Spengler, one of the outstanding German philosophers of the first half of the twentieth century, identified eight great civilizations: ancient Egyptian, Chinese, Indian, Babylonian, Classical, Arab, Mexican, and the current Western civilization. He distinguished these civilizations in a way that differs significantly from Marx's linear understanding of history. In Spengler's view—immortalized in his still influential work *Der Untergang des Abendlandes (The Decline of the West)*, originally published in German in 1918—the essence of the development of civilizations and cultures lies in their incessant birth, development, peak, and final decline.[25] Spengler illustrates their development by analogy to the four seasons: he compares spring to the feudal stage; summer to the expansion of towns existing in harmony with the surrounding countryside; autumn to the onset of decline accompanied by centralistic tendencies, trade boom, secularization—in other words, the alienation of the idea of symbolic forms—and rapid expansion of urban forms of life. Finally, winter is marked by a decline that ushers in rampant plutocracy, loss of identity and ideals, and life in bloated urban agglomerations.

Spengler considered the main developmental stages of the eight great civilizations to be identical and claimed that this allowed predictions to be made about the direction of civilizations that were not yet defunct. He also believed that civilizations had identical life cycles and so would last approximately the same amount of time. This arose from a more general observation that civilizations developed along the same trajectory. Thus, for example, the first century in the development of the Antique civilization was from 1100 to 1000 BC. Its parallel, according to Spengler, was the first century of our own Western culture, between AD 900 and 1000. He called this "contemporaneity" (Gleichzeitigkeit), and referred to the last developmental stage of any culture as "civilization." This stage is characterized every time by, among other things, a loss of the meaning of history, artificiality and stagnation, materialism accompanied by loss of religion, the proliferation of sin and a boom of the entertainment industry, a decline of morale and art, explosions of violence, and disastrous wars. What is also remarkable is that he arrived at this position and adopted this attitude to life at the age of just thirty-eight.

Arnold Toynbee, in contrast, earned an international reputation as a result of the comparative method he used to analyze different civilizations. A Study of History, a work in ten volumes published in London between 1934 and 1954, is simply overwhelming, if only for its sheer size. It contains a detailed discussion of more than twenty civilizations, with a focus on the regularities in their development.[26] Toynbee concluded that civilizations grew from encounters with both external and internal challenges and were therefore the result of cultural and natural factors. He wrote that civilizations develop and increase in social complexity by coping with problems. Thus, for example, he suggests that ancient Egyptian civilization was formed because the population of the Nile Valley had to cope with Nile floods.

Toynbee distinguishes nineteen successful civilizations (including "our own" Western one). He then adds four abortive civilizations, which were unable to overcome the challenges they faced, and five arrested ones, characterized by castes and rigid specialization. According to Toynbee, every civilization is unique because it encountered a distinct set of problems and responded to them in specific ways. What they all have in common, however, is that the challenges are always being faced by a "Creative Minority"—a relatively small part of the population capable of seeing further ahead and finding successful solutions. At the beginning of a civilization a religious system may often make a significant contribution to successful outcomes. The moment this minority begins to stagnate and loses its ability to resolve problems, it becomes a "Dominant Minority," which consolidates its privileged status by force. It is then subjected to attack on two fronts: a dominant "internal" proletariat grows up against it within the state, while it is attacked from the outside by an "external" proletariat—a group of people living beyond its boundaries. The Universal State emerges as a result: this is the final stage that precedes the civilization's decline. The Dominant Minority consolidates its positions and a struggle against the majority begins; the minority loses both its creativity and its ability to respond to internal and external challenges.

The one serious drawback of Toynbee's overview of the development of civilizations is the largely arbitrary manner in which he distinguishes one civilization from another: for example, he presents the Sumerian and Akkadian civilizations as two different entities, but joins the Greek and Roman into a single "Hellenistic" civilization. Toynbee also reflected on the fate of contemporary civilizations—Islamic, Hindu, and Far Eastern. He believed they had two basic options for their future: to become in the end a part of the Western civilization, or to develop into a Universal State and finally to be engulfed by their internal problems.

This small selection of philosophers and historians of civilizational change illustrates that their approach to history was built on the concept of an underlying developmental trajectory, particularly as the consequence of internal factors and dynamics. One issue that they almost entirely neglected (perhaps with the exception of Toynbee) was the impact of the natural environment. This, however, can be explained through the lack of available data about the very concept of climate development and human resilience.

Fig. 2.5. View of one of the earliest dams in human history—built, but never finished, at the beginning of the Fourth Dynasty in Helwan, Sadd al-Kafara. (M. Bárta)

Multiplier Effect and 'Punctuated' History

The nature of historical processes as perceived through archaeological data provides a different perspective on the historical dynamics and the mechanisms of change. The British archaeologist Colin Renfrew published his PhD dissertation, in 1972, on the origins and history of the Cycladic society and its impact on the later Minoan, Mycenaean, and Greek civilizations.[27] The Cycladic culture characterizes prehistoric development on the Aegean Sea's Cycladic islands, which emerged around 3200 BC and disappeared during the transition between the third and second millennia BC. It went through several distinct phases as it developed.

The genesis and development of the Cycladic civilization provided Renfrew with a platform on which to demonstrate, relying on systems theory, a phenomenon known as the 'multiplier effect.' Renfrew showed that no advanced culture, society, or civilization could be taken as a homogenous continuum, but was composed of various subsystems with specific features and functions. Traditionally, we can identify subsistence, technological, social, symbolism, and trade and communication subsystems. The subsistence subsystem covers the role and function of sources of livelihood, the manner in which they are acquired and used, and the practical and symbolic importance attached to them. The technological subsystem involves the specific human actions that lead to the manufacture of artifacts or to increasingly specialized production processes. Its basic building elements are humanity's practical world of needs and symbolic world of ideas, the raw materials required to produce artifacts, and the artifacts themselves. The social system consists of the varied conduct and norms governing human interaction. The complexity of these relations grows in proportion to the complexity of the system. The symbolic system involves activities and attitudes relating to language, religion, art, science, and other ways in which humans express their state of knowledge of the world, views of the world, and attitudes toward it. And, finally, the trade and communication system involves commercial strategies and relations and the movement of goods, be they raw materials, artifacts, or know-how.[28]

Of course, these subsystems interact all the time and influence one another; any one alone would lose its purpose and ability to function. Moreover, it is difficult to clearly separate the individual subsystems. Their interfaces are usually transitional, and the same activity may fall within more than one system at the same time. More complex civilizations, like ancient Egypt, China, and others that used script, can be said to have an additional subsystem—the administration. This refers to the manner in which the society's functions are administered and represents another specific and vital sphere of human activity, which plays a key role in the civilization's rise and fall.

Renfrew's theory resembles another currently rather neglected theory, also formulated in 1972, by two Harvard paleontologists—Niles Eldredge and Steven Jay Gould. Gould may be better known to readers because of his books popularizing geology, paleontology, and natural science research in general. But both scientists concluded, by studying the fossil record of trilobites and snails and analyzing the dynamics of their development and morphological transformations, that there was no such thing as a gradualist evolutionary development. They proposed a new theory—or rather, a new view of the theory of evolution: that it proceeds

Fig. 2.6. A set of mummification pottery with preserved remains of beetles dating to the reign of Pepy I. Abusir, tomb of Inti. (M. Bárta)

in leaps. In invertebrates, a species cycle would typically take five to ten million years, while specialization changes would usually occur within a rough interval of five to fifty thousand years, and the system leaps through those time frames. This is the root of Eldredge and Gould's theory of punctuated equilibria.[29]

This theory is no longer a part of the current discourse in evolutionary biology, mainly because it ignores symbiotic events (hereditary transfer of part or all of the genome).[30] But, like Renfrew's work, it is interesting to the study of the Old Kingdom and Egyptian history because it postulates that change takes place in leaps, not in gradual progression. Renfrew's multiplier effect theory takes a similar approach. This is Eldredge and Gould's greatest contribution to the philosophy of the dynamics of long-term processes: their thesis of variable velocity of diachronic development (development in time), which is punctuated by leap moments separated by long periods of sustained development as if free of any fundamental shifts. This idea is crucial to understanding processes that for thousands of years governed the voyage of individual societies, cultures, and civilizations through time.

When studying the mechanism of the development of any society—not only its collapse—the principle of punctuated equilibria explains how the system moves from one developmental stage to another. Historical development is not linear and does not change at a constant rate; it happens in leaps. A period of uneventful stasis is followed by abrupt fundamental changes when all of Renfrew's subsystems interact.

The archaeologist and the historian should be in pursuit of the zeitgeist, the spirit of the age, which unites the community in question and sets it apart from what came before and what came after. Continuity and innovation, permanence and change, uniqueness and commonness are integral aspects of the orientation of a modern scientist in time and space in a world of defunct civilizations and cultures (and of those that still cling to life). The angle of view, range of knowledge, and preferences of the scientist are also important. We cannot succeed in understanding a society without synergy between nature and social sciences, and the archaeologist and historian must take into account all possible subsystems that together make up that society—or, more specifically, how and when these subsystems interact.

Based on the theory of punctuated equilibria, major turning points can be identified in Egypt in the third millennium BC, which we will now look at in detail. We will consider dividing the history of Egypt during the Early Dynastic Period and the Old Kingdom into stages based not on Manethonic dynasties, but on fundamental transformations within the society of the day. These periods had their rulers, of course, and we will see that the individual has always played a significant role, some to such an extent that they changed the course of history (although only when born into a context with a strong potential for change).

3 The Pharaohs and the Rising State

THIS AND THE NEXT FOUR CHAPTERS will consider the course and major features of the history of Egypt in the third millennium BC.[1] According to traditional scholarship, the third millennium saw several defining moments: the unification of Upper and Lower Egypt, the accession of King Netjerykhet Djoser to the throne at the beginning of the Third Dynasty, the beginning of the Fourth Dynasty and the reign of Sneferu, the transition between the Fourth and Fifth Dynasty, the reign of Niuserre, the late Fifth Dynasty reigns of Djedkare and Unas, the reign of Pepy I of the Sixth Dynasty, and finally the end of the Sixth—or, perhaps more important, the Eighth—Dynasty. This marked the beginning of a dramatic decline in the complexity of the ancient Egyptian state and its disintegration into smaller, largely separate entities, which signified the end of the first unified state in the history of ancient Egypt.[2]

The centuries-long process outlined above was not a linear sequence of historical events or singular personal achievements: this period saw real changes in the nature and character of Egyptian society and state, and evidence gleaned from archaeology, literature, and the natural sciences suggests that these changes followed a pattern of punctuated equilibria. The evidence allows us to pinpoint major turning points that shaped and changed society in the third millennium.

In doing so, we will focus on periods when major changes took place, typically in a leap-wise fashion. Nevertheless, the traditional dynasties may be shown not to be wholly without value. Our understanding of these has relied significantly on the writings of an Egyptian priest called Manetho, from Sebennytus in the Nile Delta, who compiled a history of ancient Egypt for the early Ptolemaic rulers.[3] And it is possible that Manetho's sources really did reflect the way the ancient Egyptians perceived the significant events of their time rather than simply transitions between royal lineages.

Changing Perspectives of the Period

This book proposes the following periodization of third-millennium BC Egypt, based on points at which significant changes may be detected:

1. The beginning of the First Dynasty and the accession of Narmer, who unified Upper and Lower Egypt into one state, followed by Hor-Aha.
2. Rule of King Den in the middle of the First Dynasty, when he carried out a fundamental administrative transformation of the country, removed the political elites in Nubia, and made important strategic decisions that changed Egypt's relations with the Near East.
3. The beginning of the Second Dynasty, when Hetepsekhemwy had to pacify both lands of Upper and Lower Egypt again as a consequence of political instability at the end of the First Dynasty.
4. The beginning of the Third Dynasty and the rule of King Djoser, during which the development of script was completed, the state administration grew substantially more complex, and the first monumental stone tomb complex was built.
5. The period of the reigns of Kings Shepseskaf and Userkaf at the end of the Fourth and beginning of the Fifth Dynasty, marked by the rise of nonroyal officials to the highest levels of state bureaucracy and by many other related changes taking place in religion, art, architecture, and state administration.
5. The reign of King Niuserre, which saw a democratization of the afterlife, an expansion of the power and influence of nonroyal officials, and a rise in the importance of nepotism.

6. The reign of Kings Djedkare and Unas toward the close of the Fifth Dynasty and the introduction of essential reforms, especially in the sphere of the symbolic presentation of the king.

7. The reign of King Pepy I, when the status of the center and the provinces changed fundamentally.

8. The final phase of the reign of Pepy II, whom most scholars consider to be the last ruler of the Old Kingdom.

9. The gradual decline of the Old Kingdom form of government and state during the Seventh and Eighth Dynasties.

Of course, it is not possible to separate one historical era from the next with surgical precision. After all, several millennia separate us from the Early Dynastic Period (First to Second Dynasties) and the Old Kingdom (Third to Eighth Dynasties). What is more relevant is that despite the progress made by contemporary multidisciplinary Egyptology, we still cannot identify all the reasons for these changes (granted that this is a problem all historians face).

Here we will try to demonstrate that in every turning point defined along the punctuated equilibria model, there is much evidence that sudden changes in the Old Kingdom were critical and numerous, and affected many aspects of ancient Egyptian society, from administration and religion to monumental architecture—with its symbolic forms that often represent the basic pillars of the society's ideology and organization—and finally, to the level of material culture. Monumental architecture in particular—royal and nonroyal—is significant and characteristic of the specific context and development of ancient Egyptian society, and as such it will also be frequently used in this study. Hence the German term *Architektur der Macht*—'architecture of power.'[4]

It should be noted that there is a relative paucity of evidence from the First and Second Dynasties. We must therefore rely more heavily on architecture, together with the meager written sources (mostly title sequences of individual officials) to identify the ground-breaking changes in the development of the ancient Egyptian state and society during this period.

One might object that changes may only *appear* to take place at a particular time because we have incomplete archaeological and historical evidence: there may be a lack of data for the periods before and after the moment we have identified as the point when the equilibrium was disturbed. While this is always a possibility, it does not seem likely to apply to Egypt in the third millennium BC, as most of this period is relatively well known and the general picture has not yet been changed by discoveries made in recent years. This does not mean, of course, that we cannot expect any modifications in the future.

White Walls

Around the end of the fourth millennium BC, it is generally agreed that the region from the First Cataract in the south to the Mediterranean Sea in the north was controlled by a single chieftain of Thinis (near modern Girga).[5] This was a moment when essential decisions had to be made, whose impact on the geopolitical and economic situation was immediate and substantial.

The location of the then-capital of Upper Egypt, Thinis, was impractical in terms of controlling the northern part of Egypt, as well as its economic flows, administration, and foreign trade. As a result, a new capital was established for unified Egypt in the region lying east of the present-day pyramid fields of Abusir and Saqqara. It was given the name 'White Walls' (in ancient Egyptian *inbw-ḥḏ*, the first phase of the city classically called Memphis, nowadays believed to have been near the modern village at Kom Fakhry in Mit Rahina). We know it existed some two or three generations before the unification of the country, as attested by a rock inscription in Wadi Ameyra, Sinai, dating to the period of the Predynastic ruler Iry-Hor.[6] The shifting of the capital led to a major leap in the quality and sophistication of the way in which the country was administered.

The town-like agglomeration—or this is at least what we Egyptologists tacitly suppose—was situated west of the main river channel of the Nile, where it became the heart of the unified state. Later tradition, as preserved by Manetho, had it that the town was founded by a King Menes, who is sometimes considered to be identical to Hor-Aha (see further below).[7] According to Manetho, it was Menes who diverted the flow of the Nile to allow a city to be built on the reclaimed land, strategically located on the border between Upper and Lower Egypt. The

Fig. 3.1. The White Walls of Memphis probably originally referred to the white cliffs of the North Saqqara cemetery. (M. Bárta)

most recent paleohydrological study of the Nile riverbed suggests that the individual distributaries of the Nile started branching exactly around White Walls and that this was where the Nile Delta began in the earliest times, some twenty-five kilometers south of the modern division.[8]

The name 'White Walls' presents an interesting uncertainty. It could imply a single meaning or several simultaneous ones. The toponym definitely referred to a clearly delineated area, probably a smaller fortified settlement or citadel, surrounded by an extensive and largely agricultural settlement. The walls would presumably have been built of mud bricks and plastered white. But the name may also have reflected the fact that the settlement was founded by rulers from Hierakonpolis, in Upper Egypt, traditionally depicted wearing the White Crown. The name would thereby have expressed the supremacy of Upper Egypt in the region and been visible symbolic proof of the outcome of the battles for unification. If that is the case, it might have been Iry-Hor of Upper Egypt—or an even earlier king—who ordered the city to be built, possibly to exercise some kind of supervision over the Nile Delta. The name may also have referred to the naturally white limestone plateaus of North Saqqara, where the tombs of the governors appointed by the Upper Egyptian rulers were later located and which must have been an impressive sight when observed from the valley.

The broader archaeological context of the city's origin is important as well. As far as is known, there was no earlier settlement in the immediate vicinity. Meanwhile on the eastern bank, although no settlement has yet been found, the Egyptian archaeologist Zaki Youssef Saad (1901–82) explored a necropolis at Helwan from 1942 to 1954. The locality contained more than ten thousand graves.[9] This important cemetery has since been further excavated and studied by an Australian expedition led by Christiana Köhler.[10] It is only now that the importance of these finds can be fully understood in the context of other archaeological discoveries made around Abusir and Saqqara.

The vast majority of the Helwan tombs are simple pit graves approached from the surface by stairs cut into the bedrock. There were only a few dozen richer tombs with more spacious subterranean areas and limestone components, such as ceiling blocks and lined burial chambers. The tombs differed on the surface, too—their elevated parts were made of mud bricks and were decorated with the palace façade motif (niching). The built-up area of the tombs (250–400 m^2) also suggests that they were primarily built for persons of relatively low status. At Saqqara, the tombs cover areas of more than 600 m^2 and some an area of more than 1,000 m^2.

Very little can be said about the social status of the owners of the Helwan tombs, which would have been important testimony in view of the growing social complexity of the then-capital city and its environs. All we know through archaeological excavation is this: some fifty tombs were originally equipped with stelae showing the owner of a tomb sitting before an offering table. An important part of each stela's decoration consisted of the owner's name and titles. Although several dozen stelae have been preserved, only a few are in a good condition. Men's tombs outnumbered those of women by approximately 2:1. An interesting finding was that two of the women bore the title of Royal Daughter. In the other women's tombs, the titles have not been preserved; we can

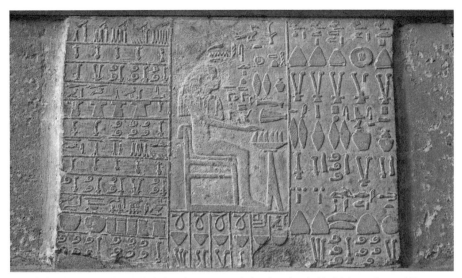

Fig. 3.2. So-called ceiling stela belonging to a royal daughter buried in Helwan, Second Dynasty. Egyptian Museum, Cairo. (M. Bárta)

only assume that the interred were the wives of officials, women of the royal court, or women of the harem. In any case, the number of socially significant women's tombs (judging by the sheer size of the tombs, their structure, and their position in the cemetery) is high, especially compared to the cemetery at Saqqara from the same period. More titles were listed in the tombs of men: one was a prince and the son of a king, two others were court officials, four were artisans, and the same number were priests. But on the whole, the record is sparse.[11]

There are fewer sources than one would wish to reconstruct the history of the First Dynasty. Indeed, as late as 1895 Egyptologists had no inkling that ancient Egypt existed before the reign of King Sneferu at the beginning of the Fourth Dynasty. The reason was simply the absence of sources.[12]

Yet that was the time when the solid foundations of the political system and administration of the ancient Egyptian state were laid.[13] We owe much to seal impressions from the tombs at the cemetery of Umm al-Qaab at Abydos, in particular those dated to the reigns of Kings Den and Qaa. Thanks to these seals, we know the sequence of the First Dynasty kings. There were eight altogether, who seem to have ruled for some 170 years in total. The first ruler of unified Egypt was apparently Narmer, followed by Hor-Aha, Djer, Djet, Den, Anedjib, Semerkhet, and Qaa.

Catfish on the Throne

Based on his monumental palette from Hierakonpolis (see below), King Narmer has generally been regarded as the first ruler of unified Egypt. His name was written as the hieroglyphic sign for catfish *(n'r)* and the sign for a hoe *(mr)*. According to tradition, Narmer, also referred to as 'Menes,' the 'unifier' of Egypt, came from Thinis, the capital of Upper Egyptian rulers.[14] Narmer's reign is also documented by monuments bearing his name in several sites lying to the northeast of Egypt—Arad, Nahal Tillah, and Tell Erani—and at several places in the Egyptian Delta and southern Egypt.[15] Until the time of Den, the Egyptians apparently secured physical control of trade with the Near East by maintaining their own small trading outposts in southern Palestine. King Narmer seems to have been regarded by his successors as the founder of their line, as indicated by the seal of King Qaa mentioned above, which was discovered by a German expedition in Umm al-Qaab.[16] It is curious that not a single monument bearing the name of Narmer, apparently the first ruler of unified Egypt, has been found in Memphis, unless we count a jar coming from the subterranean part of Djoser's pyramid complex.[17]

A unique monument from Narmer's time has survived: the Narmer Palette found in Hierakonpolis.[18] It depicts the main pillars of Egyptian royal dogma and iconography but dates from a period when temples and sacred precincts were not yet decorated with reliefs on stone walls. A large part of temple decoration may have been movable, like this palette. It was found in 1898 in what is known as the Main Deposit in the much-rebuilt temple of the god Horus at Hierakonpolis. Common practice in ancient Egyptian temples was that from time to time, older, disused items would be removed from shrines and buried with reverence because they had been dedicated to the god and never lost their divine nature. This was the fate of the Narmer Palette and many other valuable artifacts.[19]

The 63.5-cm-high palette is made of greyish siltstone and adorned on both the obverse and reverse sides. At the top of each side is a decoration featuring the goddess Bat, with two cow heads with horns curved inward. Bat later merged with Hathor due to their similar nature and primary

Fig. 3.3. (a and b) Recto and verso of the Narmer palette from Hierakonpolis. (S. Vannini, Laboratoriorosso)

status as mother of the king. Perhaps equally important was that they were considered to symbolize the sky. The obverse of the palette is dominated by two serpopards, mythical animals with the long necks of snakes or giraffes and the bodies and heads of leopards; two men are reining in the animals. This is a typical Near Eastern motif borrowed by Egyptian iconography. In the middle of the palette, the necks of the serpopards form a circle inside which cosmetics powder was supposed to be ground, although the more decorated palettes are thought to have been given as offerings and never used. The register above the animals shows the king walking out of his palace. The palace is depicted on the very left as a rectangular building. The king's sandal-bearer strides behind the king; in front of the king there is first a man—possibly the vizier—and then, on the right, four standard-bearers. The king is barefoot, which may indicate that he is walking on sacred soil. He is wearing a short kilt and the Red Crown of Lower Egypt. In his right hand he holds a scourge, in his left a mace.

On the left proper is a scene composed of several elements. There are two vertical rows of five bound captives each with their severed head lying between their feet. A sickle-shaped boat hovers above them, above which is a falcon holding a harpoon. To its left, next to one leaf of a double-leaved door, there is another bird—maybe a plover. The palette is topped with depictions of two bovine heads, symbolizing Bat. Between them there is the motif of the palace façade containing Narmer's name. The bottom part of the palette has a depiction of a bull, the personification of the king, demolishing the walls of a settlement with his horns. The settlement has an oval ground plan. In its middle there is a rectangular mound with two protrusions—perhaps a central construction, perhaps a temple precinct? The inhabitants of the conquered settlement are being trampled under the bull's hooves.

The reverse side of the palette is dominated by the standing king wearing a kilt reaching above his knees and adorned with a bull's tail. On his head he has the White Crown generally associated with Upper Egypt.[20] Behind him, depicted on a much smaller scale, is the sandal-bearer. The ruler is again barefoot. In his right hand he is wielding his mace and with his left he is clutching the hair of a subdued Asiatic whose skull he is about to crush. Above the captive there is the symbol of the Delta papyrus thicket, again with the head of a northerner—indicating Lower Egyptian affiliation—held on a rope by the god Horus in his falcon form. The top part of the palette is identical with the obverse. The bottom part contains a depiction of a pair of slaughtered northerners, each accompanied by a hieroglyphic symbol, which may indicate their place of origin.

For many decades, Egyptologists have been obsessed with finding the specific meaning of the individual scenes on the palette, although the literal interpretation is currently taking a back seat. It seems increasingly likely that this was not a depiction of one or more specific historical events, but rather a timeless message pointing to the symbolic status of the ruler and his role in maintaining divine order and driving off the forces of chaos.[21] David O'Connor has expressed the view that the palette contains not only a timeless message, but also a very specific testimony about certain religious ideas existing in Narmer's time.[22] Diana Patch has noted that the image of Narmer wearing the Upper Egyptian crown and especially the kilt and amulet in the shape of a swallow, and the symbolic elements such as the Nile Delta papyrus thicket and net patterns, correspond with a later tradition relating to the daily rebirth of the sun god Re.[23] While it is true that evidence of Re in this period is lacking, here these could simply be references to a solar deity.

Moreover, she suggests that the Red Crown may not refer to Lower Egypt here, but because of its color might evoke the image of glittering light or the blush of dawn, or the atmosphere of a bloody predawn battle.[24] In her study, Patch mentions a scene similar to the one on the Narmer Palette, albeit hailing from a much later period: the barque of the sun god Re floating in the morning through a double-winged door into this world.[25] In this sense, the boat in the Narmer Palette could be interpreted as the sun barque entering a new day with the help of the king, who is slaying the enemies of Re (the two rows of beheaded captives), who in later tradition are also decapitated. In any case, there is no doubt that the palette is imbued with timeless symbolic and religious meaning referring to basic traits of nascent Egyptian kingship.

Thus, at the very beginning of the unified state, we see sophisticated iconography (probably developed earlier, during the Predynastic era) that was later elaborated in the symbolic world of the ancient Egyptians. The ruler crushing the heads of enemies stands out very distinctly in the Narmer Palette, and this iconic expression of the sovereign authority of the ruler and the cosmic force of *maat* continues to appear, for example, on temple façades through Greco-Roman times.

The Reformer King

The Egyptian ruler bearing the name Den may be seen as one of the outstanding figures of ancient Egyptian history. He reigned in about the middle of the First Dynasty and seems to have radically changed the administration, collection of taxes, foreign policy, and aspects of religious practice, reflected especially in the construction of tombs of the elite. Unfortunately, as with the Early Dynastic Period in general, we have far less information about his reign than we would like.

What we do know is that his predecessor-but-one, Djer, had realized certain preconditions for the reforms that Den later implemented. We also know that during Djer's reign a large military campaign took place that eliminated the A-Group elite, thus suppressing a dangerous political opponent on Egypt's southern border. The famous Gebel Sheikh Suleiman relief, from the region of the Second Cataract, depicts Nubian captives. At the same time, the two toponyms featuring prominently on the rock suggest that Djer was assisted by two important cities of Upper Egypt: Hierakonpolis and Naqada.[26]

As for the political history of Den's rule, we know that he set out against the 'archers,' as the Nubians were then called, to the land south of the First Cataract and was instrumental in finally bringing peace to the region. Meanwhile, the former Egyptian trading colonies in the region of present-day Palestine and Israel had apparently ceased to exist, and the Egyptians had withdrawn to their home territories.[27] This may have happened under the pressure of growing urban civilizations and the organized nature of the society in this area. The Palermo Stone contains the oldest mention of the existence of the sacred bull Apis kept in the capital city. Among Den's reforms were the foundation of farms in the northwestern part of the Delta and a population census of the eastern Delta.

It may have become evident during his reign that Egypt's booming administration of the country required basic reform to be effective. The state was expanding in many ways, which placed increasing demands on the state administrators and officials. At the same time, it was necessary to carry out essential changes to the way the state administration was managed. It appears that Den succeeded in all these steps.[28] He reorganized the royal court so that it, and therefore the whole country, was sustained by three basic pillars. The first was the administrative department in charge of organizing and recording the delivery of hunted game to the court; the second was the scribes' office; and the third was the department responsible for the households of the princes and royal wives. Den also founded a permanent residential palace that included the royal office, *pr-nsw*, with its most important department—the royal treasury. One significant consequence of the reforms was that individual members of the royal family ceased to run independent households and were instead placed under a unified system that supplied the royal court and its members.

The settlements surrounding the court provided a wealth of agricultural products for the members of the royal family and for the officials—both high-ranking royals and a small number of commoners.

The philosophy of managing and providing supplies to the court was highly innovative. Provisioning was concentrated in departments with specialized functions—*ḥwt* in ancient Egyptian. To our knowledge, there were at least seventeen such units. There were the departments of 'the two pots' with an attached pig-slaughtering facility, a leather- and shoe-making department, departments of scribes, weavers, gardeners, matting, fine textiles, gold, flax, bread, and others. The names show that the tasks of the individual departments were clearly defined. The activities were coordinated by an official bearing the title Inspector of the Royal House (*ḥrp-ꜥḥ pr-ꜥꜣ*) who was subordinated to the highest-ranking prince. The royal court also employed artisans, personal servants, dog guards, keepers of the seal (who controlled the flow and amount of goods to which they attached royal seals), butchers, supervisors, and dwarves. It was probably from these groups that the unfortunate individuals were recruited to be put to death with their master in the 'secondary graves' of the Abydos cemetery.[29]

The activities of the departments were organized by the Treasury, which controlled all departmental economic processes, especially the recording of all goods entering and leaving the system. The Treasury redistributed the goods among the king and his court, the high officials, and the provinces, as well as using them to pay workers hired for state-sponsored projects. The fact that the oldest known evidence relating to the Treasury comes from Den's reign suggests that he was the founder of this institution, which for thousands of years would be the hub of the ancient Egyptian redistribution and taxation system. The oldest evidence for the Treasury is the title Overseer of the White House.[30] The terms 'White House' and 'Red House' were used interchangeably during several dynasties as an apparently generic term meaning 'treasury,' before the term 'White House' came into common use.

An important component of the king's entourage was the group of 'friends' (*smrw*) assigned to provide personal services to the king. These assistants must initially have been appointed from among members of the royal family, given the sensitive nature of the service and the vital information to which they may have had access. It was not until much later, toward the close of the Fourth Dynasty, that posts in the closest vicinity of the ruler came to be held by individuals of nonroyal descent.[31]

The outcome of the reforms during Den's reign was a large rise in the number of officials, and thus also of nonroyal tombs. The foundation of a new cemetery in Abu Rawash also seems to have been partly a consequence of the growing number of people at the royal court and in the state. Around thirty officials' tombs are known from this period at this cemetery.[32]

The royal title *nsw-biti* (The One Who Belongs to the Sedge and the Bee) is often assumed to denote Upper and Lower Egypt, but the meaning is probably more complex than this. It appeared for the first time during Den's rule, and according to contemporary interpretations it seems likely that both elements referred in a specific way to the person of the ruling king.[33] The attributes of the ancient Egyptian ruler were expressed by, among other things, the royal titulary, which eventually comprised five names denoting various aspects of the king's divine rule over Egypt. They included the name of the god Horus (Horus, the falcon, was the protector of the king on earth), which was the oldest documented regnal name placed in a *serekh*—a rectangle standing on its short side, with the bottom part filled with an adornment resembling the niched façade of a royal palace and upper part containing the regnal name. It was surmounted by a falcon, Horus. The second regnal name was the *nsw-biti*, with the third, found from the Fifth Dynasty onward, *s3-R^c* (Son of the God Re; the sun god was the most important god of the latter part of the Old Kingdom and, simultaneously, the symbolic divine father of the earthly king). The fourth was the *biti nbti* (Of the Two Ladies; the king was also under the protection of the major heraldic goddesses of Upper and Lower Egypt, Nekhbet and Wadjet), and the fifth was the *Ḥr/bik-nbw* (Golden Horus/falcon), of uncertain meaning and import.[34]

The title *nsw-biti* symbolized the ruling king and his extraordinary position in both parts of the unified country. One of the highest-ranking court officials, the king's secretary and Keeper of the Royal Seal, was titled *ḥtmw-biti* (Sealer of the King, or "Chancellor"). The title was of Upper Egyptian origin and its roots undoubtedly lie in the victory of the Upper Egyptian rulers at the time of the unification battles.[35]

The royal seal was immensely important because it represented the confirmation of a royal decision or control. Available sources suggest that the function of the bearer of this office was probably similar to that of chancellors of European feudal monarchs. A typical example would be Jan IX of Středa, who served the Holy Roman Emperor Charles IV. It is not without interest that after the death of the emperor, his seal was broken in two to mark the end of the chancellor's authority, and that the chancellery itself was closed. Other titles documented from the time of Den onward are ꜥḏ-mr and ḥrp, which refer to the officials overseeing the operation of farms in the Delta that fell under central administration.[36] Den is also the ruler under whom Egypt was divided into individual nomes or provinces.[37]

Den's title nsw-bity also has important and straightforward political connotations. It may indicate that during his reign both Upper and Lower Egypt were brought under real political and economic control. It appears that originally the two components of this regnal name were independent and referred to the chieftain (later king) being the most notable and prominent of the elite.[38] It is important to note in this context that the oldest known evidence of the iconographic Double Crown— the White Crown of Upper Egypt and the Red Crown of Lower Egypt merged into one—dates from Den's reign, providing further evidence that it was during his time that Egypt became a truly united country, with all the associated consequences.[39]

Den was no doubt a great statesman and apparently ruled long enough to enforce all the new measures. A fragment of a limestone vessel from Den's tomb in Umm al-Qaab has an inscription that confirms that the king celebrated a second sed festival.[40] This was one of the most significant festivals connected with a king.[41] It traditionally took place after thirty years of reign and served as a ritual regeneration of the king's vitality and physical powers. The king thus demonstrated symbolically that he remained fit and able to rule his people.

Den was buried at the traditional royal cemetery at Abydos. His tomb is the most complex construction project of the entire First Dynasty.[42] It also contains further key evidence that this era was groundbreaking in many ways, including in relation to technology, architecture, and symbolism. As with earlier kings' burials at the site, Den's tomb was constructed at the bottom of a large pit dug six meters below the ground level of the surrounding terrain, but it incorporated many innovations. The side walls of the pit were lined with mud brick covered with matting. The

Fig. 3.4. Tomb of Den in Abydos, Umm al-Qaab, with clearly marked shaft tombs for the entourage of the king. (M. Bárta)

burial chamber was enormous: the ground plan measured 9 × 15 m, and the floor was paved with meticulously laid stone blocks of red and black granite. This is the oldest evidence of an architectural use of such a hard stone. The middle of the burial chamber contained a wooden structure measuring 12 × 6 × 3 m, which concealed the royal burial. Originally, dozens of imported jars were placed around this structure.

A key innovation in the tomb's architecture was the descending entrance corridor to the burial chamber from the east. The entrance to the chamber itself was blocked by a large limestone block (which served as a portcullis). This technical solution allowed a far-reaching change in the construction of royal tombs and funerary preparations. In previous royal tombs the aboveground parts of the tomb could only be completed after the actual burial of the king, but thanks to Den's architect a new practice was adopted, making the burial chamber accessible via a roofed stairway. The remaining part of the tomb, including aboveground structures, could thus be completed independently of the time of the burial.[43]

Another new component to Den's tomb was a southwestern extension connecting the underground part of the tomb with the surrounding terrain via a separate stairway that led to the desert surface. This extension contained a room that once sheltered a seated royal statue, perhaps symbolizing the reborn king. At the end of the rebirth ritual, which took place inside the tomb, the king would have departed through here, via the west-facing stairway, to join the Egyptian gods in the afterlife. In the specific topography of the Abydos cemetery this would have meant setting out for the large valley, the 'Great Wadi,' in a southwest direction. In the minds of the ancient Egyptians, this valley, enclosed on both sides by a high rock massif, may have conveyed the impression of the heavenly horizon, the *akhet*, where they believed the sun 'died.' The sun was then reborn at the break of dawn on the eastern horizon.

This belief probably originated not later than the rule of King Djer as, starting with his tomb, the royal tombs in Abydos have a vacant space in the southwestern corner, without subsidiary burials, to secure the uninterrupted departure of the king for the western horizon. It is thus probably not by chance that for thousands of years it was Djer's tomb that, in ancient Egypt, was considered the place of the burial and subsequent cult of the god Osiris.[44] And it is this never-ending cycle of dying and rebirth that may be reflected in the Narmer Palette described above.

One of the outstanding monuments dating to Den's era is Saqqara tomb S 3035, which belonged to the chancellor Hemaka. This tomb exemplifies the progress Egypt had made under Den's rule.[45] The base of the tomb measured 57.30 × 26 m and the aboveground construction had forty-five storage areas for diverse funerary equipment. Once the tomb was completed and its owner laid in the burial chamber, most of the stores were no longer accessible. The discovered funerary equipment that deserves mention here includes small disks made of stone, copper, and ivory; game pieces; weapons (arrows); and tags with inscriptions of the names of King Den and his predecessor Djer, important evidence of the symbolic world of the time. There were also remnants of textiles, wooden cabinets, stone and ceramic vessels, and seal imprints. The external brick walls of the tomb were adorned with niches imitating a palace and implying the idea of eternal residence in the afterlife. The most important individual finds include a papyrus scroll that, though unused, is a clear indication that Egypt was already a civilization with a developed system of writing. No similar early document has, however, been found so far.

A stairway led from the east to a burial chamber measuring 9.50 × 4.90 m. It was closed in three places with large limestone blocks. Despite this obstacle, the burial chamber was apparently robbed in ancient times. The chamber was oriented south–north and lay almost twelve meters below the ground. Remnants of two limestone pillars designed to support the chamber's ceiling structure were found inside. This represents the earliest evidence of building stone used in a nonroyal tomb. The walls of the room were meticulously plastered and still contained pitiful remains of Hemaka's body when the chamber was entered in modern times.

Slaughtered Servants?

The tomb complex of King Den, like that of the other burials of First Dynasty rulers at Abydos, includes a remarkable component: the so-called subsidiary burials. The custom of burying servants, apparently killed or obliged to kill themselves after the monarch's death, is demonstrated by some 130 burials arranged in double or triple rows along the perimeter of the king's tomb.

In this, Den followed a tradition introduced by Hor-Aha, if not earlier. Hor-Aha's tomb was surrounded by three rows of 36 burials. For Queen Merneit there were 41, for Djer 318 (and an additional 269 secondary burials around his funerary enclosure), Djet 174, Anedjib 64, Semerkhet 68, and Qaa 26. It is evident that the number of sacrificed individuals declined during the First Dynasty. During the Second Dynasty the custom disappeared altogether: only in Khasekhemwy's tomb was at least one buried servant found. Subsidiary human burials were usually placed in brick-lined pits arranged in regular rows and containing the remains of mostly young men, twenty to twenty-five years old. It has still not been satisfactorily proven that the people were all put to death at once, at the time of the ruler's funeral.[46]

Some iconographic evidence of ritual sacrifice during the First Dynasty, including a small ebony tag formerly attached to an oil jar, was found in the tomb of the chancellor Hemaka at Saqqara.[47] The engraved surface is divided into three horizontal registers. The purpose of the scenes was to demonstrate some of the ritual episodes that were important for the ruler and his court. Generally, they depict processions of servants bearing gifts and oblations that were probably connected with funeral activities. From our perspective, the top register is the most important. On the extreme right, just under the opening where the heraldic plants of Upper and Lower Egypt—lotus and papyrus—were attached, there is a hieroglyphic sign meaning 'to accept.' Below the sign there is a pair of men. The one on the left is plunging a long object into the torso of the other, whose arms are bound behind his back. The first man is holding a bowl in his left hand, probably to catch the blood. Further to the left there is a procession of men carrying (from right to left): a lance, a bird (ibis?), a catfish, a statue in the form of a mummy (or Osiris? although he is not otherwise attested before the end of the Fifth Dynasty), and at the end of the group there is a man holding an unidentified object (ladder? large censer?). On the extreme left there is the *serekh* of King Djer with Horus on top, facing right, receiving the whole procession. Other such scenes of the sacrifice of captives are known from this time.[48]

This was not, however, a new custom created for royal funerals. Evidence of sacrificial burials comes from cemeteries in Naqada and Hierakonpolis, and from the Western Cemetery in Adaima. The practice is also known to have existed in other cultures, for example at the 'Death Pits' of the roughly contemporary third-millennium royal tombs at Ur in Mesopotamia, in the Kerma Culture of Sudan (2500 to 1500 BC), and in the Chinese Shang Dynasty (1600 to 1046 BC), as well as in the more recent suttee ritual in India. It is usually assumed that ritual human sacrifice was practiced in the early stages of states, when ritual death was meant to eliminate violence, strengthen the ruling ideology, and secure a specific social status in the next world for those killed in this way.[49]

The First Crisis of the Unified State

The state continued to develop after the long and successful reign of King Den, but there was growing potential for conflict, which finally broke out at the end of the First and beginning of the Second Dynasty. The proof is in the name of the Second Dynasty king Hetepsekhemwy—'The One Who Reconciles the Two Powers.' This has been taken to indicate that at the beginning of his reign the new king had to reunify Upper and Lower Egypt.[50]

Den had been succeeded by Anedjib, who is generally remembered because tomb S 3038, belonging to a high official, was built at Saqqara during his reign. The stepped form of the inner casing over its burial chamber has been cited as a precursor of the Step Pyramid (see chapter four). The reign of Semerkhet, the dynasty's penultimate ruler, was short, while Qaa, its last king, celebrated two *sed* festivals and thus apparently ruled for quite a long time.[51] Evidence suggests that two ephemeral rulers followed Qaa, although they are not mentioned in any later Egyptian king lists and so may have been usurpers. They are known as Ba and Sneferka from material bearing the Horus names, although it has also been suggested that the latter might have been an alternate Horus name of King Qaa.[52] The presence of short-lived kinglets is, of course, potentially indicative of political instability.

As already noted, the first ruler of the Second Dynasty was Hetepsekhemwy. Seals bearing his name were found in the Abydos tomb of the last king of the First Dynasty, Qaa,[53] which suggests a smooth transition (and that there were in fact no intervening usurpers). As to why Manetho placed a dynastic division at this point, it could have been a break in the male line. Or perhaps the burial of the first three Second Dynasty kings at Saqqara reflects political instability: does the location of their tombs suggest that their rule was restricted to Lower Egypt? Alternatively, Hetepsekhemwy may have been guided by a need to balance the differences between Upper and Lower Egypt and therefore to be closer to the center of the state's political life. Whatever the reason for its location at Saqqara, his tomb manifests distinct changes in the concept of the royal grave.[54] Instead of a relative orientation on the basis of the local topography, as was the practice in Abydos, the tomb is formally oriented north–south. This can be deduced from its subterranean part, as the superstructure has not been preserved, the site having been overbuilt by the funerary complex of the Fifth Dynasty king Unas. The substructure was not built in an open pit in the tradition of the First Dynasty but was largely tunneled into the bedrock. Seals belonging to the owner of the tomb were found here, as were examples bearing the name of his successor, Raneb, suggesting that he carried out the funeral.

The site of Raneb's tomb remains unknown, but that of *his* successor, Ninetjer, is very well known.[55] It confirms that later Second Dynasty rulers preserved the changes to tomb architecture that Hetepsekhemwy had introduced, creating a subterranean palace of eternity, with bedrooms, banquet and reception halls, and even a toilet and a bathroom.[56]

Aside from details of innovations in tomb architecture, we know relatively little about the reigns of the first three Second Dynasty kings. It seems that in administration and religion, everything continued in line with the trends that started in the time of King Den. The political activities of Hetepsekhemwy, Raneb, and Nynetjer appear to have been limited to the region of Lower Egypt. After Nynetjer's death, Egypt evidently broke into its southern and northern parts and was ruled by several ephemeral kings such as Weneg, Sened, and Nubnefer. The end of the Second Dynasty was marked by the reigns of Peribsen and Khasekhem, who later changed his name to Khasekhemwy.[57]

In his Horus name, Peribsen replaced the protective figure of the god Horus in his *serekh* with the god Sutekh (Seth), who, equally with Horus, was considered the patron of Upper Egypt. Peribsen and his ultimate successor, Khasekhem(wy), withdrew to the south and had their tombs built at Abydos, in the traditional burial site of the First Dynasty kings. This may have been a symbolic gesture indicating the king's preference for Upper Egypt. It is not known why exactly Peribsen returned to the traditional burial ground at Abydos or why he explicitly demonstrated his close ties with the god Sutekh. But the fact that current evidence for this king is limited to Upper Egypt may be one reason for his veneration of this particular god.

The last Second Dynasty king, Khasekhem, began his reign with a Horus-*serekh*, but after changing his name to Khasekhemwy had *both* Horus and Sutekh placed on his *serekh*. That this may have been an act of reconciliation after a period of civil war is suggested by the records on two statues of Khasekhem from Hierakonpolis, which document the capture of 47,209 northern (Lower Egyptian) enemies.[58] Having presumably been victorious and restored the political unity of the two lands, the king extended his name to Khasekhemwy (The Two Powers Have Appeared), his *serekh* showing Sutekh with the Lower Egyptian crown and Horus with the Upper Egyptian crown or the Double Crown of Upper and Lower Egypt. Sometimes Sutekh has no crown at all. The king's name was also extended by the phrase 'The Two Lords [meaning Horus and Sutekh] Are at Peace in Him,' which reinforces the idea of post-conflict reconciliation. From then on, both gods were portrayed as protective deities of the king and were often depicted during his coronation and uniting the heraldic plants of the two lands.

Khasekhemwy had an impressive tomb built for himself at Abydos in the architectural style of the First Dynasty royal tombs, but with a linear layout reminiscent of the Saqqara tombs of the earlier part of the Second Dynasty.[59] The burial chamber was innovative in that it was faced with dressed limestone blocks. The tomb was associated with a large brick enclosure, known as Shunet al-Zebib. This was built close to the valley to serve as the sacred precinct during the funerary rites; similar enclosures had been built for most, if not all, of Khasekhemwy's predecessors, at both Abydos[60] and Saqqara,[61] but his was the last example of its kind.

Khasekhemwy is also known for his great construction projects in Hierakonpolis, where he had a temple built containing blocks of red granite with decoration and inscriptions,[62] as well as a large brick 'fort,' although it has been suggested that the latter was actually a funerary construction.[63] Two statues mentioned above were also found at the site.[64] A relatively recent analysis of the stone fragments from Hierakonpolis from his reign shows that two cult structures must have existed here—one was represented by the temple of Horus itself, the other apparently stood in the southeastern part of the 'fort,' near its entrance.[65]

Khasekhemwy's wife was named Nimaathap. Her son, according to Manetho, was the first ruler of the Third Dynasty—Netjerykhet Djoser. As the preceding pages suggest, not much changed in the development of state and society from the end of the First Dynasty through most of the Second. The only reliable evidence is monumental architecture and a few surviving written documents. It appears that after the death of King

Fig. 3.5. Red granite relief from the reign of Khasekhemwy, who reigned under the protection of both state divinities—Horus and Sutekh. Egyptian Museum, Cairo. (M. Bárta)

Den, there was no other significant figure until Khasekhemwy. But he laid the groundwork for the reign of his son to become a real milestone in the development of Egyptian civilization, which was recognized by the ancient Egyptians themselves.

It is clear that during this era there were at least four remarkable leaps that affected most aspects of society and of ideology: the beginning of the First Dynasty, the reign of King Den, the beginning of the Second Dynasty, and the end of the Second Dynasty under King Khasekhemwy. Each of these leaps was, however, immediately preceded by a period of increasing tension and gradual accumulation of potential for a major change, which then culminated in a specific event—a leap—which was then again followed by a longer period of stasis. This pattern will be frequently encountered in the Old Kingdom as well.

4 The Foundation of the Empire

NO VIEW OF THE OLD KINGDOM LANDSCAPE is more beautiful than the one from the top of the pyramid of Neferirkare at Abusir. If the weather is good, one can see the pyramids of Giza and the sun temples at Abu Ghurab to the north; and, to the south, the royal cemetery at Abusir, including the pyramid complex of King Raneferef; the southern part of the Abusir necropolis; the Saqqara burial ground, dominated by Djoser's funerary complex and accompanied by its younger siblings, the pyramids of Userkaf, Unas, and Teti; and finally the pyramids of South Saqqara and the two legendary pyramids of King Sneferu at Dahshur. All this from a single spot.

The apex of a pyramid is the symbol par excellence of ancient Egyptian civilization. This was the first place that was touched by the rays of the rising sun god Re. For ancient Egyptians this was a clear message that the sun god had fought his battle against the forces of evil in the netherworld and emerged victorious so that he could be (re)born on the eastern horizon. The pyramid, as such, was also the manifestation of the power and skill of the Egyptians of the third millennium BC, who from the Third to Fifth Dynasties developed a state that remains the symbol of civilization even now. It is Djoser's funerary complex, built by the legendary architect Imhotep, that marks the start of this glorious period, and it seems likely that the era's decline began with the end of the rule of King Niuserre, who was the last 'sun' ruler to be buried at Abusir and arguably one of the outstanding personalities of this time.

The Threshold of a New Era

The Third Dynasty was preceded by some three hundred years of Egypt as a unified nation, during which the country experienced different rates of change. There were key moments associated with the rulers Narmer, Den, Hetepsekhemwy, and Khasekhemwy when quick and substantial changes were felt across society and state. Unfortunately, we know far less than we would like about the Third Dynasty, whose character was shaped particularly by its first king, Netjerykhet, who later came to be known as Djoser.[1]

The time of King Djoser was marked by remarkable qualitative leaps in the fields of architecture (and thus technology) and writing, as well as in the administration and organization of the state. Djoser's reign is generally considered to mark the beginning of the Third Dynasty, though it is not entirely clear why. Preserved seals of Queen Nimaathap reveal that Djoser was her son, which also makes him the son of King Khasekhemwy. Seals in Khasekhemwy's tomb show that Djoser prepared his funeral at Abydos. Similarly, inscriptions made using the same technique appear on stone jars in the tombs of both kings, indicating that the vessels came from the same atelier for luxury goods. A vessel bearing Khasekhemwy's name was even found in the substructure of Djoser's mortuary complex at Saqqara. And one of the fragments from the temple or chapel that Djoser built in Heliopolis refers to Sutekh, the god that Khasekhemwy placed next to Horus as the head of the Egyptian pantheon.[2] The close relationship between Khasekhemwy and Djoser is also suggested by two seals in tomb K1 at Beit Khallaf cemetery: both seals have identical texts that refer to a "house of provisioning of the vineyards of Memphis," but one seal bears Djoser's name, the other Khasekhemwy's.[3]

Thus, in terms of the continuity of a royal lineage, there appears to be no reason to consider Djoser's reign to be the start of a new dynasty—perhaps with the exception that his reign marked a return of the royal cemetery to the Memphite region. But most historical sources, including the Palermo Stone and Turin Royal Canon, seem to mark out Djoser as the founder of a new era.[4] This may be explained only if we take into

Fig. 4.1. The pyramid complex of Djoser was built completely out of limestone, without any significant evolution of stone architecture before him. Saqqara. (M. Bárta)

consideration all his known achievements: looked at in that light, Djoser's influence and legacy overshadow all other Third Dynasty rulers.

Djoser's rule can be explored through the surviving material culture of his time. For example, the first documented sentence containing a verb dates to his reign.[5] The first known stone temples of that period were built at Heliopolis in the north, and Gebelein in the south. Djoser also left traces on Elephantine Island, where a large settlement already existed when he came to power, and sent expeditions to the Wadi Maghara region of Sinai from where the much-desired turquoise was imported.[6]

The Turin Canon records that Djoser reigned for nineteen years. The author of that papyrus has, most unusually, marked Djoser's name uniquely in red, presumably to indicate that something was fundamentally different about this ruler. Djoser's era does seem to be groundbreaking in many respects. It was Djoser who finally ended the tradition of burying rulers at Abydos and transferred the kingly necropolis definitively to the cemeteries of the capital city, White Walls. The move began an unprecedented expansion of the Saqqara cemeteries, as well as laying the groundwork for the emergence and expansion of later royal necropoleis at Dahshur, Zawyat al-Aryan, Abusir, Giza, and Abu Rawash. It is unclear what prompted Djoser do this, but it might have been the general geopolitical situation and an ambition to create a true royal capital for the unified state.

As noted in the previous chapter, Djoser's father appears to have had to fight a civil war against a Lower Egypt enemy to reunify the kingdom. The need to control the northern part of the country more effectively may have been one of the reasons to move the capital there—for both the living and the dead. Kinship matters may also have been a factor: according to Manetho, Djoser's family was connected to the Memphite region. Whatever lay behind the decision to transfer the royal residence to White Walls, it certainly had its benefits. Not least of these was that the ruler could physically attend to matters in the capital city, which was increasingly important in view of the growing complexity of the apparatus of the state, contacts with foreign lands, and the need for better supervision over Lower Egypt.

For example, there is unambiguous documented evidence that one of the first viziers in Egyptian history dates to the period of Djoser's reign. The term 'vizier' comes from Arabic; it designated an office like that of a modern prime minister and is therefore indicative of a more complex state administration. In ancient Egypt the vizier represented the ruler, and in practice the whole country was subordinated to him. In ancient Egyptian his title was *ʒiti ʒti (n) zʒb*.[7] The vizier in question was Kaimen, paradoxically not known from any stela or tomb, but from twenty-one inscriptions preserved on stone jars from the substructure of Djoser's complex in Saqqara.[8]

The builder of King Djoser's royal mortuary complex was the renowned Imhotep. A high royal official (perhaps of royal descent, though no evidence survives), Imhotep was an architect, a physician, and a Heliopolitan high priest of the sun god Re.[9] There are few documents dating to Imhotep's time and confirming his existence. One is the plinth of a statue of Djoser found near the southeastern corner of the king's mortuary complex.[10] The front part of the plinth bears the name of the king; to its left is a hieroglyphic inscription that reads:

Keeper of the Seal of the King of Upper Egypt,[11] Custodian of Royal Domains, Master of the Large Estate, Prince, High Priest of Heliopolis, Imhotep, Supervisor of Sculptors, Craftsmen, and Artisans making stone vessels.

The statue was probably first situated within a small cult area in the entrance to the complex. Although found as early as 1926, it continues to be the subject of debate.[12] There is also evidence of Imhotep's existence in the underground galleries of Djoser's complex: his title of Chief Lector Priest appears several times on stone vessels apparently donated by Imhotep to his king.[13]

Despite the enormous influence Imhotep unquestionably had on Egypt in his time, his career can only be reconstructed today using circumstantial evidence. Imhotep was probably already active as a builder at the end of the Second Dynasty, under Khasekhemwy, who was, as far as we know, the first ruler to give his architects small assignments for stone buildings. One such work was a shrine at Hierakonpolis built partly of red granite (see "The First Crisis of the Unified State" in chapter 3). But Imhotep's art reached its peak during the reigns of Djoser and his successor, Sekhemkhet.

The Architecture of Power

Ancient Egyptian monumental architecture—both its philosophy and its specific forms—often reveals valuable details about the character of its time. This certainly applies to King Djoser's pyramid complex at Saqqara, which is a unique monument surpassing anything that came before and to which no other Third Dynasty royal monument can compare. The monumental scale of its plan, the unparalleled forms and concepts, would suffice in themselves to justify the ancient Egyptian notion of Djoser as the founder of a new era.

The architect was Imhotep, who was also involved in the construction of Sekhemkhet's pyramid complex after Djoser's death.[14] Djoser's grand tomb was undoubtedly conceived to symbolize his eternal afterlife, where the king-god would meet with the other gods of the Egyptian pantheon. These meetings were depicted all around the pyramid complex, and particularly in the open court with its sanctuaries dedicated to the gods of

Upper and Lower Egypt.[15] The complex was even called "The Refreshment of the Gods."[16] Imhotep overcame numerous technical constraints when he decided to build the complex entirely of stone: small, regular limestone blocks were used in place of more traditional materials, such as brick, wood, reeds, and mats. This innovation is reflected in a Ramesside inscription that refers to Djoser as the "opener of stone."[17] The limestone blocks were still very small—the size of larger mud bricks. The architecture of the complex included three-quarter columns with trunks partly anchored in the masonry, as if the builders were concerned about letting the columns stand freely in space. The architect often replicated with stone the building methods typically used with wood and reeds.

This was the king's symbolic residence and at the same time the mortuary complex that his soul would dwell in after his death, and that priests and followers would visit. In the minds of the ancient Egyptians, this was the place where the terrestrial physical world met the transcendental world of the gods—the ancient Egyptian *axis mundi*. It is therefore no surprise that it was designed and built with such care, as were similar complexes built by Djoser's successors. These complexes guaranteed rulers' afterlife existence, their exit from the profane world and accession to the realm of Egyptian gods. The perfection and completion of the pyramid complexes had to guarantee that the earthly world created by the gods would continue and that *maat* would be preserved. *Maat* was a concept of the balanced cosmic order and of the divine and therefore legitimate ruler whose main task was to maintain justice, as well as a set of generally accepted norms of conduct and behavior.[18] As such, *maat* was the principal measure of law and cosmic order represented and maintained by the king on behalf of the god Re. For the king to be able to dwell there, the complex had to contain all (or at least most of) the elements that were a part of his earthly residence. The pyramid itself comprised a system of mostly independent architectonic entities with different but complementary functions.

The very existence of this pyramid complex is proof of Egypt's potential at the beginning of the Third Dynasty. It is also indicative of the consolidation of political circumstances of its time, and testifies to the intricately devised and multiple forms of ancient Egyptian religion, symbolism, and presentation of power and authority: the structure includes

Fig. 4.2. *Serdab* statue of Djoser from the Step Pyramid complex in Saqqara. Egyptian Museum, Cairo. (Archive of the Czech Institute of Egyptology, Charles University, M. Zemina)

stage sets for the celebration of religious holidays, buildings commemorating the unification of Upper and Lower Egypt, a mortuary temple for the afterlife cult of the king, an altar where offerings were presented to the sun god, and also the *serdab*, a sealed room with a statue of the king, seated and looking through narrow apertures toward the sky. This was analogous to the place in the royal tombs at Abydos through which the soul of the king left the tomb and departed for the world of the gods.

Djoser's huge complex is one of the main reasons that his reign is considered to be truly radical. It heralded the transition to symbolic stone architecture and singular monumentalization, when the individual architectural components began to speak in a clearer figurative language. And it is Djoser's pyramid complex that best illustrates these new features. Scholars of the complex have suggested that it was originally modeled on a primeval mound, reflecting earlier *mastaba* tombs, but that the design gradually expanded.[19] Then it fundamentally changed: the original idea was abandoned and the Step Pyramid was born. Many interpretations of this new form have been proposed, but which is correct? To judge from the later Pyramid Texts, the design may have been a staircase by which the ruler would ascend to the heavens. Or it may have been a mechanical repetition of earlier designs that comprised a single step or monumental primeval mound. One of the astronomical theories is based on the formal resemblance between the pyramid's stepped silhouette and the shape of the sun at sunrise and sunset under certain atmospheric conditions. Is the pyramid itself thus an early solar symbol?

Whatever the answer, Djoser's innovations determined the character of Egypt for several decades. Half a century later, the founder of the Fourth Dynasty would emerge and Egypt would take another great leap.

Lord of the Cosmic Order of *Maat*

Sneferu was the first king of the Fourth Dynasty, the unrivaled builder of Egyptian pyramids in the third millennium BC.[20] The beginning of this new dynasty probably marks a new royal lineage that lasted for about a century, as no evidence links Sneferu by blood with his predecessor, Huni.

Sneferu's mother may have been Queen Meresankh I, although this is not entirely certain.[21] Nor is the oft-repeated claim that Sneferu's wife was Hetepheres (I). Meresankh appears not to have been Huni's

Fig. 4.3. Stela of the 'Lord of Maat,' King Sneferu, from the Bent Pyramid temple in Dahshur. Egyptian Museum, Cairo. (M. Bárta)

principal royal wife, so Sneferu may have struggled to be seen as a legitimate king at the start of his reign (a problem which did arise at the end of the Fourth and the beginning of the Fifth Dynasty, as we will see in chapter 5). Hetepheres's title 'God's Daughter of His Body' may be taken to mean that she was a daughter of Huni. If that was the case, then Sneferu's marriage to her may have been a crucial way to cement his legitimacy. It has also been suggested that Hetepheres was the mother of Khufu, Sneferu's son and successor, because her tomb was found at Giza (G 7000x), and Khufu may have been responsible for the establishment of the deposit (without a corpse).

Sneferu's reign lasted for at least thirty years[22] and introduced a number of significant changes. It was Sneferu who consolidated and strongly modified the form of government in Egypt.

During the First and Second Dynasties the ruler traveled throughout the country to run it in person, not unlike the early medieval monarchs of Europe. This trip along the Nile was called the *šmsw Ḥr*, 'following of Horus' (Horus being a reference to the king), because he would, of course, be traveling with his retinue; 'The Followers of Horus' remained an honorific title until the end of the Old Kingdom. Toward the end of the Second Dynasty, official records start referring to a property census occurring every two years, and it is from the start of Sneferu's reign that cattle appear as the main item of interest to officials. These censuses were used in Egypt to date the years of reign of the individual rulers.[23]

Such journeys stopped at select locations, generally places connected with the cult of an important deity and having a strong economic potential. It was probably Sneferu who built small pyramids at such sites.[24] These pyramids would be visible from afar and so marked what could be called 'exclusive' royal domains. A closer look at the location of these little pyramids highlights the religious and economic significance of the regions in question and provides insight into the overall geopolitical situation during Sneferu's lifetime.

These prominent sites, listed from south to north, were Elephantine on what was then Egypt's southernmost border, Edfu, Hierakonpolis, Nubt (Ombos), Abydos, Zawyat al-Mayyitin, and Seila, near Meidum. In most cases, these pyramids occupied elevated sites visible from afar, even though the individual small pyramids were no higher than 4 to 8.[25]

meters.[25] From older studies of irrigation in Egypt at the end of the nineteenth and beginning of the twentieth centuries, so prior to the building of dams on the Nile,[26] it becomes apparent that these small pyramids are situated in the most important lowlands irrigated by the Nile floods (Arabic: *hawdu*).[27] The detailed geomorphological and water regime maps from pre-dam eras are important in that they reflect the original ancient Egyptian landscape, and thus provide insight into ancient thinking in relation to the Nile cycle.[28] These areas that were so important at the rise of the ancient Egyptian state would, paradoxically, later become the centers of independent provincial development during and after its collapse at the end of the Old Kingdom.

The distribution of these local centers is indicative of another feature of the ancient Egyptian state in this period: an administration based on an asymmetric relationship between the capital Memphis and several prominent local centers. This may explain why, until the end of the Fifth Dynasty, the tombs of high officials were concentrated almost exclusively around the capital. This did not change until the Sixth Dynasty.

Sneferu's steps were important in the governance of the state as a whole, whose administration continued to grow. According to the French Egyptologist Michel Baud (1963–2012), Sneferu reorganized the administration of the entire country, one of the outcomes of which was the now fully conceptualized office of the vizier.[29] As discussed above, this office existed at least as early as the Third Dynasty: it was then held by Kaimen, who served under Djoser. However, neither his tomb nor anything else about him is known. It was not until the reign of Sneferu that the office of vizier and of the individuals holding it began to be properly documented, even though by that time the vizier had become the king's deputy in practically all spheres of state administration. Indeed, during the Fourth Dynasty, this office was held only by the closest members of the royal family, usually the king's uncles or brothers—but not his sons, as they were potential heirs to the Egyptian throne until their father's death.

Under Sneferu's rule, an enormous leap occurred not only in the administration of the state, but also in monumental architecture. Sneferu was the greatest third-millennium exponent of big construction projects, not his son Khufu, despite his enormous pyramid at Giza. As well as his country-wide network of small pyramids, Sneferu built three

Fig. 4.4. Wooden panel of Hesyra, who was a high official during the later Third to early Fourth Dynasty, from his tomb in Saqqara. His titles indicate the complexity of state administration during this period. Egyptian Museum, Cairo. (after Quibell 1913, pl. XXIX)

full-size pyramids as successive candidates for his tomb: one at Meidum and two others at Dahshur. Besides the pyramid complexes themselves, there were also several large cemeteries built in Meidum and Dahshur for the members of his family and high court officials. There is no doubt that these construction activities sapped a significant amount of the country's economic potential. As a reflection of the economic and political state of Egypt under his reign, this achievement marks out Sneferu as the outstanding ruler of the Fourth Dynasty, if not of the Old Kingdom as a whole.[30]

The Three Pyramids of Sneferu

Sneferu's first pyramid lies on the most direct route between the Nile Valley and the Faiyum, which from time immemorial had played a major role in the economy of ancient Egypt. The Faiyum had a dense network of settlements. This together with the enormous agricultural potential of the region—and thus the availability of economic resources and people—may have been what attracted Sneferu to the site.[31]

The Meidum pyramid represents a historical turning point in several respects. It moves definitively from the rectangular enclosure-based scheme of the Third Dynasty rulers Djoser and Sekhemkhet in Saqqara to the one that would become the standard:[32] the valley temple that formed the gateway to the complex and the Nile Valley; the ascending ramp (which would quickly develop into a roofed causeway) that connected the valley temple with the mortuary temple where the daily cult for the king was performed; and the pyramid that served as the king's actual tomb. An extensive cemetery of *mastaba*s (trapezoidal built tombs) of high officials unfolded like a ribbon to the north, set out in a way that may intentionally have emulated the shape of the First and Second Dynasty burial ground on the limestone cliffs of North Saqqara.

At some stage, however, Sneferu decided to be buried much closer to the capital at Memphis. Sneferu's second pyramid was thus built at Dahshur, less than five kilometers from White Walls, a distance that workers could walk every day from their nearby settlements. This may explain why no large pyramid town has yet been found in the vicinity of this pyramid, nor for that matter near the other cemeteries directly adjacent to Memphis. In fact, the only such town known from the Old

Fig. 4.5. The pyramid and cult temple of Sneferu in Meidum. (M. Bárta)

Kingdom is the one established at Giza under the Fourth Dynasty kings, probably only built because there was no settlement network close by, so the infrastructure necessary for the construction of the tombs had to be developed on the spot.

Sneferu's new pyramid at Dahshur differed from all earlier examples in being smooth-sided ('true'), rather than stepped, with a distinctive change of angle giving it its modern name: the Bent Pyramid. It seems to have suffered structural problems while still under construction, prompting both efforts to convert the Meidum pyramid to 'true' form and the construction of a second monument at Dahshur, known as the Red or Northern Pyramid (while the Meidum project was still unfinished). Fragments of a false door of red granite discovered near the mortuary temple at the eastern foot of the Red Pyramid, together with pieces of an Old Kingdom mummy, suggest that this pyramid was the actual site of Sneferu's burial.[33] The false door distinguishes the Red Pyramid from earlier royal tombs (including the Bent and Meidum pyramids), where all known cult places were defined by a pair of stelae.[34]

It has been suggested that Sneferu's Dahshur pyramids were complementary, with the northern one (the Red) serving as the king's true tomb, and the southern (Bent) pyramid, also fully functional during the Old Kingdom, serving as a sun temple.[35] The causeway to the Bent Pyramid approaches it from the northeast, where a small temple stands to this day. Although it was generally thought to be the valley temple, the latest research suggests it was simply a cult construction on the road to the pyramid—a stop for the processions from the Nile Valley to the desert plateau, perhaps built for the celebration of the king's thirty years on the throne of Egypt.

The layout of the chambers inside the Meidum pyramid was also very different from earlier examples. The burial chamber was no longer placed below ground or at the natural ground level, but high above the base of the pyramid—although this is not true of its two antechambers. Finally, the Medium pyramid represents a great technological leap forward: the use of the corbelled vault, which was introduced in the construction of the interior spaces, allowed for higher ceilings while at the same time being a very effective way to distribute the pressure of the surrounding stone. This same technique was used in apparently unique relieving cavities filled with loose material such as sand or construction debris above the pyramid's corridor and antechambers.

Some of the changes in the architecture of royal mortuary complexes during Sneferu's reign reflected the development of underlying religious ideas. Previously, worship of the god Horus led to buildings being oriented according to the stars, in a north–south direction: this is seen in the Step Pyramid, for example, and is taken to imply an astral destination for the dead king. But the early Fourth Dynasty saw devotion shift to the sun god, Re. Monuments such as the new complex at Meidum were accordingly oriented east–west, implying a solar destiny along the path of the sun. It is probably due to this shift in religious thinking that, although the actual burial chambers of the Meidum and Bent pyramids were still oriented north–south (like the tombs of earlier kings), that of the Red Pyramid lay east–west, as did those of all later kingly burials in the Old (and Middle) Kingdoms.

The transition to the sun cult at the beginning of the Fourth Dynasty was symbolized by the shape of the pyramid, the transfer of the cult temple to the eastern foot of the pyramid, and the change of the orientation of the king's burial chamber. It is reinforced by the names of Sneferu's two pyramidal complexes at Dahshur. The solar implications of 'Sneferu Is Rising South' and 'Sneferu Is Rising North' seem clear, the verb in both cases being $ḫ^c$, written with a hieroglyph depicting a stylized sun rising over a mountain, used for the 'rising' of the sun and the 'appearance' of the king.[36] Sneferu's rule also saw innovation in regnal names. His was the first to be regularly written in a cartouche,[37] an oval, symbolized by a protective loop (šn) and suggestive of the infinite, one expression of which is the eternally repeating solar cycle.

The cult of the sun god Re is probably connected with the first evidence—in written sources, as no physical trace has yet been found—of a *mrt* shrine dating to the period of Sneferu's rule, where the goddess Hathor, the sun god Re, and the king were worshiped.[38] The written evidence suggests that this sort of temple would have been found near a royal residence or at the entry to a burial ground, near a valley temple. In a *mrt* shrine, the king would be considered the spouse of the goddess Hathor, and their wedding would probably take place there. That is why the shrine was called 'The House of Love' in ancient Egyptian. It is certainly interesting to note that references to the *mrt* shrine do not appear again until the time of King Userkaf at the beginning of the Fifth Dynasty: this was the high point of the sun cult, which the kings of that dynasty used to promote their political objectives.

The evolution of monumental architecture during Sneferu's rule suggests that it was a period of major change. His building efforts clearly leveraged the country's enormous economic potential. He was also engaged in intensive land development. A procession of human personifications of funerary estates preserved from the decoration of the Bent Pyramid's 'valley temple' illustrates his internal colonization and the founding of many new settlements (*grgwt*) and estates (*ḥwwt*) in the central part of Egypt and especially in the eastern Delta, which at that time was still very marshy land.[39] The biographical inscriptions of the high officials Pehernefer and Metjen refer to nineteen settlements (*grgwt*) being founded by Sneferu on the territories of the First, Second, Fifth, and Sixth Lower Egyptian nomes.[40] He also consolidated the administration of the country and ensured its viability by establishing a

Fig. 4.6. One of the major innovations in architecture in the time of Sneferu was the corbelled roof. Bent Pyramid in Dahshur. (M. Bárta)

number of estates (*ḥwwt*) that produced rich resources for payment in kind of state officials. By the end of the Fourth Dynasty, most of these officials, especially those in the highest posts, seem to have come from the many branches of the royal family. The offices they held included the maintenance of the regular mortuary cult in the temple complexes, which was fully funded by the state—in reality, the ruler.

No less important were Sneferu's efforts to standardize aspects of the burials of the royal family and dignitaries. This is evident in the Meidum cemeteries west of his pyramid, where the size of some *mastaba*-type tombs becomes more regular, based on affiliation and social status. The same uniformity is plainly visible in Dahshur, in the East Mastaba Field, and culminates a generation later in Giza, during the reign of Sneferu's son Khufu.[41] A similar tendency to order is reflected in the tomb inscriptions in these cemeteries. It is apparently not by accident that the first *ḥtp-di-nsw* offering formulae appear at this time. These refer to the king as the principal donor of various offerings for the owner of the tomb.[42] The texts eventually became omnipresent in the tombs, and the power of magical words of the offering formulae was considered more than sufficient to make up for real offerings. In fact, these magical texts to a large extent replaced lavish and expensive offerings.[43]

Modernizations were also made in the material culture of mortuary cults which, like the offering formulae, were undoubtedly connected with a drive to economize. Thus, we find the masses of stone vessels found in earlier tombs replaced by 'Meidum ware' (named for the first appearance of the ware at the site)—a high-quality ceramic with high red polish, which imitated the shapes of stone vessels.[44] There were also miniature ceramic bowls and cups, used extensively in offering chapels to hold symbolic amounts of foodstuffs and beverages deemed essential in the afterlife. Their tiny size was meant to ensure economy in provisioning the cult.[45] It is the manufacture of these miniatures that is particularly relevant. The bottoms of the pots show quite clearly that they were made on a rotating potter's wheel, which is not known to have existed before the Fifth Dynasty. But the type of ceramic they are made from indicates that this technology must have been developed much earlier. The unifying context of all the innovations we have seen allows us to suppose that they instigated significant technological innovation that had far-reaching impact.[46]

Fig. 4.7. The first well-attested vizier in Egyptian history was Nefermaat, buried in Meidum. Egyptian Museum, Cairo. (Archive of the Czech Institute of Egyptology, Charles University, M. Zemina)

Fig. 4.8. Innovations by Sneferu also influenced nonroyal tombs. A new type of sunk reliefs with compartments to maintain the color pastes made a brief appearance, too. Tomb of Nefermaat, Meidum, Egyptian Museum, Cairo. (Archive of the Czech Institute of Egyptology, Charles University, M. Zemina)

Economic Prerequisites of Building the State

In view of the spectacular rise of the state during the reign of King Sneferu, reflected especially in the new forms and monumentality of sacral architecture, it is natural to ask how such ostentatious, expensive, and logistically demanding projects were financed. Thousands of people must have been involved in the building. Hundreds of others were needed to maintain the mortuary cults. All of them were paid in kind, receiving commodities produced by estates and workshops all over the country. Enlightening in this regard is a comparison of two sites, illustrated with calculations, that was published in 2013 by Richard Redding, an archaeologist and archaeozoologist who has been researching pyramid builders' settlements in the Giza pyramid field for many years.[47] This microscosm of the economic background of large-scale projects of the era reveals the general outlines of the underpinnings required by the highly complex Old Kingdom state.

Before he joined the Giza project, which was led by the American archaeologist Mark Lehner, Redding was part of a team studying the remnants of an Old Kingdom settlement dated to the Fifth Dynasty at Kom al-Hisn in the eastern Delta. This site has been occupied for several thousand years up to the present day. In ancient times, the goddesses Sekhmet and Hathor were worshiped here. Apart from the standard village-like settlement, the site is interesting due to the large quantity of domesticated faunal remains found there. Exploring the site gives the impression that it was one of the many farms that produced the commodities needed to support the ancient state and state-run projects, especially the construction of pyramid complexes, which consumed significant resources and labor.

Most of the animal bones studied were, perhaps surprisingly, from pigs. Archaeologists found the bones of 717 pigs, 614 sheep and goats, and 29 cattle. The cattle to pig ratio was 0.04:1; cattle to sheep and goats, 0.05:1; sheep and goats to pigs, 0.86:1. Pigs were thus twice as important in this locality as sheep and goats, the advantage further enhanced because a pig gives roughly 1.5 times more meat than a sheep or a goat. The reproduction figures are also interesting: one sow can produce up to 14 piglets in a year, compared to 1.2 kids per female goat and 0.8 lambs per ewe. It can thus be estimated that at this site there were 14.3 goats and

Fig. 4.9. Cult temple of Sneferu in Dahshur, Red Pyramid. (M. Bárta)

sheep to one pig. The large number of goat and sheep bones found indicates that, next to pigs, these were the most frequently consumed species; most of the animals were female and over two years old. The young sheep and goats—apparently male—were evidently taken away by the central authorities and that is why there were so few of their bones here.

There may be a similar reason for the very small number of cattle bones found. An analysis of organic macro-remains has pointed to intensive cattle rearing. This finding emerged from the waste layers left behind by these animals.[48] Redding believes the disparity between the indirect evidence of intensive cattle rearing and the absence of actual cattle bones is quite easy to explain: the largest proportion of the cattle was taken by the central state authorities and was not designated for local consumption. The main source of meat for the local population, who were livestock keepers, was pigs—not least because they could not be herded long distances and so from the state's point of view were unsuitable as a form of liquidity. Beef was, moreover, considered a relatively expensive commodity in ancient Egypt; this is true even today in rural areas of Egypt, where this meat is usually consumed as a special meal only on Friday, the day of rest.[49]

So, we have available to us an analysis of a livestock estate that produced resources used by the state to support and feed the laborers and officials working at pyramid building sites. But to understand the role of these farms in the state activities or, to be more specific, in sustaining the workforces working on them, which were deployed all over the country, one must closely examine the most famous site of the Old Kingdom, the Giza pyramid field.

The modern visitor whose attention is fixed exclusively on the three gigantic pyramids will probably be unaware of the unassuming settlement nearby, which has contributed so much to our understanding of the essential principles of the ancient Egyptian economy and pyramid building.

The aim of the Giza project was to explore and perform a contextual multidisciplinary interpretation of a large settlement—preserved to the immediate southeast of the pyramid plateau—that housed builders and laborers who worked on the late Fourth Dynasty pyramid of Menkaure.[50] The site is separated from the pyramid necropolis proper by a massive wall called Heit al-Ghurab (Wall of the Crow), built of large limestone blocks and running for 200 meters in the east–west direction. The wall is 10 meters wide at its base and 10 meters high. The massif of the wall is broken only in one place by a large underpass, which allowed passage in the north–south direction and connected the necropolis to the pyramid builders' settlement.

The settlement occupied an area of at least 200 × 300 meters and comprised several clearly distinguishable parts, all built of mud brick and preserved to a height of only a few dozen centimeters. There were galleries housing the pyramid builders, bakeries, workshops, inspection sites, and a large, enigmatic columned hall. To the southwest of the laborers' galleries there was the Western Town, where the local elite resided. To the southeast was the Royal Administrative Building. This is where the warehouses and five large silos were located. East of the settlement was the Eastern Town, which was probably part of a local, more permanent settlement and had little to do with the construction of the Giza complex itself; this is the main reason why the plan of this settlement is more organic.

Remnants of livestock bones were found practically all over the area of the settlement at different floor levels. It is analysis of these finds that helps us to identify the basic components of the staple diet of the ancient Egyptian population of that time. It also allows quantitative and qualitative distinctions to be drawn between different parts of the settlement, which leads to inquiries about the social status of the people who lived there.[51]

Altogether 25,000 pieces of sheep and goat bones, 8,000 cattle bones, and 1,000 pig bones have been analyzed so far. The ratio of cattle to sheep and goat bones indicates that the smaller animals played a much larger role in the diet of the settlement's inhabitants. The fact that the meat yield from a young beef carcass is eight to ten times higher than from a goat or sheep means that there was three to four times more beef in the locality than mutton. Most cows were relatively young; roughly half were less than 18 months old at the time of slaughter and only 20 percent lived to the age of two. The sheep to goat ratio was 3:1, with half the animals being slaughtered before they were 16 months old and 10 percent by age two. The proportion of pigs was also very small; there were eight times more cattle than pigs, and twenty-three times more sheep and goats.

Comparing these details to the analysis from Kom al-Hisn shows relatively clearly that the Giza settlement was created and supported by the state, given that it was almost totally reliant on food from the outside. This is reflected in the age, sex, and bone distribution of the individual types of livestock. There is also an absence of the small mammals and hunted animals that are found in other types of settlement.[52] The number of pigs in each settlement is interesting: whereas there were very few at Giza, the ratio of pigs to sheep and goats in Kom al-Hisn was practically 1:1. The conclusion is simple: pork was an important part of the ancient Egyptian diet, but since pigs could not be driven long distances as a herd, they would always be animals of local importance, consumed at the place where they were bred.

This site also answers the question as to why it is unique among the settlements we have found so far. Three-quarters of the pyramid complexes were built within five kilometers of the Old Kingdom capital, which we presume lay to the east of North Saqqara (next to the modern village of Kom Fakhry). That being the case, there was no need to build central camps for the workforce: they already lived on the outskirts of the capital.

Fig. 4.10. To economize on funerary cults, miniature plates and cups for symbolic amounts of food and drink began to be used in the reign of Sneferu. Abusir. (Archive of the Czech Institute of Egyptology, Charles University, M. Frouz)

Giza (and presumably the even more remote but little-investigated Abu Rawash) was much more isolated, so it was necessary to bring in workers and provide them with food, housing, and tools. The approximate figures quoted above give some indication of the size of the administration at the time and the material demands of people employed by the state, be they officials, priests, or laborers. Estates providing the financial support for state expenditures were spread across the country. It was necessary to ensure highly efficient production of agricultural products, to tap the country's potential, to record the goods that were produced and transfer them to the place where they were needed, to distribute remuneration in kind, and much else. By now the reader must suspect that the ancient Egyptian state had reached the height of human ability to control a highly sophisticated system with relatively simple tools.

We can thus extrapolate that an overwhelming part of Egypt's population at that time depended directly or indirectly on pyramid building. Estimates commonly arrive at a population of around one million during the Old Kingdom, compared to about 100,000 to 200,000 inhabitants at around 3000 BC.[53] Considering, hypothetically, that every man had a wife and several children at home, and was probably also partly responsible for aging parents, we easily come to a figure of 200,000 to 250,000 individuals who may have had a direct or indirect income from a pyramid building

Proteins and Pyramid Building

In his 2013 study of the settlement at Kom al-Hisn, which relies on both archaeology and natural sciences,[55] Redding asks about the economic aspects of rearing livestock, the numbers needed to feed the people working at the construction site of a pyramid complex, the amount of farmland needed to rear livestock, the number of people employed in that sort of farming, and so on.

According to Egyptological analyses, some 25,000 people were occupied at the building site for Menkaure's pyramid during the Nile floods (from June to September). This was a quarter of the number cited by the 'Father of History,' Herodotus, when he wrote about the pyramid of Khufu in Giza. These workers were brought in primarily to transport building stone to the site: during the floods it was relatively easy to get a large amount of building material close to the site on rafts. For the other eight months of the year there were only about ten thousand workers at the same site. Several centuries later, when the brick pyramid of Amenemhat III was being built in Dahshur, 'only' five thousand laborers were needed.

If we accept that 10,000 people were needed to build the Great Pyramid, the following figures would apply. A person doing hard labor requires at least 45–50 g of protein per day. Fish, beef, and pork contain around 75 percent protein. This means that a male worker doing hard physical work will need to consume at least 67 g of fish, beef, or pork protein. Due to the content of fat, water, ash, fiber, and other components, there are 18 g of protein per 100 g of meat. This translates to 370 g of meat per person per day. Of course, ancient Egyptians could acquire a substantial amount of protein from foods other than meat or fish. Eggs were out of the question—chickens had not yet been domesticated—but other good sources of protein were beans and other legumes. If only half of the protein came from meat, then 1,850 kg of meat per day would have been needed for 10,000 people.

Today, a slaughtered cow in Egypt provides roughly 120 kg of meat, a sheep or goat about 16 kg. The proportion of sheep and goats to cattle in the workers' galleries at Giza was 12:1. At a place called North Street Gate House, the proportion was 0.8:1 because the actual site manager lived there, which resulted in an average ratio of 3.5:1 across Kom al-Hisn as a whole. It is evident that beef was considered a luxury and that entitlement to beef rations differed according to the social status of the consumer. To ensure daily deliveries of meat, 10.5 head of cattle and 36.8 sheep or goats had to be slaughtered. To cover the demands of a ten-day working week, 105 head of cattle and 368 sheep and goats were required—3,833 head of cattle and 13,414 sheep and goats for a year. Considering the proportion of male animals to female, reproduction rates, and birth rates, maintaining that annual supply would require a herd of 21,900 head of cattle and 54,750 sheep and goats. Some 21,920 hectares (ha) of land would be needed to feed the cattle, as well as 18,250 ha for the goats and sheep. That is a total of roughly 40,000 ha, plus additional land to support those who took care of the animals. It is thus easy to arrive at a figure of 120,000 ha, which is 5 percent of the present-day area of farmland in the Delta. Although the colonized and reclaimed area of the Delta was much smaller then, this was still not a very large acreage.

According to common analogies, some 3,650 herdsmen would have to look after the cattle and 1,095 after the sheep and goats. Thus, besides the ten thousand laborers working at the pyramid building site, the central state administration had to provide for nearly five thousand herders—as well as fishermen, farmers, bakers, and all the other people needed to run a small town. The estimate that for most of the year at least twenty thousand people, and many more during the flood season, worked at and around the building site, will not be far from the truth. Moreover, available studies do not include the number of people working in the stone quarries.

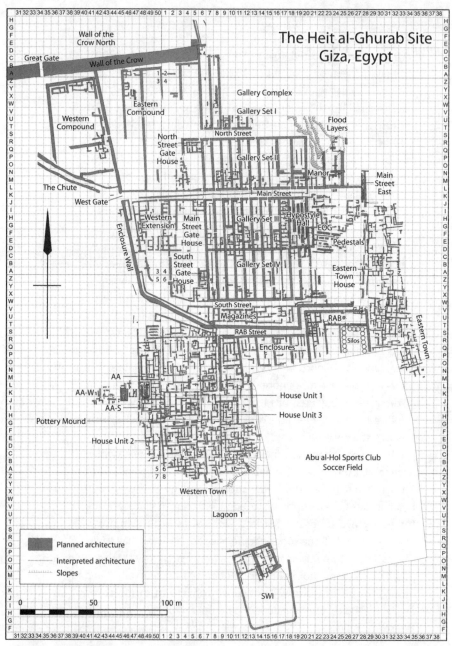

Fig. 4.11. Ground plan of the pyramid city in Giza shows the extent and complexity of the construction works and logistics during the Fourth Dynasty. (courtesy of Ancient Egypt Research Associates, Boston)

project that lasted for several decades. Thus, it is not surprising that it was really the ruler who provided for nearly everyone's welfare. Of course, the building of a pyramid complex was not the only state-funded project; other temples, palaces, and drainage canals were built, expeditions financed, and so forth. And it is interesting to note that Mark Lehner concluded, based on his excavations of the workers' settlement in Giza, that the Fourth Dynasty was a period of exceptional intervention by the state, in the form of internal levies, for extended periods of time.[54] By the close of the Sixth Dynasty, the ideology that underpinned the divine right of kings and the cosmological order was in crisis. What emerges from the historical and archaeological data is that by this time the king had lost control of state affairs; this was at the core of the ideological crisis and a major contributing factor in the fall of the Old Kingdom.

5 The Empire of the Sun God

A Retreat of the Royal Family

The reader may ask why, as we move from Sneferu to the end of the Fourth Dynasty, or rather, to the start of the Fifth Dynasty, we did not dwell on Khufu, Sneferu's son, familiarly known as the builder of the largest pyramid in Egyptian history. He is left aside here as our primary objective is to identify major periods of change, whereas Khufu's reign was a continuation of the policies initiated by his father. The same is essentially true of his successors, up to the end of the Fourth Dynasty.

In contrast, the ascent of the Fifth Dynasty rulers to the throne in the second half of the twenty-fifth century BC did herald significant shifts in the cultic topography, history, characteristics of state administration, ideology, art, and religion of the pharaonic state. The last ruler of the Fourth Dynasty, Shepseskaf, eschewed the now-traditional site of the royal necropolis at Giza. He decided instead to situate his tomb—for reasons at first glance obscure—at South Saqqara, which, until then, had no tradition of royal tombs, thereby founding an entirely new royal necropolis. Moreover, the superstructure of his tomb resembled a *mastaba*, or perhaps a huge sarcophagus.[1] Shepseskaf's reasons for taking this dramatic step may have been the consequence of processes that had come to a climax during his reign.

One of the pillars of Fourth Dynasty rule, as it had probably been since the unification of Egypt, was that members of the royal family occupied the highest offices in the state administration.[2] The vizierate, and other high posts, were usually taken by the king's uncles or cousins.

The potential for the changes seen in the transition from the Fourth to the Fifth Dynasty arose as early as the reign of Menkaure, who was both the last Fourth Dynasty king to build a pyramid as a royal tomb and the last king to build at Giza.

The complexity of the state apparatus was now intensifying and growing in administrative complexity due to the expansion of the state. It became necessary to employ increasing numbers of officials and priests, with the result that toward the end of the Fourth and beginning of the Fifth Dynasty, officials of nonroyal descent began to penetrate the highest levels of the bureaucracy: the royal family was simply no longer capable of servicing the complicated machinery of the state. The last vizier who was certainly of royal descent was Sekhemkara, a son of King Khafre and Queen Hekenuhedjet. His tomb (LG 89) is in the Khufu and Khafre Quarry in Giza, near the tomb of his brother Inumin (LG 92).[3] The inscriptions inside Sekhemkara's tomb list the various offices he held, including that of vizier, and the kings whom he served: Khafre, Menkaure, Shepseskaf, Userkaf, and Sahure.[4] This former quarry contains also other rock tombs of viziers from the end of the Fourth Dynasty—Nebemakhet (LG 86), Nikaura (LG 87), and Ankhmara—none of whom apparently had royal blood.[5] The last known viziers of royal descent were all sons of Khafre. This means that a generation later, Menkaure's sons were the first royal family members who were not in charge of the office of the vizier. Therefore by the end of the Fourth Dynasty, and even more at the beginning of the Fifth, it is clear that the office of the vizier was not held exclusively by the representatives of the royal family but also by officials of nonroyal origin. This trend prevailed completely from the Fifth Dynasty onward.

The Sun Kings: New Era, New Politics

The beginning of the Fifth Dynasty was a transitional period, with the viziers Duaenra, Babaf (probably Duaenra's son), and Seshathotep Heti all being of nonroyal descent but closely connected to the king, as their titles show;[6] Hratch Papazian calls it a period of "administrative

Fig. 5.1. Scribes dominated the administration of the Egyptian state, particularly from the beginning of the Fifth Dynasty, when the state began to be run by increasing numbers of officials of nonroyal origin. Statue of Nefer, Abusir, reign of Niuserre. (Archive of the Czech Institute of Egyptology, Charles University, M. Frouz)

calibration."[7] A large number of new settlements emerged, especially in the Delta, undoubtedly influenced by the rising complexity of the state and the growing number of officials.[8]

A possible indicator of the rise of the number of officials is the quantity of scribal statues that can be dated to this period. These statues, which depict a high official sitting with legs crossed and unrolled papyrus scrolls in the lap, had appeared sporadically since the beginning of the Fourth Dynasty, the earliest datable examples belonging to Khufu's eldest son, Kawab, who was one of the few royal sons to hold the office of vizier during his father's reign. A dozen more can be dated to the Fourth Dynasty. But the number rises sharply from the start of the Fifth Dynasty: some thirty-seven scribal statutes have been documented from that time, and they are particularly common in the second half of the dynasty. This pattern corresponds to the rising number of statues in general at that time. Then in the Sixth Dynasty the number drops off to just nine.[9] These are of course approximate figures, especially given the vagaries of dating, yet they do seem to demonstrate a trend, which may represent a fluctuation in the number of senior officials in the state apparatus and a decline in the Sixth Dynasty, perhaps indicative of a royal policy of curtailing bureaucratic power and autonomy to focus trust in a small number of selected officials, whose loyalty was ensured by marriage into the royal house.

The new strategy of filling both lower and higher posts with nonroyal officials may not have been implemented without opposition. The biography of a high official named Ptahshepses, buried at Saqqara, who served in high office at the end of the Fourth and beginning of the Fifth Dynasty, offers a picture of the period under discussion.[10] Ptahshepses was brought up at the royal court of Menkaure and later served under Shepseskaf. The first king of the Fifth Dynasty, Userkaf, then gave him his daughter Khamaat in marriage, a decision that inaugurated a new strategy for Egyptian kings, who henceforth used the instrument of matrimonial relationship to ensure the loyalty of high state officials of nonroyal descent.

Ptahshepses's career is also proof that the transition from the Fourth to the Fifth Dynasty was not entirely about change. Ptahshepses served at court in a number of posts until the reign of Niuserre in the middle of the Fifth Dynasty, a period of some forty years. This suggests a desire for continuity in a time of transition. Based on calculations made by Peter Dorman, Ptahshepses may have been born five years before the death of King Menkaure, was about sixteen years old when Userkaf died, thirty-one when Neferirkare ascended the throne, fifty-eight at the ascension of Raneferef, and sixty-nine when Niuserre became king.[11]

The fates of the rulers at the turn of the Fifth Dynasty indicate that this was a time of change. Menkaure's family was steadily losing supreme control of the state's administration, and Menkaure himself began a trend for building substantially smaller pyramids. To make up for the loss of monumentality, from now on a trend toward richer decoration becomes discernible. Menkaure's principal wife was apparently Khamerernebti (II); their son Khuenra probably died before he could succeed his father. It has been argued that Khentkaus (I) was a daughter of Menkaure, and that she became the main representative of the royal family after Khuenra's early death.[12] She was in any case important in the changing social climate of Egypt at the end of the Fourth and beginning of the Fifth Dynasty.

Viziers in the Time of Change

Comparing the group of titles typical of viziers of the Fourth Dynasty with those of the Fifth and Sixth Dynasties, one finds differences, of course, but also titles that survived throughout that period.[13] All the Fourth Dynasty viziers had honorific titles associated with the royal family, a formal recognition of the fact that they were all of royal descent. However, some of the titles typical among Fourth Dynasty viziers ended with Sekhemkara, the last vizier of royal descent: Nobleman, Embalmer of Anubis, Overseer of the King's House, The Eldest Son of the King, King's Chancellor, King's Son of His Body—in other words, titles that were completely beyond the reach of commoners.

A different set of titles is typical among Fifth Dynasty viziers. Most appear during the reign of King Neferirkare, whose vizier was Washptah,[14] and the most common were Pillar, Spokesman of the People, The One Who Belongs to the Chapel of Nekhen, Superior of the Scribes of Royal Documents, Inspector of the Court, Priest of Maat, Keeper of All Secrets, Inspector of Scribes, and Overseer of the Royal Estate. The title of Nobleman does not appear during the Fifth Dynasty before the vizier Ptahhotep Desher, who served during the reign of Djedkare. The list shows that a large part of the title related to the more profane aspects of life and work at the royal court. Some, of course, had an honorific meaning: titles like Pillar, Spokesman of the People, The One Who Belongs to the Chapel of Nekhen had no factual definition but only referred to the social status of their bearers. They also pointed to the viziers' plebeian origin, their authority, and their symbolic role, as indicated by the reference to Nekhen (Hierakonpolis).

Despite these social shifts, many of the duties of the office of vizier remained virtually unchanged. This involved the act of applying seals, being present at the palace—in the House of Morning—during the king's morning toilet and breakfast, and managing state building projects, the administration of silos, and the treasury. These were all roles relating to governing the state and its affairs; other duties included agricultural work and the collection and redistribution of taxes.[15]

The shifting structure of viziers' titles ended, as noted above, during the reign of King Neferirkare, when Washptah held the office of vizier. One of the titles that particularly reflected this shift was Spokesman (of the People), which suggests a certain democratization of the state administration.[16] Another historically, although not formally, important title was Keeper of Secrets.[17] A diachronic analysis shows that use of this title was quite limited during the Fourth Dynasty and became increasingly frequent only with the onset of the Fifth Dynasty. The stress on keeping secrets seems only to have been thought necessary when non–family members were involved in government, whereas family members could be trusted implicitly. In due course, new strategies for rank emulation would have to be invented.[18]

Her famous tomb, sometimes referred to as the 'Fourth Pyramid of Giza,' is situated in a former quarry, north of Menkaure's valley temple. An inscription preserved on a pillar in front of her chapel is generally read as referring to Khentkaus as the "Mother of Two Kings of Upper and Lower Egypt." The most plausible explanation based on available data seems to be that Khentkaus was the mother of two consecutive rulers at the turn of the Fifth Dynasty: Shepseskaf and Userkaf.[19] If Khentkaus was married to a man of nonroyal descent, this may have resulted in her sons having to struggle with issues of royal legitimacy. This could have motivated their strategy for consolidating power, which found its full expression in monumental architecture and in their positions on the politico-religious scene of that time.

The relationship between Menkaure, Khentkaus, and Shepseskaf is manifested clearly in the design of the similar substructures of their tombs, even though their superstructures were very different.[20] In all three, the ceiling of the burial chamber is carved in the shape of a vault, and there is a room with six niches off an access corridor or antechamber.[21] Since no original inscriptions or physical remains have been found in these niches, their purpose can only be surmised, but there can be no doubt that their presence must have had a strong religious meaning, otherwise they would not have been a consistent part of royal burials of the time.

Fig. 5.2. Tomb of Shepseskaf in South Saqqara, viewed from the north. (M. Bárta)

Fig. 5.3. Tomb of Shepseskaf in South Saqqara. (M. Bárta)

Older scholarship suggested that Shepseskaf's decision not to be buried at Giza arose from disputes within the royal family.[22] However, there may have been a more prosaic reason: there was no more room on the Giza plateau for another pyramid complex, so he decided to return to a point between the ancient pyramid fields of Saqqara and Dahshur. We can only speculate as to why he chose to build the superstructure of his tomb to resemble a *mastaba* or sarcophagus. One reason might be that the rising number of nonroyals gaining access to offices of state, and the king's own not quite pure lineage, prompted him to build his tomb to resemble a *mastaba* similar in form to the tombs of the newly emerging elite. Another reason may have been that from the north—from ancient Memphis—the view of the tomb would evoke the impression of the sun setting between two mountain peaks. The 'peaks' were the two Dahshur pyramids of King Sneferu.[23] And Shepseskaf may have planned this impression to make it clear that he was upholding the legacy of King Sneferu and his Fourth Dynasty family. Shepseskaf also took care to have the individual rooms in the underground part of his tomb laid out in a way that corresponded with the current royal tradition, as seen in the tombs of Menkaure and Khentkaus.

The Birth of the Realm of *Maat*

Shepseskaf's probable brother Userkaf, the first king of the Fifth Dynasty, took the Horus name Iry-Maat, 'The One Who Performs *Maat*.' This was a significant symbolic statement. It implied on the one hand that the era before Userkaf's rule was disorganized and, on the other, that he would be the one to reintroduce law and order (the attributes of *maat*). He also used the symbolic connotations of the landscape and the distribution patterns of royal tombs in a significant way. His tomb lies in a place that is illogical at first glance: the whole complex is squeezed into a space close to the northeastern corner of Djoser's sacred precinct. It lay within Djoser's 'Dry Moat,' which forced Userkaf's architect to move the outer parts of his pyramid temple south of the pyramid. This all suggests that Userkaf wished to link himself with the legacy of the founder of the Old Kingdom. It is also interesting that the center of his pyramid is precisely aligned with that of Shepseskaf's tomb, and with Sneferu's Bent Pyramid at Dahshur. The relationship between Userkaf and Shepseskaf is evident, but let us return for a moment to Sneferu.[24]

It is interesting that Sneferu's Horus name was Nebmaat, 'Lord of Maat.' This meant that, like Userkaf, Sneferu linked his policy to the order of the goddess Maat. He was also the ruler to whom later generations of Egyptian kings would turn in the hope of acquiring religious and political legitimacy,[25] often drawing on the goddess Maat, guarantor of divine order and authority, and a connection to the Bent Pyramid. In the pyramid complex of King Raneferef at Abusir, for example, Sneferu's Horus name is the name that most frequently appears on stone cult vessels.[26]

Sneferu's Bent Pyramid played an important role throughout the Old Kingdom, including the reign of Pepy II. This last important Old Kingdom king centered his pyramid on an axis connecting Djoser's pyramid and the Bent Pyramid. This is not a surprising decision. At a time of political instability, such alignments could be a symbolic way of linking with the legacy of great ancestors. Upholding Sneferu's legacy was, as mentioned above, considered a good way of consolidating one's own position.

Userkaf also relied heavily on religion as a means of consolidating his political line. In ancient Egypt, religion deeply permeated the governance of the state. It was quite common, for instance, for important state

Fig. 5.4. Pyramid complex of Userkaf at the northeast corner of the complex of Djoser. (M. Bárta)

officials to simultaneously hold high positions in religious institutions. The merging of individual—secular, from our modern point of view— and religious institutions led, naturally, to the blending of interests. To dominate, a ruler had to assume control of both spheres. And this was certainly Userkaf's intention.[27]

One of the features of Userkaf's reign was a renewed interest in provincial matters, which the king seems to have demonstrated from the moment he took the throne. This was reflected in a new wave of building activity, with temples being built under the auspices of the king all over the country, including at Medamud and Tehna, and new settlements being founded, especially in Lower Egypt.[28] Userkaf evidently wanted not just to consolidate his power, but also to demonstrate that it was he who was restoring *maat*. The new temples boosted the number of sacral buildings in different parts of Egypt, but also, more significantly, they allowed the king to exert greater control over the country's economic processes in the country: temples had both economic and religious functions and therefore served as political centers.[29]

Userkaf's reign marked the beginning of the construction of innovative sun temples whose plans closely resembled those of royal pyramid complexes, sharing such features as a valley temple, a causeway, and a main temple housing a cult area, which in the sun temples was not a chapel, but a large pedestal supporting an obelisk—the symbol of the sun god Re. Unlike most cult temples, these were located on the west bank of the Nile, not far from the pyramid complexes of the Fifth Dynasty kings.

The existence of six such temples is documented, although the physical remains of only two, belonging to Kings Userkaf and Niuserre, have been preserved in the Abu Ghurab/Abusir region.[30] Although still virgin when Userkaf built his sun temple there, this area would soon become the principal cemetery of the Fifth Dynasty kings.

In the Name of Re—A New Strategy of Faith

Userkaf's sun temple[31] owed its genesis largely, if not entirely, to the political context at the beginning of the Fifth Dynasty. As discussed above, Shepseskaf and Userkaf were probably brothers, sons of Khentkaus by a nonroyal father. Both would therefore have had to find ways to consolidate their legitimacy as rulers. Building a solar temple might have been one way to do this, by emphasizing the royal relationship with the sun god.

In Userkaf's sun complex, the form of the valley temple may have been inspired by the *heb-sed* temple of Sneferu at Dahshur, situated on the causeway leading to his Bent Pyramid. If so, this would be another example of how important Sneferu's prestige and influence were for Userkaf. Unlike Sneferu's temple at Dahshur, which was oriented north–south, Userkaf's was oriented northeast–southwest, as was the causeway. It is difficult to reconstruct the temple as a whole because substantial parts, especially to the south, were badly damaged in ancient times. Herbert Ricke (1901–76), who studied the monument and its architecture, proposed a reconstruction of the temple that included a large open courtyard with sixteen columns, and seven chapels at its northern end. The famous head in the Egyptian Museum, probably part of the king's statue,[32] was found right next to the temple.

The causeway ran up to the desert plateau from the southern part of the valley temple. This was an open ramp, bordered on both sides by a low wall made of mud brick, that joined the east–west oriented upper cult temple at its northeastern corner; it was not decorated in any way. The upper, cult temple was built in four stages. In the first, the temple was enclosed by a large wall made of white-plastered mud brick. The corners of the enclosure were rounded and probably recalled the main temple at Hierakonpolis, Nekhen, which by then was already ancient. Hierakonpolis had been, since Predynastic times, one of the major religious and political centers of Upper Egypt dominated by the cult of Horus, the divine protector of all Egyptian kings. It is not by chance that Userkaf's sun complex was called *Nḥn-Rˁ*, 'The Fort of Re'—or rather 'Re's Nekhen'—as the principal site of the cult of the god Re. According to Ricke, at this first stage the interior of the temple, which was presumably intended to resemble the temple at Heliopolis, was simple, maybe even austere. There was a wooden column, perhaps adorned with a sun disk on top (judging from contemporary inscriptions, where the oldest documents use a standing obelisk capped with a disk as the determiner of the temple), and a cult site by its eastern foot.

During the second stage of building the temple was expanded and acquired a square plan. Instead of the wooden column, a six- to seven-meter-high limestone pedestal was built to support an obelisk of red granite. It now lies in thousands of fragments scattered across the temple floor, which is one reason why it is so difficult to determine its original height. It is also almost impossible to determine what exactly was on the very tip—whether the obelisk was capped with a copper or gold sheath, or whether the cap was in the form of a sun disk. Evidence for these options comes from an inscription in the tomb of a priest of the sun god, Neferiretenef,[33] which refers to the sun temples of Userkaf and Niuserre in the list of the priest's titles. The name of Userkaf's temple is determined by a column with a sun disk on top, while that of Niuserre's has the determinative of a plain obelisk.[34] At this stage the obelisk may have had a small north–south oriented room, likely a chapel, by its eastern foot, built inside the base of the obelisk. North and south of the altar there were small chapels, probably consecrated to Re and Hathor, the two deities to whom, along with the king, the complexes were dedicated.

During the third, penultimate stage, the temple was extended on its east and west sides, with storage chambers built of mud brick being added in the western part. South of the temple, a closed complex was added made

Fig. 5.5. Satellite image of Abusir, Saqqara, and Dahshur, showing the alignment of the pyramids of Sneferu (the Bent Pyramid), Shepseskaf, and Userkaf. (compiled by M. Bárta)

up of small rooms, also built of brick, and divided into two symmetrical parts. These areas may have served as temporary accommodation for the priests. There was only one entrance to these rooms—from the temple.

Finally, during the last stage, a brick altar was built to the east of the obelisk, shadowed on all four sides by short walls. In the eastern part of the temple, along its axis, mud brick benches were added, where offerings were probably laid out during the sacrificial ritual. After this 'solarization'—consecration to the sun deity by the ruler—the offerings were sent on to their destinations, to individual funerary installations. A final touch, carried out at the wish of King Djedkare, was to install a stone altar in place of the brick one; this is documented in an inscription found in Sinai, in the Wadi Maghara quarries.[35]

But what was it that inspired Userkaf to build such an unorthodox and costly complex? Although there is no express evidence of his reasons, various sources suggest that his main concern was to gain control of the economic and political affairs of the Residence as he had done in the provinces. From the Palermo Stone it can be inferred that the cult of the sun god was not as strong at the beginning of the Fifth Dynasty as some have believed. Userkaf, Sahure, and Neferirkare took much care to support the cult of many other deities of the pantheon, especially by allocating land. Prominent among them were the "Souls of Heliopolis," Hathor and Horus (together with Re, of course), worshiped in the sun temples, and also Nekhbet, Wadjet, and some others.[36]

By creating a specific centralized place for the cult of the god Re, alongside Horus, Hathor, and in a certain sense also himself, Userkaf followed a Fourth Dynasty trend, begun when Radjedef, Khufu's successor, added the attribute 'Son of Re' to the royal titulary and was the first to declare himself as such, and when Menkaure boldly supported the cult of Hathor, the symbolic mother and spouse of the king, as evidenced in his famous triads.[37] He also gained considerable control not only over contemporary ideology of the period, but also over the economy.[38]

The emerging sun temples had a very specific economic role. The papyrus archives from Abusir confirm that all the commodities coming from the Residence and intended to supply the pyramid temples of the ancient Egyptian kings were delivered first to the sun temple of the ruling king, where they were consecrated and purified by the sun—solarized ('solarization' means that offerings were symbolically left exposed to the energy of the sun for some limited time)—and only then sent on to their final destinations. There is no need to point out that these resources were also used to pay the officials employed in the temple complexes.[39] This model is supported by the existence of sacrificial platforms or benches in Userkaf's sun temple and large and small stone altars in Niuserre's temple. These were to facilitate the solarization of the many items that had to be exposed to this process. The daily flow of offerings making their way to the sun temple before being reallocated to the individual pyramid complexes must have been heavy.

The Residence played a key role in supplying the sun temples, being the original source of many of the commodities in question. But the sun temples were also allocated their own land by the king. For instance, insofar as the details on the Palermo Stone can be trusted, we know that Userkaf had two bulls and two geese sent to his sun temple every day. Moreover, he had forty-four arourae (one aroura was approximately 2,500 m²) of land somewhere in Lower Egypt—unfortunately the entry does not specify exactly where—allotted to Re and Hathor, the gods to whom the sun temple was devoted.[40] These two deities were, on a mythological level, the parents of kings. These data come from the Third Cattle Census, which represents Year 5 or 6 of the king's reign, during the second stage of the construction of the sun temple; it was already in full operation.

Each necropolis employed hundreds of officials and priests whose livelihoods depended on the king's bounty; their loyalty was ensured economically, and it was under the king's direct control, subject to his whims and preferences. In this way the king considerably curtailed the priests' influence. Everyone was in one way or another on the payroll of the Egyptian gods headed by Re. And everything started and ended with a decision made by the king.

The new sun temples were also significant rivals of the temple of Re in Heliopolis. This is indicated by the fact that the principal title of the Heliopolitan high priest, *wr m33* (Greatest of Seers), is not found after the reign of King Shepseskaf, and *wr m33 Twnw* (Greatest of Heliopolitan Seers) is seen for the first time under Sahure. The sun temples are last documented during the reign of Teti at the beginning of the Sixth

Fig. 5.6. False door of Ptahshepses, from Saqqara. He is believed to be the first nonroyal official to marry a royal daughter. His false door also features the god Osiris for the first time. British Museum. (M. Bárta)

Dynasty, shortly after the reappearance of the unqualified *wr m3̄3* title for the Heliopolitan high priest under Unas; it then continues to be used until the end of the Old Kingdom.[41] These shifting titles suggest a power struggle to control religious ideology.

As the ruler began to bring the country's economic processes, and thus also divine cults, under his control, the structure of the priesthood in the sun temples changed. Some of the priests employed in the sun temples also worked in the royal mortuary complexes at Abusir and did not belong among the highest social strata of court officials. They were in fact a closed community of officials, almost entirely dependent on the pharaoh's decisions and thus—presumably—fully loyal to the king.

As such they would certainly have supported him in many symbolic and religious matters.

A closer look at the composition of the clerks and priests employed in Userkaf's sun temple reveals two basic groups: the *ḥm-nṯr* priests and the *wʿb* priests.[42] The titles including *ḥm-nṯr* were mostly linked to the gods of the Egyptian pantheon, for instance the *ḥm-nṯr Rʿ m Nḫn-Rʿ*; we also find *ḥm-nṯr* of Re and Hathor, of Horus, and of the deities in the temple.

The other titles held by officials employed in the sun temples highlight an interesting fact: temple service was not a full-time job, but an activity performed for a certain period.[43] Recall, too, that an official could perform multiple functions and hold multiple offices at the same time, and that priestly and administrative offices were not mutually exclusive; indeed they were often combined in various ways. Of course, although we know the titles of many ancient Egyptian officials from tomb inscriptions on false doors, tracking an individual's career is complicated by their habit of listing every title they ever held.

So, a look at the other activities of the forty-five men who we know had various functions in Userkaf's sun temple reveals that these officials had certain things in common. Fifteen temple priests held very specific courtly offices with honorific titles (in this context, titles expressing how close the officials were to the king, but not implying any real function) such as Property Custodian of the King and Sole Friend, and similar variations on that theme. Nineteen priests, almost half of the documented priests in the temple, held the office of Scribe. Around a third provided personal services to the ruler—as royal barbers, manicurists, chamberlains, and guards. Sixteen priests were Keepers of Secrets, twenty-one worked at pyramid complexes, ten served at the court of justice (albeit only from the reign of Niuserre onward); twenty-eight were priests of deceased monarchs.[44]

Control over the economic flows in the country and the remuneration of state officials provided the kings at the beginning of the Fifth Dynasty with an effective system of supervision over the expanding nonroyal bureaucratic apparatus. It is certainly interesting in this context that officials holding the office of vizier are completely absent from the lists of sun temple personnel.

A millennium later, a similar policy was imitated, consciously, by Akhenaten, at a time when the power of the priests of Amun permeated all parts of the country and state, and the king was looking for a way of constraining this power and finally eliminating it altogether. This gave birth to Akhenaten's religious reform, sometimes seen as a form of monotheism, which was based on the cult of the sun god and fully under the control of the king, who was represented by just a few loyal officials. The architecture of the temples of Aten was also based on the legacy of the sun temples of the Fifth Dynasty kings, small sacrificial altars and offerings that were subsequently redistributed as remuneration to the temple priests and officials.[45]

A New Policy for the "Great Good"

The king would not have been able to enforce this policy alone. He needed allies in the form of loyal dignitaries. That is why it was probably Userkaf who created a special group of high officials holding the office of r-Nḫn (Spokesman of Nekhen). This title appears at the beginning of the Fifth Dynasty and its most important aspect is its social context.[46] The office holders usually served at the royal court and/or the court of justice. Today we know of thirty-six bearers of this title, who had seventy-five more titles between them. The most common were Priest of Maat (twelve references in all) and smsw-ḥȝit, 'Elder of the ḥȝit-hall' (also twelve references). Most of the evidence referring to holders of this office was found in the pyramid complexes of Kings Neferirkare and Raneferef, and in the sun temples of Userkaf, Neferirkare, and Niuserre. Roughly a third of the bearers of the title are dated to the Fifth Dynasty, the rest to the Sixth Dynasty. An interesting point is that there was only ever one office holder with this title at one time. This situation may have changed during the Sixth Dynasty, however, especially in view of the large number of known holders of the title.

There is probably an important link between the title Spokesman of Nekhen, which emphasizes the status of Nekhen, and the name of the sun complex of Userkaf, whose name, Nḫn-Rˤ, could be translated as either 'Stronghold of Re' or 'Hierakonpolis of Re.' Nekhen itself, as has been stated earlier, the Upper Egyptian city of Hierakonpolis, was one of the most important centers in Egypt on the cusp of its unification. It was the center of the cult of the protector of Upper Egypt, the god Horus,

Fig. 5.7. Relief fragment from Userkaf's complex in Saqqara. Unlike the Fourth Dynasty, which preferred sheer monumentality for royal monuments, the subsequent Fifth and Sixth Dynasties largely reduced the scale and focused on the elaboration of decoration and symbolism of the tomb complexes of the kings. Saqqara. Egyptian Museum, Cairo. (Archive of the Czech Institute of Egyptology, Charles University, M. Zemina)

A New Policy for the "Great Good" 119

and simultaneously a significant religious center, whose importance lasted throughout the Old Kingdom. The reference to Nekhen in the title Spokesman of Nekhen recalls its status as the symbol of a prominent religious center with Horus at its head in a way that appears designed to strengthen the religio-political significance of Userkaf's sun sanctuary.

This suggested link between Userkaf's sun temple and the Upper Egyptian religious center could be confirmed by other discoveries relating to the Hierakonpolis temple. It was explored more than a hundred years ago, which led to the discovery of the Main Deposit, a cache of cult artifacts (including the Narmer Palette) dating to the Late Predynastic, Archaic, and Old Kingdom periods.[47] The temple was surrounded by a large mud brick enclosure wall, inside which was a high sand mound sheathed with limestone blocks.[48] This is strikingly similar to the sun temples of Userkaf and Niuserre: within the main temple there was a sand mound evoking the idea of the primeval hill where life was conceived. Sun temples with an obelisk on a stone base are not known to have existed prior to Neferirkare's reign.[49] This idea of the primeval mound may have been enhanced by the rounded corners of the enclosure wall of the main temple of Userkaf's sun complex. Indeed, perhaps the entire upper temple was intended to evoke the idea of the primeval mound.

At the beginning of the Fifth Dynasty a new title appears, Priest of Maat, which implied that its bearers were responsible for establishing and maintaining order in the name of the goddess of justice, in accordance with the wishes of the king, executor of the goddess's will on earth.[50] This is reminiscent of the incorporation of 'Maat' into the Horus names of Userkaf and Sneferu. The consolidation or reintroduction of 'Maat' by the king and priests appears to have been an axiom of the beginning of the Fifth Dynasty.

The goddess Maat never had her own temple in Egypt. Her priests must have been dignitaries who subscribed to the concept of order and justice at a more symbolic level, though if a ruler claimed allegiance to Maat, these priests would have been his extended arm. They would have comprised a core group, close to the king, that enforced the interests of the ruling elite.[51] In the absence of this sort of arrangement, it would be difficult to imagine what purpose was served by priests of a goddess without temples or cult places of any kind.

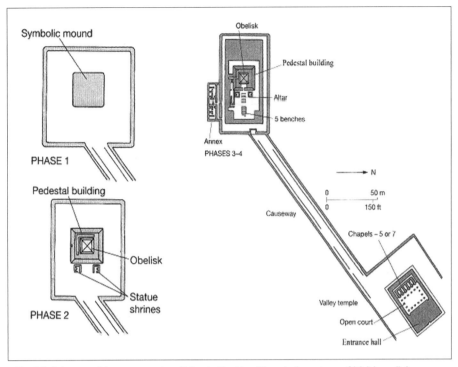

Fig. 5.8. Scheme of the sun temple of Userkaf in Abu Ghurab. (courtesy of M. Nuzzollo)

If we return to the meaning of the title 'Spokesman of Nekhen,' we see that it refers to a specific group of dignitaries formed at the beginning of the Fifth Dynasty in connection with the new religio-political reality, with the clear role of supporting the king. They were to be assisted in this by allusion to the order of the goddess Maat and the ancient religious center of Horus at Hierakonpolis, and by the newly emerging form of monumental architecture, represented in Userkaf's case by his sun temple.

An important final observation is that there is no evidence for the office of the High Priest of Heliopolis at Heliopolis, where the mysterious Benben Stone, the symbol of the sun god Re, was located for much of the Fifth Dynasty—from the start and for almost the entire time that sun temples were being built. This may confirm the hypothesis that these temples were built to bring the cult of the sun god Re under the king's control.[52]

A result of this policy was that all the rulers who built the sun complexes incorporated the sun god into their regnal name: Sahure's name meant 'He Who Is Close to Re'; Neferirkare's, 'Beautiful Is the *Ka* of Re'; Raneferef's, 'Beautiful Is Re'; Niuserre's, 'The One Who Belongs to the Power of Re'; and Djedkare's, 'Eternal Is the *Ka* of Re.' Exceptions are the founder of the Fifth Dynasty, Userkaf, whose name meant 'Powerful Is His *Ka*,' and Menkauhor, 'Enduring Are the *Ka*s of Horus,' who ruled immediately after Niuserre. This may be proof that the policy, initiated by Userkaf, only began to be enforced after he became king.

To close this chapter, let us add, by reference to the reign of King Sneferu, that it was Userkaf who restored the tradition of building *mrt* shrines, where the cults of the ruler, the god Re, and the goddess Hathor were celebrated. It appears that the king presented himself as a child of Re and Hathor in these temples, which as we have seen are known by inscriptions from the time of Sneferu and then, after a hiatus, only from the Fifth Dynasty and early Sixth Dynasty. They played a significant role in promoting the king's exclusive connection with the sun god Re, in a way that would be echoed much later by Akhenaten.[53]

6 The Sun at Its Zenith

Niuserre, the Last King of the Abusir Dynasty

Niuserre is another king of the famous Fifth Dynasty—the 'sun' dynasty—during whose reign both the society and many of its founding principles were transformed. As we have seen, the key question for the first Fifth Dynasty rulers was how to consolidate the relatively unstable position and lack of legitimacy that resulted from their mixed lineage. Part of the answer was to seek support from the growing nonroyal sphere of high officials. A king could not achieve these objectives without controlling huge economic resources. These processes determined the nature of the Fifth Dynasty and, in a certain sense, were put to good use during the reign of King Niuserre.

Niuserre ruled for a relatively long time: the *sed* festival decoration in his sun temple almost certainly proves that he celebrated thirty years on the throne. As with previous kings, evidence from various spheres of ancient Egyptian society document not only the ways in which Niuserre's reign was exceptional, but also the depth to which the times had changed. The principal changes in the fields of monumental architecture, religious ideology, artifacts, iconography, texts, and hierarchy (as reflected in intricate titulary, rituals, and behavioral strategies) might briefly be described as "the rhetoric of power."[1] This allows the ruling elite to maintain—and possibly consolidate—their power, status, and position with the help of 'public relations.' Players of this 'power game' are motivated to adapt to the changing social environment by the attractive potential for significant reward, which grows in proportion to the intensity of their participation. This creates a system of positive reinforcement and at the same time spreads rapidly in an 'us' and 'them' environment. We saw this effect during the reign of King Userkaf, with the emergence of interest groups of priests of the goddess Maat and Spokesmen of Nekhen.[2] The mechanism was also at work under King Niuserre.

Niuserre was a younger brother of King Raneferef.[3] Their parents were Neferirkare and Queen Khentkaus (II), whose tomb lay to the south of her husband's pyramid. Niuserre did not just build his own funerary complex and the second—archaeologically documented—sun temple in Abu Ghurab, he also oversaw the completion of his mother's pyramid complex and the completion of his father's to a simplified design. Moreover, thanks to Lehner's research at Giza, there is growing evidence relating to Niuserre's building activities on this site for which we still have no satisfactory explanation.[4]

Most of the evidence pointing to fundamental changes in Niuserre's time is provided by monumental architecture. The funerary complex of King Niuserre at Abusir bore the name *Mn-swt-Ny-wsr-R^c* (The Places of Niuserre Endure.) In line with Old Kingdom tradition, this name covered all the main components of the complex. It also underlines both their importance and the fact that in the eyes of the ancient Egyptians, this was truly an eternal project that symbolized the permanence and unchangeability of Niuserre's rule. His complex was the last royal tomb built in the pyramid necropolis at Abusir. It had the standard components—valley temple, causeway, pyramid temple, and the pyramid proper—but still it differs from its predecessors in some important ways.[5]

In the first place, Niuserre's architect had to deal with the problem of where to put it. Until then, the kings buried at Abusir had situated their pyramids to align the northwest corner with the temple of the sun god Re in Heliopolis. The three kings buried at Giza engaged in a similar practice, symbolically aligning the southeastern corner of their pyramids with the same temple.[6] But for Niuserre to follow suit would have meant building his pyramid complex deep in the desert southwest

Fig. 6.1. Pyramid necropolis of Abusir with the pyramid of Niuserre in the center. (M. Bárta)ollo)

of his brother's.[7] It was decided therefore to squeeze the new complex into an area lying northeast of the complex of their father, Neferirkare. This was, indeed, the only feasible solution in the rapidly filling pyramid necropolis. What is surprising in this context is the orientation of the Abusir pyramids toward the Heliopolis sacred precinct, which seems to conflict with the real politics of the Fifth Dynasty kings.

Niuserre's valley temple had two entrances divided by columns. The principal entrance, oriented to the east, contained two rows of papyrus columns of red Aswan granite. The second was in the southwest, roughly oriented toward Abusir Lake, the direction of the main entrance to the Abusir and Saqqara necropolis; it was also embellished with a single row of columns. The entrance could not be oriented directly to the southeast because there was a port there, which anyone arriving from the settlement of the capital city had to circumvent from the southwest. The entrances were complemented by two ramps starting near the harbor, from which emerged the material goods that supported the daily functioning of the mortuary cult. The floor was paved with black basalt to

Fig. 6.2. Pyramid temple and causeway of Niuserre from the top of his pyramid. (M. Bárta)

evoke the impression of the Nile Delta, where the god Horus, whom the ancient Egyptian king was believed to personify, was miraculously conceived. In roughly the center of the temple there was a room with three niches for the king's statues. Although the temple was badly damaged in the Middle Ages, fragments of reliefs were preserved that depicted such themes as the ruler defeating his enemies, and a scene of Hathor nursing the king. Remnants of statues of captive enemies of Egypt were found, as well as fragments of lion sphinxes and an alabaster head of Queen Reputnebu, one of Niuserre's wives.[8]

The causeway was a little less than 400 m long, with its upper end roughly 28 m higher than the valley temple. Its eastern part (the first two-thirds) made use of Neferirkare's unfinished causeway. Beyond this, the line of the causeway was diverted to the northwest, with a newly built section to join it to the entrance to the king's pyramid temple. Unlike Sahure's causeway, this one appears to have been undecorated, as neither Borchardt nor the later Czech archaeologists have found any fragments of reliefs that may have come from there.[9]

The most interesting part of the complex is the mortuary temple adjacent to the pyramid's eastern entrance. The ground plan of the temple is different from typical Fifth Dynasty temples and has an inverted T shape. This was an unavoidable design, because the temple and the pyramid were located in a part of the necropolis already occupied by older tombs, which the ruler decided to respect. The eastern part of the temple comprised a long, arched passageway, the *pr-wrw* (House of the Great Ones), which is generally considered to be the place where the court elite bade farewell to their dead king. Along each side of this hall, in the north and the south, were five storage rooms. After the hall came the open courtyard, the *wsht*, paved with black basalt and lined by sixteen red granite columns with papyrus-shaped capitals. The architecture of the courtyard was intended to evoke the Nile Delta and the myth of Osiris, one of the most important myths from the point of view of the king's life in the netherworld. The shafts of the columns were decorated with the king's titular and depictions of the heraldic protective goddesses of Egypt, with the cobra goddess Wadjet on the north and the vulture goddess Nekhbet on the south. The passageway around the courtyard was roofed with limestone slabs adorned with stars, painted in imitation of the night sky.

After the courtyard came the internal, 'intimate' part of the temple, which started with a transverse corridor—called in Ancient Egyptian *ʿrrt*. In its western wall was a niche containing a statue of a lion, to safeguard the entrance to this most sacred part of the temple. Then came a room with five niches in which the king's statues were probably placed. After this was an architectural innovation in temple design, the *antichambre carrée*, a room with a square floor plan and a single column in the center, the walls adorned with processions of gods. This was followed by the central part of the temple, an east–west oriented chapel with an altar and cult stela in the form of a false door. An important innovation in Niuserre's complex was the strongly accented corner structures, called *Eckbauten*, found at the northeastern and southeastern corners of the pyramid temple. The prevailing opinion is that they were prototypes of the pylons that would later become temple gateways as we know them, for example from the New Kingdom temples at Luxor and Karnak.[10]

The burial place of the ruler was hidden in the pyramid itself, with the burial chamber at its center. The pyramid was built in seven stages of construction on a base with sides 78.5 meters long; it was 50 meters high. The entrance to the pyramid was at ground level, in the middle of the northern wall. This is where the corridor started and then gradually descended southward to the burial chamber. Approximately halfway down the corridor was a granite portcullis. From this point the corridor continued five degrees toward the southeast to reach the center of the burial chamber, which had a rectangular plan and was oriented east–west, beneath the center of the pyramid. The burial chamber itself was built in a sunken pit with a ceiling made of three saddle roof layers built of massive blocks of limestone, each separated by a layer of limestone chippings for a more even distribution of pressure on the ceiling. Unfortunately, the chamber was repeatedly robbed and damaged in ancient times. The current state of the interior of the pyramid of Niuserre is such that it cannot be entered; it is thus quite possible that someday we will learn much more about this pyramid.

The Delight of Re

'The Delight of Re' was the name (in ancient Egyptian, *šsp-ib-Rꜥ*) of the sun temple of Niuserre, located just a few hundred meters north of Userkaf's temple at Abu Ghurab—and still standing today.[11] Its structure, building materials, decoration, and symbolism made this temple the perfect manifestation of the idea of the sun temple—the place of the cult of the god Re, where the king demonstrated his exclusive status as the guarantor of *maat*. The design was based on the same principles as earlier sun temples. But because of its condition and the degree to which it has been studied, Niuserre's temple has become the modern exemplar of this form.

Niuserre's complex, like Userkaf's, comprised a valley temple, causeway, and upper temple. There were three entrances to the valley temple: a main entrance facing east and divided by four columns of red granite with palmiform capitals; and two side entrances (north and south), flanked with two granite columns each. All three entrances opened into a spacious hall leading to the causeway in the direction of the main temple. On the walls of this hall there probably used to be a list of all the feasts celebrated in the complex, though only tiny fragments of it survive.[12] In close proximity to the temple there was a large settlement that reached the

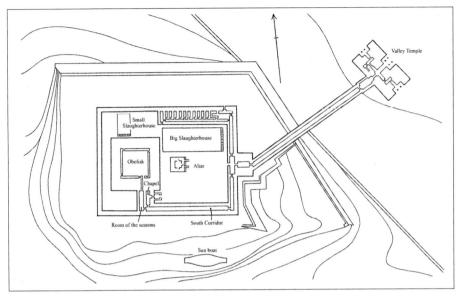

Fig. 6.3. Plan of the sun temple of Niuserre. (courtesy of M. Nuzzollo)

edge of the main temple with the obelisk. The size of the settlement can be estimated based on its western enclosure wall, which was some three hundred meters long. The presence and significant size of the settlement indicate that Niuserre's sun complex was a truly significant establishment, which played an important role in the context of the Memphis necropolis and its religious, politico-symbolic, and economic aspects.

The architect of the main temple made use of the local topography and situated the construction on a small mound, in a place where the Western Desert plateau dips into the Nile Valley. The size of the complex required considerable adjustment of the terrain, but the site of the main temple was not chosen for practical reasons alone. The local topography of the pyramid fields shows that it—or more precisely the center of the base of the obelisk—stands on a line connecting the center of Userkaf's pyramid in Saqqara and that of the Great Pyramid (Khufu's) at Giza.[13] Thus, here too, Niuserre employed the same strategy as Userkaf, who used local spatial relations at the Memphis necropolis to symbolically follow in the steps of his famous ancestors, and from this derive legitimacy and authority. It was a matter of principle for Niuserre to demonstrate his relationship with Userkaf (and through Userkaf with Sneferu), and also with Khufu—the god, Sneferu's son, the builder of the biggest pyramid ever constructed in Egypt.

The main temple of the sun complex had a rectangular plan oriented east–west. Its eastern part consisted of a large entrance gate leading to a spacious open courtyard. Today there are large alabaster altars (basins?) arranged along its eastern wall where offerings used to be placed to be solarized before being sent on to the individual royal mortuary complexes in the necropolis. The arrangement of these altars evokes the bench altars in the courtyard of the main temple of Userkaf's sun complex. Clearly, a large number of offerings were brought in every day. Another row, this time of smaller sacrificial basins, was situated in the western part of the temple, north of the base of the obelisk. Along the northern wall of the court there was a series of storage rooms. The courtyard itself was evidently used for the preparation of offerings for further redistribution to their final destinations. In the western part of the court, there was a unique alabaster altar consisting of a central circular element representing the sun and four offering altars in the shape of the *hetep* (offering) sign radiating from the disk, oriented in the four cardinal directions. The circular element could be read as *Re*, referring to the sun god; the whole altar could therefore be interpreted to mean 'Re's offerings from everywhere' (or 'from all directions').

The western part of the temple was dominated by a large obelisk platform 20 m high. The base had slanting sides and supported an obelisk, 36 m high, built of limestone blocks. Unfortunately, the pyramidion that crowned the obelisk is lost, so it is unknown whether it was gold or copper plated. The height of the obelisk, together with the base and the terrain elevation, was 72 m above the surrounding Nile Valley.[14]

A corridor with depictions of the religious festivities relating to the *sed* festival ran along the southern side of the courtyard. This festival played an enormous role in ancient Egyptian royal ideology, as it served as the symbolic restoration of the king's supernatural divine powers. As previously mentioned, these rituals usually took place on the thirty-year jubilee of the king's ascension to the throne. Its depiction in this temple points to the significant position that the king and his cult had in this place too.[15]

Fig. 6.4. View of the open court, altar, and obelisk platform in the sun temple of Niuserre. (M. Bárta)

An important part of the area south of the obelisk base was the Chamber of the Seasons, with depictions portraying the three seasons of the ancient Egyptian year. Only two have been preserved in fragments of the relief—inundation and harvest. These are the seasons that reflect the absolute, limitless function of the sun god Re as the creator of the world and provider of life.[16] When excavations finished at this site, the reliefs were taken to the Berlin Museum, where they sustained serious damage during the Second World War. It is thus theoretically possible that a third, planting season was also represented here. But it is more likely that there were only two seasons on these reliefs, one on each of the long walls of the chamber.[17] The selection of the two seasons of the year would then be a consequence of the spatial arrangement of the room. The massive foundation of the obelisk contained an unlit spiral corridor that led to its top, and ended at the obelisk's foot. South of the main temple there was a large brick model of the sun barque buried in a pit and intended for the symbolic journey of the sun god Re across the sky.

Much of what is known about this sun temple comes from ancient texts. The most significant include the "foundation inscription" published in 1977 by Wolfgang Helck,[18] which reveals the special dynamism connected with the sun temples. Architectural evidence and graffiti from Userkaf's reign point to the speed with which the first stage of his sun temple—and probably of the others—was built using easily available mud bricks. The temples were later extended, with mud bricks being replaced by limestone and, to a more limited extent, by more valuable materials like alabaster and red granite. This two-stage construction suggests that the essential requirement of each new ruler was for the sun temple to be completed and start fulfilling its basic role in the offering cycle as soon as possible.

The reconstruction of the initial brick temple is also mentioned in the foundation inscription. This provides valuable details about the components of the temple, which included, among other things, a pond and a mysterious building covering an area of some 3,500 m². The inscription also refers to a significant enrichment of the temple inventory and equipment: Niuserre donated statues of Re and Hathor to the temple as well as 107 gold and 19 silver vessels, 8 bronze altars, a cult barque lined with green stone, 10 *wekha* standards adorned with lapis lazuli, and 100 cedarwood vessels. The list is far from complete and it is regrettable that only a part of the inscription has been preserved. Details of the economic aspects of temple operations are provided elsewhere in the inscription, which refers to the gift of estates (evidently comprising villages and people, who worked the fields and took care of the cattle and poultry). The yields of these estates were the exclusive property of the sun temple. The items on the preserved part of the inscription include an annual yield of 100,000 loaves of bread and units of beer (which works out to 274 a day), 1,000 pieces of confectionery, more than 1,000 head of cattle, 1,000 birds, game from the Western Desert, milk, honey, and much else.

However, many questions concerning this complex have not been fully answered—for instance, what happened to the offerings solarized here? Were they sent on to the individual mortuary temples at the necropolis immediately, or through the mediation of the Residence, or dispersed elsewhere? We also do not know for certain whether the

Fig. 6.5. Scene from the *sed* festival of Niuserre in his sun temple. (courtesy of M. Nuzzolo)

priests serving here and organized in phylae (working gangs) were the same individuals who served in the rulers' mortuary temples, although the evidence we have suggests this was the case, as indicated by the titles preserved, especially in the tombs at Abusir, Saqqara, and Giza.

Evidence points to a total of twenty-five dignitaries serving in the sun temple of King Niuserre, which is roughly half the number who served in Userkaf's. Most of them held the office of Priest of Re in the Sun Temple of Niuserre. Half also held court offices serving the king. This group included Niankhkhnum and Khnumhotep, famous for their tomb at Saqqara. Both served as manicurists and appear on reliefs in the tomb of Vizier Ptahshepses at Abusir.[19] Nine of the dignitaries also held the office of scribe, twelve had honorific courtly titles, and fifteen had the title of Keeper of Secrets, mentioned earlier in the context of the start of the Fifth Dynasty. Finally, twelve of the officials had functions relating to the king's cult and thirteen to the cult in the royal complexes. According to Gay Wilson, the absence of the gods Horus and Re-Horakhty in the titles of priests connected with the sun temple may point to a significant shift in the religious sphere. And, of course, from here it is not far to Osiris and his cult, which is documented for the first time in this period.[20]

Ptahshepses, the Father of Lobbyists

From the preceding overview of the major monuments linked to Niuserre at the pyramid fields, it is clear that this was a highly dynamic period in architecture. But the innovations were not limited to royal structures.

Niuserre's reign was characterized by the rising power of many high officials of nonroyal descent. This trend had deep roots going back to the end of the Fourth and beginning of the Fifth Dynasty, which were marked by a retreat of members of the royal family from various top administrative offices. The most prominent representative of this trend was a dignitary and later vizier named Ptahshepses, whose tomb is, coincidentally, also at Abusir and was explored in the 1960s and 1970s by a Czechoslovak team. The tomb, individual texts, reliefs, and architecture helped gradually to reconstruct the career of this extraordinary man and of members of his family.[21] Unlike his namesake buried at Saqqara, the Abusir Ptahshepses was at least twenty-five years younger and was buried in a monumental, multichambered tomb built in a completely different style.

Ptahshepses's Abusir tomb, discovered by the French archaeologist Jacques de Morgan at the end of the nineteenth century, was developed in several stages, incorporating elements that had hitherto been exclusive to royal pyramid complexes. This was possible thanks to his extraordinary career, which started when he served at the royal court and was in personal service to the king—and was probably also the royal hairdresser. At that time Ptahshepses, as befitted his status at court, started building a smaller stone *mastaba* located northeast of Niuserre's complex. Its location, however, indicates that he had an extraordinary position at the court even before he was appointed vizier. This appointment was made not long after Niuserre became king. Thus, while simultaneously holding many other offices, Ptahshepses became the overseer of all royal works in the country, overseer of the royal palace, and the king's confidant. As far as we know, he also became only the second dignitary of nonroyal descent to marry a pharaoh's daughter, following his namesake in the reign of Userkaf who was buried at Saqqara. As mentioned earlier, intermarriage was a tool used by the kings of the Fifth Dynasty, and also the Sixth, when they needed to secure the loyalty of influential dignitaries and their families and thereby consolidate their own power.

The exploration of the tomb and of the different stages of its construction has provided reliable proof that Ptahshepses employed many elements of royal architecture, such as a monumental, almost ten-meter-high front with columns; a room with three niches for the cult of three statues of the owner; a large open courtyard surrounded by huge limestone pillars with

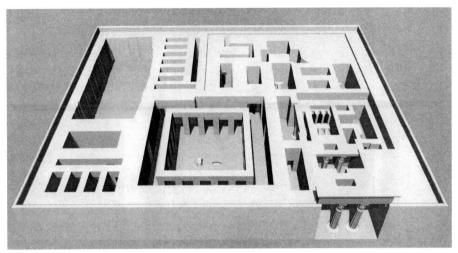

Fig. 6.6. 3D reconstruction of the *mastaba* complex of Ptahshepses in Abusir. (after Krejčí 2009, pl. XVII)

the standing figures of the owner of the tomb; an east–west oriented cult chapel with a false door in the western wall and bench along the northern wall; a room in the shape of a boat for journeys to the netherworld; and a saddle roof above the burial chamber. Two red granite sarcophagi made in the royal workshops, intended for the owner of the tomb and his second wife, Princess Khamerernebti, still stand in the burial chamber. The original decoration of the tomb was very rich; only one-fifth of the decoration has been preserved, covering around sixty square meters. It is regrettable that more of the depictions have not been preserved, since the few that have are of considerable historical interest, showing pottery manufacture, market, desert, and palanquin scenes, and many others.[22]

Nonetheless, even the remaining decoration suffices to form a relatively accurate idea of how influential and powerful the highest-standing officials in the country had become even then. The new strategy of these dignitaries was to promote the male members of their families to high positions, especially in offices over which they had control. This, of course, had a long-term impact on the character of the state administration, as well as on the situation at court. Ptahshepses is a typical example. As far as we know, he was married twice—the second time to a royal daughter of Niuserre. The marriages produced probably seven

Fig. 6.7. Pillared court in the *mastaba* complex of Ptahshepses in Abusir. (M. Bárta)

sons, most of whom began their careers as royal court officials. Many of them acquired the title of Sole Companion, Lector Priest, and Priest of the *'Ist* Chamber. These titles guaranteed a safe source of income. Ptahshepses Junior II was the most successful son, which is evident from his other titles, such as The One in Charge of the Diadem and Inspector of the Palace. These were offices requiring considerable skill and personal commitment. The peak of his court career was the title Overseer of Upper Egypt, as documented by inscriptions in his tomb, which is located to the east of his father's.[23]

Ptahshepses's example sparked the next development: a contemporary high official named Ti imitated Ptahshepses's portico, but instead of columns used pillars, which later became much more popular in nonroyal architecture, maybe due to the simplicity of their form.[24] After Ti, Ptahshepses's example was followed by the viziers Senedjemib Inti and Senedjemib Mehu at the Giza necropolis, west of the Great Pyramid.[25] During Niuserre's rule, the tombs of these officials grew significantly in size, the number of rooms in each individual tomb complex rose, often to more than ten, and the decorative program became richer, with images covering not only the walls of cult chapels, but also the walls of the corridors, storage rooms, and open spaces including the courtyard. Large, open courtyards became a major component of these tombs.

For the other changes that took place in this period we can look to one example that speaks for all: Ti's tomb at Saqqara includes depictions of altogether about 1,800 figures (roughly 90 percent male), with Ti himself depicted almost one hundred times. Funerary priests dominate in the reliefs (more than 560 depictions), followed by boatmen and fishermen (about 180), cattle rearers (about 150), scribes and overseers (150), family members (118), and peasants (108). The number of figures and the way they are divided by affiliation and trade clearly points to the enormous attention paid to the decoration plan of the tomb and the degree to which this can be considered to reflect the real lives of the ancient Egyptians.

Architecture of Power

Major changes that took place in the transition from the Fourth to the Fifth Dynasty are documented in certain features associated with the construction of pyramid complexes: the size of the pyramids, the scale of relief decorations, and the size of the storage areas.

As to size, the largest pyramids were conceived at the beginning of the Fourth Dynasty—the side of the base of Sneferu's Meidum pyramid was 144 m long, his Red Pyramid 220 m. This trend culminated with the largest pyramid, built by Sneferu's son Khufu, at 230.4 m, and the Pyramid of Rakhef, at 215.5 m. The first ruler of the Fifth Dynasty, Userkaf, had a pyramid built whose side was just one-third as long—73.3 m. Most of the Fifth Dynasty pyramids have bases with sides of about 78 m. So, while the size of a king's pyramid was of major importance during the Fourth Dynasty, this later changed for various reasons.

An opposite trend is evident in the way relief decoration developed in the individual pyramid complexes of Old Kingdom rulers. Here we can observe a marked trend toward more elaborate treatment. To put it briefly: as the pyramids diminished in size, the emphasis on the symbolic role of the pyramid complexes and their decoration increased. While Sneferu's mortuary complex in Dahshur had approximately 64 running meters of decoration, Khufu's 100 m, and Userkaf's 120 m, Sahure's complex had several times more—370 m—and the trend continued to rise during the Fifth and Sixth Dynasties. To what can this trend be attributed? As usual, there is no single answer. It seems to have been the result of several factors acting together: resources were limited and needed elsewhere around the capital city; the local bedrock could not support pyramids as big as those built during the Fourth Dynasty; and there was a greater emphasis on expressing and communicating the symbolic and religious aspects of the king's rule via texts and reliefs.

The third and last specific feature of the diachronic development of pyramid complexes is the function and size of storerooms. From the Fifth Dynasty onward this was a characteristic part of the mortuary temple, a place where all the commodities designated for the altar offerings and subsequently for the use of the individual officials and priests employed in the temple were

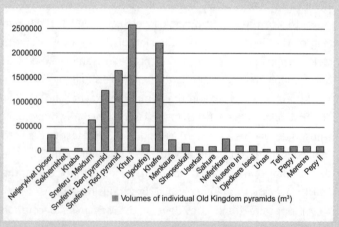

Fig. 6.8. Sizes of the Old Kingdom pyramids. (compiled by M. Bárta)

stored. In Egyptology this cycle is called the reversion of offerings. A closer look at the transformation of these stores over time would reveal some essential dynamics. The mortuary temple of the Red Pyramid of King Sneferu in Dahshur covered an area of approximately 800 m² and had practically no storage space. The same was true of Khufu's temple, which took up more than 2,000 m² but also had virtually no storerooms. At the outset of the Fifth Dynasty, under King Sahure, storage areas comprised just over a fifth of a total temple area of 4,250 m²; in the temple of Pepy II in South Saqqara, they occupied more than half of the total. How can this expansion be explained? The trend most likely reflects what we know about the Fifth Dynasty, which is probably also true of the Sixth. As in modern states, the growing number of officials exerted pressure on the budget due to the size of the payroll and individual benefits. These payments in kind had to be stored before they were distributed, so as the number of officials grew, so did the space required for storage. Maybe the ancient Egyptians thought—as many of us still do today—that this linear trend would go on forever, but events following the Sixth Dynasty quite quickly opened their eyes.[26]

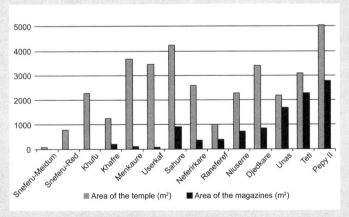

Fig. 6.9. Increasing sizes of the storage-room areas in the pyramid complexes of the Old Kingdom kings, in relation to the built area of the pyramid complexes. (compiled by M. Bárta)

From the very beginning, large courtyards formed an essential part of nonroyal tombs and often occupied a substantial part of the built-up area. These courtyards were the place of important offering ceremonies, which were held to ensure the tomb owner's undisturbed life after death, as confirmed by numerous sacrificial altars found in these places. The courtyards had a function similar to the *ws t* courtyards, which were a stable part of royal funerary temples, where burnt offerings were made to the spirit of the dead king. The courtyards were also closely connected to statues of the tomb owner, to his idealized portraits, as frequent finds in these locations attest. In most cases, as with cult chapels, the courtyards were interconnected with *serdab*s via narrow apertures through which the owner (by means of his statue) could observe what was happening in the courtyard or elsewhere.

During Niuserre's reign, dignitaries' large tombs developed into so-called family tombs, which are exactly the opposite of the opulent tombs of the wealthy officials of the time. The family tombs are usually built of mud bricks on a relatively small ground plan. The superstructure usually consists of one small chapel and one or more rows of shafts incorporated in the brick massif west of the chapel. The shafts were used for the burials of the individual members of the family to which the tomb belonged. The size and depth of the shafts and the properties of the burial chambers themselves are indicative of the status of the buried individuals. Their social status was of course also reflected in the details of the burial—the deceased could be buried in a plain reed mat or in a wooden coffin—and in the composition of the funerary equipment, though this was always very modest.[27]

As far as the chapel is concerned, this may have been the main cult site with the stela of the highest-status owner of the tomb. It often contained a limestone false door with his name and titles. Sometimes there would be undecorated niches, which served as modified cult places for other members of the family. The niches would usually correspond with the main shafts in the first row. The further a shaft was to the west, the lower the social status of the individual buried there. These tombs were used for male, female, and child burials. The idea of such tombs emerged, typically, during the reign of King Niuserre as a consequence of the greater emphasis placed on kinship relations, which were becoming an increasingly relevant and indeed dominating factor in the appointment of individuals to high posts, and thus in the entitlement to receive payments in kind as a result of such an appointment. It goes without saying that a large majority of such tombs were usually devoid of any decoration.[28]

Another of the many innovations occurring in Niuserre's reign involved the new themes that started to be depicted on the walls of nonroyal tombs. We can only speculate about the reason, but it may have been connected to the democratization of the afterlife cult and the rise of the middle class, which started assuming more rights and powers. The new themes also seem to be derived from the Chamber of Seasons in Niuserre's pyramid complex. They included, for example, market scenes portraying barter transactions among professional groups in the capital and its environs, where there was more specialization than in the provinces.[29] Other scenes showed the owner of the tomb being carried in a litter, usually during inspections at the building site, or had a desert theme.[30]

Fig. 6.10. Detail of the name of Osiris from the false door of Neferinpu in Abusir. (Archive of the Czech Institute of Egyptology, Charles University, M. Frouz)

A New God with a Goatee

The era of Niuserre's reign coincided with the rise of a new deity, which was a rare occurrence in the history of ancient Egypt. The name of the god was Osiris, and we know little about either his genesis or the meaning of his name. In any case, this was a large change for the Egyptians of that time. Suddenly—at least that is how it appears today—their pantheon was enriched by a god who became the master of the netherworld that would contain the souls of all the dead, not just of the king. It was a kind of democratization of the afterlife, in the sense that every Egyptian could hope for a blissful existence after death.[31] Returning to the theory of punctuated equilibria, the roots of the "limited democracy" of the netherworld were present already during the reign of Niuserre, although Mark Smith, for example, suggests that it did not begin in earnest until the Sixth Dynasty.[32]

Gwyn Griffiths interprets Osiris's name to mean 'Mighty.'[33] David Lorton, in contrast, suggests that it ought to be understood as 'State of Performance,' in the sense of a performed and completed mummification ritual.[34] This would make sense in the context of the rites relating to the funerary acts and the magical revival of the dead.

The first available documentation of this god is in the *htp-di-nsw* formula of the high official Ptahshepses buried at Saqqara, whose false door is displayed today in the British Museum in London.[35] This dignitary was the one who also married the royal princess Khamaat, daughter of Userkaf. What matters here is that Ptahshepses died during the reign of King Niuserre, which gives us the latest date by which his stela—with its mention of Osiris—could have been completed. It may have been made even earlier, as an official of such high standing, and especially one who lived so long, is likely to have had his tomb prepared far in advance. The oldest evidence of the god Osiris may thus have predated Niuserre's reign. Osiris also appears in the tomb of the aforementioned priest Neferiretenef, who served in the sun temples of Sahure and Neferirkare.[36] In both Ptahshepses's and Neferiretenef's tombs, Osiris is mentioned in the offering formula "An offering made by Osiris . . ." and the determinative of his name is the sign of a sitting man with a goatee and wearing a close-fitting cloak. The possibility that Neferiretenef's tomb predates Niuserre has also been suggested both by Nigel Strudwick and by Bernard Mathieu, in his latest work on the beginnings of the cult of Osiris.[37]

The cult of Osiris is also reflected in the iconography of the 'offer-ings scene,' where the owner of the tomb is depicted sitting at a table with sliced loaves of bread in front of him. This is a classical image from Early Dynastic stelae that gradually passed to the Old Kingdom. It was the central scene on every false door. Over time, as the scene developed, the shape of the bread changed: the loaves became ever more elongated until—in Niuserre's time—they were transformed, due to a formal simi-larity of shape, into reeds. One of the earliest depictions of the two forms occurring side by side, before reeds finally replaced the bread altogether, can be found in the Saqqara tomb of Ti, which also dates to Niuserre's reign.[38] From that moment, the offering scene acquired a stronger sym-bolic meaning and started to refer to the Osiris myth—to his rebirth in the papyrus thickets of the Nile Delta. Since this scene appeared in every tomb with an offering place, we can truly speak about a democratization of the ideas related to the afterlife thus symbolized,[39] although even the poorest decorated tombs belonged to relatively well-off officials. Most ancient Egyptians could only afford a simple pit grave with an offering emplacement, often of mud, so it was a limited democracy at best.

Osiris was often given the attribute Nebmaat (Lord of Maat). This is another expression of the theological climate at the start of the Fifth Dynasty, a period that, as we have seen, also witnessed the expanding cult of the goddess Maat and the priests of Maat, and the Horus names of Sneferu (Lord of Maat) and Userkaf (The One Who Accomplishes Maat), whose daughter was Khamaat (Maat Appears).[40]

The God Osiris and His Assassination

The Osirian myth is, to begin with, a myth concerning the first ruler of Egypt. It is recorded in the earliest texts of a more or less continuous nature, the Pyramid Texts, which first appeared in the pyramid of Unas at the end of the Fifth Dynasty. Initially, only the ruler would be resurrected as Osiris after death. As we have already seen, the beginnings of the myth have been traced to the Fifth Dynasty, based on the first known inscriptions that include Osiris's name. The Pyramid Texts still make a distinction between the ruler and Osiris, but later the deceased king merges with Osiris. The whole Osirisian myth was a significant component of the ancient Egyptian concept of coming to terms with death and the dominant view of the eternal institution of the king, who represented the Egyptian gods on earth. But no source has yet been found that contains the myth in its entirety, so what we have today is a multilayered story with sometimes contradictory details, much of which is derived from Greek and Roman transmissions. For ancient Egyptians, death did not mean the end, but a very intricate rite of transition for which one had to prepare well in advance.

The myth as we know it is this: Osiris was a king ruling on earth. His parents were Geb, the god of the earth, and Nut, the goddess of the sky. They had three children besides Osiris—his brother Sutekh and his sisters Isis and Nephthys. Osiris took Isis as his wife, and Sutekh took Nephthys. Sibling marriages were quite common in the royal families of ancient Egypt, as they guaranteed the integrity of the family line.

Osiris and Sutekh argued. Sutekh murdered his brother and flung his remains across Egypt. Isis and Nephthys secretly gathered the scattered pieces and hid with them in the papyrus marshes of the Nile Delta. They managed to reassemble the whole body and revive Osiris for a brief time so that he could impregnate Isis. Osiris then departed for the next life, where he became the lord of the netherworld and ruler of the kingdom of the dead. Isis meanwhile secretly gave birth to and raised Osiris's son Horus. When Horus matured, he challenged his uncle Sutekh for dominance of the world, to take up his father's legacy that was rightfully his. After a series of battles, Horus defeated Sutekh and came to rule the human world. He became the ruler of the fertile Nile Valley, while his uncle ruled the desert regions surrounding Egypt as well as the countries beyond. From that time on, Horus was identified as both the living king and the god who protected him, while Osiris was identified as the dead king.

The ancient Egyptians commemorated Osiris's death every year at the beginning of the Nile flood, which for them was the symbol of productive forces and rebirth, akin to Osiris's impregnating Isis after being reborn in the Egyptian Delta. This is the background to the reed symbol in the offerings scene. In the tombs of high officials, the reeds in this scene also indicate that they too would be reborn and journey to the netherworld to join Osiris.

Moreover, it is likely that the promulgation of the cult of Osiris was linked to the dignitaries of the royal court in the first half of the Fifth Dynasty.[41] In this way, they affirmed their social status in life while at the same time securing a degree of exclusivity for life in the netherworld, which was (and had to be) different from the one reserved for the king.

Niuserre and Loyalty Acquired through Daughters

Niuserre's reign also introduced the practice of marrying royal daughters to representatives of influential noble families, which later became an integral part of the political court scene.[42]

Nineteen marriages have been documented of women bearing the title Royal Daughter or variants such as Royal Daughter of His Body or Eldest Royal Daughter.[43] With one exception, these women were buried in cemeteries near the capital of the day (the exception is lady Ifi, buried in al-Hamamiya in Upper Egypt). At least thirteen of these royal daughters married dignitaries of nonroyal descent. The first documented case of this policy dates to the beginning of the Fifth Dynasty, when, as we have seen, King Userkaf gave his eldest daughter, Khamaat, in marriage to Ptahshepses, a high official.[44] Princess Ifi was the second royal daughter to follow this policy. She married a dignitary, Kakhenet, and was the only one to be buried away from the Memphis pyramid field.[45] Both these princesses were the forerunners of a practice that flowered under King Niuserre and his successors; we know of at least ten such marriages in the second half of the Fifth Dynasty alone.

We know the names of two officials who married Niuserre's daughters during his reign: Vizier Ptahshepses was married to Princess Khamerernebti, who was even buried in his tomb (Abusir tomb AC 8),[46] and the dignitary Sekhemankhptah married Princess Bunefer (Giza tomb G 7152).[47] Niuserre's third daughter, Sheretnebti, also wed a high official of nonroyal descent, but his name is unknown.

In some cases, there is no evidence that the husbands of royal daughters held high office in their own right. It is possible to prove, however, that they came from powerful families. For example, Princess Nubibnebti married a priest Sankhuptah, as documented in the tomb of his father and also by his statues.[48] His father was the official Akhtihotep—buried at Saqqara, southeast of Djoser's complex—who held, among other posts, the office of Priest of Khnum, First of the House of Life[49] in All Its Places.[50] Similarly, Princess Meresankh married the official Wepemneferet Wepa (G 8882), who is not known to have held any high post despite titles like Administrator of the (Town of) Pe and Administrator of the Domain of Horus (sb3w ḥnt(i) pt), and his role as the official in charge of distributing rations in the House of Life. Meanwhile, it is documented that in three marriages of royal daughters to nonroyal officials, the sons-in-law received the honorific title Royal Son even though they were not biologically related to the king. Who were the three husbands? They all lived during the Fifth Dynasty and the one with the highest standing was our Abusir vizier Ptahshepses; the others were Seshemnefer (III) and Khufukhaf (II). It is likely that the eldest son of an important family was chosen for marriage to a royal princess.

Excavations carried out by the Czech Institute of Egyptology at Abusir in 2012 discovered, in the southern part of their concession (Abusir South), the rock tomb of Princess Sheretnebti, who was the third of Niuserre's daughters to be married to a high official. Today, this is the most thoroughly researched complex of a royal princess in Egyptian archaeology.[51] Although the complex had already been damaged by robbers in ancient times, the individual burial chambers dug out in the floor of the rock chapel are well preserved. The burial chambers of the princess and especially of her husband point to the latter having been a dignitary of very high status. This is reflected in the incredibly beautiful execution of his limestone sarcophagus. It has also been possible to

Fig. 6.11. Statue of Princess Sheretnebti, daughter of King Niuserre. She was married to an anonymous official buried in Abusir South. (Archive of the Czech Institute of Egyptology, Charles University, M. Frouz)

Fig. 6.12. Tomb of Ti, reign of Niuserre. Ti built his lavish tomb in Saqqara. His tomb features depictions of about 1,800 figures (roughly 90% are male). Funerary priests dominate in the reliefs (more than 560 depictions), followed by boatmen and fishermen (about 180), cattle keepers (about 150), scribes and overseers (150), family members (118), and ordinary peasants (108). Many of them are labeled not only with their titles and professions, but also with names. (courtesy of S. Vannini and Laboratoriorosso)

reconstruct part of the princess's badly damaged false door. And finally, the *serdab* proved a sensational find, containing the limestone statues of the princess, her husband, and their children.

One interesting element in the context of this practice of political marriages to princesses is the remarkable rise, which dates to King Niuserre's rule, in names created specifically for princesses. These are personal names, where one part is the word *nbti*, which means 'two ladies' and refers to the two protective goddesses of Upper and Lower Egypt, Nekhbet and Wadjet, imbuing the name with significant religious and political connotations. Such names had previously been reserved for persons of royal descent, but under Niuserre, we see both a general increase in the number of documented names of this type and their use in the nonroyal sphere, which would grow increasingly common.[52] The most likely reason for this trend is further, albeit still limited, democratization. Explicit worship of the most important deities in the state became accessible also to the lower strata of the elite, similar to the faith in Osiris.

We can thus see how Niuserre's reign ushered in significant changes, leaving Egypt a different country in many respects. Niuserre's successor was King Menkauhor, whose reign was very short and who left behind an unfinished pyramid complex in Central Saqqara. He was succeeded by Djedkare Isesi, who ruled for some four decades. Djedkare's reign corresponds approximately with the close of the Early Bronze Age III in the Near East and the start of Stage IV. This was not a chance divide, at least in the region of Syria–Palestine and Mesopotamia. It was around the middle of the twenty-fourth century that the Near East entered a period of instability that saw most towns disappear or decline and a large part of the population revert to a nomadic way of life.[53] Unsurprisingly, the Old Kingdom entered a new, this time final, stage of development at about the same time.

7 Kings and Kinglets

THE REIGN OF DJEDKARE OPENS another chapter of Egyptian history. Djedkare abandoned the pyramid necropolis of the sun kings at Abusir and founded a new cemetery in South Saqqara. He also ended the long tradition of building sun temples, and with it the focus on this expression of the cult of the sun god and the king. However, the king's regnal name means 'The Soul of Re Is Permanent,' which suggests that despite the growing tendency toward the cult of Osiris,[1] there was still a desire to maintain the cult of the sun god Re. It must be stressed that these tendencies were not mutually exclusive.

Djedkare's reign also saw some of the provinces (nomes) start to become less dependent on the center, including nomes 15, 20, and 21, for which we have records of local deputies of the king, nomarchs.[2] The first list of the Upper and Lower Egyptian nomes is known from the time of Niuserre,[3] but the nomarchs' rise in influence was made possible by the steps Djedkare took to decentralize the Egyptian administration. Being at some distance from the Residence and the king, nomarchs soon became increasingly independent. Many succeeded in making their office hereditary, and Sixth Dynasty kings were kept busy trying to contain their power and influence. As we will see, the growing independence of the provinces would become one of the reasons for the eventual fall of the Old Kingdom.

It is not by chance that during Djedkare's reign such features had already begun to appear: they were typical of a declining centralized state.[4] Parallels existed in other declining civilizations, including the Aztec and Inca. Alongside the shifting balance of power from the imperial center to the provinces, other factors emerged one by one and had a cumulative impact on the state. These included bolstering, emulation, resistance, exodus and internal population movement, information control, appropriation, complicity, and assimilation, which we will define and examine in the next paragraphs.[5]

To better understand the specific events that took place in Egypt, it might be helpful to look at the mechanism of decline in general terms. It begins with *bolstering*, when the elites and local dignitaries cooperate with the center with the aim of consolidating their own positions. This is related to *emulation*, when the local elites in the provinces emulate the status, style, and customs associated with the ruling elite. Then comes *resistance*, efforts by the local elites to reduce the center's control over local affairs—or end it altogether. Next come *exodus* and *internal population movement*, when ordinary members of society or members of the local elites who have been removed from their posts withdraw to areas beyond the influence of the center, or try to enhance their standard of living in other ways. This may be the only factor that has not been identified in Egypt in this period. After that is *information control*, whereby the local population strives to prevent the flow of information toward the center. The ensuing *appropriation* process concerns the activities of the provincial population aimed at usurping or modifying the procedures and institutions coming from the center and using them for their own purpose. The last two factors, *complicity* and *assimilation*, refer to local elites and sometimes ordinary people cooperating with the center, especially in the economic sphere, to consolidate their own interests, and ultimately trying to integrate into the social, economic, and identity spheres of the dominant society.

These factors manifested themselves toward the latter part of the Old Kingdom, beginning in Djedkare's time, but not as a homogeneous continuum. We have seen that already under King Niuserre, the independence of high officials was growing, as evidenced by the marriage of the king's daughters to several men of nonroyal descent, and the elites

Fig. 7.1. Pyramid of Djedkare. (M. Bárta)

had begun to emulate the king's status and specific royal manifestations, as seen in the architectural components of Ptahshepses's *mastaba*. This eventually led to the emergence of the initial factors of decline, *bolstering of power* in the provinces and *emulation*. Niuserre's successors, Djedkare and Unas, reacted by adopting several measures[6] intended to suppress the personal ambitions of the increasingly independent high officials.

The Race for Social Status

In this period, the *status race* phenomenon was clearly already in full swing. The basic contours of this trend can be mapped not later than the beginning of the First Dynasty (and probably earlier), and it continues throughout ancient Egyptian history. It involved an ongoing competition between the royal domain and the nonroyal members of the elite. The king was constantly seeking new ways to set himself apart from the other members of the ever-expanding ruling class.[7] However, no sooner had he introduced a new way to symbolize his power and superiority (for examples, see further below) than nonroyals began to take it for themselves. The king was then obliged to look for some new way to set himself apart. The best evidence we have of this ancient Egyptian arms race is in cemeteries, texts, two- and three-dimensional art, and iconography. The way this race developed over time and the patterns it followed during the third millennium BC—starting with the Third Dynasty—can be summarized as follows.[8]

1. Old Kingdom royal tombs were typically placed in the dominant location within the cemetery. They formed the center around which the tombs of members of the royal family and of high officials of nonroyal descent were concentrated.[9] Burial close to the king was a privilege. The First Dynasty practice of sacrificing retainers when the king died had been abandoned, but access to the afterlife was still derived from proximity to the king.[10] This had changed by Niuserre's time, when high officials started to build their own monumental tombs away from the king's. These increasingly became centers of local burial clusters for the officials' own dependents.[11]

2. The superstructure of the royal tomb gradually acquired its final pyramidal shape at the beginning of the Third Dynasty, which distinguished it from nonroyal tombs (apart from some of the nonroyal mud tombs of workers at Giza).[12] The practice of building pyramids atop nonroyal tombs would not be adopted until the New Kingdom.

3. From the First Dynasty onward, royal and nonroyal tombs were distinguished by size, form, and materials. In the first three dynasties, building with stone was the king's prerogative, as he owned all the sources of that material. Officials could thus use stone for their tombs only with the king's consent. The first *mastaba*s (tombs of nonroyal officials) built entirely of limestone appeared relatively late, not before the beginning of the Fourth Dynasty.[13] Other types of stone, such as black basalt, red granite, and alabaster, were used exclusively in the construction of royal complexes and temples.[14]

4. As the royal complex developed over time, new means of expressing the king's unique status were devised, including distinctive architectural and decorative elements that emphasized the king's role. These were adopted and incorporated into the design of nonroyal tombs, albeit always with a delay of several generations.

Examples of this trend are as follows:

- During the First and Second Dynasties, the Abydene tombs of kings differed from nonroyal tombs not only in their size, but especially in the layout of the substructure. They had in common the building materials used (mud brick, wood, mats, to some extent limestone), a tumulus above the burial chamber, and stelae with the details of the owner of the tomb. Unlike the stelae of officials, however, royal stelae were always erected in pairs and were much larger, bearing the Horus name of the king. There was also a striking difference in the amount and quality of funerary equipment.[15]
- During the Third Dynasty royal tombs moved to Saqqara and were built of limestone, while the tombs of high officials continued to be built of mud brick and smaller blocks of stone.[16] The chapels of nonroyal tombs were occasionally lined with limestone. The overall concept of the royal tomb, especially its superstructure, diverged completely from nonroyal tombs, and during the reign of Djoser began to be built in the shape of a stepped pyramid. While royal tombs were designed to facilitate the king's ascent to the sky, the officials' life after death took place within the tomb, or possibly west of the burial ground.
- During the Third Dynasty, the emphasis in royal tombs was on the substructure, which was designed to store copious amounts of funerary equipment; nonroyal tombs started showing signs of conspicuous economization, reflected in the smaller size and shrinking number of the underground burial spaces, which often consisted of just one room. While the superstructures of the royal tombs continued to grow in size through the late Fourth Dynasty, nonroyal tombs became standardized at the beginning of the Fourth Dynasty and started to grow only in the reign of Niuserre.[17]
- A sudden change can be observed at the beginning of the Fourth Dynasty: the underground areas of pyramids were reduced to contain the burial chamber and a couple of other rooms used as stores or, possibly, entrance areas. In the same period, the classical pyramid shape started to appear.

- During the Fourth Dynasty, the decoration of the walls of the individual parts of the royal complex developed. The oldest evidence comes from the Bent Pyramid of King Sneferu at Dahshur.[18] During this period, the tombs of the highest officials and members of the royal family also started being decorated in a limited way.[19] It was only in the Fifth Dynasty that decoration of nonroyal tombs became common, with the quality and scope of the decoration depending on the wealth and status of the tomb owner.[20]

- At the end of the Fifth Dynasty another distinct feature appeared in the decoration of pyramids: the Pyramid Texts. They appeared first on the walls of the antechamber and burial chamber, and expanded during the Sixth Dynasty into other parts of the substructure.[21] This decorative element was later adopted by several consorts of Pepy I and II, and then used in Coffin Texts by high officials during the Middle Kingdom.[22] The first decorated funeral chambers of high royal dignitaries, such as those of Kaiemankh, Rawer (III), Senedjemib Inti, and Seshemnefer (IV), all located at Giza, appeared at the same time as the Pyramid Texts, if not even earlier.[23] Perhaps this was not just a chronological coincidence.

Djedkare, Unas, and the Magical Manual for the Netherworld

Djedkare Isesi was the first in a series of kings who ruled at the end of the Fifth Dynasty and throughout the Sixth, who implemented bold administrative reforms in an attempt to fight the progressive deterioration of the state apparatus, the growing bureaucracy, the decline of the king's authority, and centrifugal trends in the provinces (all of which appeared first under Niuserre and heralded trouble to come). This period is, in a way, a prime example of a system sinking ever deeper into its internal problems. The initial reaction was to introduce a reform that would offer some respite, at least in the short term. As that attempt failed, a new reform would be tried in its place, and so on ad infinitum. In Egypt, as in neighboring areas, this was probably aggravated by an external factor—climate change.[24]

To counteract the loss of royal power and prestige at the end of the Fifth Dynasty, Djedkare established the special office of Governor of Upper Egypt to try to control what was happening south of the capital, and to prevent it eroding the authority of the central administration. He simultaneously introduced the office of a second vizier whose seat was not in the capital, but in Akhmim—an important political and economic center from which it was possible to control other significant areas.[25] The oldest documented burials of provincial dignitaries date to Djedkare's time. Additionally, the viziers of that time ceased to bear the title of Overseer of the Mortuary Priests of the Pyramid Complex of King XY and acquired the title of Overseer of the Pyramid Complex of King XY. It is not easy to unravel the implications of this change, but maybe the more general designation meant that the vizier exerted control over not just the staff of a pyramid complex, but everything related to it. Djedkare was, moreover, the first king to move the site of his pyramid complex to South Saqqara. It is still not clear why. Perhaps it was because Memphis was developing toward the south and the king wished to keep his eternal residence as close to the administrative center as possible.[26]

His successors Unas and Teti must have felt differently, as they built their pyramid complexes close to Djoser's, at the traditional Old Kingdom Saqqara burial ground. Teti's successors, Pepy I, Merenre, and Pepy II, followed Djedkare's example and built their tombs in South Saqqara, as did the Eighth Dynasty 'rulers' whose pyramids were also discovered in this area.

The last king of the Fifth Dynasty was Unas. Not much is known about his lineage and there is speculation that he was of nonroyal descent and hailed from the Nile Delta.[27] Unas's wives were Nebet and Khenut, both apparently of nonroyal descent and buried in a double *mastaba* east of their husband's pyramid temple.[28] Unas's regnal name, with no mention of Re, may signal a departure from the ideology of the sun god, who had been so prominent during the Fifth Dynasty. There is some disagreement as to whether Unas ruled for fifteen or thirty years, but in any event his reign was not insignificant.[29]

Unas's building activities have been documented in the settlement on Elephantine Island in Aswan. Reliefs from Unas's causeway depict cargo boats laden with palmiform columns of red granite, being brought from

Fig. 7.2. Burial chamber of Unas in Saqqara, with the Pyramid Texts. (M. Bárta)

Aswan to form part of his funerary complex. Unas built his pyramid in Central Saqqara, south of Djoser's. His causeway starts from the valley temple situated west of a large harbor and mooring area (located next to the road near the present-day entrance to the Saqqara site). On its way to the pyramid, the causeway had to circumvent limestone cliffs and therefore has several bends. Its path was blocked by the *mastaba* tombs of earlier dignitaries, many of which Unas had dismantled or removed and used as building materials for his own tomb complex. He must have had good reason to choose this awkward and built-over location. Its proximity to Djoser's pyramid, which would have created a link with the past and conferred a degree of legitimacy and continuity upon Unas, may have been a deciding factor.

Unas himself has no extraordinary place in history, based on the current evidence—with one exception. The burial chamber and antechamber of his pyramid were inscribed with the Pyramid Texts, the earliest of these texts to have yet been found.[30] They are religious compositions whose primary objectives are to ensure the king's safe journey to the netherworld and magically protect his person after death. The texts are a disparate collection of spells of varying nature, origin, and age. Why Unas, of all the kings, brought in this innovation is an unanswered question, but it is clear that it was done to retain and emphasize the king's unique position in this world and the next. Already Egypt's highest officials had bridged much of the distance between ruler and elite when Ti at Saqqara and Ptahshepses at Abusir incorporated into their tombs architectural features previously reserved to the king.[31] But after the Pyramid Texts were introduced, it took only three generations before their use began to spread, first to other members of the royal family, then—transformed into Coffin Texts—to officials of the First Intermediate Period and the Middle Kingdom.[32]

Unas tried to deal with the growing independence of high officials in his own way (many centuries later, during the Middle Kingdom, his method was emulated by Senwosret III—perhaps unintentionally). Unas recalled the second vizier and provincial officials to the capital, where they would be under his control. Central administration again dominated the provinces, and—somewhat surprisingly—there is no evidence of high officials being buried in the provinces during Unas's reign. But

Fig. 7.3. Burial chamber of Unas in Saqqara, detail of the Pyramid Texts. (M. Bárta)

these effects did not last, and the kings of the Sixth Dynasty continued to introduce new measures in what would prove to be a futile attempt to control the provinces.[33]

The Way Back

Until the end of the Old Kingdom the state was able to plan, finance, and carry out physically and financially demanding expeditions. We know of journeys to the Sinai Peninsula, to Hatnub in the Eastern Desert, and to the more distant regions of Nubia because they are documented by inscriptions bearing the names of the rulers who funded them or the men who led them.[34] And for 150 years, Egypt appears to have been relatively stable. Yet viewed more closely, the entire Sixth Dynasty exhibits signs typical of the final stage of the decline of social systems.

The Sixth Dynasty lasted from around the beginning of the twenty-third century BC to the middle of the twenty-second, and during this time the power structures typical of the earlier Old Kingdom began to disintegrate. The state administration fell into decline, central powers

Fig. 7.4. Pillared hall in the mastaba of Mereruka. Saqqara. (M. Bárta)

retreated to make way for local centers, the power of provincial officials and their families increased, and affiliation of specific families with hereditary offices began to limit development. The king's office and his divine status were exposed to gradual abrasion, and the fight for power and influence at the royal court intensified. Court intrigues included a failed assassination attempt on King Pepy I and, according to a later report related by Manetho, a successful one on Teti.[35] (However, we know of these only from circumstantial evidence; no direct historical sources have been found.)[36] The state, or rather the king, responded to all this by introducing successive administrative reforms—changing the vizirate, marriage policy, attitudes to the provinces—but they were largely ineffective.[37]

The first king of the Sixth Dynasty was Teti. His paternal ancestry is unknown. His mother was Queen Sesheshet (I); his father is nowhere to be found.[38] The tombs of many dignitaries of his time were subjected to *damnatio memoriae* to erase all physical trace of the owner's name and thereby erase the individual from memory. Some tombs were even reassigned to different persons. This was a very cruel punishment, because an Egyptian who had lost his name and his tomb could not hope to have a life after death in the netherworld.[39] These acts show that the ruler faced opposition in his own court, which is suggested also by one of Teti's regnal names, Seheteptawy, meaning 'He Who Pacifies the Two Lands.' Teti ruled for not more than twelve years, as confirmed by Annals from South Saqqara.[40]

Teti's principal wives included Iput, daughter of Unas and mother of Pepy I—indicating a certain continuity between the Fifth and the Sixth Dynasties—and Khuit, evidently the mother of Userkare, an ephemeral king who ruled after Teti. Teti's reign was also the time of two notable viziers: Kagemni and Mereruka. Both were his sons-in-law. Kagemni was married to Sesheshet Nubkhetnebti, and Mereruka to Sesheshet Waatetkhethor. Clearly, the name of Teti's mother was very popular in the royal court at that time. It is also evident that Teti was a great follower of Niuserre's policy of reinforcing the loyalty of high officials by marrying them to his daughters.

Like Unas, Teti redesigned some aspects of the state apparatus. Teti, too, had two viziers residing in the capital city. Unlike those of Unas, they each had defined powers in the provinces: one oversaw tax collection, the other all royal works (meaning the planning and management of construction projects funded by the state). Also, under Teti, the seat of the vizier was established in what is now Edfu. Manetho records that it was Teti who, after a reign of almost thirty years, was finally murdered by his palace guards in a harem plot, though evidence from contemporary sources is lacking.[41]

Teti was succeeded on the throne by Userkare. Userkare's reign, which lasted for a few years at most, was a very short intermezzo from a historical point of view—not even his tomb is known today.[42] His name, which means 'Strong Is the *Ka* of Re,' may be indicative of the inner strife at the court focusing around the solar cult of the god Re, as it does not follow the usual pattern of royal names used by the kings of the Sixth Dynasty, which generally omit the god Re. His successor was Pepy I, the son of Queen Iput and Teti.

Pepy I's pyramid complex in South Saqqara, Men-nefer-Pepy (Eternal Is the Beauty of Pepy), gave its name to the entire settlement area

Fig. 7.5. Granaries and taxation of grain were among the pillars of the ancient Egyptian economy. Tomb of Mereruka, Saqqara. (M. Bárta)

originally called White Walls (p. 50). It lay to the east of the Saqqara pyramid field and came to be known as Mennefer (or 'Memphis' in its later Greek form).

Pepy I took in marriage two daughters of the Abydos dignitary Khui and his wife Nebet. He evidently did so to retain (or regain) control over Upper Egypt. These daughters are known by their regnal names, Ankhenespepy I and II. According to Yannis Gourdon, their names take the form of an oath and express the king's allegiance—or allegiance to the king: 'As Pepy Lives for Her' or 'She Has Taken an Oath on Pepy.'[43] Khui and Nebet also had a son, Djau, who became vizier, evidently as a reward of the union between the royal and his Abydos family. This is revealed by the so-called Djau Pillar, which depicts Djau and two sisters, both of whom who are designated as royal wives.[44] This may explain why for quite a long time the seat of the vizier's office was at Abydos after it was moved there from Edfu. This was an important juncture in efforts to preserve the administration and royal offices of the Old Kingdom, which would have repercussions as late as the Eighth Dynasty.

Pepy I also became the target of a harem plot, headed by one of his wives. Luckily for him, the plot was foiled in time. We do not know the fate of the conspirators, who included some of the high officials of the time and perhaps the vizier Rawer. This might explain why the vizier did not take part in the investigation, which was conducted by the high official Weni.[45] This was such an important and unique event, and such an uncommon expression of the king's trust, that Weni could not resist including the following on the biographical inscription in his tomb at Abydos:

When there was a legal case in secret in the royal harem against the
    royal wife, the "great of affection,"
his majesty had me proceed to hear it on my own.
(11) No vizier or official was present apart from myself
because I was excellent, I was rooted in his heart,
and his heart was full of me. I alone, together
(12) with (just) one other judge and mouth of Nekhen put it down
    in writing,
    although I was (just) of the rank of overseer of the $ḫnty$-$š$ of the
    Great House;
never before had anyone like me heard the secrets of the royal
    harem, and yet his majesty let me (13) hear (them) . . . .[46]

It is curious that both Teti and Pepy I were targeted for assassination. Perhaps it shows that the times were changing and the king had to fight on many fronts, including the royal harem. It is also possible that similar attempts had been made before—or even regularly—but are hidden from view by the absence of historical sources from earlier periods. Intrigues at court and around the country were certainly rife, and there is no doubt that the ruler's many children became strong competitors for the throne amid all the uncertainty, clientelism, and waning influence of the ruler and his hand-picked officials.

Pepy I's successor Merenre was the son of Queen Ankhenespepy I. This did not prevent him, after he became king, from marrying his aunt, Ankhenespepy II, wife of the late Pepy I, who became the mother of Pepy II. Merenre's rule is marked by the emergence and development of numerous local necropoleis for high officials in the provinces of Upper Egypt: Elephantine, Edfu, Thebes, Coptos, Dendara, Qasr al-Sayad,

Fig. 7.6. Sixth Dynasty tombs of high officials in Qubbet al-Hawa, Aswan, included landing facilities and causeways remotely resembling royal pyramid complexes of the period. (M. Bárta)

Abydos, Akhmim, Deir al-Gabrawi, Meir, al-Sheikh Said, Zawyat al-Mayyitin, Kom al-Ahmar, and Deshasha.[47]

Texts from this time indicate a substantial degree of royal authority across the country, as attested by two references to the trips that Merenre led to the Aswan region. Here the Egyptian king met with the chiefs of the Nubian tribes, Irtjet, Medjat, and Wawat, to receive their homage and tribute.[48]

After Merenre's relatively short reign, his son, Pepy II, took the throne. He is the ruler traditionally associated with the end of the Old Kingdom and the Sixth Dynasty. The length of Pepy II's reign is unclear. There is a short inscription found on Elephantine Island that mentions the second anniversary of his *sed* festival celebration.[49] There is also an inscription referring to the Year after the Thirty-first Count, First Month of Shemu, day 20, from Hatnub graffito No. 7, which is the highest contemporary date for his reign found so far.[50] Therefore, it seems that he must have ruled for at least sixty-two or sixty-four years, based on the biennial census. A much later tradition (the Turin Canon) has it that Pepy II reigned for ninety years; Manetho puts it at ninety-four. The current opinion, however, is that just over sixty years is most likely.[51]

The period of the reign of Pepy II was marked by many reforms, carried out in several distinct stages. During the first half of his rule the office of vizier was held by members of the Khui family at Abydos. This was clearly the consequence of the policy put in place under Pepy I and his marriages to daughters of that family. Between the twenty-fifth and thirty-fifth year of Pepy II's reign, the office of the governor of the south was abolished; from then on, the title could be used by all the nomarchs of Upper Egypt. All these local chiefs were responsible and subordinated to the 'southern vizier.' The king had central granaries built in Thebes, Meir, and probably Abydos to collect taxes (paid in grain). The nomarchs in those locations then acquired, quite logically, the title of Overseer of the Granaries.[52]

In the second half of Pepy II's rule the nomarchs proceeded to bring the control of local priests under their administration, as indicated by their new title, Overseer of Priests. At the same time, however, the title Overseer of the Southern Lands was restricted to the nomarch of Meir.[53]

These shifts in the use of important administrative titles suggest that the state was incessantly changing its strategy for governing remote southern provinces and collecting taxes from them. The fact that these measures were implemented uniformly, however, suggests that the state still had a degree of autonomy, strength, and various coercive methods at its disposal.

Rulers from Edfu

The nomarchs of Edfu, the traditional center of the cult of the falcon god Horus, where one of the best-preserved temples of ancient Egypt stands to this day—albeit in its later, Ptolemaic form—are typical of their time. The site lies near Aswan, then Egypt's southern border. Many expeditions departed from Edfu for the Eastern Desert where Wadi Barramiya began, with its profusion of rock engravings dominated by depictions of prehistoric Naqada boats. Edfu was also one of the few places where the Nile Valley opened and offered a larger area of rich fertile soil for agriculture. It was therefore an important economic center, and it was in the interests of the rulers to keep it under their control.

One of the prominent nomarchs of Edfu was the dignitary Isi, who was in office already under King Teti.[54] Isi was bound to Teti through marriage to Teti's daughter Sesheshet Sathathor. Isi was then succeeded by his son, Meryrenefer Qar. Qar grew up at Teti's court, reached adulthood under Pepy I, and inherited the office of nomarch of Edfu from his father during the reign of Merenre. All this is related in his biography, whose form and content anticipate the boastful texts of local rulers during the First Intermediate Period.

The Self-Confident Meryrenefer Qar

This biography helps us to understand the essence of the deep social changes that took place toward the close of the Old Kingdom and permeated the whole society. It contains the following—for us the most interesting—passage:

> I was a youth who tied the headband in the time of Teti,
> and (then) I was taken to Pepy (I),
> to be given an education among the children of the chiefs.
> I was promoted to sole companion and the overseer of
>   ẖnty-š of the Palace in the time of Pepy (I).
> Then the majesty of Merenre had me go south, to the
>   second nome of Upper Egypt
> as a sole companion and great chief of the nome
> and as overseer of the grain of Upper Egypt and overseer of
>   priests,
> through my excellence and my noble status in the heart of
>   (his) majesty.
> It fell to my lot to be the lord at the head of all the chiefs of
>   the totality of Upper Egypt.
> I was the one who judged for the whole of Upper Egypt.
> I saw to it that the cattle of this nome were more (numerous) than the cattle in the stables of the foremost part
>   of the whole of Upper Egypt.

The fact is that it was not found that (anything comparable
    was done by) the chief who was previously in this nome;
This was through my vigilance,
through my excellence in controlling matters for the
    Residence.
I was the keeper of secrets of all matters
Which were brought from the narrow doors in the foreign
    lands.
I gave bread to the hungry and clothes to the naked
Whom I found in this nome.
I gave a jug of milk from my own hand;
I measured out the grain of Upper Egypt from my funerary
    estate for a hungry man whom I found in this nome;
with regard to any man whom I found in this nome
burdened down with a loan of grain from another,
I paid back his creditor from my funerary estate.
I buried every man of this nome who had no son
With linen from the property of my estate.
I propitiated all foreign lands for the Residence
In accordance with my excellence
and in accordance with my vigilance in relation to this,
and I was favoured in respect of it by my Lord.
I rescued the helpless one from one who was more powerful
    than he,
and I judged litigants to their satisfaction.

I am the beloved one of his father,
and the favoured one of his mother, whom his siblings love.
O you who live upon earth and who shall pass by this tomb
    (of mine),
if you love the king, then you shall say
a thousand of bread, a thousand of beer,
a thousand oxen, for the sole companion Meryrenefer.[55]

The unique text of Meryrenefer Qar includes valuable details about the circumstances in Egypt, particularly in the provinces south of the capital, during the Sixth Dynasty. From the very beginning it is relevant that Qar relates that as the young son of Isi, an important dignitary, he was brought up at the royal courts of Teti and Pepy I. This was a royal policy that aimed to engender absolute loyalty in officials by raising them with connections to the royal family and court. These children came from old and influential families on whom the king bestowed hereditary offices, passed down for two or three generations.

The subsequent passages relate how Merenre sent Qar to the Second Upper Egyptian nome with its main seat in present-day Edfu. Qar presents himself, in his own words, almost as an autocrat disposing of all the assets, both land and livestock, adjudicating disputes, intervening on behalf of the hungry and indigent or those burdened by debt. Qar even states he had a role in international diplomacy.

Probably already during the reign of Pepy II, but obviously at its end, one of the local chiefs in the southern part of Upper Egypt, Khui, nomarch of the Thirteenth Upper Egyptian nome, started to insert his name in a royal cartouche. This is an unequivocal indication that he considered himself an autocratic ruler. He also had himself buried in a tomb that conspicuously resembles a pyramid and is located at what is now Dara. It seems that Khui brought the centers in Meir and Deir al-Gabrawi (Upper Egyptian nomes 8, 12, and 14), formerly governed by strong local noble families, under his authority. If the time of Khui is correctly dated—and there has been little doubt about that so far—this is proof that the symbolism and incontestability of the royal office were challenged in unprecedented ways during the second part of Pepy II's reign.[56]

In the context of the growing power and influence of some of the nomarchs, it is crucial to look at the distinct geomorphology of the individual sections of the Nile between Aswan and Cairo. Besides regions of Edfu and Hierakonpolis, there are several stretches where the Nile Valley widens significantly. Moving from south to north with Edfu as the point of departure, there is first the Great (Qena) Bend with Thebes as its natural political center; then come Sohag (with its center in Abydos), Akhmim, Asyut, Minya, and finally the Faiyum.[57] These ancient centers are likely to have heavily influenced the modern territorial division south

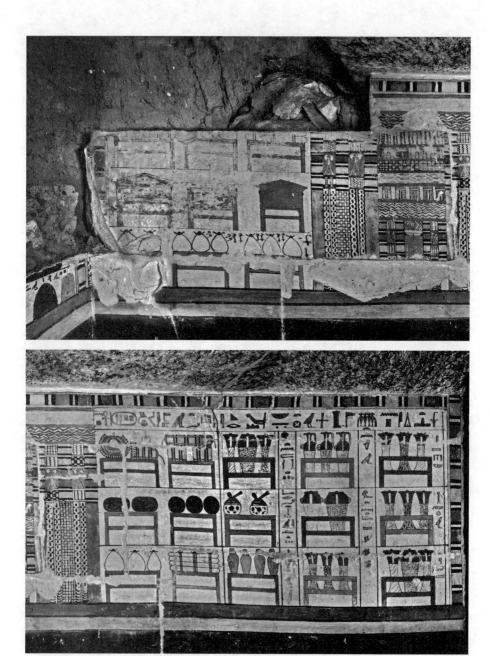

Fig. 7.7. Decorated wall from the burial chamber of Pepyankh in Saqqara. (courtesy M. Megahed)

of Cairo, as proposed in 1889 by the French engineer J. Barrois. This simply reflects the logic and driving forces of landscape, environmental, and geopolitical properties. It is therefore no surprise that these places were also important power centers during the Sixth Dynasty.[58]

It is as essential to be aware that most of these centers were the starting points of major trade routes to the Eastern Desert. The valley near Edfu has already been mentioned; others included the valley leading to the Eastern Desert from al-Kab (Hierakonpolis lay on the western bank opposite al-Kab), and Wadi Hammamat starting in the Qena Bend, which connected the Nile Valley to the Red Sea.[59]

Seventy Kings and the End of the Era of Pyramid Builders

The very long reign of Pepy II had an uncommon effect that aggravated an already complicated situation after his death. His more than sixty years on the throne and numerous wives, who gave him even more numerous offspring and potential male heirs, may have been why the Seventh Dynasty was marked by instability and frequent changes of ruler. According to official tradition as related by Manetho (or, more precisely, by later authors who preserved a part of his work on the history of Egypt), the Seventh Dynasty lasted seventy days and was ruled by seventy kings. Another source puts it at five rulers reigning for seventy-five days.[60] This is why the Seventh Dynasty does not feature much in works on the history of the Old Kingdom.

Pepy I and Pepy II entered into many marriages with a variety of elite women, which may have increased instability at court and helped to create factions and interest groups, ultimately weakening the state apparatus. Pepy I had seven or eight wives.[61] Pepy II had eight that are documented. The marriages of Pepy II produced at least four kings of the Eighth Dynasty: Neferkare (II) Nebi, Merenre Nemtyemsaf II, Nedjerkare (sometimes erroneously referred to as Nitokris),[62] and Nefer Neferkare.[63]

After the chaos of the Seventh Dynasty, the Eighth Dynasty was calm, if brief. It lasted about thirty-two years, a little longer than one (modern) human generation. The basic source for the determination of the chronology of the Eighth Dynasty is found in the Abydos King List in the temple of the Nineteenth Dynasty king and father of Rameses II, Sethy

I. The Abydos King List names seventy-five predecessors of Sethy I since the unification of the country shortly after 3000 BC.[64] Kings of the Eighth Dynasty are, of course, listed too. They are in the fortieth to fifty-sixth positions. At first glance, seventeen rulers in the Eighth Dynasty period seems excessively high, especially when matched against the total number of kings on this list. But most of the listed kings are also known from other historical sources, such as the Turin King List or even Manetho; this supports the accuracy of the Abydos King List and helps to determine the chronology of this period.[65] The practically contemporaneous monument discovered in 1861 in the Saqqara tomb of the dignitary Tjenry, the Saqqara Tablet, does not list a single king between Pepy II and Mentuhotep II, the unifier of Egypt at the beginning of the Middle Kingdom.[66] This may indicate that, for the tablet's author, the time between the traditional end of Old Kingdom (the Sixth Dynasty) and the beginning of the Middle Kingdom was of no particular significance.

Several kings on the list from the Abydos temple of Sethy I are, moreover, documented as the direct descendants of the Sixth Dynasty, of Pepy II, and belong to the Eighth Dynasty rulers. The first of these is Neferkare (II) Nebi, who was the son of Pepy II and Ankhenespepy IV. It is also known that Neferkare (II) Nebi had built—or at least started to build— a complex named Djedankhneferkara.[67] The other direct descendants include Nemtyemsaf (Merenre II), the son of Pepy II and Queen Neith; Neferkare, son of Pepy II and Ankhenespepy III; and Neferkara Pepyseneb (Pepy-is-healthy), whose name evidently refers to his probable father, Pepy II. It seems logical to place Pepyseneb at the beginning of the Eighth Dynasty.[68] Another significant ruler was Kakare Ibi, who had a pyramid complex built near the causeway of Pepy II.[69] It is no wonder that five rulers of the Eighth Dynasty bear the component Neferkare as part of their names—positively referring to Pepy II Neferkare.

There are good reasons for considering the Eighth Dynasty to be part of the Old Kingdom. According to available sources, the kings of the Seventh and Eighth Dynasties continued to reside in the Memphite area; at least some of them continued building pyramid complexes, especially in South Saqqara, and they maintained royal titles and iconography. They were largely able to control Upper Egypt—perhaps with the help of their Abydos relatives—and to issue royal decrees that applied

Fig. 7.8. View of several queens' complexes of Pepy I in South Saqqara. Each of them is represented by a miniaturized complex similar to the complex of the king. (M. Bárta)

to some of the temples in the provinces, especially the temple of Min at Coptos.[70] But their sphere of control was significantly less than those of their predecessors. Meanwhile, the powers of the viziers grew at the end of the Old Kingdom, partly because they were not subordinated directly to the king, but above all because there were far fewer officials with real power in the central administration—and far less money.

The fact that a blood relationship existed between some of the kings of the Eighth Dynasty and Pepy II establishes that this dynasty was the legitimate heir to the tradition of the Old Kingdom.[71] Marriage politics also played a major role at Abydos, in the case of an influential family living there in the Eighth Dynasty. We are informed by historical sources that Nebet, the daughter of one of the Eighth Dynasty kings, Neferkauhor, married an official named Shemai, from the family at Abydos.[72] According to Hratch Papazian, the high incidence of specific personal names in the family of Khui of Abydos (names such as Khui, Shemai, Idi, and Nebet) is a relatively reliable indicator that this family, thanks to its bond with the royal family, had created a local ruling dynasty that became a major pillar supporting royal interests in the provinces.[73] This was also reflected in the large number of royal decrees Neferkauhor issued in favor of Abydos dignitaries and the local temple of the god Khontamenti.[74] Moreover, Neferkauhor appointed Idi, Shemai's son, to the office of governor of Upper Egypt, which in practice governed the First to Seventh Upper Egyptian nomes.[75]

Other local centers, for instance in Mo'alla, developed in parallel to Abydos. This is confirmed by a report stating that the governor of Upper Egypt from Abydos set out with his council, *qnbt*, to Mo'alla, to consult with the local ruler Hetep.[76] Incidentally, it was this Hetep who would become the father of one of the most important independent rulers of Upper Egypt during the First Intermediate Period, Ankhtify.[77]

The fact that numerous royal decrees were issued during the Eighth Dynasty is another strong argument supporting the claim that the rulers in Memphis, despite their limited economic and political power, were still able for some time to continue implementing Old Kingdom policy across many parts of Egypt. This included ordering expeditions (for instance, to Wadi Hammamat), or building pyramid complexes, though little evidence is available of the latter. There is physical evidence of only one complex in South Saqqara belonging to Kakare Ibi, which was small compared to the classical Old Kingdom pyramid standard, or even to Sixth Dynasty complexes. The side of the base of Kakare's pyramid measured only 31.5 m. By way of comparison, the same measurement in the pyramid of Pepy II, a mere three generations earlier (if a generation lasts about twenty years), was 76 m, and even in the pyramids of his wives it was 21 to 24 m. There is also indirect epigraphic evidence (in the form of their names) of at least three other pyramid complexes of the Eighth Dynasty. These were probably also located somewhere in South Saqqara.[78]

Clearly the short duration of the Seventh Dynasty (on the order of months) applies to a rather chaotic period, when the numerous royal progeny contended for the throne. Pepy II's wives (he had at least eight) certainly gave birth to several royal sons. The Eighth Dynasty seems to have brought some calm and a few stable rulers, a number of whom were also related to Pepy II. The approximately thirty years of the rule of this dynasty marked a return to the symbolic presentation of the king and his reign in line with the Old Kingdom tradition.

Fig. 7.9. Remains of the small pyramid of King Ibi in Saqqara, Eighth Dynasty. (M. Bárta)

However, some of the negative Sixth Dynasty trends persisted. The country continued to fall under the growing influence of powerful local families, and the treasury had to cope with lower and more erratic revenues, the consequence of insecure political and climatic environments. Little wonder that late in the twenty-second century BC, the country disintegrated, for a relatively short period, into smaller and more politically and economically autonomous parts dominated by local dignitaries and their families—the First Intermediate Period. This period includes the Ninth, Tenth, and part of the Eleventh Dynasties, which ruled different parts of the country. While the Herakleopolitan Ninth and Tenth Dynasties, comprising about forty rulers, overpowered the Memphite kings and largely dominated Lower Egypt, Upper Egyptian territory was split among local warlords who exerted their power over several nomes, Ankhtify of Mo'alla south of Thebes being probably the best known of them.

It seems that during this period Egypt was also plagued by a relatively longer spell of low Nile floods which were making the living conditions of the majority of the population still more difficult.[79] This is reflected in one monument of the period apparently documenting years of famine. It is the stela of Djari, from the time of the reign of Intef I of the Theban area,[80] in which the owner clearly refers to a year when famine struck, and when he had to provide for the people in his town or region. It appears he had the means to do so, as the text on another stela linked to him indicates that Djari held high posts in the service of Intef II.[81] He not only fought by the king's side, but was also assigned to procure Upper Egyptian barley to supply the region between Elephantine and Aphroditopolis (the territory of the First to Tenth Upper Egyptian nomes), which equates roughly to the territory stretching from Aswan to Luxor.

There is thus no reason to doubt that there had been famines, and if they did strike in the period after the fall of the Old Kingdom, it would have been local rulers in the regions who would have had to deal with the consequences and provide for local communities. There is another iconographic detail that stands out in this context: it is not until the First Intermediate Period that large numbers of weapons appear in the depictions of owners of stelae. The most popular is a bow, which was one of the most common weapons at that time; it was a typical symbol of the discharge of the office of local chief, who often had to deal with contentious or dangerous issues with the help of weapons and soldiers.

As early as 1885, Adolf Erman proposed that the decline of the Old Kingdom had been precipitated by a long-term crisis of the state that could be traced back to the reign of Pepy I, when provincial officials and their families started to gain more independence.[82] A similar view was expressed two years later by Ernst Meyer, who traced the seeds of the crisis back to the Fifth Dynasty and described the Sixth Dynasty as a period when nobles won out over the kingship.[83] This tendency to suppress the effect of external influences led Jan Assmann, in 1996, to state that he saw the rise and fall of the Old Kingdom as the result of a single endogenous process.[84]

It would take more than a century for Egypt to generate new momentum and set out on the road to reunification by joining northern elements into the Ninth and Tenth Dynasty polity of the Herakleopolitans, and the south into the Head of the South under the Theban Eleventh Dynasty—and then true reunification of Upper and Lower Egypt under Mentuhotep II.[85]

Fig. 7.10. Ruins of the pyramid of Djau in Dara, late Sixth Dynasty. (M. Bárta)

Fig. 7.11. First Intermediate Period stela showing the owner with weapons. Unlike the Old Kingdom, this period often depicts weapons on funerary stelae. Egyptian Museum, Turin. (M. Bárta)

8 The Land Turned like the Potter's Wheel

AN ANCIENT EGYPTIAN SAGE NAMED IPUWER described the situation in Egypt following the demise of the Old Kingdom as "the land turned like the potter's wheel."[1] As argued in the preceding chapters, the history of the Old Kingdom could be seen as a model of the processes of rise, decline, and fall encountered in most civilizations. What these processes show is that societies are anything but static, and their character is determined by largely symbolic norms and the changing dynamics of development. Thus, the rise and fall of the Old Kingdom cannot be attributed to isolated events. It resulted from a specific context molded by processes within the society—evolution of the elites, administration of the country, and religious changes, to name but a few—alongside external constraints, such as geographical location and climate change.

There was a similar state of affairs during the Middle and New Kingdoms. In the Middle Kingdom, which emerged after the collapse of the Old Kingdom, the reign of Senwosret III is clearly the major turning point, like Niuserre's in the Fifth Dynasty.[2] Senwosret III also had to contend with the erosion of royal power and the rising influence of certain powerful and influential families in the provinces. He chose to contain their influence by moving their offspring to the royal court at the Residence (exactly as Pepy I had done before him) and to carry out major administrative reforms.[3] The benefits were short-lived. Thus, despite evidence that

Egypt was invaded at the end of the Middle Kingdom, it appears that the mechanism of its decline was already in place. As in the Old Kingdom, several internal factors destabilized the country over the long term, affecting its administration, economy, and governance, and the legitimacy of its elites. These weakened the state to such an extent that it was unable to sustain concurrent external stresses, in this case migrating ethnic groups.

Indeed, the final demise of the Middle Kingdom appears to have been induced by external influences—especially the large influx of Asiatics, the Hyksos, into the Nile Delta, which they then controlled for several generations, or approximately 150 years. As a result, Egypt split into southern and northern parts (Upper and Lower Egypt) with centers in Avaris and Thebes.[4] The story was repeated toward the end of the Twentieth Dynasty, whose decline was hastened by incursions by Libyan tribes.[5] The first major external stress came substantially earlier, in the reign of Rameses III, who was able to drive off the Sea Peoples attacking Egypt.[6] However, in both cases these external factors precipitated change in a system that had already been weakened from within.

The impact of migrating populations is a popular theme in archaeology. Already in 1894 Flinders Petrie surmised that the Old Kingdom had been disrupted by incursions of Asian populations; he could not otherwise explain the decline of the era of the pyramid builders. To prove his point, he used the so-called knob sealings finds, which, because of their assumed foreign origin, were supposed to provide unambiguous evidence of this invasion.[7] In more recent literature, however, the hypothesis that alien incursions contributed to the collapse of the Old Kingdom is practically absent. It may have been the misapprehension of endogenous social processes and of the exogenous role of climate that led Karl Jansen-Winkeln, like Petrie, to attribute the collapse of the Old Kingdom to an incursion from Asia.[8] Nevertheless, there is no substantial evidence to support this theory. Only toward the end of the First Intermediate Period do we read in *The Instruction for Merikare* about battles against the Asiatics in the Delta.[9] And it is likely that the infiltration of the Delta by the foreign elements was facilitated by the anarchy that existed after the fall of the Old Kingdom: it was a consequence instead of a cause.

A certain degree of famine caused by climate change has also been proposed as an ultimate cause of the collapse of the Old Kingdom. Food

Fig. 8.1. Tired and pessimistic face of the Middle Kingdom ruler Senwosret III. (Fitzwilliam Museum, Cambridge, UK)

shortages are certainly a motif appearing in texts from the First Interme-diate Period. Such a phenomenon would, of course, be placed into the context of extraordinarily high or low Nile floods. The hypothesis was tested in detail by Barbara Bell and others (as we will see in more detail below).[10] It must be said, however, that periods of famine in the period following the end of the Old Kingdom need not have coincided with Nile floods. They may have been due to the breakdown of the adminis-trative structures that were essential to keeping the country running at times of flood and harvest and for the effective subsequent redistribution of produce. Yet the proxy data combined with the historical information do indicate that internal crisis and low Nile floods may had been related, at least to some extent.

Fig. 8.2. First Intermediate Period stela of Djari, which makes reference to a low Nile flood. The Royal Museums of Art and History, Brussels. (M. Bárta)

Despite the environmental evidence, the multiple causes for the weakening, decline, and eventual demise of the Old Kingdom must be sought in its internal dynamics and changing patterns of development. Some of these causes have been traced as far back as the end of the Fourth or the beginning of the Fifth Dynasty. For example, Miroslav Verner has suggested that the relatively small dimensions of Shepseskaf's funerary monument at the end of the Fourth Dynasty may be indicative of the declining economic and political power of the kings of the late Fourth Dynasty. Verner places the next stage of the Old Kingdom's disintegration in the mid–Fifth Dynasty, during the reign of Neferirkare, and sees its causes in the rise of officials and priests in numbers and steady weakening of the king's power.[11]

Renate Müller-Wollermann also attributes the fall of the Old Kingdom exclusively to internal factors. She relies on a theory of internal crisis, similar to Marx's theory of the crisis of capitalism, and posits that the real reasons for the decline of the Old Kingdom were these:[12]

1. Crisis of identity, meaning that the individuals and groups tasked with ruling the country did not identify with their role and official tasks;
2. Crisis of legitimacy, whereby the governing institutions and individuals were not accepted as such by the majority in the society;

3. Crisis of participation, in which certain individuals or groups attempted to secure disproportionate power;
4. Crisis of penetration, because power and authority were limited and unable to control the whole state;
5. Crisis of distribution, where difficulties in distributing or redistributing commodities led to great inequalities of wealth between the affluent elite and the majority.

All these factors were direct consequences of the status race discussed earlier in the book, the hypertrophy of the bureaucracy, and the advancing rise of powerful families both in the Residence and in the provinces. According to Müller-Wollermann, the principal cause of the fall of the Old Kingdom was a crisis of penetration, reflected especially in the state's smaller presence and declining authority in the provinces. The second most important was a crisis of distribution, which was the result of the continuous expansion of the bureaucratic apparatus at a time of shrinking resources coveted by a growing number of players: this created a self-reinforcing loop leading to ever-dwindling supply amid ever-growing demand.

Müller-Wollermann pointed to the rising number of decorated nonroyal tombs as specific evidence of these factors. Yet some caution is needed here: this trend could reflect the growing complexity of state administration, which would have led to more high officials having the means not only to ensure a comfortable life for themselves, but also to make arrangements for their journey to the next world by building lavish tombs.[13]

Alongside the factors identified by Müller-Wollermann we must place a crisis of land tenure, which flowed from the increasing amounts of land that were assigned to individual temples (see the Palermo Stone and individual donations of land to temples during the Fifth Dynasty).[14] And, last but not least, we must not forget the climate depredations at the end of the Old Kingdom.

Nadine Moeller has approached the decline of the Old Kingdom by comparing archaeological, environmental, and historical sources.[15] At the outset of her study, she made it clear that her intention was to rebut earlier sources that focused exclusively on Nile floods as the cause for that decline. A key merit of her study is that it offers a reliable synthesis of earlier findings on the decline of the Old Kingdom, and her conclusions rely on documented facts—that the fall of the Old Kingdom was not sudden but the outcome of long-term processes and protracted crises, also observable elsewhere, and that there is rich evidence to suggest it coincided with increasing drought and intensifying aeolian activity.

Moeller's insistence on multiple correlated triggers contrasts with Barbara Bell's position: "The cause I postulate as 'historical reality' is drought—widespread, severe, and prolonged, lasting for several decades and occurring more or less simultaneously over the entire Eastern Mediterranean and adjacent lands."[16] While Bell does not deny the significance of contemporary political and social factors, she asserts that a climatic and economic deterioration of sufficient magnitude can set in motion forces beyond the power of any society to sustain (let alone control).

To a large extent Bell has followed a path cut by Rhys Carpenter in a 1966 study, in which he offered, as one of the first scientists in the field of archaeology, a similar explanation for the cultural collapse of Mycenaean Greece and the Hittite Empire.[17] Bell's thoughts have recently been revived by Fekri Hassan.[18] The Nile's substantial role in Egyptian history is unarguable.

A glance at statistics of relatively recent floods shows that whether Nile floods were excessively high or inadequately low, the result was basically the same—a disaster with severe impact. The consequences of an 1877 flood that was two meters lower than average are well known: more than 35 percent of farm land remained unirrigated; in the Qena and Girga provinces it was 62 to 75 percent of the fields.[19] As that year's statistics show, this was not restricted to Egypt; signs of scarcity and stress were discernible in other parts of the world as well.[20]

Archaeological sources reflect the phenomenon of the drying environment toward the end of the Old Kingdom through thicker layers of wind-deposited sand. This has been well documented by investigations carried out at Dahshur. Probe samples were collected over a period of several years to enable the investigation of sediment formations many meters thick at this pyramid field. The examined cross-sections pointed to a residential settlement contemporaneous with the early Fourth Dynasty (of course in a place with a continuous history of settlement until the Sixth Dynasty), located at a depth of 6 to 6.5 meters with a

Fig. 8.3. Massive aeolian sand layers in Dahshur—causeway of the Bent Pyramid. (M. Bárta)

1- to 1.5-meter-thick layer of aeolian sand sitting immediately on top of it. Above this sand was another cultural layer, dated on the basis of pottery to approximately the era of Senwosret III.[21] Meanwhile, findings made over many years by a British expedition working in the Abusir and Saqqara area showed that the large areas of the valley temples of the pyramid complexes had been partly filled with wind-blown sand as early as during the Old Kingdom.[22]

Research carried out by the Czech Institute of Egyptology in the area of the Abusir Lake has provided similar results.[23] In 2007, four large trenches were opened and examined in different parts of the lake to map its history over the last five thousand years, with special focus on the third millennium BC, when this principal entryway to the Abusir and Saqqara necropolis was frequented most. Among the major discoveries were remains of a landing ramp documented in Trench A. A brick platform was found at a depth of two meters. It was oriented northeast–southwest and terminated by several steps at its northern end. This may have been a landing ramp for boats carrying visitors to the necropolis either for cult purposes or to perform funeral ceremonies. The structure may have been built as early as the Third Dynasty (dated on the basis of pottery shards). Sediment cross-sections to a depth of 1.8 to 3.2 m below ground level were mapped in three trenches, and they confirm that a general trend of the period was spells of drought followed by sudden flash floods.

The sediments from the ancient Memphis pyramid fields tell the following story: The landing harbor ramp discovered on the shore of the Abusir Lake roughly 18 m above sea level is about 4 m above the reconstructed Old Kingdom flood surface level, which in the Memphite region was approximately 14 m above sea level.[24] If the average height of the Nile flood was 1.5 m, we could expect the lowest settlement level to be about 15.5 m above the current sea level.[25] This is confirmed by the results of the probes drilled in Dahshur, which located a Fourth Dynasty settlement at a height of 16–17.5 m—we must not forget that there is evidence of very high floods at the beginning of the Fourth Dynasty, which could be why the ramp is so high relative to the Nile floodplain. At some time during—or possibly after—the Fifth and Sixth Dynasties, layers were formed as a result of heavy rain. These were later covered by even thicker layers of wind-deposited sand, which is proof of intensive aeolian activity and thus also of deepening drought.[26]

One more remark must be made here. While most of the scholars favoring low Nile floods as a cause of the Old Kingdom's fall argue for an 'event-like' climate change, this may not be the best approach. What emerges from the available proxy data and environmental record is a more gradual deterioration of the climate coupled with the tendency for lower Nile floods and occasional torrential rains. The desert scenes reappearing in tomb decorations dated to Niuserre's reign are illustrative of this trend. The same has been suggested by a recent study by Joanne Clarke and her team, which shows that climate changes in the Near East and North Africa during the sixth to fourth millennia BC were a relatively long process—from the human perspective—lasting for a century or two.[27] Thus the idea of a climate change event over a short span of years appears unlikely.[28]

Nile floods, or more precisely their varying and mostly decreasing absolute heights over the course of the third millennium BC, are not the only environmental key to understanding the dynamics of ancient

Fig. 8.4. Trench A in the Lake of Abusir in 2007. (M. Bárta)

Egyptian history. Paradoxically, rains also played a role. We learn about them mostly through indirect evidence. There is not a single depiction of rain on the reliefs or in the extant images dating to the Old Kingdom. We know that in ancient Egyptian religion, rain was considered a hostile manifestation of the powers of Sutekh, the god of the desert. (Even today rain is not one of the best-loved natural phenomena.) Egyptian architecture also suggests an aversion to rain. Under the floor of Sahure's pyramid temple at Abusir, dating to the early Fifth Dynasty, an intricate web of small channels was cut in the limestone blocks of the temple to divert rainwater from it. The causeway to the temple was drained in a similar way; thanks to the damaged floor any present-day visitor can see the channels.[29] Similarly, at the upper edge of Niuserre's causeway we can see the mouth of a drainage system aiming away from the temple. The stone channel here terminates with a lion's paw, which diverted the water into a large, round stone tank adjoining the ascending path on the outside.[30] The lion's paw here was meant to symbolize control over the potentially evil and destructive forces of the rainwater.

We can conclude at least that it did rain in ancient Egypt, even to such a degree that measures had to be taken inside the temples to neutralize the effects of the rain water. This was so at least from the beginning of the Fifth Dynasty. But did it rain often, or rarely? Evenly, or haphazardly? Softly, or in downpours? In the winter, or in summer? And especially: Did it rain more at the beginning of the Old Kingdom than at the end, or was it the other way around? To find even partial answers to these questions we must look elsewhere.

One of the difficulties in studying the history of climate change in Egypt lies not only in the contrast between the desiccation of the desert and the fertility of the Nile Valley, but also in the contrast between the drier south and the wetter north, which benefited from more frequent precipitation thanks to the Mediterranean coastline, the North Atlantic Oscillation (NAO), and the variable influence of the Intertropical Convergence Zone (ITCZ), which affected the climate of Egypt in a north–south direction. While in the northern part of Egypt the current annual precipitation rate is 200 millimeters, in the south it may rain only once in several years.[31]

The mechanism of the gradual desiccation of the desert has been discussed elsewhere; what is germane here are the long-term precipitation trends. These have a direct impact also on the hydrological regime of the Nile itself. During the humid phase of the Middle Holocene (7500–4000 BC), Ethiopia lay in the summer monsoon band. This contributed to the abundance of water in the Nile, as one of its main tributaries was the Blue Nile flowing from this region. After roughly 4000 BC the monsoons started weakening, which led to a corresponding drop in the height of annual Nile floods that continued until 2200 BC. This was documented in another study that measured the proportion of strontium isotopes in Nile River sediments. This research indicated that there was a steep drop in Nile floods around 2500 BC. In the Faiyum Lake evidence, this was called the Qadrus Recession. The $^{87}Sr/^{86}Sr$ ratio was lowest around the year 2200 BC, which was due to lower rainfall in Ethiopia contributing to greater soil erosion. This trend had a direct impact on the build-up in the Nile Delta sediments of a layer up to five centimeters thick containing manganese-iron hydroxide, which has been dated to this period.[32]

The Abusir and Saqqara tombs, which are the best documented in relation to traces left by rains in the Old Kingdom, may serve as the key. Some of the Old Kingdom tombs in Abusir contained relatively thick layers of mud, but there were no thin microlayers which might have indicated that the muddy sediment had been deposited in stages. To the contrary, all the evidence points to more solid layers having been deposited as the result of intensive rainfalls, which triggered a mighty muddy runoff from the tombs' earthen surfaces. These rains then created conspicuous mud layers in the subterranean parts of the tombs, which were robbed and consequently left open at the end of the Old Kingdom, allowing their open underground parts to be penetrated by the rain and mud.

At Saqqara, this trend has been observed in the places where burial pits built mostly during the Sixth Dynasty were found; the dating of the very strong evidence of rains is even more accurate. Layers of sand built up as a consequence of subsequent aeolian activity settled on the displaced layers of mud and quartzite grains originating from the local bedrock. We thus have very interesting material evidence that torrential rains did occur during the Old Kingdom and created a typical stratigraphic record. At the same time, data on the height of floods, stratigraphy of sediments (settled layers of aeolian sand), analysis of faunal remains, iconographic depictions, isotope analysis, and other evidence point to declining Nile flood levels and the gradual desiccation of the country combined with intensive soil erosion. It may be that these simultaneous processes were caused by two climatic phenomena: the NAO in the northern part of the country, reaching here from the eastern Mediterranean and bringing monsoon rains; and the ITCZ, which contributed to the severity of the drought in the region south of the Egyptian border and had an effect on decreasing precipitation in the Ethiopian mountains, which was reflected directly in reduced Nile flooding rates. It almost seems as if NAO and ITCZ were complementary, although there is no solid evidence to support this. But while the idea that increasing drought and falling Nile floods were accompanied by higher rainfall seems counterintuitive, perhaps this was precisely what happened at the close of the Old Kingdom.

A text from the Saqqara tomb of Kaiemtjenenet, dating to the reign of Djedkare, contains a unique description of a heavy rain that hit the king and his entourage:

(2) It happened that [a storm and darkness] arose,

(3) . . . and I could not find a man who could follow the route because of the storm.

(4) [Nonetheless His Majesty ordered that the voyage continue] on the river (Nile), on that day of desperately foul weather.

(5) [His Majesty said: You have sailed the vessel] to the delight of My Majesty over it. Certainly you are a true sailor

(6) [and you are not fearful] of a great storm on the river.

(7) [His Majesty backed me in this difficult journey] from beginning to the end, and it went well for Him, and nothing happened to Him.

(8) [When we reached the Residence, His Majesty favoured me] very greatly. Then His Majesty said: It was like a voyage of Re on the Great Lake. . . .[33]

Business as Usual?

There is another tendency in the debates around the collapse of the Old Kingdom, this time to say that there was no collapse at all and everything continued as usual.[34] This, however, is a part of a broader intellectual discourse occupying a specific place in Western scholarly research, which now and then succumbs to the temptation to interpret, for example, the decline of the Roman Empire during the fifth century as progress.[35]

According to this approach, all that happened was that toward the end of the Sixth Dynasty, the royal office passed into the hands of local families in Upper Egypt and everything carried on but at a lower level of complexity. Here lies the root of the misapprehension of the term 'kingship' (German *Königtum* and French *royauté*) by proponents of this theory, and of the concept of "power" as applied by the German sociologist Heinrich Popitz.[36] Kingship as a sacred office with which the gods have entrusted the king, and the king's maintenance of the world order created by gods, cannot by its nature be held by just any chief or be shared among families on the mere basis of their wealth. The German Egyptologist Malte Römer may be right to say that no "crisis of the economy" could have occurred in ancient Egypt as there was no economy per se, in the sense defined by our modern capitalist world. But while we can agree as a general rule that using twenty-first-century concepts to try to understand ancient history may not be entirely helpful, it is nonetheless possible that the end of the Old Kingdom was precipitated by a crisis relating to the management of the state's subsistence strategies, and that this crisis was due to both internal and external causes, namely the inability of the state to mobilize the construction of drainage and irrigation canals and dams and to redistribute economic potential, and the lower heights of the annual Nile floods.

The French scholar Juan Carlos Moreno García published a study in 2015 concerning the development of ancient Egypt immediately after the collapse of the Old Kingdom. The study is largely based on the work of Nadine Moeller. It also responds to earlier literature on collapse,[37] and it is clear that Moreno García understands 'collapse' to be absolute destruction, ruin, and annihilation. We know, however, that collapse is a process, and as such is more like a deep transformation that penetrates all spheres of society, accompanied by a loss of complexity, reduction of vertical structures, and disintegration into smaller units. Moreno García is also in sharp disagreement about the important role that both internal factors and external ones like climate change or reduced annual floods played in the fall of the Old Kingdom. In this respect, he refers to an earlier study by Stephan Seidlmayer, who maintained a positive view of the events and processes that characterized the First Intermediate Period (decentralization, disintegration, proliferation of local cultures, appearance of specific artistic styles, emergence of local elites, and similar).[38]

Moreno García's line of reasoning implies a tendency to view the processes that followed the end of the Old Kingdom as manifestations of a certain type of globalization, typified by free movement of goods and persons—in Egypt and beyond—and flowing from multiculturalism.[39] In reality, the First Intermediate Period was a continuation of processes that had begun during the Old Kingdom, only at a much lower level of complexity and with the participation of local communities and regions rather than states. Trade was organized not just by settled populations, but also by nomadic ethnic groups, and in fact international contacts and trade proliferated.

Moreno García's work is helpful in that it shows that the decentralization that followed the decline of the Old Kingdom was not an obstacle to continued long-distance trade. A study published in 1996 by Mordechai Haiman supports this conclusion.[40] Haiman points out that after the end of the Sixth Dynasty, trade continued between Egypt (the Egyptian Delta) and the copper-mining region of Wadi Feynan on the territory of present-day Jordan. By mapping transitory Bedouin camps between these two regions, Haiman provided unequivocal proof that it had been the nomads in the region who took over the trade in, and evidently also the mining of, copper at a time when all other dominant structures were absent. But this in itself is not sufficient grounds to conclude that in the First Intermediate Period, smaller regions prospered independently, trade flourished, and people lived happily free of conflict or of economic and environmental stresses.

After the Old Kingdom

There appear to have been two dominant power centers in post–Eighth Dynasty Egypt—one in Thebes and the second in Herakleopolis in the Faiyum region. The two were engaged in a power struggle, which led in the end to the reunification of Egypt and a continuation of the glorious tradition of the Old Kingdom rulers.

One man who gained a regional reputation during these battles was a dignitary named Ankhtify.[41] His biographical inscription vividly describes his expedition against the town of Edfu, center of the Theban nome and of the cult of Horus, protective deity of ancient Egyptian kings. The text describes Ankhtify's conquest of Edfu. The ruler of Armant later asked Ankhtify to relieve the Theban siege of his city. Ankhtify set out toward Thebes and the enemy's army fled before him.

In the post–Eighth Dynasty period, the Memphite region faded from importance, materially and spiritually. People continued to live there, of course, but there were no more monumental royal tombs, monuments bearing the names of kings, divine temples, or significant residential cemeteries for the elite, even though a large complex of nonroyal monuments is known from this period.[42] This decline is linked to the move of power centers to places like Herakleopolis or Thebes in Upper Egypt which had previously not played an important geopolitical role. Their rulers would adopt elements of royal iconography to consolidate their own power and legitimacy.

Simultaneously, two things vanished: the concept of royal power as the guarantor of stability, and the idea of an administrative and symbolic

Fig. 8.5. Chapel of Ankhtify in Mo'alla, First Intermediate Period. (M. Bárta)

center that was home to king and court and birthplace of the culture's symbols, ideology, and values.[43] These changes, which bore a striking resemblance to pre-unification Egypt, flowed from a dissatisfaction with the very concept of the state among dignitaries and high officials.[44] They preferred the idea of segmented territories of a size that reflected the amount of influence one provincial chief could wield. Each chief in his chiefdom replaced the king as guarantor of the divine order, heart of administration and religion, and symbol of order, permanence, and stability.[45] The period after the Old Kingdom is thus a kind of negation of the sociological concept of rule. While the Old Kingdom—and especially the Fifth Dynasty—represented the peak of 'rule' in the sense of growing depersonalization, increasing formalization, and mounting integration, the decline and demise of the Old Kingdom was marked by completely opposite tendencies: increased personalization, multiplication, and disintegration.

What emerges is that immediately after the end of the Old Kingdom (at the end of the Eighth Dynasty) and the decline of central authority,

Lower and Upper Egypt started developing differently. This is evident especially in the material culture.[46] It is also visible in the cemeteries, where the new social reality is reflected in the tombs of a new kind of leader and their retinues of followers and sympathizers. Local burial grounds provide a good opportunity to study the relationship between dominant graves and the poorer ones linked to them by chronology and location.[47] The same relationship is implied in contemporaneous texts. They clearly identify the patrons who played a protective role in the society and derived from it authority and status—probably similar to that of a chief—and at the local level represented and substituted the original authority of the state.[48]

In the same vein, there is no reference to the kingship in any inscription in the period immediately following the end of the Eighth Dynasty—the institution as such had ceased to exist. Instead, the inscriptions of individual local rulers in Upper Egypt describe how they took care of their people at a time when famine was rife everywhere else. Moreover, in most cases it is difficult to find a link between the elites we know existed toward the end of the Old Kingdom and those in the provinces during the First Intermediate Period.[49]

The mechanism of transformation of power at that time has not yet been subjected to deeper study, but what we can observe is that while in the Old Kingdom state administration was based on the individual regions (nomes) headed by a nomarch referred to as the 'great overlord' (ḥry-tp-ꜥꜣ), after the end of the Old Kingdom traditionally powerful settlements (one could even call them towns) and their outskirts became the new centers headed by governors (ḥꜣty-ꜥꜣ).[50] This is a clear indication that the country had disintegrated into several more or less independent regions with no central authority.

Conclusion

From all that has been described, it follows that the fall of the Old Kingdom was the consequence of several concurrent and mutually amplifying trends. First, there was the slow erosion of the effectiveness of the centralized state accompanied by steady growth of the administrative apparatus. This led to a slow rise, probably during the reign of Niuserre, in the power, wealth, and independence of prominent individuals and

Fig. 8.6. Painting from the First Intermediate Period tomb of Ity in Gebelein. Most probably, Ity is represented as a ruler smiting head of his enemy—an iconographically exclusive royal motif of the Old Kingdom. Egyptian Museum, Turin. (M. Bárta)

several regions over Egypt's political territory. This was a time when powerful families started to usurp more and more power from the central administration and when several local centers started to become more and more independent. As the king's power and reach beyond the capital eroded, the country's economy declined—as did its social stability. This was exacerbated by reduced Nile floods and advancing drought combined with occasional torrential rains. Then toward the end of the Sixth Dynasty the ruling structure collapsed like a house of cards. It had a limited and short-lived resurgence during the Eighth Dynasty, after which Egypt broke into distinct provinces each ruled by an independent chieftain. These would eventually form the basis of Egypt's reunification, the Middle Kingdom.

It is clear that the ultimate collapse of many forms characteristic of the Old Kingdom did not leave an entire void. Although the centralized state apparatus, unifying power, and monumental architecture disappeared, a new and simpler way of life grew in their place, as reflected in contemporary material culture, the proliferation of local forms of administration and arts, and a rise in local conflicts. It is certainly not by chance that many tomb owners of the First Intermediate Period are represented with weapons, a feature which was virtually absent during the Old Kingdom. The situation, not dissimilar to the period before the unification of Egypt around 2950 BC, was ripe and the Old Kingdom aftermath was in fact necessary for a new take-off.

The Old Kingdom, which lasted almost five centuries, is nothing else but a laboratory of a complex societal evolution which displays—perhaps surprisingly—quite distinct and modern features despite their actual distance from our own world. Their study sheds light on inner dynamics of the society: its priorities and trends, combined with external phenomena such as climate change, represent a vivid picture, full of inspiration even today. The way the ancient Egyptians coped with increasing bureaucracy, mandatory expenses, an increasingly complex society, the legitimacy of increasingly ineffective elites, access to resources, nepotism and interest groups, religious priorities and politics, management and use of energy (provided by the annual Nile floods and the sun), and last but not least, environmental change—all of these features represent a world which may be used as a mirror to reflect our own. Despite the current level of our knowledge of ancient Egyptian civilization and of complex civilizations in general, our study of them is far from complete. Yet even at this stage it is possible to combine the information provided by dozens of archaeological projects all over Egypt and build more general theories, elucidating not only some specifics of Egyptian history but of the human past in general. Ancient Egyptians believed firmly that if their name survived, they would be granted immortality. It has been my main ambition to contribute to their belief.

Notes

Notes to Preface

1 Braudel 1980.
2 On the rise of bureaucracy, see Olson 1982 and Fukuyama 2015. On elites, see Savage et al. 2008; Rothkopf 2009; Rothkopf 2012; Stark and Chance 2012. On energy consumption and its importance, see Homer-Dixon 2006; Strumsky, Lobo, and Tainter 2010; Hall, Lambert, and Balogh 2014; and most recently Smil 2018.
3 Bárta 2018; Bárta and Kovář 2019.
4 Mitchell 2008; Haldon et al. 2018.
5 Christian et al. 2011; Motesharrei, Rivas, and Kalnay 2014; Bárta 2018.
6 Fergusson 2010; Morris 2013; Morris 2014.
7 Tainter 1988; S.P. Huntington 1993; Acemoglu and Robinson 2012; Smith et al. 2012, to name but a few.
8 Bárta 2016b.
9 On cycles, see Turchin 2012.

Notes to Chapter One

1 S.P. Huntington 1993: 24.
2 Morgan 1877: 12.
3 Woods 2010; Stauder 2010.
4 Trigger 2003: 43.
5 Childe 1950.
6 Toynbee 1934–54.
7 Childe 1950.
8 Trigger 2003: 40–48.
9 See discussion in Sanderson 1995.
10 Renfrew 1972: ch. 2.

11   *Contra* Wengrow 2015.

12   Bárta 2013c.

13   Dreyer et al. 1998.

14   Naqada II was a prehistoric culture on the territory of Upper and to some extent Lower Egypt. It is dated to 3500–3200 BC.

15   To name but a few: Pardey 1976; Kanawati 1980; Strudwick 1985; Kemp 1989; Papazian 2012.

16   S.P. Huntington 1993: 23.

17   Renfrew 1972: 3–8.

18   Wengrow 2010 for an overview.

19   Wright and Johnson 1972.

20   For city-states in the Near East, cf. Leick 2002.

21   Wright and Johnson 1972; Bárta 2013c.

22   Aristotle, *Politics*, Book 1, Part 1.

23   Cf. Claessen and Skalník 1981a.

24   Hobbes 1968.

25   Rousseau 1939: [I.6].

26   Rousseau 1939: [I.7].

27   Weber 1972: 29.

28   Cf. Claessen and Skalník 1981a; 1981b.

29   Childe 1942.

30   Carneiro 1970: 734.

31   Scott 2017.

32   Hafsaas-Tsakos 2015.

33   Carneiro 1967.

34   North, Wallis, and Weingast 2013.

35   Compare also the 2010 English translation of an original 1980 work by the French anthropologist Pierre Clastres, *Archaeology of Violence*, Ian Morris's 2014 study *War! What Is It Good For? Conflict and the Progress of Civilization, from Primates to Robots*, or the latest exhibition on the phenomenon and role of war in human history displayed in Halle, Germany (Meller and Schefzik 2015).

36   Rappaport 1968: 116.

37   Johnson and Earle 2000: 246.

38   Carneiro 1970.

39   Lanning 1967: 64.

40   Compare Homer-Dixon 2006; Hall, Lambert, and Balogh 2014.

41   D'Altroy 2007: 36–41.

42   Chagnon 1983.

43   Blanton and Fargher 2009.

44   Cf. Bussmann 2014 and Warden 2014, with earlier literature.

45   See Snape 2014; Baines 2015; Moeller 2016.

46   See Claessen and Skalník 1981a: 469–510; for geographical constraints, Kaplan 2012; Roberts 1989; Burroughs 2005; for the latest discussion of effects of climate, Kerner, Dann, and Bangsgaard 2015; for energy issues, Homer-Dixon 2006.

47   See Trigger 2003.

48   Translation Lichtheim 2006: 205–206.

49 Dalley 2008: 24–26.

50 Dove 2014: 55–66.

51 *The Spirit of the Laws* (published in 1748).

52 E. Huntington 1913; 1917.

53 Dendrochronology as a scientific method is much older: Leonardo da Vinci already knew that rings form every year and that their features depend on external conditions. By the nineteenth century it was evident that annual rings and dendrochronology could be used successfully to reconstruct climate development (Twining 1833).

54 Willett 1953.

55 Bond et al. 1997.

56 Bond et al. 1997: 1257–58, 1264.

57 Dansgaard et al. 1984.

58 Roberts 1989: 121–54; for a more general framework of climate change within the eastern Sahara region, see also Pachur and Altmann 2006.

59 Dalfes, Kukla, and Weiss 1997.

60 National Research Council 2002: 41–42, with an overview of literature and debates.

61 The literature on collapse is enormously rich and varied. See for example a pivotal study by Tainter (1988) and Middleton (2017), with further references.

62 Ryan and Pitman 2000; Lewis 2006; Finkel 2014; Nunn and Reid 2016.

63 Dalley 2008.

64 Atrahases, translation Dalley 2008: 110–13.

65 Guilhou 2010; translation Lichtheim 2006: 198–99.

66 Bárta 2013e. For the latest general study on kings, kingship, and the elites see Graeber and Sahlins 2017.

67 For this last point see Jansen-Winkeln 2010.

Notes to Chapter Two

1 Kuper and Kröpelin 2006; Butzer 2012; Bárta 2015c, with references to earlier literature.

2 Dalfes, Kukla, and Weiss 1997.

3 For an overview see Meller, Arz, Jung, and Risch 2015.

4 E.g., Butzer 1976; Faure and Williams 1980; Issar and Brown 1998; McIntosh, Tainter, and McIntosh 2000; Scarborough 2003; Issar 2003; Mackay, Battarbee, Birks, and Oldfield 2005; Bollig, Bubenzer, Vogelsang, and Wotzka 2007; Dove 2014; Kerner, Dann, and Bangsgaard 2015.

5 Willcocks 1889; Toussoun 1925; Popper 1951; Butzer 1976; Sezgin 2001; Seidlmayer 2001; with earlier literature.

6 T.A.H. Wilkinson 2000a; Baud and Dobrev 1995.

7 The largest, 43 cm high and 26 cm wide, is in the Archaeological Museum in Palermo, Sicily. Of the remaining six, five much smaller fragments are in the Egyptian Museum in Cairo, and one is in the Petrie Museum in London. For a full publication and bibliography of the fragments, see T.A.H. Wilkinson 2000a.

8 Tallet 2017: 160.

9 Tallet 2017: 150.

10   Bell 1970; 1971.

11   F.A. Hassan 1981, and later, F.A. Hassan 1997.

12   Toussoun 1925: 302.

13   Seidlmayer 2001: 92.

14   Bell 1970: 572.

15   T.A.H. Wilkinson 2000a.

16   Macklin et al. 2015.

17   Macklin et al. 2015: 113.

18   Raue, Seidlmayer, and Speiser 2013.

19   Ziermann 1993: 138–40 and fig. 15; Seidlmayer 2001: 81–82, 90, table 7.

20   Macklin et al. 2015.

21   Bárta and Bezděk 2008.

22   Welc and Marks 2013.

23   Rosenthal 2015: 137.

24   Marx 1887.

25   Spengler 1918: 1922.

26   Toynbee 1934–54.

27   Renfrew 1972.

28   Renfrew 1972: 22–23.

29   Eldredge and Gould 1972.

30   Sapp 2003.

Notes to Chapter Three

1   See, for instance, W.S. Smith 1962; Kemp 1989; Vercoutter 1992; Vandersleyen 1995; T.A.H. Wilkinson 1999; Shaw 2000.

2   Bárta 2015e; 2016b.

3   Waddell 1940.

4   Rheidt and Schwander 2004; now see Warburton 2012.

5   T.A.H. Wilkinson 2000b.

6   Tallet and Laisney 2012.

7   Waddell 1940.

8   Bunbury 2010.

9   Saad 1947; 1951; 1957; 1969; T.A.H. Wilkinson 1996.

10   Köhler 2005; Köhler and Jones 2009; Köhler 2014; Köhler et al. 2017.

11   T.A.H. Wilkinson 1996.

12   Emery 1962: 21.

13   Emery 1962; A.J. Spencer 1996; T.A.H. Wilkinson 1999; Wengrow 2006.

14   T.A.H. Wilkinson 1999: 67–70.

15   See T.A.H. Wilkinson 1999: 69.

16   Dreyer et al. 1996: 72, fig. 26; for more on chronology see Hassan, Serrano, and Tassie 2006.

17   Lacau and Lauer 1959: 9, pl. 1[1].

18   Cairo JE32169=CG14716 (Porter and Moss 1937: 193–94).

19   Bussmann 2010: 53–58.

20   Goebs 2008.

21   Baines 2007: 122.
22   O'Connor 2011.
23   Patch 1995.
24   Goebs 2008: 163 n.371.
25   Patch 1995: 111, fig. 14.
26   Somaglino and Tallet 2015.
27   Braun 2011.
28   Helck 1987.
29   Helck 1987 *passim*.
30   Petrie 1900: pl. xxii[35], xxiii[40].
31   Helck 1987.
32   T.A.H. Wilkinson 2000b.
33   Schneider 1993.
34   For a general discussion of the problems and issues see Förster 1997.
35   Jones 2000: 763–64, with references.
36   Engel 2013: 29–31.
37   Engel 2006; Helck 1974.
38   Cf. Schneider 1993.
39   Edwards 1971: 26.
40   Dreyer et al. 1990: 80, fig. 9, pl. 26d.
41   Hornung and Staehelin 1974; 2006; Bárta 2015c.
42   Tomb T (Porter and Moss 1937: 83–85; Dreyer et al. 1990: 72–79; 1993: 57–61;
     2000: 97–118; 2003: 88–107).
43   Bárta 2011a: 70–71.
44   Effland and Effland 2013.
45   Emery 1938.
46   Crubézy and Midant-Reynes 2005, with overview of earlier literature.
47   Emery 1938: 35, fig. 8 and pl. 17[411].
48   Crubézy and Midant-Reynes 2005: 78, fig. 3.
49   E.F. Morris 2007 n.2014; Crubézy and Midant-Reynes 2005, with summary of
     sources.
50   For the general context see Emery 1962; Edwards 1971; A.J. Spencer 1996; T.A.H.
     Wilkinson 1999.
51   Lacau and Lauer 1959: 12, pl. 8[41].
52   Ćwiek 2003, 53, fn. 211, with discussion.
53   Dreyer et al. 1996: 71–72, fig. 25, pl. 14a.
54   Lacher-Raschdorff 2014.
55   Lacher-Raschdorff 2014.
56   Bárta 2011a: 79–80.
57   Helck 1987; Dodson 1996.
58   Quibell 1900: pl. XL.
59   Porter and Moss 1937: 87; Dreyer et al. 1998: 164–66; 2000: 122–28; 2003: 108–24;
     2006: 110–27.
60   Porter and Moss 1937: 54–55; Kemp 1966; Kaiser and Dreyer 1982: 253–60;
     O'Connor 1989.
61   Dodson 2016: 6–9.

62   Porter and Moss 1937: 196.
63   Porter and Moss 1937: 196; Kemp 1963; Alexanian 1998; Friedman and Raue 2007.
64   Cairo JE32161; Ashmolean E.517 (Porter and Moss 1937: 195–96).
65   Alexanian 1998.

Notes to Chapter Four

1   On him and his reign see T.A.H. Wilkinson 1999: 95–98; Baud 2002; Bárta 2011a: 108–12.
2   Fragments of a broken naos of Djoser were discovered by Ernesto Schiaparelli in 1903 and they are now on display in the Turin Museum (Inv.Suppl. 2671), see Weill 1911–12.
3   Garstang 1903.
4   This is done in the texts by setting off Djoser's reign from the preceding part either graphically (in a new column), or by marking his name in red, as in the Turin Royal Canon.
5   Regulski 2010.
6   Baud 2002, passim.
7   van den Boorn 1988.
8   Lacau and Lauer 1965: 1–2, pl. 1.
9   Helck 1987: 255–58.
10   Cairo JE49889 (now in the Imhotep Museum).
11   But cf. discussion in chapter 3.
12   For the original publication see Firth and Gunn 1926. For a more recent discussion, see Baud 2002: 119–23.
13   For overview see Wildung 1977: 9–10.
14   Goneim 1957: 4.
15   Baud 2002: 105–15.
16   Porter and Moss 1974: 399–415.
17   Wildung 1969: 82–84.
18   Assmann 1990, passim.
19   For the evolution and significance of the complex, see Verner 2002: 108–40.
20   For overview, with older literature, Nikolova 2004; Verner 2002: 159–89.
21   Callender 2011: 59.
22   Hornung, Krauss, and Warburton 2006: 490.
23   Nolan 2005.
24   Dreyer and Kaiser 1980; Bárta 2005b.
25   Radwan 2003: 111.
26   The first being that at Aswan, completed in 1902.
27   Lehner 2000: 298–307.
28   Willcocks and Craig 1913.
29   Baud 1999: 312.
30   On his monuments, see Verner 2002: 153–89.
31   Ćwiek 1997: 17–22; Zecchi 2001: 89–91.
32   It is possible that the Layer Pyramid at Zawyat al-Aryan may have initiated the change (Dodson 2000: 87).
33   Stadelmann 1983: 232.

34 Which Stadelmann has argued imply cenotaphs (Stadelmann 1983: 237–41; 1985: 85–86), although this is not a widely held view.
35 Nuzzolo 2015a.
36 Nikolova 2004: 84.
37 Although the earliest use of a cartouche to surround the regnal name is dated to the reign of the Third Dynasty king Nebka, the Horus Sanakht. For a detailed discussion, including the doubtful cases, see Ćwick 2003: 28–29, n. 95.
38 Verner 2014: 227–32.
39 Moreno García 1999.
40 Junker 1939; Gödecken 1976.
41 Bárta 2005b.
42 Barta 1968.
43 Bárta 2011a: 132.
44 Petrie 1892.
45 Bárta 1995b.
46 For a more general reflection on the social aspects of pottery at the time of the Old Kingdom see Bárta 1996, and more recently Arias Kytnarová 2014.
47 Redding 2013.
48 Moens and Wetterstrom 1988.
49 Ikram 1995.
50 Lehner 2002; 2015.
51 For details see Redding 2013.
52 von den Driesch and Boessneck 1985.
53 Butzer 1976: 83, table 4; Mortensen 1991.
54 Lehner 2015: 401.
55 Redding 2013.

Notes to Chapter Five

1   Jéquier 1928.
2   Bárta 2013e.
3   Jánosi 2005: 375–79.
4   Strudwick 1985: 136.
5   Strudwick 1985: 59, 74, 106–108; Jánosi 2005: 406.
6   Schmitz 1976: 166; Strudwick 1985: 312–13.
7   Papazian 2012: 111.
8   Papazian 2012.
9   G.D. Scott 1989; statistics based on the Catalogue.
10 Dorman 2002.
11 Dorman 2002.
12 Callender 2011: 149–53.
13 Dulíková 2011.
14 Dulíková, Mařík, Bárta, and Cibuľa 2018.
15 Strudwick 1985.
16 Bárta 2016a.
17 Rydström 1994.

18   Bárta 2016b.

19   Stadelmann 2000: 531 n.10; for other possible genealogies see S. Roth 2001: 360 and Gundacker 2010.

20   Verner 2001a: 245; Bárta 2016a: 58, fig. 3.

21   Jéquier 1928: pl. II.

22   S. Hassan 1943: 63–67.

23   Magli 2013: 123, fig. 5.2.

24   Bárta 2016a.

25   Graefe 1990.

26   Vlčková 2006: 83–86 and 85, fig. 5.2.

27   For Userkaf's reign see Verner 2014: 29–36.

28   Bussmann 2010: 109–16, 509–12.

29   Goedicke 1979; Papazian 2012.

30   Bissing 1905; Kaiser 1956; Winter 1957; Ricke 1965; Bárta 2013a.

31   Ricke 1965; Verner 2014: 199–207.

32   Cairo JE 90220 (Verner 2017: 20–26).

33   Now in the Musées royaux d'Art et d'Histoire in Brussels.

34   Walle 1930: 53.

35   Kammerzell 2001.

36   R.H. Wilkinson 2003: 148–80.

37   Seidel 1996: 25–49.

38   Helck 1984.

39   For more on the papyrus archives in Abusir see Posener-Kriéger 1976 and Posener-Kriéger, Verner, and Vymazalová 2006.

40   Strudwick 1985: 70.

41   Wilson 2001: 377.

42   Wilson 2001: 48–88; Voss 2004: 54.

43   A.M. Roth 1991.

44   Wilson 2001: 90–94.

45   Laboury 2010: 123.

46   Bárta 2013b.

47   Quibell 1900: 6, pl. 4; Quibell and Green 1902: pl. 72.

48   T.A.H. Wilkinson 1999: 309–11; McNamara 2008.

49   Kaiser 1956: 111–12; Mariette 1889: 101 (determinative in tomb of Ifefi).

50   Bárta 2013b.

51   Bárta 2013b.

52   Moursi 1972; Wilson 2001; Bárta 2013b.

53   Verner 2014: 227–32.

Notes to Chapter Six

1   Cannadine and Price 1987: 3.

2   Bárta 2013d.

3   On his reign see Bárta 2005c; Bárta and Dulíková 2015; Verner 2014: 61–75.

4   Personal communication from Mark Lehner.

5   For details on this complex see Borchardt 1907 and Verner 2002: 311–19.

6 Goedicke 2000.
7 Verner, Posener-Kriéger, and Jánosi 1995.
8 Verner 2002: 311–19 with details.
9 Krejčí 2012.
10 Arnold 1994.
11 For more on this construction see Bissing 1905; Verner 2014: 212–18; and literature.
12 Helck 1977b.
13 Bárta 2016a.
14 Verner 2014: 215.
15 Nuzzolo 2015b.
16 Edel and Wenig 1974.
17 Verner 2014: 214.
18 Helck 1977b.
19 Moussa and Altenmüller 1977; Krejčí 2009.
20 Wilson 2001: 143–60.
21 Verner 1977; Vachala 2004; Krejčí 2009.
22 Vachala 2004.
23 Bárta 2000.
24 Épron 1939.
25 Brovarski 2001.
26 For details on the development of all the three features discussed in this box see Bárta 2005a.
27 Bárta 2002.
28 Bárta 2002; Bárta 2005c; Bárta 2006.
29 Bárta 1998.
30 A.M. Roth 1994, or see Bárta 2015c for depictions of scenes with a desert theme.
31 Griffiths 1980; Begelsbacher-Fischer 1981: 124–25.
32 M. Smith 2009.
33 Griffiths 1980: 60–61.
34 Lorton 1985.
35 Mathieu 2010: 78, fig. 1.
36 van de Walle 1978: 24, no. 70 and pl. 1.
37 Strudwick 2005: 304; Mathieu 2010: 77.
38 Bárta 1995b.
39 Bárta 1995b.
40 Mathieu 2010: 85–87.
41 For their list see Dulíková 2016.
42 Bárta and Dulíková 2015; the examples below are based on this study.
43 Schmitz 1976: 109–33, 340–42; Baud 1999: 185–89, 333–46; Callender 2002: 133–55.
44 Dorman 2002.
45 El-Khouli and Kanawati 1990: 26–66.
46 Verner 1977.
47 Badawy 1976: 15–24.
48 Cairo CG37 and CG196.

49 In ancient Egypt the House of Life was a center of learning and texts. Only men—initiated priests—were allowed to enter it. See Bárta 2015e.
50 Ziegler 2007.
51 Bárta, Vymazalová, Dulíková, Arias Kytnarová, Megahed, and Varadzinová 2014; Vymazalová and Dulíková 2012; Vymazalová and Dulíková 2014.
52 Bárta and Dulíková 2015 and other literature.
53 Bárta 2013d.

Notes to Chapter Seven

1 Megahed 2016.
2 Sinclair 2013: 125.
3 Altenmüller 2001: 597.
4 Stark and Chance 2012.
5 Stark and Chance 2012.
6 Kanawati 1980: 11–21.
7 Bárta 2016b.
8 Bárta 2011a.
9 A.M. Roth 1993.
10 Albert and Midant-Reynes 2005.
11 Bárta 2006.
12 For the Third Dynasty pyramids see Baud 2002.
13 Bárta 2005b.
14 See Lehner and Hawass 2017.
15 Bestock 2009; O'Connor 2011.
16 Baud 2002; Bárta 2005b.
17 Bárta and Dulíková 2015.
18 Fakhry 1959.
19 Harpur 1987; 2001; Bárta 2005b.
20 Bárta and Dulíková 2015.
21 J.P. Allen 2005.
22 Willems 2008.
23 Kanawati 2010.
24 Bárta 2015b; Weiss 2017.
25 Kanawati 1980; Brovarski 2013.
26 Bárta 2005a.
27 Verner 2014.
28 Munro 1993.
29 Stasser 2013.
30 J.P. Allen 2005.
31 Bárta 2005c.
32 Willems 2008.
33 Kanawati 1980: 16–17.
34 Eichler 1993.
35 Kanawati 2003.
36 Kanawati 2003.

37 Kanawati 1980; Bárta 2015e.
38 For more on her role see Stasser 2013 and Callender 2011.
39 Kanawati 2003.
40 Baud and Dobrev 1995.
41 Stadelmann 1994.
42 Gourdon 2016: 65–68.
43 Gourdon 2016: 99.
44 Cairo CG 1431, Mariette 1869: pl. 2a.
45 Strudwick 2005: 377.
46 Strudwick 2005: 353.
47 See Elsner 2004; Dodson and Ikram 2008, with further references to individual
    sites.
48 Strudwick 2005: 133–34[50, 51].
49 Sethe 1903: 1:115.
50 Spalinger 1994: 308.
51 Hornung, Krauss, and Warburton 2006: 134.
52 Kanawati 1980: 62–87.
53 Kanawati 1980: 88–99.
54 Moreno García 1998.
55 Sethe 1903: 1:251–55; Moreno García 1998; Strudwick 2005: 342–44.
56 Kamal 1912: 132, fig. 9; Weill 1958: 79; Kanawati and McFarlane 1992: 151–52.
57 Cf. Barrois 1889: pl. 1–3; Lyons 1908: pl. 1.
58 Barrois 1889: pl. 1.
59 Baines and Málek 1986: map on 41.
60 Papazian 2015: 395.
61 Callender 2011: 344 [Genealogy 6]; Labrousse 2010.
62 Ryholt 2000.
63 Callender 2011: 344 [Genealogy 7]; Labrousse 2010.
64 Kitchen 1976.
65 Details in Papazian 2015.
66 Mariette 1864.
67 Jéquier 1933: 53, fig. 31.
68 Papazian 2015: 414–15, 416, tab. 10.2.
69 Jéquier 1935; Verner 2002: 378.
70 Goedicke 1967; 1980.
71 Cf. Ryholt 2000.
72 Fischer 1964: 35–38.
73 Papazian 2015.
74 Goedicke 1967: 165–213.
75 Goedicke 1967: 178–83.
76 Kanawati and McFarlane 1992: 157–62.
77 Vandier 1950; Bárta 2003.
78 Papazian 2015: 420, tab. 10.3.
79 F.A. Hassan 1997; Stanley, Krom, Cliff, and Woodward 2003.
80 Brussels E.4985 (Schenkel 1965: 99–101; Landgráfová and Navrátilová 2011: 7–8).
81 Cairo JE 41437 (Schenkel 1965: 99–101; Landgráfová and Navrátilová 2011: 8–9).

82   Erman 1885: 66.

83   Meyer 1887: 131–33.

84   Assmann 1996: 63.

85   Vandersleyen 1995: 11–31.

Notes to Chapter Eight

1   Gardiner 1909.

2   Tallet 2005.

3   Franke 1991.

4   Bietak 1996; Oren 1997; Ryholt 1997: 293–95.

5   Jansen-Winkeln 2002.

6   Cline 2014.

7   Petrie 1894: 117–18; Frankfort 1926.

8   Jansen-Winkeln 2010.

9   Helck 1977b.

10   Bell 1970; 1971; F.A. Hassan 1981; 1997; Stanley, Krom, Cliff, and Woodward 2003; Málek 2000; Seidlmayer 2000; T.A.H. Wilkinson 2010: 97.

11   Verner 2001b: 588–89.

12   Müller-Wollermann 1986: 20–25.

13   Jánosi 2006; Bárta 2011a.

14   Cf. Gundlach 1998: 227–28.

15   Moeller 2005.

16   Bell 1971: 2.

17   Carpenter 1966.

18   F.A. Hassan 1997.

19   Moeller 2005: 154.

20   Walford 1879: 18.

21   Alexanian and Seidlmayer 2002.

22   Jeffreys 1997, with earlier literature.

23   Cílek et al. 2012.

24   Jeffreys and Tavares 1994: 150.

25   Willcocks 1889: 44.

26   Cílek et al. 2012: 8.

27   Clarke et al. 2016.

28   Bárta 2015c.

29   Borchardt 1910: 29–30.

30   Borchardt 1907: 45, fig. 28.

31   Welc and Marks 2013.

32   Stanley, Krom, Cliff, and Woodward 2003.

33   Strudwick 2005: 285.

34   Römer 2011.

35   Cf. Ward-Perkins 2006.

36   Popitz 1986.

37   Moreno García 2015.

38   Seidlmayer 2000.

39 Moreno García 2015: 10, fig. 6.
40 Haiman 1996.
41 Vandier 1950.
42 Daoud 2005.
43 Shils 1972.
44 Cf. Morony 1987.
45 Kurth 1992; Baines and Yoffee 1998; Bárta 2013b.
46 Seidlmayer 1990: 439.
47 Seidlmayer 1990: 441.
48 For more on the patron–client relationship in ancient Egypt see Lehner 2000; on the texts see Franke 2006.
49 Schenkel 1965.
50 Pardey 1976: 211.

Bibliography

Abbreviations

Ä&L   *Ägypten und Levante: Zeitschrift für ägyptische Archäologie und deren Nachbargebiete* (Vienna: Verlag der Österreichischen Akademie der Wissenschaften)

ArOr   *Archiv Orientální* (Prague: Charles University)

ASAE   *Annales du Service des antiquités de l'Égypte* (Cairo: Institut français d'archéologie orientale/Supreme Council of Antiquities Press)

BACE   *Bulletin of the Australian Centre for Egyptology* (North Ryde: Australian Centre for Egyptology, Macquarie University)

BASOR   *Bulletin of the American Schools of Oriental Research* (New Haven: American Schools of Oriental Research)

BIFAO   *Bulletin de l'Institut français d'archéologie orientale du Caire* (Cairo: Institut français d'archéologie orientale)

BMSAES   *British Museum Studies in Ancient Egypt and Sudan* (London: British Museum)

BSEG   *Bulletin de la Société d'Égyptologie de Genève* (Geneva: Société d'Égyptologie de Genève)

BSFE   *Bulletin de la Société française d'égyptologie (Paris: Société française d'égyptologie)*

211

CAJ	*Cambridge Archaeological Journal* (Cambridge: McDonald Institute for Archaeological Research)
ÉNiM	*Égypte nilotique et méditerranéenne (Lyon: Université Paul Valéry)*
GM	*Göttinger Miszellen* (Göttingen: Universität Göttingen. Ägyptologisches Seminar)
JARCE	*Journal of the American Research Center in Egypt* (New York: American Research Center in Egypt)
JEA	*Journal of Egyptian Archaeology* (London: Egypt Exploration Fund/Society)
JNES	*Journal of Near Eastern Studies* (Chicago: University of Chicago Press)
Kmt	*Kmt: A Modern Journal of Ancient Egypt* (San Francisco: Kmt Communications)
MDAIK	*Mitteilungen des Deutschen Archäologischen Instituts, Kairo* (Mainz am Rhein: Philipp von Zabern/Berlin: De Gruyter)
PES	*Prague Egyptological Studies* (Prague: Charles University)
PNAS	*Proceedings of the National Academy of Sciences of the United States of America* (Washington: National Academy of Sciences)
RdE	*Revue d'égyptologie* (Leuven: Peeters)
SAK	*Studien zur altägyptschen Kultur* (Hamburg: H. Buske Verlag)
VarAeg	*Varia Aegyptiaca* (San Antonio: Van Siclen Books)
ZÄS	*Zeitschrift für Ägyptische Sprache und Altertumskunde* (Berlin: Akademie Verlag)
ZPE	*Zeitschrift für Papyrologie und Epigraphik* (Cologne: Universität zu Köln)

Bibliography

Acemoglu, D., and J.A. Robinson. 2012. *Why Nations Fail: The Origins of Power, Prosperity, and Poverty*. New York: Crown Business.

Albert, J.-P., and B. Midant-Reynes, eds. 2005. *Le sacrifice humain en Égypte ancienne et ailleurs*. Paris: Soleb.

Alexanian, N. 1998. "Die Reliefdekoration des Chasechemui aus dem sogenannten Fort in Hierakonpolis." In *Les critères de datation stylistiques à l'Ancien Empire*, edited by N. Grimal, 1–29. Cairo: Institut français d'archéologie orientale.

Alexanian, N., and S. Seidlmayer. 2002. "Die Residenznekropole von Dahschur: Erster Grabungsbericht." *MDAIK* 58: 1–28.

Allen, J.P. 1992. "Re'-wer's Accident." In *Studies in Pharaonic Religion and Society in Honour of J. Gwyn Griffiths*, edited by A.B. Lloyd, 14–20. London: Egypt

Exploration Society.

———. 2005. *The Ancient Egyptian Pyramid Texts*. Atlanta: Society of Biblical Literature.

Allen, R. 1997. "Agriculture and the Origins of the State in Ancient Egypt." *Explorations in Economic History* 34/2: 135–54.

Almásy, L.E. 1998. *Schwimmer in der Wüste*. Munich: Deutscher Taschenbuch Verlag.

Altenmüller, H. 2001. "Old Kingdom: Fifth Dynasty." In *The Oxford Encyclopedia of Ancient Egypt*, edited by D.B. Redford, 597–601. Oxford: Oxford University Press.

Anderson, W. 1992. "Badarian Burials: Evidence for Social Inequality in Middle Egypt during the Early Predynastic Era." *JARCE* 29: 51–80.

Andrews, P. 2005. *Tarawera and the Terraces*. Rotorua: Bibiophil and the Buried Village.

Arias Kytnarová, K. 2014. "Pottery." In *Abusir XXIII: The Tomb of the Sun Priest Neferinpu*, by M. Bárta, Y. Abe, K. Arias Kytnarová, P. Havelková, L. Hegrlík, L. Jirásková, P. Malá, I. Nakai, V. Novotný, E. Ogidani, A. Okoshi, Z. Sůvová, M. Uchinuma, and H. Vymazalová, 109–43. Prague: Charles University in Prague.

Arnold, D. 1994. *Lexikon der ägyptischen Baukunst*. Zurich: Artemis.

———. 1999. *Temples of the Last Pharaohs*. New York: Oxford University Press.

Assmann, J. 1990. *Ma'at: Gerechtigkeit und Unsterblichkeit im alten Ägypten*. Munich: Beck.

———. 1996. *Ägypten: eine Sinngeschichte*. Munich: Hanser.

———. 2006. *Ma'at: Gerechtigkeit und Unsterblichkeit im alten Ägypten*. 2nd ed. Munich: Beck.

———. 2011. *Steinzeit und Sternzeit: altägyptische Zeitkonzepte*. Munich: Wilhelm Fink.

Badawy, A. 1976. *The Tombs of Iteti, Sekhem'ankh-Ptah, and Kaemnofert at Giza*. Berkeley: University of California Press.

Baines, J. 1995. "Kingship, Definition of Culture, and Legitimation." In *Ancient Egyptian Kingship*, edited by D. O'Connor and D.P. Silverman, 3–47. Leiden: Brill.

———. 2007. *Visual and Written Culture in Ancient Egypt*. New York: Oxford University Press.

———. 2015. "Ancient Egyptian Cities: Monumentality and Performance." In *The Cambridge World History*, III: *Early Cities in Comparative Perspective, 4000 BCE—1200 CE*, edited by N. Yoffee, 27–47. Cambridge: Cambridge University Press.

Baines, J., and J. Málek. 1986. *Atlas of Ancient Egypt*. Oxford: Phaidon.

Baines, J., and N. Yoffee. 1998. "Order, Legitimacy, and Wealth in Ancient Egypt and Mesopotamia." In *Archaic States*, edited by G.M. Feinman and J. Marcus, 199–260. Santa Fe, NM: School for Advanced Research Press.

Barrois, J. 1889. *Irrigation in Egypt*. Washington: Government Printing Office.

Bárta, M. 1995a. "Archaeology and Iconography: bd3 and 'prt Bread Moulds and 'Speisetischszene' Development in the Old Kingdom." *SAK* 22: 21–35.

———. 1995b. "Pottery Inventory and the Beginning of the IVth Dynasty." *GM* 149: 15–24.

———. 1996. "Class-Type Interpretation of Pottery: Pottery Finds from the Pyramid Temple of Raneferef and Their Significance." *Památky archeologické* 87: 137–60.

———. 1998. "Die Tauschhandelszenen aus dem Grab des Fetekty in Abusir." *SAK* 26: 19–34.

———. 2000. "The Mastaba of Ptahshepses Junior II at Abusir." *Ä&L* 10: 45–66.

———. 2002. "Sociology of the Minor Cemeteries during the Old Kingdom: A View from Abusir South." *ArOr* 70(3): 291–300.

———. 2003. *Sinuhe, the Bible and the Patriarchs*. Prague: Set Out.

———. 2005a. "Architectural Innovations in the Development of the Non-Royal Tomb during the Reign of Nyuserra." In *Structure and Significance: Thoughts on Ancient Egyptian Architecture*, edited by P. Jánosi, 105–30. Vienna: Verlag der Österreichischen Akademie der Wissenschaften.

———. 2005b. "Location of the Old Kingdom Pyramids in Egypt." *CAJ* 15(2): 177–91.

———. 2005c. "The Transitional Type of Tomb at Saqqara North and Abusir South." In *Texte und Denkmäler des ägyptischen Alten Reiches*, edited by S.J. Seidlmayer, 69–89. Berlin: Achet-Verlag.

———. 2006. "Non-Royal Tombs of the Old Kingdom at Abusir." In *Abúsír: Tajemství pouště a pyramid / Abusir: Secrets of the Desert and the Pyramids*, edited by H. Benešovská and P. Vlčková, 122–45. Prague: National Museum.

———. 2009. *Abusir XIII: Tomb Complex of the Vizier Qar, His Sons Qar Junior and Senedjemib, and Iykai: Abusir South 2*. Prague: Dryada.

———. 2011a. *Journey to the West: The World of the Old Kingdom Tombs in Ancient Egypt*. Prague: Charles University in Prague, Faculty of Arts.

———. 2011b. *Swimmers in the Sand: On the Origins of Ancient Egyptian Mythology*. Prague: Dryada.

———. 2013a. "Abu Gurob." In *The Encyclopedia of Ancient History*, edited by R. Bagnall, K. Brodersen, C. Champion, A. Erskine, and S. Huebner, 1:7–9. Malden: Wiley–Blackwell.

———. 2013b. "Egyptian Kingship during the Old Kingdom." In *Cosmos, Politics, and the Ideology of Kingship in Ancient Egypt and Mesopotamia. Philadelphia, November 5–11, 2007*, edited by J.A. Hill, P. Jones, and A. Morales, 257–83. Philadelphia: University of Pennsylvania Museum of Archaeology and Anthropology.

———. 2013c. "Radiocarbon Dates for the Old Kingdom and Their Correspondences." In *Radiocarbon and the Chronologies of Ancient Egypt*, edited by J.A. Shortland and R.C. Bronk, 218–23. Oxford: Oxbow Books.

———. 2013d. "The Sun Kings of Abusir and Their Entourage: 'Speakers of Nekhen of the King.'" In *Diachronic Trends in Ancient Egyptian History: Studies Dedicated to the Memory of Eva Pardey*, edited by M. Bárta and H. Küllmer, 24–31. Prague: Faculty of Arts, Charles University in Prague.

———. 2013e. "Zrychlování tempa: Svět bohů, králů a monumentů (4000–1000 př. Kr.)." In *Civilizace a dějiny: Historie světa pohledem dvaceti českých vědců*, by M. Bárta and M. Kovář, 111–43. Prague: Academia.

———. 2014. "Vertikalita. Co se stalo?" In *Něco se muselo stát: Nová kniha proměn*, edited by V. Cílek, 378–85. Prague: Novela Bohemica.

———. 2015a. "Ancient Egyptian History as an Example of Punctuated Equilibrium. An Outline." In *Towards a New History for the Egyptian Old Kingdom: Perspectives on the Pyramid Age*, edited by P.D. Manuelian and T. Schneider, 1–17. Leiden: Brill.

———. 2015b. "Long Term or Short Term? Climate Change and the Demise of the Old Kingdom." In *Climate and Ancient Societies*, edited by S. Kerner, R.J. Dann, and P. Bangsgaard, 177–95. Copenhagen: Museum Tusculanum Press.

———. 2015c. "Makrohistorie a přerušované rovnováhy: O dynamice dějin." In *Povaha změny: Bezpečnost, rizika a stav dnešní civilizace*, edited by M. Bárta, M. Kovář, and O. Foltýn, 18–37. Prague: Vyšehrad.

———. 2015d. "The Oldest Mythological Run in Egyptian Western Desert? On the Possible Origins of the Sed Feast in Ancient Egypt." In *Forgotten Times and Spaces: New Perspectives in Paleoanthropological, Paleoethnological and Archeological Studies*, edited by S. Sázelová, M. Novák, and A. Mizerová, 487–93. Brno: Institute of Archaeology of the Czech Academy of Sciences.

———. 2015e. "Tomb of the Chief Physician Shepseskafankh." *PES* 15: 15–27.

———. 2016a. "'Abusir Paradigm' and the Beginning of the Fifth Dynasty." In *The Pyramids: Between Life and Death, Proceedings of the Workshop Held at Uppsala University*, edited by I. Hein, N. Billing, and E. Meyer-Dietrich, 51–74. Uppsala: Uppsala Universitet.

———. 2016b. "Temporary and Permanent: Status Race and the Mechanism of Change in a Complex Civilisation; Ancient Egypt in between 2900 and 2120 BC." In *From Crisis to Collapse: Archaeology and the Breakdown of Social Order*, edited by J. Driessen and T. Cunningham, 289–305. Louvain le Neuve: Aegis.

———. 2018. "Heraclitus' Law, Punctuated Equilibria and the Dynamics of the Contemporary World." *Terrorism: An Electronic Journal and Knowledge Base* 7 (3 December): 7–14.

Bárta, M., Y. Abe, K. Arias Kytnarová, P. Havelková, L. Hegrlík, L. Jirásková, P. Malá, I. Nakai, V. Novotný, E. Ogidani, A. Okoshi, Z. Sůvová, M. Uchinuma, and H. Vymazalová. 2014a. *Abusir XXIII: The Tomb of the Sun Priest Neferinpu (AS 37)*. Prague: Charles University in Prague, Faculty of Arts.

Bárta, M., and A. Bezděk. 2008. "Beetles and the Decline of the Old Kingdom: Climate Change in Ancient Egypt." In *Chronology and Archaeology in Ancient Egypt (The Third Millennium BC): Proceedings of the Conference Held in Prague (June 11–14, 2007)*, edited by M. Bárta and H. Vymazalová, 214–22. Prague: Czech Institute of Egyptology.

Bárta, M., and V. Brůna. 2006. *Satelitní atlas pyramid: Abú Ghuráb, Abúsír, Sakkára, Dahšúr / Satellite Atlas of the Pyramids: Abu Ghurab, Abusir, Saqqara, Dahshur*. Plzeň: Dryada.

Bárta, M., and V. Dulíková. 2015. "Divine and Terestrial: Power Rhetorics in Ancient Egypt (Case of Nyuserra)." In *7. Symposium zur Königsideologie / 7th Symposium on Egyptian Royal Ideology: Royal versus Divine Authority. Acquisition, Legitimization and Renewal of Power*, edited by F. Coppens, J. Janák, and H. Vymazalová, 31–48. Wiesbaden: Harrassowitz.

Bárta, M., and M. Kovář. 2011. *Kolaps a regenerace: cesty civilizací a kultur: minulost, současnost a budoucnost komplexních společností*. Prague: Academia.

———. 2013. *Civilizace a dějiny: historie světa pohledem dvaceti českých vědců*. Prague: Academia.

Bárta, M., and M. Kovář, eds. 2019. *Civilisations: Collapse and Regeneration; Rise, Fall and Transformation in History*. Prague: Academia.

Bárta, M., M. Kovář, and O. Foltýn, eds. 2015. *Povaha změny: bezpečnost, rizika a stav dnešní civilizace*. Prague: Vyšehrad.

Bárta, M., H. Vymazalová, V. Dulíková, K. Arias Kytnarová, M. Megahed, and L. Varadzinová. 2014. "Exploration at the Necropolis at Abusir South in the Season of 2012: Preliminary Report." *Ä&L* 24: 17–40.

Barta, W. 1968. *Aufbau und Bedeutung der altägyptischen Opferformel*. ÄF 24. Glückstadt: Augustin.

Baud, M. 1999. *Famille royale et pouvoir sous l'Ancien Empire égyptien*. Cairo: Institut français d'archéologie orientale.

———. 2002. *Djéser et la IIIe dynastie*. Paris: Pygmalion.

Baud, M., and V. Dobrev. 1995. "De nouvelles annales de l'Ancien Empire égyptien. Une 'Pierre de Palerme' pour la VIe dynastie." *BIFAO* 95: 23–92.

El-Baz, F. 2003. "Geoarchaeological Evidence of the Relationships between the Terminal Drought in North Africa and the Rise of Ancient Egypt." In *Egyptology at the Dawn of the Twenty-first Century: Proceedings of the Eighth International Congress of Egyptologists, Cairo, 2000*, 1: *Archaeology*, edited by Z. Hawass and L.P. Brock, 64–72. Cairo: American University in Cairo Press.

Begelsbacher-Fischer, B.L. 1981. *Untersuchungen zur Götterwelt des Alten Reiches im Spiegel der Privatgräber der IV. und V. Dynastie*. Freiburg: Universitätsverlag.

Bell, B. 1970. "The Oldest Records of the Nile Floods." *Geographical Journal* 136: 569–73.

———. 1971. "The Dark Ages in Ancient History, I: The First Dark Age in Egypt." *American Journal of Archaeology* 75/1: 1–26.

Bestock, L. 2009. *The Development of Royal Funerary Cult at Abydos: Two Funerary Enclosures from the Reign of Aha*. Wiesbaden: Otto Harrassowitz.

Bietak, M. 1996. *Avaris: The Capital of the Hyksos: Recent Excavations at Tell el-Dab'a*. London: British Museum Press.

Bissing, F.W. von. 1905. *Das Re-Heiligtum des Königs Ne-woser-re*, I: *Der Bau*. Berlin: Duncker.

Blanton, R.E., and L.F. Fargher. 2009. "Collective Action in the Evolution of Pre-Modern States." *Social Evolution & History* 8/2: 133–66.

Bollig, M., O. Bubenzer, R. Vogelsang, and H.-P. Wotzka, eds. 2007. *Aridity, Change and Conflict in Africa: Proceedings of an International ACACIA Conference Held at Königswinter, Germany, October 1–3, 2003*. Colloquium

Africanum. Cologne: Heinrich-Barth-Institut in Kooperation mit
Universität zu Köln.

Bond, G., W. Showers, M. Cheseby, R. Lotti, P. Almasi, P. deMenocal, P.
Priore, H. Cullen, I. Hajdas, and G. Bonani. 1997. "A Pervasive Millennial-
scale Cycle in North Atlantic Holocene and Glacial Climates." *Science*
278/5341: 1257–66.

Bonnet, H. 1952. *Reallexikon der ägyptischen Religionsgeschichte*. Berlin: Gruyter.

Borchardt, L. 1907. *Das Grabdenkmal des Königs Ne-user-re'*. Leipzig:
Hinrichs'sche Buchhandlung.

———. 1910. *Das Grabdenkmal des Königs Sáḥu-re*. 2 vols. Ausgrabungen der
Deutschen Orient-Gesellschaft in Abusir 1902–1908. Leipzig: J.C. Hinrichs.

Bradley, D.G., D.E. MacHugh, P. Cunningham, and R.T. Loftus. 1996.
"Mitochondrial Diversity and the Origins of African and European Cattle."
PNAS 93/10: 5131–35.

Braudel, F. 1980. *On History*. Chicago: University of Chicago Press.

Braun, E. 2011. "Early Interaction between Peoples of the Nile Valley and
the Southern Levant." In *Before the Pyramids: The Origins of Egyptian
Civilization*, edited by E. Teeter, 105–22. Chicago: Oriental Institute.

Breasted, J.H. 1912. *Development of Religion and Thought in Ancient Egypt:
Lectures Delivered on the Morse Foundation at Union Theological Seminary*.
London: Hodder and Stoughton.

Brovarski, E. 2001. *The Senedjemib Complex, 1: The Mastabas of Senedjemib
Inti (G 2370), Khnumenti (G 2374), and Senedjemib Mehi (G 2378)*. 2 vols.
Boston: Museum of Fine Arts.

———. 2013. "Overseers of Upper Egypt in the Old to the Middle Kingdoms.
Part 1." *ZÄS* 140: 91–111.

Brunton, G. 1937. *Mostagedda and the Tasian Culture (British Museum Expedition
to Middle Egypt, First and Second Years 1928, 1929)*. London: Quaritch.

Brunton, G., and G. Caton-Thompson. 1928. *The Badarian Civilisation and
Predynastic Remains near Badari*. London: Quaritch.

Buchanan, M. 2000. *Ubiquity: The Science of History . . . Or Why the World Is
Simpler Than We Think*. New York: Crown Publishers.

Bunbury, J. 2010. "The Development of the River Nile and the Egyptian
Civilization: A Water Historical Perspective with Focus on the First
Intermediate Period." In *History of Water*, series II, 2: *Rivers and Society:
From Early Civilizations to Modern Times*, edited by T. Tvedt and R. Coopey,
52–71. London: I.B. Tauris.

Bunsen, C.C.J. 1845–57. *Aegyptens Stelle in der Weltgeschichte: Geschichtliche
Untersuchung in fünf Büchern*. Hamburg: Perthes.

Burroughs, W.J. 2005. *Climate Change in Prehistory: The End of the Reign of
Chaos*. Cambridge: Cambridge University Press.

Bussmann, R. 2010. *Die Provinztempel Ägyptens von der 0. bis zur 11. Dynastie:
Archäologie und Geschichte einer gesellschaftlichen Institution zwischen Residenz
und Provinz*. Leiden: Brill.

———. 2013. "The Social Setting of the Temple of Satet in the Third
Millennium BC." In *The First Cataract on the Nile: One Region, Different*

Perspectives, edited by D. Raue, S.J. Seidlmayer, and P. Speiser, 21–34. Berlin: De Gruyter.

——. 2014. "Scaling the State: Egypt in the Third Millennium BC." *Archaeology International* 17: 79–93.

Butzer, K.W. 1976. *Early Hydraulic Civilization in Egypt: A Study in Cultural Ecology*. Chicago: University of Chicago Press.

——. 2012. "Collapse, Environment, and Society." *PNAS* 109/10: 3632–39.

Callender, V.G. 2002. "Excursus I. The Princesses and Their Burial Comparations; Excursus II. Observations on the Position of Royal Daughters in the Old Kingdom." In *Abusir IV: Djedkare Family Cemetery*, by M. Verner and V.G. Callender, 133–55. Prague: Charles University in Prague, Czech Institute of Egyptology.

——. 2011. *In Hathor's Image I: The Wives and Mothers of Egyptian Kings from Dynasties I–VI*. Prague: Charles University, Faculty of Arts in Prague.

Campagno, M. 2004. "In the Beginning Was the War: Conflict and Emergence of the Egyptian State." In *Egypt at Its Origins: Studies in Memory of Barbara Adams*, edited by S. Hendrickx, R.F. Friedman, K.M. Ciałowicz, and M. Chłodnicki, 689–703. Leuven: Peeters.

Cannadine, D., and S. Price, eds. 1987. *Rituals of Royalty: Power and Ceremonial in Traditional Societies*. Cambridge: Cambridge University Press.

Carneiro, R.L., ed. 1967. *The Evolution of Society: Selections from Herbert Spencer's Principles of Sociology*. Chicago: University of Chicago Press.

Carneiro, R.L. 1970. "A Theory of the Origin of the State." *Science* NS 169/3947: 733–38.

Carpenter, R. 1966. *Discontinuity in Greek Civilization*. Cambridge: Cambridge University Press.

Caton-Thompson, G. 1927. "Explorations in the Northern Fayum." *Antiquity* 1/3: 326–40.

Černý, J. 1973. *A Community of Workmen at Thebes in the Ramesside Period*. Cairo: Institut français d'archéologie orientale.

Chagnon, N.A. 1983. *Yąnomamö: The Fierce People*. 3rd ed. New York: Holt, Rinehart, and Winston.

Childe, V.G. 1942. *What Happened in History*. Harmondsworth: Penguin Books.

——. 1950. "The Urban Revolution." *Town Planning Review* 21/1: 3–17.

Chłodnicki, M., K.M. Ciałowicz, and A. Maczyńska. 2012. *Tell El-Farkha I: Excavations 1998–2011*. Poznań: Poznań Archaeological Museum.

Christian, D., et al. 2011. *Maps of Time: An Introduction to Big History*. California World History Library 2. Berkeley: University of California Press.

Cílek, V., M. Bárta, L. Lisá, A. Pokorná, L. Juříčková, V. Brůna, A.M.A. Mahmoud, A. Bajer, J. Novák, and J. Beneš. 2012. "Diachronic Development of the Lake of Abusir during the Third Millennium BC, Cairo, Egypt." *Quaternary International* 266: 14–24.

Claessen, H.J.M., T. Bargatzky, G.L. Cowgill, I.M. Diakonoff, R.R. Hagesteijn, F. Hicks, J.-C. Muller, D.T. Potts, M. Rowlands, A.C. Sinha, and J.-P. Warnier. 1984. "The Internal Dynamics of the Early State." *Current Anthropology* 2/4: 365–79.

Claessen, H.J.M., and P. Skalník, eds. 1981a. *The Study of the State*. The Hague: Mouton Publishers.

Claessen, H.J.M., and P. Skalník. 1981b. "Ubi sumus? The Study of the State Conference in Retrospect." In *The Study of the State*, edited by H.J.M. Claessen and P. Skalník, 469–510. The Hague: Mouton Publishers.

Clarke, J., N. Brooks, E.B. Banning, M. Bar-Matthews, S. Campbell, L. Clare, M. Cremaschi, S. di Lernia, N. Drake, M. Gallinaro, S. Manning, K. Nicoll, G. Philip, S. Rosen, U.-D. Schoop, M.A. Tafuri, B. Weninger, and A. Zerboni. 2016. "Climatic Changes and Social Transformations in the Near East and North Africa during the 'Long' 4th Millennium BC: A Comparative Study of Environmental and Archaeological Evidence." *Quaternary Science Reviews* 136: 96–121.

Clastres, P. 2010. *Archaeology of Violence*. Los Angeles, Cambridge, MA, and London: Semiotext(e).

Cline, E.H. 2014. *1177 BC: The Year Civilization Collapsed*. Princeton: Princeton University Press.

Crubézy, E., and B. Midant-Reynes. 2005. "Les sacrifices humains à l'époque prédynastique: l'apport de la nécropole d'Adaïma." In *Le sacrifice humain en Égypte ancienne et ailleurs*, edited by J.-P. Albert and B. Midant-Reynes, 58–81. Paris: Soleb.

Cuvier, G. 1813. *Essay on the Theory of the Earth*. Edinburgh: Printed for William Blackwood, South Bridge-Street; and John Murray, Albemarle-Street, and Robert Baldwin, Paternoster-Row, London.

———. 1834. *Barona Gjřjho Cuviera Rozprava o přewratech kůry zemnj, a o proměnách w živočistwu gimi způsobených, w ohledu přjrodopisném a děgopisném*. Prague: Knížecj arcibiskupská knihtiskárna.

Ćwiek, A. 1997. "Fayum in the Old Kingdom." *GM* 160: 17–22.

———. 2003. "Relief Decoration in the Funerary Complexes of the Old Kingdom: Studies in the Development, Scene Content, and Iconography." PhD diss., Warsaw University.

Dalfes, H.N., J. Kukla, and H. Weiss, eds. 1997. *Third Millennium BC Climate Change and Old World Collapse*. Berlin: Springer.

Dalley, S. 2008. *Myths from Mesopotamia: Creation, the Flood, Gilgamesh, and Others*. Oxford: Oxford University Press.

D'Altroy, T.N. 2007. *The Incas*. London: Blackwell.

Dansgaard, W., S.J. Johnsen, H.B. Clausen, D. Dahl-Jensen, N. Gundestrup, and C.U. Hammer. 1984. "North Atlantic Climatic Oscillations Revealed by Deep Greenland Ice Cores." In *Climate Processes and Climate Sensitivity*, edited by J.E. Hansen and T. Takahashi, 288–98. Washington: American Geophysical Union.

Dansgaard, W., S.J. Johnsen, H.B. Clausen, D. Dahl-Jensen, N.S. Gundestrup, C.U. Hammer, C.S. Hvidberg, J.P. Steffensen, A.E. Sveinbjörnsdottir, J. Jouzel, and G. Bond. 1993. "Evidence for General Instability of Past Climate from a 250-kyr Ice-Core Record." *Nature* 364: 218–20. doi: 10.1038/364218a0.

Daoud, K. 2005. *Corpus of Inscriptions of the Herakleopolitan Period from the*

Memphite Necropolis: Translations, Commentary and Analyses. Oxford: Hadrian Books.

Darnell, D. 2002. "Gravel of the Desert and Broken Pots in the Road: Ceramic Evidence from the Routes between the Nile and Kharga Oasis." In *Egypt and Nubia: Gifts of the Desert*, edited by R. Friedman, 156–77. London: British Museum Press.

———. 2008. "The Rayayna Crossroads: Life, Death and the Divine in the Upper Egyptian Desert." In *Abstracts of Papers Presented at the Third International Colloquium on Predynastic and Early Dynastic Egypt*, edited by R. Friedman and L. McNamara, 40–45. London: The British Museum.

Darnell, J.C. 2002. *Theban Desert Road Survey in the Egyptian Western Desert. Volume I.: Gebel Tjauti Rock Inscriptions 1–45 and Wadi el–Hol Rock Inscriptions 1–45*. OIP 119. Chicago: Oriental Institute.

Davis, W. 1992. *Masking the Blow: The Scene of Representation in Late Prehistoric Egyptian Art*. Berkeley: University of California Press.

Debono, F., and B. Mortensen. 1990. *El Omari: A Neolithic Settlement and Other Sites in the Vicinity of Wadi Hof, Helwan*. Mainz am Rhein: Philipp von Zabern.

Dee, M., D. Wengrow, A. Shortland, A. Stevenson, F. Brock, L. Girdland Flink, and C. Bronk Ramsey. 2013. "An Absolute Chronology for Early Egypt Using Radiocarbon Dating and Bayesian Statistical Modelling." *Proceedings of the Royal Society A* 469/2159: 1–10.

Diamond, J.M. 2005. *Collapse: How Societies Choose to Fail or Survive*. London: Allen Lane.

Dieter, A. 1994. *Lexikon der ägyptischen Baukunst*. Munich: Artemis.

Dillery, J. 1999. "The First Egyptian Narrative History: Manetho and Greek Historiography." *ZPE* 127: 93–116.

Dodson, A. 1996. "The Mysterious 2nd Dynasty." *Kmt* 7/2: 19–31.

———. 2000. "The Layer Pyramid of Zawiyet el-Aryan: Its Layout and Context." *JARCE* 37: 81–90.

———. 2003. *The Pyramids of Ancient Egypt*. London: New Holland.

———. 2016. *The Royal Tombs of Ancient Egypt*. Barnsley: Pen & Sword.

Dodson, A., and S. Ikram. 2008. *The Tomb in Ancient Egypt: Royal and Private Sepulchres from the Early Dynastic Period to the Romans*. London: Thames & Hudson.

Donker van Heel, K. 2012. *Djekhy & Son: Doing Business in Ancient Egypt*. Cairo: American University in Cairo Press.

———. 2014. *Mrs. Tsenhor: A Female Entrepreneur in Ancient Egypt*. Cairo: American University in Cairo Press.

Dorman, P. 2002. "The Biographical Inscription of Ptahshepses from Saqqara: A Newly Identified Fragment." *JEA* 88: 95–110.

Dove, M.R., ed. 2014. *The Anthropology of Climate Change: An Historical Reader*. Chichester: Wiley–Blackwell.

Dreyer, D., and W. Kaiser. 1980. "Zu den kleinen Stufenpyramiden Ober- und Mittelägypten." *MDAIK* 36: 43–59.

Dreyer, G., J. Boessnek, A. von den Driesch, and S. Klug. 1990. "Umm el-Qaab: Nachuntersuchungen im frühzeitlichen Königsfriedhof, 3/4 Vorbericht." *MDAIK* 46: 53–90.

Dreyer, G., U. Hartung, and F. Pumpenmeier. 1993. "Umm el-Qaab: Nachuntersuchungen im frühzeitlichen Königsfriedhof, 5./6. Vorbericht." *MDAIK* 49: 23–62.

Dreyer, G., E. Engel, U. Hartung, T. Hikade, E.C. Köhler, F. Pumpenmeier, A. von den Driesch, and J. Peters. 1996. "Umm el-Qaab: Nachuntersuchungen im frühzeitlichen Königsfriedhof, 7/8 Vorbericht." *MDAIK* 52: 11–81.

Dreyer, G., and M. Fischer. 1998. *Umm el-Qaab I: Zu den kleinen Stufenpyramiden Ober- und Mittelägypten*. Mainz am Rhein: Philipp von Zabern.

Dreyer, G., U. Hartung, T. Hikade, E. Christiana Köhler, V. Müller, and F. Pumpenmeier. 1998. "Umm el-Qaab: Nachuntersuchungen im frühzeitlichen Königsfriedhof, 9./10. Vorbericht." *MDAIK* 54:77–167.

Dreyer, G., A. von den Driesch, E.-M. Engel, R. Hartmann, U. Hartung, T. Hikade, V. Müller, and J. Peters. 2000. "Umm el-Qaab: Nachuntersuchungen im frühzeitlichen Königsfriedhof, 11./12. Vorbericht." *MDAIK* 56: 43–129.

Dreyer, G., R. Hartmann, U. Hartung, T. Hikade, H. Köpp, C. Lacher, V. Müller, A. Nerlich, and A. Zink. 2003. "Umm el-Qaab: Nachuntersuchungen im frühzeitlichen Königsfriedhof, 13./14./15. Vorbericht." *MDAIK* 59: 67–138.

Dreyer, G., A. Effland, U. Effland, E.-M. Engel, R. Hartmann, U. Hartung, C. Lacher, V. Müller, and A. Pokorny. 2006. "Umm el-Qaab: Nachuntersuchungen im frühzeitlichen Königsfriedhof, 16./17./18. Vorbericht." *MDAIK* 62: 67–129.

Driesch, A. von den, and J. Boessneck. 1985. *Die Tierknochenfunde aus der Neolithischen Siedlung von Merimde–Benisalame am Westlichen Nildelta*. Munich: Universität München.

Driessen, J., and C.F. MacDonald. 2000. "The Eruption of the Santorini Volcano and Its Effects on Minoan Crete." In *The Archaeology of Geological Catastrophes*, edited by W.J. McGuire, D.R. Griffiths, P.L. Hancock, and I.S. Stewart, 81–93. London: Geological Society.

Drioton, É., and J.-P. Lauer. 1939. *Sakkarah: Les monuments de Zoser*. Cairo: Institut français d'archéologie orientale.

Droux, X. 2005. "Une représentation de prisonniers décapités en provenance de Hiérakonpolis." *BSEG* 27: 33–42.

Drower, M.S. 1995. *Flinders Petrie: A Life in Archaeology*. 2nd ed. Madison: University of Wisconsin Press.

Dulíková, V. 2011. "Institue vezirátu: Několik poznámek k vezírům Staré říše." *Acta Fakulty filozofické Západočeské univerzity v Plzni* 3: 113–31.

———. 2016. "The Reign of King Nyuserra and Its Impact on the Development of the Egyptian State." PhD diss., Charles University, Prague.

Dulíková, V., R. Mařík, M. Bárta, and M. Cibuľa. 2018. "Invisible History: Hidden Markov Model of Old Kingdom Administration Development and Its Trends." In *Old Kingdom Art and Archaeology 2017*. Milan: Sala

Napoleonica-Palazzo Greppi, Università degli Studi di Milano.

Edel, E. 2008. *Die Felsgräbernekropole der Qubbet el-Hawa bei Assuan*, I/1: *Architektur, Darstellungen, Texte, archäologischer Befund und Funde der Fräber QH 24—QH 34 p.* Paderborn: Schöningh.

Edel, E., and S. Wenig. 1974. *Die Jahreszeitenreliefs aus dem Sonnenheiligtum des Königs Ne-user-re.* Berlin: Akademie Verlag.

Edwards, I.E.S. 1971. "The Early Dynastic Period in Egypt." In *Cambridge Ancient History*, I/2: *Early History of the Middle East*, edited by I.E.S. Edwards, C.J. Gadd, and N.G.L. Hammond, 1–70. Cambridge: Cambridge University Press.

Effland, U., and A. Effland. 2013. *Abydos: Tor zur ägyptischen Unterwelt.* Mainz am Rhein: Philipp von Zabern.

Eichler, E. 1993. *Untersuchungen zum Expeditionswesen des ägyptischen Alten Reiches.* Wiesbaden: Harrassowitz.

Eiwanger, J. 1982. "Die neolithische Siedlung von Merimde–Benisalame." *MDAIK* 38: 67–82.

———. 1984. *Merimde–Benisalame I: Die Funde der Urschicht.* Mainz am Rhein: Philipp von Zabern.

———. 1988. *Merimde–Benisalame II: Die Funde der mittleren Merimdekultur.* Mainz am Rhein: Philipp von Zabern.

———. 1992. *Merimde–Benisalame III: Die Funde der jüngeren Merimdekultur.* Mainz am Rhein: Philipp von Zabern.

Eldredge, N., and S.J. Gould. 1972. "Punctuated Equilibria: An Alternative to Phyletic Gradualism." In *Models in Paleobiology*, edited by T.J.M. Schopf, 82–115. San Francisco: Freeman, Cooper and Co.

Elsner, P. 2004. *Die Typologie der Felsgräber: strukturanalytische Untersuchung altägyptischer Grabarchitektur.* Frankfurt am Main: P. Lang.

Emery, W.B. 1938. *The Tomb of Hemaka.* Cairo: Government Press.

———. 1949. *Great Tombs of the First Dynasty.* Cairo: Government Press.

———. 1962. *Archaic Egypt.* Harmondsworth: Penguin Books.

Engel, E.-M. 2006. "Die Entwicklung des Systems der ägyptischen Nomoi in der Frühzeit." *MDAIK* 62: 151–60.

———. 2013. "The Organisation of a Nascent State: Egypt until the Beginning of the 4th Dynasty." In *Ancient Egyptian Administration*, edited by M.G. Juan Carlos, 19–40. Leiden: Brill.

Enmarch, R. 2005. *The Dialogue of Ipuwer and the Lord of All.* Oxford: Griffith Institute.

Épron, L. 1939. *Le tombeau de Ti.* Cairo: Institut français d'archéologie orientale.

Erman, A. 1885. *Aegypten und aegyptisches Leben im Altertum.* Tubingen: H. Laupp.

Eyre, C. 2002. *The Cannibal Hymn: A Cultural and Literary Study.* Liverpool: Liverpool University Press.

Fakhry, A. 1959. *The Monuments of Sneferu at Dahshur.* Cairo: General Organization for Government Printing Offices.

Faulkner, R.O. 1985. *The Ancient Egyptian Book of the Dead.* London: British Museum Publications.

Faure, H., and M.A.J. Williams. 1980. *The Sahara and the Nile: Quaternary Environments and Prehistoric Occupation in Northern Africa*. Rotterdam: Balkema.

Feinman, G.M. 2012. "Comparative Frames for the Diachronic Analysis of Complex Societies: Next Steps." In *The Comparative Archaeology of Complex Societies*, edited by M.E. Smith, 21–43. Cambridge: Cambridge University Press.

Fergusson, N. 2010. "Complexity and Collapse: Empires on the Edge of Chaos." *Foreign Affairs* March/April 2010. https://www.foreignaffairs.com/articles/united-states/2010-03-01/complexity-and-collapse

———. 2013. *The Great Degeneration: How Institutions Decay and Economies Die*. London: Penguin Books.

Finkel, I. 2014. *The Ark before Noah: Decoding the Story of the Flood*. London: Hodder & Stoughton.

Fiore Marochetti, E. 2013. "Gebelein." In *UCLA Encyclopedia of Egyptology*, edited by W. Wendrich, 1–20. Los Angeles. http://digital2.library.ucla.edu/viewFile.do?contentFileId=2260825

Firth, C.M., and B.G. Gunn. 1926. *Teti Pyramid Cemeteries*. 2 vols. Excavations at Saqqara. Cairo: Imprimerie de l'Institut français d'archéologie orientale.

Firth, C.M., J.E. Quibell, and J.-P. Lauer. 1935. *The Step Pyramid*. Cairo: Institut français d'archéologie orientale.

Fischer, H.G. 1964. *Inscriptions from the Coptite Nome: Dynasties VI–XI*. Rome: Pontificium Institutum Biblicum.

———. 1977. *Egyptian Studies II: The Orientation of Hieroglyphs*, I: *Reversals*. New York: The Metropolitan Museum of Art.

Flannery, K., and J. Marcus. 2012. *The Creation of Inequality: How Our Prehistoric Ancestors Set the Stage for Monarchy, Slavery and Empire*. Cambridge, MA: Harvard University Press.

Förster, F. 1997. "Die 'Reichseinigung': Stand, Probleme und Perspektiven eines ägypt(olog)ischen Phänomens." MA thesis, Universität zu Köln.

Förster, F., H. Riemer, and R. Kuper. 2012. "The 'Cave of Beasts' (Gilf Kebir, SW Egypt) and Its Chronological and Cultural Affiliation: Approaches and Preliminary Results of the Wadi Sura Project." In *Chronological and Palaeoenvironmental Issues in the Rock Art of Northern Africa*, edited by D. Huyge, F. Van Noten, and D. Swinne, 197–216. Brussels: Royal Academy of Overseas Sciences.

Fowles, S. 2016. "Writing Collapse." In *Social Theory in Archaeology and Ancient History: The Present and Future of Counternarratives*, edited by G. Emberling, 205–30. Cambridge: Cambridge University Press.

Franke, D. 1991. "The Career of Khnumhotep III of Beni Hassan and the so-called 'Decline of the Nomarch.'" In *Middle Kingdom Studies*, edited by S. Quirke, 51–68. New Malden, UK: SIA Publishing.

———. 2006. "Fürsorge und Patronat in der Ersten Zwischenzeit und im Mittleren Reich." *SAK* 34: 159–85.

Frankfort, H. 1926. "Egypt and Syria in the First Intermediate Period." *JEA* 12: 80–99.

Friedman, R.F., ed. 2002. *Egypt and Nubia: Gifts of the Desert*. London: British Museum Press.

Friedman, R.F., and P.N. Fiske, eds. 2011. *Egypt at Its Origins 3: Proceedings of the Third International Conference "Origin of the State. Predynastic and Early Dynastic Egypt," London, 27th July—1st August 2008*. Leuven: Peeters.

Friedman, R.F., and D. Raue. 2007. "New Observations on the Fort at Hierakonpolis." In *The Archaeology and Art of Ancient Egypt: Essays in Honor of David B. O'Connor*, edited by Z.A. Hawass and J.E. Richards, 1:309–36. Cairo: Supreme Council of Antiquities.

Frobenius, L. 1897–98. "Der westafrikanische Kulturkreis." *Petermanns Mitteilungen* 43/44: 225–71.

Fukuyama, F. 2015. *Political Order and Political Decay: From the Industrial Revolution to the Globalization of Democracy*. New York: Farrar, Straus and Giroux.

Gardiner, A.H. 1909. *The Admonitions of an Egyptian Sage from a Hieratic Papyrus in Leiden (Pap. Leiden 344 recto)*. Leipzig: Hinrichs'sche Buchhandlung.

———. 1959. *The Royal Canon of Turin*. Oxford: Oxford University Press.

Garstang, J. 1903. *Mahâsna and Bêt Khallâf, Egypt Research Account*. London: Quaritch.

Geertz, C. 1980. *Negara: The Theatre State in Nineteenth-century Bali*. Princeton: Princeton University.

Gill, C. 2017. *Plato's Atlantis Story: Text, Translation and Commentary*. Liverpool: Liverpool University Press.

Ginzburg, C., J.A. Tedeschi, and A. Tedeschi. 1980. *The Cheese and the Worms: The Cosmos of a Sixteenth-Century Miller*. London: Routledge & Kegan Paul.

Gödecken, K.B. 1976. *Eine Betrachtung der Inschriften des Meten im Rahmen der sozialen und rechtlichen Stellung von Privatleuten im Ägyptischen Alten Reich*. Wiesbaden: Harrassowitz.

Goebs, K. 2008. *Crowns in Egyptian Funerary Literature: Royalty, Rebirth, and Destruction*. Oxford: Griffith Institute.

Goedicke, H. 1967. *Königliche Dokumente aus dem Alten Reich*. Wiesbaden: Harrassowitz.

———. 1979. "Cult-temple and 'State' during the Old Kingdom." In *State and Temple Economy in the Ancient Near East: Proceedings of the International Conference Organized by the Katholieke Universiteit Leuven from the 10th to the 14th of April 1978*, 2 vols., edited by E. Lipiński, 113–31. OLA 5. Leuven: Departement Oriëntalistiek.

———. 1980. "Koptosdekrete." In *Lexikon der Ägyptologie*, III, edited by W. Helck, 740. Wiesbaden: Harrassowitz.

———. 2000. "Abusir—Saqqara—Giza." In *Abusir and Saqqara in the Year 2000*, edited by M. Bárta and J. Krejčí, 397–412. Prague: Oriental Institute.

Goldman, I. 1970. *Ancient Polynesian Society*. Chicago: University of Chicago Press.

Goneim, M.Z. 1957. *Horus Sekhem-khet: The Unfinished Step Pyramid at Saqqara*. Cairo: Institut français d'archéologie orientale.

Gould, S.J. 2002. *The Structure of Evolutionary Theory*. Cambridge, MA: Belknap Press of Harvard University Press.

Gourdon, Y. 2006. "Le nom d'épouses abydiennes de Pépy Ier et la formule de serment à la fin de l'Ancien Empire." *BIFAO* 106: 89–103.

———. 2016. *Pepy Ier et la VIe Dynastie*. Les grand pharaons. Paris: Pygmalion.

Graeber, D., and M.D. Sahlins. 2017. *On Kings*. Chicago: Hau Books.

Graefe, E. 1990. "Die gute Reputation des Königs 'Snofru.'" In *Studies in Egyptology: Presented to Miriam Lichtheim*, edited by S. Israelit-Groll, 1:257–63. Jerusalem: Hebrew University.

Grafenstein, U. von, H. Erlenkeuser, A. Brauer, J. Jouzel, and S.J. Johnsen. 1999. "A Mid-European Decadal Isotope-Climate Record from 15,500 to 5000 Years B.P." *Science* 284/5420: 1654–57.

Griffiths, J.G. 1980. *The Origins of Osiris and His Cult*. Leiden: Brill.

Guilhou, N. 2010. "Myth of the Heavenly Cow." In *UCLA Encyclopedia of Egyptology*, edited by J. Dieleman and W. Wendrich, 1–7. https://escholarship.org/uc/item/2vh551hn.

Gundacker, R. 2010. "Ein Beitrag zur Genealogie der 4. Dynastie, Teil 2: Die späte und ausgehende 4. Dynastie." *Sokar* 20: 30–44.

Gundlach, R. 1998. *Der Pharao und sein Staat: die Grundlegung der ägyptischen Königsideologie im 4. und 3. Jahrtausend*. Darmstadt: Wissenschaftliche Buchgesellschaft.

Gunn, J. 2000. *The Years without Summer: Tracing AD 536 and Its Aftermath*. Oxford: Archaeopress.

Hafsaas-Tsakos, H. 2009. "Hierarchy and Heterarchy: The Earliest Cross-cultural Trade along the Nile." In *Connecting South and North: Sudan Studies from Bergen in Honour of Mahmoud Salih*, edited by H. Hafsaas-Tsakos and A. Tsakos, 19–40. Bergen: BRIC.

———. 2015. "War on the Southern Frontier of the Emerging State of Ancient Egypt." PhD diss., University of Bergen.

Haiman, M. 1996. "Early Bronze Age IV Settlement Pattern of the Negev and Sinai Deserts: View from Small Marginal Temporary Sites." *BASOR* 303: 1–32.

Haldon, J., et al. 2018. "History Meets Palaeoscience: Consilience and Collaboration in Studying Past Societal Responses to Environmental Change." *Proceedings of the National Academy of Sciences* 115/13: 3210.

Hall, C.A.S., J.G. Lambert, and S.B. Balogh. 2014. "EROI of Different Fuels and the Implications for Society." *Energy Policy* 64 (January 2014): 141–52.

Harpur, Y. 1987. *Decoration in Egyptian Tombs of the Old Kingdom: Studies in Orientation and Scene Content*. London: Kegan Paul International.

———. 2001. *The Tombs of Nefermaat and Rahotep at Maidum: Discovery, Destruction and Reconstruction*. Prestbury: Oxford Expedition to Egypt.

Harriet, C., ed. 2007. *Regime Change in the Ancient Near East and Egypt: From Sargon of Agade to Saddam Hussein*. Oxford: Oxford University Press.

Hassan, F.A. 1981. "Historical Nile Floods and their Implications for Climatic Change." *Science* 212/4499: 1142–45.

———. 1997. "Nile Floods and Political Disorder in Early Egypt." In *Third Millennium BC Climate Change and Old World Collapse*, edited by H.N. Dalfes, G. Kukla, and H. Weiss, 1–23. Berlin: Springer.

Hassan, F.A., A.J. Serrano, and G.J. Tassie. 2006. "The Sequence and Chronology of the Protodynastic and Dynasty I Rulers." In *Archaeology of Early Northeastern Africa: In Memory of Lech Krzyżaniak*, edited by K. Kroeper, M. Chłodnicki, and M. Kobusiewicz, 687–722. Poznan: Archaeological Museum.

Hassan, S. 1943. *The Excavations at Giza*, 4: *1933–1934*. Cairo: Government Press.

Hawass, Z., and A. Vannini. 2007. *The Royal Tombs of Egypt: The Art of Thebes Revealed*. Cairo: American University in Cairo Press.

Helck, W. 1974. *Die altägyptischen Gaue*. Wiesbaden: Dr. Ludwig Reichert.

———. 1977a. *Die Lehre für König Merikare*. Wiesbaden: Otto Harrassowitz.

———. 1977b. "Die 'Weihinschrift' des Neuserre." *SAK* 5: 47–77.

———. 1984. "Heliopolis und die Sonnenheiligtümer." In *Sundries in Honour of Torgny Säve-Söderbergh*, edited by R. Holthoer, 67–72. Uppsala: Almqvist & Wicksell International.

———. 1987. *Untersuchungen zur Thinitenzeit*. Wiesbaden: Harrassowitz.

Hendrickx, S., R.F. Friedman, K.M. Ciałowicz, and M. Chłodnicki, eds. 2004. *Egypt at Its Origins: Studies in Memory of Barbara Adams: Proceedings of the International Conference "Origin of the State Predynastic and Early Dynastic Egypt," Kraków, 28.8.–1.9. 2002*. Leuven: Peeters.

Herbich, T., and A. Jagodziński. 2008. "Geophysical Investigation of the Dry Moat of the Netjerykhet Complex in Saqqara." In *Man—Millennia—Environment, Studies in Honour of Romuald Schild*, edited by Z. Sulgostowska and J. Tomaszewski, 273–79. Warsaw: The Institute of Archaeology and Ethnology, Polish Academy of Sciences.

Hesiod. 1988. *Hesiod's Works and Days*. Edited by R. Hamilton, E. Rainis, and R. Ruttenberg. Bryn Mawr, PA: Thomas Library, Bryn Mawr College.

Hobbes, T. 1968. *Leviathan*. Edited by C.B. MacPherson. Harmondsworth: Penguin Books.

Hoffman, M.A. 1991. *Egypt before the Pharaohs: The Prehistoric Foundations of Egyptian Civilization*. London: O'Mara.

Holdaway, S., W. Wendrich, and R. Phillipps. 2010. "Identifying Low-level Food Producers: Detecting Mobility through Lithics." *Antiquity* 84: 184–94.

Homer-Dixon, T. 2006. *The Upside of Down: Catastrophe, Creativity, and the Renewal of Civilization*. Washington: Island Press.

Hornung, E. 1963. *Das Amduat: Die Schrift des verborgenen Raumes*. Wiesbaden: Harrassowitz.

———. 1979. *Das Totenbuch der Ägypter*. Zürich: Artemis.

———. 1997. *Altägyptische Jenseitsbücher: ein einführender Überblick*. Darmstadt: Primus Verlag.

Hornung, E., R. Krauss, and D.A. Warburton. 2006. *Ancient Egyptian Chronology*. Leiden: Brill.

Hornung, E., and E. Staehelin. 1974. *Studien zum Sedfest*. AH 1. Geneva: Edition de Belles-Lettres.

———. 2006. *Neue Studien zum Sedfest*. AH 20. Basel: Schwabe.

Hrozný, B. 1940. *O nejstarším stěhování národů a o problému civilisace proto-indické*. Prague: Orientální ústav ČSAV.

Huntington, E. 1913. "Changes of Climate and History." *The American Historical Review* 18/2: 213–32.

———. 1917. "Climatic Change and Agricultural Exhaustion as Elements in the Fall of Rome." *Quarterly Journal of Economics* 31/2: 173–208.

Huntington, S.P. 1993. "The Clash of Civilizations?" *Foreign Affairs* 72/3: 22–49.

Ibn Khaldun. 2015. *The Muqaddimah: An Introduction to History—Abridged Edition*. Edited by N.J. Dawood. Princeton: Princeton University Press.

Ikram, S. 1995. *Choice Cuts: ctpw Meat Production in Ancient Egypt*. Leuven: Peeters.

Issar, A.S. 2003. *Climate Changes during the Holocene and Their Impact on Hydrological Systems*. International Hydrology Series. Cambridge: Cambridge University Press.

Issar, A.S., and N. Brown. 1998. *Water, Environment and Society in Times of Climatic Change: Contribution from an International Workshop within the Framework of International Hydrological Program (IHP) UNESCO, held at Ben-Gurion University Sede Boker, Israel from 7–12 July 1996*. Dordrecht: London Kluwer Academic.

Jánosi, P. 2005. *Giza in der 4. Dynastie: die Baugeschichte und Belegung einer Nekropole des Alten Reiches*. Vienna: Verlag der Österreichischen Akademie der Wissenschaften.

———. 2006. *Die Gräberwelt der Pyramidenzeit*. Zaberns Bildbände zur Archäologie. Mainz am Rhein: Verlag Philipp von Zabern.

Jansen-Winkeln, K. 2002. "Ägyptische Geschichte im Zeitalter der Wanderung von Seevölkern und Libyern." In *Die nahöstlichen Kulturen und Griechenland an der Wende vom 2. zum 1. Jahrtausend v. Chr.*, edited by E.A. Holzinger and H. Matthäus, 123–42. Möhnesee: Bibliopolis.

———. 2010. "Der Untergang des Alten Reiches." *Orientalia Nova Series* 79/3: 273–303.

Jaspers, K. 1949. *Vom Ursprung und Ziel der Geschichte*. Zürich: Artemis.

Jeffreys, D. 1997. "Fieldwork 1997: Excavations and Survey East of Saqqara–Abusir Escarpment." *JEA* 83: 2–4.

Jeffreys, D., and A. Tavares. 1994. "The Historic Landscape of Early Dynastic Memphis." *MDAIK* 50: 143–73.

Jéquier, G. 1928. *Le Mastabat Faraoun*. Cairo: Institut français d'archéologie orientale.

———. 1933. *Les pyramides des reines Neit et Apouit*. Cairo: Institut français d'archéologie orientale.

———. 1935. *Fouilles à Saqqarah: La pyramide d'Aba*. Cairo: Institut français d'archéologie orientale.

Johnson, A.W., and T. Earle. 2000. *The Evolution of Human Societies*. Stanford: Stanford University Press.

Johnston, S., and J. Mazo. 2013. "Global Warming and the Arab Spring." In *The Arab Spring and Climate Change: A Climate and Security Correlations Series*, edited by C.E. Werrell and F. Femia, 15–21. Washington: Center for American Progress. https://climateandsecurity.files.wordpress.

com/2012/04/climatechangearabspring-ccs-cap-stimson.pdf.

Jones, D. 2000. *An Index of Ancient Egyptian Titles, Epithets and Phrases of the Old Kingdom*. 2 vols. Oxford: Archaeopress.

Juglar, C. 1862. *Des crises commerciales et de leur retour périodique en France, en Angleterre et aux États-Unis*. Paris: Guillaumin.

Junker, H. 1939. "Pḥrnfr." *ZÄS* 75: 63–84.

Kaiser, W. 1956. "Zu den Sonnenheiligtümern der 5. Dynastie." *MDAIK* 14: 104–16.

Kaiser, W., and G. Dreyer. 1982. "Umm el-Qaab. Nachuntersuchungen im frühzeitlichen Königsfriedhof: 2. Vorbericht." *MDAIK* 38: 211–69.

Kamal, B. 1912. "Fouilles à Dara et à Qoçéir El-Amarna." *ASAE* 12: 128–42.

Kammerzell, F. 2001. "'. . . within the Altar of the Sun': An Unidentified Hieroglyph and the Construction of the Sun Temple Nḫn-R'w." In *Structuring Egyptian Syntax: A Tribute to Sarah Israelit-Groll*, edited by O. Goldwasser and D. Sweeney, 153–64. Göttingen: Seminar für Ägyptologie und Koptologie.

Kanawati, N. 1980. *Governmental Reforms in Old Kingdom Egypt*. Modern Egyptology Series. Warminster, England: Aris & Phillips.

———. 2003. *Conspiracies in the Egyptian Palaces: Unis to Pepy I*. London: Routledge.

———. 2010. *Decorated Burial Chambers of the Old Kingdom*. Cairo: Supreme Council of Antiquities.

Kanawati, N., and A. McFarlane. 1992. *Akhmim in the Old Kingdom*. Sydney: Australian Centre for Egyptology.

Kaplan, R.D. 2012. *The Revenge of Geography: What the Map Tells Us about Coming Conflicts and the Battle against Fate*. New York: Random House.

Kay, J.J. 2000. "Application of the Second Law of Thermodynamics and Le Chatelier's Principle to the Developing Ecosystem." In *Handbook of Ecosystem Theories and Management*, edited by S.E. Jørgensen and F. Müller, 235–60. Boca Raton, FL: Lewis Publishers.

Kemp, B.J. 1963. "Excavations at Hierakonpolis Fort, 1905: A Preliminary Note." *JEA* 49: 24–28.

———. 1966. "Abydos and the Royal Tombs of the First Dynasty." *JEA* 52: 13–22.

———. 1989. *Ancient Egypt: Anatomy of a Civilization*. London: Routledge.

Kenoyer, J.M. 1997. "Trade and Technology of the Indus Valley: New Insights from Harappa." *World Archaeology* 29: 262–80.

Kerner, S., R.J. Dann, and P. Bangsgaard, eds. 2015. *Climate and Ancient Societies*. Copenhagen: Museum Tusculanum Press.

El-Khouli, A., and N. Kanawati. 1990. *The Old Kingdom Tombs of El-Hammamiya*. Sydney: Australian Centre for Egyptology.

Kitchen, K.A. 1973. *The Third Intermediate Period in Egypt (1100–650 BC)*. Warminster: Aris and Phillips.

———. 1976. *Ramesside Inscriptions: Historical and Biographical*, I: *Ramesses I, Sethos I, and Contemporaries*. Oxford: Blackwell.

Köhler, E.C. 2005. *Helwan I: Excavations in the Early Dynastic Cemetery: Season*

1997/98. Heidelberg: Heidelberger Orientverlag.

———. 2010. "Theories of State Formation." In *Egyptian Archaeology*, edited by W. Wendrich, 36–54. Chichester: Wiley–Blackwell.

———. 2014. *Helwan III: Excavations in Operation 4, Tombs 1–50*. Rahden: Verlag Marie Leidorf.

Köhler, E.C., and J. Jones. 2009. *Helwan II: The Early Dynastic and Old Kingdom Funerary Relief Slabs*. Rahden: Verlag Marie Leidorf.

Köhler, E.C., C. Marshall, A.M.A. Ali, H. Böhm, and M. Abd El Karem. 2017. *Helwan IV: Excavations in Operation 4, Tombs 51–100*. Rahden: Verlag Marie Leidorf.

Kondrashov, D., Y. Feliks, and M. Ghil. 2005. "Oscillatory Modes of Extended Nile River Records (AD 622–1922)." *Geophysical Research Letters* 32/10: doi 10.1029/2004GL022156.

Krejčí, J. 2009. *Abusir XI: The Architecture of the Mastaba of Ptahshepses*. Prague: Czech Institute of Egyptology.

———. 2012. "Nyuserra Revisited." In *Abusir and Saqqara in the Year 2010*, edited by M. Bárta, F. Coppens, and J. Krejčí, 513–24. Prague: Czech Institute of Egyptology.

Kuper, R., and S. Kröpelin. 2006. "Climate-controlled Holocene Occupation in the Sahara: Motor of Africa's Evolution." *Science* 313/5788: 803–807.

Kurth, A. 1982. "Nut." In *Lexikon der Ägyptologie* 4, edited by W. Helck and W. Westendorf, 535–41. Wiesbaden: Harrassowitz.

———. 1992. "Usurpation, Conquest and Ceremonial: From Babylon to Persia." In *Rituals of Royalty: Power and Ceremonial in Traditional Societies*, edited by D. Cannadine and S. Price, 20–55. Cambridge: Cambridge University Press.

Laboury, D. 2010. *Akhénaton*. Paris: Pygmalion.

Labrousse, A. 2010. "Huit épouses du roi Pépy Ier." In *Egyptian Culture and Society: Studies in Honour of Naguib Kanawati*, edited by A. Woods, A. McFarlane, and S. Binder, 297–314. Cairo: Supreme Council of Antiquities.

Lacau, P.L., and J.-P. Lauer. 1959. *La pyramide à degrés, IV: inscriptions gravées sur les vases*. Cairo: Institut français d'archéologie orientale.

———. 1965. *La pyramide à degrés, 5: inscriptions à l'encre sur les vases*. Cairo: Institut français d'archéologie orientale.

Lacher-Raschdorff, C.M. 2014. *Das Grab des Königs Ninetjer in Saqqara: Architektonische Entwicklung frühzeitlicher Grabanlagen in Ägypten*. Wiesbaden: Harrassowitz Verlag.

Lacina, B., and N.P. Gleditsch. 2005. "Monitoring Trends in Global Conflict: A New Dataset of Battle Deaths." *European Journal of Population* 21/2: 145–66.

Landgráfová, R., and H. Navrátilová. 2011. *It Is My Good Name That You Should Remember: Egyptian Biographical Texts on Middle Kingdom Stelae*. Prague: Faculty of Arts, Charles University in Prague, Czech Institute of Egyptology.

Lanning, E.P. 1967. *Peru before the Incas*. Englewood Cliffs: Prentice-Hall.

Lauer, J.-P., and P. Lacau. 1936–39. *La pyramide à degrés*. Cairo: Institut français d'archéologie orientale.

Lawler, A. 2010. "Collapse? What Collapse? Societal Change Revisited." *Science* 330/6006: 907–909.

Lehner, M. 1985. *The Pyramid Tomb of Hetep-heres and the Satellite Pyramid of Khufu*. Mainz am Rhein: Philipp von Zabern.

———. 2000. "Fractal House of Pharaoh: Ancient Egypt as a Complex Adaptive System, a Trial Formulation." In *Dynamics in Human and Primate Societies: Agent-based Modeling of Social and Spatial Processes*, edited by T.A. Kohler and G.J. Gumerman, 257–353. Oxford: Oxford University Press.

———. 2002. "The Pyramid Age Settlement of the Southern Mount at Giza." *JARCE* 39: 27–74.

———. 2008. *The Complete Pyramids*. London: Thames & Hudson.

———. 2015. "Labor and the Pyramids: The Heit el-Ghurab 'Workers Town' at Giza." In *Labor in the Ancient World*, edited by P. Steinkeller and M. Hudson, 397–522. Dresden: ISLET-Verlag.

Lehner, M., and Z. Hawass. 2017. *Giza and the Pyramids*. London: Thames and Hudson.

Leibovich, M. 2014. *This Town: Two Parties and a Funeral—Plus, Plenty of Valet Parking!—in America's Gilded Capital*. New York: Blue Rider Press.

Leick, G. 2002. *Mesopotamia: The Invention of the City*. London: Penguin Books.

Lepsius, C.R. 1858. *Königsbuch der alten Ägypter*. Berlin: Besser.

Lesko, B. 1999. *The Great Goddesses of Egypt*. Norman: University of Oklahoma Press.

Lewis, M.E. 2006. *The Flood Myths of Early China*. Albany: State University of New York Press.

Li, F. 2013. *Early China: A Social and Cultural History*. Cambridge: Cambridge University Press.

Lichtheim, M. 2006. *Ancient Egyptian Literature: A Book of Readings*, 2: *The New Kingdom*. Los Angeles: University of California Press.

Lorton, D. 1985. "Considerations on the Origin and Name of Osiris." *VarAeg* 1/3: 113–26.

Luttwak, E.N. 1976. *The Grand Strategy of the Roman Empire from the First Century AD to the Third*. Baltimore: Johns Hopkins University Press.

Lyons, H.G. 1908. *The Cadastral Survey of Egypt 1892–1907*. Cairo: Ministry of Finance.

MacGregor, N. 2012. *A History of the World in 100 Objects*. London: Penguin Books.

Mackay, A., R. Battarbee, J. Birks, and F. Oldfield, eds. 2005. *Global Change in the Holocene*. New York: Arnold.

Macklin, M.G., W.H.J. Toonen, J.C. Woodward, M.A.J. Williams, C. Flaux, N. Marriner, K. Nicoll, G. Verstraeten, N. Spencer, and D. Welsby. 2015. "A New Model of River Dynamics, Hydroclimatic Change and Human Settlement in the Nile Valley Derived from Meta-analysis of the Holocene Fluvial Archive." *Quaternary Science Reviews* 130: 109–23.

Magli, G. 2013. *Architecture, Astronomy and Sacred Landscape in Ancient Egypt*. New York: Cambridge University Press.

Málek, J. 1982. "The Original Version of the Royal Canon of Turin." *JEA* 68: 93–106.

————. 2000. "5. The Old Kingdom (c. 2686–2125 BC)." In *The Oxford History of Ancient Egypt*, edited by I. Shaw, 89–117. Oxford: Oxford University Press.

Malville, J.M., R. Schild, F. Wendorf, and R. Brenmer. 2008. "Astronomy of Nabta Playa." In *African Cultural Astronomy: Current Archaeoastronomy and Ethnoastronomy Research in Africa*, edited by J.C. Holbrook, R.T. Medupe, and J.O. Urama, 131–43. Berlin: Springer Verlag.

Manuelian, P.D., and T. Schneider, eds. 2015. *Towards a New History for the Egyptian Old Kingdom: Perspectives on the Pyramid Age*. Leiden: Brill.

Mariette, A. 1864. "La table de Saqqarah." *Revue archéologique* 10: 168–86.

————. 1869. *Abydos: description des fouilles exécutées sur l'emplacement de cette ville*. Paris: A. Franck.

————. 1889. *Les mastabas de l'Ancien Empire*. Paris: F. Vieweg.

Marouard, G., and H. Papazian. 2012. "The Edfu Pyramid Project: Recent Investigation at the Last Provincial Pyramid." *Oriental Institute News and Notes* 213: 3–9.

Mařík, R., and V. Dulíková. 2015. "Matematické vyjádření complexity společnosti." In *Povaha změny: Bezpečnost, rizika a stav dnešní civilizace*, edited by M. Bárta, M. Kovář, and O. Foltýn, 98–129. Prague: Vyšehrad.

Marx, K. 1887. *Capital: A Critical Analysis of Capitalist Production*. 2 vols. London: Swan Sonnenschein.

Mathieu, B. 2010. "Mais qui est donc Osiris? Ou la politique sous le linceul de la religion." *ÉNiM* 3: 77–107.

McAnany, P.A., and N. Yoffee. 2010a. *Questioning Collapse: Human Resilience, Ecological Vulnerability, and the Aftermath of Empire*. Cambridge: Cambridge University Press.

————. 2010b. "Questioning How Different Societies Respond to Crises." *Nature* 464: 977.

————. 2010c. "Why We Question Collapse." In *Questioning Collapse: Human Resilience, Ecological Vulnerability, and the Aftermath of Empire*, edited by P.A. McAnany and N. Yoffee, 1–17. Cambridge: Cambridge University Press.

McGuire, W.J., D.R. Griffiths, P.L. Hancock, and I.S. Stewart, eds. 2000. *The Archaeology of Geological Catastrophes*. London: Geological Society.

McIntosh, R.J., J.A. Tainter, and S.K. McIntosh. 2000. *The Way the Wind Blows: Climate, History, and Human Action*. Historical Ecology Series. New York: Columbia University Press.

McNamara, L. 2008. "The Revetted Mound at Hierakonpolis and Early Kingship: A Re-interpretation." In *Egypt at Its Origins 2: Proceedings of the International Conference "Origin of the State, Predynastic and Early Dynastic Egypt," Toulouse (France), 5th–8th September 2005*, edited by B. Midant-Reynes and Y. Tristant, 901–36. Leuven: Peeters.

Meadows, D.H., D.L. Meadows, J. Randers, and W.W. Behrens III. 1972. *The Limits to Growth: A Report for the Club of Rome's Project on the Predicament of Mankind*. New York: Universe Books.

Meadows, D.H., J. Randers, and D.L. Meadows. 2004. *The Limits to Growth: The 30-year Update*. White River Junction: Chelsea Green Publishing Company.

Megahed, M.A.M. 2016. "The Pyramid Complex of Djedkare–Isesi at South Saqqara and Its Decorative Program." PhD diss., Charles University, Prague.

Meller, H., H.W. Arz, R. Jung, and R. Risch, eds. 2015. *Ein Klimasturz als Ursache für den Zerfall der alten Welt? 2200 BC—A Climatic Breakdown as a Cause for the Collapse of the Old World? 7. Mitteldeutscher Archäologentag vom 23. bis 26. Oktober 2014 in Halle (Saale).* Halle: Landesmuseum für Vorgeschichte.

Meller, H., and M. Schefzik, eds. 2015. *Krieg: eine archäologische Spurensuche: Begleitband zur Sonderausstellung im Landesmuseum für Vorgeschichte Halle (Saale), 6. November 2015 bis 22. Mai 2016.* Darmstadt and Halle: Landesamt für Denkmalpflege und Archäologie Sachsen-Anhalt, Konrad Theiss Verlag, Imprint der WBG (Wissenschaftliche Buchgesellschaft).

Meyer, E. 1887. *Geschichte des alten Aegyptens.* Berlin: Grote'sche Verlagsbuchhandlung.

Midant-Reynes, B. 2000. *The Prehistory of Egypt: From the First Egyptians to the First Pharaohs.* Oxford: Blackwell.

Midant-Reynes, B., and Y. Tristant, eds. 2008. *Egypt at Its Origins 2: Proceedings of the International Conference "Origin of the State: Predynastic and Early Dynastic Egypt," Toulouse (France), 5th–8th September 2005.* Leuven: Peeters.

Middleton, G.D. 2012. "Nothing Lasts Forever: Environmental Discourses on the Collapse of Past Societies." *Journal of Archaeological Research* 20/3: 257–307.

———. 2017. *Understanding Collapse: Ancient History and Modern Myths.* Cambridge: Cambridge University Press.

Mitchell, P. 2008. "Practising Archaeology at a Time of Climatic Catastrophe." *Antiquity* 82: 1093–1103.

Moeller, N. 2005. "The First Intermediate Period: A Time of Famine and Climate Change?" *Ä&L* 15: 153–67.

———. 2016. *The Archaeology of Urbanism in Ancient Egypt: From the Predynastic Period to the End of the Middle Kingdom.* Cambridge: Cambridge University Press.

Moens, M.-F., and W. Wetterstrom. 1988. "The Agriculture Economy of an Old Kingdom Town in Egypt's West Delta: Insights from the Plant Remains." *JNES* 47/3: 159–73.

Moiso, B. 2015. "The Tomb of Iti and Neferu." In *Museo Egizio*, edited by P. Bonacini, 62–69. Modena: Franco Cosimo Panini Editore.

Montesquieu, C.L. de S., A.M. Cohler, B.C. Miller, and H.S. Stone. 1989. *The Spirit of Laws.* Cambridge: Cambridge University Press.

Moreno García, J.C. 1998. "De l'Ancien Empire à la Première Période Intermédiare: L'autobiographie de Q3R d'Edfou—entre tradition et innovation." *RdE* 49: 151–60.

———. 1999. *Ḥwt et le milieu rural égyptien du 3e millénaire: économie, administration et organisation territoriale.* Paris: Champion.

———. 2015. "Climatic Change or Sociopolitical Transformation? Reassessing Late 3rd Millennium BC in Egypt." *Tagungen des Landesmuseums für Vorgeschichte Halle* 13: 1–16.

Morenz, S. 1960. *Ägyptische Religion*. Stuttgart: Kohlhammer.

Morgan, L.H. 1877. *Ancient Society: or, Researches in the Lines of Human Progress from Savagery through Barbarism to Civilization*. Chicago: Charles H. Kerr.

Morony, M.G. 1987. "'In a City Without Watchdogs the Fox Is the Overseer': Issues and Problems in the Study of Bureaucracy." In *The Organization of Power: Aspects of Bureaucracy in the Ancient Near East*, edited by M. Gibson and R.D. Biggs, 7–18. Chicago: Oriental Institute.

Morris, E.F. 2007. "Sacrifice for the State: First Dynasty Royal Funerals and the Rites at Macramallah's Rectangle." In *Performing Death: Social Analyses of Funerary Traditions in the Ancient Near East and Mediterranean*, edited by N. Laneri, 15–37. Chicago: Oriental Institute.

———. 2014. "(Un)Dying Loyalty: Meditations on Retainer Sacrifice in Ancient Egypt and Elsewhere." In *Violence and Civilisation: Studies of Social Violence in History and Prehistory*, edited by R. Campbell, 61–93. Oxford: Oxbow Books.

Morris, I. 2013. *Why the West Rules—for Now: The Patterns of History and What They Reveal about the Future*. London: Profile Books.

———. 2014. *War! What Is It Good For? Conflict and the Progress of Civilization, from Primates to Robots*. New York: Farrar, Straus and Giroux.

Mortensen, B. 1991. "Change in the Settlement Pattern and Population in the Beginning of the Historical Period." *Ägypten und Levante/Egypt and the Levant* 2: 11–37.

Motesharrei, S., J. Rivas, and E. Kalnay. 2014. "Human and Nature Dynamics (HANDY): Modeling Inequality and Use of Resources in the Collapse or Sustainability of Societies." *Ecological Economics* 101: 90–102.

Mourad, A.-L. 2011. "Siege Scenes in the Old Kingdom." *BACE* 22: 135–58.

Moursi, M.I. 1972. *Die Hohenpriester des Sonnengottes von der Frühzeit Ägyptens bis zum Ende des Neuen Reiches*. Münchner ägyptologische Studien 26. Munich: Deutscher Kunstverlag.

Moussa, A.M., and H. Altenmüller. 1977. *Das Grab des Nianchchnum und Chnumhotep*. Mainz am Rhein: Philipp von Zabern.

Müller-Wollermann, R. 1986. "Krisenfaktoren im ägyptischen Staat des ausgehenden Alten Reichs." PhD diss., Eberhard-Karls-Universität Tübingen.

Munro, P. 1993. *Der Unas-Friedhof Nord-West: Topographisch-historische Einleitung: das Doppelgrab der Königinnen Nebet und Khenut*. Mainz am Rhein: Philipp von Zabern.

Murray, C. 2003. *Human Accomplishment: The Pursuit of Excellence in the Art and Sciences 800 BC to 1950*. New York: Harper Collins Publishers.

National Research Council. 2002. *Abrupt Climate Change: Inevitable Surprises*. Washington: National Academy Press.

Neustupný, E. 2007. *Metoda archeologie*. Plzeň: Aleš Čeněk.

Nikolova, D. 2004. "The Reign of Sneferu: Some Aspects of the Historical and Religious Development." *Journal of Egyptological Studies* 1: 61–88.

Nolan, J.S. 2005. "The Original Lunar Calendar and Cattle Counts in Old Kingdom Egypt." In *Basel Egyptology Prize 1: Junior Research in Egyptian*

History, Archaeology, and Philology, edited by S. Bickel and A. Loprieno, 75–97. Basel: Schwabe.

―――. 2010. "Mud Sealings and Fourth Dynasty: Administration at Giza." PhD diss., University of Chicago.

North, D.C., J.J. Wallis, and B.R. Weingast. 2013. *Violence and Social Orders: A Conceptual Framework for Interpreting Recorded Human History*. Cambridge: Cambridge University Press.

Nunn, P.D., and N.J. Reid. 2016. "Aboriginal Memories of Inundation of the Australian Coast Dating from More than 7000 Years Ago." *Australian Geographer* 47/1: 11–47.

Nuzzolo, M. 2007. "The Sun Temples of the Vth Dynasty: A Reassessment." *SAK* 36: 217–47.

―――. 2015a. "The Bent Pyramid of Snefru at Dahshur: A Project Failure or an Intentional Architectural Framework?" *SAK* 44: 259–82.

―――. 2015b. "The Sed-Festival of Niuserra and the Fifth Dynasty Sun Temples." In *Towards a New History of the Egyptian Old Kingdom: Perspectives on the Pyramid Age*, edited by P.D. Manuelian and T. Schneider, 366–92. Leiden: Brill.

O'Connor, D.B. 1989. "New Funerary Enclosures (Talbezirke) of the Early Dynastic Period at Abydos." *JARCE* 26: 51–86.

―――. 2009. *Abydos: Egypt's First Pharaohs and the Cult of Osiris*. London: Thames & Hudson.

―――. 2011. "The Narmer Palette: A New Interpretation." In *Before the Pyramids: The Origins of Egyptian Civilization*, edited by E. Teeter, 145–52. Chicago: Oriental Institute.

Olson, M. 1982. *The Rise and Decline of Nations: Economic Growth, Stagflation, and Social Rigidities*. New Haven: Yale University Press.

Oren, E.D. 1997. *The Hyksos: New Historical and Archaeological Perspectives*. Philadelphia: University of Pennsylvania Museum of Archaeology and Anthropology.

Pachur, H.-J., and N. Altmann. 2006. *Die Ostsahara im Spätquartär: Ökosystemwandel im größten hyperariden Raum der Erde*. Berlin and Heildeberg: Springer Verlag.

Papazian, H. 2010. "The Temple of Ptah and the Economic Contacts between Memphite Cult Centers in the Fifth Dynasty." In *8. Ägyptologische Tempeltagung: Interconnections between Temples. Warschau, 22–25. September 2008*, edited by M. Dolińska and H. Beinlich, 137–53. Wiesbaden: Harrassowitz.

―――. 2012. *Domain of Pharaoh: The Structure and Components of the Economy of Old Kingdom Egypt*. HÄB 52. Hildesheim: Gebrüder Gerstenberg.

―――. 2015. "The State of Egypt in the Eighth Dynasty." In *Towards a New History for the Egyptian Old Kingdom: Perspectives on the Pyramid Age*, edited by P.D. Manuelian and T. Schneider, 393–428. Leiden: Brill.

Pardey, E. 1976. *Untersuchungen zur ägyptischen Provinzialverwaltung bis zum Ende des Alten Reiches*. Hildesheim: Gerstenberg.

Parkinson, R.B. 1999. *Cracking Codes: The Rosetta Stone and Decipherment*. London: British Museum.

Patch, D. 1995. "A 'Lower Egyptian Costume': Its Origins, Development and Meaning." *JARCE* 32: 93–116.

Petrie, W.M.F. 1892. *Medum*. London: Nutt.

———. 1894. *A History of Egypt*, I: *From the Earliest Kings to the XVIth Dynasty*. London: Methuen.

———. 1900. *The Royal Tombs of the First Dynasty*. London: Egypt Exploration Fund.

———. 1901. *The Royal Tombs of the Earliest Dynasties II*. London: Egypt Exploration Fund.

Petrie, W.M.F., and J.E. Quibell. 1896. *Naqada and Ballas*. London: Quaritch.

Piotrovsky, B. 1967. "The Early Dynastic Settlement of Khor-Daoud and Wadi Allaki: The Ancient Route of the Gold Mines." In *Fouilles en Nubie (1961–1963)*, 127–40. Cairo: Organisme général des imprimeries gouvernementales.

Pokorný, P., and M. Bárta, eds. 2008. *Něco překrásného se končí: kolapsy v přírodě a společnosti*. Prague: Dokořán.

Popitz, H. 1986. *Phänomene der Macht: Autorität, Herrschaft, Gewalt, Technik*. Tübingen: J.C.B. Mohr.

Popper, W. 1951. *The Cairo Nilometer: Studies in Ibn Taghrî Birdî's Chronicles of Egypt*. Los Angeles: University of California Press.

Porter, B., and R.L.B. Moss. 1937. *Topographical Bibliography of Ancient Egyptian Hieroglyphic Texts, Reliefs, and Paintings V: Upper Egypt: Sites (Deir Rîfa to Aswân, excluding Thebes and the Temples of Abydos, Dendera, Esna, Edfu, Kôm Ombo and Philae)*. Oxford: Clarendon.

———. 1974. *Topographical Bibliography of Ancient Egyptian Hieroglyphic Texts, Reliefs, and Paintings III: Memphis. Part I: Abû Rawâsh to Abûsîr*. 2nd ed. Oxford: Oxford University Press; Griffith Institute.

Posener-Kriéger, P. 1976. *Les archives du temple funéraire de Néferirkarê-Kakaï (Les papyrus d'Abousir): traduction et commentaire*. 2 vols. Bibliothèque d'étude/Institut français d'archéologie orientale du Caire. Cairo: Institut français d'archéologie orientale du Caire.

Posener-Kriéger, P., M. Verner, and H. Vymazalová. 2006. *Abusir X: The Pyramid Complex of Raneferef: The Papyrus Archive*. Prague: Czech Institute of Egyptology.

Possehl, G.L. 1990. "Revolution in the Urban Revolution: The Emergence of Indus Urbanization." *Annual Review of Anthropology* 19/1: 261–82.

———. 1998. "Sociocultural Complexity without the State: The Indus Civilization." In *Archaic States*, edited by G.M. Feinman and J. Marcus, 261–91. Santa Fe: School of American Research.

———. 2002. *The Indus Civilization: A Contemporary Perspective*. Walnut Creek, CA: AltaMira.

Quibell, J.E. 1898. "Slate Palette from Hieraconpolis." *ZÄS* 36: 81–84.

———. 1900. *Hierakonpolis*, I. London: Quaritch.

———. 1913. *Excavations at Saqqara, 1911–12: The Tomb of Hesy*. Cairo: Imprimerie de l'Institut français d'archéologie orientale.

Quibell, J.E., and F.W. Green. 1902. *Hierakonpolis*, II. London: Quaritch.

Quigley, C. 1979. *The Evolution of Civilizations*. Indianapolis: Liberty Fund.

Quirke, S. 2001. *The Cult of Ra: Sun-worship in Ancient Egypt*. London: Thames and Hudson.

Radwan, A. 2003. "The Step Pyramids." In *The Treasures of the Pyramids*, edited by Z. Hawass, 86–111. Cairo: American University in Cairo Press.

Raikes, R.L. 1964. "The End of the Ancient Cities of the Indus." *American Anthropologist* 66/2: 284–92.

Rappaport, R.A. 1968. *Pigs for the Ancestors: Ritual in the Ecology of a New Guinea People*. 9th printing. New Haven: Yale University Press.

Raue, D. 2008. "Who Was Who in Elephantine of the Third Millennium BC?" *BMSAES* 9: 1–14. http://www.britishmuseum.org/research/publications/online_journals/bmsaes/issue_9/raue.aspx.

Raue, D., S.J. Seidlmayer, and P. Speiser. 2013. *The First Cataract of the Nile: One Region—Diverse Perspectives*. Berlin: de Gruyter.

Redding, R.W. 2013. "A Tale of Two Sites: Old Kingdom Subsistence Economy and the Infrastructure of Pyramid Construction." In *Archaeozoology of the Near East X: Proceedings of the Tenth International Symposium on the Archaeozoology of South-Western Asia and Adjacent Areas*, edited by B. De Cupere, V. Linseele, and S. Hamilton-Dyer, 307–22. Leuven: Peeters.

Redford, D.B., ed. 2001. *The Oxford Encyclopedia of Ancient Egypt*. Oxford: Oxford University Press.

Regulski, I. 2010. *A Palaeographic Study of Early Writing in Egypt*. Leuven: Peeters.

Reinold, J. 2010. "Kadruka." In *Sudan: Ancient Treasures: An Exhibition of Recent Discoveries from the Sudan National Museum*, edited by D.A. Welby and J.R. Anderson, 42–48. London: British Museum.

Reinold, J., and L. Krzyzaniak. 1997. "6,000 Years Ago: Remarks on the Prehistory of the Sudan." In *Sudan: Ancient Kingdoms on the Nile*, edited by D. Wildung, 9–34. Paris: Flammarion.

Reisner, G.A., and W.S. Smith. 1955. *A History of the Giza Necropolis*, II: *The Tomb of Hetep-heres the Mother of Cheops*. Cambridge: Harvard University Press.

Renfrew, C. 1972. *The Emergence of Civilisation: The Cyclades and the Aegean in the Third Millennium BC*. London: Methuen.

Rheidt, K., and E.L. Schwander, eds. 2004. *Macht der Architektur—Architektur der Macht: Diskussionen zur archäologischen Bauforschung*. Mainz am Rhein: Philipp von Zabern.

Ricke, H. 1965. *Das Sonnenheiligtum des Königs Userkaf*. 2 vols. Cairo: Schweizerisches Institut für Ägyptische Bauforschung und Altertumskunde.

Rizkana, I., and J. Seeher. 1990. *Maadi 4: The Predynastic Cemeteries of Maadi and Wadi Digla*. Mainz am Rhein: Philipp von Zabern.

Robbins Schug, G., K.E. Blevins, B. Cox, K. Gray, and V. Mushrif-Tripathy. 2013. "Infection, Disease, and Biosocial Processes at the End of the Indus Civilization." *PLoS ONE* 8(12). 10.1371/journal.pone.0084814

Roberts, N. 1989. *The Holocene: An Environmental History*. Oxford: Basil Blackwell.

Römer, M. 2011. "Was ist eine Krise? oder: Wie ist das Alte Reich (nicht) untergegangen?" *GM* 230: 83–101.

Rosenthal, F. 2015. *Ibn Khaldun. The Muqaddimah. An Introduction to History. Abridged and edited by N.J. Dawood.* Bollingen Series. Princeton: Princeton University Press.

Rossi, C. 2004. *Architecture and Mathematics in Ancient Egypt.* Cambridge: Cambridge University Press.

Roth, A.M. 1991. *Egyptian Phyles of the Old Kingdom: The Evolution of a System of Social Organization.* Studies in Ancient Oriental Civilization 48. Chicago: The Oriental Institute of the University of Chicago.

———. 1993. "Social Change in the Fourth Dynasty: The Spatial Organization of Pyramids, Tombs, and Cemeteries." *JARCE* 30: 33–55. doi: 10.2307/40000226

———. 1994. "The Practical Economics of Tomb Building in the Old Kingdom: A Visit to the Necropolis in a Carrying Chair." In *For His Ka: Essays Offered in Memory of Klaus Baer,* edited by D.P. Silverman, 227–40. Chicago: Oriental Institute.

Roth, S. 2001. *Die Königsmutter des Alten Ägypten von der Frühzeit bis zum Ende der 12. Dynastie.* Wiesbaden: Harrassowitz.

Rothkopf, D. 2009. *Superclass: The Global Power Elite and the World They Are Making.* New York: Farrar, Straus and Giroux.

———. 2012. *Power, Inc.: The Epic Rivalry between Big Business and Government—and the Reckoning That Lies Ahead.* New York: Farrar, Straus and Giroux.

Rousseau, J.-J. 1939. *The Social Contract.* New York: Carlton House.

Ryan, W., and W. Pitman. 2000. *Noah's Flood: The New Scientific Discoveries about the Event That Changed History.* New York: Touchstone.

Rydström, K.T. 1994. "HRY SŠTA 'In Charge of Secrets': The 3000-year Evolution of a Title." *Discussions in Egyptology* 28: 53–94.

Ryholt, K.S.B. 1997. *The Political Situation in Egypt during the Second Intermediate Period c. 1800–1550 BC.* Copenhagen: Museum Tusculanum Press.

———. 2000. "The Late Old Kingdom in the Turin King-list and the Identity of Nitocris." *ZÄS* 127: 87–100.

Saad, Z.Y. 1947. *Royal Excavations at Saqqara and Helwan (1941–1945).* Cairo: Institut français d'archéologie orientale.

———. 1951. *Royal Excavations at Helwan (1945–1947).* Cairo: Institut français d'archéologie orientale.

———. 1957. *Ceiling Stelae in Second Dynasty Tombs from the Excavations at Helwan.* Cairo: Institut français d'archéologie orientale.

———. 1969. *The Excavations at Helwan: Art and Civilization in the First and Second Egyptian Dynasties.* Norman: University of Oklahoma Press.

Sadr, K. 1991. *The Development of Nomadism in Ancient Northeast Africa.* Philadelphia: University of Pennsylvania Press.

Sallaberger, W., and A. Westenholz. 1999. *Mesopotamien: Akkade-Zeit und Ur III-Zeit.* Freiburg: Universitätsverlag Freiburg.

Sanderson, S.K. 1995. *Civilizations and World Systems: Studying World-historical Change*. London: AltaMira Press.

Sapp, J. 2003. *Genesis: The Evolution of Biology*. Oxford: Oxford University Press.

Savage, M., et al. 2008. *Remembering Elites*. Malden, MA, and Oxford: Blackwell.

Scarborough, V.L. 2003. *The Flow of Power: Ancient Water Systems and Landscapes*. Santa Fe, NM: SAR Press.

Schenkel, W. 1965. *Memphis, Herakleopolis, Theben: die epigraphischen Zeugnisse der 7.–11. Dynastie Ägyptens*. Wiesbaden: Harrassowitz.

———. 1978. *Die Bewässerungsrevolution im alten Ägypten*. Mainz am Rhein: Philipp von Zabern.

Schmidt, K. 2006. *Sie bauten die ersten Tempel: das rätselhafte Heiligtum der Steinzeitjäger*. Munich: C.H. Beck.

Schmitz, B. 1976. *Untersuchungen zum Titel S3–NJSWT "Königssohn."* Bonn: Rudolf Habelt Verlag.

Schneider, T. 1993. "Zur Etymologie der Bezeichnung 'König von Ober- und Unterägypten.'" *ZÄS* 120: 166–81.

———. 2008. "Periodizing Egyptian History: Manetho, Convention, and Beyond." In *Historiographie in der Antike*, edited by K.-P. Adam, 183–97. Berlin: Walter de Gruyter.

Schwartz, G.M., and J.J. Nichols, eds. 2006. *After Collapse: The Regeneration of Complex Societies*. Tucson: University of Arizona Press.

Scott, E.P. 2005. "Are We Collapsing? A Review of Jared Diamond's Collapse: How Societies Choose to Fail." *Journal of Economic Literature* 43/4: 1049–62.

Scott, G.D. 1989. "The History and Development of the Ancient Egyptian Scribe Statue, II: Catalogue Numbers 1–150." PhD diss., Yale University.

Scott, J.C. 2017. *Against the Grain: A Deep History of the Earliest States*. New Haven: Yale University Press.

Seidel, M. 1996. *Die königlichen Statuengruppen, I: Die Denkmäler vom Alten Reich bis zum Ende der 18. Dynastie*. Hildesheim: Gerstenberg.

Seidlmayer, S.J. 1990. *Gräberfelder aus dem Übergang vom Alten zum Mittleren Reich: Studien zur Archäologie der Ersten Zwischenzeit*. Heidelberg: Heidelberger Orientverlag.

———. 2000. "The First Intermediate Period (c. 2160–2055 BC)." In *Oxford History of Ancient Egypt*, edited by I. Shaw, 118–47. Oxford: Oxford University Press.

———. 2001. *Historische und moderne Nilstände: Untersuchungen zu den Pegelablesungen des Nils von der Frühzeit bis in die Gegenwart*. Berlin: Achet-Verlag.

Sethe, K. 1903. *Urkunden des Alten Reichs*. Leipzig: J.C. Hinrichs'.

Sezgin, F. 2001. *The Cairo Nilometer: Texts and Studies*. Frankfurt am Main: Institute for the History of Arabic–Islamic Science at the Johann Wolfgang Goethe University.

Shaw, I., ed. 2000. *The Oxford History of Ancient Egypt*. Oxford: Oxford University Press.

Shils, E. 1972. "Center and Periphery." In *The Constitution of Society*, edited by E. Shils, 93–109. Chicago: University of Chicago Press.

Shirai, N. 2010. *The Archaeology of the First Farmer-herders in Egypt: New Insights into the Fayum Epipalaeolithic and Neolithic*. Leiden: Leiden University Press.

Silverman, D.P., and D.B. O'Connor, eds. 1995. *Ancient Egyptian Kingship*. Leiden: Brill.

Sinclair, N. 2013. "The Development and Decline of Provincial Rule from the Old to the Middle Kingdom: An Analysis of the Tombs and Titles of the Senior Officials of Upper Egypt." MA thesis, Macquarie University, Sydney.

Smil, V. 2018. *Energy and Civilization: A History*. Cambridge, MA: MIT Press.

Smith, M. 2009. "Democratization of the Afterlife." In *UCLA Encyclopedia of Egyptology*, edited by J. Dielman and W. Wendrich, 1–16. Los Angeles. http://digital2.library.ucla.ed u/viewItem.do?ark=21198/zz001nf62b

Smith, M.E. 2012. *The Comparative Archaeology of Complex Societies*. Cambridge: Cambridge University Press.

Smith, M.E., et al. 2012. "Archaeology as a Social Science." *Proceedings of the National Academy of Sciences* 109/20: 7617.

Smith, W.S. 1962. "The Old Kingdom in Egypt and Beginning of the First Intermediate Period." In *Cambridge Ancient History*, 1/14. Cambridge: Cambridge University Press.

Snape, S. 2014. *The Complete Cities of Ancient Egypt*. London: Thames & Hudson.

Somaglino, C., and P. Tallet. 2015. "Gebel Sheikh Suleiman: A First Dynasty Relief after All . . . ." *Archéo-Nil* 25: 123–34.

Sorokin, P.A. 1945. *The Crisis of Our Age: The Social and Cultural Outlook*. New York: Abingdon-Cokesbury Press.

Spalinger, A. 1994. "Dated Texts of the Old Kingdom." *SAK* 21: 275–319.

Spencer, A.J., ed. 1996. *Aspects of Early Egypt*. London: British Museum Press.

Spencer, P. 2011. "Petrie and the Discovery of Earliest Egypt." In *Before the Pyramids: The Origins of Egyptian Civilization*, edited by E. Teeter, 17–24. Chicago: Oriental Institute.

Spengler, O. 1918, 1922. *Der Untergang des Abendlandes: Umrisse einer Morphologie der Weltgeschichte*. 2 vols. Munich: C.H. Beck.

Stadelmann, R. 1983. "Die Pyramiden des Snofru in Dahshur: Zweiter Bericht über die Ausgrabungen an der nördlichen Pyramide." *MDAIK* 39: 225–41.

———. 1985. *Die ägyptischen Pyramiden: vom Ziegelbau zum Weltwunder*. Mainz am Rhein: Philipp von Zabern.

———. 1994. "König Teti und der Beginn der 6. Dynastie." In *Hommages à Jean Leclant*, edited by C. Berger, G. Clerc, and N. Grimal, 327–35. Cairo: Institut français d'archéologie orientale.

———. 2000. "Userkaf in Saqqara und Abusir: Untersuchungen zur Thronfolge in der 4. und frühen 5. Dynastie." In *Abusir and Saqqara in the Year 2000*, edited by M. Bárta and J. Krejčí, 529–42. Prague: Academy of Science of the Czech Republic, Oriental Institute.

Stanley, J.-D., M.D. Krom, R.A. Cliff, and J.C. Woodward. 2003. "Short Contribution: Nile Flow Failure at the End of the Old Kingdom, Egypt: Strontium Isotopic and Petrologic Evidence." *Geoarchaeology* 18/3: 395–402.

Stark, B.L., and J.K. Chance. 2012. "The Strategies of Provincials in Empires."

In *The Comparative Archaeology of Complex Societies*, edited by M.E. Smith, 192–237. Cambridge: Cambridge University Press.

Stasser, T. 2013. *La mère royale Seshseshet et les débuts de la VIe dynastie*. Brussels: Safran.

Stauder, A. 2010. "The Earliest Egyptian Writing." In *Visible Language: Inventions of Writing in the Ancient Middle East and Beyond*, edited by C. Woods, 137–48. Chicago: Oriental Institute Museum.

Steindorff, G. 1926. *Die Blütezeit des Pharaonenreiches*. Bielefeld: Verlag von Velhagen & Klasing.

Stenberg, T. 2013. "Chinese Drought, Wheat, and the Egyptian Uprising: How a Localized Hazard Became Globalized." In *The Arab Spring and Climate Change: A Climate and Security Correlations Series*, edited by C.E. Werrell and F. Femia, 7–14. Washington: The Center for American Progress. https://climateandsecurity.files.wordpress.com/2012/04/climatechangearabspring-ccs-cap-stimson.pdf

Stevenson, A. 2016. "The Egyptian Predynastic and State Formation." *Journal of Archaeological Research* 24/4: 421–68.

Stock, H. 1942. *Studien zur Geschichte und Archäologie der 13. bis 17. Dynastie Ägyptens: unter besonderer Berücksichtigung der Skarabaen dieser Zwischenzeit*. Gluckstadt: J.J. Augustin.

Strudwick, N.C. 1985. *The Administration of Egypt in the Old Kingdom: The Highest Titles and Their Holders*. London: Kegan Paul International.

———. 2005. *Texts from the Pyramid Age*. Atlanta: Society of Biblical Literature.

Strumsky, D., J. Lobo, and J.A. Tainter. 2010. "Complexity and the Productivity of Innovation." *Systems Research and Behavioral Science* 27: 496–509.

Swelim, N. 1988. "The Dry Moat of the Netjerykhet Complex." In *Pyramid Studies and Other Essays Presented to I.E.S Edwards*, edited by J. Baines, T.G.H. James, A. Leahy, and A.F. Shore. 12–22. London: The Egypt Exploration Society.

———. 2006. "The Dry Moat, the South Rock Wall of the Inner South Channel." In *Timelines: Studies in Honour of Manfred Bietak*, edited by E. Czerny, I. Hein, H. Hunger, D. Melman, and A. Schwab, 363–76. Leuven: Peeters.

Szabo, B.J., C.V. Haynes, and T.A. Maxwell. 1995. "Ages of Quaternary Pluvial Episodes Determined by Uranium-series and Radiocarbon Dating of Lacustrine Deposits of Eastern Sahara." *Palaeogeography, Palaeoclimatology, Palaeoecology* 113/2–4: 227–42.

Tainter, J.A. 1988. *The Collapse of Complex Societies*. Cambridge: Cambridge University Press.

———. 2006. "Social Complexity and Sustainability." *Ecological Complexity* 3/2: 91–103.

Taleb, N.N. 2001. *Fooled by Randomness: The Hidden Role of Chance in Life and in the Markets*. New York: Random House and Penguin.

Tallet, P. 2005. *Sésostris III et la fin de la XIIe dynastie*. Lonrai: Pygmalion.

———. 2014. "Des papyrus du temps de Chéops au Ouadi el-Jarf (Golfe de Suez)." *BSFE* 188: 25–49.

———. 2017. *Les papyrus de la Mer Rouge*. Cairo: Institut français d'archéologie orientale.

Tallet, P., and D. Laisney. 2012. "Iry-Hor et Narmer au Sud-Sinaï (Ouadi 'Ameyra): Un complément à la chronologie des expéditions minières égyptiennes." *BIFAO* 112: 381–98.

Tassie, G.J. 2014. *Prehistoric Egypt: Socioeconomic Transformations in North-East Africa from the Last Glacial Maximum to the Neolithic, 24,000 to 6,000 cal BC.* London: Golden House Publications.

Teeter, E., ed. 2011. *Before the Pyramids: The Origins of Egyptian Civilization.* Chicago: Oriental Institute.

Toussoun, O. 1925. *Mémoire sur l'histoire du Nil.* Cairo: Institut français d'archéologie orientale.

Toynbee, A.J. 1934–61. *A Study of History.* 10 vols. Oxford: Oxford University Press.

Trenberth, K.E., P.D. Jones, P. Ambenje, R. Bojariu, D. Easterling, A. Klein Tank, D. Parker, F. Rahimzadeh, J.A. Renwick, M. Rusticucci, B. Soden, and P. Zhai. 2007. "Observations: Surface and Atmospheric Climate Change." In *Climate Change 2007: The Physical Science Basis. Contribution of Working Group I to the Fourth Assessment Report of the Intergovernmental Panel on Climate Change*, edited by S. Solomon, D. Qin, M. Manning, Z. Chen, M. Marquis, K.B. Averyt, M. Tignor, and H.L. Miller, 235–36. Cambridge: Cambridge University Press.

Trevor-Roper, H.R. 1972. "Fernand Braudel, the Annales, and the Mediterranean." *Journal of Modern History* 44/4: 468–79.

Trigger, B.G. 2003. *Understanding Early Civilizations: A Comparative Study.* Cambridge: Cambridge University Press.

Turchin, P. 2012. "Dynamics of Political Instability in the United States, 1780–2010." *Journal of Peace Research* 49/4: 577–91.

Twining, A.C. 1833. "On the Growth of Timber—Extract of a Letter from Mr. Alexander C. Twining, to the Editor, dated Albany, April 9, 1833." *American Journal of Science* 24: 391–93.

Vachala, B. 2004. *Abusir VIII: Die Relieffragmente aus der Mastaba des Ptahschepses in Abusir.* Prague: Set Out.

van den Boorn, G.P.F. 1988. *The Duties of the Vizier: Civil Administration in the Early New Kingdom.* London: Kegan Paul International.

Vandersleyen, C. 1995. *L'Égypte et la vallée du Nil, 2: De la fin de l'Ancien Empire à la fin du Nouvel Empire.* Paris: Presses universitaires de France.

van de Walle, B. 1930. *Le mastaba de Neferirtenef aux Musées royaux d'art et d'histoire à Bruxelles (Parc du cinquantenaire): Notice sommaire.* Brussels: Édition de la Fondation égyptologique reine Élisabeth.

———. 1978. *La chapelle funéraire de Neferirtenef.* Brussels: Musées royaux d'art et d'histoire.

Vandier, J. 1950. *Mo'alla: la tombe d'Ankhtifi et la tombe de Sébekhotep.* Cairo: Institut français d'archéologie orientale.

Vercoutter, J. 1992. *L'Égypte et la vallée du Nil, 1: Des origines à la fin de l'Ancien Empire 12000–2000 av. J.-C.* Paris: Presses universitaires de France.

Verner, M. 1977. *Abusir I: The Mastaba of Ptahshepses.* Prague: Charles University.

————. 2001a. "Old Kingdom." In *The Oxford Encyclopedia of Ancient Egypt*, edited by D.B. Redford, 2:585–91. Oxford: Oxford University Press.

————. 2001b. *The Pyramids: A Complete Guide*. New York: Grove Press.

————. 2002. *The Pyramids: Their Archaeology and History*. London: Atlantic Books.

————. 2014. *Sons of the Sun: Rise and Decline of the Fifth Dynasty*. Prague: Charles University in Prague, Faculty of Arts.

————. 2017. *Abusir XXVIII: The Statues of Raneferef and the Royal Sculpture of the Fifth Dynasty*. Prague: Charles University, Faculty of Arts.

Verner, M., P. Posener-Kriéger, and P. Jánosi. 1995. *Abusir III: The Pyramid Complex of Khentkaus*. Prague: Charles University.

Vischak, D. 2015. *Community and Identity in Ancient Egypt: The Old Kingdom Cemetery at Qubbet el-Hawa*. New York: Cambridge University Press.

Vlčková, P. 2006. *Abusir XV: Stone Vessels from the Mortuary Complex of Raneferef at Abusir*. Prague: Czech Institute of Egyptology.

Voss, S. 2004. "Untersuchungen zu den Sonnenheiligtümern der 5. Dynastie: Bedeutung und Funktion eines singulären Tempeltyps im Alten Reich." PhD diss., Universität Hamburg.

Vymazalová, H., and V. Dulíková. 2012. "Sheretnebty, a King's Daughter from Abusir South: Preliminary Report of the 2012 Spring Season." *ArOr* 80: 339–56.

————. 2014. "New Evidence on Princess Sheretnebty from Abusir South." *ArOr* 82: 1–19.

Waddell, W.G. 1940. *Manetho*. Loeb Classical Library. London.

Walford, C. 1879. *The Famines of the World: Past and Present. 2 Papers Read before the Statistical Soc. of London, and Repr. from Its Journal*. London.

Warburton, D. 2012. *Architecture, Power, and Religion: Hatshepsut, Amun and Karnak in Context*. Beiträge zur Archäologie 7. Vienna: Lit Verlag.

Warden, L.A. 2014. *Pottery and Economy in Old Kingdom Egypt*. Leiden: Brill.

Ward-Perkins, B. 2006. *The Fall of Rome and the End of Civilisation*. Oxford: Oxford University Press.

Warren, E. 1897. "An Investigation on the Variability of the Human Skeleton: With Especial Reference to the Naqada Race Discovered by Professor Flinders Petrie in His Explorations in Egypt." *Philosophical Transactions of the Royal Society B: Biological Sciences* 189: 135–227.

Way, T. von der, and J. Boessneck. 1997. *Tell el-Fara'în—Buto: Ergebnisse zum frühen Kontext Kampagnen der Jahre 1983–1989*. Mainz am Rhein: Philipp von Zabern.

Weber, M. 1972. *Wirtschaft und Gesellschaft: Grundriss der verstehenden Soziologie*. 5th ed. Tübingen: J.C.B. Mohr.

Weill, R. 1911–12. "Un temple de Noutirkha-Zosir à Héliopolis." *Sphinx* 15: 9–26.

————. 1958. *Dara: campagnes de 1946–1948*. Cairo: Organisme général des imprimeries gouvernementales.

Weiss, H. 2015. "Megadrought, Collapse, and Resilience in Late 3rd Millennium BC Mesopotamia." In *Ein Klimasturz als Ursache für den Zerfall der alten Welt? 2200 BC—A Climatic Breakdown as a Cause for the Collapse of* the Old World? 7. Mitteldeutscher Archäologentag vom 23. bis 26. Oktober 2014 in Halle (Saale), edited by H. Meller, H.W. Arz, R. Jung, and R. Risch, 35–52. Halle: Landesmuseum für Vorgeschichte.

———. 2017. *Megadrought and Collapse: From Early Agriculture to Angkor*. New York: Oxford University Press.

Weiss, H., M.-A. Courty, W. Wetterstrom, F. Guichard, L. Senior, R. Meadow, and A. Curnow. 1993. "The Genesis and Collapse of Third Millennium North Mesopotamian Civilization." *Science* 261/5124: 995–1004.

Welc, F., and L. Marks. 2013. "Climate Change at the End of the Old Kingdom in Egypt around 4200 BP: New Geoarchaeological Evidence." *Quaternary International* 324: 124–33.

Wells, R.A. 1992. "The Mythology of Nut and the Birth of Ra." *SAK* 19: 305–21.

Wengrow, D. 2006. *The Archaeology of Early Egypt: Social Transformations in North-East Africa, 10,000 to 2,650 BC*. Cambridge: Cambridge University Press.

———. 2010. *What Makes Civilisation? The Ancient Near East and the Future of the West*. Oxford: Oxford University Press.

———. 2015. *Goody Lecture 2015: Cities before the State in Early Eurasia*. Halle: Max Planck Institute for Social Anthropology.

Wenke, R.J. 2009. *The Ancient Egyptian State: The Origins of Egyptian Culture (c. 8000–2000 BC)*. Cambridge: Cambridge University Press.

Werrell, C.E., and F. Femia. 2013a. "Climate Change before and after the Arab Awakening: The Cases of Syria and Libya." In *The Arab Spring and the Climate Change: A Climate and Security Correlations Series*, edited by C.E. Werrell and F. Femia, 23–32. Washington: Center for American Progress. https://climateandsecurity.files.wordpress.com/2012/04/climatechangearabspring-ccs-cap-stimson.pdf

Werrell, C.E., and F. Femia, eds. 2013b. *The Arab Spring and Climate Change: A Climate and Security Correlations Series*. Washington: Center for American Progress. https://climateandsecurity.files.wordpress.com/2012/04/climatechangearabspring-ccs-cap-stimson.pdf

Wetering, J. van. 2017. "The Cemeteries of Nubt, Naqada Region, Upper Egypt." In *Egypt at Its Origins 5: Proceedings of the Fifth International Conference "Origin of the State. Predynastic and Early Dynastic Egypt," Cairo, 13th–18th April 2014*, edited by B. Midant-Reynes and Y. Tristant, 521–49. Leuven: Peeters.

Wildung, D. 1969. *Die Rolle ägyptischer Könige im Bewusstsein ihrer Nachwelt*. Berlin: B. Hessling.

———. 1977. *Imhotep und Amenhotep: Gottwerdung im alten Ägypten*. Munich: Deutscher Kunstverlag.

Wilkinson, R.H. 2003. *The Complete Gods and Goddesses of Ancient Egypt*. London: Thames and Hudson.

Wilkinson, T.A.H. 1996. "A Re-examination of the Early Dynastic Necropolis at Helwan." *MDAIK* 52: 337–54.

———. 1999. *Early Dynastic Egypt*. London: Routledge.

———. 2000a. *Royal Annals of Ancient Egypt: The Palermo Stone and Its Associated*

Fragments. Studies in Egyptology. London: Kegan Paul International.

———. 2000b. "Political Unification: Towards a Reconstruction." *MDAIK* 56: 377–95.

———. 2010. *The Rise and Fall of Ancient Egypt: The History of a Civilisation from 3000 BC to Cleopatra*. London: Bloomsbury.

Willcocks, W. 1889. *Egyptian Irrigation*. London: E. & F.N. Spon.

Willcocks, W., and J.I. Craig. 1913. *Egyptian Irrigation*. 3rd ed. 2 vols. London: E & F.N. Spon; New York: Spon & Chamberlain.

Willems, H. 2008. *Les textes des sarcophages et la démocratie: éléments d'une histoire culturelle du Moyen Empire Égyptien*. Paris: Éditions Cybèle.

———. 2014. "The First Intermediate Period and the Middle Kingdom." In *A Companion to Ancient Egypt*, edited by A.B. Lloyd, 81–89. London: Blackwell.

Willet, H.C. 1953. "Atmospheric and Oceanic Circulation as Factors in Glacial–Interglacial Changes of Climate." In *Climate Change, Evidence, Causes, and Effects*, edited by H. Shapley, 51–71. Cambridge, MA: Harvard University Press.

Williams, B.B. 1986. *Excavations between Abu Simbel and the Sudan Frontier Part 1: The A-group Royal Cemetery at Qustul: Cemetery L*. Chicago: Oriental Institute.

———. 2011. "Relations between Egypt and Nubia in the Naqada Period." In *Before the Pyramids: The Origins of Egyptian Civilization*, edited by E. Teeter, 83–92. Chicago: Oriental Institute.

Wilson, E.G. 2001. "The Cult of Re in the Old Kingdom." PhD diss., Macquarie University, Sydney.

Winter, E. 1957. "Zur Deutung der Sonnenheiligtümern der 5. Dynastie." *Wiener Zeitschrift für die Kunde des Morgenlandes* 54: 222–33.

Wittfogel, K.A. 1957. *Oriental Despotism: A Comparative Study of Total Power*. New Haven: Yale University Press.

Wood, G. 2014. *Tambora: The Eruption That Changed the World*. Princeton: Princeton University Press.

Woods, C. 2010. "The Earliest Mesopotamian Writing." In *Visible Language: Inventions of Writing in the Ancient Middle East and Beyond*, edited by C. Woods, 33–50. Chicago: Oriental Institute Museum.

Wright, H.T., and G.A. Johnson. 1972. "Population, Exchange, and Early State Formation in Southwestern Iran." *American Anthropologist* 77/2: 267–89.

Yeakel, J.D., M.M. Pires, L. Rudolf, N.J. Dominy, P.L. Koch, P.R. Guimarães, and T. Gross. 2014. "Collapse of an Ecological Network in Ancient Egypt." *PNAS* 111/40: 14472–477.

Zandee, J. 1960. *Death as an Enemy: According to Ancient Egyptian Conceptions*. Leiden: Brill.

Zecchi, M. 2001. *Geografia religiosa del Fayyum: dalle origini al IV. secolo a.C.* Imola: La Mandragora.

Zhang, D.D., H.F. Lee, C. Wang, B. Li, Q. Pei, J. Zhang, and Y. An. 2011. "The Causality Analysis of Climate Change and Large-scale Human Crisis." *PNAS* 108/42: 17296–301.

Ziegler, C. 2007. *Le mastaba d'Akhethetep*. Paris: Musée du Louvre Editions.
Ziermann, M. 1993. *Elephantine XVI: Befestigungsanlagen und Stadtentwicklung in der Frühzeit und im frühen Alten Reich*. Mainz am Rhein: Philipp von Zabern.

Index

Names of kings of Egypt are given in CAPITALS

247

Zawyat al-Mayyitin (Sultan) 80, 165

inbw-ḥḏ (White Walls) 50; *see also* Memphis
'Ist chamber 136

'rrt-corridor 127
'd-mr (official title) 61

wr-m33 (Greatest of Seers) 115
wr-m33 'Iwnw (Greatest of Heliopolitan Seers) 115
wsḫt hall 127

biti nbti (kingly title) 60

pr-wrw (House of Great Ones) 127
pr-nsw (royal office) 58

mrt shrine 86, 122

Nḥn-Rꜥ (sun-temple of Userkaf) 118
nsw-biti (kingly title) 60, 61

r-Nḫn (Spokesman of Nekhen) 118

h3it-hall 118

ḥ3ty-ꜥ3 (governor) 194
ḥwt (department) 59
ḥwwt (estates) 86, 88
Nḥn-Rꜥ priest 117
ḥm-nṯr Rꜥ m Nḥn-Rꜥ (Priest of Re in Nḥn-Rꜥ) 117
ḥry-tp-ꜥ3 (Great Overlord) 194
ḥtp-di-nsw offering formula 88, 142
Ḥr/bik-nbw (kingly title) 60

ḫnty-š (overseer) 164
ḫrp (official title) 61
ḫrp-ꜥḥ pr-ꜥ3 (Inspector of the Royal House) 59
ḫtmw-biti (Sealer of the King/ Chancellor) 60

s3-Rꜥ (kingly title) 60
sb3w ḫnt(i) pt (Administrator of Domain of Horus) 146
smsw-h3it (Elder of *h3it*-hall) 118
smrw (friend) 59

šmsw Ḥr (Following of Horus) 80

grgwt (settlements) 86